D1315159

Energy Law and Policy for the 21st Century

The Energy Law Group

James E. Hickey, Jr.
Professor of Law and Director of International Programs
Hofstra University
School of Law

Suedeen G. Kelly
Keleher & McLeod Professor of Law
University of New Mexico

Marla E. Mansfield
Professor of Law and Professorial Fellow, NELPI
University of Tulsa
College of Law

Joseph P. Tomain
Dean and Nippert Professor of Law
University of Cincinnati
College of Law

Donald N. Zillman
Godfrey Professor of Law and Interim Provost
University of Maine

Rocky Mountain Mineral Law Foundation
Denver, Colorado
2000

PREFACE

This work reflects the collective wisdom of the authors' involvement in energy matters. We have practiced, taught, consulted, researched, and written in the field since energy law first took shape in the wake of the OPEC embargo and oil price increases of 1973. We have also intersected as colleagues in numerous situations over the last twenty years. Thus, The Energy Law Group seems fitting title for our collective efforts.

As good colleagues will do, we differ on matters of energy law and policy. We agree, however, on certain fundamentals that provide a useful place from which to start a study of energy law. First, law does not exist in a vacuum. Law operates in a world influenced by laws of science and engineering and the less precise precepts of economics, sociology, and politics. Second, energy law operates at local, state, national, and international levels. Third, energy law is an evolving body of law. It may be formed by common law property doctrines that date back five hundred years in English law. It may also be governed by federal regulations approved last week and subject to change after the next election.

Our objective is to provide a concise examination of energy law for the student of law or public policy or for the attorney or policy maker who is new to the field. We are more primer than treatise. We want to provide fundamentals of the field rather than the latest regulations or court decisions. Specific treatises, various news services and internet data bases supply these materials.

We have tried to emphasize information rather than opinion. If you leave the work uncertain whether we favor or oppose the continued development of nuclear power, the growth of federal regulation of electricity, or a crash program to address global warming, we will have accomplished our mission to provide you with the basics to help you form your conclusions on these important matters of law and public policy.

The five of us are equal contributors to the work. Chapter authors are identified and should be the point of contact for questions or suggestions about the individual chapters. Throughout the text we draw on our predecessor texts, Zillman and Lattman, ENERGY LAW (1983) and Tomain and Hickey, ENERGY LAW AND POLICY (1989) in the preparation of this work. But these books are dated and this stands as a new work, not simply an updating of older texts. Our thanks go out to several decades of students, research assistants, and administrative staff who have helped to shape the present product.

The text is composed of two broad sections. The first section examines energy from a variety of perspectives. These sections are not specific to a single energy source (e.g., oil, coal, nuclear power). They emphasize that law, economics, and policy are close companions in the field. The energy professional who understands the relevance of only one discipline usually does not serve her client well whether that client is an individual, an energy business, a government office, or a non-governmental organization.

You should approach these materials in a way that best reflects your expertise and preferences. Chapter One begins with an overview of the world of energy. What is energy? In what forms does it appear? How is it used? What decisions result from those facts? This introduction should allow the novice to the field to understand the "big picture." It should also allow those familiar with one aspect of energy to understand its other dimensions.

Chapter Two provides a layperson's introduction to the role of economics in energy decisions. In the energy field, law is best made or interpreted if parties understand economics and public policy. Persons expert, or familiar, with this material can move rapidly or delete. Persons approaching these disciplines for the first time are encouraged to read more widely in some of the materials cited.

Chapter Three introduces the structure of energy law in the United States. A substantial portion of the chapter examines the key constitutional provisions —the Commerce Clause, the Supremacy Clause, the Due Process and Equal Protection Clause, the Takings Clause —that have governed government regulation of energy for a century and a half. We provide sufficient extracts from some of the significant cases to allow individual case discussion. The concluding sections of Chapter Three address the federal legislative process and the administrative process. Much energy law comes from these sources. Law students, whose first year experience has been shaped by the appellate judicial decision, may need to be introduced, or reintroduced, to these essential realms of lawmaking.

Chapter Four continues the introduction to law by moving to the international sphere. Although this is not an international resources law text, the domestic energy lawyer needs to appreciate the growing importance of transnational activity. The chapter provides an introduction to some of the ways in which international law is likely to intersect with national law.

Chapter Five introduces another theme that runs throughout modern energy law —environmental protection. Environmental law grew up around energy industries. Some of the classic environmental harms have been a consequence of energy's successes in the modern world. Fossil fuel combustion for electric generation and transportation fouls the air. Coal mining disturbs land surfaces. Hydroelectric dams change the ecological communities in their river systems. A nuclear power accident threatens massive radiation release that brings cancers and genetic deformations in its wake.

Much of environmental law has consisted of trying to make the energy industries control their undesired pollution. As the economist would phrase it, we wish "to internalize the externalities." We introduce you to some of the legal approaches to controlling these environmental harms. A further section introduces some of the prominent pollution control laws that will play a role in the development of many energy projects.

Chapter Six concludes the first half of the text with a blending of history and public policy. We identify some of the grand themes that have driven United States energy policy over the last century. Not surprisingly energy decisions are often a part of larger issues facing the American economy and American society. The study suggests that "everything comes in cycles" as periods of governmental intervention in the energy economies give way to periods of government encouragement of business and deregulation. The chapter sets the stage for many of the laws and policy decisions highlighted in the resource specific chapters that follow.

Chapter Seven begins a resource by resource consideration of the primary energy sources. We begin with petroleum, the most versatile of energy fuels. The initial sections of the chapter discuss the discovery and extraction of both oil and natural gas. Similar laws govern the property rights to extract the two fossil fuels. The remaining sections of the oil chapter address oil.

Chapter Eight addresses the distinctive features of natural gas. These primarily concern the regulation of the shipment and use of the gas resource once it is extracted from the ground.

Chapter Nine studies the third of the fossil fuels, coal. Coal is the fuel that powered America at the turn of the last century —heating homes and businesses, fueling the railroads, ships and industries. Today, coal's primary use is for the fuel to run electric generating plants. Coal today poses one of the dilemmas of energy policy. U.S. coal is plentiful and relatively inexpensive. However, it is also the most polluting of the fossil fuels and a major worldwide contributor to global warming.

Chapter Ten address nuclear power, the least predictable of the major fuel sources today in terms of its future. The world of 2050 could be substantially powered by nuclear generated electricity. Alternatively, nuclear power could have vanished from the world's energy mix. Legal decisions have combined with policy matters to raise this nuclear uncertainty. In the next decade or two, public opinion will likely be more important than law in deciding nuclear's future.

Chapter Eleven examines hydroelectric power, another energy source that is predominantly useful for the generation of electricity. Hydropower law in the United States was shaped by the contest between private and public interests seeking the development of waterpower. Today, environmental concerns also play a part in the further development of the power of falling water.

Chapter Twelve addresses that invaluable secondary source of energy —electricity. While nature does create electricity as lightning and in other forms, most useable electricity is the product of the operation of an electric generator powered by the burning of a fossil fuel, the force of falling water, or the energy released by the nuclear process. Electricity has been one of the primary subjects of public utility regulation at both the state and federal levels. As that economy changes, new legal and policy approaches must be addressed. The chapter places you in the midst of this fast-moving evolution in energy law.

Chapter Thirteen concludes the text with a look at some of the alternatives to the present fossil fuel, nuclear, and hydro world. Alternatives is a widely inclusive term that includes ancient energy sources like wood burning and ultra-modern ones like fusion. Despite government encouragement over the last twenty years, the use of alternatives in the United States has grown only modestly. However, those decades have provided an opportunity to identify and address the legal problems that the technologies raise. That knowledge contributes to intelligent predictions about the alternatives' likely contributions to energy use in 2010, 2020, or 2050.

Summary of Contents

Table of Contents

Chapter Three: The Legal Framework
by Donald N. Zillman

Chapter Four: International Law
by James E. Hickey, Jr.

Chapter Six: Toward a Sustainable Energy-Environmental Policy
by Joseph P. Tomain

Chapter Seven: Oil
by Marla E. Mansfield and James E. Hickey, Jr.

Chapter Thirteen: Alternative Energy Sources
by Suedeen G. Kelley

Table of Cases*

(reference is to chapter-page)

*Professor Hickey would like to thank his research assistant, Omayra Perez, for her work on the Table of Cases.

CHAPTER ONE

An Introduction to Energy

by Donald N. Zillman

I.   PERSPECTIVES ON ENERGY

This text introduces you to energy—its forms, its uses, and its legal control. Energy pervades our lives. As a consequence, contemporary Americans are likely to take energy for granted.

A moment's reflection on modern education emphasizes our dependence on energy. You are probably reading this text in a heated or cooled library, business office, classroom or residence. If it is night, you will be using electric light. Your trip to the classroom has probably relied on a petroleum powered car or bus. The existence of petroleum powered airplanes has made it possible for your classmates from California and New York and Alabama and Hong Kong and Berlin to meet face to face in one classroom. Electric power runs dozens of devices essential to education from personal computers to photocopy machines to janitorial equipment. The marvels of the world wide web, computer retrieval services, and electronic mail depend on reliable electricity. The oil and gas that can be used as fuels can also serve as product components. Most of the chairs, tables and floor coverings in a classroom or library are formed in part from petrochemical raw materials.

Defined broadly, energy is the ability to do work. While work has several popular meanings, it is technically defined as the mathematical product of a force multiplied by the distance this force moves along the line of application. A force of one pound moving a distance of one foot produces one foot-pound of work.

Energy may be potential or kinetic. A frequently cited example of the difference between potential and kinetic energy is a hydroelectric plant. Water stored behind a dam is not working but has the potential to work when it is released. When it drops due to the action of gravity, it possesses kinetic energy because of its motion. The motion may be used to turn turbines and generators to produce electric energy.

Energy occurs in a wide variety of forms, such as mechanical, chemical, electrical, nuclear, and heat. These forms can be converted from one to another. The various forms of energy are measured and expressed in different units or values. Some of the units of measurement are based on the metric system (kilograms, meters) and others on the English system (pounds, feet). For example, heat energy can be measured both in calories (one calorie is the heat needed to raise the temperature of one gram of water one degree Celsius at 15 degrees centigrade) and in British Thermal Units (one BTU is the heat needed to raise the temperature of one pound of water one degree Fahrenheit at 59.5 degrees Fahrenheit). The consumption of electrical energy is measured in kilowatt-hours (KWH). Nuclear energy is measured in millions of electron volts (mev) or billions of electron volts (bev).

The total of all energy and matter in the universe is constant. Energy and matter (mass) cannot be created from nothing and cannot be destroyed. Although the sum of both energy and matter in the universe is constant, matter can be converted to energy and vice versa. The conversion of mass to energy is the basis of nuclear energy, and is governed by Einstein's famous equation $E=mc^2$—where E is energy, m is mass, and c is the velocity of light. In non-nuclear reactions, the law of conservation of energy and mass holds. In other words, in processes not generating nuclear energy, the total amount of energy at the end of the process will be the same as at the beginning. If work is done during the process, however, the energy available to do work is greater at the beginning than at the end; energy will be converted from more useful to less useful forms. An example illustrates the point.

A steel block is lifted above the ground to be dropped to drive a spike. The elevated block has potential energy. As the block falls, this potential energy is converted to kinetic energy because the block has mass and is in motion. As the potential energy is converted to kinetic energy, some energy is lost in overcoming air resistance to the falling block. This energy is used to generate heat by friction between the falling block and the air and cannot later be used to drive the spike. When the block hits the spike, the block will deform slightly. This internal deformation generates heat which also is energy unavailable for driving the spike. A sound is produced when the block hits the spike—further loss of useful energy. The total energy delivered to drive the spike, plus all the losses, equals the total potential energy possessed initially by the elevated block. No energy has been created or lost, but not all the potential energy has been converted to useful work. Due to such energy losses, no energy conversion process utilizes all the energy available, i.e., the efficiency of energy conversion is not 100%.

A major challenge to technology is to increase the efficiency of energy conversion. Such increases in efficiency result in more work being accomplished from the same available energy. Automobile transmissions offer a familiar example. A car equipped with a standard transmission, if driven properly, will get better gas mileage than a car equipped with an automatic transmission. The fluid coupling in an automatic transmission loses energy as heat (slippage) to a greater extent than a dry clutch. Thus, the potential energy of gasoline, converted to mechanical energy by the engine, is less fully used to do the work of driving the car if an automatic transmission is used.

These natural laws force tradeoffs in energy conversion. Thus, some of the anti-pollution equipment and specifications of modern automobile engines reduce the efficiency of conversion of the energy in the gasoline. Lower gas mileage results from this lower efficiency, but pollution is reduced. Similar trade-offs occur in power generation and industrial processes. Obviously, heat is not always useless energy or lost in the system. In burning coal, for example, heat is the energy form we wish to obtain.

II. SOME HISTORY

It is useful to reflect on the use of energy at different historical periods. We can compare energy in the United States in 1800, 1900, 1950 and 2000. The very different civilizations of these four eras are explained in part by the energy resources available to American citizens.

In 1800 the United States was entering its second decade as a nation. We had added a few new states to the original thirteen. However, our borders stopped at the Mississippi River. The work of America was primarily on the farm. Most Americans lived in small towns or in rural areas. Such essentials of modern life as electricity, telecommunications, the automobile, the railroad, and the airplane had not been invented.

Human and animal power, wood, and wind were the essential energy sources of 1800 America. Transportation was by foot or slow stagecoach over primitive roads on land. Sail power along the lengthy east coast of the United States provided considerable movement of people and goods. Travel and communication were typically measured in weeks or months rather than days or hours.

Ordinary living, whether in city, town or on the farm, could be a struggle. Burning wood supplied the only source of warmth in cold climates. The multiple fireplaces in early 19th century houses reflected necessity rather than decoration. Wood heat also was necessary for cooking and for what warm water bathing was done. The absence of electricity helped attune Americans to a cycle of reliance on daylight. Candle or oil lighting provided a poor contrast to the light of the sun.

Work relied heavily on human and animal (primarily horse) power. Physical labor marked almost every aspect of farming, the production of goods, or homemaking in 1800. There was nothing unusual about a 50 year old man or woman worn down by a life of physical labor. The heavy dependence on human labor also helped explain America's ugly tolerance of human slavery until the end of the Civil War.

A century later, enormous changes had taken place in America. By 1900, the country stretched across the continent. Following the Spanish-American War in 1898, overseas possessions had become part of an American empire. The years following the Civil War had seen an enormous growth of an industrial America. Most Americans still lived and worked on farms, but major industries had developed around American cities.

The energy fuel of 1900 was coal, extracted in large amounts from the Appalachian region. Coal provided the energy for powered transportation—the railroads and much of shipping. (The automobile of 1900 was barely out of the experimental stage.) Coal furnaces were common for heating urban properties. Coal provided the heat to power much of the industrial work of America. Coal, converted to gas, provided a good deal of lighting. Electricity was only gradually beginning to take over the lighting market.

By 1950, American energy use had changed markedly. Coal's role was diminished. Petroleum and electricity had taken over several sectors of the market. By 1950, the use of electricity (generated by one of the primary energy fuels) was widespread throughout America. Petroleum had helped create the transportation revolution led by the automobile and the airplane. The former gave individual flexibility in transportation and allowed the growth of the suburbs. The latter put every part of the United States within a day's travel from another part of the country. It also set the stage for higher speed jet travel which would similarly shrink the world.

Home and business were now likely to be heated by petroleum or natural gas. Electricity, and the wondrous range of labor-saving devices that it encouraged, changed lifestyles profoundly for Americans of all social classes. Imagine the wonder with which a middle class American of 1800 or 1900 or even 1950 would view the modern contemporary home equipped with a television, a refrigerator, an electric range, a washer and dryer, and increasingly, a personal computer. Just as electricity has reshaped the home, so too has it shaped the workplace. Electricity powers innumerable machines on the assembly line. It drives the white collar office whose output is considered service rather than product. Soon, it may even power our cars. Table I shows the sources from which Americans obtain their electricity.

In 1996, 3077 billion kilowatt hours of electricity were produced in the United States. Six hundred seventy-five billion kilowatt hours of electricity were produced from nuclear power (21.9%) and 1737 billion kilowatt hours of electricity from coal-fired generation (56.5%). Hydroelectric produced 11%, gas another 9% and petroleum 2%. In 1996 retail sales of electricity

---

[1] Energy Information Administration (EIA), ELECTRIC POWER ANN. (1996).
[2] *Id.*

exceeded total net generation by 7 billion kilowatt hours. The difference was accounted for by import of electricity from Canada.[3]

Table I. Percentage Share of United States Electric Utility Net Generation By Source			
Energy Source	1996	1992	1987
Coal	56.5	56.2	56.9
Nuclear Power	21.9	22.1	17.7
Hydro Electric	10.7	8.6	9.7
Natural Gas	8.5	9.4	10.6
Petroleum*	2.2	3.2	4.6
Geothermal and other**	.2	.4	.5

Petroleum includes distillate fuel oil, residual fuel oil including crude oil burned as fuel, jet fuel and petroleum coke.
**Other includes wood, waste water, photovoltaic and solar thermal energy used to generate electricty for distribution.*
Source: Energy Information Administration, Annual Report–Coal EIA Form-759

In 1996 domestic coal consumption rose to a high of 983 million short tons (mst), up 4% from 1995. This increase is due to electric utility consumption of coal.[4] United States' coal production increased to 1062.9 million short tons of coal in 1996. Americans consumed 1006.2 mst of coal, exporting approximately 90.5 mst and importing 7.1 mst. Distribution of coal use was: the electric power industry consumed 897.2 million short tons, other industry and miscellaneous 71.3 mst, coke plants 31.3 mst, and residential and commercial consumed the remaining 6.0 mst.[5]

In 1997, nuclear power accounted for 17.8% of U.S. electricity generation, second only to coal in the U.S. electricity generation mix, but down from 19.4 % in 1996. The long term (through 2015) nuclear power outlook in the United States is for nuclear capacity to decline sharply, with no new nuclear units expected to come on-line during the forecast time frame. By 2015, the United States is expected to have 59 nuclear units (compared to 110 at the end of 1996) providing only 10% of total electric generation. As of late 1997 several U.S. nuclear plants remained offline due to safety concerns.[6]

---

[3] *Id.*

[4] *Id.* COAL INDUSTRY ANN. (1996).

[5] *Graphical Summary of the Annual Energy Review Coal Data. Graphical Summary of U.S. Coal Production and Consumption* (visited Feb. 26, 1998) <http://www.eia.doe.gov/emeu/aer/aergs/coal.html>.

[6] EIA, UNITED STATES OF AMERICA 9 (Nov. 1997).

As you will see, America has diversified its mixture of energy sources as we near the year 2000. Coal, petroleum, natural gas, nuclear power and hydro power will all provide significant shares of American energy in 2000. They are joined by such old standbys as wind power and wood burning and such emerging technologies as solar photovoltaic, geothermal, and fusion energy.

Since 1950, we have also recognized that energy development is not an unqualified good. Our energy-dependent society demands the sacrifice of scarce and often non-renewable resources. The natural gas that is burned to heat a home or power an electrical generator cannot be used to make fertilizer. We also pay for energy use with dirty air, injured workers, damaged landscapes and the disruption of human relationships. Particularly in the area of environmental harms, society and government face hard choices between costs and benefits of energy.

An understanding of energy law is vastly assisted by an understanding of the energy raw materials and the ways in which they are processed and used. Law rarely operates in a vacuum. The laws that govern an energy industry will reflect technology (e.g., can coal be extracted from a particular formation), economics (e.g., is the price of petroleum sufficient to encourage expensive off-shore exploration and production), politics (e.g., do sufficient states benefit from petroleum production to encourage favorable national tax legislation), and psychology or sociology (e.g., are sufficient numbers of Americans uncomfortable with nuclear power to discourage its further development?).

Most energy decisions involve a variety of the disciplines mentioned. As an example, coal miners in the United States are influenced by the geography of Australian harbors. Since both American and Australian coal companies may compete to export coal to Japan, Taiwan, or Korea, harbor expansion may be necessary before larger quantities of coal can be shipped out of the Australian ports. A prohibitively expensive excavation and dredging project in Australia may mean more coal contracts and more mining jobs in the Western United States.

Our focus so far has been on the United States. The rest of the industrialized world mirrors the American patterns of energy use. The inventories of resources and uses will vary from country to country. Often the local presence of raw materials will determine the energy mix. Germany and China have significant coal reserves. Norway is rich in hydro power. Parts of the Middle East are awash in petroleum and natural gas. Local consumption patterns will reflect the local product. Political, psychological, and sociological factors may drive other decisions. France and Japan are more comfortable with nuclear power than the United States or Scandinavia. Cheap coal may take a back seat to the need for clean air. Conversely, government may make decisions to favor local extractive industries that do not make sense when viewed from an international economic perspective.

In non-industrialized or "third world" nations, energy patterns may vary considerably from those in Tokyo, Los Angeles or Paris. Transport may still be primitive. The average citizen may not own a car and may travel long distances only by bus or rail. Homes are heated mostly by wood, dung or low grade coal. Electricity remains foreign to some rural areas and of questionable reliability in other areas. Much productive work may still be the product of human and animal labor.

III. ENERGY PRODUCTION AND CONSUMPTION

The average citizen does not think in terms of the laws of energy conservation or resource inventories. To him or her, energy is the gallon of gasoline in the fuel tank, the heat from the natural gas furnace, the electrically lighted room, the booming stereo set or quiet computer, or the reliable industrial machine. The energy that drives these useful products is produced from a limited number of natural resources. Students of energy law need to understand the sources and uses of energy.

For over two decades the United States Energy Information Administration (EIA) has gathered and published data about U.S. energy production and consumption. We have examined some already. Various private services offer similar statistics. The EIA data usually describe U.S. energy in terms of BTUs. The BTU reference permits a comparison of different types of energy units (tons of coal, barrels of oil, therms of natural gas). A BTU is equivalent to 252 calories. A kilowatt hour is equal to 3413 BTUs. As points of reference, one gallon of unleaded gasoline contains 115,000 BTUs, one pound of bituminous coal has about 12,000 BTUs and one gram of fissionable U-235 has 74 million BTUs. To reduce the need for large numbers, large scale energy use is measured in quads or quadrillion BTUs.

The present dominant sources of American energy are the fossil fuels, so named because they are derived from prehistoric animal and vegetable life. The fossil fuels are coal, natural gas, and petroleum (liquid hydrocarbons). Crude oil is actually a mixture of petroleum (liquid hydrocarbons) and some dissolved natural gas. The remaining sources of United States energy are hydro-power, nuclear power, and the variety of old and new technologies that may be lumped under the heading alternatives. As we note later, these primary sources do not include electricity, one of the most beneficial of energy uses. Electricity is a secondary source produced from the combustion of a fossil fuel or the use of the nuclear chain reaction or the power of falling water.

Table II shows the production of American energy by type from 1950 to present. Table III shows United States consumption of energy by type for the same years. Differences between the two figures reflect imports and exports. The most notable import is petroleum. The figures reflect that the United States consumes about twice as much petroleum as it produces domestically.

Table II.			U.S. Production of Energy by Type 1950-1996				
Year	Coal	Natural Gas	Petroleum & Natural Gas Plant Liquids	Hydro-Power	Nuclear Power	Geo-thermal	Total Gross Energy Production
1950	14.62	6.23	12.27	1.42	0	0	34.55
1960	11.12	12.66	16.39	1.60	0.01	0	41.78
1970	15.05	21.67	22.91	2.63	0.24	0.01	62.51
1980	18.83	19.70	20.52	2.91	2.70	0.11	64.82
1987	20.14	17.14	19.88	2.63	4.91	0.25*	64.95
1992	21.59	18.38	17.58	2.57	6.61	3.23*	69.96
1996	22.61	19.53	16.27	3.59	7.17	3.44*	72.61

All figures are in Quadrillion BTU's
*The geothermal figures for 1987, 1992 and 1996 include geothermal, biofuel and solar.
Source: EIA, Annual Report to Congress 1980, Vol.2, p.5 and EIA Coal Industry Annual 1996

What energy sources, both foreign and domestic, were used to provide the 93.81 quads of energy consumed in 1996? In that year the United States derived 22.4 % from coal, 24% from natural gas, 38% from petroleum, 7.6% from nuclear, and 7.8% from hydro-power and other renewables, including human and animal power. The fact that 84.4% of this total comes from petroleum, natural gas, and coal reflects our dependence on the non-renewable fossil fuels.[7]

---

[7] *Graphical Summary of the Annual Energy Review Data* (visited Feb. 27, 1998) <http://www.eia/doe/gov/emeu/aer/aergs/aer2.html>.

Table III.	U.S. Consumption of Energy by Type 1950-1996						
Year	Coal	Natural Gas	Petroleum & Natural Gas Plant Liquids	Hydro-Power	Nuclear Power	Geo-thermal	Total Gross Energy Consumption
1950	12.89	8.97	13.32	1.44	0	--	33.62
1960	10.12	12.39	19.92	1.65	0.01	--	44.08
1970	12.66	21.79	29.52	2.65	0.24	--	66.83
1980	15.67	20.44	34.25	3.13	2.70	--	76.27
1987	18.01	17.74	32.87	3.12	4.91	0.25*	76.90
1992	19.21	20.33	33.53	2.89	6.61	2.86*	85.43
1996	20.99	22.59	35.72	3.88	7.17	3.48*	93.81**

All figures are in quadrillion BTUs
* The figures for the 1987, 1992 and 1996 geothermal column include geothermal, biofuel, solar and wind. Net import of coal categories are eliminated.[8]
** Minor variation in total consumption due to rounding.
Source: EIA, Annual Report to Congress 1980, Vol.2, p.7 and EIA Coal Industry Annual 1996

How did Americans use the 93.81 quads of energy? Thirty-six percent was used for residential and commercial purposes, which most notably includes the oil and natural gas used in furnaces to heat buildings. Thirty-eight percent was used in the industrial sector as fuel or raw materials to create the great variety of American industrial products. These two categories include energy used for the generation of that most valuable secondary source of energy, electricity. Lastly, 26% of the energy was used for transportation—the motor gasoline, diesel fuel and jet fuel that allow Americans to be the most mobile people in the history of the world.[9]

In 1996, the United States consumed 18.3 million bbl/d of oil: 7.9 million bbl/d (or 43% of the total) was motor gasoline, 3.4 million bbl/d (18%) distillate fuel oil, 1.6 million bbl/d (9%) jet fuel, and 850,000 bbl/d (5%) residual fuel oil. U.S. oil demand is expected to increase by about 300,000 bbl/d (1.6%) in 1997, and another 270,000 bbl/d (1.5%) in 1998.[10]

Where do we get the 93.81 quads of energy? The United States is one of the world's major energy producers. The 1996 figures show a total domestic production of 72.61 quads. The major contributors are coal (22.61

[8] *Id.* COAL INDUSTRY ANN., *Table, U.S. Energy Overview, Selected Years, 1987, 1992-1996*, X (1996).

[9] *Graphical Summary of the Annual Energy Review Data* (visited Feb. 27, 1998) <http://www.eia/doe/gov/emeu/aer/aergs/aer2.html>.

[10] EIA, UNITED STATES OF AMERICA 3 (Nov. 1997).

quads), natural gas (19.53 quads) and petroleum (16.27 quads). Nuclear power contributed an additional 7.17 quads, and hydro-power contributed 3.62 quads with the remaining forms contributing less than 3.41 quads.[11]

   Tables II, III and IV show the heavy American reliance on imported petroleum. In 1950, U.S. petroleum production was roughly equal to consumption. By 1960 imported petroleum was needed to supply demands. In 1980 the United States consumed over 34 quads but produced 20.52 quads. We imported about 40% of our petroleum needs, a percentage that President Jimmy Carter stated was intolerable. Yet fifteen years later the percentage of petroleum has risen still higher to almost 50%.

Table IV. Petroleum Imported to the United States 1960-1996							
Year	Saudi Arabia	Iran	Vene-zuela	Libya	Indo-nesia	Algeria	Nigeria	Total OPEC
1960	84	34	911	0	77	1	0	1314
1970	30	39	989	47	70	8	50	1343
1978	1144	555	645	654	573	649	919	5751
1980	1252	8	460	550	337	481	846	4233
1990	1339	0	1025	0	114	280	800	4296
1996	1363	0	1676	0	59	256	617	4211

All figures in thousand barrels per day.[12]
Source: EIA, Annual Report to Congress 1980, Vol 2, p. 55 and EIA Petroleum Supply Annual 1996, Vol. 1)

   Petroleum imports by themselves are not a bad thing. Calls for energy independence (i.e., no reliance on imports) in the early 1970s made little economic or political sense. However, United States' policy may vary according to the country of export. Table IV shows the changing nature of our petroleum imports over the last four decades. Heavy dependence on nations of the Organization of Petroleum Exporting Countries (OPEC) in the early 1970s was widely seen as a foreign policy concern. Since then, we have diversified our imports but the OPEC Middle East remains a major source of both petroleum and political volatility.

   In the first eight months of 1997, U.S. net imports of crude oil and refined petroleum products were 9.0 bbl/d, up 4.7% from the same period in

---

   [11] *Graphical Summary of the Annual Energy Review Data* (visited Feb. 27, 1998) <http://www.eia/doe/gov/emeu/aer/aergs/aer2.html>.
   [12] 1 EIA, PETROLEUM SUPPLY ANNUAL, *Table S3, Crude Oil and Petroleum Product Imports.*

1996. These imports represented 48% of U.S. oil consumption. Slightly less than half of this oil came from OPEC nations, with Persian Gulf sources accounting for about 19% of U.S. oil imports during the period. Overall, the top suppliers of oil to the United States for January-August 1997 were Venezuela (1.7 million bbl/d), Canada (1.45 million bbl/d), Saudi Arabia (1.4 million bbl/d), and Mexico (1.4 million bbl/d).[13]

Tables V and VI show imports and exports by type for the years, 1987, 1992 and 1996. Table V reflects an overall increase in energy imports since 1987 of approximately eight quadrillion BTUs.

Table V. United States Imports by Type			
Type	1996	1992	1987
Crude Oil	16.24	13.25	10.07
Petroleum Products	3.86	3.71	4.10
Natural Gas	2.90	2.16	.99
Coal	.18	.30	.04
Other	.50	.43	.57
TOTAL	23.68	19.66	15.76

All figures are in Quadrillion BTUs[14]
Source: EIA Coal Industry Annual, Table ES1. U.S. Energy Overview, Selected Years, 1987, 1992-1996 (1996).

Table VI. United States Exports by Type			
Type	1996	1992	1987
Coal	2.37	2.68	2.09
Crude Oil	2.06	2.01	1.63
Other	.26	.33	.13

All figures are in Quadrillion BTUs[15]
Source: EIA Coal Industry Annual. Table ES1. U.S. Energy Overview, Selected Years, 1987, 1992-1996 (1996)

---

[13] EIA, UNITED STATES OF AMERICA 3 (Nov. 1997).

[14] EIA COAL INDUSTRY ANN., *U.S. Energy Overview, Selected Years, 1987, 1992-1996*, X (1996).

[15] *Id.* COAL INDUSTRY ANN., Table ES1, U.S. Energy Overview, Selected Years, 1987, 1992-1996, X (1996).

Figures 1 and 2 provide further perspectives on the worldwide energy picture. The United States and some countries of the former Soviet Union are among the few countries that are both major producers and consumers of energy. China is rapidly reaching that state. Countries like Saudi Arabia and Kuwait are major producers but modest consumers. Such major industrial powers as Japan, France, and Italy have almost no domestic production. Their economies depend on imported energy, most significantly, petroleum.

Figure 1.   World Primary Energy Production[16]

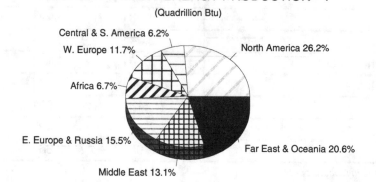

WORLD PRIMARY ENERGY PRODUCTION - 1
(Quadrillion Btu)

Central & S. America 6.2%
W. Europe 11.7%
North America 26.2%
Africa 6.7%
E. Europe & Russia 15.5%
Far East & Oceania 20.6%
Middle East 13.1%

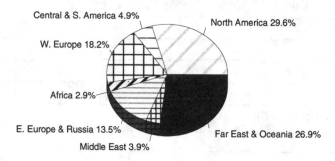

WORLD PRIMARY ENERGY CONSUMP
(Quadrillion Btu)

Central & S. America 4.9%
W. Europe 18.2%
North America 29.6%
Africa 2.9%
E. Europe & Russia 13.5%
Far East & Oceania 26.9%
Middle East 3.9%

Source: EIA International Energy Database.
Table F1. World Primary Energy Production (Btu) 1987-1996
Table E1. World Primary Energy Consumption (Btu) 1987-1996.

---

[16] *Id.* INTERNATIONAL ENERGY DATABASE. *Table F1, World Primary Energy Production 1987-1996; Table E1, World Primary Energy Consumption 1987-1996.*

Figure 2.   World Petroleum Consumption and Crude Oil Production[17]

World Petroleum Consumption - 1996
World Total: 71,254 Mb/d

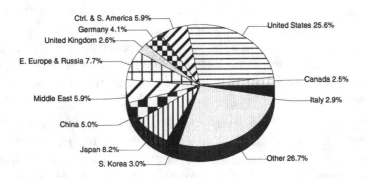

World Crude Oil Production - 1996
World Total: 64,054 Mb/d

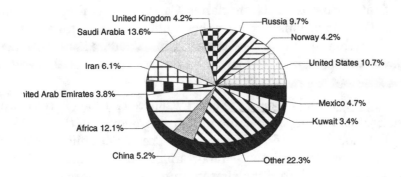

Source: EIA, International Energy Database.
Table 1.2 World Petroleum Consumption, 1987-1996.
Table 2.2 World Crude Oil Production. 1987-1996.)

---

[17] *Id.* INTERNATIONAL ENERGY DATABASE. *Table 1.2, World Petroleum Consumption 1987-1996; Table 2.2, World Crude Oil Production 1987-1996* (Dec. 1997).

IV. THE ENERGY RESOURCES

Each of the primary energy sources offers distinct legal and political concerns. Petroleum is the versatile energy source. Petroleum makes contributions to all of the end-use categories. Petroleum *is* transportation. Virtually all of our cars, planes, and ships run on petroleum. Petroleum also remains an option for heating residential and commercial properties, for running many industrial processes, and for fueling electric generating plants. In addition to serving as a fuel, petroleum and the other hydrocarbons are useful product components. Household products, clothing, fertilizers, and medicines depend in part on the fossil fuels for raw materials. The massive petrochemical industry is evidence of this fact.

Natural gas has evolved from an undesired by-product of petroleum production into a major contributor to world energy supplies. Developments in long-distance pipelines and, more recently, in the ocean shipment of liquefied natural gas have enhanced natural gas' geographic range. You can produce the product in one place and use it thousands of miles distant. Gas is a very clean burning fuel, which makes it the most attractive fossil fuel for some industrial processes. It also makes natural gas the least air polluting of the burned fossil fuels. While gas does not contribute to transportation to any significant extent, it is a major contributor to the residential, commercial, industrial, and electric utility sectors. The major gas producing nations are the United States, Russia, the Netherlands, Canada, the United Kingdom and China. The OPEC nations are also beginning to undertake significant production from their gas reserves. In the United States, a half dozen states—Texas, Louisiana, California, Kansas, Oklahoma, and New Mexico provide most of the United States' natural gas.

The third fossil fuel is coal—*the* energy source of 1900. Three countries the United States, Russia, and China produce a majority of the world's coal. Germany, Poland, the United Kingdom, the Czech Republic, South Africa, India, and Australia also contribute important amounts. Some are significant exporters of their coal. Within the United States, coal is more widely distributed than oil and gas. Such geographically diverse states as Wyoming, West Virginia, Illinois, and Texas are coal producers. While coal remains an important energy fuel, it has lost important markets over the last decades. Coal has ceased to be a part of transportation. Coal's use in home heating is greatly reduced from 1900 or even 1950. Coal's primary uses today are for industrial processes and for the generation of electricity. Coal burning, however, can often be the most environmentally damaging of the fossil fuel uses. Lastly, coal's bulk makes it the most expensive fuel to transport. Transporting coal from the mine to the power plant at which it is burned often costs as much as the coal.

In certain situations, it may be economical or essential to convert coal to a petroleum or gas product. In World War II, Germany met its petroleum needs by deriving petroleum liquids from coal. South Africa has experimented with similar technologies. United States efforts to stimulate a synthetic fuels industry have failed for economic reasons. The cost of producing the synthetic gas or petroleum from coal is more expensive than the extraction and production of petroleum or natural gas.

The nuclear process is a fourth source of energy. The primary peaceful use of nuclear energy is to generate large amounts of electricity. The raw material of nuclear energy is uranium oxide, which is mined in the United States, Russia, Zimbabwe, South Africa, Australia, and Canada. Most United States uranium mining has been carried out in Colorado, New Mexico, Utah, Texas, and Wyoming. The raw uranium oxide is processed into nuclear fuel that can power a nuclear reactor. The controlled nuclear reaction is desired for the same reasons the combustion of hydrocarbons is desired—to produce heat. The splitting of atoms (fissioning) in the reactor produces enormous amounts of heat. The heat produces steam to turn a turbine that runs an electric generator. About 20 nations have nuclear electric generating plants. Among the major nuclear consumers are the United States, Russia, Japan, France, the United Kingdom, Germany, Canada, and Sweden.

The fifth energy source is hydro-power—the energy content of falling water. Hydro-power is used today for electrical generation. Hydro-power projects range from small run-of-the-river installations to giant multipurpose projects such as Grand Coulee, Hoover, or Glen Canyon Dams. The United States, Russia, and Canada are the largest hydro-power producers. Norway, Sweden, France, Brazil, and China also have significant production. Brazil and the Scandinavian countries rely on hydro-power for a major contribution to total energy needs. In the United States, the Pacific Northwest and the Tennessee Valley have relied on hydro-power for substantial electric generation.

Despite ambitious predictions in the 1970s, alternative and renewable fuels will provide only a small percent of United States energy use in the year 2000. For all the discussion of exotic new fuel sources, wood burning may be the most used of the alternatives today. The limited present use of alternatives should not discourage their study by policy makers and lawyers. Solar, geothermal, and fusion power have the potential to supply significant portions of world energy needs. Economic, environmental, or political changes may push these technologies to the forefront within the lifetime of the readers of this book.

All of the primary energy sources are useful in the production of that most valuable secondary source, electricity. An electric power plant converts mechanical energy into electrical energy. The electricity is produced by an electric generator which works on the basic principle that an electrical conductor, e.g., a copper wire, will develop a flow of electricity if moved through a magnetic field. All electric generators use conductors that rotate in the magnetic field so that a rotational force is required for an electric generator to function. The rotational energy required is supplied in all large modern electric power plants by turbines whose shafts are usually directly coupled to the shaft of the generator. In large power plants the turbines which turn the generators are driven either by steam (coal, oil, or gas fired plants or nuclear plants) or by moving water (hydroelectric plants). In small power plants, or those made to be portable, the rotational energy may be supplied by an internal combustion engine, or perhaps by a windmill.

The voltage of an alternating current can be stepped-up or stepped-down by means of transformers. These highly efficient devices are used to raise (step-up) the generator output voltage for transmission over long distances. Other transformers at sub-stations or at the place where the electrical power is to be used then step-down the voltage to that which is required. The high voltages on the transmission lines are used to reduce transmission losses.

The electric power distribution grid is a complex system of generating facilities, transmission lines, control devices, protective equipment, and transformers. Such grids are commonly interconnected among generating points so that electric power from several generating stations can be fed into a distribution grid.

Energy law and policy are rich in predictions and projections. What will be the price of petroleum in 2005? How many new electric generating plants will be needed to supply customers in 2010? How much petroleum remains in Texas? In dealing with projections and predictions related to energy, certain usages must be borne in mind. The terms "resource" and "reserve" are incorrectly used interchangeably. A mineral "resource" is an accumulation of naturally occurring solid, liquid or gaseous material in the earth that has been found by exploration (such as drilling) or is surmised and which may become available for use if economically or legally obtainable. Mineral "reserves" are resources which are known and can now actually be legally and economically extracted. The status of a "resource" may change to a "reserve" depending on technology of extraction, market price, legal restraints, and environmental factors. For example, coal may be a reserve in some areas only if it is within 3000 feet of the surface.

This distinction is particularly significant when dealing with the many published predictions and projections of resources and needs. Estimates of "reserves" may be based on present market value or technology. Hence, they are suspect when used for prediction. "Resource" estimates, if accurate, indicate total ultimate availability. The bias of the predictor should be considered in examining such projections.

V.   THE BUSINESS OF ENERGY

Our examination of energy sources and uses has so far ignored how we get from raw material (the coal in the ground, the petroleum under the seabed, the water falling in a river) to the useable product (the gasoline for the tank, the electricity to run the air conditioner). Much of energy law and policy are influenced by the nature of the raw resources and the nature of the industries that have developed to move the product from natural state to consumer.

For all of the resources we have discussed, use of the raw material requires a number of steps. These are discovery, extraction, refining or other processing, transportation, and distribution. In addition, law or policy may require the elimination of the undesirable side effects (e.g., air pollution, disrupted land surfaces) of any of these steps.

Discovery involves the recognition that a resource is valuable, its identification and location, and usually an estimation of the amount present. Burning wood to produce heat has been used since the dawn of civilization. Knowledge of controlled nuclear fission is a product of the 20th century. An appreciation of the energy content of falling water would persuade a lay person that the Colorado River was an energy source. Substantial scientific and technical skill was needed to discover oil and gas in the North Sea and on the Alaska North Slope.

A second step is extraction of the resource. In familiar terms, this is the mining of the coal or uranium, the operation of the oil and gas well, or the construction and operation of the hydroelectric dam and power plant. Two generalizations cut across all industries. First, extraction makes substantial demands on property rights. Often, property uses (e.g., farming, ranching, recreational use) have been established well before energy resources were discovered. Rich coal seams may underlie valuable farming land. Offshore oil and gas development may conflict with fishing areas. These intrusions may require the law to resolve land use conflicts. Second, the extraction activities commonly tend to be expensive and demand a large investment before usable energy is returned—if it ever is. Coal mining equipment, oil and gas production platforms, nuclear reactors, and hydroelectric dams and facilities can be multimillion or billion dollar ventures.

A third step is refining and processing the raw material. The crude oil extracted from the ground cannot power an automobile. Raw uranium oxide would not fuel a nuclear electric generating plant. Despite our references to the five energy raw materials (coal, petroleum, natural gas, nuclear power, hydropower), there are great varieties within individual fuels. Not all coal or crude oil is identical. Chemical and physical variations may make significant differences in the cost of preparing a product for end use and in the end use of the product. For example, pollution standards limiting sulphur content of fuel may give a substantial advantage to a low sulphur coal or crude oil. The refining stage will remove product impurities and prepare the raw material for its end use. The nuclear process requires several processing stages. The modern petroleum refinery may separate crude oil into a number of different end products. As with raw material extraction, refining and processing operations may be costly.

A fourth step involves the transportation of the product from its source to the place of end use. Mankind is at nature's mercy. The richest petroleum reserves in the world are located in a sparsely populated area thousands of miles from major petroleum consuming nations. Superb hydroelectric sources are typically a great distance from electricity users. Western United States coal may be chemically superior to eastern coal, but it is burdened with expensive transportation costs. Clearly, there are options in transportation. Should Saudi Arabian crude oil be refined in Saudi Arabia or shipped to distant refineries? Should an electric generating plant be located next to the coal mine or next to the population center that will eventually consume the electricity? Economics, technology, law, and politics all play a part in these decisions.

A fifth step is the sale of the processed and transported product to the eventual consumer. The consumer may be an individual homeowner, a major private manufacturer, or some arm of government. Often several distributors may handle the product before it is consumed.

A final factor in assessing energy processing and use are the undesirable side-effects. Every energy use causes some harm to the natural and human environment. Energy industries have given rise to some of the most prominent pollution in American society and in consequence have helped to create much of American environmental pollution law. The popular reaction to the Santa Barbara and Exxon Valdez oil spills, Appalachian strip mining, Three Mile Island, and smog over major cities has forced energy industries to internalize many of the negative aspects of their products.

In the United States, private enterprise plays the major role in most of the energy exploration, production, processing, and sale decisions that we have discussed. Most Americans purchase their electricity, motor gasoline, and natural gas from a private corporation whose objective is to return a profit to its shareholders. At different times and for different reasons in American history, national, state or local governments have undertaken some of the work in distributing the energy products. Government remains the owner of major reserves of fossil fuel in the Western United States and under the offshore Outer Continental Shelf. Government has built hydro-electric facilities. Government has been involved in the processing of nuclear fuel. Government has also chosen to be involved in the production, transmission, and distribution of electric energy.

In addition to an ownership role, governments regulate the workings of the energy markets in a variety of ways. Much of this text will examine the reasons and the consequences of governmental involvement in the workings of the market. The most extensive regulation has been in the context of government regulation of the energy public utility. Large segments of the natural gas and electric energy industries have seen government as an active participant in making such traditional business decisions as which customers are to be served, what investment shall be made in the business, and what price shall be charged for the service. A major topic for energy law and policy over the past two decades has been the degree to which the industries should be "deregulated" in the expectation that market competition will better distribute scarce resources than would government mandate. However, even in a substantially more deregulated energy economy, government will likely continue to set and enforce standards for environmental pollution, consumer protection, and worker health and safety.

The last two decades have seen a worldwide growth in the operation of energy businesses by private, for-profit businesses. The collapse of the Communist economies of the former Soviet Union and Eastern Europe removed a substantial portion of government run energy businesses from the world economy. But, just as significant has been the movement away from government ownership in many western democracies including our close legal ancestor, the United Kingdom. British privatization of energy industries has been followed by many other countries.

Private enterprise in energy has become increasingly multinational. The most visible examples are the major multinational oil companies. These corporations like Exxon, Shell, and British Petroleum operate globally. Their wealth exceeds that of most nations in the world. They are integrated in most phases of energy activity. Their employees include petroleum geologists, drillers and well operators, refiners, and sales personnel for the refined products. The major multinationals increasingly are diversified over several energy resources. "Oil" companies will own coal, natural gas, and uranium reserves. They may be involved in research and development in alternative fuel sources.

While giant multinationals dominate the news in the energy industries, energy businesses can also be small "mom and pop" operations. Generalizations about an energy "industry" need to be attentive to the different types of businesses that are a part of it.

Subsequent chapters will elaborate on the matters discussed in this Introduction. For now, it should suffice to say that the energy lawyer will need a familiarity with technology, economics, and politics as well as law. Additionally, the energy lawyer's work is increasingly likely to cross national boundaries in the 21st Century. The cross-disciplinary and cross-boundary nature of energy law are what help to make it a fascinating field of study and work. ❦

CHAPTER TWO

Energy-Environmental Economics and Regulation

by Joseph P. Tomain

I.   INTRODUCTION

In Chapter 6, we describe the general energy-environmental policy for the United States. To better appreciate that policy, it is important to understand our mixed economy. In other words, the student of policy must understand the interaction of government regulation and markets, because it is this interaction that generates the energy and environmental policies that affect us as lawyers, politicians, policymakers and the like.

In this Chapter, we present the basics of our market economy and the economic principles underlying that economy. Further, we discuss when and why markets fail to achieve their objectives and how those failures can be corrected with government regulation. Finally, we explain the central economic and non-economic goals behind energy-environmental policies and we identify the regulatory tools employed by government to achieve those goals.

II.   THE REGULATORY PROCESS[1]

Making public policy in the United States is a tricky enterprise.[2] The principal difficulty is to separate a lay understanding of policy from the political reality of it. A lay understanding is that public policy is a series of purposive actions to achieve an articulated goal. In other words, a policy is

---

[1]*See generally* Joseph P. Tomain & Sidney A. Shapiro, *Analyzing Government Regulation*, 49 ADMIN. L. REV. 377, 385-389 (1997); *see also* Sidney A. Shapiro & Joseph P. Tomain, REGULATORY LAW AND POLICY (2d ed. 1998).

[2]*See, e.g.*, David L. Weimer & Aidan R. Vining, POLICY ANALYSIS: CONCEPTS AND PRACTICE (2d ed. 1992); Aaron B. Wildavsky, SPEAKING TRUTH TO POWER: THE ART AND CRAFT OF POLICY ANALYSIS (1979); William I. Jenkins, POLICY ANALYSIS: A POLITICAL AND ORGANIZATIONAL PERSPECTIVE (1978); James Q. Wilson, *The Politics of Regulation* in THE POLITICS OF REGULATION (1980); Laurence H. Tribe, *Policy Science: Analysis or Ideology* 2 PHIL. & PUB. AFFAIRS 66 (1972).

articulated, then implemented. In the private sector, in a corporation for example, it may be the case that policy is set by a board and senior management, and employees are then charged with the responsibility to implement that policy.

Public policy, especially in a market-oriented democracy, works differently. It is an easier task to describe policy as the outcome of the regulatory process rather than as a set of pre-determined goals to be achieved. Another way of putting this distinction is that in a centrally planned economy, policy is articulated by government officials and agencies are required to carry out those policies.[3] Because there is no central planning in the United States, public policy is the outcome of a series of decisions made by several public and private institutions and actors. Most significantly, public policy is the consequence of the interaction of government and market.

A simple description of the regulatory process involves the intersection of law, politics, and policy and can be graphically depicted. The law circle encompasses the Constitution, as well as statutes, regulations, and judicial decisions. These are discussed in Chapter 3. The politics circle denominates the partisan, interest group influences that compete for attention in legislatures. And, the policy circle represents the rational, often empirical, arguments made to support particular policy or political positions. The shaded area constitutes valid public policies. In other words, a policy proposal must be supported

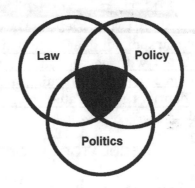

Figure 1: Regulatory Variables

by law, sustained by policy arguments, and satisfy partisan politics. Otherwise, it will not survive the policymaking process.

The basic understanding of public policy is that it emanates from administrative agencies. This basic understanding is partial, however. A better understanding of public policy incorporates the interaction between agencies and the legislature as well as judicial review of the actions of both branches. Simply stated, agencies cannot act without legislative authoriza-

---

[3]*See, e.g.*, Daniel Yergin & Joseph Stanislaw, THE COMMANDING HEIGHTS: THE BATTLE BETWEEN GOVERNMENT AND THE MARKETPLACE THAT IS REMAKING THE MODERN WORLD, chs. 5 and 6 (1998).

tion. Most frequently, legislatures pass broad statutes directing an agency or agencies to act. In short, the legislature sets the general policy objectives and the agencies "fill in the details." The reason why legislative action does not fully constitute public policy is because individual legislative action most often only addresses a part of a social problem. The Clean Air Act Amendments, as an example, affect electric utilities but say nothing about retail wheeling which requires further legislation. Thus, at one level, public policy is the product of the interaction between a legislative allocation of authority and its implementation by administrative agencies.

A refinement of Figure 1 shows public policy in the legislature as the product of the interaction of politics, policy, and constitutional law (see Figure 2 below). The politics circle represents legislative proposals that have political support. The policy circle represents those regulatory alternatives for which rational policy arguments can be made. The constitutional law line prevents the adoption of some alternatives (those below the line) that have political support but lack constitutional authority. As an example of an invalid legislative decision, policymakers, producers, and consumers may all favor a more competitive electric power industry. However, the Fifth Amendment takings clause limits government's ability to undermine prior private investment decisions made

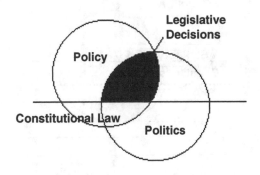

Figure 2: Legislative Decisions

with the approval or encouragement of the government. The treatment of such "stranded costs" may give rise to constitutional questions needing resolution by the United States Supreme Court.[4] Legislative proposals must fit into the overlap between the policy analysis and politics circles in order to be held valid.

Figure 3 depicts the relationship of policy, politics, and statutory and constitutional law in administrative agencies. As in the legislature, an agency's regulatory decisions are influenced by the interaction of law, politics, and policy. An agency, however, has less discretion to react to these influences than does a legislature because its enabling statute prevents it from adopting some regulatory alternatives that have policy and political support. For example, the economic climate might be such that electricity

---

[4]*See, e.g.,* J. Gregory Sidak & Daniel F. Spulber, DEREGULATORY TAKINGS AND THE REGULATORY CONTRACT (1997).

or natural gas rates could be allowed to float to the market price without federal oversight. However, both the Federal Power Act[5] and the Natural Gas Act,[6] require that rates be set by the Federal Energy Regulatory Commission at "just and reasonable" levels. Thus, a valid policy decision is one that satisfies constitutional and statutory law and that has political and policy support. These decisions are located in Figure 3 in the intersection of the policy and political circles that is located above the two legal baselines established by statutory and constitutional law constraints.

Finally, an agency's capacity to act is affected by its institutional framework, which includes legal constraints, but more generally consists of the institutional arrangements, capacities, and incentives present in any administrative environment. Agency decisions will be affected by such non-legal factors as institutional routines, agency agendas, presidential politics, congressional oversight, bureaucratic culture, professional training, and agency resources. Due to limited resources, for example, the Environmental Protection Agency is incapable of cleaning up all identified hazardous waste sites.

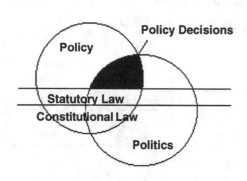

Figure 3: Policy Decisions

The regulatory process model depicts the interaction of the variables and reveals certain patterns. All proposals must satisfy the legal baselines. Further, the policy and politics variables interact in certain ways. When a final proposal makes strong policy sense, there is a powerful inference that it is the product of a deliberative process rather than interest group politics. Alternatively, when the policy rationale is substantially weak, the lack of a rationale supports the conclusion that a program is the result of political behavior. Most policies, however, fall somewhere in between these extremes. Thus, public policies are determined by the efficacy of the policy evidence, the political feasibility of the supporting arguments, including the impact of institutional influences, and the limitations of legal authority. Therefore, in order to

---

[5]Federal Power Act, 16 U.S.C. § 824d(a) (1994).
[6]Natural Gas Act, 15 U.S.C. § 717c(a) (1994).
[7]Garry Mucciaroni, REVERSALS OF FORTUNE: PUBLIC POLICY AND PRIVATE INTERESTS (1995); *see generally* James G. March & Johan P. Olsen, REDISCOVERING INSTITUTIONS: THE ORGANIZATIONAL BASIS OF POLITICS (1989); James Q. Wilson, BUREAUCRACY: WHAT GOVERNMENT AGENCIES DO AND WHY THEY DO IT (1989).

make a credible policy argument either to a legislature or to an agency, that argument must have sound bases in law, politics, and policy.

III. THE LIFE CYCLE OF GOVERNMENT REGULATION

The regulatory process that we have just described indicates which variables are necessary at any point for the success of a policy proposal. The interaction of these variables is also affected by the temper of the times. Our country has experienced regulatory cycles throughout its history. There are some periods, the New Deal can be considered the primary example, during which government intervention in the private markets was very active and expansive. There have been other times during our history, such as the Reagan Revolution, in which government intervention has waned. As it happens, these regulatory periods fall into an historical pattern. Roughly every thirty years there is an expansion or contraction of government regulation.[8] Another way of describing this ebb and flow is to view government regulation as a "life cycle,"[9] which falls into six more or less identifiable stages as depicted in Figure 4. Because government regulation and private markets are so closely interconnected, the life cycle also affects and is affected by the growth and development of specific industries.[10] This interconnection is described in more detail in Chapter 6 when we discuss U.S. energy-environmental policy.

Figure 4: Life Cycle of Government Regulation

The first stage of the regulatory life cycle, the *free market*, adopts a version of laissez-faire or of limited government. During this period, government intervention is absent from a particular industry or market. It can be persuasively argued that the free market is the preferred form of

---

[8]*See* Shapiro & Tomain, *supra* note 2 at ch. 3; Arthur Schlesinger, Jr., THE CYCLES OF AMERICAN HISTORY (1986).

[9]*See* Marver Bernstein, REGULATING BUSINESS BY INDEPENDENT COMMISSION (1955).

[10]The electricity industry provides a nice example. *See* Joseph P. Tomain, *Electric Restructuring: A Case Study in Government Regulation*, 33 TULSA L. REV. 827 (1998); Robert L. Bradley, Jr., *The Origins of Political Electricity: Market Failure or Political Opportunism*, 17 ENERGY L.J. 59 (1996).

social ordering because resource use is efficient, maximized, and fairly allocated as we discuss later in this chapter. Initially, electric and natural gas utilities, as two examples, were unregulated industries and were very competitive.

If the market is functioning properly, in other words, if the market is efficient and fair, then government intrusion cannot improve the situation. In the face of a well-working market, government regulation will at least add unnecessary administrative costs, thus reducing allocative efficiency, and may cause inequitable distributions of resources.

Achieving or maintaining a free market, however, is difficult because often a necessary characteristic for a competitive market is absent. If, for example, a market comes to be dominated by a single producer, as subsequently happened in the electric industry and with natural gas pipelines, then monopoly power can be exercised with its consequent ills, a topic explained in detail below.

Stage 2 of the regulatory life cycle, then, is the recognition of a *market failure* or market imperfection such as the presence of monopoly power or of a negative externality such as pollution. This stage is the situation of a market in disequilibrium. The market is perceived as inefficient (i.e., wasteful), unfair, or both. In Stage 2, once a failure, such as a pollution externality or a maldistribution of resources, is identified, then a regulatory response from government is invited. In other words, the existence and the identification of a market failure becomes the justification for government intervention into private enterprise, thus moving regulation into the next stage.

Stage 3 is the imposition of *government regulation* or, in other words, the implementation of public policy. In order to reach this stage, a justification for government intervention must be given. Generally, two justifications exist. Government intervenes to promote economic efficiency, that is, to correct an economic market failure. Or, government attempts to promote a non-economic value, such as distributional equity. More often than not, these two justifications are mixed.

Such justifications for government intervention are necessary but insufficient conditions for government regulation, because the government must respond to the perceived market failure with the correct regulatory tool or policy. The correct form of regulation must correspond with the identified market failure. The consequence of using the wrong regulatory tool, using price supports to correct an externality, for example, may worsen a situation rather than improve it. The wrong tool may make regulation more costly or impose the costs more unfairly than the market defect. The use of an inadequate or incorrect regulation thus creates *regulatory failure*, or Stage 4.[11] A crude test of regulatory failure is if the cost of regulation outweighs its benefits.

For nearly a century, electricity and natural gas rates were set by government. In the 1970s, federal ratemaking in the natural gas market greatly disrupted the production and consumption of natural gas and is considered a classic example of regulatory failure.[12] The regulation of the electric industry is another example of regulatory failure. The traditional rate formula contributed to excess generation capacity[13] starting in the mid-1960s. When regulators tried to correct the excess, investments in utilities declined.[14] These distortions in electricity regulation complicate the current restructuring of the industry.[15]

There are two possible reactions to regulatory failure. In the last two stages of the life cycle, government can respond by fixing the failure through *regulatory reform* at Stage 5, such as modifying existing regulations. FERC initiatives to open access to natural gas and electricity transmissions systems are examples of regulatory reforms. Alternatively, in the sixth and final stage of the regulatory life cycle, government can extract itself from the market altogether by complete *deregulation*. Thus, by eliminating regulations, the cycle reverts back to Stage 1, the free market.

IV. ECONOMIC REGULATORY GOALS

Having described the key variables of the regulatory process and the life cycle of government regulation, it is proper to ask: What purposes or goals does government regulation serve?

As mentioned earlier, regulatory policies are based on economic and non-economic goals. In this section, we identify those goals in more detail by first presenting the economic goals and the market operations that are intended to achieve those goals. Next, we present some non-economic goals.

---

[11]Stephen Breyer, *Analyzing Regulatory Failure: Mismatches, Less Restrictive Alternatives, and Reform*, 92 HARV. L. REV. 549 (1979).

[12]Stephen Breyer & Paul MacAvoy, *The Natural Gas Shortage and the Regulation of Natural Gas Producers*, 86 HARV. L. REV. 941 (1973); M. Elizabeth Sanders, THE REGULATION OF NATURAL GAS: POLICY AND POLITICS, 1938-1978 (1981); Arlon R. Tussing & Connie C. Barlow, THE NATURAL GAS INDUSTRY: EVOLUTION, STRUCTURE AND ECONOMICS (1984).

[13]Harvey Averch & Leland L. Johnson, *Behavior of the Firm Under Regulatory Constraint*, 52 AM. ECON. REV. 1052 (1962).

[14]Peter Navarro, THE DIMMING OF AMERICA: THE REAL COSTS OF ELECTRIC UTILITY FAILURE (1985).

[15]*See* Sidak & Spulber *supra* note 4.

We hasten to add that the non-economic goals are better illuminated by a discussion of the inadequacy of the economic goals. The single most important economic goal is efficiency. Efficiency can be seen either as maximizing resources or eliminating waste. Yet, even efficient markets can have harmful distributional consequences requiring government intervention for non-economic reasons. "Lifeline" telephone rates that provide essential service for customers too poor to pay the full cost of service would be an example of a non-economic regulation.

When a market works competitively, society obtains a number of important benefits. Because markets match supply and demand, they are efficient in the sense that they maximize wealth and minimize waste. Markets conserve scarce resources by moving resources to their highest valued uses. Competitive markets also reduce the surpluses and shortages of goods and services. Further, markets also stimulate firms to lower costs and engage in technological innovation. In a perfectly competitive market, no consumer will pay more money for a product or service when the same product or service is being sold at a lower price. By reducing costs, however, a firm can gain additional business if it can charge less than its competitors. Moreover, if a firm can produce a new product, or improve a product, it has the opportunity to increase its sales. Consumers will be willing to pay more for the new or improved product because it is not identical to other similar products. In this way, producers maximize market share. In short, competitive markets maximize consumer satisfaction and producer profits.

Another way of stating this advantage is to say that a perfectly competitive market maximizes social wealth. The market is able to accomplish this feat because it produces a *consumer surplus*. Consider Figure 5A. At the equilibrium price (P), many consumers are able to purchase a product for less money than the maximum price they would be willing to pay for it. Consumers have different preferences for a product, and some persons will pay more for it than others will pay. The demand curve reflects this reality. At higher prices, that is, along line A-E, there are consumers willing to pay more than P for a good. This means that all of those persons who are willing to pay more than P get a benefit. They can

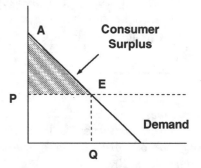

Figure 5A: Consumer Surplus

spend or invest the money that they would have paid for the product if it had cost more than P. Thus, competition generates a consumer surplus by lowering the price that many consumers have to pay to less than the maximum price that they are willing to pay for a good. In Figure 5A, this *consumer surplus* is represented by the large triangle (A-E-P).

Similarly, *producer surplus* is created when there are producers willing to supply goods to a market below the equilibrium price. Just as there is a range of consumers willing to pay more than the equilibrium price, there is

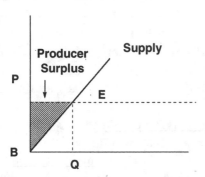

a range of producers willing to put goods on the market below the equilibrium price along the line B-E. Perhaps an individual producer's costs are lower or something happened in the market to increase the value of a producer's existing stock. The total producer surplus from these goods is represented in Figure 5B by the shaded triangle (B-E-P).

Figure 5B: Producer Surplus

The trick of the competitive market is to maximize both producer surplus and consumer surplus. Similarly, it is the economic goal of government regulation to maximize such surplus when markets fail to do so.

⟨We can understand how competitive markets achieve their benefits and maximize consumer and producer surplus through economic analysis.⟩ Economic analysis involves first, defining economics; second, identifying basic economic assumptions; and, third, becoming familiar with how the market operates.

A.   Economics Defined

Economics can be defined as: "[T]he study of how people and society choose to employ scarce resources that could have alternative uses in order to produce various commodities and to distribute them for consumption, now or in the future, among various persons and groups in society."[16]

⟨Economic analysis presents a model for explaining human behavior relative to the acquisition and transfer of resources, particularly resources which can be traded in a hypothetical perfectly competitive market.⟩It is a useful tool for understanding the production, distribution, and consumption of scarce natural resources and for illuminating questions about energy goals or purposes. Economic analysis also helps explain the negative environmental consequences that occur along the fuel cycle.

---

[16]Paul A. Samuelson & William D. Nordhaus, ECONOMICS 4 (12th ed. 1985).

Before reviewing the limiting assumptions economists make about human behavior, it is important to acknowledge a distinction about the statements economists make. Sometimes, and properly so, economic statements simply describe the phenomena which are being analyzed. The fact that the domestic rate of inflation rises in proportion to the rise in price for a barrel of oil is an example of a descriptive statement. When economics is used to make descriptive statements, it is called positive economic analysis. Positive analysis is what economists are trained to do.

Economists, however, also make statements which go beyond simple description and evaluate economic phenomena. The statement "oil import fees are good for the domestic economy" is an example of an evaluative statement. When economists make evaluative statements, it is called normative economic analysis.[17] The central idea behind all normative analysis (economic or otherwise) is that the analyst is making a claim about the best state of the world—the way the world should or ought to operate rather than the way the world appears to operate in fact. In other words, the normative analyst offers an opinion about what constitutes a good policy.

The distinction between positive statements and normative statements is extremely significant. An economist is specially trained to make technical, positive statements about economic activities. An economist is *not* trained in any special way to make normative statements about economic policy—that is the role of the policy analyst or politician. Put slightly differently, from a technical standpoint, an economist is no better situated to assess or evaluate energy-environmental policy than a lawyer.

From an economic perspective, there are two broad normative categories into which energy-environmental laws or policies can be assigned. First, it can be said that a good energy-environmental law or policy is one which maximizes wealth or is efficient. Or, it can be said that a good energy-environmental law or policy is one which results in a fair distribution of wealth or resources or is equitable. These normative categories of efficiency and equity may facilitate energy-environmental policy discussions at a general level. They may also be supported (or criticized) with technical, positive economic data. Still, it is extremely important to distinguish these statements from positive economics which describes how wealth and resources are or will be distributed in fact, not whether the resulting distribution is good or bad.

---

[17]Joseph E. Stiglitz, ECONOMICS 21-23 (2d ed. 1997).

B.   Economic Assumptions

Economic analysis operates on specific assumptions to make its model work. This section explores three of those assumptions. First, specific characteristics of property are identified. Second, this section looks at an assumption economists make about human behavior, specifically, that people are rational maximizers of their individual self interest. Third, the characteristics of the free market are noted. Later in the chapter, when the assumptions are relaxed, this preliminary analysis helps identify market imperfections which often require government regulation to correct.

1.   *Property*

One undeniable aspect of the human condition is that we live in a world of scarce natural resources. Scarcity exists when human desires are greater than the availability of the means to fulfill them. Economics, as noted, is the study of how humans make choices in a world of scarcity. Another way of discussing the economic allocation and distribution of scarce resources is by talking about property rights.

Economic analysis works best when the traditional notions of private property prevail. Traditionally, private property has attributes of completeness, exclusion, and transferability. In other words, the traditional concept of private property means that the full range of property rights and duties can be defined fully (completeness); property owners can keep others from using their property (exclusion); and, property interests can be moved easily from one person to another (transferability). These property attributes can be illustrated by reference to a mined ton of coal. The owner of the mined ton of coal knows the precise amount of the resource, can legally prevent others from using the coal, and can transfer or sell it to another person. All natural resources are not so easily treated, however.

In important respects, some natural resources have characteristics that distinguish them from traditional notions of private property as defined above. No one, for example, owns solar power, air, or water in the same way that someone owns a ton of coal. Consequently, it is difficult to define completely someone's property rights in these resources. Because ownership in solar energy, air, and water cannot be defined clearly and they are much more freely open to use by many consumers, they are what economists call public goods. It is difficult to exclude consumers from using public goods and they cannot be priced accurately. As a result, public goods are frequently undervalued and overconsumed. In other words, public goods are inefficiently utilized in an unregulated market.

Oil and natural gas in the ground, as other examples, are impossible to measure accurately, are depletable, and are increasingly costly to produce. Further, because they are migratory resources, it is also difficult for one property owner to exclude another from capturing the benefits of these natural resources. In fact, because of these defects, such fugacious resources, without government intervention, will be overconsumed resulting in a Tragedy of the Commons,[18] i.e., the inefficient depletion of a resource. The inability to exclude other users means that ownership of that resource is incomplete and that the full, efficient use, and fair distribution of these resources may not be accomplished by a free market. Government regulation is used to overcome the property rights defects in natural resources which result in inefficient uses and unfair distributions.

2. *Individual-Rational-Maximization*

Economic analysis assumes that voluntary exchanges take place between individual self-interested actors in orderly markets for the purpose of maximizing wealth. There are two general classes of actors on the market stage—consumers and producers. Economists assume that both consumers and producers are rational maximizers of their individual self-interest. Broadly put, producers will produce goods from the least costly resources available in order to maximize their profits and consumers will pay less for an item rather than more in order to maximize the use of their money. In these ways, consumer surplus and producer surplus are maximized.

This fundamental idea about *Homo Economicus* or Economic Man, that people are rational maximizers of their individual self-interest, is a significant assumption about human behavior and its limitations should be noted. One might be put off by what seems to be the selfishness and greed of the wealth maximizing motivations being attributed to people. It should be acknowledged that economic analysis does not deal with the behavior of every individual all of the time. Rather, the economist speaks generally. All people are not solely motivated by a desire to maximize wealth all of the time. Over the long run, however, it is fair to say that people tend to prefer more of something rather than less.

Another objection is that all people do not act rationally all of the time and make uneconomic choices. While this may be true, at times, for any given individual, the alternative assumption of irrational behavior over the whole range of human conduct makes any analysis unworkable and does not conform with experience. Thus, economists assume rationality.

---

[18]Garrett Hardin, *The Tragedy of the Commons*, 162 SCIENCE 1243 (1968).

A third objection frequently leveled at the rational-maximization assumption is that it takes little or no account of altruistic behavior. People certainly act in their self-interest; they also act in the interest of others despite adverse economic consequences. The objection that economic analysis disregards altruistic behavior seems right, unless one defines altruism as one person acting for the benefit of someone else because it makes the actor feel good. Such an expansive definition, however, is tautological.

Finally, the idea of consumers and producers as rational maximizers of their individual self-interest also leaves little room for a conception of collective action. If collective action is defined as action by a group of individuals whose end product is the sum of the end products of the individual actors, then there is no conflict with the economic concept of individual wealth maximization. If, however, collective action is defined as having an end product that is greater than the sum of the end products of the individual actors (synergy) then an economic model based on individual wealth maximization has nothing to say about such collective action.[19] Still, most often individuals are making choices most often for their own benefit and occasionally for the benefit of the group. Thus, the individualistic assumption seems sound.

3.   The Market

The marketplace may be viewed as the stage on which producers and consumers reveal their economic preferences and act out their desires through the mechanism of exchange. To function properly as an exchange mechanism, the marketplace stage must have certain props:

(1)   there must be numerous buyers and sellers;

(2)   there must be a large enough quantity of goods so that no single buyer or seller perceives that he or she can affect price by varying either the quantity demanded or supplied;

(3)   the product must be homogenous;

(4)   there must be accurate and complete product information for buyers and sellers; and,

(5)   there must be freedom of entry and exit from the marketplace.

With the stage thus set, market exchanges among consumers (buyers) and producers (sellers) result in an efficient allocation of resources in that goods and resources are allocated to those uses which maximize total

---

[19]*See* Lester Thurow, DANGEROUS CURRENTS (1983).

wealth. <u>In colloquial language, efficiency is the state in which the size</u> of the <u>pie is as big as it can get.</u> ⟨As an incident of a wealth maximizing strategy, the market encourages the optimum use of resources by moving resources to their most valued uses.⟩ Electricity, for example, will be generated from coal rather than nuclear power when it is cheaper to burn coal. ⟨Furthermore, the market encourages innovation as an adjunct of allocating resources to their highest and best use.⟩ The increased contribution of co-generation to the supply of electricity is an example of a technological innovation.

These several ideas: <u>that economic analysis employs simplifying assumptions about the world and about human behavior; that it can</u> be <u>applied descriptively (positively) or evaluatively (normatively); and, that it</u> can be used to derive statements about wealth maximization (efficiency) or fair distribution (equity) are fundamental to understanding public policy discussion.

<u>These ideas become operational in markets to which we now turn.</u> ⟨First, the basic microeconomic operations of the perfectly competitive market are described.⟩ Then the market is examined more closely for flaws. <u>The closer examination reveals that there are imperfections in real markets.</u> ⟨These imperfections are referred to as market failures and a general list of market failures is presented.⟩ Next, <u>it will be seen that the presence of a market failure serves as a justification for government intervention.</u> We, therefore, discuss the regulatory tools that government uses to correct those failures.

C.   Market Operations

If one imagines the trading floor of the New York Stock Exchange or a shopping center during the holiday season, then markets may appear to be disorganized, chaotic places. This inference would be mistaken. Instead, markets which exhibit the above characteristics are orderly, obey the laws of demand and supply, and attain economic efficiency. The following market operations explain how and when efficiency is achieved.

1.   Demand

<u>There is one irrefutable (and unprovable) assumption which underlies the concept of demand. As a matter of human behavior, the more one has of a good the less another unit of the good is valued.</u> That is, the more one has of a good, the less one is willing to pay for an additional unit of the same good. Having purchased 15 gallons of unleaded gasoline for $1.00 per gallon, a rational wealth maximizing consumer will not pay $1.25 for an additional

gallon unless something is wrong in the market. Occasionally, the counter example of prestige goods is suggested in which people would be willing to pay more for a good, such as an imported car, when an equivalent car can be acquired for less money. This is not a valid counter example. The economist's response is that the value of a good is what matters and a good has monetary and non-monetary values. People pay more for prestige goods because they believe that such a purchase will make them feel better, healthier, sexier, stronger, etc. Therefore, the value or price of the prestige good includes non-monetary as well as monetary attributes. Consequently, the consumption of so-called prestige goods obeys the same law of demand as the consumption of ordinary goods.

The law of demand is represented in Figure 6. Figure 6 demonstrates the law of demand by showing that at a price P_1 ($2.00/gallon), there is only a demand for a quantity Q_1 (10 gallons of gasoline). Similarly, the demand at P_2 ($.50/gallon) is Q_2 (40 gallons of gaso-line). Simply stated, consumers are willing to buy more as prices decline. Conversely, consumers will purchase (demand) less as prices increase.

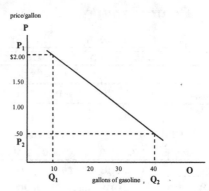

Thus, the demand curve always slopes downward and to the right because as the quantity increases, the price decreases. A more technical way of stating this phenomenon is to say that a consumer's marginal utility decreases as consumption increases. The downward sloping phenomenon is true for individ-

Figure 6: Demand Curve

uals and for markets because the market demand curve is downward sloping and represents the aggregate of many individual consumers' demand curves.

2.   *Supply*

In its simplest formulation, a supply curve is the mirror image of the demand curve. Just as there is a law of demand (people pay less for additional units), there is a law of supply. As prices rise, producers are encouraged to consign (supply) more goods to the market. This behavior is shown graphically in Figure 7. Figure 7 indicates that as the price of oil rises, more oil is placed on the market. Producers are motivated to enter the market because they will find it more profitable to supply oil rather than supply some other lower-priced product.

The relationship between the price and the supply of oil can be the basis of an energy policy. If, for example, an energy policy decision is made to increase the amount of domestic oil available in the market, then

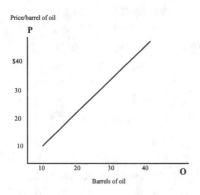

Figure 7: Supply Curve

government regulations, such as oil import fees which have the effect of raising oil prices to or above the world oil price, will result in more domestic oil being placed on the market by domestic oil producers. This scheme is beneficial to producers but not to consumers. In order to encourage domestic oil producers to increase production or to undertake new or expanded exploration of oil fields, consumers must pay the higher price for oil. After a while, however, consumers will slow their consumption in response to price rises. Thus, producers experience declining marginal productivity as consumption slows just as consumers experience declining marginal utility in their consumption of goods when prices rise.

The dramatic fall of oil prices in the 1980s after the oil price increases in the 1970s demonstrates the opposite effect on domestic oil producers. As prices fell from an excess of $30 per barrel to less than $10 per barrel, oil producers left the market and put their resources to use elsewhere. Not surprisingly, domestic oil producers, particularly independent producers, wanted the government to impose oil import fees to reverse the fall in domestic oil prices for the express purpose of keeping them in the market rather than having consumers buy less expensive foreign oil.

3. *Equilibrium*

Orderly markets operate by moving towards their equilibrium point. General equilibrium is defined as the state of the economy in which all goods and services are properly priced and there is no pressure to change conditions by increasing or decreasing supply. Partial equilibrium relates to the state of only one market. The following discussion concerns partial equilibrium.

In Figure 8, point E, where the demand and supply curves intersect, is called the equilibrium point. For a firm in a competitive market, the equilibrium point is the point at which its marginal costs equal its marginal revenue thus enabling the firm to maximize its profit. The equilibrium point also indicates the proper (efficient) price and the proper (efficient) quantity of goods to put on the market.

⟨Figure 8 represents a market in oil. In the figure, **E** indicates that 30 barrels of oil (Q_1) will be sold at $10 per barrel ($P_1$). Imagine a group of producers who want to sell oil at $20 per barrel ($P_2$). Indeed, at a price of $20 there would be 40 barrels (Q_2) supplied because the supply curve tells us that at that price producers would put that quantity on the market. If the market is at equilibrium, however, those suppliers are foolish to produce oil to be sold at $20 per barrel because at that price the demand for oil is only 10 barrels (Q_3). More to the point, in a competitive market, current demand is satisfied at $10 per barrel and individual price-taking firms cannot affect price by altering supply⟨Consequently, if producers put 40 barrels of oil on the market to be sold at $20/barrel, there would be an oversupply, or glut, of oil because it would not all be consumed. ⟩ ⟨And, by the way, those producers will go broke because they cannot sell their oil at that price because consumers in a market at equilibrium can satisfy their demand at $10.⟩

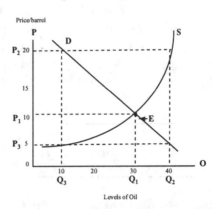

Figure 8: Equilibrium Point

Naturally, oil producers may speculate that the price of oil will rise. If the price of oil does not rise as speculating suppliers hope and they are mistaken in their gamble, then any oil placed on the market in excess of the 30 barrels demanded at $10 is surplus or waste. Similarly, it is economically irrational for producers to offer oil at $5 per barrel. At $5 ($P_3$), the demand by consumers for the product is 40 barrels but at that price producers are only willing to supply 10 barrels because that is all they can profitably produce. This excess demand for oil at $5 per barrel can be called a shortage because consumers want more oil than producers are willing to produce.

The concepts *surplus* and *shortage* are artificial and alien to pure economic analysis. In a strict, technical sense, there can be no shortage or surplus because quantity (supply) is a function of price (demand). Individual consumers will buy oil when the price is right for them. In other words, at $2.50 per gallon gasoline at the pump, people will buy less gas than when the price is $1.00 per gallon. According to economic analysis, there is no shortage of gasoline because that price simply reflects a reduced consumer demand. Likewise, when a gallon of gasoline is priced at $.50, then more gas will be consumed. Rather than label these situations as shortages and surpluses, it is more accurate from an economic standpoint to say that at $2.50 per gallon, consumers would prefer lower prices and at $.50 gallon producers would prefer higher prices.

The interaction of supply and demand (price and quantity) thus moves competitive markets toward the equilibrium point. The equilibrium point, therefore, reveals much about the market. It identifies the efficient price and quantity. Relatedly, it also identifies the efficient consumer demand and the efficient producer supply. At equilibrium, production matches consumption and profits cannot be increased by shifting resources from one good to another or from one industry to another.

4.   Costs

A market becomes unprofitable for any given producer when its costs exceed its revenues resulting in financial losses. A producer's costs determine whether the producer stays in the market. In a competitive market, if an individual producer's unit costs exceed the unit price of a good, then the producer is forced to exit the market. In essence, an individual producer's cost curve becomes its supply curve. Similarly, the cost curve for an industry is the aggregate of the cost curves of the several firms in the industry. Costs, then, are related directly to supply because the number of units sold depends on production costs.

For producers, production costs follow a law of their own. They fall for a period and then rise. This can be understood by realizing a distinction between *fixed* and *variable costs*. *Total costs* are comprised of fixed costs and variable costs. The cost of the first barrel of oil supplied by a producer equals the total costs (fixed and variable) of exploration and drilling. The cost of the second barrel is simply the additional cost (variable) of maintaining production of the already constructed well. The second and all additional barrels of oil produced from a certain well at a certain depth do not add exploration, drilling, or additional fixed costs. Thus, the cost or the price per barrel for succeeding barrels of oil falls over the life of the well as more barrels are produced because total costs are spread over more units of production. This decline in costs per barrel continues until it becomes necessary to incur additional fixed costs by drilling deeper or by drilling another well. At this point, the costs per barrel of oil begin to rise as additional fixed expenses are incurred, thus demonstrating the law of diminishing returns. The initial decrease in costs and latter increase in costs can be illustrated by the cost curves in Figure 9.

Figure 9 depicts the law of diminishing returns for two cost curves — the *marginal cost* curve (**MC**) and the *average cost* curve (**AC**). Average cost is defined simply as total costs divided by total quantity. For example, if an oil well produces 1,000 barrels of oil and it costs $18,000 to produce that oil, then the average cost per barrel is $18. If the well produces 1,001 barrels and it costs $18,019 to produce that quantity, then the average cost per barrel is $18,019 divided by 1,001 or $18.001.

Because producers must make a profit in order to stay in business, profit is included in total costs as well. A good must be priced to cover total costs including profit, otherwise the firm will sustain a financial loss. Average cost gives a simple indication whether total costs are being covered by all units of production. Average costs, however, do not accurately indicate the current costs of the resources used in the production process. For a more accurate calculation of the current cost of resources used in production, economists use the concept of marginal cost.

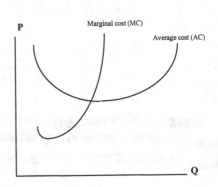

Figure 9: Marginal and Average Cost

Marginal cost is defined as the increase in total cost of production due to the last unit of output. Incremental cost is often used as a synonym for marginal cost of production. Referring back to the initial oil well example, the next barrel of oil recovered from an already producing well is less costly to produce than the barrel previously produced from that well. In this situation, the cost of producing oil at the margin (i.e., the next increment) declines. This is an example of declining marginal costs. However, if the well must be drilled deeper or if another well must be constructed, or if variable costs rise then the cost of the next marginal or incremental unit will rise.

The fact that additional money must be invested in capital construction in order to produce that next barrel is significant because it means that the costs of production are increasing and that revenues must increase accordingly in order for the oil producer to maintain the same level of profitability and, after a certain point, stay in business. If, for example, the total cost of producing 1,000 barrels of oil is $18,000 and if the total cost of producing 1,001 barrels of oil is $18,019 dollars, then the marginal cost of the last increment is $19. The oil producer should then charge $19 per barrel of oil (the producer's marginal cost) rather than average cost per barrel of $18.001 in order to maintain profitability. By relating production costs to incremental units of output, marginal costs more accurately portray the current costs of production and profitability.

Notice that in Figure 9 the two cost curves intersect. The marginal cost curve (**MC**) intersects the average cost curve (**AC**) at the latter's lowest point. This intersection of these cost curves means that if a producer prices its product based on average cost, then whenever marginal cost is greater than average cost the firm is beginning to lose money because it will be selling its most recent unit of production below the costs it incurred to produce it. The intersection of these two curves also means that as long as marginal costs are lower than average costs, the average cost curve will decline. Conversely, when marginal costs are rising, average costs will also be pulled up with them.

It is a common misconception to think that producers always price goods based on average cost. If producers did price their products in this way, then they would go out of business in the long-run since they realize negative profits when marginal costs exceed average costs. For years, federal and state rates for electricity and natural gas were based on historic average cost rather than marginal cost. Such practices caused a severe shortage in the interstate natural gas market in the late 1960s and 1970s. The practice also contributed to excess capacity in electric generation plants.

The marginal cost curve, then, becomes the individual producer's supply curve. To avoid these losses and to reflect accurately current costs, the producer should price its product based on marginal cost. These cost curves reveal the following lesson—marginal cost is a key variable to watch for profitability. Another key variable is marginal revenue.

5.   *Marginal Revenue*

Since all rational producers want to maximize their profits, they will try to sell the quantity of products having that effect. To ascertain the level of maximum profits, economists focus on *marginal revenue* rather than total revenue. It must be noted that maximizing profits does not mean maximizing total revenue. The more products a firm sells, the more revenue a firm earns. However, as the discussion of marginal and average costs indicates, the more a firm produces, the more production costs it incurs, and the more revenue it needs to cover those increased production costs. However, as our discussion of average and marginal costs demonstrated, costs will increase under certain circumstances. Profits are maximized when marginal cost equals marginal revenue. Figure 10 illustrates the relationship of revenue and profitability.

In Figure 10, column **Q** represents the number of production units sold. Column **P** is the price charged for each unit of production. Column **TR** is the total revenue and it is derived by multiplying **Q** by **P**. The **TC** column is the total costs of production of a particular number of units of production and

Q	P	TR	TC	TP	MC	MR
1	10	10	8	2		
2	9	18	10	8	2	8
3	8	24	14	10	4	6
4	7	28	16	8	2	4
5	6	30	18	12	2	2
6	5	30	20	10	2	0
7	4	28	22	6	2	-2
8	3	24	24	0	2	-4
9	2	18	26	-8	2	-6
10	1	10	28	-18	2	-8

Figure 10: Revenues and Profits

this figure is independent of the other previous variables. The **TP** column is total profits and it is derived by subtracting the total costs from the total revenue. The **MC** column represents the marginal or incremental costs of producing the next unit. **MC** represents the amount of change in the **TC** column as the quantity produced is increased by one. The last column, **MR**, is marginal revenue and it measures the changes in the **TR** column as quantity is increased by one.

Figure 10 reveals that total revenue (**TR**) is not maximized simply by selling a greater quantity (**Q**). As price (**P**) declines after 6 units, total revenue is not being maximized. Rather, the maximum total revenue of 30 is reached at either 5 or 6 units of production and begins to decline with the sale of the seventh unit. From a **TR** standpoint, it literally makes no difference whether the firm produces at 5 or 6 units because the total revenue (30) is the same. However, total profit (**TP**) is maximized between those two production levels where marginal cost (**MC**) equals marginal revenue (**MR**). At 6 units of production, **TP** = 10. At 5 units of production, **TP** = 12. Therefore, profit is maximized at 5 units of production rather than at a higher quantity which would produce a higher revenue. The most profitable production level can be identified by equating marginal cost and marginal revenue. Figure 10 indicates that at 5 units, **MC** = **MR** = 2 and total profit is at its highest point at 12. The correspondence between marginal revenue and marginal cost is significant both for producers in perfect competition and for producers possessing monopoly power because it indicates the point of profit maximization for any firm.

6.   *Firm Price and Industry Price*

In competitive markets, individual firms are called price takers and they sell their products at the price set by the industry. Remember that cost lies behind a firm's supply curve and that cost helps set the market price for a good in an industry. An industry's supply curve is simply the sum of the supply curves of all the individual firms in the industry. An industry then competes for resources among other industries. The price a firm in a competitive industry charges for its product is related to the industry's cost curve as shown in Figure 11.

Figure 11A is a picture of an industry's supply (**S**) and demand (**D**) curves and the industry's equilibrium point (**E**). Notice that the industry's equilibrium point sets the individual firm's price (Figure 11B). Notice further that the individual firm's price line is horizontal. This is because in a perfectly competitive market one firm cannot change the industry's

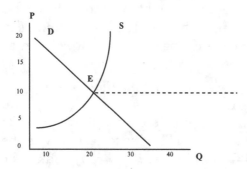

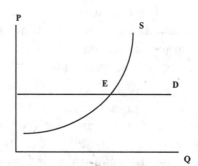

Figure 11A: Industry   **Figure 11B: Firm**

market price by definition. Thus, in Figure 11B the price line for the individual firm is set by the industry. Notice also that this line fixes the individual firm's demand curve as well as its level of marginal revenue. For an individual firm in a competitive industry, therefore $P = D = MR$. The individual firm cannot raise its prices in the hope of greater profitability because the firm will lose all of its customers to other firms in the industry. A firm may be able to lower its price, assuming that there is some cushion of profitability which there may not be, but it would be irrational for the firm to do so because in a perfectly competitive market it can sell all of its product at the prevailing market price. There is simply no need to lower price in the hope of gaining a larger market share.

The demand curve for the industry (Figure 11A) does not have this horizontal characteristic because if the prices in the industry change, then consumers will respond by buying more of the goods when the price declines or less of the goods when the price increases. In other words, consumers will move their resources from other industries in response to declining prices and to other industries in response to increasing prices. Electric utilities, for example, will switch to natural gas rather than burn coal to generate electricity when the price of coal is greater than the price of natural gas.

During the oil embargoes in the 1970s domestic oil companies were price takers at the world oil price. Integrated domestic oil companies also had their own wells which produced oil priced below the world price. As a result, such firms could charge the world price when they sold their oil to independent oil refiners while they could refine and resell their own oil more cheaply and at a greater profit.

7.   *Elasticity*

Consumers do not increase or decrease their demand evenly across all price ranges and consumers do not move all of their resources into a single industry. In fact, consumers tend to react differently to price changes in different industries. The horizontal demand curve in Figure 11B is a picture of a perfectly elastic demand. Price elasticity of demand is defined technically as the percentage change in quantity divided by the percentage change in price.

When demand is perfectly elastic, then any change in price produces an enormous shift in demand. The individual firm that raises its price above the industry price eventually goes out of business because consumer response is to stop buying that individual firm's products because they have equally satisfying goods available to them at lower price elsewhere. Imagine a street intersection with four gas stations each charging $.90 per gallon of gasoline with the same octane rating. If one of the stations raises its price to $1.00 per gallon, theoretically, it should lose all of its customers to the other three stations. This situation is an example of perfectly elastic demand.

Perfectly inelastic demand exists when consumers take the same amount of a product regardless of the price charged. To some extent, and at different income levels, the more a product is deemed a necessity the more inelastic is the response to a price rise. Do you think that goods such as water or blood would be elastic or inelastic? As a corollary, the more of a luxury a good is perceived to be, the more elastic is the response to price changes.

A traditional example of a relatively inelastic demand has been electricity, which, in modern society, is clearly a necessary and largely indispensable product. During the 1970s, as the price of electricity rose, residential consumers either slowly moved their resources away from public utility generated electricity to better (more efficient) uses (home generators or solar power as examples) or slowly started to conserve. The electric industry's experience in recent years indicates that the demand elasticity for electricity is less inelastic than it was once believed to be.

In competitive markets, that is, those markets having the characteristics listed above, the laws of supply and demand naturally move markets to their most efficient point, the equilibrium point. However, outside forces can shift supply and demand curves. Two types of outside forces are exogenous events, e.g., changes in markets other than the one under consideration, and government regulations. We turn to both types.

8.   Exogenous Events   outside forces

In a competitive market, the equilibrium point is reached as bargaining takes place between numerous buyers and sellers. However, events external to a market can occur which may alter the market and may cause a shift in supply and demand schedules and therefore shift price and quantity. Such shifts may force producers and consumers to move resources to and from different markets or to and from different industries.

The Arab Oil Embargo of October 1973 is an example of just such an exogenous event which had notable effects in several markets. The immediate consequence of the Oil Embargo was a radical reduction in world oil production. According to the laws of supply and demand, a reduction in production has the inevitable consequence of raising prices. Consistent with those laws, oil prices quadrupled as a result of the Arab Oil Embargo. For most consumers, the price rise was felt most dramatically at the gasoline pump as they waited in lines at gas stations for gasoline supplies that were rationed by the federal government.

As the price of gasoline rose during the Embargo, consumers' desire for more fuel efficient cars also rose. Figure 12 depicts a shift in demand for compact cars which was brought about by rising gasoline prices. The price rise in the gasoline market caused a rise in demand in the small car market thus moving the demand curve for the small car market to the right from **D** to **D1**.

⟨Notice the effect of this movement on the price and the quantity of small cars — both price and quantity increase from **P** to **P1** and from **Q** to **Q1** respectively.⟩In order to avoid higher gasoline prices, more consumers bought compact cars. <u>The rise in demand for compact cars resulted in a price rise for compact cars because more consumers were willing to pay more for compact cars in the belief that higher car prices</u> would be less than the long term cost of higher priced gasoline.

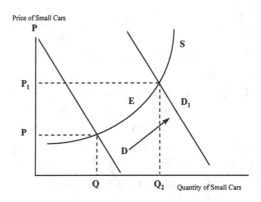

Figure 12: Demand Shift

⟨The Embargo also contributed to a shift in oil supply by reducing the quantity of available foreign oil.⟩This shift moved the supply curve to the left from **S** to **S1** as in Figure 13. When the supply curve moves in this leftward direction, the effect is to increase price from **P** to **P1** and to reduce quantity from **Q** to **Q1**.

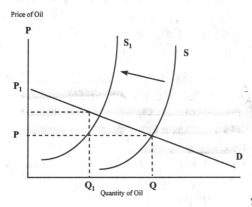

Figure 13: Supply Shift

9. Government Regulations

Think for a moment about the significance of exogenous events like the 1973 Arab Oil Embargo. ⟨The intrusion of external forces into a market can have significant effects on the price and on the quantity of products.⟩Government price regulations have similar effects. When government regulations impose price ceilings on a producer below prevailing market prices, as the government did with oil and natural gas in the 1970s, then shortages occur. ⟨A shortage is created because consumers demand more goods at restricted prices than producers are willing to produce. ⟍

<u>Figure 14 represents the situation of a price control.</u>⟨At equilibrium point (**E**), a quantity (**Q**) of goods is placed on the market at a specific price (**P**).⟩If regulators believe that **P** is too high for consumers they can restrict price with a price control setting reduced prices at **P₁**. <u>The direct conse-quences of the price control are to (1) lower prices from **P** to **P₁**; (2) re</u>duce

supply from **Q** to **Q_S**; (3) increase demand from **Q** to **Q_D**; and, consequently, (4) create a shortage from **Q_S** to **Q_D**.

Price subsidies have the opposite effect as depicted in Figure 15. Again at equilibrium the proper prices and quantities are found at **P** and **Q** respectively. If government wants to encourage supply, it can raise prices through subsidies.

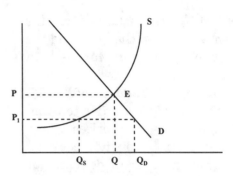

Figure 14: Price Control

In Figure 15, the subsidy has the effects of (1) increasing prices from **P** to **P_1**; (2) increasing the supply from **Q** to **Q_S**; (3) decreasing demand from **Q** to **Q_D**; and, consequently, (4) creating a surplus from **Q_S** to **Q_D**. Simply, producers supply more and consumers demand less.

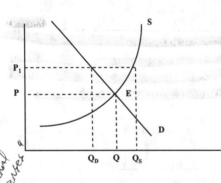

Figure 15: Price Subsidy

Eventually, the markets will respond to government regulations as they do to exogenous events by shifting the demand and supply curves to conform to price signals.

Clearly, government regulations affect the market. Not only do regulations create situations of shortage or surplus, regulations also have distributional consequences. By restricting the price of oil below the world market price, for example, billions of dollars of transfer payments were made from U.S. consumers to foreign producers because domestic oil producers could not put oil on the market and consumers bought foreign oil. The significance of this observation cannot be underestimated. Market imperfections, and changes in markets and government regulations, such as the rules implementing energy-environmental policy, have both efficiency and distributional effects. Understanding those effects is essential for evaluating the efficacy of energy-environmental laws and policies. The following section examines some non-economic rationales behind government intervention.

V.   NON-ECONOMIC REGULATORY GOALS

Chief among the non-economic goals for government regulation is the redistribution of wealth to overcome or compensate for unfair distributions.

Another problem with relying on markets to organize social relationships is that the operation of markets reflects only commodity values. It is one thing to buy and sell cars in markets, but there may be goods, such as babies, that society does not wish to see traded in markets. Because markets reflect only commodity values, they can produce results that society will consider inappropriate in terms of other preferred values such as human dignity or political representation. Society intervenes in the following contexts to conform markets to these non-economic values.

A.   Prohibited Trades

In an unfettered market economy, everything would be for sale and no activity would be forbidden. Yet, a society might object that certain market exchanges are morally objectionable and should be prohibited for that reason. For example, a market system permits the buying and selling of slaves, as long as there are willing buyers and sellers with the means to subjugate the slaves. The influence of individuals opposed to slavery depends on their financial resources and competitive positions. Drugs, prostitution, and human organ trading are all susceptible to economic analysis and can be sold in markets. The political question is: Do we prefer a society that allows legitimate markets in these goods?

If some good is to be prohibited as a matter of principle, the political system must act to limit the operation of markets. In other words, society uses regulation to prohibit some exchanges because of their morally or politically objectionable nature.

Another example of market transactions that society prohibits is trading votes for dollars. Do we want a government in which politicians freely trade their influence on a quid pro quo basis for cash?

It may be surprising to learn that there is a scholarly discipline called public choice,[20] that makes exactly that claim. Public choice theory predicts that government decisions depend on which group or groups offer the greatest rewards to legislators and administrators. The medium of exchange is the repayment of past favors or the creation of a stock of credits for obtaining future favors.

---

[20]*See* Kenneth Joseph Arrow, SOCIAL CHOICE AND INDIVIDUAL VALUES (2d ed. 1963); James M. Buchanan & Gordon Tullock, THE CALCULUS OF CONSENT: LOGICAL FOUNDATIONS OF CONSTITUTIONAL DEMOCRACY (1962); Mancur Olson, THE LOGIC OF COLLECTIVE ACTION: PUBLIC GOODS AND THE THEORY OF GROUPS (1965); Dennis C. Mueller, PUBLIC CHOICE II (1989).

The public choice model of politics is not unattractive. First, it is based upon reasonable observations that people do act in their own self interest. Second, it uses the microeconomic model which has been a very successful method in the social sciences. Third, it has certain explanatory power for the "deals" that are cut in legislatures all of the time. Finally, proponents of public choice theory admit that individuals may not always be motivated by their self-interest when they engage in politics, but they contend that relying on self-interest to explain public choices is more accurate than competing explanations.

Public choice theory has its critics.[21] The public choice perspective does not explain significant elements of the regulatory state. Industry and producer groups were unable to stop the passage of many environmental, health and safety, and consumer protection laws, and they have been unable to secure the repeal of these laws. They have also been unable to stop deregulation efforts in the airline, trucking, banking, and telecommunications industries that disfavored them, or to prevent some unfavorable tax legislation.

B.   Elimination of Price as the Basis of Trades

The distribution of wealth in a society determines which persons will acquire scarce goods and services. When goods or services are in scarce supply, many people are unable to buy them because of their high price. Society may regard this result as inequitable when certain goods or services are involved. Some regulatory programs involve replacing the allocation of scarce goods or services by markets with government allocation. For example, the government prohibits a market in which organs for transplantation would be bought and sold, and relies instead on health care providers to determine who is to receive such organs. Otherwise, human organs would go to the highest bidder and the wealthy can always outbid the poor. When gasoline or natural gas shortages appeared in the 1970s, government regulations set priorities and allocated these products based on need rather than on the desire to horde or the ability to pay.

---

[21]See, e.g., Jerry L. Mashaw, GREED, CHAOS & GOVERNANCE: USING PUBLIC CHOICE TO IMPROVE PUBLIC LAW (1997); Donald P. Green & Ian Shapiro, PATHOLOGIES OF RATIONAL CHOICE THEORY: A CRITIQUE OF APPLICATIONS IN POLITICAL SCIENCE (1994); Daniel A. Farber & Philip P. Frickey, LAW AND PUBLIC CHOICE: A CRITICAL INTRODUCTION (1991).

C.   Redistribute Wealth

The previous reason for regulation objects to market allocation because it is unfair or inappropriate to allocate a good or service on the basis of price in light of the distribution of wealth. Other regulatory programs seek to remedy the distribution of wealth produced by the operation of markets.

Some persons will prosper in a market economy, but others will not. A person may need food to survive, but if he or she lacks resources, he or she will go hungry. The market system will not recognize a person's needs without resources. By comparison, a rich person may want a third automobile. Even though that person can only drive one car at a time, the market will recognize the person's wants, because the person has the money to purchase the automobile. Thus, even an efficient market system can produce a distribution of wealth that a majority of citizens find unsatisfactory because some people are too poor to live a humane existence. Welfare and related programs reflect a collective judgment that a just society does not relegate the poorest of its citizens to conditions of degradation and despair. When utility rates were rising more rapidly than previously experienced, state utility commissioners set lifeline rates for the poor and elderly. These minimum rates were subsidized by other classes of consumers.

D.   Promote Collective Values

Some forms of regulation seek to promote collective values which a society wishes to protect and cultivate. (By comparison, an economist assumes that the aggregation of individual market decisions by consumers results in the best use of resources for the community.) For example, if no market defects are present, the economist would permit markets to determine the use and distribution of basic and valuable resources, such as air, water, and mineral rights.

Many who object to relying on markets to define resource use believe that there are some things or states of affairs that are intrinsically valuable and deserve to be protected irrespective of whether they are immediately useful or valuable.[22] For example, some laws seek to protect natural resources because market exchanges only reflect the preferences of today's consumers. The protection of endangered species reflects this commitment. So do laws protecting natural areas from environmental degradation that

---

[22]Janna Thompson, *A Refutation of Environmental Ethics*, 12 Envt'l Ethics 147, 148 (1990).

is impossible or extraordinarily expensive to repair. Laws protecting cultural artifacts or historic sites have the same motivation.

Market exchanges reflect short-term phenomena and, as *Homo Economicus* shows us, they look to the individual actor's satisfaction. Environmental protection and natural resource preservation are not short-term. Rather, they are intergenerational. Further, the benefits of saving the environment and resources may not be readily quantifiable.[23] It may take years or a generation or more to glean benefits from medical research in the Rain Forest. As such, microeconomic market theory has little to tell us about long-term phenomena.

VI. MARKET FAILURES

In the United States, the competitive market is the preferred method of social control. According to economic theory, competitive markets establish efficient quantities and prices for goods as the discussion of supply, demand, and equilibrium showed. The market, its proponents extol, is also consistent with the American spirit of liberty and individualism. No central planning office decides what producers produce or what consumers consume. Instead, allocation decisions are made through voluntary market exchanges. Market exchanges are sustained by the dollar where each dollar has an equal vote in the marketplace—one dollar, one vote. Race, gender, religion, or national origin are irrelevant in the free market because prices and quantities of goods are determined by a person's willingness to pay. This is to say that consumers and producers are measured by their dollar votes, not by their race, gender, religion, or national origin. Thus, the market maximizes individual choice just as it maximizes individual wealth. Additionally, the market by giving accurate price signals encourages innovation because producers are aware of which resources are ripe for investment and those resources, including capital, move to their most productive markets. Therefore, the virtues of the market, in the idealized form just given, include liberty, equality, opportunity, and innovation as well as economic efficiency.[24]

One does not have to venture too far into political theory to realize that the caricature of the market as the preferred method of social control does not reflect reality. For example, the one-dollar, one-vote marketplace equation assumes that every consumer vote is equal. This equation ignores

---

[23]Mark Sagoff, THE ECONOMY OF THE EARTH (1988).

[24]Milton Friedman, FREE TO CHOOSE (1980); CAPITALISM AND FREEDOM (1982); Frederick A. Hayek, THE CONSTITUTION OF LIBERTY (1960); THE ROAD TO SERFDOM (1994).

the distribution of wealth. Simply, wealthy persons have more votes than poor persons. To summarize, the market can achieve its economic benefits if its assumptions are sound and if its operations run smoothly. The reality is, however, that market defects abound.[25] A market defect becomes a justi-fication for government intervention. We examine those market defects and justifications in this section.

We earlier noted that government intervenes in markets for economic (efficiency) and non-economic (equity) reasons.[26] Economist Richard Musgrave[27] has said that government intervenes in markets for three reasons. First, the government may wish to smooth out business cycles such as recessions, depressions, or the stagflation of the 1970s. At this level, government uses Keynesian macroeconomic controls, such as expanding or contracting the supply and flow of money through changes in interest rates. This book does not address such macroeconomic controls. Second, government may want to redistribute wealth such as through a progressive income tax or a system of wage and price controls. This type of government intervention generally is referred to as social regulation and is intended to reach fair allocations and distributions of resources. Ratemaking has such distributive aspects to it. Third, the government may wish to correct market failures. Market failures can be defined as the inability of the market to allocate or to distribute resources efficiently. This type of government intervention generally is referred to as economic regulation.

Energy-environmental laws and policies generally are intended to accomplish either or both of Musgrave's last two objectives and can be seen as both economic regulation and non-economic or social regulation. First, as economic measures, energy-environmental laws and policies are intended to mimic the free market model by repairing efficiency failures. Second, as social measures, energy-environmental laws and policies also have wealth distribution and other social effects.

For the most part, the following ten examples of market failure correct market inefficiencies, although there are some distributional motives for certain regulations. This list summarizes the work of Justice Stephen Breyer.[28] These instances of market failure indicate that the free market is not achieving its optimum goal and, therefore, government intervenes either

---

[25]*See e.g.*, Robert Kuttner, EVERYTHING FOR SALE: THE VIRTUES AND LIMITS OF MARKETS (1997); Cass R. Sunstein, FREE MARKETS AND SOCIAL JUSTICE (1997).

[26]Arthur Okun, EQUALITY AND EFFICIENCY: THE BIG TRADEOFF (1975).

[27]Richard Musgrave, THE THEORY OF PUBLIC FINANCE (1959).

[28]Stephen Breyer, REGULATION AND ITS REFORM (1982); *see also* Shapiro & Tomain, *supra* note 1; Anthony Ogus, REGULATION: LEGAL FORM AND ECONOMIC THEORY (1994).

to prevent inefficient outcomes or to affect preferred distributions of wealth. Notice, then, that the existence of a market failure serves as a justification for government intervention through economic and social regulation.

A.   Control Monopoly Power

In a competitive market, the equilibrium point is reached as individual price-taking firms exchange goods at prices and at quantities which promote efficiency. No one firm can cause a change in price by either flooding the market with a product or withholding supply. A monopoly market is the opposite of perfect competition. In a monopoly market, there is one producer selling a unique product and there are significant barriers to entry into that market by other potential producers of the same product. When these conditions exist, the monopolist is in a position to raise prices, reduce output, and impose a welfare loss on society simultaneously as depicted in Figure 16.

A producer in a competitive market maximizes profits when it sets its prices at the intersection of its marginal revenue and marginal cost curves (point **A**). A monopolist's marginal revenue curve (**MR**) is downward sloping and is always below its demand curve (**D**) because a monopolist by definition, cannot engage in price discrimination by selling its product to different customers at different prices. Therefore, if a monopolist lowers its price to one consumer, it is forced to lower prices on its entire output, thus reducing total revenue. Figure 16 indicates how a monopolist sets its prices.

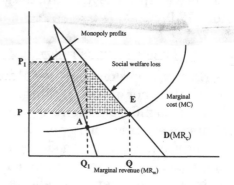

Figure 16: Monopoly Pricing

Notice that the monopolist's marginal revenue (**MR$_c$**) curve intersects the marginal cost (**MC**) curve in a different place than it intersects the demand (**D**) curve. In a competitive market, the demand and marginal revenue curves are the same and price and quantity are derived from the intersection of the **MC** and **D/MR$_c$** curves. However, the monopolist can use the intersection point of its marginal revenue (**MR$_m$**) and marginal cost (**MC**) curves to derive the price and quantity of goods for its profit maximization.

In a competitive market, goods would be priced at **P** and the quantity **Q** would be produced because **P** and **Q** are derived from the intersection of the **MC** and **D/MR$_c$** curves as the dotted lines indicate. The monopolist, however, derives its price and quantity from the intersection of its **MC** and **MR$_M$** curves at Point A, again as the dotted lines indicate. Thus, the monopolist prices at **P1** and produces the quantity at **Q1**. Notice that the result of monopoly pricing is a price increase from **P** to **P1** and quantity decrease from **Q** to **Q1**. This lower output and higher price results in monopoly profits represented by the shaded rectangle.

In addition, the dotted triangle indicates a loss of consumer surplus which is also referred to as a social welfare loss. This loss occurs because to raise prices the monopolist cuts production below the level which would have occurred in a competitive market and consumers are forced to forego consumption of the monopolized good for which their marginal benefit, represented by their willingness to pay, exceeds the marginal cost of production. In other words, there are consumers that would have been willing to buy the good along a price range from **P** to **P1** but these consumers are denied this opportunity because output has been reduced and those goods are not available for consumption. Thus, in a monopoly market consumers pay higher prices than a competitive market would dictate and they must forego some consumption opportunities. These lost opportunities are represented graphically by the dotted triangle and this loss is sometimes referred to as a deadweight loss.

Some industries are said to be natural monopolies. Utilities such as electricity, natural gas, or telephone service are often called natural monopolies because of their structure. Each industry requires large front-end capital investment in plant and equipment. Additionally, utilities are structured such that a large part of their capital investment, the distribution system, cannot be duplicated efficiently. There really is no need to run two sets of electric power lines or telephone wires into a neighborhood. Once a distribution system is established, though, it is very inexpensive, for example, to run utility lines to a single residence once the neighborhood has received utility service. Thus, after the large initial capital investment and after the distribution system is in place, it is economically efficient for one firm rather than multiple firms to provide the service.

The economic fear of natural monopoly is that competition can lead to waste. Imagine two electric utilities, which are competing to serve the same geographic market. Because it is so costly to enter the electric industry, the unsuccessful entrant will have wasted its initial capital investment because a given geographic area only needs one system of generation facilities and transmission lines to service it. Consequently, the losing competitor's capital investment is wasted. In an effort to avoid economic waste, government, often at the initiation of utilities, intervened in the electric utility industry. Governments granted utilities exclusive franchises (monopoly status) in exchange for the authority to regulate prices. Thus, through government regulation, economic waste was avoided and the exercise of monopoly power was curbed.

B.   Externalities

An externality is a production cost or benefit which is not reflected in the price of a product. If the price does not reflect all costs and benefits, then the price signal to consumers is inaccurate thus resulting in overconsumption or underconsumption of the product. Pollution is a classic example of a negative externality the cost of which is not included in the price of the product. A coal burning electric utility generates electricity as its product. It also causes air pollution. Pollution imposes costs on society and the costs must be absorbed by someone. Absent government intervention, there is no incentive for the utility to absorb pollution costs in the price of its electricity because it is cheaper to produce electricity and pollute than it is to produce electricity and install pollution control equipment. If one electric utility voluntarily installed pollution control equipment and other utilities did not, the first utility would be forced to raise prices which would reduce its profits. If the externality is harmful, as in the case of pollution, then all production costs are not reflected in the price of the product. The product is under-priced and consumers are induced to overconsume because they are receiving inaccurate, low price signals.

Externalities may also be beneficial. Research and development, for example, may result in ideas for technological improvements. However, any ideas which are not protected by patents or copyrights are disseminated to the public and the value of those ideas cannot be captured by the producer. In order to arrive at the true cost of the product, the producer must internalize the costs or benefits of the externalities. The effects of the internalization of externalities on a firm and an industry are shown in Figure 17.

The effect of forcing a firm in a competitive industry (Figure 17A) to internalize the cost of negative externalities is to reduce the firm's output from **Q** to **Q1** and thereby

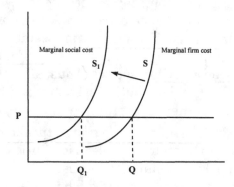

Figure 17A: Firm

lower its profits. The effect of internalization on an industry (Figure 17B) is to raise the price of the product from **P** to **P1**, and consequently, lower total industry output from **Q** to **Q1**. Government pollution regulations, through

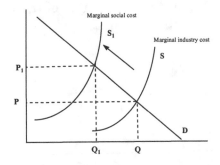

Figure 17B: Industry

standard-setting or technology-forcing as examples, make producers absorb or internalize social costs. (The difficult problem is to develop a regulation that accurately mimics what the market would do if it could force the internalization of costs.)

Negative externalities present a problem for economic analysis and for policymakers. To put it simply, there is an optimal amount of pollution that society can bear.[29] It remains for policymakers to determine where that point lies. Let us illustrate.

Imagine a coal-burning electric utility that pollutes the air. That utility's profits (marginal revenue) can be shown graphically in Figure 18. The vertical axis measures revenue, the horizontal axis measures the percentage of pollution. If the utility were forced to emit zero pollution, then its marginal revenue would also be zero (or close to it) because it would be forced to produce nothing (or close to it). If, however, there were no pollution constraints, then at 100% pollution, the utility would maximize its marginal revenue because it could produce without regard for social consequences. Therefore the **MR** curve slopes upward and to the right.

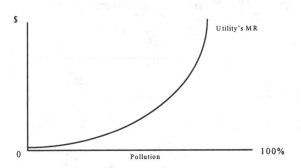

Figure 18: Utility's Marginal Revenue

Also imagine property owners surrounding the utility who are affected by the pollution generated by the utility. The value of their property can also be depicted graphically as in Figure 19. At zero pollution, the value to the

___

[29]David W. Pearce & R. Kerry Turner, ECONOMICS OF NATURAL RESOURCES AND THE ENVIRONMENT, chs. 4 and 5 (1990).

property owners is maximized. And, at 100% pollution, the value of their property moves toward zero because they suffer the costs of the pollution.

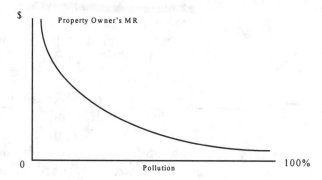

Figure 19: Property Owner's Marginal Revenue

To ascertain the optimal amount of pollution, we simply superimpose one graph on the other and the point of intersection (**OP**) is the optimal amount of pollution as shown in Figure 20.

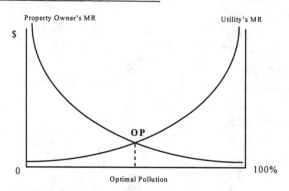

Figure 20: Optimal Pollution

Why is **OP** the point of Optimal Pollution?

The **OP** is the optimal point because a pollution level at any other point causes a social loss to be borne either by the utility or by the property owners as shown in Figure 21.

At Pollution Level One (P_1), for example, the marginal revenue to the property owners will increase from **OP** to **B**. However, the marginal revenue to the utility will recede from **OP** to **A**. Consequently, the utility will produce at **A** rather than at **OP** and there is a social loss represented by the triangle **A-B-OP** because society is denied an amount of the utility's product along the **A-OP** line.

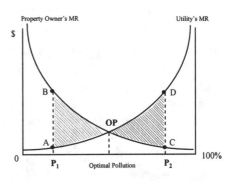

At Pollution Level Two (**P₂**), there is a shift of revenue from the property owners to the utility. As the marginal revenue to the utility rises from **OP** to **D**, the marginal revenue for the property owners falls from **OP** to **C**. The value of

Figure 21: Non-optimal Pollution

the owners' property declines along the **OP-C** line and that loss is uncompensated, thus generating a social loss represented by the triangle **OP-C-D**.

C.   Transaction and Information Costs

Transaction costs are defined as "the costs of identifying the parties with whom one has to bargain, the costs of getting together with them, the costs of the bargaining process itself, and the costs of enforcing any bargain reached."[30] Doing business by bargaining, negotiating, or litigating imposes costs on the parties which reduces the gains to be made from the transaction or trade. More importantly, the imposition of those costs on one party or the other can affect the efficiency or the fairness of the transaction.

One of the seminal articles in the field of law and economics entitled *The Problem of Social Cost*[31] argued that in a world of zero transaction costs economic factors would bargain with each other until they reached the efficient solution to their dispute. Known as the Coase Theorem, this argument has a dramatic implication for law. In short, for efficiency purposes and in a situation of zero transaction costs, the initial imposition of a legal entitlement on one party or another is irrelevant to reaching the efficient allocation of resources. Coase demonstrated that in a transaction costless world it is irrelevant whether the factory has the right to pollute or whether the property owners have the right to enjoin the pollution because the parties will bargain to the efficient solution. In short, if pollution damages are more costly than pollution control equipment, then the parties will pay the cost of the equipment. If, however, the control costs exceed the

---

[30]A. Mitchell Polinsky, AN INTRODUCTION TO LAW AND ECONOMICS 12 (1983).
[31]Ronald H. Coase, *The Problem of Social Cost*, 3 J. L & ECON. 1 (1960).

cost of pollution, then the cost of pollution will be borne by one party or the other.[32]

Needless to say, Coase caused considerable discussion in law schools[33] yet the corollaries to the Coase Theorem may be more noteworthy than the basic theorem. We do live in a world of transaction costs. And because economic actors are most often not similarly situated the initial placement of a legal entitlement has the direct effect of imposing transaction costs on one party or another and this imposition may prevent efficient bargains from taking place. In the Utility-Property Owner hypothetical above, the transaction costs to an individual property owner to challenge a utility's pollution are most likely higher than any damage the individual homeowner is likely to incur. In such a situation, transaction costs prohibit a single owner from challenging the utility. Even the transaction costs of having several homeowners organize to collectively fight the utility may be prohibitive. Therefore, bargaining may be difficult or impossible. Additionally, the imposition of the legal entitlement determines distributional issues, such as who pays whom. Government regulation can attempt to reduce or redistribute transaction costs by placing costs on those parties in the best or least costly position to avoid or absorb them.

Doing business also involves information costs. Information is often a valuable product and is an example of a positive externality. Yet, there are also often disincentives to produce that information. First, because it is a positive externality, it is hard to recoup all of the value of that information and rational economic producers are not inclined to give away information for free. Second, information can be costly to produce. Third, information may provide benefits to competitors or in the case of critical information, may harm the producers. Consequently, there are reasons not to produce information.

Yet, consumers need information to make rational economic choices and it is costly to acquire information. It is very expensive for an individual ratepayer to learn about how retail natural gas prices are set, for example.

As a matter of economic efficiency information costs should be placed on the party—consumers or producers—who can provide the information at the least cost. As a matter of policy, the government may determine either

---

[32]Shapiro & Tomain *supra* note 1 at 400-11.

[33]Guido Calabressi & Douglas Melamed, *Property Rules, Liability Rules, and Inalienability: One View of the Cathedral*, 85 HARV. L. REV. 1089 (1972); *see also* Symposium, *Property Rules, Liability Rules, and Inalienability: A Twenty-Five Year Retrospective*, 106 YALE L. J. 2091 (1997); Robert C. Ellickson, ORDER WITHOUT LAW: HOW NEIGHBORS SETTLE DISPUTES (1991).

that a certain type of information should be provided or that a certain party should bear information costs. Prohibitions against false or deceptive advertising are examples of government regulation concerning the quality of information. Gas mileage ratings on cars and electric efficiency ratings on appliances are examples of government regulations which require producers to disclose hard-to-obtain information.

Although transaction costs and information costs are inevitable, both reduce the gains to be made from trade. Nevertheless, it is important for decisionmakers to pay attention to these costs to keep them as low as possible and fairly distributed. Through economic analysis decisionmakers can learn when and how these costs can be reduced for efficiency purposes and upon whom these costs can be distributed and allocated for equity purposes.

D.   Rent Control

An economic rent is the financial return earned on a fixed supply. The term rent originally applied to land and, as can be readily seen, the supply of land is fixed. Economists have given the term a broader application and apply it to supplies other than land. During the 1973 Arab Oil Embargo, world oil production was reduced and oil prices rose. Domestic oil companies, which had available large quantities of pre-Embargo priced oil, enjoyed the rise in world oil prices because they could then sell their old oil that they had on hand to customers at the new, higher prices. The difference between the pre-Embargo price and the post-Embargo price is an example of an economic rent. Economic rents differ from monopoly rents in that the monopolist consciously raises the price of their goods because they have the market power to do so. The producer who benefits from economic rents does not necessarily have monopoly power, rather the rise in price for their stockpiled reserves can be affected by events outside their control. Domestic oil producers may not have had monopoly power during the Embargo period but they did capture economic rents when they increased the price of their previously produced or acquired domestic reserves to the world level. These domestic producers were the beneficiaries of a windfall. Government regulation is sometimes used to capture windfalls as when the Crude Oil Windfall Profits Tax of 1980[34] taxed domestic producers who raised their prices in response to the Embargo.

---

[34]Crude Oil Windfall Profits Tax, Pub. L. No. 96-223, 94 Stat. 229 (repealed 1988).

E.   Excess Competition

Excessive competition is listed as an example of market failure. This proposition is dubious, however, because excessive competition has more often been used as an argument for government regulation. The classic examples of industries employing the excess competition argument are the airline and the trucking industries. These industries sought government protection because they feared that too many entrants into their markets would erode their market shares reducing their profits. In the case of the airlines, the industry argued that excessive competition would have serious safety effects and therefore regulation was warranted. Truckers argued that national commerce would suffer from too much competition because the quality of service would erode. Similarly, utilities by asserting that they were "natural monopolies" also sought government protection in the form of exclusive franchises which eliminated other entrants into a utility's protected market. Each of these industries essentially sought restrictions on entry as well as rate relief. Justice Breyer calls the excess competition justification an "empty box"[35] because it is less an economic reason for regulation than it is a political rationalization for government protection of certain industries.

F.   Unequal Bargaining

When parties to a transaction do not have equal information or equal market power they are in an unequal bargaining situation. The most common examples of unequal bargaining occur in consumer contexts. Individual consumers often feel as if they have little or no power to negotiate the terms of their purchases. Automobile warranties, insurance policies and other contracts of adhesion put consumers at a bargaining disadvantage. The individual residential utility user is also at a bargaining disadvantage. Individual residential users do not negotiate with their utility for utility rates, nor do individual residential users have a choice of utilities among which they can choose to purchase utility service. Government regulations can attempt to equalize bargaining power by requiring administrative agencies to regulate certain industries or industry practices "in the public interest" or to designate an agency to represent the underrepresented.

---

[35]Breyer, *supra* note 28 at 29-32 and ch. 11.

G.   Rationalization

Rationalization is the imposition of uniform standards on or government control of an industry. Rationalization either can occur voluntarily such as when an industry agrees to make a uniform product such as light bulbs of uniform size and wattage or can occur through government intervention. Federal government regulation of the nuclear power industry is an example of rationalization. Through a complicated set of safety and environmental laws, the federal government attempts to regulate uniformly the construction and operation of commercial nuclear power plants. U.S. regulators, unlike their French counterparts, choose not to rationalize the types of reactors used in nuclear power plants. Instead, each utility was free to design its own reactor. As a result, construction costs grew significantly as reactor manufacturers experimented with several designs.

H.   Moral Hazard

A moral hazard is a situation in which the probability of a loss or the size of the loss may be increased because a person has less of an incentive to take precautions. This problem of moral hazard arises in all insurance cases. For example, persons with health insurance are more likely to take risks or to consume health services if someone else is paying than if they had to pay for the full cost of those health services out of their own pocket.[36] Similarly, people tend to treat themselves more lavishly when someone else pays. Such generous treatment distorts the market because true preferences are not recorded. In a sense, traditional public utility regulation is a form of moral hazard. Under the traditional ratemaking formula, utilities were encouraged to make capital expenditures knowing that those expenditures could be recouped from ratepayers. Thus, the incentive is to overspend rather than stop at the most efficient point.

I.   Paternalism

Paternalism occurs when government regulates in the belief that citizens should behave a certain way and government regulations attempt to induce that behavior. Compulsory education, government required drug testing, and proposed government sponsored prayer in schools are examples of paternalistic regulation. During the energy crisis, there was a short-lived

---

[36]Polinsky, *supra* note 30 at 54; Samuelson & Nordhaus, *supra* note 17 at 498-500.

discussion of government inspectors monitoring private thermostats so that people did not consume too much energy. Clearly, such regulation is meant to affect behavior and the not so implicit argument is that people cannot be depended upon to monitor their own use of energy.

J.   Scarcity

Scarcity exists when goods are available only in a limited supply. Most goods are scarce and must be rationed in some way. Rationing can occur through the market or through government intervention. When goods are particularly scarce, the market may be perceived as not effectively distributing goods to the places where they are thought to be most needed. At such times, government rationing rather than the market is used to allocate goods to consumers. In times of drought, or even during the oil crisis, the market was not left to allocate goods, instead goods were allocated by government. During the 1973 energy crisis, motorists were only allowed to buy gasoline every other day and government also rationed crude oil among domestic oil refiners. Another example of this sort of regulation occurred in the natural gas industry. During this period, natural gas was in short supply. The Federal Energy Regulatory Commission (FERC) required natural gas pipelines and distribution companies to file curtailment plans. These plans indicated which natural gas customers would receive reduced supplies or no supply and in what order according to a list of priorities established by FERC. Hospitals and schools, for example, would be curtailed later or less severely than industrial consumers.

VII. REGULATORY METHODS[37]

Notice the interaction between these examples of market failure and government regulation. Market failures serve as justifications for government regulation. Also notice that these individual examples of market failure are not discrete. A lack of adequate information may cause an inequality of bargaining power or serve as the reason for paternalistic intervention. It is useful, however, to identify specific market failures because once the particular failure is identified, then a particular type of regulation may best be used to correct the specific failure. If externalities present unacceptably high costs, then they can be limited through government imposed standards or taxes. If monopoly power is the market distortion, then price setting may be the appropriate response. The trick is to respond to a specific market failure with the appropriate type of

---

[37]Shapiro & Tomain *supra* note 1 at 46-48.

government regulation. Effective government regulation requires correct responses to perceived failures for both economic and non-economic reasons. Otherwise, there will be a mismatch between the illness and the cure. Efficiency or equity may suffer even more. Although regulation occurs in a wide variety of circumstances, there are only a small number of regulatory methods. Here we briefly describe five broad categories of regulatory tools. The remainder of the book will describe more specific applications of these categories.

A. Price Controls

In some circumstances the government will regulate the price charged for products or services. The most common use of price controls is in the regulation of utilities, such as electrical and natural gas distribution companies and local telephone companies. Cost of service ratemaking is the specific form of price control used in utility regulation. Price controls are also used to control the high profits (called "rents" in economics) earned by firms who control goods or services in short supply. Historically, price controls, or price ceilings, are typically used in response to rents. The government also utilizes price controls in agricultural markets, primarily through subsidies to farmers and has used subsidies to promote markets in alternative fuels known as synfuels.

B. Entry and Exit Controls

The government will also regulate the conditions of entry into or exit from a market. In utility regulation, entry and exit controls are applied to entire firms. Government regulators determine when utilities can enter new markets and when they can exit old ones. In other types of regulation, entry and exit controls are applied to individual products or services. For example, licensing is a form of entry control when nuclear power plants are licensed by the Nuclear Regulatory Commission (NRC). Nuclear plants cannot be constructed until they are approved by the NRC. The NRC also has the authority to close plants if they pose an unreasonable risk. Occupational licensing is another example of exit and entry control. Individuals cannot practice law in a state unless they are licensed to do so by a licensing board, and such boards have the authority to order an individual to stop practicing law if he or she is unfit to do so.

The control over entry and exit by government licensing has been a fertile area for deregulation, primarily in the area of the electric, natural gas, and telecommunications industries. At the same time, deregulation has created the need for additional entry controls to address bottleneck problems in those industries.

C. Standard Setting

A third regulatory tool is standard setting. It consists of the government's promulgation of a standard or a rule that has the same legal status as legislation passed by Congress or by a state legislature. Persons or firms subject to the standard have a legal duty to comply with it; they will be subject to fines, or even imprisonment, for failure to obey.

Standard setting is used in a variety of regulatory contexts. Command-and-control standards for air and water pollution and for pollution technology were routine during the 1970s. Later more flexible and market-based environmental standards have been used.

D. Allocation

Allocation refers to the distribution by the government of some benefit or entitlement. During the energy crisis the federal government ordered integrated oil companies to supply oil to independent oil refiners that were cut off from foreign supplies. The government also set priorities on which consumers were to receive natural gas and in what amount in case of a severe natural gas shortage.

E. Taxes and Other Economic Incentives

Instead of using standards to compel persons or firms to take certain actions, the government can sometimes obtain the same result by relying on taxes or other economic incentives. For example, the government could forbid a firm from emitting more than a certain amount of a pollutant. Alternatively, the government could tax the firm for emitting pollution above some minimum amount. Because taxes and other economic incentives are often discussed as potential alternatives for other forms of regulation, the possible use of this tool as part of regulatory reform is discussed in several chapters.

VIII. CONCLUSION

In this chapter we have attempted to describe how economic analysis affects public policy in the United States. In short, public policy is the result of an ongoing dialogue between government and markets. Certain generalizations can be made about the policymaking process and certain patterns of regulation can be identified as we have shown. Finally, we believe that the following graphic can be useful in understanding the remainder of the book. Earlier we have presented a list of regulatory goals and justifications for government intervention. We have also presented a brief list of regulatory methods that can be used to achieve those goals. Both are summarized in Figure 22.

To better understand why certain regulations have been imposed on energy industries or to protect the environment, it is important to identify the market failure and whether government seeks to advance efficiency or equity. Next, the analyst should determine if the regulatory tool that has been chosen accomplishes its goal. If not, are there better regulatory alternatives or should government deregulate? These issues and questions run throughout the remainder of the book. ❦

Regulatory Goals	Regulatory Methods
Address Market Failure: • Competitive Conditions • External Costs • Inadequate or Inaccurate Information • Public Goods	• Price Controls • Entry and Exit Controls • Standard Setting • Allocation • Taxes and Other Economic Incentives
Achieve Social Goals: • Prohibit Objectionable Exchanges • Eliminate Price as the Basis of Exchange • Remedy Distribution of Wealth • Subject Exchanges to Collective Values	
Figure 22: Goals and Methods of Regulation[38]	

[38]Shapiro & Tomain, *supra* note 1 at 21.

CHAPTER THREE

The Legal Framework

by Donald N. Zillman

I. INTRODUCTION

We have described the working world of energy as a series of transactions that locate, extract, refine, sell, use, and mitigate the harms of the energy raw materials (coal, petroleum, natural gas, nuclear power, hydropower, alternatives) to provide the desired energy outputs (transportation, home heating and cooling, industrial processes). The law helps decide what decisions will be made. It then facilitates those decisions by accommodating the needs of the concerned parties (land owner, mineral explorationist, raw material purchaser, government).

To illustrate the point, consider the presence of valuable petroleum under the Alaska North Slope. While we have an energy resource that could be developed, we need to answer several questions to determine the feasibility of developing the resource. First, does the technology exist to extract and move the petroleum to market? Today, the answer is "yes." A century ago such a project would have been impossible.

Second, is the project economical? To answer this question we need to know the cost of extraction and transportation. The technology may be feasible, but it may not come cheaply. We also need to know the present and predicted future price of petroleum. If petroleum is selling at $10 a barrel with little prospect of increase, our venture may not make economic sense. In practical terms, lenders will not advance money to finance the project. The company that uses its own funds to advance the project may get an angry reaction from its stockholders when exploration and extraction expenses cannot be paid back from the proceeds. On the other hand, if petroleum is selling at $25 a barrel with prospects of going even higher, the venture may be a financially sensible one.

A third consideration is political. What groups favor or disfavor the petroleum project? Here we may find environmental groups, local businesses, Native American villages, and national security advocates on different sides of the issue. Some matters may be political "no brainers." For example, how would you assess the chances of a marginally profitable mining proposal in the Grand Canyon? Other energy ventures, suggest close contests between well represented interest groups.

Political preferences may have already been expressed in legal standards. The law creating a national park may forbid energy development activity. Or, the law may command that if strip mining of coal occurs then the harm to the land should be corrected. Compliance with the law probably will add to the cost of the project. Non-compliance with the law may subject the developer to fines or jail.

One purpose of law is to order and resolve disputes between private parties. The parties may be individuals or giant corporations. The law may be created by the legislature (the United States Congress or the Legislatures of the 50 States), the courts, or the administrative agencies. Much energy law in the United States is private law arising from the common-law fields of property, contract, and tort. As an example, an energy developer suspects that a piece of farmland is underlain by valuable energy resources. Long-established rules of property, tort, and criminal law make it clear that the developer cannot simply go on the land and begin digging. He needs to reach an agreement with the farm owner. This may suggest the developer buys the land and becomes the new owner. More likely, the developer will purchase a limited privilege to explore and extract the valuable minerals. Out of this practical need, a body of law governing extractive operations on private land developed. Law aids the parties by defining who has what rights and what is needed to transfer these rights to another party. The law also allows parties to draft standard forms to perfect the transfers. This saves the cost of drafting each new agreement from the beginning. Afterwards, if a dispute arises concerning the use of the land, the courts stand ready to decide the merits of a complaint that a breach of contract has occurred, a wrong has been committed, or a property right has not been conveyed.

Even zealous advocates of smaller government probably oppose eliminating this function of the law. A dedicated believer in free markets needs the legal system (typically the courts) to establish rights in property and then to enforce promises arising out of those rights.

A second role of law, and one that appears throughout energy law, is the stating and enforcing of public policies. Here, government is more than a referee between private parties. Government, typically through the Legislature, mandates a policy. Even citizens who disagree with the policy are bound by it. Failure to comply may result in fine or imprisonment.

The assessment of government's role as public policy maker requires an understanding of the American legal system. Three crucial aspects of our system are the constitutional framework that structures American law, the law-making process carried out by the United States Congress and the fifty state legislatures, and the federal and state administrative processes. Each plays a major role in energy law. Each aspect is discussed in turn.

II.   THE CONSTITUTIONAL LAW OF ENERGY

The Constitution of the United States and the Constitutions of the fifty States are our fundamental legal documents. American constitutions typically do two things. First, they create the structure of government (legislative, executive, and judicial branches) and give powers to those bodies. Second, they provide limitations on the power of government (e.g. in the Bill of Rights). This granting and withholding of power in the constitutions reflects our historic American ambivalence about government.

The United States constitutions (national and state), with rare exception, do not *command* governmental action. The legislature and executive (President or Governor) are authorized to exercise power if they choose to do so. In particular, the constitutions do not guarantee the basic necessities of life. In this respect American constitutions differ from constitutions of other nations. Consider two examples:

Constitution of Bangladesh, article 15:

It shall be a fundamental responsibility of the State to attain . . . a constant increase of productive forces and a steady improvement in the material and cultural standards of living . . . with a view to securing to its citizens—

(a)   The provision of the basic necessities of life, including food, clothing, shelter, education, and medical care.

Constitution of Nigeria, article 16(2):

The State shall direct its policy towards ensuring . . . (d) that suitable and adequate shelter, suitable and adequate food . . . are provided for all citizens.

The concept of governmental responsibility for basic necessities is also reflected in the International Covenant on Economic, Social, and Cultural Rights, an international treaty prepared under the auspices of the United Nations.

Article 11

1. The States' Parties to the present Covenant recognize the right of everyone to an adequate standard of living for himself and his family, including adequate food, clothing, and housing, and to the continuous improvement of living conditions.

Defenders of the American way of life would argue that our social "safety net" to prevent starvation or provide shelter is as good or better than Bangladesh's or Nigeria's. The American "safety net," however, is created by the acts of the Legislature and the political will that backs them up, not the Constitution.

In theory, all provisions of the United States Constitution might have some impact on energy law. In practice, however, one or more of only half a dozen provisions are involved when an energy case reaches the courts on constitutional grounds. Each of these provisions has a rich constitutional history aside from energy cases. Our focus here on energy related disputes should not suggest that research on the question would involve only energy cases.

The Legislative Branch, Congress, is created and empowered in Article I of the United States Constitution. After mandating the creation of Congress and specifying how laws are enacted, Article I Section 8 details the powers of Congress. Congress is not given whatever legislative power it might want. Rather, Congress has enumerated powers only. Historically, however, Congress has often asserted its enumerated powers broadly. In addition, it has relied on the final clause of section 8 —the power to "make all laws which shall be necessary and proper for carrying into execution the foregoing powers, and all other powers vested by this Constitution in the Government of the United States, or in any Department or officer thereof."[1]

The United States Constitution does not address the ownership or use of specific natural resources (e.g., minerals, water). Again, the United States contrasts with other nations whose constitutions set forth government ownership of certain natural resources. The United States Government's ownership claims to certain energy resources stem from government's position as a landowner—most particularly in many of the western United States.

State Constitutions, often in the Western United States, may assert state ownership over water resources, certain lands, or other natural resources. Typically, the constitutional provision will authorize the Legislature to make necessary laws for the use of the resources. These laws may authorize development of the resources by private businesses or individuals.

A. The Commerce Clauses

The Congressional power most relevant to the energy industries is the Commerce Clause. The Clause gives Congress the power "to regulate

---

[1] U.S. CONST., art I, § 8.

commerce with foreign nations, and among the several states, and with the Indian Tribes."[2] An introductory constitutional law course will familiarize readers with many of the United States Supreme Court decisions that have given scope to the Commerce Clause. The cases have emphasized that the Clause has both an affirmative and a negative dimension.

The affirmative dimension appears clearly in the language of the Constitution. Congress is given power to regulate certain types of commercial activity. The regulation is typically to the disadvantage of one or more business enterprises or groups of consumers. For example, a regulation on strip mining may enhance land, air, and water in the surrounding area. However, it will likely prevent certain profitable mining or, at least, add to its cost.

Early Supreme Court cases like *Gibbons v. Ogden*,[3] decided in 1824 gave an expansive definition to "commerce." Chief Justice Marshall's classic opinion observed that "commerce" is more than mere "buying and selling." "Commerce, undoubtedly, is traffic, but it is something more—it is intercourse."[4]

Chief Justice Marshall's opinion continued by observing the grant of power to Congress applied "to those internal concerns which affect the states generally; but not to those which are completely within a particular State, which do not affect other states, and with which it is not necessary to interfere, for the purpose of executing some of the general powers of the government."[5] Interstate steamboat activity (the subject of *Gibbons v. Ogden*) was therefore within Congress' powers under the Commerce Clause.

Part of President Franklin Roosevelt's New Deal during the 1930s and 1940s required the assertion of broad powers of the federal government over aspects of the economy that had previously been left to regulation by state government or to no regulation at all.

Many of these Congressional enactments authorized detailed control over rather local aspects of the economy. Opponents challenged these actions as exceeding Congress' power under the Commerce Clause. *Wickard v. Filburn*, gave an expansive reading to "interstate commerce" as it upheld federal regulation of a single farmer's production of wheat, much of it grown for home consumption.[6] In essence, the Supreme Court accepted the logic that the single farmer's efforts must be combined with all other growers'

---

[2] *Id.*

[3] 22 U.S. (9 Wheat.) 1 (1824).

[4] *Id.* at 189.

[5] *Id.* at 195.

[6] 317 U.S. 111 (1942).

production. The totality of production would have an impact on interstate commerce sufficient to allow federal regulation. One year earlier in *United States v. Darby*[7] the Supreme Court had stated:

> The power of Congress over interstate commerce is not confined to the regulation of commerce among the states. It extends to those activities intrastate which so affect interstate commerce or the exercise of the power of Congress over it as to make regulation of them appropriate means to the attainment of a legitimate end, the exercise of the granted power of Congress to regulate interstate commerce.[8]

One of the best modern examinations of the scope of Congressional authority under the Commerce Clause is *Hodel v. Virginia Surface Mining and Reclamation Assn*.[9] The case resolved a constitutional challenge to the 1977 Surface Mining Control and Reclamation Act, a federal statute enacted to control the impacts of surface coal mining, popularly referred to as strip mining.

The history of the Surface Mining Act gave a sense of the constitutional issues at stake. The damage from unreclaimed strip mining had been known for years, primarily in the Appalachian States. In theory, the stream pollution, surface disruption, and other undesirable impacts of surface mining could be controlled by the states or localities in which the mining sites were located. However, economics and politics typically prevented control laws from being written or enforced. National environmental groups urged the United States Congress to correct the problems. After several failures, Congress did pass a comprehensive surface mining statute in 1977 which was signed by President Jimmy Carter.

Opponents of the federal regulation, having lost in the halls of Congress, brought their challenge to the Supreme Court. One of their arguments was that the statute exceeded Congress' power under the Commerce Clause. The opponents, whose claims were put forward by the Virginia Surface Mining and Reclamation Association, contended that what was regulated was land, hardly something "in commerce."[10] Further, the impacts of the strip mining were local and statewide, not national. Therefore, no "interstate" element entered into the question.

---

[7] 312 U.S. 100 (1941).
[8] *Id.* at 118.
[9] 452 U.S. 264 (1981).
[10] *Id.* at 275.

Justice Thurgood Marshall had little sympathy for the arguments of the Virginia Association. He observed:

The task of a court that is asked to determine whether a particular exercise of congressional power is valid under the Commerce Clause is relatively narrow. The court must defer to a congressional finding that a regulated activity affects interstate commerce, if there is any rational basis for such a finding. This established, the only remaining question for judicial inquiry is whether "the means chosen by [Congress] must be reasonably adapted to the end permitted by the Constitution."[11]

Harking back to *Wickard*, and subsequent cases, Justice Marshall quoted the Court's 1975 opinion in *Fry v. United States*: "[e]ven activity that is purely intrastate in character may be regulated by Congress, where the activity, combined with like conduct by others similarly situated, affects commerce among the States or with foreign nations."[12]

Even the Virginia Association recognized that Congress had prepared lengthy findings about the interstate impacts of uncontrolled surface mining. However, the Association seemed to assert that the purely local nature of the activity should change the result. The Court disagreed. It noted that "the power conferred by the Commerce Clause [is] broad enough to permit congressional regulation of activities causing air or water pollution, or other environmental hazards that may have effects in more than one State."[13] Further, Congress could constitutionally address the fear that leaving regulation to the States would encourage some states to sacrifice environmental objectives for increased coal production. "The prevention of this sort of destructive interstate competition is a traditional role for congressional action under the Commerce Clause."[14]

Having found the Congressional purpose constitutional, the Court turned to "the question whether the means selected by Congress were reasonable and appropriate."[15] Most of the Virginia Association's challenge focused on the claim that the Surface Mining Act standards duplicated matters regulated by other federal pollution control statutes. The Court was concise in rejecting this claim. "The short answer to this argument is that the effectiveness of existing laws in dealing with a problem identified by

---

[11] *Id.* at 276.
[12] 421 U.S. 542, 547 (1975).
[13] *Hodel* at 282.
[14] *Id.*
[15] *Id.* at 283.

Congress is ordinarily a matter committed to legislative judgment."[16] The Act was a constitutional exercise of the Commerce power.

Justice, later Chief Justice, Rehnquist concurred in the judgment. However, his concurring opinion took a skeptical look at the evolution of the Court's Commerce Clause jurisprudence:

> It is illuminating for purposes of reflection, if not for argument, to note that one of the greatest "fictions" of our federal system is that the Congress exercises only those powers delegated to it, while the remainder are reserved to the States or to the people. . . . one could easily get the sense from this Court's opinions that the federal system exists only at the sufferance of Congress.[17]

In Justice Rehnquist's view, the Court should not automatically defer to any Congressional finding that a matter concerned interstate commerce.

> Some activities may be so private or local in nature that they simply may not be in commerce. Nor is it sufficient that the person or activity reached have some nexus with interstate commerce. Our cases have consistently held that the regulated activity must have a substantial effect on interstate commerce. . . . Moreover, simply because Congress may conclude that a particular activity substantially affects interstate commerce does not necessarily make it so. Congress' findings must be supported by a "rational basis" and are reviewable by the courts.[18]

By 1995 Justice Rehnquist's cautions commanded a majority of the Court. In *United States v. Lopez*,[19] five justices struck down Congress' prohibitions on the possession of guns in school zones as unsupported by Congressional power under the Commerce Clause. The majority indicated that Congress might have been able to make a case for the connection between guns in the schools and interstate commerce. (The dissenters clearly felt Congress had done so.) However, Congress had not done so and the Court was not ready to adopt a wholly relaxed view that if Congress mentions interstate commerce, it must be interstate commerce.

The lasting impact of *Lopez* remains to be seen. But, the case is a reminder that there may be judicially enforceable limits on Congressional power under the Commerce Clause.

---

[16] *Id.*
[17] *Id.* at 307-08.
[18] *Id.* at 310-11.
[19] 514 U.S. 549 (1995).

Most Commerce Clause litigation has not involved whether Congress has the power to address a matter of interstate commerce. The more frequent concern has involved whether state or local laws should be struck down as infringing on federal authority over interstate commerce. This is the "negative commerce clause" or the "dormant commerce clause." While such a proposition is not directly stated in the constitutional language, the courts have found such a dimension to the Commerce Clause for many years.

The logic of the negative commerce clause goes back to one of the primary reasons for the creation of the new Constitution to replace the old Articles of Confederation. During and following the Revolution, states and localities often sought to impose restrictions on the movement of goods across state lines. Typically, the restriction reflected a desire to favor local businesses or to add to the revenues of local government. As example, a state might impose a tax or fee on a product brought from another state for sale in the taxing state. If the tax was paid, the treasury of the taxing state benefited at the expense of the out-of-state producer. At the same time, local manufacturers might appreciate the advantage provided to their product. A competitor's product had been made more expensive, or possibly kept out of the market altogether.

A variety of interests—importing manufacturers, transporters eager for business, customers seeking competing products at good prices, and some foresighted governments—recognized that the overall nation would suffer from such restraints of trade. The drafters of the Constitution, in a variety of provisions, supported a national market with limited restraints on interstate trade.

The energy field is particularly prone to assertions of the "negative" Commerce Clause. Many energy products move long distances from place of origin to place of use. Deposits of energy raw materials may make states and localities eager to preserve "their" coal, oil, or hydropower or at least to get the maximum value for its sale to customers "from away". The large amounts of money involved in many energy transactions make them attractive targets for government taxing schemes. It is not surprising then that over fifty significant decisions of the United States Supreme Court involve the "negative" Commerce Clause aspects of energy or natural resources.

We do not provide an exhaustive summary of the constitutional law of the "negative" Commerce Clause, even in the energy field. Nevertheless, readers should understand some of the situations in which conflicts arise, some of the factors that stimulate legislation that runs afoul of the Clause, and some of the principles of law that the Supreme Court has established.

Dormant Commerce Clause

First, what prompts legislation that may violate the negative aspects of the Commerce Clause? As the historical origins of the Clause disclose, there may be powerful incentives towards local favoritism. The legislator wanting to regulate, tax, or not subsidize a "foreign" product or to "protect" a local product may not care about larger issues of the national or international good. Local manufacturers and their employees are the voters, campaign contributors, and legislative lobbyists with the most impact on the local legislator. The complaints of an aggrieved business a thousand miles distant may be only dimly heard.

Further, the Supreme Court has recognized that states and localities can address local concerns that also impact interstate commerce. Government may be providing services that justify local taxation. Government may also see threats to local health and safety posed by the interstate commercial activity. The United States Supreme Court has earned its pay by drawing the often imprecise lines between a permissible exercise of state or local authority that involves interstate commerce and an impermissible attempt that disrupts the goal of a national economy.

An early example of interstate commercial issues in an energy context is *West v. Kansas Natural Gas Co.*[20] The Oklahoma legislature passed a statute forbidding the transportation of Oklahoma-produced natural gas outside the state. Oklahoma asserted its right to preserve Oklahoma gas for Oklahomans. The Supreme Court first distinguished gas in transport from state regulation of the production of gas from the well. Once the gas had been extracted from the well it was a commercial product like shoes or paper or lumber. The Court speculated on the harmful impact on commerce if all states could hoard their resources. The Court held the Oklahoma statute unconstitutional.

A decade later the Court reviewed a similar West Virginia statute discouraging shipment of gas out of state in the face of unmet needs in West Virginia. The Court summarized: "A state law, whether of the state where the gas is produced or that where it is to be sold, which by its necessary operation prevents, obstructs or burdens such transmission is a regulation of interstate commerce—a prohibited interference."[21]

Still more recently in *New England Power v. New Hampshire*,[22] New Hampshire attempted to forbid the export of hydroelectric energy produced in New Hampshire. The Supreme Court struck down the local preference as

---

[20] 221 U.S. 229 (1911).

[21] *Pennsylvania v. West Virginia*, 262 U.S. 553, 586-97 (1923).

[22] 455 U.S. 331 (1982).

"precisely the sort of protectionist regulation that the Commerce Clause declares off-limits to the states."[23]

A variant of these efforts at protectionism was also declared unconstitutional in *Wyoming v. Oklahoma*.[24] An Oklahoma statute required Oklahoma coal-burning electric generating plants to buy at least 10% of their coal supply from Oklahoma mines. The State of Wyoming, which benefitted from taxes on Wyoming coal sold to Oklahoma power producers, challenged the statute as a restriction on interstate commerce. The Court agreed. It observed: "When a state statute clearly discriminates against interstate commerce, it will be struck down . . . unless the discrimination is demonstrably justified by a valid factor unrelated to economic protectionism. . . ."[25] Oklahoma could not offer such a justification.

Taxation of activities with an interstate aspect have proved troubling for the Court. A 1954 case, *Michigan-Wisconsin Pipe Line Co. v. Calvert*,[26] suggests the legal contours of the field. Texas imposed a tax on the occupation of "gathering gas." Texas imposed the tax on the entire volume of gas taken and prepared for immediate interstate shipment. The pipeline companies asserted a violation of the negative Commerce Clause. The Court summarized the tensions in the field:

> The recurring problem is to resolve a conflict between the Constitution's mandate that trade between the states be permitted to flow freely without unnecessary obstruction from any source, and the state's rightful desire to require that interstate business bear its proper share of the costs of local government in return for benefits received.[27]

The Court continued: "It is now well settled that a tax imposed on a local activity related to interstate commerce is valid if, and only if, the local activity is not such an integral part of the interstate process, the flow of commerce, that it cannot realistically be separated from it."[28]

The timing of the Texas taxation was crucial to the Court. Texas had imposed the tax after the gas had been committed to the interstate shipment. "But the tax here is not levied on the capture or production of the gas, but rather on its taking into interstate commerce after production,

---

[23] *Id.* at 339.
[24] 502 U.S. 437 (1992).
[25] *Id.* at 454.
[26] 347 U.S. 157 (1954).
[27] *Id.* at 166.
[28] *Id.*

gathering and processing."[29] If all states through which the gas passed by pipeline were to attempt a similar tax "[t]he net effect would be substantially to resurrect the customs barriers which the Commerce Clause was designed to eliminate."[30] The Court held the tax unconstitutional.

Discrimination in taxation is as offensive as discrimination in the access to resources. *New Energy Company v. Limbach* is illustrative.[31] The Ohio Legislature sought to encourage the production and use of ethanol in Ohio. Ethanol (gasohol) appeared to be an attractive substitute for foreign petroleum. Unfortunately, pure economics still favored petroleum and disfavored ethanol. In order to reduce the competitive advantage the Legislature mandated a tax credit against the Ohio motor vehicle fuel sales tax for each gallon of ethanol sold by Ohio fuel dealers. However, the credit could be taken only if "the ethanol is produced in Ohio or in a State that grants similar tax advantages to ethanol produced in Ohio."[32]

The Court smelled economic protectionism—Ohio gasohol manufacturers attempting to get a competitive advantage over their non-resident counterparts. It summarized: "Thus, state statutes that clearly discriminate against interstate commerce are routinely struck down . . . unless the discrimination is demonstrably justified by a valid factor unrelated to economic protectionism . . ."[33] This did not change because only a few companies were involved nor because of the provision for reciprocity for states who welcomed Ohio produced ethanol. "The present law likewise imposes an economic disadvantage upon out-of-state sellers; and the promise to remove that if reciprocity is accepted no more justifies disparity of treatment than it would justify categorical exclusion."[34] Nor, did the Court find a "legitimate local purpose" for the statute. Suggestions that the statute promoted cleaner air (from less polluting ethanol) seemed only accidentally advanced by this statute.[35]

Discrimination means different things to different people. Witness, *Commonwealth Edison Co. v. Montana*.[36] The State of Montana imposed a severance tax on the production of coal within the State. The State produced large amounts of coal. Much of it came from federally owned land within

---

[29] *Id.* at 169.
[30] *Id.* at 170.
[31] 486 U.S. 269 (1988).
[32] *Id.* at 271.
[33] *Id.* at 274.
[34] *Id.* at 275.
[35] *Id.* at 278-80.
[36] 453 U.S. 609 (1981).

Montana. The considerable majority of the coal was sold to users (typically for electric generation) outside Montana. The severance tax rate could reach up to 30% of the contract sales price. It is not hard to imagine the Montana legislator weighing the benefits and detriments of a vote for the severance tax. The prospect of making out of state coal users pay for a considerable part of Montana government has a definite allure.

The Supreme Court observed that the current test to review a tax statute under the Commerce Clause had been set out in *Complete Auto Transit v. Brady*,[37] a case involving taxes on automobiles. The formal language of the tax statute is not determinative of its constitutionality. Rather, the "practical effect" is crucial. The Court will sustain a tax "against Commerce Clause challenge when the tax is applied to an activity with a substantial nexus with the taxing state, is fairly apportioned, does not discriminate against interstate commerce, and is fairly related to the services provided by the State."[38]

How did the Montana severance tax measure up under the *Complete Auto Transit* test? There was clearly a "substantial nexus" with the State of Montana, the site of the coal mining. The Court also had no difficulty with the "fair apportionment" test. The remaining two tests deserved more attention. The challengers of the tax asserted that it discriminated against interstate commerce since the vast majority of the coal that was taxed left the State. Here, form triumphed over practical effect. The Court held: "[T]he Montana tax is computed at the same rate regardless of the final destination of the coal, and there is no suggestion here that the tax is administered in a manner that departs from this evenhanded formula."[39] Prior precedents had not emphasized the actual impact of the burden (here, non-resident users absorbing the vast majority of the tax burden). In the Court's words: "We are not convinced that the Commerce Clause, of its own force, gives the residents of one State the right to control in this fashion the terms of resource development and depletion in a sister State."[40] The message was for Congress. If Congress became dissatisfied with Montana's approach, it could exercise its affirmative power under the Commerce Clause to control the interstate commerce aspects of Montana's taxing program. Justice White's concurrence emphasized this point.

The fourth aspect of the *Complete Auto Transit* test also troubled the Court. Was the tax "fairly related to the services provided" by Montana? The

---

[37] 430 U.S. 274 (1977).

[38] *Id.* at 279.

[39] *Commonwealth Edison* at 618.

[40] *Id.* at 619.

Court emphasized that a tax dedicated to the general support of the government need not equate the tax received to the precise government benefits rendered to the taxpayer. "Moreover, there is no requirement . . . that the amount of general revenue taxes collected from a particular activity must be reasonably related to the value of the services provided to the activity."[41] The Court elaborated: "[T]he fourth prong of the *Complete Auto Transit* test imposes the additional limitation that the measure of the tax must be reasonably related to the extent of the contact, since it is the activities or presence of the taxpayer in the State that may properly be made to bear a 'just share of state tax burden' . . ."[42]

The Montana severance tax met this requirement. The precise level of the tax was a decision for the Montana Legislature, not for the courts.

Justices Blackmun, Powell, and Stevens dissented. They found the tax to be "tailored" to take advantage of interstate commerce and to make Montana very wealthy. Technical compliance with *Complete Auto Transit*'s non-discrimination and fair-relationship-to-services requirements overlooked the practical impacts of the tax.[43]

The most frequently cited test in the negative Commerce Clause area comes from the Supreme Court's 1970 decision in *Pike v. Bruce Church, Inc.*[44] The case involved an Arizona order that forbade packing Arizona cantaloupes out of state. The practical effect of the order would have been the construction of a $200,000 packing shed in Arizona when a comparable packing shed was available across the nearby California border.

The Arizona order failed constitutional review. The Court observed that it "viewed with particular suspicion state statutes requiring business operations to be performed in the home State that could more efficiently be performed elsewhere."[45] Arizona's objective was to prevent deceptive packaging that would hurt the reputation of Arizona growers. Here, however, the order sought to assure only that Arizona's name would be on the packaging of high quality cantaloupes. This state interest was too minimal to overcome the burden on interstate commerce.

The Court offered this test: "Where the statute regulates even-handedly to effectuate a legitimate local public interest, and its effects on interstate commerce are only incidental, it will be upheld unless the burden imposed on such commerce is clearly excessive in relation to the putative local

---

[41] *Id.* at 622.
[42] *Id.* at 626.
[43] *Id.* at 638.
[44] 397 U.S. 137 (1970).
[45] *Id.* at 145.

benefits."[46] The Court continued "If a legitimate local purpose is found, then the question becomes one of degree. And the extent of the burden that will be tolerated will of course depend on the nature of the local interest involved, and on whether it could be promoted as well with a lesser impact on interstate activities."[47]

The complexity of negative Commerce Clause review in energy cases is suggested by *Northwest Central Pipeline Corp. v. Corp. Commission.*[48] As the petroleum and natural gas chapters will explain in greater detail, state governments have taken an active interest in the rates of production of their oil and gas reserves. A Kansas regulation governed the timing of production from the massive Hugoton gas field. It did so in a way that clearly encouraged producers with wells in a number of states to take the Kansas gas first. The regulation was challenged on both Commerce Clause and Supremacy grounds. The latter challenge asserted that federal government regulation of aspects of the natural gas industry forbade Kansas' action. The Court found no federal preemption of Kansas activity.

On the Commerce Clause issue, Northwest Central first claimed discriminatory economic protectionism. It contended that "[W]hatever the pipelines' reactions to the regulation, Kansas interests will benefit, and at the expense of interstate pipelines or of producers in other States."[49] The Court disagreed. It found this a "neutral" regulation that treated all gas the same whether it was headed for an intrastate or interstate market.

Alternatively, Northwest Central asked that the *Bruce Church* test be applied. The balancing test of *Bruce Church* worked in Kansas' favor in the opinion of the Court. Kansas had substantial state interests in encouraging production of its natural gas. The reduction of gas extraction from other states (the alleged harm to interstate commerce) was not "clearly excessive" when weighed against the Kansas interests.[50] Kansas' order was constitutional.

A case like *Northwest Central* indicates that while the Court can set out rules like those in *Bruce Church* or *Complete Auto Transit*, their application to specific factual situations is often not clear. Sensible legislatures may disguise their motives to avoid obvious discrimination. Often, legitimate state objectives may work a substantial harm to interstate commerce.

---

[46] *Id.* at 142.
[47] *Id.*
[48] 489 U.S. 493 (1989).
[49] *Id.* at 522.
[50] *Id.* at 525-26.

B.   Congressional Power over the Federal Lands

One of the constitutional powers of Congress of greatest significance to energy law does not appear with the Commerce Clause and the other powers spelled out in Article I Section 8. Section 3 of Article IV provides in part "The Congress shall have Power to dispose of and make all needful Rules and Regulations respecting the Territory or other Property belonging to the United States . . ."[51]

This federal lands power is of special significance in the Western United States. A bit of history is useful. The United States was formed from the thirteen original colonies. Several of those colonies had claims to lands as far west as the Mississippi River. These territories were eventually opened to settlement. Out of them were created the second generation of states admitted to the Union. In both colonies and the trans-Appalachian new States, the federal government did not assert land ownership. Most of the land surface began in or soon moved to private ownership. Accordingly, it is rare to find more than 5% of the territory of an eastern state under the ownership of the federal government. National parks, national forests, and military installations are among the exceptions to private ownership.

West of the Mississippi, a very different pattern prevailed. Here the United States first took title to the land. The federal government bought the vast Louisiana Territory (recall the Lewis and Clark Expedition designed to find out exactly what had been purchased). A war with Mexico resulted in the cession of much of the Southwest. Settlement between the United States and Great Britain added the Pacific Northwest portions of the United States. We purchased Alaska from Russia. Only Texas, which joined the Union after its own secession from Mexico, did not join the Union following initial United States' ownership and control.

At acquisition, most of the land of these territories was within the ownership and control of the United States. This was "territory . . . belonging to the United States" in the terms of Article IV Section 3. Accordingly, Congress was empowered to make "rules and regulations" respecting it.

Congress assuredly did not want to keep all of the property in federal ownership. Needs of national defense and economic development encouraged plans to invite citizens and corporations onto the land. Title was offered in return for settlement. The goal was occupation, economic development, and eventual statehood.

A half century of Congressional acts authorized one of the world's great land giveaways. Homesteaders, desert land settlers, miners, and railroad

---

[51] U.S. CONST., art. IV, § 3.

companies (whose work encouraged further development) were invited to occupy and use the land. Occupancy and use led to a grant of title from the United States to the citizen or corporate developer. Private land ownership expanded west of the Mississippi.

Congress' generosity also extended to the new states. Typically, on statehood, the new state would be granted federal lands to help the state in its economic development. Lastly, a further portion of the surface of the "federal lands" was set aside as reservations for the Native American tribes that were relocated or confined to make way for the great western expansion.

As a result of these varied developments, the map of a western state today will reflect various types of ownership—private, state, tribal, and federal. Even after the land grants, a substantial portion of the western states remained in the hands of the federal government. In some areas, lands were reserved for special federal purposes—national parks, national forests, military bombing ranges, and wildlife refuges. The largest amount of federal land, however, was not classified for any special purpose. Most of these general lands now are under the control of the Bureau of Land Management of the Department of the Interior.

All of this suggests that the Congressional power to make "rules and regulations" gives the Congress a great deal of potential control over energy matters in the western states. Are coal, uranium, oil or gas located under federal lands? If so, Congress has power over them. Is a waterway useful for hydroelectric energy production? Its proximity to federal lands may give Congress a say in its development. Does a long distance pipeline or transmission line need to cross federally owned land? The Congress, or its delegate, has a role in its development.

One of the first United States Supreme Court cases to consider natural resource issues addressed the scope of the Congressional power. In *United States v. Gratoit*[52] a dispute arose over a federal license for smelting lead ores in Illinois. The Court described the power of Article IV Section 3 as "vested in Congress without limitation."[53] That was sufficient to authorize the lease for smelting.

In *Utah Power and Light v. United States*[54] a private power company sought to use federal forest land. It claimed authority from a Utah statute which assumed a power company had a right to use federal public lands unless the federal government had specifically controlled the usage. The

---

[52] 39 U.S. (14 Peters) 526 (1840).
[53] *Id.* at 537.
[54] 243 U.S. 289 (1917).

Supreme Court disagreed: "[T]he power of Congress is exclusive and . . . only through its exercise in some form can rights in lands belonging to the United States be acquired."[55] In a further passage, the Court recognized that Congressional "rules and regulations" provided powers similar to those of the States. Congress has the power to control use "and to prescribe the conditions upon which others may obtain rights in them, even though this may involve the exercise in some measure of what commonly is known as the police power."[56]

The prominent recent statement of Congressional authority over the federal public lands appears in *Kleppe v. New Mexico*.[57] Congress sought to protect wild horses and burros on the public lands. New Mexico officials viewed the animals as nuisances to be eliminated. They sought to round-up the strays for eventual killing. New Mexico contended that the exercise of Congressional authority required a showing that either "the animals were moving in interstate commerce or damaging the public lands."[58] New Mexico sought a declaratory judgment that the federal law was unconstitutional.[59]

The Supreme Court sided squarely with Congress. While recognizing some role for judicial review, the Court observed that "determinations under the Property Clause are entrusted primarily to the judgment of Congress."[60] The Court continued: ". . . [w]hile the furthest reaches of the power granted by the Property Clause have not yet been definitively resolved, we have repeatedly observed that '[t]he power over the public land thus entrusted to Congress is without limitations.'"[61] This extensive power over the federal lands "necessarily includes the power to regulate and protect the wildlife living there."[62]

Despite the broad statement of federal power (which would imply total federal control of half the land surface of some states), the *Kleppe* opinion reflected the reality of Western land law. While the federal government could constitutionally govern every aspect of the federal lands, it does not. The reasons vary. Politics may discourage Congress from asserting too broad a jurisdiction over matters of importance to a state. Recall that United States Senators and Representatives are residents of their electoral territory and typically come with a strong grounding in local politics. Alterna-

---

[55] *Id.* at 404.
[56] *Id.* at 405.
[57] 426 U.S. 529 (1976).
[58] *Id.* at 533.
[59] *Id.* at 534.
[60] *Id.* at 536.
[61] *Id.* at 539.
[62] *Id.* at 541.

tively, economics may drive a federal decision. Would Congress really want to spend the funds to provide full police protection to millions of acres of lightly occupied lands?

Over the years a wealth of accommodations have been worked out to decide whether state, local, or federal authorities exercise the powers of government over certain territories. Further, as we have noted, a conclusion that federal or state authorities control an issue does not end the legal inquiry. The question of which agency of the government has been given the authority remains. Environmental conservation or law enforcement activities on federal land may vary widely depending on whether the land is a national park or a top-secret military installation.

C.   The Supremacy Clause

Article VI Section 2 of the Constitution sets out a principle crucial to energy law. The Supremacy Clause asserts the primacy of the federal authority within its areas of competence.

> This Constitution, and the Laws of the United States which shall
> be made in Pursuance thereof; and all Treaties made, or which
> shall be made, under the Authority of the United States, shall be
> the supreme Law of the Land; and the Judges in every State shall
> be bound thereby, any Thing in the Constitution or Laws of any
> State to the Contrary notwithstanding.[63]

The origins of the Clause go back to the unhappy experiences of the Revolution and the Articles of Confederation. Even in crucial national areas like war making and the movement of interstate commerce, the federal government's authority was subject to contrary state views. As the negative Commerce Clause cases suggest, different motives may drive a state legislature or a city council than drive the national Congress. An essential part of federal power had to be its ability to override contradictory commands from state and local governments. Thus, the Supremacy Clause.

Energy cases often assert both Commerce Clause and Supremacy Clause challenges to a state or local action. The claims arise out of different sections of the Constitution and should be assessed separately. Nonetheless, common themes appear.

Supremacy cases commonly involve conflicting federal and state (or local) laws. The message of the Supremacy Clause is clear: if there is genuine conflict within an area of federal authority, the federal authority wins

---

[63] U.S. CONST., art. VI, § 2.

wins. What makes Supremacy law interesting (and often, frustrating for government officials) is the determination of when a conflict is present.

The responsibility for such situations can be placed on Congress. As the Supreme Court has made clear, Congress can specifically address supremacy or preemption issues in the statute it writes, or, less satisfactorily, in clear legislative history. The provision of a federal statute that says: "And no state or locality shall enact any law [in this area]" probably settles the issue of who has power. Alternatively, Congress in its legislation can make clear that state or local legislation may coexist with the federal enactment. The provision "Nothing in this section shall prevent a state or locality from . . ." almost certainly preserves state capability.

Litigation about preemption may be caused by Congressional neglect to clarify the rules in an obvious preemption situation. Alternatively, an unobvious preemption situation may not have been foreseen by legislators and staff who are under time pressures and focused on the problem immediately before them. In other situations, legislative sponsors have foreseen preemption questions but not wanted to push the issue. A clear statement preempting state legislation in the federal bill may arouse lobbyists and legislative opponents prior to the bill's passage. Better to secure enactment and then let the courts, administrative agencies, or a future Congress worry about preemption.

The energy field has provided some of the significant Supremacy Clause cases. The conflict between state and federal authority over hydroelectric power development that gave rise to *First Iowa HydroElectric Coop v. FPC*[64] provides a useful beginning for studying energy preemption cases. First Iowa, complying with the Federal Power Act, filed a declaration of intent to operate a hydroelectric plant on the Cedar River in Iowa. The State of Iowa then asserted that First Iowa must also follow Iowa's process for licensing water-power projects. The Supreme Court sided with First Iowa's claim that state regulation was preempted. Iowa could not enforce its permitting provisions. In reaching that result, however, the Court found that the Federal Power Act "discloses both a vigorous determination of Congress to make progress with the development of the long idle water power resources of the Nation and a determination to avoid unconstitutional invasion of the jurisdiction of the States."[65] What resulted was "a dual system involving the close integration of these powers rather than a dual

---

[64] 328 U.S. 152 (1946).
[65] *Id.* at 171.

system of futile duplication of two authorities over the same subject matter."[66]

Ray v. Atlantic Richfield Co.[67] provides an excellent study of the law and politics of an energy preemption case. At issue was the control of oil spills from tankers navigating beautiful and often treacherous Puget Sound of Washington State. Congress' Ports and Waterways Safety Act addressed many issues of relevance to oil tanker activity. A subsequent Washington State Tanker Law sought to impose standards that were more protective of the Puget Sound environment and consequently more costly or prohibitive to the shipment of petroleum. One can imagine the different perspectives of Congresspersons (some who may never have been within two thousand miles of Puget Sound) and Washington State legislators (some of whom may draw substantial electoral and financial support from fishing and recreational interests located on the Sound).

Citing its prior precedents, the Supreme Court offered a structure for analyzing preemption cases. In a case, like this one, where the State of Washington possessed clearly recognized police powers to protect the local health, safety, and welfare, the courts should assume no preemption of the state law unless "that was the clear and manifest purpose of Congress."[68] Congress can override state police power, but it must be clear that that is what it desired.

Federal preemption can appear is several situations. First, as discussed earlier, express pre-emptive statutory language can resolve the matter. Second, federal regulation of an area may be so pervasive as to imply preemption of state or local authority. Third, the federal interest in a field may be so dominant that state or local authority is preempted. In these areas, the entire field of action is preempted even though a precise state law is not contradicted by a precise federal law.

In addition to the field preemptions, the precise federal and state laws may conflict. The most direct conflict involves the flatly contradictory provisions of federal and state law. As example, suppose a federal statute mandates a certain reclamation program for a mined property. A state statute also demanding reclamation absolutely forbids the mandated federal program. What's a miner to do? The Supremacy Clause and preemption law offers the clear advice. The state statute is not constitutional. A second type of subject area preemption involves the state law that imposes an obstacle

---

[66] *Id.*

[67] 435 U.S. 151 (1978).

[68] *Id.* at 157.

to carrying out the purpose of the federal law even though a flat-out conflict is not presented.

Ray applied these standards to several challenged provisions of the Washington State Tanker Law. A careful reading of the statutes determined that some state requirements for the provision of tanker pilots (needed to navigate in risky waters) clearly encroached on federal authority. Other pilot requirements did not.

State provisions mandating certain safety features on the tankers were struck down as conflicting with Congress' "intended uniform national standards."[69] Here, the Supreme Court was well aware of the burdens on the transportation industry of having to vary safety standards every time they crossed a state boundary. The Court observed: "The Supremacy Clause dictates that the federal judgment that a vessel is safe to navigate United States waters prevail over the contrary state judgment."[70]

Washington State, however, could impose a tugboat escort requirement. The Court viewed this as an operating requirement, rather than a preempted design specification. Further, examination of the provision under the negative Commerce Clause reached a similar conclusion favorable to Washington State regulation. There did not appear to be a compelling need for uniformity of regulation. Washington's interests in preventing oil spills were large. The financial cost of the regulation appeared modest.

Nuclear energy has given rise to some of the most interesting preemption cases of the last two decades. As the nuclear chapter will elaborate, nuclear energy has been an area of consistent federal government interest. Nonetheless, many aspects of the use of nuclear power have an impact on traditional state and local concerns. With the coming of organized opposition to nuclear power development, ample opportunities for conflict were present.

In *Pacific Gas & Electric Co. v. State Energy Commission*[71] the Supreme Court set the contours of state involvement in nuclear power regulation. A California statute conditioned the location of new nuclear electric generating plants in California on the provision of adequate storage arrangements for spent nuclear waste. At the time the statute passed, and continuing today, most spent radioactive waste is stored at the plant site. The California statute left the determination of a satisfactory waste disposal plan to the Federal Nuclear Regulatory Commission (NRC). However, it noted that the NRC determination could be overridden by a subsequent vote of the California Legislature. One remaining fact provides context for the

---

[69] *Id.* at 163.

[70] *Id.* at 165.

[71] 461 U.S. 190 (1983).

Supreme Court holding. Prior to the passage of the California statute, a California citizen initiative proposition had sought to stop further nuclear activity, primarily on the grounds that radioactivity risks made the technology unsafe.

Opponents of the California statute raised several parts of the preemption matrix in their challenge to the statute. None was wholly successful. The federal law did not expressly forbid state action. Rather, the federal statutory scheme worked a division of authority between federal and state regulators. The Court summarized: "[T]he Federal Government should regulate the radiological safety aspects involved in the construction and operation of a nuclear plant, but that . . . the States retain their traditional responsibility in the field of regulating electrical utilities for determining questions of need, reliability, cost, and other related state concerns."[72] Phrased differently: "[T]he Federal Government maintains complete control of the safety and 'nuclear' aspects of energy generation; the States exercise their traditional authority over the need for additional generating capacity, the type of generating facilities to be licensed, land use, ratemaking, and the like."[73]

Having set out the standard of review, the Court then assessed what California had done and why it had done it. The statute did not seek to "regulate the construction or operation of a nuclear powerplant."[74] This would be preempted "even if enacted out of nonsafety concerns . . ."[75] "[S]tate safety regulation is not pre-empted only when it conflicts with federal law. Rather, the Federal Government has occupied the entire field of nuclear safety concerns, except the limited powers expressly ceded to the States."[76] This area preemption assertion thus asked whether California had a non-safety basis for the enactment of the statute. Here the Supreme Court favored California. It accepted the California Legislature's declaration that its concern with radioactive waste storage was economic rather than safety-related. The Court was not inclined to delve deeply into Legislative motive. It also treated as irrelevant the failed citizen initiative that appeared to be safety focused.[77]

The challengers of the statute next sought to find a specific preemption by federal statute. The Congress had certainly addressed nuclear power regulation in detail. However, "[t]he NRC's imprimatur . . . indicates only

---

[72] *Id.* at 205.
[73] *Id.* at 212.
[74] *Id.*
[75] *Id.*
[76] *Id.*
[77] *Id.* at 215.

that it is safe to proceed with such [nuclear] plants, not that it is economically wise to do so."[78] The California statute did not interfere with the
federal statute and regulations. Nor, had Congress expressed a goal to
promote nuclear power "at all costs."[79] The Court concluded that "the legal
reality remains that Congress has left sufficient authority in the States to
allow the development of nuclear power to be slowed or even stopped for
economic reasons."[80]

The message to State Legislatures seemed clear. They could influence
nuclear development in their jurisdiction despite the broad federal powers
in the area. The key was to state their reasons as economic ("We don't think
our utility ratepayers can afford this technology.") rather than safety-related
("We are scared of the health impacts of a large scale release of radiation.")
The Court had given a practical veto to the states that undercut significant
federal legislation promoting nuclear power.

Following *Pacific Gas & Electric*, several other nuclear cases addressed
preemption in connection with individual claims for harm from the nuclear
process. *Silkwood v. Kerr-McGee Corp.*[81] upheld the award of state law
punitive damages arising out of Silkwood's contamination by the escape of
plutonium from a licensed nuclear fuels facility. The Court's majority found
that federal legislation, specifically the Price-Anderson Act on compensation
for nuclear accidents, preserved state remedies including punitive damages.
The Court noted: "Paying both federal fines and state-imposed punitive
damages for the same incident would not appear to be physically impossible.
Nor does exposure to punitive damages frustrate any purpose of the federal
remedial scheme."[82]

The tensions in the case are well identified in the opinions of the four
dissenters. Justices Blackmun and Marshall observed that the punitive
damages award in *Silkwood* was one hundred times greater than the
maximum fine that the Nuclear Regulatory Commission could have imposed
for Kerr-McGee's misdeed. This "wreaks havoc with the regulatory structure
that Congress carefully created."[83] Justices Powell and Burger joined in a
separate dissent that observed the majority opinion "authorizes lay juries

---

[78] *Id.* at 218.
[79] *Id.* at 222.
[80] *Id.* at 223.
[81] 464 U.S. 238 (1984).
[82] *Id.* at 257.
[83] *Id.* at 259.

and judges in each of the States to make regulatory judgments as to whether a federally licensed nuclear facility is being operated safely."[84]

Utility regulation, a task undertaken by both the state and federal government, has also been a regular source of Supremacy Clause law. Several cases give a flavor of the disputes. In *Arkansas Electric Cooperative Corp. v. Arkansas Public Service Commission*[85] the state regulatory commission asserted the power to control rates charged by the Cooperative for wholesale sales of power to individual retail dealers in the state. The Cooperative claimed that the Federal Power Act (FPA) and the Rural Electrification Act (REA) precluded such a state exercise of power. The Supreme Court disagreed. It found that wholesale rates of cooperatives were not subject to federal rate regulation, that the REA's legislative history recognized a place for state rate regulation, and that "a federal decision to forgo regulation in a given area may imply an authoritative federal determination that the area is best left *un*regulated, and in that event would have as much pre-emptive force as a decision to regulate."[86]

Different facts stimulated a different decision in *Mississippi Power & Light v. Mississippi ex rel. Moore*.[87] At issue was the very expensive power produced by the Grand Gulf nuclear plant. Mississippi, through its Attorney General, demanded to review the prudence of the Grand Gulf expenditures before allowing its costs to be charged to Mississippi ratepayers. However, a previous Order of the Federal Energy Regulatory Commission (FERC) had required Mississippi Power & Light to purchase 33% of the Grand Gulf output. Did the FERC Order preempt Mississippi's attempt "to set retail rates that do not recognize the costs associated with that allocation as reasonable?"[88]

The Supreme Court's prior opinion in *Nantahala Power & Light Co. v. Thornburg*, controlled.[89] In *Nantahala* the Court held that once FERC set rates for interstate sales of electric power "a State may not conclude in setting retail rates that the FERC-approved wholesale rates are unreasonable."[90] The *Mississippi Power & Light* Court reemphasized: "FERC-mandated allocations of power are binding on the States, and States must treat those allocations as fair and reasonable when determining retail

---

[84] *Id.* at 274.
[85] 461 U.S. 375 (1983).
[86] *Id.* at 384.
[87] 487 U.S. 354 (1988).
[88] *Id.* at 369.
[89] 476 U.S. 953 (1986).
[90] *Id.* at 966.

rates."[91] The Court continued: "The Supremacy Clause compels the MPSC to permit the utility to recover as a reasonable operating expense costs incurred as a result of paying a FERC-determined wholesale rate for a FERC-mandated allocation of power."[92]

The *Northwest Central Pipeline v. Corp. Commission* litigation, discussed under the Commerce Clause, also illustrates Supremacy issues in the joint state and federal regulation of natural gas. The Kansas Corporation Commission's order encouraging the faster production of gas from the Hugoton Field was challenged as infringing on federal regulation of interstate natural gas transactions. The Supreme Court concluded that the Kansas Order "regulates in a field that Congress expressly left to the States; it does not conflict with the federal regulatory scheme; hence it is not pre-empted."[93] The Kansas Order regulated gas producers' rates of production from their wells, a traditional matter of state health and safety regulation. The fact that the Order had "some impact on the purchasing decisions and hence costs of interstate pipelines does not without more result in conflict pre-emption . . ."[94] The Court continued:

> There may be circumstances in which the impact of state regulation of production on matters within federal control is so extensive and disruptive of interstate commerce in gas that federal accommodation must give way to federal pre-emption, but this is not one of them. Indeed, it appears that if [the Kansas Order] operates as a spur to greater production of low-cost Hugoton gas, this would be entirely congruous with current federal goals.[95]

The Kansas Order was constitutional.

D. Limitations on Federal Powers to Control the States

As the Supremacy Clause section illustrates the United States operates under a federal system of government. Both states and the national government are recognized as sovereign in different areas. The Constitution itself grants and denies power to federal or state governments.

On some matters, one government may have exclusive control over the issue. For example, in Article I Section 8 Congress is given the powers to

---

[91] *Mississippi Power and Light* at 371.

[92] *Id.* at 355.

[93] 489 U.S. 493, 509 (1989).

[94] *Id.* at 516.

[95] *Id.* at 518.

"establish an uniform rule of naturalization," to punish "counterfeiting the
. . . coin of the United States" and to "declare war." State ability to legislate
in these areas is almost non-existent. In other areas, by contrast, federal
and state sovereignty both are present. The negative Commerce Clause
cases and the federal lands cases provide examples of shared jurisdiction.
Conflict is controlled by both the Supremacy Clause and the negative
Commerce Clause and by political restraint by both federal and state
officials.

In recent decades, a lively controversy has developed over whether
specific amendments or general principles of federalism limit the exercise
of federal authority over certain state governmental functions. These cases
do not challenge the basic power of Congress to regulate the area. The
question rather is whether Congressional power to regulate individuals or
private corporations extends to the regulation of state and local governments.

Two cases *National League of Cities v. Usery*[96] and *Garcia v. San
Antonio Metro Transit Authority*[97] set out opposing positions in closely
divided opinions.

Both cases involved the Federal Fair Labor Standards Act that
regulated maximum hours of work and minimum pay. Applied to private
employers, the statute clearly was a constitutional application of Congress'
power over interstate commerce. However, Congress also applied the statute
to state and local governments in their relations with their employees.
Municipal governments, reluctant to have the federal government dictate
employment conditions and pay for their workers, brought suit. In *National
League of Cities*, the Supreme Court sustained the challenge of the local
governments. The Court held that Congress did not have such power over
"a coordinate element in the system established by the Framers for
governing our Federal Union."[98] The Court worried about the disappearance
of the "separate and independent existence" of the States if Congress could
exercise such power.[99] The Court held "that insofar as the challenged
amendments operate to directly displace the States' freedom to structure
integral operations in areas of traditional governmental functions, they are
not within the authority granted Congress [by the Commerce Clause]."[100]

---

[96] 426 U.S. 833 (1976).
[97] 469 U.S. 528 (1985).
[98] *National League of Cities* at 849.
[99] *Id.* at 851.
[100] *Id.* at 852.

For a decade the Supreme Court and lower courts tried to define the contours of the *National League* decision. In *Hodel v. Virginia Surface Mining and Reclamation Assn.*[101] opponents of federal surface mining legislation raised a challenge under the 10th Amendment to the Constitution. The 10th Amendment provides: "The powers not delegated to the United States by the Constitution, nor prohibited by it to the States, are reserved to the States respectively, or to the people." Looking to *National League*, the Mining Association claimed that this was an interference with the "traditional [state and local] governmental function" of regulating land use.[102] The Court identified three requirements in the *National League* holding. First, the regulation must regulate states as states. Second, it must address matters that were attributes of state sovereignty. Third, state compliance with the federal law must impair the state's ability to structure integral governmental operations. Only if all three conditions were met would the federal statute be struck down. The challenge ran aground on the first requirement. The Surface Mining Act did not regulate states; rather it regulated private mining companies. The 10th Amendment challenge failed.

A year later in *FERC v. Mississippi*[103] a second federal energy statute posed a more intriguing examination of the 10th Amendment. The Public Utility Regulatory Policies Act (PURPA) attempted to encourage a variety of energy conservation measures. As the title suggests, Congress felt that regulation of the natural gas and electric public utilities offered considerable potential for increased energy conservation. A novel federal mandate asked state utility commissions to "consider" requiring the utilities under their jurisdiction to adopt certain conservation activities and regulations. State utility commissions were not required to adopt the federally suggested programs. However, organs of state government were being directed by a federal statute.

A Court found the gentle persuasion approach of PURPA to be constitutional. The majority conceded that in PURPA "the Federal Government attempts to use state regulatory machinery to advance federal goals."[104] But, the Court believed the Congress had not overstepped its authority relative to state sovereignty. The PURPA did "not involve the compelled exercise of Mississippi's sovereign powers. And, equally import-

---

[101] 452 U.S. 264 (1981).
[102] *National League of Cities* at 852.
[103] 456 U.S. 742 (1982).
[104] *Id.* at 759.

ant, they do not set a mandatory agenda to be considered in all events by state legislative or administrative decisionmakers."[105]

Justice Powell dissented. He found the PURPA imposed "unprecedented burdens on the States."[106] The 10th Amendment forbade the prescription of "administrative and judicial procedures that States must follow. . . ."[107]

Justices O'Connor, Burger, and Rehnquist in a separate dissent elaborated. Their colorful phrase talked of PURPA "conscript[ing] state utility commissions into the national bureaucratic army."[108] The three parts of the *Hodel* test were met. "By taxing the limited resources of these commissions [with mandatory programs for "considering" the federal standards] and decreasing their ability to address local regulatory ills, PURPA directly impairs the power of state utility commissions to discharge their traditional functions efficiently and effectively."[109] The argument that Congress could have taken over the entire area of utility regulation under its Commerce Clause authority was beside the point. Congress' preemption of the field would free the states to devote their resources elsewhere. The PURPA "compromise" left the States in the utility regulation business but burdened with the federal standards. Further, the decision also undermined a virtue of the federal system, the ability of one or a few states to try new governmental initiatives which in time and with success might be adopted by other states. "PURPA, which commands state agencies to spend their time evaluating federally proposed standards and defending their decisions to adopt or reject those standards, will retard this creative experimentation."[110]

By 1985, Supreme Court scholars could conclude that the logic of *Usery* had now focused on the 10th Amendment's protection of powers "reserved to the States." But, cases like *Hodel* and *Mississippi* indicated that the Court was not eager to find further situations in which the federal government had overstepped its authority. Then, the shift of a single justice appeared to undercut the doctrinal basis for the 10th Amendment jurisprudence.

The Federal Fair Labor Standards Act returned to the Supreme Court in *Garcia v. San Antonio Metro Transit Authority*.[111] Five members of the Court overruled *National League* calling the "traditional governmental functions" test both unworkable and "inconsistent with established princi-

---

[105] *Id.* at 769.
[106] *Id.* at 771.
[107] *Id.*
[108] *Id.* at 775.
[109] *Id.* at 781.
[110] *Id.* at 789.
[111] 469 U.S. 528 (1985).

ples of federalism."[112] In a key passage, the majority observed "the principal means chosen by the Framers to ensure the role of the States in the federal system lies in the structure of the Federal Government itself" not in the specific language of the 10th Amendment.[113] State sovereignty was properly protected by "procedural safeguards inherent in the structure of the federal system [rather] than by judicially created limitations on federal power."[114]

Justices Powell, Burger, Rehnquist and O'Connor dissented to a "decision [that] substantially alters the federal system embodied in the Constitution . . ."[115] The decision "effectively reduces the Tenth Amendment to meaningless rhetoric when Congress acts pursuant to the Commerce Clause."[116]

The *Garcia* decision may have ended an expansive theory of states' rights based on the 10th Amendment. It did not end concern that Congress might overstep in its relations with the states. Another energy case, *New York v. United States*,[117] revitalized the theory of limits on federal authority.

The Federal Low Level Radioactive Waste Policy Amendments attempted to address the problem of disposal of some of the less toxic forms of nuclear waste. All parties litigating the issue agreed that Congress had the power to regulate low-level nuclear waste under the Commerce Clause. What divided the parties was Congress' capability to "direct or otherwise motivate the States to regulate in a particular field or a particular way."[118] These conclusions stemmed from the Supreme Court's formulation of the 10th Amendment law. "If a power is delegated to Congress in the Con-

stitution, the Tenth Amendment expressly disclaims any reservation of that power to the States; if a power is an attribute of state sovereignty reserved by the Tenth Amendment, it is necessarily a power the Constitution has not conferred on Congress."[119]

The Court then turned to the types of incentives Congress could use with the States to persuade them to implement federal policy choices. While Congress had certain capabilities, it could not "commandeer" the legislative processes of the States. "While Congress has substantial powers to govern the Nation directly, including in areas of intimate concern to the States, the

---

[112] *Id.* at 531.
[113] *Id.* at 550.
[114] *Id.* at 552.
[115] *Id.* at 557.
[116] *Id.* at 560.
[117] 505 U.S. 144 (1992).
[118] *Id.* at 161.
[119] *Id.* at 156.

Constitution has never been understood to confer upon Congress the ability to require the States to govern according to Congress' instructions."[120]

Two of Congress' express powers in Article I Section 8 gave Congress useful, and constitutional, tools in their dealings with the states on the low-level waste issue. The Spending Clause legitimated a Congressional program of money grants to the states for waste disposal purposes. These grants could be conditioned on the states' "attainment of a series of milestones" that advanced the federally desired goal of regional waste storage sites.[121]

A second portion of the program relied on the Commerce Clause. Congress mandated a set of incentives that raised costs of waste disposal and eventually denied access to waste disposal sites for states which had not advanced the goals of the federal disposal program. The Court observed the effect of the statute: "The affected States are not compelled by Congress to regulate, because any burden caused by a State's refusal to regulate will fall on those who generate waste and find no outlet for its disposal, rather than on the State as a sovereign."[122] A State was neither forced to spend money nor to participate in the program if it chose not to. This was a permissible "conditional exercise of Congress' commerce power."[123]

A third statute provision met a different fate. This provision mandated that if a state did not eventually satisfy Congress' goals for waste disposal, the state itself would have to "take title" to all low-level nuclear waste in its territory after a certain date. Here, a majority of the Court believed Congress had "crossed the line distinguishing encouragement from coercion."[124] Congress had unconstitutionally commandeered state legislative authority by either the command to accept ownership of the waste or by the order to regulate it according to Congressional instructions. Neither the Commerce Clause nor the Spending Clause supported such actions.

The Court observed that the take title provision

> [a]ppears to be unique. No other federal statute has been cited which offers a state government no option other than that of implementing legislation enacted by Congress. Whether one views the take title provisions as lying outside Congress' enumerated powers, or as infringing upon the core of state sovereignty reserved by the Tenth Amendment, the provision is inconsistent

---

[120] *Id.* at 162.
[121] *Id.* at 173.
[122] *Id.* at 174.
[123] *Id.*
[124] *Id.* at 175.

with the federal structure of our Government established by the Constitution.[125]

The majority concluded with language that harked back to *National League*.

> States are not mere political subdivisions of the United States. State governments are neither regional offices nor administrative agencies of the Federal Government. . . . Whatever the outer limits of that sovereignty may be, one thing is clear: The Federal Government may not compel the States to enact or administer a federal regulatory program.[126]

Dissenting Justices White, Blackmun, and Stevens noted the irony of the case. The states had urged Congress to help with solutions to the low-level waste problem and had generally endorsed this solution. In Justice White's language: "I do not understand the principle of federalism to impede the National Government from acting as referee among the States to prohibit one from bullying another."[127] Justice Stevens in separate dissent concluded there was no doubt of Congress' power to direct a state government to endorse a federal program. As example, he observed a state could be commanded to take remedial steps "if one State's radioactive waste created a nuisance that harmed its neighbors."[128]

E. The Protection of Private Rights Against Government Action: Due Process and Equal Protection

‹Previous sections have shown that questions about powers of government are often litigated by citizens or private corporations whose interests have been harmed by the assertion of government power.›Cases brought under the Commerce Clause, the Federal Lands Clause, or the Supremacy Clause illustrate this. The Court is asked to decide whether the action of government (state or federal) is constitutional. If it is, the action may constitutionally disadvantage the private party. If it is not, the private party is left free to continue its activities.

The Framers of the Constitution and the citizens who ratified it were not satisfied with only the control on the new government provided by grants of limited powers. One of the first orders of business for the newly

---

[125] *Id.* at 177.
[126] *Id.* at 188.
[127] *Id.* at 199.
[128] *Id.* at 212.

created Congress was to write, approve, and present to the states a Bill of Rights that formally incorporated a set of protections of citizen's rights against actions of the new national government. These were the first ten amendments to the Constitution.

Originally the Bill of Rights was thought to limit only the national government, not state and local governments. The Civil War changed that. The 13th, 14th, and 15th Amendments to the Constitution gave the national government, through acts of Congress, significant powers over rights at state and local level. A century of Supreme Court cases elaborated on those Constitutional grants. By the 1970s it was clear that most of the Bill of Rights applied equally to national, state, and local governments. Most state constitutions also have Bills of Rights which guarantee many of the same rights guaranteed by the United States Constitution's first ten amendments.

The citizen who thinks about the Bill of Rights at all is likely to recall it as protecting rights in the criminal process (Fourth Amendment protections against "searches and seizures"; Fifth Amendment protection against self-incrimination; Sixth Amendment requirements of a lawyer in criminal defense) or protecting freedom of speech and religion (the First Amendment). These protections may seem far removed from the work of energy lawyers.

Three provisions of the Bill of Rights and the 14th Amendment, however, are pertinent to claims of individual and corporate owners that government has taken action to disadvantage their economic interests. The Fifth Amendment provides that no "person" (which has been interpreted to include corporate entities) shall be "deprived of life, liberty, or property, without due process of law." This provision is repeated in section one of the 14th Amendment: "nor shall any State, deprive any person of life, liberty, or property, without due process of law."

Section one of the Fourteenth Amendment continues that no State "shall deny to any person within its jurisdiction the equal protection of the laws." The "equal protection" Clause does not appear in the Fifth Amendment. However, the United States Supreme Court has found "equal protection" to be a part of the Due Process protections of the Fifth Amendment against United States Government action. Thus, for practical purposes United States, state, and local government actions all must proceed in accordance with the equal protection requirements.

A third critical protection of individual and corporate rights appears in the Fifth Amendment. It provides a further protection against government: "nor shall private property be taken for public use without just compensation." This so-called Takings Clause does not appear in the 14th Amendment. However, the Supreme Court has held that it applies to control state and local government actions as part of the due process of law protected by the 14th Amendment.

The three protections—due process, equal protection, Takings Clause—are broad and imprecise in their phrasings. What is "due process of law"? What are matters of "life, liberty, or property?" What constitutes "equal protection of the law?" What is a taking of "private property . . . for public use?" What is the "just compensation" that legitimates such a taking?

The grand Constitutional language has been given life by a century of decisions from the United States Supreme Court, the lower federal courts, and the courts of the states which may be called on to interpret both the United States Constitution and the Constitution of their State. In the energy field, cases usually arise out of an attempt by government to regulate an energy business (a coal mine, an electric company, an oil and gas company). The business challenges the action of government on one or more of the constitutional bases.

Governments throughout history have written laws that govern private business. We have examined the major power of the United States Congress in the area—the Commerce Clause. State Legislatures have a general "police power" to involve themselves in a wide variety of business decisions. Despite popular understanding of "police" as the "cop on the beat", the legislative police power is a broad capability to legislate on matters of health, safety, and morals for the public good. A great many of these federal or state legislative enactments disadvantage some portion of the business community. Safety laws cost money for safer machinery and may reduce production to the detriment of the economic bottom line. Environmental pollution statutes may forbid cost-free waste disposal techniques or require expensive reclamation projects.

A century of Supreme Court opinions makes clear that many of the Court's decisions balance government's needs against private burdens. A conclusion that any economic disadvantage to business from government regulation would violate the constitution would cripple government. At the other extreme, a legislative power to make any enactment, however great the impact on business, would leave business subject to the whims of the legislative process. The courts have understandably steered towards a middle course.

St. Louis Consolidated Coal v. Illinois[129] provides an early example of constitutional review of energy regulation. Coal mine owners used the Due Process Clause to challenge Illinois' regulation of coal mine working conditions. The Supreme Court gave a strong endorsement to the power of

---

[129] 185 U.S. 203 (1902).

the Illinois Legislature to act in the area: "The regulation of mines and miners, their hours of labor, and the precautions that shall be taken to ensure their safety, health and comfort, are so obviously within the police power of the several States, that no citation of authorities is necessary to vindicate the general principle."[130] One provision of the statute allowed the State to appoint mine inspectors and make the mine owners pay their salaries. A second statutory provision allowed less rigorous inspections of mines employing five or fewer employees than for larger mines. The Court was unimpressed with the mine owner's claim of irrational discrimination or a denial of equal protection of the laws.

Five years later in *Wilmington Star Mining Co. v. Fulton*[131] another provision of the Illinois statute was sustained against a due process challenge. At issue was a provision that forced mine owners to be liable for the acts of their supervisory personnel or their inspectors. The Supreme Court held that even if common-law tort doctrines rejected owner liability in this situation, the statute could constitutionally change the rule to the disadvantage of the owners. Due process was not violated. Neither did the singling out of mine owners from other employers to bear this burden violate the equal protection clause.

Four years later in *Lindsley v. Natural Carbonic Gas Co.*[132] the Court sustained a New York statute controlling owner behavior that might deplete the common source of supply for the Saratoga Springs' mineral springs. The Court recognized the Legislature had wide scope in making distinctions in legislation for purposes of the equal protection clause. Only a purely arbitrary provision of a statute without reasonable basis should be overturned. In *Barrett v. Indiana*,[133] a case reviewing the width of mine tunnels, the Court observed: "The legislature is itself the judge of the means necessary and proper to that end, and only such regulations as are palpably arbitrary can be set aside because of the requirements of due process of law under the Federal constitution."[134]

This line of cases was decided during an era in Supreme Court history in which the Court was quite ready to overturn economic regulation on so-called "substantive due process" grounds. The landmark case, *Lochner v. New York*,[135] which declared unconstitutional New York's regulation of maximum work hours in bakeries, gave its name to the era. In essence, the Supreme

---

[130] *Id.* at 207.
[131] 205 U.S. 60 (1907).
[132] 220 U.S. 61 (1911).
[133] 229 U.S. 26 (1913).
[134] *Id.* at 29.
[135] 198 U.S. 45 (1905).

Court held that bakery owners and employees were deprived of "liberty" and "property" when government legislated maximum work hours. In practical terms, the Court held that regardless of the process provided, the state could not deprive business and employees of their "liberty" or "property."

In this context, the energy cases discussed above provide an exception to *Lochner* era assumptions. Here, distinctive aspects of the energy industries allowed state police power regulation for the benefit of public health and safety to overcome substantive due process objections. In simple terms, the Court was persuaded there was something different about a coal mine.

The *Lochner* era ended during the later years of Franklin Roosevelt's presidency. The Supreme Court has since withdrawn from any significant effort to scrutinize economic regulation by the states under the Due Process or Equal Protection Clauses. The Court usually asks no more than that there be a "rational" basis for the Legislature's actions. If there is, the legislation withstands constitutional challenge. In *Exxon Corp. v. Eagerton*, the Court summarized the "lenient standard of rationality" that applied to a challenge under the Equal Protection Clause: "Under that standard a statute will be sustained if the legislature could have reasonably concluded that the challenged classification would promote a legitimate state purpose."[136]

Several modern era energy cases give a sense of due process challenges. They also suggest the Court's willingness to defer to legislative judgments. *Usery v. Turner Elkhorn Mining Co.*[137] challenged aspects of the Federal Coal Mine Health and Safety Act of 1969 that provided for compensation for miners incapacitated by black lung disease. The mine owners challenged the requirement for compensation of miners who had ceased work in the mining industry before passage of the federal compensation program. The Court rejected the challenge. It emphasized that: "our cases are clear that legislation readjusting rights and burdens is not unlawful solely because it upsets otherwise settled expectations [that there was formerly no obligation to compensate miners with black lung]. This is true even though the effect of the legislation is to impose a new duty or liability based on past acts." (citations omitted)[138] The Court found the retroactive application of the statute "is justified as a rational measure to spread the costs of the employees' disabilities to those who have profited from the fruits of their labor—the operators and the coal consumers."[139] Justice Powell's concurrence reaffirmed the point. "Nor does the Constitution require that legislation on

---

[136] 462 U.S. 176, 195-196 (1983).
[137] 428 U.S. 1 (1976).
[138] *Id.* at 16.
[139] *Id.* at 18.

economic matters be compatible with sound economics or even with normal fairness. As a result, economic and remedial social enactments carry a strong presumption of constitutionality . . ."[140]

In *Duke Power Co. v. Carolina Environmental Study Group, Inc.*[141] opponents of nuclear power development challenged, as violative of due process, the Price-Anderson Act provisions of the Atomic Energy Act. Price-Anderson had been passed at the urging of the nuclear industry to place a limit on possible damages that could be awarded in the wake of a nuclear accident. The Act sought to address a particular dilemma posed by nuclear power. At the time of enactment, no American nuclear facility had encountered a major nuclear accident with massive release of radiation off-site. Yet, a worst case scenario for such an accident indicated damages in massive amounts. Insurers and investors were understandably cautious about committing to nuclear power under those circumstances. The Price-Anderson Act tried to solve the problem by defining certain nuclear accidents, by recognizing liability for the accidents, and, crucial for the *Duke Power* litigation, by setting a theoretical maximum amount of damages. Challengers of the statute claimed that their due process rights had been deprived by the ceiling on possible damages.

The Supreme Court sustained the statute.

> The record before us fully supports the need for the imposition of a statutory limit on liability to encourage private industry participation and hence bears a rational relationship to Congress' concern for stimulating the involvement of private enterprise in the production of electric energy through the use of atomic power. . ."[142]

The Court accepted the maximum damage amount of $560 million as a "working hypothesis" and observed that were actual damages higher than $560 million, Congress "would likely enact extraordinary relief provisions to provide additional relief, in accord with prior practice."[143] This degree of arbitrariness is "within permissible limits and not violative of due process."[144]

The Court also stressed that Price-Anderson provides "a reasonably just substitute for the common-law or state tort remedies it replaces."[145]

---

[140] *Id.* at 44.
[141] 438 U.S. 59 (1978).
[142] *Id.* at 84.
[143] *Id.* at 85.
[144] *Id.* at 87.
[145] *Id.* at 88.

The Price-Anderson Act not only provides a reasonable, prompt, and equitable mechanism for compensating victims of a catastrophic nuclear incident, it also guarantees a level of net compensation generally exceeding that recoverable in private litigation. . . . This panoply of remedies and guarantees is at the least a reasonably just substitute for the common-law rights replaced by the Price-Anderson Act. Nothing more is required by the Due Process Clause.[146]

Similar logic rejected plaintiffs' equal protection challenge.

United States v. Locke[147] looks at several aspects of a due process challenge. Congress enacted section 314 of the Federal Land Policy and Management Act to allow federal land managers to terminate undeveloped mining claims on federal lands. Thousands of such claims had accumulated over the years. Section 314 required a mining claimant who wished to retain his rights to file with the United States an annual notice of that intent "prior to December 31" of each year. Locke, who clearly wished to retain a valuable mineral claim, filed exactly on December 31. The Bureau of Land Management denied the filing as one day too late. Locke sued.

Locke first attempted to construe section 314 to what he argued was Congress' intent—get your claim in by the end of the year if you want to retain it. The Supreme Court was unpersuaded. "Prior to December 31" means December 30 at the latest.[148] That meaning was spelled out in the Bureau of Land Management's regulations governing filings.

Locke turned to constitutional argument. He urged that due process required he have an intent to abandon his claim before it could be taken away. The Court was unmoved. Congress clearly had the power (under the federal lands clause) to qualify existing property rights. "Claimants thus must take their mineral interests with the knowledge that the Government retains substantial regulatory power over those interests."[149] The government objective of clearing the public lands of stale title claims was "clearly legitimate."[150]

Locke finally claimed that he was entitled either to specific notice that his claim was about to lapse or a chance to appeal the initial denial. The Court again disagreed.

---

[146] *Id.* at 93.
[147] 471 U.S. 84 (1985).
[148] *Id.* at 84.
[149] *Id.* at 105.
[150] *Id.* at 106.

[T]he Act provides appellees with all the process that is their constitutional due. In altering substantive rights through enactment of rules of general applicability, a legislature generally provides constitutionally adequate process simply by enacting the statute, publishing it, and to the extent the statute regulates private conduct, affording those within the statute's reach a reasonable opportunity both to familiarize themselves with the general requirements imposed and to comply with those requirements.[151]

That had been done and Locke had lost his claim.

Public utility regulation has been a regular source of due process challenges for over a century. Typical public utility statutes demand that the for-profit utility company shall charge only "just and reasonable" rates for their services. Companies who feel that the "just and reasonable" rate does not provide adequate return on their investment often challenge the utility commission's decision as a denial of due process.

The modern statement from the Supreme Court appears in *Duquesne Light Co. v. Barasch*.[152] A Pennsylvania statute forbade utility companies from charging ratepayers for investments in building nuclear plants that had later been cancelled. The utilities claimed a deprivation of due process.

The Court reviewed and reaffirmed prior precedents. These emphasized that only if rates were "confiscatory" did due process enter the picture. Further, rate orders were to be reviewed for their "total effect" not piece by piece. The Court elaborated: "[W]hether a particular rate is "unjust" or "unreasonable" will depend to some extent on what is a fair rate of return given the risks under a particular rate-setting system, and on the amount of capital upon which the investors are entitled to earn [on] that return. At the margins, these questions have constitutional overtones."[153]

Here, the nuclear plant expenditures in question were only a small percentage of the total utility investment.

No argument has been made that these slightly reduced rates jeopardize the financial integrity of the companies, either by leaving them insufficient operating capital or by impeding their ability to raise future capital. Nor has it been demonstrated that these rates are inadequate to compensate current equity holders

---

[151] *Id.* at 108.

[152] 488 U.S. 299 (1989).

[153] *Id.* at 310.

for the risk associated with their investments under a modified prudent investment scheme.[154]

While the utility commission has a broad range of discretion consistent with due process, the Court speculated that there were limits of fairness: "Consequently, a State's decision to arbitrarily switch back and forth between methodologies in a way which required investors to bear the risk of bad investments at some times while denying them the benefit of good investments at others would raise serious constitutional questions."[155] That was not the case in *Barasch*. The Pennsylvania statute was sustained.

F. The Protection of Private Rights Against Government Action: Takings of Property

We have seen the Due Process Clause of both the 5th and 14th Amendments provides that no person shall be "deprived of . . . property, without due process of law" by action of government. The Due Process cases suggest both the substantive and procedural aspects of due process. Procedural due process promises that government can deprive a person of property so long as it provides due process of law. This probably requires an existing legal standard for the deprivation, notice to the owner of the pending deprivation, and an opportunity to be heard on the matter. *Memphis Light, Gas & Water v. Craft*,[156] reviewing termination of electric service, provides an example. Government could deprive plaintiff of the property right of continued electric service. However, the customer had to have notice of the termination and an opportunity to respond (for example, to contest an erroneous bill).

Substantive due process, by contrast, involves a claim that government may not deprive the owner of some rights in property under any circumstances. As we have seen, since the 1930s substantive due process arguments on matters of economic regulation have not been favored by the Supreme Court.

One might suppose that the Due Process Clauses provided sufficient protection for property interests. However, the drafters of the Fifth Amendment added the separate clause "nor shall private property be taken for public use without just compensation" immediately after the Due Process Clause. Subsequently, the United States Supreme Court held the Takings Clause binding on state and local governments as a part of the 14th

---

[154] *Id.* at 312.

[155] *Id.* at 315.

[156] 436 U.S. 1 (1978).

Amendment. Similarly, most State Constitutions provide a protection against takings that mirrors the Fifth Amendment language.

What does the Takings Clause add? Most narrowly, the Clause addresses the situation in which government wants to acquire full ownership of private property, most often land. In familiar terms, the Clause responds to the needs of Government for land for the new highway, the expanded airport runway, or the wildlife preservation area. The Clause affirms a power of government, the power of eminent domain, to acquire legally a private owner's full interest in the property and to remove the private owner. At its extreme, the Clause tells the owner that she or he cannot stay on the property in the face of government need for it and willingness to pay.

The Clause does provide two protections for the private property owner. First, Government must act for "public use." This protection calls to mind stories from elsewhere in the world of the dictator's arbitrarily seizing property for personal pleasure. This is forbidden. However, "public use" is an expandable term. In *Strickley v. Highland Boy Gold Mining Co.*[157] a Utah statute granted mining companies the State's right of eminent domain in order to secure the movement of ore to market (at issue in *Strickley* was an aerial bucket line over plaintiff's property). Plaintiff argued that this was a violation of the 14th Amendment because the taking was for a private corporation. The Supreme Court disagreed. The Constitution did not require "general public use" of the property right taken. The State of Utah could for good reason grant a right of eminent domain to a private business interest. One year earlier the Court had approved a Utah statute allowing private water companies to exercise a right of eminent domain in order to construct channels to move water from stream to place of use. There, in *Clark v. Nash*[158] the Court called the use a "public one" in light of the crucial societal importance of access to water in the desert.

The law of eminent domain is now well established. Government's ability to acquire property is conceded. The tough issue becomes "how much must government pay?" A substantial body of law has defined the contours of "just compensation." These matters have rarely reached the Supreme Court in recent decades.

The issue that has become a regular on the Supreme Court docket involves the regulatory taking. Here, government wishes to take an action that will have an impact on the property owner's total bundle of rights in property. However, government does not want to take full title to the

---

[157] 200 U.S. 527 (1906).
[158] 198 U.S. 361 (1905).

property (often land) either because such ownership is not needed for the government's purpose or because the government does not want to pay "just compensation" from a badly stretched budget. The government denies any taking has occurred that would bring the Takings Clause into play. The property owner takes a different view. Most probably, the owner would like the government to abandon the regulation and leave the owner free to enjoy "my property rights." However, if the government insists, the owner wants to be paid "just compensation" for the loss of economic value she suffers. These "inverse condemnation" or "regulatory takings" cases have provided a fertile source for Supreme Court jurisprudence in recent years.

Energy law provided one of the landmark precedents in the Takings realm. *Pennsylvania Coal Co. v. Mahon*[159] continues to be cited as authority three quarters of a century after its decision. At issue was the subsidence (collapse) of land as a consequence of underground coal mining removing support for the land. Pennsylvania Coal's mining lease under plaintiff's property gave it the right to extract the coal and provided that the surface landowner "takes the premises with the risk, and waives all claim for damages that may arise from mining out the coal."[160] That private agreement between mining company and landowner made it clear which party had property rights in the right to undermine land. However, several decades after the agreement had been reached, the Pennsylvania Legislature passed the Kohler Act. In essence, the statute prevented underground mining in circumstances where subsidence of the land threatened harm to homeowners. Pennsylvania Coal claimed the Pennsylvania Legislature had taken its right to mine coal.

Justice Oliver Wendell Holmes faced the conflict of private and public law: "[T]he statute is admitted to destroy previously existing rights of property and contract. The question is whether the police power can be stretched so far."[161] Justice Holmes continued:

> Government hardly could go on if to some extent values incident to property could not be diminished without paying for every such change in the general law . . . But obviously the implied limitation must have its limits, or the contract and due process clauses are gone. One fact for consideration in determining such limits is the extent of the diminution. When it reaches a certain magnitude, in

---

[159] 260 U.S. 393 (1922).
[160] *Id.* at 412.
[161] *Id.* at 413.

most, if not in all cases there must be an exercise of eminent domain and compensation to sustain the act.[162]

Justice Holmes' assessment of the interests on both sides suggested his conclusion.

> This is the case of a single private house. No doubt there is a public interest even in this. . . . But usually in ordinary private affairs the public interest does not warrant much of this kind of interference. A source of damage to such a house is not a public nuisance even if similar damage is inflicted on others in different places.[163]

"On the other hand the extent of the taking is great. It purports to abolish what is recognized in Pennsylvania as an estate in land . . ."[164]

Justice Holmes concluded that the Kohler Act "cannot be sustained as an exercise of the police power."[165] He then offered a ringing support of the Takings Clause. "When this absolute protection [the Takings Clause] is found to be qualified by the police power, the natural tendency of human nature is to extend the qualification more and more until at last private property disappears. But that cannot be accomplished in this way under the Constitution. . . ."[166]

Justice Holmes continued in what would become the most cited language of the case. "The general rule at least is, that while property may be regulated to a certain extent, if regulation goes too far it will be recognized as a taking."[167]

> We are in danger of forgetting that a strong public desire to improve the public condition is not enough to warrant achieving the desire by a shorter cut than the constitutional way of paying for the change. . . .this is a question of degree—and therefore cannot be disposed of by general propositions. But we regard this as going beyond any of the cases decided by this Court.[168]

---

[162] *Id.*

[163] *Id.*

[164] *Id.* at 414.

[165] *Id.*

[166] *Id.* at 415.

[167] *Id.*

[168] *Id.* at 416.

Justice Holmes ended by expressing his unease that the surface owners, having made their private bargain, now wanted to undo it in the Legislature.

> [B]ut the question at bottom is upon whom the loss of the changes desired should fall. So far as private persons or communities have seen fit to take the risk of acquiring only surface rights, we cannot see that the fact that their risk has become a danger warrants the giving to them greater rights than they bought.[169]

Justice Brandeis dissented. He began by noting the public interest in the case.

> Coal in place is land; and the right of the owner to use his land is not absolute. He may not so use it as to create a public nuisance, and uses, once harmless, may, owing to changed conditions, seriously threaten the public welfare. Whenever they do, the legislature has power to prohibit such uses without paying compensation . . .[170]

Justice Brandeis continued, distinguishing the *Mahon* facts from the intent of the Takings Clause: "The restriction here in question is merely the prohibition of a noxious use. The property so restricted remains in the possession of its owner. The State does not appropriate it or make any use of it. The States merely prevents them from making a use which interferes with paramount rights of the public."[171] Justice Brandeis was skeptical of the loss to the coal company.

> But values are relative. If we are to consider the value of the coal kept in place by the restriction, we should compare it with the value of all other parts of the land. That is, with the value not of the coal alone, but with the value of the whole property. . . . For aught that appears the value of the coal kept in place by the restriction may be negligible as compared with the value of the whole property. . . .[172]

Justice Brandeis then addressed a concept raised by Justice Holmes, the "average reciprocity of advantage."[173] The term dealt with government regulations that would burden but also advantage the economic interests of

---

[169] *Id.*
[170] *Id.* at 417.
[171] *Id.*
[172] *Id.* at 419.
[173] *Id.* at 422.

property owners. As example, a statute or local ordinance might forbid keeping barnyard animals in a residential neighborhood. A homeowner wanting to keep pigs could claim an economic loss from the prohibition. However, it is also fair to reflect that he benefitted in his property values and the enjoyment of his property because the ordinance forbade his neighbors from keeping animals also. Justice Holmes had rejected analogies to "average reciprocity of advantage"[174] holdings in *Mahon*. Justice Brandeis pursued the point: "reciprocity of advantage is an important consideration, and may even be an essential, where the State's power is exercised for the purpose of conferring benefits upon the property of a neighborhood. . . . But where the police power is exercised, not to confer benefits upon property owners, but to protect the public from detriment and danger, there is, in my opinion, no room for considering reciprocity of advantage." Other precedent cases showed no reciprocity of advantage "unless it be the advantage of living and doing business in a civilized community. That reciprocal advantage is given by the act to the coal operators."[175]

By the mid-1980s, the *Mahon* decision seemed more famous for its distinguished authors than for its precedent value. The *Mahon* majority sided with the coal company against the State of Pennsylvania. In general, most later Supreme Court and lower court regulatory takings cases sided with Government, holding that the regulatory activity was permissible without compensation i.e. that plaintiff's property had not been "taken." *Mahon's* majority language is also imprecise. To state that a government action can go "too far" and become a taking doesn't provide much guidance to property owners and government officials.

By the mid-1980s it was even a fair question whether *Mahon* remained good law. In 1987 what might be called "son of *Mahon*" (if not "grandson of *Mahon*") reached the Supreme Court in *Keystone Bituminous Coal Ass'n. v. DeBenedictis*.[176] A new Pennsylvania statute, the Bituminous Mine Subsidence and Land Conservation Act, had been enacted to respond to concerns about the impacts of strip-mining on the lands and waters of the State. Specific subsidence provisions of the Act suggested that coal companies would not be able to mine all of the coal that they owned in order to provide sufficient surface support. The Coal Association brought suit under the Takings Clause. The suit did not identify a specific parcel of land that was burdened. Rather, it challenged the statute on its face—under any application it would be unconstitutional.

---

[174] *Id.*

[175] *Id.*

[176] 480 U.S. 470 (1987).

⟨The Coal Association did not have to look far for legal precedent. This was *Mahon* revisited in its eyes. The Supreme Court should either grant it an easy win or overrule the sixty-five year old precedent.⟩

The Court did neither. Remarkably, the Court found that *Mahon* did not control the case. Harking back to Justice Holmes' statement that *Mahon* dealt with a "single private home," the Court distinguished the Bituminous Mine Subsidence Act as an enactment for a public purpose to correct "a significant threat to the common welfare."[177] By contrast, the Kohler Act reviewed in *Mahon* was for the "benefit of private parties." The Court continued by expressing its skepticism that the modern statute would be unconstitutional in every situation. The Court found no showing that the Act "makes it impossible . . . to profitably engage in their business, or that there has been undue interference with their investment backed expectations . . ."[178] The majority was also rather dismissive of the argument that the entirety of the legally recognized support estate had been taken by Pennsylvania's action.

Four dissenters disagreed with most aspects of the majority opinion. Differences between *Mahon* and *Keystone Bituminous* were trivial. Despite language about a "single house," *Mahon* had involved a statute of general applicability passed for health and safety purposes and defended by the State of Pennsylvania. Further, it was clear that the Coal Subsidence Act took the full value of coal that was required to be left in place to meet the subsidence standards. This coal had no other value to the mining company. The loss of value from the ban on mining was considerable. Further, the support estate was a recognized legal estate under Pennsylvania law.

Five-to-four Supreme Court decisions usually suggest uncertainty in an area of law. In that respect *Keystone* was a good bell-weather. An enthusiast for ample government powers unconstrained by the Takings Clause would have regarded the *Keystone Bituminous* decision as a strong endorsement of government powers in the regulatory takings area. As the dissent implied, *Keystone Bituminous* was a virtual overruling of the *Mahon* decision if not all of the language of Justice Holmes.⟩

⟨Two other decisions in the 1987 terms, however, left *Keystone Bituminous* looking more like a last assertion of broad government powers to avoid the Takings Clause than a harbinger of things to come.⟩ The other decisions began a decade in which the Supreme Court gave life to the Takings Clause well beyond what would have been expected a decade earlier.

---

[177] *Id.* at 485.
[178] *Id.*

In *First Lutheran Church v. Los Angeles County*,[179] the Court held that government's wrongful denial of a rebuilding permit could constitute a "temporary taking" for which compensation was required. Both majority and dissent made clear that the decision forced government officials to proceed at their peril. If their regulatory action was eventually held to be a taking, government would have to pay rather than simply apologize for an erroneous reading of its authority.

In *Nollan v. California Coastal Commission*,[180] and later in *Dolan v. City of Tigard*[181] the Court examined the constitutionality of conditions imposed on grants of government regulatory permission. The *Dolan* facts are illustrative. The Dolans sought a building permit from the City to expand their store. The City insisted that in return for the grant of the permit the Dolans dedicate a part of the property for flood control purposes and another part for a bicycle path. The Dolans claimed that this forced dedication ("give us the property if you want the building permit") violated the Takings Clause.

The *Dolan* Court returned to its analysis in *Nollan*. There, the Court found the requested dedication of land (a beachfront easement) was unrelated to plaintiff's requested permit to expand his house. In Justice Scalia's colorful phrasing: "In short, unless the permit condition serves the same governmental purpose as the development ban, the building restriction is not a valid regulation of land use but an 'out-and-out plan of extortion'"[182]

In *Dolan* the Court agreed there was the "essential nexus" between the expansion of the Dolans' store and parking lot and the need for more flood control land and alternatives to automobile traffic to the expanded store.[183] However, the Court insisted that the "essential nexus" was only the first question to be asked.[184] A second question was "whether the degree of the exactions demanded by the City's permit conditions bears the required relationship to the projected impact of petitioner's proposed development."[185]

To test this factor the Court adopted a "rough proportionality" test to determine compliance with the Takings Clause. "No precise mathematical calculation is required, but the city must make some sort of individualized determination that the required dedication is related both in nature and

---

[179] 482 U.S. 304 (1987).
[180] 483 U.S. 825 (1987).
[181] 512 U.S. 374 (1994).
[182] *Nollan* at 837.
[183] *Dolan* at 383.
[184] *Id.* at 386.
[185] *Id.* at 388.

extent to the impact of the proposed development."[186] The City could not do so on the record presented. Crucially, the City could not show why it needed title to the floodplain rather than a simple prohibition of development. Also the order for dedication of the bikepath lacked the precision the standard demanded. "[T]he city must make some effort to quantify its findings in support of the dedication for the . . . pathway beyond the conclusory statement that it could offset some of the traffic demand generated."[187]

The most significant recent Supreme Court takings case for energy law purposes is *Lucas v. South Carolina Coastal Commission*.[188] A beachfront landowner claimed that the South Carolina Beachfront Management Act and its application to his property forbade him from building two luxury homes. The Beachfront Act addressed significant environmental problems. Lucas conceded it was a proper exercise of the police power by the Legislature. However, he contended that the absolute prohibition of his homes constituted a compensable taking.

Justice Scalia reviewed the "regulatory takings" cases. He found two categories of cases crossed Justice Holmes' line of regulation going "too far." The first involved situations in which government actually took physical possession of plaintiff's property. This was clearly not the situation in *Lucas*. The second involved situations "where regulation denies all economically beneficial or productive use of land."[189] Justice Scalia elaborated: "[W]hen the owner of real property has been called upon to sacrifice all economically beneficial uses in the name of the common good, that is, to leave his property economically idle, he has suffered a taking."[190]

The opinion then addressed situations where government could constitutionally regulate noxious uses with no obligation to provide compensation. The Scalia opinion offered a difficult distinction involving the nature of rights acquired in property. "Where the State seeks to sustain regulation that deprives land of all economically beneficial use, we think it may resist compensation only if the logically antecedent inquiry into the nature of the owner's estate shows that the proscribed use interests were not part of his title to begin with . . ."[191] The opinion continued: "[Any] confiscatory regulations cannot be newly legislated . . ., (without compensation), but must inhere in the title itself, in the restrictions that background principles of the

---

[186] *Id.* at 391.
[187] *Id.* at 395-96.
[188] 505 U.S. 1003 (1992).
[189] *Id.* at 1015.
[190] *Id.* at 1019.
[191] *Id.* at 1027.

State's law of property and nuisance already place upon land ownership."[192] "When, however, a regulation that declares "off-limits" all economically productive or beneficial uses of land goes beyond what the relevant background principles would dictate, compensation must be paid to sustain it."[193]

The concurring and dissenting opinions found many flaws with the majority view. The finding that the land had been made valueless seemed dubious. Surely, there were values in a piece of prime beachfront property even if a house could not be built on it. The case was one that should have required Lucas to present appeals to the denial of building permits to South Carolina officials. Since Takings Clause jurisprudence has been most comfortable reviewing specific factual situations, the majority erred in trying to write a categorical rule. Lastly, the dissenters disagreed with Justice Scalia's rejection of contemporary legislation as a basis for establishing government police power constraints on property use. Such limitations could be just as valid as longstanding common law rules.

Nollan, Lucas, First Church, and *Dolan* vitalize the Takings Clause in the regulatory takings area. Valid exercises of the police power may run afoul of the requirement for "just compensation." The Court has not yet articulated an overarching theory that explains when regulation goes "too far" in *Mahon* terms. Court majorities on some of the major precedents are fragile. But, Takings law has become a check on the exercise of government power over many matters in the energy field.

III. THE LEGISLATIVE PROCESS

The Constitution provides limited guidance about how the legislative process works. Article I, Section 7, requires legislation to pass both Houses of Congress and be signed by the President or be reapproved by two-thirds majorities in Congress after a Presidential veto. State constitutions are usually no more detailed in defining the state legislative process. They are even less specific than Article I, section 8 in granting powers to the Legislature. Often, the state constitution simply notes that the "legislative power" is vested in the chambers of the Legislature. This open-ended power includes our frequently studied police power.

It is also worth recognizing that the powers of local governments (cities, counties, school districts, special purpose districts, etc.) are derived from either the State Constitution or the Legislature. While Constitutional

---

[192] *Id.* at 1029.
[193] *Id.* at 1030.

provision or legislative enactment may give considerable "home rule" to
localities, localities are not "sovereign" in the sense that States and the
United States are sovereign. The 1923 United States Supreme Court opinion
in *Trenton v. New Jersey*, makes the point clearly.

> In the absence of state constitutional provisions safeguarding it
> to them, municipalities have no inherent right of self-government
> which is beyond the legislative control of the State. A municipality
> is merely a department of the State, and the State may withhold,
> grant or withdraw powers and privileges as it sees fit.[194]

The United States Constitution makes little or no mention of some of
the essentials of modern federal legislative practice. Three such essentials
are the role of the President, the role of committees, and the role of outside
interest groups.

Article II, Section 3 of the Constitution authorizes the President "from
time to time [to] give to the Congress Information of the State of the Union,
and recommend to their Consideration such Measures as he shall judge
necessary and expedient . . ." We are familiar with the pomp of the Annual
State of the Union address by the President to both Houses of Congress.
That is merely the tip of the large iceberg that is Executive branch
involvement in the enactment of legislation.

Times change in the relations between President and Congress. The
first term of Franklin Roosevelt's New Deal and the early years of Lyndon
Johnson's Presidency were periods when Congress was more responder to
Presidential suggestions for legislation than initiator of that legislation. By
contrast, the return of Republican control to Congress in 1994, marked a
term of high legislative activity little influenced by the President.

The Executive Branch (numerically, by far the largest of the three
branches) will participate in lawmaking in a myriad of ways. Most visibly,
the President himself in the State of the Union or other public speech will
"present to the Congress" proposed legislation to remedy a perceived problem. When the President is not personally leading a campaign, specialists
in the Executive Branch will weigh in with Congressional Committees or
make their views known to key legislators. Lastly, the officers of the
Executive Branch are the closest observers within government of how well
existing legislation is working. Formal oversight hearings and less formal
contacts with Congress will suggest fine tuning of existing laws in order to
remain contemporary with the problems of the nation.

---

[194] 262 U.S. 182, 187 (1923).

The second fact of legislative life, ignored by the Constitution, is the significance of the committee process. Much of the refining of a piece of legislation is done in subcommittee or committee meetings in each house, and then in a conference committee consisting of representatives of both houses if there is disagreement on provisions of the bill. As a consequence, by the time any final vote is taken on a piece of legislation in the full Congress, the result is often predictable and the arguments perfunctory. The hard work, debate, and editing has been handled in specialized committees.

The committee system offers the advantages of developed expertise and of manageable working groups. The federal legislator is asked to deal with matters as disparate as national defense, energy regulation, health care, national parks, and taxation. No legislator can possibly be knowledgeable, let alone expert, in all of these fields. In many cases, the legislator's background before coming to Congress will not have prepared her or him for work in any of them. Therefore, the semi-permanent assignment of a legislator to a number of committees allows the acquisition of legislative expertise. The multi-term legislator has the opportunity to become a true national expert in fields of committee specialization.

The size of the Congress also compels the committee system. One hundred senators or 435 representatives considering a major piece of legislation without prior committee guidance would produce chaos. The same is true in smaller sized state legislatures.

The ample demands on Senators and Representatives (including the demands of raising funds for reelection) have encouraged the proliferation of legislative staff. Staff members may serve individual legislators or serve as members of permanent committees. In either capacity, staffers will bring or develop their own expertise that may allow their opinions to filter into legislation. An area like energy is particularly likely to see staff expertise come into play. Few legislators are likely to be confident they know about photovoltaic energy, off-shore oil drilling techniques, or global warming. The suggestion of the staff expert on the subject carries considerable weight.

The legislator is also likely to seek committee assignments according to personal expertise or constituency interest. Committees considering petroleum legislation have long had a Texas-Oklahoma-Louisiana flavor. Public lands committees are well staffed with western legislators. The undoubted expertise of these members is often coupled with substantial biases about the subject under regulation. Considerable friction will result when legislation threatens to harm the interests of the legislator's constituents.

The third major component of legislation, unmentioned in the Constitution, is the influence of private interest group representatives, popularly lobbyists. Much nonsense has been written about the influence of special interests on legislation. Typically my lobbyists educate and assist the legislative process and individual legislators. Your lobbyists mislead and corrupt it. The sensible place to begin an analysis of special interest influence is with the assumption that any legislature responds to community needs, and that such needs are often articulated by private groups.

Nor is there anything sacrosanct in the phrase "public interest group." Most of us lead our lives as members of particular groups or constituencies rather than as amorphous "public citizens." We are employees of General Motors, members of the Catholic Church, supporters of the Sierra Club or the National Rifle Association, military veterans, Mothers Against Drunk Driving, and residents of large cities or farms. Each group will have its own needs from government. Both good advocacy and a natural self-centeredness will assert our needs as "public needs." For example, the average university student, who may view herself as a supporter of many public causes, will probably rally to oppose any quadrupling of university tuition advocated by a group urging fairer distribution of resources in society.

Interest groups play a crucial role throughout the legislative process. In almost all cases, some interest group (including government departments) will have initiated legislation. As the legislation is being formed, interest groups will provide their information to legislators and staff members through formal testimony at committee hearings, letters, and personal contacts. Where opposing positions are well-represented, this process can provide a wealth of valuable factual and policy information to the legislator. The legislator (or more likely the staffer) who takes the time to digest the arguments of the National Coal Association, the National Association of Manufacturers, and the Friends of the Earth on a given piece of energy legislation will receive a considerable education on the topic.

One of the responsibilities of courts is to interpret legislation. As the discussion of *United States v. Locke* suggested, both legislative language and legislative intent may be imprecise. When adverse parties confront the imprecision, they may ask the courts to tell them "what the statute means."

Statutory interpretation deserves a treatise of its own. Easy generalizations such as finding the "plain meaning of the statute" or the "intent of the Legislature" are usually not helpful in deciding the cases that reach appellate courts. All too often, there is no one "plain meaning" or there are various views of the "intent of the Legislature." The invitation to look to "legislative history" may be no more helpful. Justice Jackson's concurrence in *United States v. California Public Utility Commission* makes the point well:

When we decide from legislative history . . . what Congress probably had in mind, we must put ourselves in the place of a majority of Congressmen and act according to the impression we think this history should have made on them. Never having been a Congressman, I am handicapped in that weird endeavor.[195]

IV. THE ADMINISTRATIVE PROCESS

Energy legislation, written by both the United States Congress and the State Legislatures, occupies hundreds of pages in the statute books. Some legislation in this field is remarkable for its specificity, often prescribing exact timetables for administrative compliance and ordering compliance with particular scientific standards.

Nevertheless, legislation only scrapes the surface in most areas. Much energy law takes the form of regulations and adjudications from some administrative agency. Depending on one's perspective, this is the evil influence of the bureaucracy or the thoroughly necessary work of the professional civil service in providing specificity to congressional generalizations.

The United States Constitution does not explicitly recognize the administrative realm of government. An extreme constitutional view would be that the legislature has no power to delegate its law-making responsibility in any fashion. The Supreme Court has rejected such an absolutist view. In 1911 *United States v. Grimaud* addressed the delegation of power to the Secretary of Agriculture.

> In the nature of things it was impracticable for Congress to provide general regulations for these various and varying details of management. Each reservation had its peculiar and special features; and in authorizing the Secretary of Agriculture to meet these local conditions Congress was merely conferring administrative functions upon an agent, and not delegating to him legislative power. The authority actually given was much less than what has been granted to municipalities by virtue of which they make by-laws, ordinances and regulations for the government of towns and cities.[196]

Congress could not confer its "legislative power." "But, when Congress had legislated and indicated its will, it could give to those who were to act under

---

[195] 345 U.S. 295, 319 (1953).
[196] 220 U.S. 506, 516 (1911).

such general provisions 'power to fill up the details' by the establishment of administrative rules and regulations."[197]

Two world wars and the New Deal later, the Court returned to the subject of delegation of legislative power in *American Power and Light v. SEC*.

> The legislative process would frequently bog down if Congress were constitutionally required to appraise before-hand the myriad situations to which it wishes a particular policy to be applied and to formulate specific rules for each situation. Necessity therefore fixes a point beyond which it is unreasonable and impracticable to compel Congress to prescribe detailed rules; it then becomes constitutionally sufficient if Congress clearly delineates the general policy, the public agency which is to apply it, and the boundaries of this delegated authority.[198]

The cases suggest two reasons why Congress is likely to delegate power to an administrative officer or agency: triviality and lack of expertise. Should the time of Congress be spent in determining the precise form to use in applying for a government license or the precise reclamation program to clean up after surface coal mining. Of equal importance, Congress, even aided by its staff experts, may be less sophisticated about scientific and technical matters than the career professionals at a government agency.

A further factor enters into the decision to delegate—politics. Congressmen and women facing reelection wish to avoid some hard questions. They may be comfortable setting general standards—the air should be cleaned up, strip mines should be reclaimed, oil spills should be avoided. In the abstract, these propositions draw considerable support and little opposition. However, the devil is in the details. Someone must determine whose polluting activity should be shut down or made more expensive in order to carry out the broad legislative goals. That unpopular job often falls to the unelected officer of the administrative agency tasked with implementing the legislation. The legislator may then rail about "bureaucracy run wild" in implementing the statute. Ultimately, if Congress does not like how its delegation of authority has been implemented it can amend the statute to make its wishes clear.

The well-drafted statute will make clear when powers are delegated to an administrative officer or agency. Once Congress has identified the problem it wishes addressed, it may authorize or mandate the Secretary or the Administrator to "make such rules and regulations as may be necessary" to implement legislative policy. Despite the identification of "the" Secretary

---

[197] *Id.* at 517.
[198] 329 U.S. 90, 105 (1946).

or Administrator, the actual regulation drafting will be done by members of the Department with special expertise in the matters to be regulated. The regulations will be issued in the name of the Secretary or Administrator. On important matters, the actual Secretary or Administrator may make policy judgments. More typically, the regulation is the project of non-political civil servants in the Department whose names would be known to only sophisticated followers of the Department's work.

Statutory guidance about the workings of the administrative process will be found in two places. The first is the particular substantive legislative act. Sections of the statute that address surface mining, atomic energy regulation, or grants for alternative energy sources will provide delegations of authority. In some cases the statute will provide rather precise guidance about how rules or regulations are to be drafted (e.g. opportunities for public notice, rights to comment about the proposed rule).

The second statutory guide appears in the Administrative Procedure Act, now codified in portions of Title 5, United States Code. This statute passed in 1946 does not address a particular subject matter (e.g. strip mining, clean air, nuclear safety). Instead the APA sets minimum requirements for the workings of the administrative process for most federal agencies.

In broad terms, the APA distinguishes between rulemakings and adjudications. No brief description can do full justice to the subtleties of the two terms. Generally, in rulemakings the agency acts like a legislature in setting standards to apply in the future to all parties involved in a matter under consideration.

By contrast, an adjudication will typically focus on a single party whose conduct is governed by a pre-existing legal standard. In adjudication, proceedings resemble the workings of a court. The affected party is normally allowed to be present, to present evidence, and to have the matter decided on the record by an administrative law judge, with further review by the agency and the courts.

While adjudications remain important in contemporary energy law, rulemaking predominates. Section 553 of the APA addresses rule makings. The shorthand description for this type of lawmaking is "notice and comment" rulemaking. Section 553 requires "general notice" of the proposed rule to appear in the Federal Register, a daily publication available to the public of the work of the federal government. The proposed rule must then "give interested persons an opportunity to participate in the rule making through submission of written data, views, or arguments with or without the opportunity for oral presentation." A significant proposed rule will often draw written comments from industries concerned, environmental and other advocacy groups, other government officers, and ordinary citizens. Section

553 requires the agency offering the rule to "consider" the comments. In practice, some comments will be adopted in full, some adopted in part, and some rejected. The entire process, however, gives those affected by the new regulation a chance to express their views and possibly to change the proposed draft.

Once the "notice and comment" process is complete, the regulations will become law. And, despite idle talk of regulations "not being real law", they can have as binding an effect as the Act of Congress or the State Legislature. Professor Kenneth Culp Davis, a leading expert on administrative law, captures the point well:

> Valid legislative rules have about the same effect as valid statutes; they are binding on courts. They are valid if (a) within the granted power, (b) issued pursuant to proper procedure, and (c) reasonable as a matter of due process.[199]

Administrative law exists at the state and local level as well as at the federal. Some states have well-defined administrative procedure acts and follow practices that resemble their federal counterpart. Other states are a good deal less formal in their proceedings. Nonetheless, all states carry out legislative mandates through officers of the state executive branch. In whatever form, agencies proceed with their tasks of setting general guidelines for the bodies they regulate and deciding specific requests (license applications, rate requests, administrative sanctions) for matters within their jurisdiction. Similar practices apply at the local level.

Our brief overview of the American legal system suggests the place of administrative law within the hierarchy of sources of law. A constitutional provision takes precedence over an inconsistent legislative or executive action. For example, neither the Congress nor a state legislature nor a city council could pass a law taking your house as part of an energy demonstration project without paying for it. The Fifth and Fourteenth Amendments control the contrary legislation.

In similar fashion, a regulation based on statutory authorization must be consistent with the statute. If the regulation conflicts with the statute or goes beyond its authority, the regulation will not be valid. Alternatively, if Congress is dissatisfied with a lawfully enacted regulation, it can overrule it by subsequent legislation.

Finally, the regulation binds the personnel of the department or agency adopting it. The government official is not free to decide the regulations are tedious or stupid or no longer serve public policy. The official is bound to

---

[199] K.C. Davis, ADMINISTRATIVE LAW TREATISE, Vol. II at 36.

follow the regulation even if she or he wrote it or has the power to change it. She or he may exercise that power to change it, but until the change takes place through legally appropriate procedures, the old regulation stands. The Supreme Court has emphasized that an agency is not free to disregard its own regulations. When such disregard occurs, an injured party (the disappointed license applicant, the disciplined company) will ask the department head or departmental review body to correct the error. If the department does not comply, the injured party can seek and receive assistance from a court. Typically, the court will order the agency to review the matter again, this time in compliance with the existing regulations.[200]

Thus the hierarchy: constitution controls statute, regulation and individual implementation. Statute controls regulation and individual implementation. Regulation controls individual implementation.

The hierarchy of legal authority defines how things work if the full resources of the legal system are called into play. In practice, the laws rarely require reference to the Constitution or the Supreme Court and often not to the Congress or state legislature. The law normally works at the regulatory or individual implementation level. As any good lawyer knows, in dealing with a low level bureaucrat, it is far better to point to a controlling provision of the office regulatory manual than to a provision of the Constitution.

Both legislatures and courts exercise significant powers over the administrative process. The legislature typically creates the administrative agency and determines the scope of its powers. What is created can be changed and a legislature that is displeased with an administrative agency has a variety of ways of making its displeasure known. The most extreme measure is to abolish the agency. Less drastic may be changes in its authority written in statute. Even if the statutory duties of the administrative agency are not changed, the legislature may send a powerful message by increasing or reducing its budget. Finally, the oversight hearing that allows influential legislators to praise or criticize the agency may be just as effective in persuading a change of agency policy as a change in the governing statute.

Courts also are an important player in administrative law. A considerable part of the work of the courts in the energy field involves review of administrative agency actions. The Administrative Procedure Act, 5 U.S.C. sec. 702 authorizes judicial review for "[a] person suffering legal wrong because of agency action." 5 U.S.C. sec. 706 authorizes the court to "decide all relevant questions of law, interpret constitutional and statutory

---

[200] United States v. Nixon, 418 U.S. 683 (1974); Vitarelli v. Seaton, 359 U.S. 535 (1959); United States *ex rel.* Accardi v. Shaughnessy, 347 U.S. 260 (1954).

provisions, and determine the meaning or applicability of the terms of an agency action." The section further specifies the reviewing court shall set aside actions (1) which are "arbitrary, capricious, an abuse of discretion, or otherwise not in accordance with law," (2) which are unconstitutional or in excess of statutory authority, (3) which do not follow "procedure required by law", or (4) which are "unsupported by substantial evidence in adjudicatory proceedings."

The relationship between specialized administrators and judges has fascinated scholars of the legal process. How intensively should a court second-guess the specialist? What procedural requirements should the administrator have to satisfy in order to enable the judge to make a meaningful review of the administrative decision? A leading case in establishing the judicial standard of review is *Citizens to Preserve Overton Park v. Volpe*.[201] In *Overton Park* the Court reversed and remanded a decision of the Secretary of Transportation to proceed with construction of an interstate highway through a Memphis park. The Court observed that in applying the "arbitrary, capricious . . ." standard of section 706 a "searching and careful" inquiry into the facts was required. The court reviewing an administrative action "must consider whether the decision was based on a consideration of the relevant factors and whether there has been a clear error of judgment." However, the court is not to "substitute its judgment for that of the agency."[202]

 A second task of the courts is to interpret whether administrative agency regulations are consistent with the legislative enactment. In *Chevron U.S.A. v. Natural Resources Defense Council*,[203] the Court offered a frequently quoted summary of the role of the judiciary in reviewing the issue:

> When a court reviews an agency's construction of the statute which it administers, it is confronted with two questions. First, always, is the question whether Congress has directly spoken to the precise question at issue. If the intent of Congress is clear, that is the end of the matter; for the court, as well as the agency, must give effect to the unambiguously expressed intent of Congress. If, however, the court determines Congress has not directly addressed the precise question at issue, the court does not simply impose its own construction on the statute, as would be necessary in the absence of an administrative interpretation. Rather, if the statute is silent or ambiguous with respect to the

[201] 401 U.S. 402 (1971).
[202] *Id.* at 416.
[203] 467 U.S. 837 (1984).

specific issue, the question for the court is whether the agency's answer is based on a permissible construction of the statute.[204]

The Court continued:

If Congress has explicitly left a gap for the agency to fill, there is an express delegation of authority to the agency to elucidate a specific provision of the statute by regulation. Such legislative regulations are given controlling weight unless they are arbitrary, capricious, or manifestly contrary to the statute. Sometimes the legislative delegation to an agency on a particular question is implicit rather than explicit. In such a case, a court may not substitute its own construction of a statutory provision for a reasonable interpretation made by the administrator of an agency.[205]

The agency's familiarity with both its governing statute and the policies it implements required a rule "that considerable weight should be accorded to an executive department's construction of a statutory scheme it is entrusted to administer . . ."[206]

The chapters that follow will provide frequent examples of the working of the administrative process. ❦

---

[204] *Id.* at 842-43.
[205] *Id.* at 843-44.
[206] *Id.* at 844.

CHAPTER FOUR

International Law

by James E. Hickey, Jr.[*]

I. INTRODUCTION

This chapter introduces the energy lawyer to some basics of international law and international law's relation to municipal (domestic) law. The premises for an international law introduction in this book are threefold. First, in the 21st century, globalization in energy sectors is very likely to increase and not decrease. Second, the law relevant to that globalization process increasingly will be "internationalized" (or at a minimum will be affected in some way by international law). Third, the domestic energy lawyer increasingly will have to deal both with "internationalized" domestic law and with "domesticized" international law.

This chapter proceeds in four sections. Section II defines public international law. Section III comments generally on the process of globalization and specifically on the globalization of energy sectors. Section IV briefly lays out the sources and evidences of international law. Section V concentrates on the relation between international law and domestic law, particularly in United States courts.

II. INTERNATIONAL LAW

The international law addressed in this chapter is primarily public international law. Public international law is the law that governs the relations of states, and the relations of states and international organizations. It creates legal rights and duties for states and international organizations and, where relevant, it binds those under the jurisdiction of states (i.e., individuals, corporations, business associations, and government agencies and instrumentalities). This is the body of international law which most reflects, *de jure* or *de facto*, energy policies that are, directly and

---

[*] Professor Hickey would like to thank his research assistant, Jessica Lombardo, for her help on this chapter.

indirectly, implemented and applied through domestic statutes, administrative regulations and court litigation.

This chapter does not directly examine private international law, comparative law, or domestic aspects of foreign relations law. Private international law refers to the law governing transnational relations among private parties (individuals, partnerships, corporations, joint ventures, and the like). Private international law is composed mostly of rules to resolve conflicts of domestic law, especially where transnational private contracts are involved. The most frequent relevant question in private international law among private parties is which *domestic* law of which state is to apply to a private, transnational relationship. In energy transactions, private international law questions often arise in the context of joint ventures and international contracts. Related, but different, public international law inquiries here are whether a state has a basis of prescriptive or enforcement jurisdiction over private persons or their activities[1] and, where two or more states each have a basis for jurisdiction, which public international law principles apply to decide which of those states *ought* to have jurisdiction.[2]

Comparative law is the discipline of examining and contrasting *domestic* legal systems. It does not involve international law except to the extent international law has been adopted by, or incorporated into, domestic law.

Foreign relations involves both the public international law that governs the *external* relations of states, and states and international organizations, and the *internal* domestic allocation of foreign relations powers (mostly an aspect of constitutional law). This chapter addresses primarily the former and examines the latter only to the extent it relates to the relationship of domestic and international law addressed in Section V.

III. GLOBALIZATION AND INTERNATIONAL LAW

A. Globalization Generally

Since the end of World War II and the founding of the United Nations, the world has moved toward increased contacts and interaction among states, international organizations, and nationals of states. That increased

---

[1] The four primary bases for an individual state to assert jurisdiction over persons or activities are the territorial principle, the nationality principle, the protective principle and the universality principle. *See* American Law Institute, 1 RESTATEMENT OF FOREIGN RELATIONS LAW (THIRD) (1987) at 230-244.

[2] *See* Timberlane Lumber Co. v. Bank of America, 549 F. 2d 597 (9th Cir. 1976) (using a jurisdiction balancing test based on a rule of reason.)

interaction, in turn, has evolved into accepted usages, habits, and practices that in many areas have hardened into norms and rules of international law.

The movement toward globalization has accelerated during the 1990s because of at least six interrelated and dramatic developments:

First, the disintegration of the Soviet Union in the early 1990s signaled the end of the political and military "empire" system of world governance—a process that began in earnest at the close of World War II with the movements to replace colonies with independent states. Second, the early 1990s also signaled the end of the Cold War and an accelerating movement toward global economic integration and political cooperation on regional and global fronts. Third, states increasingly have moved to embrace both democratic forms of government and privatized free market economies. Fourth, the computerized information age has arrived, which has made news and data of every kind and description available instantaneously to an increasing portion of the world's population. Fifth, the global problems needing global responses have increased dramatically in the last half decade in such areas as crime, energy, the environment, finance, food, human rights, intellectual property, natural resources, and trade, all of which have involved varying degrees of international effort to resolve. Sixth, the number of entities, state and non state, that have become involved in these global issues has multiplied exponentially and now collectively number in the thousands.[3]

Over the next few decades, the general direction of world affairs will likely be toward more globalization—absent a world war, global economic depression, or some other unforeseen global catastrophe. With that increased globalization, there will be a corresponding growth in the international law needed to accommodate inter-nation and transnational relationships.

B. Globalization of Energy Sectors

Globalization is taking place in energy sectors in several respects. The fuel cycles of nearly all energy sectors have become international.[4] There is also a growing appreciation that global environmental and economic consid-

---

[3] James E. Hickey, Jr., *The Source of International Legal Personality In the Twenty First Century*, 2 HOFSTRA L. & POL'Y SYMP. 1, 2 (1997).

[4] *See* Chapter One.

erations may affect local segments of the energy fuel cycle that have not expanded into other countries. Finally, the growing acceptance by the international community of the importance of energy transactions to global economic well being and global environmental health has also produced a dramatic increase in the number and kind of international actors involved in energy-related transactions.

1.   *Expansion of Energy Fuel Cycles*

The fuel cycles of most energy sectors, in one phase or another, have expanded into other countries. With the dramatic increase in the number of nuclear power plants in certain countries, the distribution and end-use phases of the nuclear fuel cycle have become internationalized. For example, France has moved in recent decades to rely primarily on French nuclear plants to meet its national energy needs. The excess power generated from those nuclear power plants often is sold to neighboring countries.

The back end of the nuclear fuel cycle has become internationalized in at least two ways. First, the dismantling and storage of high level radioactive materials at the end of a plant's life inherently engenders international concern, suggestions for disposal in other countries, or proposals for extraterritorial disposal in vitrified cylinders in the seabed under the high seas. As to the latter, the United States has established an Office of Subseabed Disposal Research in the Department of Energy to research, develop and demonstrate all aspects of subseabed disposal of high level radioactive waste and spent nuclear fuel.[5] In 1992, the Russians disclosed that they had been using the oceans of the East Arctic and North Atlantic as a dump for radioactive waste.[6] Given the status of the high seas and deep sea bed as an oceans commons in which all states have a legal interest, ocean disposal of high level nuclear waste necessarily is an international law concern. With regard to low level nuclear waste, international treaty law (The London Dumping Convention) prohibits dumping of low level radioactive waste in the oceans.[7]

Transnational nuclear waste in the form of spent nuclear fuel rods has also become an international issue. Some nations, like Great Britain, actively seek to reprocess the spent nuclear fuel rods of other countries, while the

---

[5] *See* Nuclear Waste Policy Act, 42 U.S.C.A. §1024.
   [6] *See* Walter Sullivan, *Soviet Nuclear Dumps Disclosed*, N.Y. TIMES, November 24, 1992, at C9.
   [7] INT'L ENV'T REP 839, Nov 17, 1993.

United States, for security reasons, opposes transnational reprocessing of nuclear fuel rods.

The fuel cycle of the petroleum sector (oil and natural gas[8]) has long been international in scope. Typically, an internationalized fuel cycle transaction involves oil or natural gas that is discovered and extracted in one country from wells drilled on land or on the maritime continental shelf and transported by oil tanker or pipeline to other countries where it is refined, distributed and used.

Since 1958, for example, the United States has consumed more energy than it has produced.[9] The deficit has been made up by energy, mostly oil and natural gas, imported from the Middle East, South America, Mexico, and elsewhere. In 1996, the United States imported 46 percent of the petroleum it used.[10] Those transnational petroleum transactions increasingly are the object of international law. For example, NAFTA has provisions that address energy transactions among the United States, Canada and Mexico.[11] Europe has adopted the Energy Charter Treaty which addresses the production of oil, gas and electricity in Eastern European and former USSR states that is transported or transmitted to Western European countries.[12] (Although the United States is not yet formally a party to the ECT, it is presently a participating observer in ECT matters and is eligible to join the ECT as a party). In addition, international law increasingly governs the environmental consequences of ocean transport of petroleum by tankers from countries where it is produced or refined to countries where it is used.[13]

In the hydroelectric sector, internationalization has occurred in the transportation and production phases of the fuel cycle. For example, Canada now sells hydroelectric power to consumers in Washington, New York and New England.[14]

---

[8] *See* Chapters Seven and Eight.

[9] *See* ANNUAL ENERGY REVIEW 1996, DOE/EIA-0384 (96), July 1997, at 2.

[10] *See id.*

[11] North American Free Trade Agreement Between the Government of the U.S. of America, the Government of Canada, and the Government of the United Mexican States, Dec. 17, 1992, arts. 601-609, 32 I.L.M. 289, 364 (1993) [hereinafter NAFTA].

[12] *See* The Energy Charter Treaty, Dec. 17, 1994, 34 I.L.M. 360 (1995).

[13] *E.g.,* THE UNITED NATIONS CONVENTION ON THE LAW OF THE SEA, art. 211, 21 I.L.M. 1261, 1310 (1982) [hereinafter Law of the Sea].

[14] *See* Allan R. Gold, *New York State Weighs Canceling a Huge Canadian Power Contract,* N.Y. TIMES, Aug. 29, 1991, at A5; Sam Howe Verhovek, *Vermont City Considers Fate of Hydropower Deal,* N.Y. TIMES, Oct. 8, 1991, at A4.

Even the coal sector has become internationalized at the end use phase of the fuel cycle.[15] Normally, the coal fuel cycle takes place primarily within the domestic jurisdiction of one country and involves local production (mining) and local use (burning in electric plants located near the mine). However, international concerns have arisen in the past twenty years or so about the transnational environmental effects of emissions from coal burning. Canada, for example, has complained in recent decades that emissions from United States coal-fired power plants in the Midwest are the cause of acid rain in Canada. That concern has resulted in international law, in the form of the United States Canada Air Quality Agreement, to address transboundary air pollution.[16]

2. *Global Economic and Environmental Concerns Affect Local Segments of the Energy Fuel Cycle*[17]

Air quality concerns about the energy fuel cycle are not merely bilateral or regional, but global as well. For example, in 1992, the United States signed the Climate Change Convention along with 153 other States. This Convention protects the earth's climate by stabilizing atmospheric concentrations of greenhouse gases which are made up primarily of emissions from coal-fired power plants.[18] In November 1998, the United States also signed the Kyoto global-warming accord that calls for reductions in heat-trapping gases produced by power plants and automobiles among other sources.[19]

Energy sector fuel cycles have also been internationalized in the sense that they have been the object of proceedings before international fora. For example, the International Court of Justice (ICJ) has been asked repeatedly to resolve international law disputes among opposite or adjacent coastal states over claims to jurisdiction in the continental shelf associated with the production of oil and gas under the seabed.[20] The World Trade Organization recently was asked to resolve an international trade law dispute involving

---

[15] *See* Chapter Nine.

[16] 30 I.L.M. 676 (1991).

[17] *See* Chapter Five on the Environment.

[18] 31 I.L.M. 849 (1992).

[19] *U.S. Signs Pact on Environment*, NEWSDAY, November 13, 1998, at A28.

[20] *E.g.*, *North Sea Continental Shelf* cases (Denmark, Germany and The Netherlands) [1969] ICJ Rep. 3; *Case Concerning Delimitation of The Maritime Boundary in The Gulf of Maine* (Canada and the U.S.), [1984] ICJ Rep. 246.

the application of United States gasoline standards to foreign oil imports from Brazil and Venezuela.[21]

3. The Increase in International Actors Involved in Energy Fuel Cycles

As mentioned above, the nuclear power sector has become globalized especially at the back end of its fuel cycle. It also has become internationalized in other phases of the nuclear fuel cycle. In the production phase, nuclear technical expertise used to build nuclear power plants now involves multinational engineering and construction corporations and even multinational law firms involved in the planning and construction of nuclear power plants all around the world. While the nuclear power industry in the United States is now moribund,[22] there exists a continuing involvement of United States companies that sell and apply their nuclear expertise in nuclear power plant projects in many countries.

In the electricity sector, internationalization has taken place, not so much in the energy fuel cycle of the commodity itself, but in the activities of electric companies. For example, increasingly United States electric utilities are buying and investing in electric facilities in Europe, Asia and the Americas. Similarly, foreign companies and investors increasingly are acquiring ownership stakes in United States electric utilities.[23]

In addition to private corporate actors, a number of international organizations have become directly involved in the nuclear sector. For example, the International Atomic Energy Agency (IAEA) provides a global forum for international cooperation in the use of nuclear energy. In addition, regional international organizations have become involved in the nuclear sector.[24] The European Atomic Energy Community (EURATOM) fosters the

---

[21] *See* U.S. Standards for Reformulated Gas, WT/DS2, WT/DS4 (complaints by Brazil and Venezuela) Report of the Panel and Appellate Body Adopted on May 20, 1996.

[22] *See* Chapter Ten. *See also* James E. Hickey, Jr. *Mississippi Power and Light Company: A Departure Point for Extension of the "Bright Line" Between Federal and State Regulatory Jurisdiction over Public Utilities*, 10 J. OF ENERGY L. & POL'Y 57, 63-64, 90 (1989), reprinted in XII PUBLIC UTILITIES LAW ANTHOLOGY, 307 (1989).

[23] *E.g., General Electric to Build Central Asian Dam*, N.Y. TIMES, Oct 14, 1992, at D1; *Energy is Buying Two-Thirds Stake in Bulgarian Utility*, N.Y. TIMES, Oct. 15, 1998, at C1; and *Statoil of Norway Invests in New York Power Stations*, N.Y. TIMES, May 23, 1998, at D1.

[24] *See* Statute of the International Atomic Energy Agency, I The International Law of Nuclear Energy, Basic Documents at 3 (Nuclear Energy). The United States is a party to the Statute.

peaceful and cooperative "growth of nuclear industries."[25] The organization of American States (OAS) created the Inter-American Nuclear Energy Commission (IANEC) "to foster and facilitate Inter-American cooperation for the development of peaceful uses of nuclear energy."[26] The Organization for Economic Co-operation and Development (OECD) created the Nuclear Energy Agency to "further the development of the production and uses of nuclear energy . . . for peaceful purposes."[27] Other global and regional organizations involved in varying degrees in the nuclear sector include the United Nations and its specialized agencies like the Food and Agricultural Organization (FAO), the United Nations' Environment Program (UNEP), the International Labor Organization (ILO), the International Maritime Organization (IMO), and the Arab Energy Agency.

Other actors in the form of nongovernmental organizations (NGOs) are exerting increasing influence over the international law applicable to energy sectors. For example, in the hydroelectric fuel cycle activities, the construction of very large hydroelectric facilities, in Brazil and in China (Three Gorges Dam), have been opposed by international environmental NGOs.[28]

A recent and misguided involvement of an NGO in energy fuel cycles occurred in the Brent Spar incident in 1995.[29] Here, the British branch of the NGO Greenpeace opposed an arrangement between the multinational oil company, Royal Dutch Shell and the British Government. The arrangement was to dispose of an oil platform erected over the British continental shelf in the Outer Hebrides by sinking it in the deep sea. Greenpeace claimed that thousands of tons of oil sludge would contaminate the North Sea in the process and demanded that the Brent Spar be towed to Norway and cut up and disposed of on land. Greenpeace then organized a press campaign, a helicopter harassment of the Brent Spar activity, and a consumer boycott in Germany. Shell relented and agreed to do what Greenpeace asked. It later turned out that Greenpeace was wrong about the oil sludge contamination and that disposal at sea of the Brent Spar might have been the soundest and environmentally least intrusive disposal method after all.

---

[25] Article 1 of the EURATOM Treaty, Nuclear Energy, *supra* note 24 at 32. (Nuclear Energy).

[26] Article 1 of the IANEC Statute, Nuclear Energy, *supra* note 24 at 118. The U.S. is a party to additional Protocols I and II.

[27] Article 1 of the Statute of the OECD Nuclear Energy Agency, Nuclear Energy, *supra* note 24 at 22. The United States is a member of the OECD.

[28] *See* Chapter Eleven on Hydroelectricity.

[29] *See* Articles cited at 9-7-95 WLN 1739, Sept. 7, 1995.

The Brent Spar incident also demonstrates the growing relevance of international law in energy fuel cycles.[30] Here, although the Brent Spar oil platform was located within British jurisdiction (its continental shelf) and governed by international contracts (joint operating agreements), international law questions remain. For example, Article 60(3) of the 1982 Law of the Sea Treaty requires in part:

> Any installations or structures which are abandoned or disused shall be removed to ensure safety of navigation, taking into account any generally accepted international standards established in this regard by the competent international organization. Such removal shall also have due regard to fishing, the protection of the marine environment and the rights and duties of other States. Appropriate publicity shall be given to the depth, position and dimensions of any installations or structures not entirely removed.[31]

Article III 1(a)(I) of the London Dumping Convention,[32] which applies to all ocean waters, defines dumping to be "any deliberate disposal at sea of . . . platforms or other manmade structures at sea."

Regionally, the 1992 Convention for the Protection of the Marine Environment of the North Atlantic in Annex III, Article 5, provides:[33]

> No disused offshore installation or disused offshore pipeline shall be left wholly or partly in place in the maritime area without a permit. . . . No such permit shall be issued if the disused offshore installation or disused offshore pipeline contains substances which result or are likely to result in hazards to human health, harm to living resources and marine ecosystem. . . ."

Even international "soft law" might come into play.[34] The 1989 International Maritime Organization (IMO) Guidelines and Standards require

---

[30] *See* Samir Mankabady, *DeCommissioning of Offshore Installations*, 28 J. MAR. L. & COM. 603 (1997).

[31] *Supra* note 13.

[32] 26 U.S.T. 2403.

[33] 32 I.L.M. 1069 (1993). The Convention was signed by North-East Atlantic States including the United Kingdom and the Netherlands.

[34] *See discussion infra*, at 17.

that certain offshore installations be removed and give coastal states the discretion to leave certain other installations in place.[35]

IV.   SOURCES AND EVIDENCES OF INTERNATIONAL LAW[36]

Where does the energy lawyer find international law that may be relevant to transnational energy fuel cycle transactions or to local segments of energy fuel cycles that may be affected by international law? Traditionally, one looks to four sources for relevant international law: treaties; custom; general principles of law; and judicial decisions and the work of writers. Article 38 of the Statute of the International Court of Justice puts it this way:

> The Court, whose function is to decide in accordance with international law such disputes as are submitted to it, shall apply:
>
> a. international conventions, whether general or particular, establishing rules expressly recognized by the contesting states;
>
> b. international custom, as evidence of a general practice accepted as law;
>
> c. The general principles of law recognized by civilized nations;
>
> d. [j]udicial decisions and the teachings of the most highly qualified publicists of the various nations as subsidiary means for the determination of rules of law.[37]

A.   International Conventions or Treaties

Treaties are international agreements governed by international law that are entered into by two or more states or other international persons,

---

[35] *See* Richard J. McLaughlin, *Coastal State Discretion, U.S. Policy, and The New IMO Guidelines For The Disposal of Offshore Structures: Has Article 5(5) of the 1958 Continental Shelf Convention Been Entirely Removed?* 1 TERR. SEA J. 245 (1991).

[36] *See generally* Ian Brownlie, PRINCIPLES OF PUBLIC INTERNATIONAL LAW 1-30 (5th ed. 1998); 1 Oppenheim's INTERNATIONAL LAW (Peace) 22-52 (Jennings and Watts eds. 1992); American Law Institute, 1 RESTATEMENT (THIRD) OF THE FOREIGN RELATIONS LAW OF THE UNITED STATES 24-39 (1987).

[37] 1995 U.N.Y.B. 1535, U.N. Sales No. E.96.1.1.

like state-created international organizations.[38] Treaties come in a variety of forms all of which fit the general definition of treaty. The *form* of a treaty generally is immaterial to its legal effect as a treaty. Forms include bilateral treaties, multilateral treaties, conventions, agreements, protocols, concordats, charters, statutes, covenants, pacts, etc. Thus, such energy-related instruments as the Energy Charter Treaty,[39] the 1982 Law of the Sea Convention,[40] the Protocol to Amend the 1963 Vienna Convention on Civil Liability for Nuclear Damage, [41] and the North American Free Trade Agreement[42] are all treaties under international law.

Today, treaties are the international law source of choice among states and international organizations because they have several attributes which make them distinctly attractive to use. Treaties are express manifestations of international obligations and they are in writing. This makes it relatively easy to analyze a treaty's words and to determine the nature and scope of international law rights and duties. Treaties also may be concluded relatively rapidly in response to problems that need to be swiftly addressed. They are very flexible instruments which are adaptable in form and substance to virtually any occasion. Once treaties come into force, they may be amended, suspended and terminated in response to changing conditions. Finally, they are on deposit with the United Nations which makes them very easy to find.[43] Not surprisingly, the number and scope of treaties is expanding geometrically. In the mid 1950s the United Nations had registered with it about 3,500 treaties. Today, that number has grown to over 30,000.[44]

From a source of law standpoint, the most important international treaties are the so-called "law-making treaties." These treaties attempt to codify or to progressively develop the body of international law related to some particular subject matter and are meant to apply to as many states as possible. Law-making treaties may, in varying degrees, apply even to states and other international legal personalities that are not a party to them to the extent they codify or reflect customary international law. In contrast,

---

[38] *See* 2 ILC YEARBOOK 31 (1962).

[39] Energy Charter Treaty, *supra* note 11.

[40] Law of the Sea, *supra* note 12.

[41] The Protocol to Amend the 1963 Vienna Convention on Civil Liability for Nuclear Damage, Sept. 12, 1997, 36 I.L.M. 1454 (1997).

[42] NAFTA, *supra* note 10.

[43] Article 102 of the U.N. Charter requires registration and publication of all treaties by all U.N. members.

[44] *The UN Treaty Collection—Overview* (visited November 9, 1998) <http://www.un.org/Depts/Treaty/overview.htm>.

other treaties are meant to apply only to a few states and may involve a narrow range of duties and rights.

Finally, it should be mentioned that there is a body of international law on the law *of* treaties generally that is itself contained in a treaty—the Vienna Convention on the Law of Treaties.[45] Here one finds the generally accepted rules governing making treaties, changing treaties, ending treaties, and interpreting treaties.

B.   Customary International Law

If there is no specific treaty in force that addresses a particular international law problem, the search for applicable international law turns to customary international law (custom). For example, in the North Sea Continental Shelf cases (involving coastal state jurisdiction over potential oil resources in the continental shelf of the North Sea), the ICJ resorted to custom to find applicable international law. One of the disputants, the Federal Republic of Germany (FRG), was not a party to a treaty (the 1958 Geneva Convention on the Continental Shelf) which might otherwise have resolved the jurisdictional dispute among Denmark, The Netherlands and the FRG.[46]

Finding customary international law is a little like Justice Potter Stewart's observations about obscenity—"I can't define it but I know it when I see it."[47] Here, the definition of custom is straightforward. The problem is knowing custom when one sees it. The application of the definition in particular settings presents the difficulties for international lawyers.

Custom is defined simply as the general practice of states accepted as law. It is the international law governing state relations based on what states do and what they accept as binding legal obligations. An analogue to custom in United States law is the common law, which, of course, is the

---

[45] 1155 U.N.T.S. 331; 8 I.L.M. 679 (1969); *see also* Ian Sinclair, THE VIENNA CONVENTION ON THE LAW OF TREATIES (1984).

[46] *See supra* note 20. The rule of custom spelled out by the ICJ was that, failing agreement, lateral delimitation of continental shelf among the disputant states was:

> "[t]o be effected in accordance with equitable principles, and taking account of all relevant circumstances, in such a way as to leave as much as possible to each party all those parts of the continental shelf that constitute a natural prolongation of its land territory into and under the sea, without encroachment on the natural prolongation of the land territory of the other."

[47] Jacobellis v. Ohio, 378 U.S. 184, 197 (1964).

body of law that is derived from usages and customs of the people confirmed by judicial decisions (in contrast to statutes).

At an earlier time in history, many areas of international law had customary international law as their primary source. For example, the law of the sea[48] and the law of diplomatic privileges and immunities[49] were derived almost entirely from custom. Today, however, the role of custom as the primary source of international law has diminished. Many subject areas previously addressed by custom have now been "codified" in treaties. For example, the law of the sea is now reflected, for the most part, in the four 1958 Geneva Conventions on the Law of the Sea[50] and in the 1982 Convention on the Law of the Sea.[51] In addition, emerging and new international problems that need international law to address, more often than not, are the object of treaties and not custom. For example, the problems of climate change, ozone layer depletion, acid rain, transport of hazardous wastes, and civil liability for nuclear accidents have all been addressed by treaty and not by custom. In general, it can be expected that new international law affecting energy fuel cycles will probably come in the form of treaties rather than custom.

There are several reasons for the shift away from custom as a source of international law and toward treaties. First, custom is unwritten law while treaties are written law. Customary international law often is difficult to determine and often does not produce particularly precise details of law that may be needed to resolve specific questions of international relations. Written law in treaties, by contrast, makes the content of international law principles generally easier to determine and apply. Second, treaties, more often than not, address international law problems more swiftly.[52] Nonetheless, custom remains a significant source of international law. For example,

---

[48] *See* James E. Hickey, Jr., *Custom and Land-Based Pollution of the High Seas*, 15 SAN DIEGO L. REV. 409 (1978).

[49] *See* James E. Hickey, Jr. and Annette Fisch, *The Case to Preserve Criminal Jurisdiction Immunity Accorded Foreign Diplomatic and Consular Personnel in the U.S.*, 41 THE HASTINGS L.J. 351 (1990).

[50] The Convention on the Territorial Sea and the Contiguous Zone, 516 UNTS 205; the Convention on Fishing and Conservation of the Living Resources of the High Seas, 559 UNTS 285; the Convention of the Continental Shelf, 499 UNTS 311; and the Convention on the High Seas, 450 UNTS 11.

[51] Law of the Sea Treaty, *supra* note 12.

[52] Sometimes the reverse is true. For example, the international law rules permitting satellites to pass over the sovereign territory of states as a matter of right arose in "hot house" fashion quite rapidly with the 1957 launch of Sputnik and the immediate acquiescence in its orbit by the world community. By contrast, it took states 15 years from 1967 to 1982 to agree to the Law of The Sea Convention.

in *The Texaco/Libya Arbitration*,[53] the sole arbitrator applied customary international law rules on expropriation to uphold oil concession contracts between the Libyan Government and two oil companies. The customary international law found by the arbitrator required that a governmental nationalization or expropriation had to be for a public purpose and required appropriate compensation to the companies whose property was nationalized or expropriated. Under custom the taking must also be non-discriminatory.[54]

Customary international law is comprised of two components, the general practice of states and the acceptance of that practice as law. These components require some comment.

1.   The General Practice of States

a.   The "of States" Component of Practice

Traditionally, international law governs the relations of sovereign states. That is, since States are sovereign entities and subjects of international law, they are both the law makers and law obeyers. It is their practices that form binding legal obligations and assertable rights. Traditionally, the practice of non-state entities such as corporations, international organizations, and non-governmental organizations (NGOs) did not constitute practice directly relevant to the formation of custom. Of course, the reaction of states to non-state practices in the form of diplomatic protests, endorsements, actions, and votes by states representatives to international bodies, etc., all are acts of state practice that are directly relevant to custom formation.

A relatively recent complication to the custom formation equation is the emergence of new, non-state subjects of international law having international legal personality.[55] For example, the United Nations has been acknowledged to have the international law right to bring claims for injuries

---

[53] 17 I.L.M. 1 (1978).

[54] *See* Banco Nacional de Cuba v. Sabbatino, 376 U.S. 398, 429 (1964). ("There is, of course, authority, in international judicial and arbitral decisions, in the expressions of national governments, and among commentators for the view that a taking is improper under international law if it is not for a public purpose, is discriminatory, or is without provision for prompt, adequate, and effective compensation.")

[55] Hickey, *supra* note 3.

to its personnel.[56] Specialized U.N. agencies like the World Health Organization (WHO) and the International Monetary Fund (IMF) have the right to seek advisory opinions of the I.C.J.[57] In these circumstances, it seems reasonable to ascribe more direct significance in custom formation to non-state international legal personalities than otherwise might be the case.

b.   The Generality Requirement

This component in the definition of custom requires that a certain "amount" of state practice must exist to establish customary international law. The question is how much state practice is needed to satisfy the generality requirement? The term "general" certainly refers to something less then complete uniformity, but how much less than unanimous acceptance of a practice by states and other international legal personalities is permissible depends on the circumstances. For example, the generality requirement for custom could be met by only a handful of states that are capable of engaging in a particular practice coupled with acquiescence of the remaining majority of states. This is what happened when the customary international law rule arose in the late 1950s that states had a right to orbit satellites over the territory of other states. At the time that the customary rule formed, only two states, the United States and the U.S.S.R., were capable of engaging in the practice of orbiting satellites. Other states either did not object or acquiesced in the practice and the customary international law rule was born. The generality requirement may also implicate so-called regional custom where a limited number of states in a common geographic area or who share common interests generate a rule among them without the involvement of the larger community of states. For example, the notion of asylum in churches is a regional customary rule unique to South American States and is not a practice engaged in by the majority of states in the world.

2.   The Acceptance of the Practice as Law

The second requirement of custom is the so-called psychological element of custom referred to in international law circles as *opinio juris sive necessitatis*. This means that the practice is engaged in or not engaged in out of a belief that law requires it. This element separates mere usages and habits engaged in by states from state practices undertaken as a matter of

---

[56] Reparation for Injuries Suffered in the Service of the U.N., [1949] I.C.J. REP 174.

[57] Article 96 (2) of the U.N. Charter.

legal obligation. For example, the habit of states to uniformly give a visiting head of a state a 21-gun salute does not amount to customary law because of the absence of *opinio juris*. That is, no state would consider that, if it gave only a 20-gun salute to a visiting head of state, it would be violating a *legal* obligation. On the other hand, the practice of states to grant criminal jurisdiction immunity to resident diplomatic agents clearly fulfills the *opinio juris* requirement.[58] That is, states are obliged as a matter of customary international law to uphold criminal jurisdiction immunity. If they do not, they understand that they have violated international law. That said, it is sometimes very difficult to empirically establish the existence of *opino juris* and for that reason it sometimes may be implied or inferred. This difficulty in establishing *opino juris* has led some to challenge the need for *opino juris* in customary international law making. Under this view, the emphasis would be on establishing only the "generality" of the practices of states and other international legal personalities.

C. General Principles of Law

If there is no treaty, custom, judicial decision or authoritative international legal writings on point, the ICJ may rely on municipal (domestic) law as needed. That is, in cases where there is a gap or vacuum in international law, resort may be had to a general principle of municipal law. The most often invoked predicate for application of municipal law is that the general principle at issue is shared in common among most states. For example, the ICJ in the *Barcelona Traction Case*[59] resorted to municipal law to deal with Belgium's assertion of Belgian shareholder claims to a Canadian corporation's assets seized by the Spanish government in a Spanish forced-bankruptcy proceeding:

> [t]he present case essentially involves factors derived from municipal law—the distinction and the community between the company and the shareholder—which the Parties, however widely their interpretations may differ, each take as the point of departure of their reasoning. If the Court were to decide the case in disregard of the relevant institutions of municipal law it would, without justification, invite serious legal difficulties. It would lose touch with reality, for there are no corresponding institutions of

---

[58] *See* Hickey and Fisch, *supra* note 49. The customary international law of diplomatic privileges and immunities is so settled that it was codified in the 1964 Vienna Convention on Diplomatic Relations, 500 U.N.T.S. 95.

[59] Case Concerning the Barcelona Traction, Light and Power Co., Limited, Second Phase, Belgium v. Spain, [1970] I.C.J. 3.

international law to which the Court could resort. Thus the Court has, as indicated, not only to take cognizance of municipal law but also to refer to it. It is to rules generally accepted by municipal legal systems which recognize the limited company whose capital is represented by shares, and not to the municipal law of a particular State, that international law refers.

In the *Corfu Channel Case* (Merits),[60] the ICJ determined the scope of liability of Albania for damage done to British warships by mines struck in Albanian territorial waters. The Court invoked municipal law to deal with questions about the use of circumstantial evidence:

> [T]he other State, the victim of the breach of international law is often unable to furnish direct proof of facts giving rise to responsibility. Such a State should be allowed a more liberal recourse to inferences of fact and circumstantial evidence. This indirect evidence is admitted in all systems of law, and its use is recognized by international decisions. It must be regarded as of special weight when it is based on a series of facts linked together and leading logically to a single conclusion.

D. Judicial Decisions and The Writings of Scholars

This source is referred to in Article 38 of the Statute of the I.C.J. as a "subsidiary" source of international law. This may seem curious to an energy lawyer in a jurisdiction where judicial decisions and the work of scholars (especially in formulating restatements of the law), may dominate as the source of law that applies to a given situation.

In traditional international law, the role of the judge and the scholar indeed is "subsidiary" in the senses both that they are not states and that they usually exercise their judgements or express their opinions after consulting, construing or referring to treaties, custom and general principles of law. In addition, international court judges traditionally are not " law-makers". They are law-interpreters and law-appliers. That said, the fact remains that judicial decisions and the work of writers are frequently invoked by states and international courts and cited regularly as the source for international law. The role of international courts in the future evolution of international law is likely to be greater than it has in the past, if for no other reason than that the number of international decision making bodies

---

[60] [1949] I.C.J. Rep. 4.

created by states is increasing in such areas as international trade, human rights and the environment.

E.   A Note on Hard Law and Soft Law

In international law, there is now a distinction made between so-called "hard" law and "soft" law. Hard law is comprised of binding obligatory international commitments. Thus, treaties in force, clear customary international law principles, decisions of international courts and the like reflect hard law. Soft law refers to non-binding legal instruments that set voluntary standards, declare principles and goals, or articulate the future aspirations of the drafters. Soft law instruments include state-generated instruments like UN General Assembly Resolutions (e.g., the Resolution adopting the Universal Declaration Human on Rights in 1948)[61] and declarations of international institutions and conferences (e.g., the 1972 Stockholm Declaration on the Environment).[62]

The generation of "soft" law is not confined to states but may be crafted by non-state actors. In the energy field, this would include the 1990 Valdez Principles on corporate environmental conduct produced by the Coalition for Environmentally Responsible Economics, comprised of individual and corporate investors and environmental organizations.[63] It would also include guidelines issued by the International Maritime Organization (IMO) like its 1989 Guidelines and Standards for the Removal of Offshore Installations and Structures on the Continental Shelf and on the Exclusive Economic Zone.[64]

Sometimes soft law may be embedded in particular aspirational provisions of hard law instruments (like treaty preambles) or in provisions seeking to move toward hard law at a future date. The tendency is that states obey hard law instruments and not soft law instruments. This merely reflects that states generally only agree to hard law commitments that they are fully prepared to obey and that they leave more ambitious undertakings

---

[61] Sometimes U.N.G.A. Resolutions are asserted to reflect hard law. However, the better view is that they only do so when they repeat accepted hard law because U.N.G.A. Resolutions are not legislative enactments, statutes or other "hard law" creating instruments.

[62] *See* Chapter Five.

[63] *See* Daniel H. Pink, *The Valdez Principles: Is What's Good for America Good for General Motors?*, 8 YALE L. & POL'Y REV. 180 (1990); *see also* Mary Page Polly, *Are International Institutions Doing Their Job? Plenary Panel: Non-Binding Norms and The Problems of Compliance*, 90 AM. SOC'Y INT'L L. PROC. 348 (1996).

[64] IMO Assembly Res. A. 672, MSC 57/27 Add. 2, Annex 31 (October 19, 1989).

to non-binding soft law instruments which they are not presently prepared
to obey except when it suits them to obey. Nonetheless, soft law instruments
can be very important because they begin the process of hard law formation
and provoke responses by states, by international organizations, and by
other non-state international actors all of which help to shape future acceptable obligations.

V. THE RELATION BETWEEN INTERNATIONAL LAW AND DOMESTIC LAW

The domestic energy lawyer of the 21st century will need a knowledge
of international law in domestic energy law practice. For example, in 1992
the Wisconsin Public Service Commission required local electric utilities, in
making filings relating to rates at which electricity would be sold in
Wisconsin, to anticipate future international law obligations of the United
States. Specifically, the Wisconsin PSC required utilities to put a dollar
amount on greenhouse gases emitted by electric power plants and to embed
that dollar amount in rates in *anticipation* of international greenhouse gas
rules:[65]

> Because of widespread concern about the risks of global warming
> at state, national and international levels, future regulations are
> likely to require the utility industry to limit its release of these
> gases. If so, utilities would incur real economic costs in order to
> comply with these regulations.
>
> ***
>
> A national and international consensus to regulate greenhouse
> gas emissions is emerging. When the likelihood of future regula-
> tion is high, it is reasonable to estimate the cost of compliance to
> utilities. Ignoring this financial risk would be imprudent.
>
> ***
>
> Monetizing the risk of greenhouse gas regulation is a prudent
> means of reducing utility business risk, by hedging against the
> future . . . [and] considering the likelihood of . . . international
> greenhouse gas regulations.

Such invocations of international standards, international rules and
international law by domestic legislators, courts, and administrative deci-
sion-makers can be expected to increase in energy matters in the decades

---

[65] Re Advanced Plans for Construction of Facilities, 136 Pur 4th, 153 (Wisconsin P.S.C. 1992).

ahead. A domestic energy lawyer must have an enhanced appreciation of the relationship between international law and domestic law. In globalized energy transactions, a relevant question will be: How do local courts and local legislative and administrative bodies deal with international energy law?

This question is not one so much about *foreign* law before United States courts as those mainly concern conflicts of the *domestic* laws of states and private international law. Foreign law questions may involve the act of state doctrine (foreign acts of states taken over property located in the foreign state should be respected by United States courts as a matter of public policy[66]), sovereign immunity (foreign sovereigns and their acts will not fall under United States court jurisdiction as a matter of comity[67]) and *forum non conveniens* (public and private interests dictate that a foreign forum ought to have jurisdiction over a case[68]).

The focus here is on the *internal* effect of public international law. *Externally*, of course, international law generally has primacy over domestic law if a conflict arises between the two.[69]

A.   Treaties

Most international law disputes that wind up in court are litigated before domestic courts rather than before international fora. Most international law issues in those disputes involve treaties or custom.

International law in the form of treaties may come before United States courts in several contexts and in several forms. The United States constitution provides simply in Article VI that:

> [a]ll Treaties made . . . under the authority of the United States,
> shall be the supreme Law of the Land; and Judges in every state

---

[66] *See* Banco Nacional de Cuba v. Sabbatino 376 U.S. 398, 428 (1964) ("[t]he Judicial Branch will not examine the validity of a taking of property within its own territory by a foreign sovereign government, extant and recognized by this country at the time of suit in the absence of a treaty or other unambiguous agreement regarding controlling legal principles, even if the complaint alleges that the taking violates customary international law.")

[67] *See* The Schooner Exchange v. McFaddon, 11 U.S. (7 Cranch) 116 (1812). Limited sovereign immunity has been codified in The Foreign Sovereign Immunities Act of 1976, 28 U.S.C. §§1602-1605.

[68] *See* Piper Aircraft Co. v. Reyno, 45 U.S. 235 (1981).

[69] *See The Alabama Claims* (U.S.-Great Britain Arbitration, 1872, 4 Papers Relating to the Treaty of Washington 49 (1872). (Moore International Arbitrations 4057: A state may not invoke domestic law as an excuse for failure to carry out international law obligations).

shall be bound thereby, anything in the constitution or Laws of any State to the Contrary notwithstanding.

Article VI establishes two guiding constitutional predicates for dealing with treaties in United States courts. The first is that treaties are on a par with federal statutes. Both apply equally as the "law of the land". The second is that conflicting state law falls to an applicable treaty.[70]

Not addressed by Article VI is the problem of conflicts between treaties on the one hand and the United States Constitution and federal statutes on the other hand. It is clear that the internal effect of treaties under the treaty making power of the United States does not "authorize what the Constitution forbids".[71] If a treaty and federal statute conflict, a rule of convenience is used that applies the latest in time; that is, the last one in date (treaty or federal statute) will control.[72]

United States courts, in considering the internal effect of international law, also must distinguish between self-executing treaties, non self-executing treaties and executive agreements, something many other nations and their courts need not do. Self-executing treaties are treaties that, once ratified, are automatically effective internally because nothing more needs to be done legislatively for the treaty objective to be realized. For example, the United States-Panama Treaty that ceded the Panama Canal to Panama was held to be a self-executing agreement, despite a challenge by the House of Representatives, because the treaty, once ratified, executed passage of title automatically.[73] Examples of non-self executing treaties which required United States implementing legislation in order for them to have internal effect are the United Nations Charter[74] and the Migratory Bird Treaty of 1916 (United States and Great Britain).[75] Executive Agreements are entered into by the President and technically are not treaties. Thus, they do not need to come before the Senate for ratification approval under Article II of

---

[70] *See* Asakura v. City of Seattle, 265 U.S. 332 (1924). (Seattle ordinance that violated a U.S.-Japan bilateral treaty held invalid.)

[71] *Id.* at 341(*citing* Geofroy v. Riggs, 133 U.S. 258, 267 (1890). *See also* Reid v. Covert, 354 U.S. 1, 16 (1957) ("no agreement with a foreign nation can confer power on the Congress, or on any other branch of government, which is free from the restraints of the Constitution").

[72] *See* Whitney v. Robertson 124 U.S. 190, 195 (1888) ("The duty of the courts is to construe and give effect to the latest expression as sovereign will.")

[73] *See* Edwards v. Carter, 580 F. 2nd. 1055 (D.C. Cir. 1978), *cert. denied,* 436 U.S. 907.

[74] *See* Sei Fuji v. California, 38 Cal. 2d 718 (1952). Articles 55 and 56 (the human rights provisions of the U.N. Charter held to be non self-executing).

[75] *See* Missouri v. Holland, 252 U.S. 416 (1920).

the Constitution.[76] In *United States v. Belmont*, the Supreme Court upheld the validity of an executive agreement as the law of the land.[77] There are hundreds of such agreements.

Most new international law that will affect the energy industry in the 21st Century and come before United States courts is likely to be in the form of non-self executing treaties that will require implementing Congressional legislation of some sort to administer or to fund the purpose of the treaty.

Another way in which treaties may have internal effect before United States courts is when they are used to interpret domestic statutes. For example, in *United States v. Maine* (Rhode Island and New York Boundary Case),[78] the Supreme Court used the 1958 Geneva Convention on the Territorial Sea and Contiguous Zone to determine the meaning of the term "bay" in the Submerged Lands Act.[79]

B.   Custom

As a general matter, United States courts have accepted that in the right circumstances they will apply customary international law. In *The Paqueta Habana* case, for example, the United States Supreme Court applied customary international law to hold that a seizure of small fishing boats under the laws of prize by the United States Government was illegal because it conflicted with customary international law.[80] It opined specifically on custom in United States Courts:

> International law is part of our law, and must be ascertained and administered by the courts of justice of appropriate jurisdiction, as often as questions of right depending upon it are duly presented for their determination. For this purpose, where there is no treaty, and no controlling executive or legislative act or

---

[76] The President "shall have the Power, by and with the Advice and Consent of the Senate, to make Treaties, providing two thirds of the Senators present concur."

[77] 301 U.S. 324 (1937). The Roosevelt-Litvinov Agreement recognizing the U.S.S.R. was held superior to New York law.

[78] 469 U.S. 504 (1984).

[79] 43 U.S.C. §§ 1301-1315 (1982).

[80] 175 U.S. 677 (1900) ("[c]oast fishing vessels, with their implements and supplies cargoes and crews, unarmed, and honestly pursuing their peaceful calling of catching and bringing in fresh fish, are exempt from capture as a prize of war [as a matter of custom]).

judicial decision, resort must be had to the customs and usages of civilized nations. . . .[81]

Thus, when there is no applicable United States "law" and there is applicable custom, United States courts must apply custom. But what about circumstances where United States "law" and custom potentially conflict? Does the *Paqueta Habana* case stand for the proposition that if there is an applicable executive order, federal statute, or court decision resort to custom will not be had? Here, the answer is uncertain. In *Sale v. Haitian Centers Councils, Inc.*,[82] the Supreme Court upheld an executive order permitting the interdiction and return of Haitian refugees on the high seas by the United States Coast Guard without mention of customary international law principles on freedom of navigation on the High Seas, exclusive flag state jurisdiction over high seas vessels, or the limited rights of visit on flagless vessels.[83] And in the face of the act of state doctrine, the Supreme Court has explicitly refused to apply custom even if that refusal was " offensive to the public policy of this country":

> [t]he Judicial Branch will not examine the validity of a taking of property within its own territory by a foreign sovereign government, extant and recognized by this country at the time of suit, in the absence of a treaty or other unambiguous agreement regarding controlling legal principles, *even if the complaint alleges that the taking violates customary international law.*[84] (emphasis added)

C.   Court-Made Rules

The treatment of treaties and custom in United States courts may also be influenced by court-made rules.

Our courts operate under certain presumptions and burdens of proof, which may come into play when international law issues are posed. One presumption is that there is no conflict between United States law and international law.[85] Of course, if there is no conflict then the court may apply either or both bodies of law. Sometimes courts employ this presumption by focusing on the international law to presume it is consistent with

---

[81] *Id.* at 700.

[82] 509 U.S. 155.

[83] The 1958 Geneva Convention on the High Seas codified these customary international law principles.

[84] *See* Banco Nacional De Cuba v. Sabbatino, 376 U.S. 398, 428 (1964).

[85] *See* United States v. Alvarez Machain, 504 U.S. 655 (1992).

United States law.[86] Sometimes courts analyze the United States law to see if it is inconsistent with international law. In cases where American law is asserted to apply extraterritorially and where international law might apply, United States courts may begin their analysis with the presumption that United States law does not apply outside our territory.[87] In other circumstances, a court may employ the burden of proof rule that the party asserting a conflict of United States and international law has the burden to establish the conflict.

If those presumptions are not overcome or if the burden of proof is not met, our courts may avoid grappling with problems of the relationship between international law and United States law. Of course, if the presumptions are overcome and the burdens are met, then our courts must deal with the substance of the international law.

Thus, United States courts have a variety of ways to justify either rejecting or applying international law. They may characterize a problem as one of treaty or custom, of conflict with state, federal, or constitutional law, of legislative or court jurisdiction, or of statutory or court interpretation. ❦

---

[86] *See id.*

[87] *See* Hartford Fire Insurance Co. v. California, 509 U.S. 764, 814 (1993) (Scalia, J., dissenting).

CHAPTER FIVE

Environmental Protection and Energy Development

by James E. Hickey, Jr.[*]

I. INTRODUCTION

Environmental law as a body of laws, regulations, judicial decisions, treaties, and legal instruments has only become relevant to energy industries in the past 30 years or so. Prior to this time, environmental harms, for the most part, were a topic of domestic tort law. The legal focus typically was on determining, case by case, the presence of a legal duty, a breach of that duty, and damages, all of which were dealt with as a purely private matter. Energy companies sometimes were shielded through limited liability from traditional tort law exposure for environmental harm associated with energy fuel cycles. For example, before the Oil Pollution Act of 1990 was enacted, United States government regulation of oil spills was minimal. The legal liability of the oil industry for environmental harm caused by oil spills from tankers, barges and off shore facilities was extremely limited.[1] In part, liability was limited to protect the United States shipping industry as a matter of maritime law and policy. Even as late as 1980, the federal Superfund Act, which was aimed at identifying and cleaning up hazardous waste dump sites, and which generally broadened the legal liability of polluters, exempted oil from its definition of "hazardous substances."[2]

Energy industries today, however, cannot operate in any resource area, in any energy market, or in any phase of the energy fuel cycle without taking into account domestic and international environmental law. This chapter introduces some of those domestic and international environmental

---

[*] Professor Hickey would like to thank his research assistant, Jessica Lombardo, for her help on this chapter.

[1] *See In re* Exxon Valdez, 1994 WL 182856 (D. Alaska) (not reported in F. Supp.); Union Oil Company v. Oppen, 501 F. 2d 558 (1974); Robins Dry Dock and Repair Company v. Flint, 275 U.S. 303 (1927).

[2] Comprehensive Environmental Response, Compensation and Liability Act, 42 U.S.C.A. § 960 (14) (CERCLA).

law considerations. It addresses United States environmental law in Section II, and international environmental law in Section III.

II. UNITED STATES ENVIRONMENTAL LAW

The United States, over the past thirty years or so, has adopted a highly comprehensive, complex and increasingly stringent set of environmental laws to control pollution and to enhance the quality of the environment. Most of those laws have an impact on energy fuel cycles. In the past, the implementation of these laws has cost billions of dollars. In the future, implementation will cost tens of billions of dollars more. The high stakes involved (the human health and economic welfare of the nation) have resulted in great debate, controversy, and considerable litigation. The result has been an improved environment, a healthier population, and a more enlightened public about environmental matters.

Prior to World War II, damage to the environment in the U.S. was treated mostly as a matter for state law and state courts. There were few local, state or federal ordinances, statutes or regulations directly addressed to pollution or to environmental quality. Environmental questions, especially regarding pollution, were addressed primarily by courts applying common law tort principles on a case by case basis. In general, the courts applied the principles of nuisance and negligence to limit pollution that originated on a person's land.[3]

The movement toward state and federal environmental statutes after World War II sought to supplement the limited ability of the courts and the common law to protect the environment. Reliance on courts and the common law alone turned out to be inadequate for several reasons. First, the overall quality of the environment is a question of public order rather than a question of private local injury. Second, courts mostly act on a case by case basis and after damage is done. Third, civil courts primarily compensate for injury rather than prevent its occurrence. The most effective method of dealing with pollution, of course, is to prevent it rather than to simply assign post delictual liability.

The states began to realize that effective protection of the environment required more than decisions issued by state courts in private law cases.

---

[3] For example, the common law of nuisance makes a person liable when he or she damages another person's property. This nuisance principle has been applied by state courts to abnormal dangers from harmful chemicals, smoke, water, and sewage. Similarly, Roman law used the prohibition of *immissio*—that water, smoke, fragments of stone and the like were not allowed to be introduced from one person's property to a neighboring property.

Effective environmental protection, states realized, required cooperation among the executive branches of state governments because pollution does not respect state boundaries, and because discrete ecosystems (forests, river basins, wetlands, etc.) often cross state borders. Meaningful environmental management, it was realized, also required government administration, political negotiations, scientific study, and the publication of reliable and specific information about the effects of human activities on the environment. Local and state courts lack the jurisdiction, the physical capability or the scientific expertise to enter into these areas.

In the late 1940s and the 1950s, the federal government began to pass statutes to make federal funds available to the states to help them regulate discrete segments of the environment. It was not until the 1960s and 1970s that the Congress began to pass laws that were addressed directly to the protection and preservation of environmental quality in the country as a whole.[5]

Environmental laws and policies in the United States that affect energy industries are too complex to present in detail. For example, federal environmental statutes affecting the oil industry alone include the following:

1. Alaska National Interest Land Conservation Act.
2. Clean Air Act Amendments of 1990.
3. Coastal Zone Management Act.
4. Comprehensive Environmental Response, Compensation and Liability Act.
5. Deepwater Port Act.
6. Endangered Species Act.
7. Federal Land Policy and Management Act.
8. Federal Water Pollution Control Act.
9. Fishery Conservation and Management Act.
10. Marine Mammal Protection Act.
11. Marine Protection, Research, and Sanctuaries Act.
12. National Environmental Policy Act.
13. National Forest Management Act.
14. National Park System Mining Regulation Act.
15. National Petroleum Reserve in Alaska.
16. National Wildlife Refuge System Act.

---

[4] Two such federal statutes were the 1948 Federal Water Pollution Control Act and the 1955 Clean Air Act.

[5] Examples of the initial national environmental laws include the Wilderness Act of 1964, the Land and Water Conservation Act of 1965, the Solid Waste Disposal Act of 1965 and the Wild and Scenic Rivers Act of 1968.

17. Natural Gas Pipeline Safety Act.
18. Occupational Safety and Health Act.
19. Oil Pollution Act of 1990.
20. Outer Continental Shelf Lands Act Amendments of 1978.
21. Resource Conservation and Recovery Act.
22. Safe Drinking Water Act.
23. Shore Protection Act.
24. Trans-Alaska Pipeline Act.
25. Wild and Scenic Rivers Act.

What follows is thus a conceptual and thematic introduction to environmental law.

A.   Models of United States Environmental Regulation[6]

There are four models of environmental regulation of the energy industry used in the United States today.

1.   The Environmental Impact Assessment Model

The environmental impact assessment model is enshrined in the 1969 National Environmental Policy Act (NEPA).[7] This model has now been adopted in various forms to regulate the environment in Europe and in other countries around the world. NEPA, in section 102, requires that environmental values must be considered by every federal agency in every substantial federal action that has a significant impact on the environment.[8] The key provision is section 102(2)(C) which forces federal agencies to prepare a detailed, written explanation of the environmental consequences of its significant actions and to make that explanation available to the public.[9] The critical language of section 102(2)(C) that mandates an environmental impact statement (EIS) provides:

(2)   all agencies of the federal government shall:

(c)   include in every recommendation or report on proposals for legislation and other major Federal actions significantly affecting the quality of the

---

[6] The models of environmental regulation are drawn directly from William H. Rodgers, Jr., ENVIRONMENTAL LAW, 1.4 (2d. ed. 1994 and Supp. West 1998).

[7] 42 U.S.C.A. §§ 4321-4370(d) (West 1994).

[8] 2 U.S.C.A. § 4332(2) (West 1994).

[9] Id.

human environment, a detailed statement by the responsible official on:

(I)   the environmental impact of the proposed action,

(ii) any adverse environmental effects which cannot be avoided should the proposal be implemented,

(iii) alternatives to the proposed action,

(iv) the relationship between local short-term uses of man's environment and the maintenance and enhancement of long-term productivity, and

(v)   any irreversible and irretrievable commitments of resources which would be involved in the proposed action should it be implemented.

The requirement that federal agencies prepare and publish an EIS has two primary effects. It operates before action is taken and it generates useful information for other government agencies, for legislatures and courts, and for citizens and industry.

However, the EIS model does not touch all segments of the energy industries alike. The EIS model for many years has had little impact on the production phase of the oil fuel cycle. For well over a decade, the petroleum industry, in obtaining onshore and offshore production leases from the U.S. government, escaped close environmental scrutiny under section 102 either because no EIS was prepared or, if prepared, an EIS was done in a comparatively relaxed fashion. In significant part, that lack of rigorous insistence by government regulators on a comprehensive EIS relating to petroleum leases was due to the belief of reviewing courts that there were other opportunities available to assess environmental effects later in the fuel cycle. For example, in *Sierra Club v. Morton*, a federal appellate court, reviewing an EIS prepared for a government lease sale of tracts in the outer continental shelf, ruled:[10]

What we hold today is that where shortcomings in a major federal action can be corrected or minimized when and if they surface, the EIS upon which such action is authorized may meet NEPA's objectives with some less detail and analysis than would otherwise be required.

---

[10] 510 F.2d 813, 828 (5th Cir. 1975).

2. The "Best Technology" Model

This model of environmental regulation presumes that pollution is a social wrong and that society should use the best technology to avoid it. The best technology model depends neither on proof of damages nor on favorable cost benefit analysis (i.e., the benefits of a clean environment outweigh the costs of achieving it). This is because the questions whether to regulate, and, if so, what form that regulation should take, already have been decided upon when the statutory or regulatory selection of the best technology model of regulation was made. A well known statutory example of this model is the 1972 Federal Water Pollution Control Act.[11] This statute combines a "best technology" model with the requirement that industries and cities get a permit from the Environmental Protection Agency before discharging into United States waters. This approach has achieved great improvement in water quality over the past two decades. The best technology model also has been enshrined in other statutes, such as the Clean Air Act Amendments of 1990[12] and the Resource Conservation and Recovery Act (RCRA).[13]

3. Risk Assessment Model

The risk assessment model of environmental regulation compels government agencies to assess the risks to human health and/or to the environment of the polluting activity being regulated. The premise is that legislators and regulators need to make hard choices about what amount of pollution is acceptable. The risk assessments operate as predicates for imposing subsequent restrictions on polluting activities. Risk assessment studies, when required, are prepared by a federal agency and most often address the pollution exposure, the adverse effects of the exposure, a determination of probabilities of exposure, and a calculation of the overall risk.

The risk assessment model has been implicated in various stages of energy fuel cycles. For example, it has been applied to the end use phase of the fuel cycle of the petroleum industry in the United States to control automobile tail pipe emissions, to the production phase to control the mining of minerals and to maintain adequate health and safety conditions in the workplace. This model continues to be used even though it has not been very

---

[11] 33 U.S.C.A. §§ 1251-1387 (West 1986 & West Supp. 1995). The FWPCA, among other things, regulates wastewater discharges from oil refineries which must obtain a discharge permit from the government.

[12] 42 U.S.C.A. §§ 7401-7671(q) (West 1995).

[13] 42 U.S.C.A. §§ 6901 *et seq.* (West 1995).

successful, largely due to substantial and continuing confusion over methodology.

CERCLA

4.   *Strict Liability Model*

Environmental statutes increasingly reflect a strict liability model, especially for corrective measures designed to deal with very dangerous conditions and materials. For example, with the passage of the Superfund law[14] in 1980, discharges of "hazardous substances" are subject to a sweeping strict liability standard to clean up hazardous waste sites. This standard is applied in addition to liability standards for damage caused by "hazardous" substances. Here, owners, former owners, operators, transporters and waste generators (so called responsible parties) that discharge or help discharge hazardous substances at specific sites or facilities are liable for clean-up costs. The only defenses to liability are for acts of God. Significantly, the petroleum industry was exempted from the 1980 Superfund law. The Oil Pollution Act of 1990 now regulates the petroleum industry under the strict liability model of regulation.

5.   *Emerging Patterns*

Three refinements to the models of environmental regulation mentioned above are emerging and becoming embedded into the regulatory mix. The first is the integration refinement which does not allow pollution prevention to be achieved in one area (for example, control of air emissions) by increasing pollution in another area (for example, by dumping waste that otherwise would have been burned into rivers, streams, or oceans). The second refinement is the use of economic incentives to achieve pollution control. These include discharge permit fees, taxes (like gasoline taxes or President Clinton's failed BTU tax bill),[15] and the creation of pollution markets premised on a statutorily created right to pollute within a cap of allowable emissions (like the emission trading scheme of the Clean Air Act Amendments of 1990). The third refinement to existing domestic environmental regulation models is to take into account both international treaty

---

[14] Comprehensive Environmental Response, Compensation and Liability Act (CERCLA), 42 U.S.C.A. §§ 9601-9675 (West 1995). The statute is aimed at identifying and cleaning up hazardous waste dump sites around the United States. CERCLA gets its popular name from provisions that establish a fund to pay for site clean-up (i.e., "the Superfund").

[15] *See United States President Calls for Broad-Based Tax on Fuels' BTU Content, Pressure Seen on Japan*, 16 INT'L ENVTL REP. (BNA) No. 4, p. 115 (Feb. 24, 1993).

obligations (like the environmental side agreement of NAFTA or the Climate Change Convention) and the international effects of domestic polluting activities (like CFC[16] emissions, carbon dioxide emissions, and ocean dumping).

Today, federal regulation of the environment is almost complete.[17] When the federal government acts on environmental issues, state laws and regulations must yield in cases of conflict. If a conflicting state law interferes with the intent of Congress reflected in federal environmental laws signed by the President, the state law very likely will be found to be unconstitutional.[18] However, state and local environmental law remains valid and enforceable if it does not conflict with federal law or is not otherwise unconstitutional. Generally, no conflict exists if the state law imposes more stringent environmental standards than the federal law. For example, the State of California imposes more stringent air pollution standards than those imposed by federal clean air laws. Federal environmental laws often compel the states to implement and to enforce federally-imposed standards through their state environmental offices.

B.   Environmental Law Sectors

1.   Water

Prior to 1972, the quality of water in rivers, lakes and streams in the United States was generally free from government regulation. Not surprisingly, industrial, municipal, and agricultural sources of water pollution in the United States increased. Organic wastes and other nutrients, toxic chemicals and other hazardous substances, heated water and sediments, all entered United States waterways in ever increasing amounts. By the late 1960s, the quality of the water in American rivers, lakes and streams had become a very serious problem. For example, in Washington, D.C., residents

---

[16] CFC stands for chlorofluorocarbons which appear, for example, in refrigeration and aerosol products.

[17] The only area where federal power to regulate the environment is uncertain is in the few instances where the federal government tries to regulate the activities of state officials themselves.

[18] The U.S. Constitution provided in Article VI, Clause 2 that federal laws are supreme:

"This Constitution, and the laws of the United States shall be . . . the supreme Law of the Land; and the Judges in every State shall be bound thereby, any Thing in the Constitution or Laws of any State to the Contrary notwithstanding."

were prohibited from fishing or swimming in the Potomac River because of severe pollution. And a river in Ohio became so polluted that it caught fire.

In 1972, the Congress enacted the Clean Water Act (CWA).[19] The CWA established a system of pollution standards, discharge permits and enforcement mechanisms aimed at making the navigable waters of the United States safe for swimming and fishing.[20] The CWA has been amended several times.

The control of water pollution under the CWA is addressed in two complementary systems of regulation. First, the CWA regulates discharges of pollutants at their point of entry into navigable waters. For example, pipes, ditches, tunnels, and wells are all "point" sources for pollutants. The CWA requires that those who discharge to navigable waters at those points must get permits to discharge. The permit issued by the EPA restricts the types and amounts of discharges allowed. If there is no permit issued, there is no permission to discharge.

This permit system, the National Pollutant Discharge Elimination System (NPDES), requires that the permit holder meet EPA standards. To obtain a permit, a discharger must demonstrate to the EPA that he is using the best "practicable" technology available for dealing with water pollutants. Later, the discharger must show that he is using the best "available" technology economically capable of being achieved to deal with polluting material (a much higher standard).

The second system to control water pollution is through overall water quality standards established by the EPA. These standards are used, instead of the NPDES permit system, where a body of water is receiving such large amounts of discharges that using either a best "practicable" or a best "available" technology discharge permit test does little or nothing to preserve existing water quality. Here, rather than use the NPDES permit system, the EPA establishes a "total maximum daily load" of waste that a particular water body may receive. Then, for that body of water, the EPA allocates to each discharger a portion of "total maximum daily load" that it may discharge.

---

[19] 33 U.S.C.A. §§ 1251 *et seq.* (as amended).

[20] The federal government's superior authority over state governments here rests on the Commerce Clause of the United States Constitution:
> "The Congress shall have Power . . . [t]o regulate Commerce
> . . . among the several States."

U.S. CONST., art I, § 8.

The term "navigable waters" in the CWA effectively has come to apply to all waters in the United States and federal authority under the CWA is complete.

Under the CWA, the enforcement of the EPA "total maximum daily load" standards and the NPDES permits is left to the states. However, the CWA does allow the EPA to inspect facilities and to monitor both discharges and overall water quality. In addition, interested citizens are allowed to sue in civil court to enforce EPA standards and permits. Citizens may sue violators and even the EPA itself for failure to carry out its statutory duties. Such citizen suits become very important to enforcement during periods of budget deficits when funds for government enforcement (either state or federal) are reduced or eliminated.

The largest quantity of uncontrolled water pollution does not come from "point" sources and is not regulated by the federal government. It is from "non-point" sources. Non-point sources of water pollution include discharges from agricultural runoff (like soil and pesticides) and urban runoff (like road tars). These "non-point" sources of water pollution are not covered by the CWA primarily because they are very difficult to control or to regulate. The CWA passes this difficult task of non-point source regulation to the states. It requires each state to develop a program to manage non-point sources of water pollution. However, there is no statutory penalty imposed by the CWA if a state fails to develop such a program. Perhaps, the lack of a federal penalty for the failure of a state to develop a program reflects, in part, the difficulty in effectively controlling water pollution from non-point sources.

Another federal statute dealing with water pollution that deserves mention is the Safe Drinking Water Act.[21] Under this statute, the EPA sets quality standards for the type and amount of pollutants contained in drinking water provided by public water systems (like cities and counties). The EPA does this by making a list, based on scientific studies, of potentially harmful substances (like lead and benzine) in drinking water. The EPA then sets an allowable concentration (parts per million) for each substance that may be present in safe drinking water. Water that has listed substances in greater concentrations than allowed by EPA is unsafe for drinking.

Much of the drinking water in the United States that comes from water underground (groundwater) is seriously threatened. Groundwater often becomes contaminated because it is a final resting place for pollutants like toxic chemicals, pesticides, oil, and landfill wastes that seep through the ground to the groundwater. Many of these substances that seep into groundwater, which is used for drinking water, have been associated with cancer, central nervous system damage, and harm to the liver and kidneys of humans.

---

[21] 42 U.S.C.A. §§ 300f *et seq.*

2.   Air

Air quality is especially affected by energy fuel cycles. The main sources of air pollution in the United States which threaten human health are automobiles, industrial smokestacks, and fossil fuel electric power plants. These sources release harmful pollutants like carbon monoxide, sulfur oxides, nitrogen oxides, and particulates. Those pollutants cause respiratory diseases (such as emphysema and bronchitis), heart problems (such as arteriosclerosis), and higher rates of cancer in humans. In addition, air pollutants harm the environment through acid rain, offensive odors, ozone and global warming, and smog.

In 1990, the federal government significantly amended the existing Clean Air Act (CAA).[22] The 1990 amendments are the first comprehensive revision of the CAA since the 1970s. The CAA was passed by Congress in 1955 and was amended several times in the 1960s and 1970s to increase federal government authority over air pollution. There were no changes to the CAA in the 1980s in part because of conflicts over state responsibility for air pollution and air quality among states from different regions of the United States (especially states from the Northeast, Midwest and the West), in part because of opposition by industries, and in part because President Ronald Reagan was not sympathetic to strengthening the CAA.

The 1990 CAA amendments are 314 pages long and affect nearly all the previous aspects of clean air laws in the United States. Many provisions are complex and highly technical.

The CAA addresses air pollution in several ways. Among the significant provisions are: (i) the creation of national air quality standards; (ii) restrictions on air pollution from stationary sources (for example, smokestack emission from industrial and electric power plants); (iii) restrictions on air pollution from mobile sources (for example, automobile exhausts); (iv) regulation of hazardous air pollutants that cause serious human illness at low concentrations; and (v) control of acid rain.

a.   National Ambient Air Quality Standards (NAAQS)

The CAA requires the EPA to establish air quality standards for the nation. This elaborate and technical system for improving the nation's air quality has evolved over the past 35 years. The basic structure is built around NAAQS and on allocation of responsibility among the states and the federal government. The EPA establishes NAAQS for air pollutants that

---

[22] 42 U.S.C.A. §§ 7401 *et seq.*

endanger public health (for example, carbon monoxide, sulfur dioxide, hydrocarbons, lead, and ozone). The NAAQS define the amount of a pollutant that will make air unsafe. States in geographic areas of the United States that have clean air which meets or exceeds the NAAQSs must meet a strict requirement to "prevent significant deterioration" of air quality.

note

Geographic regions which meet the NAAQSs, as a practical matter, fall into one of two classes. Most areas of the United States are Class II areas. Class II areas are areas in which moderate increases of pollutants might be allowed as long as the increases do not exceed a NAAQS for that pollutant. Class I areas are areas where very little deterioration of air quality is allowed. These areas usually include large national parks and wilderness areas (see discussion of land preservation below).

The NAAQSs standards are established by the EPA but are implemented by the 50 states. Each state submits a plan to implement and maintain each NAAQS set by the EPA. Once a state implementation plan is approved by the EPA, it is enforceable by states and by the federal government.

permits ✱

Generally, one who discharges significant amounts of a pollutant subject to a NAAQS must have a permit to discharge. To obtain a permit, the discharger must show that its emissions will not violate a NAAQS and that it will use the best available pollution control technology to control all its pollutants.

b.   Stationary Air Pollution Sources

Air pollution from stationary sources includes pollution from industrial factories and electric power plants (especially those using coal and oil). The CAA classifies air pollution from stationary sources in two categories—existing factories and plants, and new factories and plants. Existing factories and plants in geographic areas with dirty air (so-called "non-attainment" areas in which concentrations of pollutants exceed NAAQSs), in general, must use "reasonably available control technology" to comply with air emission standards set by EPA within a reasonable length of time (usually 2 or 3 years).[23] States must produce implementation plans to meet NAAQSs in regions with dirty air ("non-attainment" areas). If states do not produce satisfactory implementation plans, the EPA must then issue its own implementation plan which states must implement.

old plants use

note

------

[23] At the end of 1987 over 70 United States Cities did not "attain" the NAAQS for ozone and carbon monoxide.

Once NAAQSs are set and state implementation plans are approved, the CAA requires the EPA to deal with new stationary factories and plants that are built (or physically changed in a way that increases air pollution). Here, the EPA must adopt air quality standards for these new stationary sources of air pollution. The EPA requires construction and operation permits if a new factory or new electric power plant is built in a geographic area that already has dirty air (a "non-attainment" area in which one or more NAAQSs are not met). Permit requirements are more stringent in geographic areas where the air quality is better than the NAAQSs in order to prevent any deterioration.

The CAA permit system creates a private market in emission rights for new stationary sources of air pollution in "nonattainment" areas (dirty air areas). For example, suppose a private electric utility wants to build a new coal-fired power plant in an area that does not meet the NAAQSs for power plant emissions (like sulfur and particulates). The addition of a new plant usually means that the total emissions from existing and new stationary sources will increase for that area, if nothing else changes. However, under the CAA, the owner of the utility could go to a neighboring utility or to an industry that emits sulfur and particulates (like a steel company) and pay them money either to reduce their production or to shut down a furnace or boiler to offset the emissions of the new electric power plant in the non-attainment area. The EPA also allows governments in a geographic region that loses factories or plants to "bank" the resulting reduction in air pollution and to use those banked emissions in the future by giving them to new industries as an incentive to locate in that region. The new industry then withdraws those banked emission reductions and uses them to offset its polluting activities. For some time environmental groups have bought pollution rights in the commodity market and have permanently "retired" them. Local governments also may use banked emission rights to attract new industry.

c.   *Mobile Sources of Air Pollution*

The CAA uses three methods to control air pollution from automobiles, trucks, trains, ships and heavy construction vehicles (all addressing the end-use phase of the oil fuel cycle). First, it sets standards that control the amount and type of emissions from the tail pipe exhausts of vehicles. Every new car in the United States, to meet the emission standards, is fitted with a catalytic converter that cleans emissions before they leave the exhaust tail pipe. Second, standards are imposed on the gasoline and diesel fuel used in vehicles to remove lead, sulfur and other potential air pollutants. As a result, gasoline in the United States has been reformulated. Lead has been removed from all gasoline sold and some oil companies now offer "gasohol" which uses alcohol or ethanol from corn mixed with lead-free gasoline to meet fuel quality standards.[24] Third, in heavily polluted areas, programs promote the use of special clean fuel vehicles such as electric automobiles that produce no tailpipe emissions, or vehicles that burn natural gas instead of gasoline.

d.   Hazardous Air Pollutants

The CAA, in its 1990 amendments, placed hazardous sources of air pollution on a list which now has around 190 chemicals on it. Hazardous air pollutants are those that are very dangerous to human health even at low doses. Companies using chemicals on the list must use the "maximum achievable (air emission) control technology." The CAA allows adoption of even stricter emission standards if it is needed to protect public health or to avoid adverse environmental effects.

e.   Acid Rain

Acid rain is caused when sulfur emissions (especially from coal-fired electric power plants) combine with oxygen to produce sulfur dioxide which washes out in rain into forests and lakes, rivers, and waterways. Acid rain kills trees and fish and animals that feed on trees and fish. Canada over recent decades has complained that sulfur dioxide emissions from coal-fired electric utility plants in the Midwestern states of Ohio, Indiana and Illinois are carried by air currents to Northeast Canada and wash out as acid rain, which damages Canadian forests, lakes, and fish. Similar complaints are made by upstate New York.

The CAA controls acid rain through a system of allowances established by the EPA. The EPA "allows" each utility to discharge only a certain total amount of sulfur dioxide to the atmosphere. Those utilities that discharge less than their allowed total may sell the difference to a neighboring utility that is emitting more sulfur dioxide than is permitted. The neighboring utility thus may continue to pollute at the same level but its cost of business has increased. The utility that sold its allowances reduces its cost of doing business and increases its profit and competitiveness. In this way, the cleaner utilities are rewarded financially and the dirtier utilities are financially punished for their excesses, while at the same time the United States as whole stays within clean air limits.

---

[24] This "gasohol" also has the benefit of reducing United States dependence on foreign oil, although it produces additional, different, emissions.

3. Land Preservation

Beginning with President Theodore Roosevelt almost 100 years ago, the United States began to preserve its wilderness areas (including wetlands and coastal areas).[25] Since then, many millions of acres of land have been preserved by state and federal governments as wilderness, preserves, forests, and parks. About 20% of the nation's commercial forests and large amounts of oil, natural gas, coal, and commercial minerals are located on public lands. These lands are sought by both developers and conservationists.

The decisions to protect these lands are reflected in state and federal land preservation laws. Land preservation in the United States is approached differently depending on whether the land in question is private land or public land. Most of the land in the United States, of course, is privately-owned and it is developed and used as the owner wishes (subject to local zoning laws, etc.). However, there is also a vast amount of public land owned by the federal government, especially in the Western States and Alaska. About one-third of the land area of the United States (nearly 700 million acres) is public land. It is used both for commercial development of oil, natural gas, minerals, wood, and for preservation in its natural condition as national parks, forests, and wilderness areas.

The United States Constitution provides that no person shall be "deprived" of "property without due process of law . . . nor shall private property be taken for public use, without just compensation."[26] Thus, when a state government or the federal government acts to restrict private land use (for example, by preventing development or the destruction of environmentally sensitive wetlands or marshes) the constitutional issues of whether that restriction amounts to a "taking," whether due process of law was followed, and whether "just compensation" has been awarded are often raised and litigated before government agencies and before federal courts.

The federal government and state governments may have partial property rights in land underlying waterways, coastal zones and wetlands. At the state level, these partial or quasi-property rights legally come under "the public trust" doctrine. At the federal level, they come under the "navigational servitude" doctrine. The public trust in these sorts of lands cannot be relinquished by government and must be carried out in the public interest. Under these doctrines, federal and state governments have limited the

---

[25] President Roosevelt set aside around 230 million acres of land as national parks and national forests to be protected.

[26] U.S. Const., amend. v.

rights of private property owners to use these lands. For example, attempts to fill-in environmentally sensitive marshes and wetlands, to build private marinas and boat docks, to dry up lakes, to fence in or change beach fronts, or to dredge rivers and bays, all have been restricted under the public trust or navigational servitude doctrines.

The policy of the federal government towards public land has shifted back and forth from commercial use to preservation depending on the economic and political philosophies of those in office, on the market for individual natural resources, and on the health of the United States economy as a whole.

Early federal laws governing the use of public land territory encouraged the commercial extraction of natural resources. For example, the Mining Law of 1872 promotes commercial development of minerals.[27] It is not concerned with land preservation. It allows the private acquisition of mineral deposits on government-owned land. Any person who finds a mineral deposit has a right to secure extraction rights in that mineral deposit. A person who obtains a claim to a public land mineral deposit also may eventually acquire title to the land itself.

In the 1970s, environmental laws began to address the protection, preservation and economical use of public lands and their natural resources. Today, the Secretary of the Interior may prevent degradation of public lands and the Secretary of Agriculture now must have land management plans for national forests.

In addition, the President and Congress independently may withdraw public land from commercial resource development to "preserve" public land "values" that might be lost if commercial development were permitted. Vast areas of public land in Alaska were withdrawn and preserved from commercial resource development in the 1970s and 1980s through the use of executive and legislative withdrawal powers.

The legal and environmental protection for public lands is dealt with differently for submerged offshore Continental Shelf lands. The federal government owns all the seabed and subsoil under the ocean from 3 miles seaward to 200 miles offshore. This area contains thousands of square miles of submerged outer continental shelf which is rich in oil and natural gas.[28] The federal government recovers oil and gas from the outer continental

---

[27] *See* Laura S. Ziemer, *The 1872 Mining Law and the 20th Century Collide: A Rediscovery of Limits on Mining Rights in Wilderness Areas and National Forests*, 28 ENVTL L. 145 (Spring 1998).

[28] The submerged coastal lands from shore (the lower water mark) to 3 miles seaward is under state jurisdiction.

shelf, especially in the Gulf of Mexico and off the California coast, by entering into leases with private companies that successfully outbid other companies for the lease. The lease permits the private company to explore and exploit sections of the continental shelf for oil and natural gas for a period of years. The environmental dangers of oil and gas development in these coastal areas are that if a spill occurs—in drilling oil wells, in extracting oil or gas, or in transporting oil or gas from the outer continental shelf—coastal areas, fish, sea mammals, and seabirds may be harmed. In 1969, an oil well blowout in the continental shelf offshore near Santa Barbara, California killed seabirds and shell fish, ruined beaches and coastal property, and harmed fishing activities and recreation. In 1989 the oil tanker *Exxon Valdez* crashed in Prince William Sound Alaska and spilled over 11 million gallons of oil. Under the 1978 Outer Continental Shelf Lands Act and NEPA, the federal government is now required to consider "environmental values," "environmental risks," "marine productivity" and the "environmental sensitivity" of marine areas in all phases of the oil and gas development, from exploration through production and transportation.

4. Toxic Wastes

Toxic substances such as pesticides (like DDT and dieldrin), industrial chemicals (like vinyl chloride and benzene), and metals (like mercury) have been used by American farmers, companies, and factories for many decades to produce food and goods for American society. Toxic substances present a very serious danger both to the public health and welfare of humans that are exposed to them and to the environment. In recent years, the sale and use of toxic and hazardous substances have been increasingly regulated by the federal government. For example, the Federal Insecticide, Fungicide and Rodenticide Act, and the Federal Environmental Pesticide Control Act provide a comprehensive framework for regulating the sale and distribution of pesticides in the United States.

In addition, a special environmental problem has arisen, which has begun to be addressed only in the last 15 years or so. This is the very serious problem of the disposal of toxic and hazardous waste. The EPA estimates that in 1981 alone 290 million tons of hazardous wastes were produced in the United States and that there are up to 50,000 inactive sites containing hazardous and toxic wastes.

There are two federal laws that are relevant to toxic wastes. One law, the Resource Conservation and Recovery Act (RCRA), addresses the disposal of toxic and hazardous waste. The other law, the Comprehensive Environmental Response, Compensation and Liability Act (CERCLA), addresses the cleanup of existing toxic and hazardous waste disposal sites.

RCRA provides "cradle to the grave" federal regulation of the process of disposing of hazardous wastes. Under RCRA, the EPA prepares a list of toxic and hazardous substances and imposes standards of care on those that make the listed substances, transport them, use them and dispose of them. The companies and personnel dealing with toxic substances must keep detailed records and make written reports to EPA. Disposal of toxic wastes requires a permit from the EPA. Recent amendments to RCRA now also require that toxic wastes must be treated before they are disposed of to reduce their toxicity. In addition, severe restrictions are now placed on the disposal of hazardous wastes in order to encourage the treatment of wastes.

CERCLA is the well known "Superfund" law and has a serious impact on energy industries. The federal government has put billions of dollars into a fund, the Hazardous Substances Trust Fund, to pay for the removal and cleanup of hazardous waste sites listed by EPA on a National Priorities List. The amount in the fund has grown from 1.6 billion dollars in 1980 to 8.5 billion dollars through 1991. CERCLA gives the federal government authority to respond to emergencies where hazardous wastes need to be removed from waste sites in a hurry.

In cleaning up waste sites, CERCLA aims to hold private parties responsible for generating the waste, and also for the cleanup. Another aim of CERCLA is to have the individual states take the lead responsibility to assure that hazardous sites are cleaned up. In 1989, there were 1,219 sites on the National Priorities List and only a small percentage of those sites had been cleaned up since CERCLA became law in 1980. New hazardous sites are being uncovered every year and many lawsuits have arisen over who is the party responsible for cleanup. The problem of toxic waste is far from being resolved as a matter of environmental law or policy. One of the difficult issues is how to provide effective insurance coverage against being found liable for the cleanup of a hazardous waste site.[29]

III. INTERNATIONAL ENVIRONMENTAL LAW[30]

Three broad trends make the emergence of a body of international environmental law increasingly relevant to all segments of the energy industry. Those trends are the process of global integration of energy fuel

---

[29] *See* Hartford Fire Insurance Co. v. California, 509 U.S. 764 (1993) (dealing with boycott by London reinsurers of United States insurers in part because of concern about environmental liability.)

[30] *See* P. Sands, PRINCIPLES OF INTERNATIONAL ENVIRONMENTAL LAW (1995); Ved Nanda, INTERNATIONAL ENVIRONMENTAL LAW AND POLICY (1995); Pat Birnie and Alan Boyle, INTERNATIONAL LAW AND THE ENVIRONMENT (1992).

cycles and markets,[31] the internalization of environmental consequences of the energy fuel cycle into the cost component of energy prices, and the acceptance that, collectively, human and corporate activity may cause cumulative harm to a global environment increasingly under stress.[32] Those trends are reflected not only in increased attention to isolated transborder environmental events involving accidents, discharges, and spills, but also in a growing number of environmental problems of global concern many of which implicate the energy industry.) These concerns include global warming, ozone layer depletion, sea level rise, nuclear radiation, marine pollution, deforestation, and biodiversity.

A.   Historical Signposts

There are five historical signposts in the evolution of international environmental law that deserve mention: the 1941 *Trail Smelter Arbitration;* the 1972 Stockholm Conference; the 1982 Law of The Sea Treaty; the World Commission on Environment and Development; and the 1992 Rio Conference.

1.   *The Trail Smelter Arbitration*

International environmental law began with the *Trail Smelter Arbitration*[33] in 1941. In this case, the United States claimed that $2 million in compensation was owed by Canada for damage caused to land and other interests in Washington State by a privately-owned Canadian company's lead and zinc smelting operations in Canada, about ten miles from the United States-Canadian border. The damage came from smokestack emissions of sulfur carried by air currents in the form of sulfur dioxide to Washington. Canada and the United States agreed to submit the case to the International Joint Commission for arbitration. The arbitration tribunal allowed part of the United States claim and also dealt with the specific question of whether the Trail Smelter should be required to refrain from causing damage in the State of Washington in the future and, if so, to what extent. The 1941 Report of the Tribunal addressed that issue as follows:

---

[31] *See* Chapter Four on International Law.

[32] *See generally* J.E. Lovelock, GAIA: A NEW LOOK AT LIFE ON EARTH (New York: Oxford University Press 1979); THE ENVIRONMENT: GLOBAL PROBLEMS, LOCAL SOLUTIONS (Hickey and Longmire, eds., 1994); James E. Hickey, Jr., *The Globalization of Domestic Environmental Law*, 14 ENV'TL L. SECTION J. 15 (NYSBA 1994).

[33] The Trail Smelter Arbitration (United States v. Canada), 3 R.I.A.A. 1905 (1949), 35 AM. J. INT'L L. 684 (1941).

No state has the right to use or permit the use of its territory in such a manner as to cause injury by fumes in or to the territory of another or the properties or persons therein, when the case is of serious consequence and the injury is established by clear and convincing evidence.

The notion of State responsibility for environmental harm articulated in the *Trail Smelter* decision is a refinement of one of the broader premises upon which all international State responsibility rests. That premise is embodied in the traditional principle of international law that "one must so use his own as not to do injury to another" (*sic utere tuo ut alienum non laedas*).[34] The principle has been applied, *inter alia*, to international rivers, outer space, hostile expeditions, and the oceans.[35] The International Court of Justice, in opining on the legality of the threat or use of nuclear weapons in 1996, confirmed that this principle is now part of international environmental law:[36]

> The existence of the general obligation of states to ensure that activities within their jurisdiction and control respect the environment of other states or of areas beyond national control is now part of the corpus of international law relating to the environment.

Several observations about the international environmental law standard set out in *Trail Smelter* are in order. First, it confirmed the exclusive territorial jurisdiction of states as a matter of state sovereignty.[37] Second, state sovereignty over territory included the state duty to prevent the use of state territory from causing injury to neighboring state territories. Third, no state responsibility arose until after injury occurred. Fourth, the injury, to trigger state responsibility, had to be both "serious" and proved by "clear and convincing evidence." Fifth, state responsibility extended not only to purely *state* activities but to acts of private parties as well (i.e., the lead smelter was a private company). Sixth, the standard is applied on a case by

---

[34] Corfu Channel Case, [1949] I.C.J. 4, 22.

[35] *See* James E. Hickey, Jr., *Custom and Land-Based Pollution of The High Seas*, 15 SAN DIEGO L. REV. 409 (1978).

[36] Advisory Opinion to the UN General Assembly on the Legality of the Threat or Use of Nuclear Weapons [1996] ICJ Reports 226, 241-2, 35 I.L.M. 809, 821 (1996).

[37] Territorial sovereignty goes to the very definition of a state in international law (one of the definitional requirements for statehood is a defined territory) and is especially significant when dealing with natural resources like petroleum, coal, and uranium.

case basis (in the absence of some specific treaty regime addressing the environmental obligations of states).

Much of the development of international environmental law in the ensuing decades affecting, *inter alia,* the energy industry has involved adjustments to the *Trail Smelter* standards.

2.   *The Stockholm Conference on the Human Environment*

The 1972 Stockholm Conference on the Human Environment began the movement to place generic environmental concerns on the international environmental law agenda in addition to case by case incidents. It was the first coordinated effort by the international community as a whole to address the conservation and preservation of the environment. Prior to this, there had been only a few isolated treaties dealing with environmental problems that did not, viewed together, represent a cognizable body of international environmental law. The Stockholm Conference produced the now familiar Stockholm Declaration which articulated that both rights and duties of states (and non states) extend generally to the conservation and protection of the environment now and for future generations. It also generated an action plan for the future.[38] These *Stockholm Conference* instruments were non-binding soft law but nevertheless influenced greatly the evolution of international environmental law.[39]

The Stockholm Declaration, for the most part, did not disturb traditional concepts of state sovereignty. It preserved, the post-delictual approach to state responsibility for acts of pollution. For example, marine "pollution" was defined in the Declaration in a way that tracked the *Trail Smelter* standard. Substances discharged to the sea had to "result" in "deleterious effects" before they would be considered marine pollution.[40] If no harm occurred, no state responsibility arose. Tracking the *Trail Smelter* standards further, the Stockholm Conference Report eliminated *potential* deleterious effects or the *likelihood* of deleterious effects from the ambit of the marine pollution definition. That is, actual deleterious effects had to be established by demonstrably certain scientific evidence before marine pollution could be said to have occurred. The definition preserved the after-the-fact approach to legal duty.[41] The now famous Principle 21 of the

---

[38] 11 I.L.M. 416 (1972).

[39] *See* discussion of hard law and soft law in Chapter Four on International Law.

[40] Report of the United Nations Conference on the Human Environment, U.N. Doc. A/Cont 48/14 and Corrigenda 1 (1972).

[41] *Id.* at 22-24.

Stockholm Declaration affirmed both the continued sovereignty of states over "their own resources" and the need for actual damage as a predicate to state responsibility for extraterritorial environmental harm:[42]

> States have, in accordance with the Charter of the United Nations and the principle of international law, the sovereign right to exploit their own resources pursuant to their own environmental policies, and the responsibility to ensure that activities within their jurisdiction or control do not cause damage to the environment of other States of other States or of areas beyond the limits of national jurisdiction.

Principle 21 expanded state responsibility from other states' territory to global commons like the high seas or Antarctica ("areas beyond the limits of national jurisdiction"), but otherwise essentially preserved the *Trail Smelter* standard.

The value of the Stockholm Conference on the evolution of a body of international environmental law was four fold. First, it made environmental concern both part of international process and the object of international cooperation. Prior to Stockholm, there were only a few dozen multilateral agreements addressing the environment, mostly dealing with ocean pollution and migratory species. Today, there are over 1,000 international environmental legal instruments and dozens of international mechanisms and regimes dealing with environmental issues. Second, participating states recommended the establishment of the United Nations Environment Programme (UNEP) which is based in Nairobi, Kenya, and which has served as a source of issue formulation, information, and study. The UNEP also has drafted several important treaties dealing with transnational or extraterritorial environmental problems especially in the area of marine pollution. Third, the Stockholm Conference linked the scope of state responsibility for the environment generally to economic development. (Principle 8 of the Declaration stressed that "economic and social development is essential for ensuring a favorable living and working environment for man and for creating conditions on earth that are necessary for the improvement of the quality of life.")[43] Fourth, the Conference linked environmental quality to human rights. (Principle 1 provided that "Man has the fundamental right to freedom, equality and adequate conditions of life, in an environment that permits a life of dignity and well-being.")[44]

---

[42] *Id.* at 3-5.

[43] *See* discussion of sustainable development *infra* at V-27-8.

[44] *Supra* note 39.

3.   The 1982 Law of the Sea Convention[45]

The third signpost in the evolution of international environmental law is the 1982 Law of the Sea Convention. This is a multilateral umbrella treaty that addresses public order for the oceans. It entered into force in 1994. (The United States is not yet a party.)

This treaty is significant from an environmental standpoint for several reasons. First, its subject matter covers roughly three quarters of the earth. The law of the sea thus physically serves as a surrogate or model for the global environmental treaties that have followed. Second, it specifically addresses in its articles the environment of the oceans as a matter of hard treaty law rather than soft law. Third, it addresses pollution from virtually every phase of the fuel cycle because it considers both land-based and ocean-based sources of pollution. It addresses pollution that reaches the oceans from land-based power plants via the air or through direct discharges to the sea, or from gasoline road run-off from trucks and cars or from auto exhaust emissions to the air. This implicates both the production and end use phases of energy fuel cycles. It also addresses ocean-based sources of pollution like accidental oil tanker spills, intentional oil tanker discharges (like tanker washings and operational vessel discharges which implicate the transportation phases of fuel cycles). It also addresses pollution from oil wells on the continental shelf (the production phase).

In Article 1 (4), the Law of the Sea Convention defines marine pollution in more specific terms than the Stockholm Declaration and expands the *Trail Smelter* standard. It also specifically includes energy as a pollution source:

> [t]he introduction by man, directly or indirectly, of substances or *energy* into the marine environment, including estuaries, which results or is likely to result in such deleterious effects as harm to living resources and marine life, hazards to human health, hindrance to marine activities, including fishing and other legitimate uses of the sea, impairment of quality for use of sea water and reduction of amenities.[46] (emphasis added)

This definition retains the substantiality requirement for discharges to qualify as marine pollution. It requires that effects of discharges must be "deleterious" in the sense of being harmful or hazardous, or of being a

---

[45] United Nations Convention on the Law of the Sea (UNCLOS), 21 I.L.M. 1261 (1982).

[46] Third United Nations Conference on the Law of The Sea, 21 I.L.M. 1261, 1271 (Dec. 10, 1982).

hindrance to the use of the oceans, or of impairing marine environmental quality. It significantly expands the definition to include substances that are "likely to result" in deleterious effects. By implication, this definitional expansion introduces pre-delictual behavior into the state responsibility and international environmental law equation. That is, under this marine pollution definition, states would appear to have an implied duty to exercise precaution and to refrain from engaging in activities that are potentially deleterious.[47]

4.   *World Commission on Environment and Development*

In 1983, the U.N. General Assembly created the World Commission on Environment and Development (WCED or The Bruntland Commission).[48] The significance of the WCED is the introduction of the "problematic and nebulous" concept of sustainable development into the international environmental law equation. As the literature reveals, the concept is "protean in character" from a policy and law standpoint.[49]

5.   *The 1992 Rio Conference*

The 1992 Rio Conference[50] is praised for its wide participation by 180 countries and by many environmental NGOs for producing three soft law instruments (the Rio Declaration on Environment and Development[51], Agenda 21[52], and the Statement on Forest Management[53]) and for providing the occasion during which the Climate Change Convention[54] and the Biodiversity Convention[55] were signed.

---

[47] *See* discussion of the precautionary principle, *infra* at V-28-9.

[48] Named for Gro Bruntland, the Chair of the Commission. The Commission produced a report, *Our Common Future* in 1987.

[49] Ian Brownlie, PRINCIPLES OF INTERNATIONAL LAW (4th ed. 1990) at 287.

[50] The formal name is the United Nations Conference on Environment and Development (UNCED) and its popular name is "The Earth Summit."

[51] 31 I.L.M. 874 (1992).

[52] *See* Nicholas Roboman (ed), AGENDA 21 & THE UNCED PROCEEDINGS, Vols. 1-6, (1992).

[53] *Non-legally Binding Authoritative Statement of Principles for a Global Consensus on the Management, Conservation and Sustainable Development of All Types of Forest*, U.N. Doc. A/Conf. 151/26, v.3 (1992).

[54] United Nations Framework Convention on Climate Change, 31 I.L.M. 849 (1992).

[55] Convention on Biological Diversity, 31 I.L.M. 818 (1993).

However, the Rio Conference also is criticized on several counts by environmentalists. First, it articulated a right of states to develop even if this results in transfrontier pollution.[56] Second, it weakens the Stockholm Declaration's duty to conserve. Third, it calls for states to avoid taking "unilateral actions" beyond state borders and beyond state jurisdiction to address environmental problems.[57]

The historical signposts mentioned above are reflected both in specific binding treaties affecting energy fuel cycles and in emerging, overarching, principles of international environmental law.

The scope, variety and number of international treaties that impose legal rights and duties on states regarding the environment and energy fuel cycles preclude detailed treatment in this chapter on international environmental law. Some of the more significant global environmental treaties in alphabetical order are:

1.   Basel Convention on the Control of Trans-boundary Movements of Hazardous Wastes and their Disposal (Basel Convention), 28 IBM. 667 (1992).

2.   Convention on Assistance in the Case of a Nuclear Accident or Radiological Emergency (Assistance Convention) 25 I.L.M. 1377, (1986), Convention on Biological Diversity (Biodiversity Convention), 31 I.L.M. 818 (1993).

3.   Convention on the Early Notification of a Nuclear Accident (Notification Convention), 25 I.L.M. 1369 (1986).

4.   Convention on the Liability of Operators of Nuclear Ships, 67 A.J.I.L. 268 (1962).

5.   Convention on Long-Range Transboundary Air Pollution 18 I.L.M. 1442 (1979).

6.   Convention on Nuclear Safety, 33 I.L.M. 1614 (1994).

7.   Convention for the Prevention of Marine Pollution by Dumping from Ships and Aircraft (1972 Oslo Convention), 932 U.N.T.S. 3.

8.   Convention on the Prevention of Marine Pollution by Dumping of Waste and Other Matter (1972 London Convention), 1046 U.N.T.S. 120.

9.   International Convention for the Prevention of Pollution from Ships (MARPOL Convention) 12 I.L.M. 1319 (1973).

---

[56] *See* discussion of sustainable development, *infra* at V-27-8.
[57] Principle 12 of the Rio Declaration, *supra* note 50.

10. Convention on Third Party Liability in the Field of Nuclear Energy (Brussels Convention) Jan.31, 1963, 2 I.L.M. 685 (1963).

11. Convention on Third Party Liability in the Field of Nuclear Energy (Paris Nuclear Liability Convention), 956 U.N.T.S. 2G1.

12. International Convention on Civil Liability for Oil Pollution Damage, 9 I.L.M. 45 (1970).

13. International Convention on Oil Pollution Preparedness Response and Co-operation (OPRC), 30 I.L.M. 773 (1990).

14. International Convention on the Establishment of an International Fund for Oil Pollution Damage 1971 U.N. Jur. Y.B. 103.

15. International Convention Relating to the Intervention on the High Seas in Cases of Oil Pollution Casualties (Intervention Convention), 26 U.S.T. 766.

16. Protocol to the 1979 Convention on Long-Range Transboundary Air Pollution on Reduction of Sulphur Emissions or Their Transboundary Fluxes by at Least 30 Percent 27 I.L.M. 707.

17. Protocol to the 1979 Convention on Long-Range Transboundary Air Pollution Concerning the Emissions of Nitrogen Oxides or their Transboundary Fluxes, 22 I.L.M. 212 (1988).

18. Protocol to the 1979 Convention on Long Range Transboundary Air Pollution Concerning the Control of Emissions of Volatile Organic Compounds or Their Transboundary Fluxes, 31 I.L.M. 568 (1991).

19. United Nations Convention on the Law of the Sea 21 I.L.M. 1261 (1982).

20. United Nations Conference on Environment and Development: Framework Convention on Climate Change, 31 I.L.M. 849 (1992).

21. Vienna Convention for the Protection of the Ozone Layer (Vienna Convention on Ozone), Mar. 22, 1985, 26 I.L.M. 1629 (1988), 8, 45, 54, 57, 157.

22. Vienna Convention on Civil Liability for Nuclear Damage (1963) Vienna Convention), May 21, 1963, 7 I.L.M. 727 (entered into force Nov. 12, 1977), 55, 391.

In addition, there are many regional environmental treaties that have an impact on energy fuel cycles.

B. Emerging Principles

1. *Sustainable Development*

The concept of sustainable development is that nations, especially developing nations, can both progress economically and protect the environment for present and future generations. Energy industries and fuel cycles, of course, play a key role both in the level of Gross National Product (GNP) and in the degree of environmental quality enjoyed by nations. This promise of sustainable development has been pursued actively by the international community through the World Commission on Environment and Development (WCED)[58] in the 1980s, and by the United Nations Conference on Environment and Development (UNCED) in the 1990s. While the former successfully placed sustainable development on the international environmental law agenda, the latter did much to negate the promise of sustainable development.

In one of the key instruments produced by UNCED, The Rio Declaration on Environment and Development,[59] sustainable development as a policy concept arguably was dismantled. For example, while principle 1 declares that "Human beings are at the centre of concerns for sustainable development" Principles 2 and 3 largely gut the environmental conservation foundations laid down by the Stockholm Conference, eliminate the limitations on development inherent in the Report of the WCED, and scuttle state responsibility for transborder environmental damage:

Principle 2
States have, in accordance with the Charter of the United Nations and the principles of international law, the sovereign right to exploit their own resources pursuant to their own environmental *and developmental policies*, and the responsibility to ensure that activities within their jurisdiction or control do not cause damage to the environment of other States or of areas beyond the limits of national jurisdiction. (emphasis added)

Principle 3
The *right to development* must be fulfilled so as to *equitably meet developmental* and environmental needs of present and future generations. (emphasis added)

---

[58] *See* WCED, OUR COMMON FUTURE (1987).
[59] 31 I.L.M. 874 (1992).

These principles now largely replace the implied right to a safe and healthy environment of the Stockholm Declaration with a right to develop. In addition, states under the Rio Declaration arguably might now be able to cause transborder environmental damage by right if the "sovereign right [of states] to exploit their own resources pursuant to their own . . . developmental policies" outweighs their responsibility not to cause such damage. Finally, the Rio Declaration seems to scuttle even the fundamental sustainable development notion of rejecting present economic development if the environment for future generations is harmed. Under the Rio Declaration states may exercise a "right to develop" to meet the "developmental needs" of "future generations." Thus, while the term "sustainable development" remains in the lexicon of international environmental law, there is presently little of substance left to drive either law or policy formation.[60]

2.   The Precautionary Principle[61]

Another nascent notion in international environmental law is the precautionary principle. This principle is now regularly inserted into hard and soft international environmental law instruments. The basic idea here is to extend the *Trail Smelter* standard of state responsibility from a state duty to compensate for actual extraterritorial environmental damage to a duty to prevent extraterritorial environmental harm, even in circumstances where there is a lack of scientific information. However, the articulations of the precautionary principle to date reveal a vague, ambiguous, and variable principle of indeterminate binding effect.

Clarity and consistency are needed in the articulations of the precautionary principle before it can be said that it is a generally understood and accepted principle of international environmental law. The most that can be presently concluded about the principle is that, where it appears, it tends to shift the burden of proof from the victim of pollution harm (to

---

[60] *See* Marc Pallemaerts, *International Environmental Law in the Age of Sustainable Development: A Critical Assessment of the UNCED Process*, 15 J.L. & COM. 623 (Spring 1996); for an early spirited criticism of sustainable development *see* Johan Galtung, *Beyond Brundtland: Linking Global Problems and Local Solutions*, Chapter 3, in James E. Hickey, Jr. and Linda Longmire, THE ENVIRONMENT: GLOBAL PROBLEMS, LOCAL SOLUTIONS (1994) at 3.

[61] *See* THE PRECAUTIONARY PRINCIPLE AND INTERNATIONAL LAW, THE CHALLENGE OF IMPLEMENTATION (David Freestone and Ellen Hey, eds., 1996); James E. Hickey, Jr. and Vern Walker, *Refining the Precautionary Principle In International Environmental Law*, 14 VA. ENVTL L.J. 423 (Spring 1995).

demonstrate by clear and convincing evidence that actual environmental harm has occurred) to the polluter (to demonstrate that a potential activity will not cause environmental harm).The shift in burden of proof most likely operates to require the potential victim to establish something akin to a *prima facie* case for state responsibility. To meet that *prima facie* burden, clear and convincing evidence may not be needed, especially if there is potential for serious irreversible environmental harm.

3.   *The Duty to Cooperate*

On a more optimistic note, a requirement has emerged firmly in international environmental law that states must cooperate with other states and international bodies in international environmental law problems, especially where problems are regional or global in character. This cooperation requirement embraces a state duty to inform other states of imminent environmental harm, especially where natural disasters or other serious emergencies exist.[62] Increasingly, the duty of cooperation is also understood to require states to make environmental impact assessments similar to the obligation of United States government bodies to prepare an environmental impact statement under Section 102 of NEPA and to make that assessment available, especially to the potential victims of environmental harm.

---

[62] *E.g.*, International Atomic Energy Agency: Conventions on Nuclear Accident (entered into force October 27, 1986) 20 I.L.M. 1369 (1986).

CHAPTER SIX

Toward a Sustainable
Energy-Environmental Policy

by Joseph P. Tomain

> *"[Public policy is] anything a government chooses to do or not to do."*
> Thomas R. Dye, UNDERSTANDING PUBLIC POLICY 2 (1972).
>
> *"Public policy is a complex phenomenon consisting of numerous decisions made by numerous individuals and organizations."*
> Michael Howlett & M. Ramesch, STUDYING PUBLIC POLICY: POLICY CYCLES AND POLICY SUBSYSTEMS 7 (1995).

I.   INTRODUCTION

What is the energy-environmental policy of the United States? The mission statement for the Department of Energy attempts to capture what our national energy-environmental policy ought to be. That mission statement reads:

> *To foster a secure and reliable energy system that is environmentally and economically sustainable, to be a responsible steward of the Nation's nuclear weapons, to clean up our facilities, and to support continued United States leadership in science and technology.*[1]

Articulating an energy-environmental policy based on that mission statement and based on the work of the Department of Energy would be a relatively easy task. The reality, however, is much more complicated. Not only does the Department of Energy have responsibility for this field, so does the Environmental Protection Agency, the Department of the Interior, and the Department of Agriculture. Federal subagencies, such as the Federal Energy Regulatory Commission, the Economic Research and Development Administration, the Energy Information Administration, the Bureau of Land Management, the Mines Safety and Health Administration,

---

[1] U.S. Department of Energy, STRATEGIC PLAN: PROVIDING AMERICA WITH ENERGY SECURITY, NATIONAL SECURITY, ENVIRONMENTAL QUALITY, SCIENCE LEADERSHIP 7 (Sept. 1997).

the Council on Environmental Quality, and the Nuclear Regulatory Commission among others also play crucial policymaking roles. These agencies, with the exception of independent regulatory agencies, are Executive Branch institutions. These federal administrative agencies directly implicate the Legislative Branch in the policymaking process because the administrative agencies can act only pursuant to Congressional directives. Finally, the Judicial Branch has review authority of both branches and therefore also has an important role in public policymaking.

To complicate matters further, because the United States is a federal system, state energy and environmental institutions also play significant roles in shaping energy-environmental policy. Perhaps the most striking contemporary example of state influence on energy policy is the fact that state public utility commissions are taking the lead in restructuring the electric industry from generation to retail delivery. In addition to government actors, private firms and public interest groups also directly affect policy formation.

In this Chapter, we identify the dominant energy-environmental policy in the United States by examining the legal and political variables as well as the regulatory proposals which have constituted that policy over the last century.[2] Based on that description, we can then surmise what future policy will be. The reason that United States' energy-environmental policy is best described retrospectively rather than prospectively resides in the nature of our polity. The United States is not a centrally planned economy which relies on government-mandated directions for society to follow.[3] Rather, as a nation of democratic capitalism, the United States believes that the market is the preferred form of social ordering. As explained in Chapter 2, there are occasions when the market does not function properly and generates either inefficient or unfair consequences. In the face of such market failures, government regulation is introduced into private markets.

The United States is also referred to as a mixed-economy, that is, an economy in which government and market both play important roles in shaping the social order.[4] It is true that throughout our history[5] government

---

[2] Charles E. Lindblom, THE POLICY-MAKING PROCESS 3-6 (1968).

[3] Daniel Yergin & Joseph Stanislaw, THE COMMANDING HEIGHTS: THE BATTLE BETWEEN GOVERNMENT AND THE MARKETPLACE THAT IS REMAKING THE MODERN WORLD (1998).

[4] Charles E. Lindblom, POLITICS AND MARKETS: THE WORLD'S POLITICAL ECONOMIC SYSTEMS (1977).

[5] Sidney A. Shapiro & Joseph P. Tomain, REGULATORY LAW AND POLICY 77-91 (2d ed. 1998); Herbert Hovenkamp, ENTERPRISE AND AMERICAN LAW 1836-1937 (1991); Morton Keller, REGULATING A NEW ECONOMY: PUBLIC POLICY AND ECONOMIC

intervention in private markets has ebbed and flowed. It is also true that markets would not exist without government support.[6] The relationship between government and markets is central to the development of U.S. energy-environmental policy in general and of the U.S. energy industries in particular. In fact, both government and market interrelate in shaping energy-environmental policy in discernable ways. In this chapter, then, we discuss U.S. energy-environmental policy as it has developed over the course of this century. We conclude by suggesting what the future holds for that policy.

II.   U.S. ENERGY-ENVIRONMENTAL POLICY[7]

The United States, and most countries in the world, are currently entrenched in the second phase of the production and use of energy. Prior to the mid-19th century, energy was generated from renewable natural resources. In addition to harnessing the occasional stream to grind grain or a windmill to do the same, wood, together with animal and human labor were the primary energy resources. During that period, the country's population was small, and land and resources were plentiful. Any significant official policy of environmental protection was a century away.[8] With Colonel Drake's discovery of petroleum in Titusville, Pennsylvania on

---

CHANGE IN AMERICA, 1900-1933 (1990); REGULATING A NEW SOCIETY: PUBLIC POLICY AND SOCIAL CHANGE IN AMERICA, 1900-1933 (1994); William J. Novak, THE PEOPLE'S WELFARE: LAW AND REGULATION IN NINETEENTH CENTURY AMERICA (1996); Robert L. Rabin, *Federal Regulation in Historical Perspective*, 38 STAN. L. REV. 1189 (1986); Mark Alan Eisner, REGULATORY POLITICS IN TRANSITION (1993).

[6] In brief, to work well markets require property (see Chapter 2 *supra*) and property is defined and protected by common law rules. *See e.g.*, Richard A. Epstein, SIMPLE RULES FOR A COMPLEX WORLD (1995); Barbara H. Fried, THE PROGRESSIVE ASSAULT ON LAISSEZ FAIRE: ROBERT HALE AND THE FIRST LAW AND ECONOMICS MOVEMENT (1998); William J. Novak, THE PEOPLE'S WELFARE: LAW AND REGULATION IN NINETEENTH-CENTURY AMERICA (1996); Cass R. Sunstein, FREE MARKETS AND SOCIAL JUSTICE (1997).

[7] *See generally* Joseph P. Tomain, *The Dominant Model of United States Energy Policy*, 61 UNIV. COL. L. REV. 355 (1990); *Interest, Ideology and Imagination*, 5 J. MIN. L. & POL. 115 (1989-90); *Energy Policy Advice for the New Administration*, 46 WASH. & LEE L. REV. 63 (1989); John G. Clark, ENERGY AND THE FEDERAL GOVERNMENT: FOSSIL FUEL POLICIES, 1900-1946 (1987); Richard H. K. Vietor, ENERGY POLICY IN AMERICA SINCE 1945: A STUDY IN BUSINESS GOVERNMENT RELATIONS (1984); William F. Fox, Jr., FEDERAL REGULATION OF ENERGY (1983).

[8] Nevertheless, environmentalists can point to such literary personages as Ralph Waldo Emerson and Henry David Thoreau for the first stirrings of an environmental ethic.

August 27, 1859 and Thomas Edison's generation and distribution of electricity at Pearl Street Station in New York City on September 4, 1882, the United States experienced a transition from wood and other renewable resources to our present pattern of energy use that relies principally on fossil fuels and electricity.

Over the last century, the United States government has fairly consistently implemented energy policies that are guided by efficiency, that support private energy industries and markets, and that seek to correct defects in those markets. Also, since 1970, the country has developed an elaborate environmental policy. Today, the challenge remains to coordinate the two.

It is a slight mischaracterization to apply the phrase "energy law" to any period prior to the mid-1970s. The flurry of legislative activity that resulted as a reaction to the Arab Oil Embargo in 1973 and the Iranian Revolution of 1979 is generally considered to constitute the primary body of what is now referred to as energy law. This corpus of law, implementing governmental policy preferences, generally concerns the federal regulation of the exploitation of natural resources used for the production of energy and for the industrial structure used to transmit and distribute energy products. Similarly, environmental law dates its history to the National Environmental Policy Act effective January 1, 1970.

Although energy law and environmental law have only emerged recently, both have identifiable antecedents. Since the Industrial Revolution, energy regulation has been used to control the production and distribution of the social necessity called energy. It has paralleled—and supported—the growth and development of energy industries and markets. Indeed, perhaps the most significant observation about the history of energy regulation is to note the symbiotic relationship between private energy industries and public energy regulation.[9] Environmental regulation began with, and continues to have its roots in, an ethic of natural resources preservation and protection. The tension between energy production for economic growth and environmental protection for resource preservation constitutes the central, and deep, tension in any energy-environmental policy. What follows is a historical description of U.S. energy-environmental policy for the last century.

---

[9] *See* John G. Clark, ENERGY AND THE FEDERAL GOVERNMENT: FOSSIL FUEL POLICIES, 1900-1946 (1987); Richard H. K. Vietor, ENERGY POLICY IN AMERICA SINCE 1945: A STUDY OF BUSINESS-GOVERNMENT RELATIONS (1984).

A. 1887-1900

The beginning of modern energy law started in the next to the last decade of the nineteenth century with the United States Supreme Court's 1887 opinion in *Munn v. Illinois*.[10] Although the case concerned the regulation of grain elevators, *Munn* helped to create a major principle in energy law. The Court recognized the existence of natural monopolies and ruled that government could enter private markets and regulate industries in those markets. It established the principle that government would not tolerate the unlimited private exercise of market power and that such an exercise could be restrained by government price-setting. Also in that year, the Interstate Commerce Commission (ICC) was established. It is the prototype of the modern administrative agency.

At the end of the nineteenth century, energy was produced on a local or regional basis and production and distribution companies were largely unregulated.[11] At that time, there was no overarching energy policy coordinating the development and use of natural resources. Instead, specific resources like oil, coal, and natural gas were regulated independently of one another and that pattern of separate treatment largely persists.

During this period the transition from wood to coal and oil was completed, and the transition to widespread use of electricity began. The 19th century transition was also a transition from local and state to regional and national markets (and, subsequently, to government regulation), thus mirroring industry development. The role of the federal government during this period was that of a promoter. Statutes such as the Coal Entry Act,[12] the General Mining Act,[13] and the Homestead Act[14] opened federal lands to the exploration and production of resources such as oil, coal, and minerals as an aid to the expansion of the frontier.

B. 1900-1920

During the first two decades of the twentieth century, modern energy industries, energy markets, and federal energy regulations developed. As the production and distribution of energy moved from local to state to

[10] 94 U.S. 113 (1876).

[11] Leonard S. Hyman, AMERICA'S ELECTRIC UTILITIES: PAST, PRESENT AND FUTURE (6th ed. 1997); Werner Troesken, WHY REGULATE UTILITIES: THE NEW INSTITUTIONAL ECONOMICS AND THE CHICAGO GAS INDUSTRY, 1849-1924 (1996).

[12] Coal Entry Act, ch. 205, 13 Stat. 343 (1864).

[13] 30 U.S.C. §§ 22-54 and §§ 71-76 (1994).

[14] Homestead Act, ch. 75, 12 Stat. 392 (1862).

regional to national and, finally, to international markets, industry firms changed accordingly. So did government policy. Energy law and policy developed as a series of rules emanating from the fundamental tension between an energy delivery system based on private ownership and its regulation for the public good.[15] The country experienced the end of a low energy society and the beginning of a high energy one dependent on large-scale, capital-intensive, centralized, interstate energy production and distribution, first in oil, then in natural gas, and then in electricity. The general intent of federal regulation was to promote energy production and industrial stability and, occasionally, to smooth out gross social and economic distortions.

Coal reigned king during the Industrial Revolution and still maintains a significant place in the country's energy profile because of its great abundance. The United States has roughly 35 percent of the world's proved recoverable coal.[16] Production of coal increased until 1918, when it peaked at 678 million tons. Throughout this period, however, oil and natural gas markets expanded, signaling a transition from coal to the other fossil fuels. The oil and natural gas markets were expanded because new end uses such as refined petroleum products for automobiles increased demand. Because of coal's reputation as a dirty burning fuel, the cleaner alternatives of oil and natural gas were preferable. By 1925, oil constituted almost one-fifth of the energy market. But the country never abandoned coal during the transition from the solid to the liquid and gaseous fossil fuels. Instead of allowing the transition to occur in the market unimpeded, the government intentionally promoted the use of coal to buoy the industry.

Structurally, the coal, oil, and natural gas industries had similarities and differences which affected government regulation and policy. The basic difference concerned the degree of competition within each industry and the demand for each resource. The basic similarity was that each industry had a transportation bottleneck. In the oil and natural gas industries, pipelines were the bottleneck, and in the coal industry railroads were the bottleneck.[17] Of the three industries, coal was, and continues to be, the most competitive. Indeed, bottlenecks persist in the electricity and natural gas industries and to a much lesser extent in the coal industry.

---

[15] Charles F. Phillips, THE REGULATION OF PUBLIC UTILITIES: THEORY AND PRACTICE (2d ed. 1988).

[16] Larry McBride & John Pendergrass, *Coal* in Celia Campbell-Mohn, Barry Breen & J. William Futrell, ENVIRONMENTAL LAW: FROM RESOURCES TO RECOVERY, ch. 14 (1993).

[17] United States Department of Justice, COMPETITION IN THE COAL INDUSTRY 123 (1978).

During the first two decades of the twentieth century, oil became the paradigm of big industry. In 1911, the Standard Oil Company and related entities controlled 64% of the market (down from 90% in 1900 due to the federal government's successful antitrust litigation).[18] Still, in 1919, thirty-two firms controlled 60% of production, and, in 1920, the thirty largest oil firms controlled 72% of the country's refining capacity.

The natural gas industry was less concentrated during these early years because natural gas was seen as a nuisance by-product of oil exploration. It was wasted through venting into the atmosphere or burned off through flaring rather than exploited. Before the turn of the century, small natural gas companies were the rule. By the end of the first third of the century, however, natural gas was seen as a valuable commodity and the transportation network became dominated by a handful of interstate pipeline companies. This development, like the market power of the oil pipelines, led to federal regulation of the natural gas industry.

During this formative period, energy markets moved from local and state to regional and national levels. Federal intervention into private energy industries was episodic, allowing interindustry and interfuel competition to develop and later flourish. Whenever there were serious blips in energy markets, primarily when production was not flowing smoothly or when distribution was congested, the government would intervene in an attempt to smooth out the market blip. In general, pre-war intervention was motivated by a sense of progressivism colored by antitrust sentiment. The Hepburn Act[19] (which curtailed big oil's control of interstate pipelines), the Interstate Commerce Commission, the Federal Trade Commission, and the rise of state public utility commissions were all aimed at curtailing market power. Similarly, controls aimed at loosening the railroads' grip on coal hauling were also instituted.

During this period natural resources conservation programs began. In the first decade of the century, millions of acres of federal lands were withdrawn from oil leasing and later earmarked as naval reserves.[20] Also, during this period conservationists perceived coal as an exhaustible resource and millions of acres of federal lands were withdrawn from coal leasing. These withdrawals were intended to preserve natural resources and to keep

---

[18] *Standard Oil Co. of N.J. v. United States*, 221 U.S. 1 (1911).

[19] Hepburn Act, ch. 3591, 34 Stat. 584 (1906) (codified in scattered sections of 49 U.S.C. (1994)).

[20] Robert L. Bradley, Jr., 1 OIL, GAS, AND GOVERNMENT: THE U.S. EXPERIENCE 83-84 (1996).

government lands in pristine condition such as through the creation of national parks.

The Great War in 1914-1918 only slightly shook the country out of its Golden Age complacency. Professor John Clark argues that the First World War solidified the position of private energy industries. He states, "For business, the war in Europe opened great opportunities for profit through an expanding foreign trade. As many businessmen viewed it, American's entrance into the conflict provided no compelling reasons for a swollen federal economic role."[21] Although the federal government did establish the United States Fuel Administration (USFA), the first energy agency with the power to regulate prices, transportation, and distribution, the USFA did not exercise these powers. The agency was administered locally, and its principal goal was to mobilize natural resources for the war, not to coordinate energy industries.

The USFA, symbolic of the first decades of federal energy regulation and not unlike the present Department of Energy, did not use its full power to coordinate and establish a national energy plan. Instead, a muted form of corporatism took hold. Coal successfully kept government out of its industry except to support it. Natural gas was too nascent an industry to generate much concern about federal regulation, and the oil industry, with its history of concentration, was expanding into foreign markets and was showing signs of greater industrial concentration.

Coal production did not appreciably increase during the war, pricing policies were a failure, rail carriers moved coal to the highest bidders first, and coal allocation regulations were conducted on an uncoordinated regional zone basis. At the height of World War I, coal was being replaced by oil and natural gas. Nevertheless, the federal government continued to support the coal industry.

Federal oil and natural gas policies followed a pattern similar to coal regulation. During World War I, several restrictions on oil and natural gas were implemented, including fuel-switching, licensing, price and production controls, and rationing. However, these controls were not integrated in an overall energy policy, and they ended with the Armistice. Clark argues that World War I had a profound effect on future energy regulation by positioning major energy industries for years to come. The regulatory experience from 1900-1920 firmly established industry-government relations.[22]

---

[21] Clark *supra* note 7 at 50.
[22] *Id.* at 107.

Thus, in the initial two decades of the twentieth century, energy markets were structured by:

(1)   seemingly inexhaustible supplies of oil, natural gas, and coal;
(2)   a shift from local to regional and interstate resource production and distribution;
(3)   continuous growth in markets and in energy efficiency;
(4)   increasing industrial concentration, integration, and large-scale production; and
(5)   transportation bottlenecks in each industry.

❰Regulators did not treat energy industries either coordinately or comprehensively❭ Instead, the coal, oil, natural gas (and electricity) industries were regulated separately by tracking each resource through its fuel cycle from production and processing through distribution and marketing.

C.   1920-1933

The Roaring Twenties were important years for energy policy. Coal reached the end of its prominence as the nation's energy supplier, yielding this position to oil, yet still playing a major role. Mine operators, naturally, were interested in maintaining their market shares. With the industry in decline due to excess capacity and reduced demand, cutthroat competition, pressure for wage reduction, and miners' strikes resulted. Coal's shrinking market and consumers' growing preference for oil and natural gas underscored the significance of fuel substitution.

To encourage the development of oil, the common law developed the rule of capture: oil belongs to the person who captures it.[23] The rule of capture promotes production, but it also promotes waste, as producers will capture as much as they can before their neighbors do. In order to reduce such waste, the states enacted gas and oil conservation statutes to limit the amounts of gas and oil that could be extracted thus stabilizing the market and protecting resources for the future.[24]

❰At the federal level, the Federal Oil Conservation Board (FOCB), a regulatory agency, was instituted to look into the perceived weaknesses of the oil industry❭ The primary weaknesses were waste, declining reserve estimates, and price instability due in part to the occasional flush field.

---

[23] Howard R. Williams, Richard C. Maxwell, & Charles J. Meyers, CASES AND MATERIALS ON THE LAW OF OIL AND GAS 13 n. 1 (4th ed. 1979).

[24] Northcutt Ely, THE OIL AND GAS CONSERVATION STATUTES (1933); *The Conservation of Oil*, 51 HARV. L. REV. 1209 (1938); Bradley, *supra* note 20 at chs. 3 and 4.

Instead of curbing production, the FOCB responded by promoting the oil depletion allowance and by opening up the public domain under the Mineral Land Leasing Act of 1920.[25] Both responses favored industry. In short, the FOCB pressed for government controls in order to stop waste and stabilize prices as a form of oil industry protectionism. The FOCB also allowed large firms to control production and reduce the amount of oil on the market, which allowed these firms to capture economic rents. Thus the FOCB regulatory efforts worked to the great benefit of the major oil companies.

By the end of the decade the fossil fuel industries (oil, natural gas, and coal) were well entrenched. Energy markets were expanding. In addition, interfuel competition and concentration were increasing. By 1929 the split in the oil industry between the majors and the independents was deep. Twenty-one majors controlled 60% of oil production, ten firms controlled 60% of the refining, and fourteen firms controlled 70% of the pipelines. In the natural gas industry, eight holding companies controlled 85% of production. Similarly, twenty-two electricity holding companies generated 61% of the country's electricity. The coal industry was less concentrated. The seventeen largest bituminous companies controlled only 20% of the mines, but eight anthracite companies controlled 70% of the mines.[26] Indeed, in the coal industry, the major problem was not concentration; it was survival. The primary conflict was not between major and independent firms; it was between labor and capital.

The 1930s brought with them a peculiar test of the nation's energy policies. Not only did the country experience a national economic depression that put a downward pressure on prices, but rich oil fields were discovered in the oil producing states, most notably in eastern Texas. These discoveries flooded the market with remarkably cheap oil, with prices dropping below ten cents per barrel. As a result, the majors pushed for firm production controls to keep prices up. In addition, global oil markets were developing, giving the east coast refiners the option to buy cheap foreign oil. Here again, the majors sought government intervention in the form of import tariffs to protect their markets.

D.   1933-1945

On the eve of the New Deal, the nation's energy industries, markets, and their regulation had developed a pattern which continues to dominate energy planning. Oil replaced coal as the primary fuel, and large, integrated

---

[25] *See* Mineral Lands Leasing Act of 1920, Pub. L. No. 99-64, 99 Stat. 156 (codified as amended at 30 U.S.C. (1994)).

[26] Clark, *supra* note 7, at 184-85.

domestic firms continued to prosper. The New Deal did little to alter that pattern. Although, interstate distribution was federally regulated, further efforts to coordinate energy production and distribution failed despite efforts to centralize national economic planning. The primary purpose of the New Deal was to promote economic stability and centralized planning appeared to be an attractive approach. The National Industrial Recovery Act[27] was promulgated to bring about that stabilization by allowing major industries and manufacturers to set pricing and production policies for themselves without threat of antitrust prosecution. Nevertheless, provisions of the NIRA concerning the oil[28] and poultry[29] industries were held to be unconstitutional delegations of authority. Similarly, provisions of the Bituminous Coal Conservation Act,[30] were held unconstitutional,[31] thus thwarting efforts to centralize energy markets.

Just prior to the New Deal, the electricity and natural gas industries experienced concentration. That concentration put pressure on government regulators to prevent these industries from exercising market power to the detriment of consumers. In the electricity industry, firms realized that economies of scale could be achieved and that market share could be captured. From 1922 to 1927 over 1600 privately owned electric systems were eliminated as the industry concentrated.[32] Further, as generation and transmission capacities increased, so did consolidation. Entrepreneurs, like Samuel Insull and Henry Villard, created holding companies to hasten consolidation so that by the mid-1920s, 16 holding companies controlled 85 percent of the nation's electric industry.[33] These holding companies helped advance economies of scale but at a real cost to consumers. The electric trusts, like the oil trusts before them, were susceptible to stock manipulation and shareholder abuses.[34] Similarly, natural gas pipelines were also showing their market muscle. The public reacted sharply to the electricity

---

[27] National Industrial Recovery Act, Pub. L. No. 73-67, 48 Stat. 195 (1933).

[28] Panama Refining Co. v. Ryan, 293 U.S. 388 (1935).

[29] A.L.A. Schechter Poultry Corp. v. United States, 295 U.S. 495 (1935).

[30] Bituminous Coal Conversion Act, ch. 824, 49 Stat. 991 (1935) (repealed 1937).

[31] Carter v. Carter Coal Co., 298 U.S. 238 (1936).

[32] Peter C. Christensen, *Overview of Electricity Generation and the Industry*, in THE ELECTRIC INDUSTRY: OPPORTUNITIES AND IMPACTS FOR RESOURCE PRODUCERS, POWER GENERATORS, MARKETERS, AND CONSUMERS at 1-2 (Rocky Mtn. Min. Law Fdn., 1996).

[33] *Id.* at 1-4; *see also* Michael E. Parrish, SECURITIES REGULATION AND THE NEW DEAL 149 (1970); Douglas W. Hawes, UTILITY HOLDING COMPANIES § 2.03 (1987).

[34] Hawes, *supra* note 33 at § 2.05.

trusts and pipeline concentration and both industries came under scrutiny by state and federal politicians.⟩

At the state level, politicians were drawn to retail ratesetting in order to protect consumers.[35] At the federal level politicians were drawn to curbing trust abuses and making electric and gas services universally available.

The specific legislative reaction to the abuse of the energy trusts was the Public Utility Holding Company Act of 1935[36] (PUHCA). ⟨PUHCA is fundamentally a registration act requiring holding companies whose subsidiaries are engaged in either the electric utility business or in the business of the retail distribution of natural gas to register with the Securities and Exchange Commission⟨Under the Act, the SEC was authorized to examine the corporate and operational structures of the holding company to simplify and integrate operations for the purpose of avoiding abuses of shareholders. The SEC also has the authority to order divestiture where operations of utility and non-utility operations pose the potential for financial abuse.

⟨The year 1935 witnessed two significant energy regulation events. First, Congress passed Part II of the Federal Power Act[37] to regulate interstate wholesales of electric power. Part II of the FPA gave the then Federal Power Commission the authority to set the rates of interstate sales of electricity. In other words, the heart of the national electric industry, generation and transmission, came under federal power.⟩

⟨Also in that year the Federal Trade Commission issued a report[38] noting the monopoly power of natural gas pipelines.⟩Three years later, Congress passed the Natural Gas Act.[39] Patterned after Part II of the Federal Power Act, the Natural Gas Act gave the Federal Power Commission ratemaking authority over interstate sales of natural gas.

⟨The intellectual justification of the federal regulation of these industries was twofold. First, both gas and electricity were deemed to be in the public interest and highly desirable as consumer products. The idea that the federal government should promote consumption was a dramatic shift in economic thinking which surrounded the New Deal⟩Prior to the New Deal, laissez-faire reigned as courts, most notably the United States Supreme

---

[35] Hyman *supra* note 11 at ch. 17.

[36] Public Utility Holding Company Act (PUHCA) of 1935, 15 U.S.C. § 79 (1994).

[37] Federal Power Act, Part II, 16 U.S.C. § 824 (1994).

[38] Report of the FTC to the U.S. Senate, S. Doc. No. 92, 70th Cong., 1st Sess. (1936).

[39] 15 U.S.C. § 717 (1994).

Court,[40] maintained a hands-off stance towards industry. The New Deal dramatically changed that stance.[41] Now, public policy was based upon the idea that government had a role to play, not only of national economic stability, but of promoting economic growth and product consumption.[42] The New Deal experiment introduced federal regulation into nearly every sector of the national economy. Roosevelt's economic philosophy was industrial revitalization through market stabilization and business support. To this end, government played an active role in promoting the use and development of energy products.

The second idea that drove energy regulation was based on the economic notion that utilities had characteristics of a natural monopoly. Simply put, natural monopoly theory holds that one firm can more efficiently deliver a product at a lower cost than multiple firms.[43] Multiple firms cause unnecessary duplication, for example, by constructing multiple transmission and distribution systems. Such duplication is wasteful and therefore it is better to promote one firm than to have wasteful competition from a multiplicity of firms. In such a market, government regulation is necessary because if unchecked, the strongest natural monopoly firm will consolidate until it has monopoly market power and then can visit the sins of monopoly on consumers.

Federal oil policies during this period attempted to regulate production, but efforts failed as new oil production flooded the market in 1937-1938. Big oil was again the big winner of New Deal regulation. In 1937, twenty companies controlled 70% of the proven reserves and 76% of the refining capacity. In 1941, the Temporary National Economic Committee (TNEC) reported the findings of its investigation into the oil industry and concluded that the "major integrated oil companies markedly increased their pre-depression control of reserves and crude production and maintained a great supremacy in refining capacity, refining output, pipeline ownership, and marketing."[44]

---

[40] *See, e.g.*, Lochner v. New York, 198 U.S. 45 (1905).

[41] *See* Herbert Hovenkamp, ENTERPRISE AND AMERICAN LAW 1836-1937 105-204 (1991).

[42] Alan Brinkley, THE END OF REFORM: NEW DEAL LIBERALISM IN RECESSION AND WAR (1995).

[43] Formal definitions can be found in: I Alfred E. Kahn, THE ECONOMICS OF REGULATION: PRINCIPLES AND INSTITUTIONS 11-12 and II Kahn at 2-3 (1988); Stephen Breyer, REGULATION AND ITS REFORM 15-19 (1982) W. Kip Viscusi, John M. Vernon & Joseph E. Harrington, Jr., ECONOMICS OF REGULATION AND ANTITRUST 76-87 (2d ed. 1995).

[44] Clark *supra* note 7 at 245-46.

Coal's troubles continued during the New Deal. The bituminous industry was plagued by productive overcapacity, underemployment of miners, poor working conditions, and chaotic pricing. Instead of recognizing and accepting the declining fortunes of the coal industry, New Deal coal policies attempted to increase wages and promote job security. The result was a labor-sensitive coal policy that did not address the real capital problems facing the industry nor the need to reduce production to reflect market demand. The coal codes of the National Recovery Administration, like the oil codes before them, were to be administered by the industry in the fields and were not centralized in Washington. In a declining coal industry, government could not keep mines open and increase miners' wages, even though these were the goals of the New Deal. Nevertheless, the government attempted to pull off the impossible by trying to coordinate prices to the satisfaction of mine operators, mine workers, and consumers. To this end, two National Bituminous Coal Commissions were created to promulgate minimum prices and enforce codes of unfair trade practices.

Coal improved its position slightly during the war. Production increased and, more importantly, coal found the market that would serve as its largest customer until the present day, electric utilities. Although utility consumption of coal did not completely offset coal losses in the railroad, commercial, and residential sectors, electric utilities maintained a market for coal. After the war, though, coal's recurrent ills—poor labor management relations, deteriorating working conditions, resistance to federal regulation, competitive producers, and government reluctance to fix prices—continued to threaten the industry.

Also during this time and leading up to World War II, New Deal administrators attempted to engage in national energy planning. The National Resources Planning Board was charged with the long-term planning for and coordination of natural resources issues. An outgrowth of the NIRA, Interior Secretary Harold Ickes established the National Planning Board in 1933 to engage in research about population trends, housing, industry, and resources that would culminate in a "plan of national planning."[45] In 1934, the National Planning Board was incorporated into an independent agency, the National Resources Board, which later became the National Resources Planning Board, which reported to the President. World War II changed the mission of the NRPB from long-term planning to establishing a social security system and to promoting full employment. The

---

[45] Alan Brinkley, THE END OF REFORM: NEW DEAL LIBERALISM IN RECESSION AND WAR, 246 (1995).

NRPB had an ambitious agenda and as the war progressed and as FDR's fortunes changed, the Board lost its legitimacy and was disbanded in 1943.[46]

The federalization of energy policy remained uncoordinated and came predominantly in the form of the regulation of interstate energy sales.[47] This period experienced the nationalization of energy markets. The objective of promoting large-scale energy facilities had not changed even though an economic crisis threatened the country.

If the New Deal was not up to the challenge of coordinating energy policy in the 1930s, did World War II stimulate such a movement? Not really. The basic regulatory agencies, the Petroleum Administration for War and the Solid Fuels Administration for War, were divided between oil and coal and continued the old pattern of being guided by the industries themselves. Obviously, energy resources, particularly oil, needed to be mobilized, and, as during the Great War, energy policies were greatly influenced by the industries themselves. Worse, industrial concentration continued and war policies favored the larger firms as major oil companies received the bulk of federal largess being dispensed to build $1 billion of new refineries.

The New Deal response to economic problems was to encourage and support industry by stimulating the market. Regulatory objectives consisted of encouraging production, stimulating growth, and providing economic stability for energy industries as a means of supporting the economy as a whole. By limiting objectives to energy production and industrial stability—both in the name of efficiency—there was little room for either energy planning or redistribution of wealth from producers to consumers.

E.   1945-1973

The period from the end of World War II until 1965 has been called the "golden age" of the electric industry.[48] It was also the golden age for all energy industries and for the economy as a whole. The energy sector grew at a steady, predictable pace along with the economy. Such predictability made energy planning easy for individual industries. Still, the country formulated no comprehensive energy policy.[49] Regulators had little to do

---

[46] *Id.* at 245-64.

[47] *See* Natural Gas Act of 1938, Pub. L. No. 95-617, 92 Stat. 3173 (codified as amended in 15 U.S.C. (1994)); Federal Power Act, Pub. L. No. 97-375, 96 Stat. 1826 (codified as amended in 16 U.S.C. (1994)).

[48] Hyman, *supra* note 11 at 119-130.

[49] ENERGY POLICY IN PERSPECTIVE: TODAY'S PROBLEMS, YESTERDAY'S SOLUTIONS (Crauford D. Goodwin, ed., 1981) (An examination of national energy

other than monitor the ongoing growth of these industries. Underneath this placid scene, however, technological, economic, and political forces were changing in ways that culminated in a worldwide energy crisis which still affects our energy planning.

There were four notable events in energy development between World War II and the energy cataclysm of the 1970s. First, although the coal industry had long lost its prominence, it found a new stable market in the electricity industry. Second, the natural gas industry was destabilized and, beginning in 1954, entered a period of confusion from which it has yet to emerge. Third, the domestic oil industry went from surplus to shortage as the government attempted to rationalize domestic production and foreign imports. Fourth, the entire country enthusiastically jumped headlong into the commercial nuclear market, a market that today is stagnant. At the end of this period, although the energy market generally was transformed from a market of cheap abundant resources to one of more costly energy and conservation efforts, brownouts, gas lines, and curtailments were short-lived. The ability of the country to recover from significant market changes attested to the strength of the dominant energy policy.

While coal production remained relatively stable during the period at about 500 million tons per year, production shifted from eastern coal, which was mined from deep pits, to western coal, which was surface mined. This shift had dramatic environmental consequences, ultimately culminating in the Surface Mining Control and Reclamation Act[50] passed in 1977 to protect topsoil and surrounding land from the ravages of coal mining. Although coal prices were not directly set by government, government health and safety regulations made the coal business more expensive. Regulations protecting miner health and safety and the environment raised the cost of doing business. These increased costs raised industry concerns about its ability to maintain its market share when nuclear generated electricity was being touted as "too cheap to meter."[51]

The natural gas story is a favorite of pro-market advocates because government intervention has been judged a gross failure.[52] There is fairly

___

policy from the Truman Administration through the Carter Administration.)

[50] 30 U.S.C. §§ 1201-1328 (1994).

[51] Hank Schilling, *Energy Efficiency* in Celia Campbell-Mohn, Barry Breen & J. William Futtrell, ENVIRONMENTAL LAW: FROM RESOURCES TO RECOVERY, ch. 10 (1993).

[52] *See* Arlon Tussing & Connie C. Barlow, THE NATURAL GAS INDUSTRY: EVOLUTION, STRUCTURE, AND ECONOMICS (1984); Joseph P. Kalt & Frank C. Schuller, DRAWING THE LINE ON NATURAL GAS REGULATIONS (1987); M. Elizabeth Sanders, THE REGULATION OF NATURAL GAS: POLICY AND POLITICS 1938-1978 (1981).

straightforward language in the Natural Gas Act exempting producers from federal regulations[53] while regulating interstate pipelines. The clarity of this language notwithstanding, the reality of the industry and the Congressional intent of the Act were to protect consumers from the market power of interstate pipelines. The structure of the industry is such that pipelines constitute a transportation bottleneck. Pipelines purchase and transport gas from producer to distributor or end user. Consequently, without producer price regulation, any prices charged by the producer to the pipeline is fully passed through to consumers. Because of this automatic pass through, consumer pressure was brought to regulate producer prices. First, the Supreme Court ruled that producers that were affiliated with interstate pipelines could be federally regulated.[54] Once that camel's nose was in the tent, producer regulation was not far off. In 1954, the Court justified federal regulation of producer prices in *Phillips Petroleum Co. v. Wisconsin*.[55]

Phillips sent the natural gas industry into convulsions from which it has yet to recover. The direct effect of the *Phillips* ruling was to subject thousands of individual producers to trial-type ratemaking hearings before the Federal Power Commission (FPC). In the estimation of President Kennedy's Landis Commission, it would have taken the Federal Power Commission 13 years to clear its 1960 docket and taken until the year 2043 to hear the cases that accumulated during that time even if the staff tripled.[56] The FPC was just unable to administer the increase in its docket with disastrous consequences for the market. Natural gas ratemaking was transferred from individual adjudications to area ratemaking[57] then to national ratemaking[58] through rulemaking.[59] Area and national ratemaking were based on the concept of vintaging or two-tier pricing in which "old" gas prices were based on historic or embedded costs and "new" gas prices were allowed to float to market levels. The effect of two-tier pricing and cost-based ratemaking kept federally regulated natural gas prices down while

---

[53] Natural Gas Act, 15 U.S.C. § 717(b) (1994).

[54] Interstate Natural Gas Co., Inc. v. Federal Power Comm'n, 331 U.S. 682 (1947).

[55] 347 U.S. 672 (1954).

[56] U.S. Senate Comm. on the Judiciary, 86th Cong., Report on Regulatory Agencies to the President-Elect 6 (Comm. Print 1960).

[57] *Permian Basin Area Rate Cases*, 390 U.S. 747 (1968).

[58] Shell Oil Co. v. Federal Power Comm'n, 520 F.2d 1061 (5th Cir. 1975), *reh'g denied*, 525 F.2d 1261 (5th cir. 1976), *cert. denied*, 426 U.S. 941 (1976).

[59] *See* Richard J. Pierce, *The Choice Between Adjudicating and Rulemaking for Formulating and Implementing Energy Policy*, 31 HASTINGS L.J. 1 (1979); David L. Shapiro, *The Choice of Rulemaking or Adjudication in the Development of Administrative Policy*, 78 HARV. L. REV. 921 (1965).

intrastate prices floated to the market. Recalling our earlier discussions contrasting marginal and average costs, federal regulators were setting natural gas prices based on average costs and non-federal regulators, specifically the world market, set prices at marginal cost. A dual natural gas market was thus created when marginal cost exceeded average cost.

The dual market was further aggravated by strict abandonment rules that prevented federally regulated producers of gas dedicated to the interstate market from selling their gas in the more lucrative intrastate market.[60] Depressed federal pricing naturally reduced domestic production and caused an artificial natural gas "shortage." This regulatory structure hamstrung the industry and had to be dismantled. The first governmental response was not deregulation, however, rather an extremely complicated pricing scheme set out in the Natural Gas Policy Act of 1978 (NGPA).[61] The express intent of the NGPA was to unify the dual markets and to deregulate prices over a period of time. The reality was that the NGPA was a hodgepodge of legislative compromises intended to satisfy various producer, consumer, and regulator interest groups.[62]

During World War II oil emerged as the dominant energy resource, largely a result of oil's key role in fueling the transportation sector. Shortly after the war, however, imports exceeded exports, causing concern among domestic producers and raising national security issues as consumption became dependent on foreign oil. In order to shore up the domestic industry, government was importuned to place quotas on imports to raise prices for producers. Consistent with past practices, government first relied on the market and volunteerism to limit imports.[63] Not surprisingly, voluntarism was not an effective way to cut imports because imported oil was cheaper than domestically produced oil. During the 1950s, various political and rhetorical arguments were made to reduce imports for national security reasons, but the economic reality tilted in favor of cheap oil. At the end of the 1950s, oil import quotas were made mandatory, and they continued until the early 1970s when domestic production peaked, making them superfluous.

---

[60] *See* California v. Southland Royalty Co., 436 U.S. 519 (1978); United Gas Pipe Line Co. v. McCombs, 442 U.S. 529 (1979).

[61] Pub. L. 95-621, 92 Stat. 3350 (codified at 15 U.S.C. §§ 3301-3432, 42 U.S.C. § 7255 (1994)).

[62] James McManus, *Natural Gas* in David J. Muchow & William A. Mogel, 2 ENERGY LAW AND TRANSACTION § 50.02[4] (1998).

[63] Vietor, *supra* note 7, at 94-99.

The 1970s also caught oil in an unfamiliar setting—price regulation. Oil prices were set as part of President Nixon's wage and price controls.[64] These regulations took on a life of their own, lasting a decade after the Nixon economic stabilization program ended. Oil price regulations required an elaborate and costly bureaucratic machinery for their administration. Not surprisingly, the complexity of the regulations opened the way for opportunistic behavior, i.e., cheating.[65] Like natural gas price regulation before them, oil price controls were assessed as having distorted the market rather than having stimulated it,[66] and they were ultimately dismantled.[67]

Perhaps the single most notable energy event in the post-World War II period was the overwhelming commitment of capital to commercial nuclear power. The several hundred billion dollar industry began at the end of World War II as a way to channel the destructive force of nuclear power into more benign and beneficial commercial uses. In 1946, the Atomic Energy Act[68] was passed for the purpose of moving nuclear power away from the military and into civilian hands. The Act, however, still allowed the government a monopoly on controlling uranium. That monopoly existed until the Act was significantly amended in 1954[69] to permit private ownership of uranium. This control of uranium was crucial for private sector investment. Investment became substantial in 1957 with the passage of the Price-Anderson Act,[70] which limited the liability of nuclear facilities in the case of accidents.

After the passage of the Price-Anderson Act thousands of megawatts of generating capacity were ordered by private utilities. The expansion of commercial nuclear energy continued throughout the 1960s and into the

---

[64] Robert L. Bradley, Jr., 1 OIL, GAS, AND GOVERNMENT: THE U.S. EXPERIENCE, ch. 9 (1996).

[65] *Id.* at 485-86. In *United States v. Exxon Corp.*, 773 F.2d 1240 (TECA, 1985), for example, a U.S. District Court judgment of $1.6 million against Exxon for violating the pricing regulations was affirmed. The DOE estimated that they identified nearly $3 billion in overcharges from major oil companies, U.S. Department of Energy, Office of General Counsel, Program Status Report (1981).

[66] *See* Joseph P. Kalt, THE ECONOMICS AND POLITICS OF OIL PRICE REGULATION: FEDERAL POLICY IN THE POST-EMBARGO ERA (1993); David Glasner, POLITICS, PRICES AND PETROLEUM: THE POLITICAL ECONOMY OF ENERGY (1984).

[67] Exec. Order No. 12,287, 3 C.F.R. 124 (1982), *reprinted in* 15 U.S.C. 757 (1994).

[68] Atomic Energy Act of 1946, Pub. L. No. 79-585, 60 Stat. 755 (1946).

[69] Atomic Energy Act of 1954, Pub. L. No. 83-703, 68 Stat. 919 (codified as amended at 42 U.S.C. §§ 2011-2296 (1994)).

[70] Atomic Energy Damages Act (Price-Anderson), Pub. L. No. 85-256, 71 Stat. 576 (codified in scattered sections of 42 U.S.C. (1994)).

early 1970s, spurred by a pro-nuclear consensus. Private producers had a new, modern, "safe and clean" technology; consumers were pleased to receive a cheap product; and, the government was happy to find beneficial civilian uses for this technology of the future.

Towards the end of the 1960s and into the 1970s, however, the promise that had built the pro-nuclear consensus showed signs of failing. Instead of being safe, clean, cheap, and abundant, the nuclear enterprise contained large social costs involving enormous environmental, health, safety, and financial risks. Today the industry is moribund. No new nuclear plants have been ordered since 1978 and all plants ordered since 1974 have been canceled. Although there are approximately 105 plants in operation, nuclear power, particularly large scale plants of 1000 megawatts and more, seems destined to have no future.[71]

F.   1973-1992

The golden age of energy ended with an energy crisis that shook world markets and reshaped the way policymakers think about energy. Three events contributed to this reassessment. First, utilities reached a technological plateau and the post-World War II pattern of predictably expanding energy markets ended. Second, federal and state governments became heavily involved with the environment with President Nixon's signing of the National Environmental Policy Act. The third factor was the growing political power of the Organization of Petroleum Exporting Countries (OPEC). One political response to these events was to engage in national energy planning activities. These efforts failed and the dominant model of energy policy persisted.

Starting in approximately 1965, the marginal costs for the production of electricity and natural gas began to exceed their average costs resulting in a profitability squeeze for utilities. As previously noted, electricity and gas rates were based on historic (average) costs. However, increasing marginal costs meant lower profits for utilities. When marginal cost exceeded average cost then utilities were losing money until rates were set at marginal cost.[72] Also, the traditional rate formula encouraged capital investment and plant expansion because returns were calculated on capital investment. In other words, the traditional rate formula contributed to

---

[71] *See generally*, Joseph P. Tomain, NUCLEAR POWER TRANSFORMATION (1987); Union of Concerned Scientists, SAFETY SECOND: THE NRC AND AMERICA'S NUCLEAR POWER PLANTS (1987); Luther J. Carter, NUCLEAR IMPERATIVES AND PUBLIC TRUST: DEALING WITH RADIOACTIVE WASTE (1987).

[72] *See, e.g., In re* Madison Gas & Electric Co., 5 P.U.R. 4th 28 (1974).

excess capacity as utilities over-invested in new plants, especially nuclear power plants. Overinvestment and decreasing profitability was the beginning of the end of a system of utility regulation lasting nearly a century.[73]

During this period, utilities, with the rest of the economy, faced inflation, rising labor costs, the collapse of the nuclear power industry, and the OPEC and Iranian Oil Embargoes. As punishment to those countries that supported Israel during the Yom Kippur War in October, 1973, OPEC literally, closed the valve on oil entering the world market. Not only did oil prices rise, so did general economic inflation which only compounded domestic economic shifts as a result of winding down the Vietnam Conflict.

This series of events had a significant impact on national energy policies directed by the White House. In response, President Nixon who had already instituted price controls on oil as a part of general wage and price controls, signed into law the Emergency Petroleum Allocation Act of 1973[74] giving the president additional authority to regulate crude oil prices.) Also in 1973, President Nixon initiated a comprehensive review of the nation's energy goals and options called Project Independence.[75] Nixon left the White House before Project Independence saw the light of day and the project continued into the Ford Administration.

Initially, Project Independence involved three primary issues: independence from foreign oil including conservation; the role of the market in setting energy prices; and, alternatives to traditional fossil fuels. As it turned out, Project Independence never reached alternative energy sources. Issued in November, 1974, the Project Independence Report was converted to an omnibus bill entitled the Energy Independence Authority Act of 1975.[76] The legislative proposal contained thirteen titles that addressed the first two issues and strongly favored a free market in energy.[77]

An important aspect of President Ford's energy policy was the decontrol of oil and gas prices. Yet public sentiment and Democratic politics were such that immediate decontrol of oil prices was too threatening to consumer interests. Instead, the debate concerned how soon decontrol was

---

[73] Joseph P. Tomain, *Electricity Restructuring: A Case Study in Government Regulation*, 33 TULSA L. REV. 827 (1998).

[74] Pub. L. 93-159, 87 Stat. 627 (1973).

[75] Neil De Marchi, *Energy Policy Under Nixon: Mainly Putting Out Fires* in Goodwin *supra* note 49 at 458-66.

[76] H.R. 2633, H.R. 2650; S. 594.

[77] Neil De Marchi, *The Ford Administration: Energy as a Public Good* in Goodwin *supra* note 49 at 486-89.

to take place. Eventually, a compromise over prices and timing between the Ford Administration and the Democratic Congress was reached in the passage of the Energy Policy and Conservation Act[78] on December 22, 1975.

Ford tried to cobble together a national energy policy that centralized some pricing decisions such as tariffs and quotas in the Executive Branch; moved most energy pricing decisions into the market; and achieved independence through oil reserves. At the margins his policies touched coal and electricity but there was no great amount of coordination. Instead, that challenge was left to President Jimmy Carter.

President Carter neatly capsulized his energy policy in his memoirs:

> We desperately needed a comprehensive program that would encourage conservation, more fuel production in the United States, and the long-range development of alternate forms of energy which could begin to replace oil and natural gas in future years. These goals were complicated by the need to protect our environment, to insure equity of economic opportunity among the different regions of our country, and to balance the growing struggle between American consumers and oil producers.[79]

The President responded with four significant energy initiatives. First, Carter centralized energy administration in the cabinet level Department of Energy (DOE). The DOE was unable, however, to design a comprehensive national energy plan because energy decisionmaking and policymaking responsibilities were scattered over several branches of the federal government, and even within the DOE itself authority was fragmented.[80]

Second, Carter's "moral equivalent of war" speech on April 18, 1977,[81] outlined the substantive principles of his energy policy and led to the passage of the National Energy Act in October of the following year.[82] The

---

[78] Pub. L. 94-163, 98 Stat. 871 (1975).

[79] Jimmy Carter, KEEPING FAITH 92 (1982).

[80] Joseph P. Tomain, *Institutionalized Conflicts Between Law and Policy*, 22 HOUSTON L. REV. 661 (1985); Alfred C. Aman, Jr., *Institutionalizing the Energy Crisis: Some Structural and Procedural Lessons*, 65 CORNELL L. REV. 491 (1980).

[81] President's Address to the Nation, PUB. PAPERS 656 (April 11, 1977).

[82] The National Energy Act consists of five pieces of major legislation: the National Energy Conservation Policy Act, Pub. L. No. 95-618, 29 Stat. 3206 (codified as amended in scattered sections of 12, 15, 26, 31, and 42 U.S.C. (1994)); the Powerplant and Industrial Fuel Use Act of 1978, Pub. L. No. 95-620, 92 Stat. 3298 (codified as amended in scattered sections of 15 and 42 U.S. C. (1994)); the Natural Gas Policy Act of 1978, Pub. L. No. 95-621, 92 Stat. 3350 (codified at 15 U.S.C. §§ 3301-3432 & 42 U.S.C. § 7255 (1994)); the Public Utilities Regulatory Policies Act

Act addressed conventional fuels as it tried to move the country away from a dependence on foreign oil, promote the use of coal, increase energy efficiency, modernize utility ratemaking, stimulate conservation, encourage the creation of a new market in electricity, and restructure a distorted market in natural gas. In short, the National Energy Act was directed at correcting perceived market imperfections in the dominant markets of conventional fossil fuels with a tip of the hat to conservation.

The third major initiative was President Carter's energy address on April 5, 1979,[83] which stressed the need to decontrol oil prices as a means of increasing domestic oil production. The address led to the passage of the Crude Oil Windfall Profits Tax[84] designed to capture the economic rents realized by domestic oil producers as a result of the rise in world oil prices.

Finally, on July 15, 1979,[85] the President delivered his second major energy address in which he returned to his moral equivalent of war rhetoric. Again, Congress responded, this time with the passage of the Energy Security Act of 1980.[86] The Energy Security Act was a dramatically conceived package of legislation that turned energy policy away from conventional resources and toward the development and promotion of synthetic oil and gas from coal, oil shale, and tar sands. This segment of the Act focused on substitutes for fossil fuels. In addition, the Act attempted to

---

of 1978, Pub. L. No. 95-617, 92 Stat. 3117 (codified as amended in scattered sections of 15, 16, 26, 42, and 43 U.S.C. (1994)); and, the Energy Tax Act of 1978, Pub. L. No. 95-618, 92 Stat. 3174 (codified as amended in scattered sections of 26 and 42 U.S.C. (1994)).

[83] President's Address to the Nation, PUB. PAPERS 609 (April 5, 1979).

[84] Pub. L. No. 96-223, 94 Stat. 229 (codified as amended in scattered sections of 7, 12, 15, 19, 26, 31, 42, and 43 U.S.C. (1994)).

[85] President's Address to the Nation, PUB. PAPERS 1235 (July 15, 1979).

[86] The Energy Security Act, Pub. L. No. 96-294, 94 Stat. 611 (1980), also consists of several pieces of legislation including: the Defense Production Act Amendments of 1980, 94 Stat. 617 (codified in 50 U.S.C. §§ 2061-2166 (1994)); the United States Synthetic Fuels Corporation Act of 1980, Pub. L. No. 96-294, 94 Stat. 633 (codified as amended in scattered sections of 42 U.S.C. (1994)); the Biomass Energy and Alcohol Fuels Act of 1980, Pub. L. No. 96-294, 94 Stat. 683 (codified as amended in scattered sections of 7, 15, 16, and 42 U.S.C. (1994)); the Renewable Energy Resources Act of 1980, Pub. L. No. 96-294, 94 Stat. 715 (codified as amended in scattered sections of 16 and 42 U.S.C. (1994)); the Solar Energy and Energy Conservation Act of 1980, Pub. L. No. 96-294, 94 Stat. 719 (codified as amended in scattered sections of 12 and 42 U.S.C. (1994)); the Geothermal Energy Act of 1980, Pub. L. No. 96-294, 94 Stat. 763 (codified in scattered sections of 16 U.S.C. (1994); and the Acid Precipitation Act of 1980, Pub. L. No. 96-294, 94 Stat. 770 (codified in 42 U.S.C. §§ 8901-8905, 8911-8912 (1994)).

stimulate an energy transition from fossil fuels to renewable resources such as solar, biomass, alcohol, and geothermal steam while making conservation a larger part of the country's energy planning. The Act also attempted to stimulate the alternative fuels, market their research and development, and provide tax breaks, guarantees, and subsidies.

The legislation that emerged during the Carter Administration did not achieve long term success, did not achieve the intended result of coordinating national energy policy, and did not stimulate an energy transition from fossil fuels to renewable resources and conservation. Stated simply, Carter's energy program went contrary to the country's entrenched model of energy policy and contrary to the market. In short, the market controlled the production and consumption of energy because conventional fuels were cheaper than alternatives. The transition failed because of the country's reliance on the market to signal a move into other resources.

Carter's initiatives, however, were not without beneficial consequences. Deregulation of oil and natural gas prices began. The capacity of the electric industry to restructure was discovered as new sources of generation were found[87] and the role of the market in directing energy policy was reaffirmed.

If President Carter's highly centralized, pro-government energy policy failed, it would seem to follow that President Reagan's private sector, supply-side, anti-government deregulation efforts would succeed and that the DOE would be dismantled as he promised during his campaign. This scenario did not come to pass, although there clearly was greater federal reliance on the market and less on centralized planning. President Reagan made his energy intentions clear in one of his first acts in office by decontrolling oil prices on January 28, 1981.[88] The oil price decontrol was largely symbolic, however, because they were scheduled to terminate on October 1st of that year.

The Reagan deregulation program did not spring from whole cloth.[89] Natural gas deregulation, like oil deregulation, was scheduled to occur under a phased deregulation by the Natural Gas Policy Act of 1978

---

[87] Public Utilities Regulatory Policies Act of 1978, Pub. L. No. 95-617, 92 Stat. 3117 (codified as amended in scattered sections of 15, 16, 26, 42 and 43 U.S.C. (1994)).

[88] Exec. Order No. 12, 287, 3 C.F.R. 124, *reprinted in* 15 U.S.C. § 757 note (1994).

[89] Coal conversion legislation, the Powerplant and Industrial Fuel Use Act of 1978, Pub. L. No. 95-620, 92 Stat. 3289 (codified as amended in scattered sections of 15 and 42 U.S.C. (1994)), was largely repealed during the Reagan Administration.

(NGPA).[90] Similarly, although President Reagan campaigned to dismantle the United States Synthetic Fuels Corporation, the synfuels program failed because the market was unable to support it. Synfuels producers were not able to process coal into natural gas or reap oil from tar sands or from oil shale at costs competitive with oil and natural gas on the market.[91] Today, the Department of Energy is still with us and, ironically, with it a part of President Reagan's legacy continues. The Federal Energy Regulatory Commission, an independent agency within DOE, has been the leader in deregulating the electricity and natural gas industries.

Even though energy policy had a prime role during these two decades, environmental policy was the new star. The field of environmental law, like that of energy law, is a child of the 70s.[92] The first major act, the National Environmental Policy Act,[93] was signed into law effective January 1, 1970 by President Nixon, who also created the Environmental Protection Agency by executive order. Also, like energy law, environmental law has a series of common law antecedents as well as a series of state laws and federal laws directed to conservation and the creation of public parks reaching back to the turn of the century.

Environmental law is not a completely tight, well-ordered whole. Rather, it is the product of several statutes, such as the Clean Air Act, the Clean Water Act, the Endangered Species Act and the Surface Mining Control and Reclamation Act, to name just a few. Further, these statutes are administered by a number of federal agencies in addition to the EPA, such as the Department of the Interior, the Department of Agriculture, the U.S. Army Corps. of Engineers and an array of subagencies.

During the decade from 1970 to 1980 and continuing to the present, environmental law has gone through a significant transformation. The transformation is marked by two characteristics. First, in the beginning environmental law was a body of law independent of energy law and uncoordinated with it. It might even be said that environmental law was the antithesis of energy law insofar as environmental law sought to protect the natural resources that energy law sought to exploit. The motivating forces

---

[90] Pub. L. No. 95-621, 92 Stat. 3350 (codified as amended at 15 U.S.C. §§ 3301-3432 and 42 U.S.C.§ 7255 (1994)).

[91] *See, e.g.*, U.S. General Accounting Office, GAO/RCED-88-52FS, SYNTHETIC FUELS: STATUS OF THE GREAT PLAINS COAL GASIFICATION PROJECT (1987) (concluding that the project was not financially feasible).

[92] J. William Futrell, *The History of Environmental Law* in ENVIRONMENTAL LAW: FROM RESOURCES TO RECOVERY (Celia Campbell-Mohn, Barry Breen & J. William Futrell, eds., 1993).

[93] 42 U.S.C. §§ 4321-4370a (1994).

behind the modern environmental ethic were embodied in such texts as *Silent Spring,*[94] *Limits to Growth,*[95] and *A Sand County Almanac.*[96] These texts warned about pending destruction of natural environments and ecosystems and led to a very protectionist set of laws. The second characteristic which described early environmental laws was that they were resource specific. As noted above, individual statutes were passed in order to address specific problems, such as protecting air, water, land, or species, as examples.

The environmental law movement also embodied something unique and transformative in the administrative state[97]—organized public participation. Non-governmental organizations such as the Sierra Club, the Environmental Defense Fund, the Natural Resources Defense Council, and the Nature Conservancy became effective advocates for environmental policy and could not be ignored by lawmakers or policymakers.

In the mid-1980s, environmental policy began to undergo a significant transition that continues to this day. Briefly, policymakers both domestically and internationally began to acknowledge linkages between environmental and energy policies and those linkages are recognized in the phrase "sustainable development."

What is significant about the concept of sustainability which will be discussed in more detail below, is that it is a conscious coordination between energy and environmental policies. Sustainability recognizes that the fuel cycle links environmental and energy policies. As natural resources are harvested for the production of energy, it is recognized throughout that cycle, that environmental consequences follow. Consequently, environmentalists and energy policymakers not only are aware of each other but they must take pains to be able to talk with each other. Recent laws and policies recognize this need. Environmental regulations such as emissions trading, for example, use market-based tools. Energy laws such as conservation incentives in ratemaking, as another example, are intended to protect the environment from unnecessary externalities.

The story of energy in the 1980s was marked by more than a touch of irony. Oil prices were decontrolled, and OPEC lost its death grip on the

---

[94] Rachel Carson, SILENT SPRING (1962).

[95] Club of Rome, THE LIMITS TO GROWTH: A REPORT FOR THE CLUB OF ROME'S PROJECT ON THE PREDICAMENT OF MANKIND (1975).

[96] Aldo Leopold, A SAND COUNTY ALMANAC, AND SKETCHES HERE AND THERE (1949).

[97] Richard B. Stewart, THE REFORMATION OF AMERICAN ADMINISTRATIVE LAW, 88 HARV. L. REV. 1667 (1975).

global oil market with the ironic consequence that domestic oil prices fell to what many believe to be dangerously low levels. Low oil prices, naturally, threatened the oil industry and raised concerns about national security as imports continued to exceed domestic production. This sensitivity regarding national security was reflected in Operation Desert Shield/Desert Storm.

Natural gas prices were largely deregulated, and although the market was clearing as more natural gas was available and as prices began to drop, many customers of natural gas pipelines were unable to purchase lower priced gas because they were locked into long-term contracts with onerous take-or-pay penalties. Demand for electricity leveled off, and growth steadied at between 2% and 3% per year, as most electric utilities were able to weather the storm of nuclear plant cancellations. Yet the electricity industry entered the 1990s confronting potentially large needs for power after what some analysts saw as a period of financial austerity regarding investment in new generation.[98] Adding another twist to the tale, nuclear power's primary competitor, coal, comes with plenty of problems. Although coal is the most abundant domestic resource for the production of electricity, threats to the environment and to human health raise the private and social costs of its use. Finally, energy industries, with the exceptions of the nuclear industry and some independent oil producers, have generally enjoyed increasing economic stability.

Nevertheless, the energy crisis contained several important lessons. First, the heavy hand of government price setting through traditional ratemaking outlived its usefulness. The electricity and natural gas industries, as examples, were set to begin restructuring. Second, the environmental consequences of a hard path energy policy could not be ignored. And, third, energy-environmental policy would increasingly be played out on the world stage.

The 1970s and 1980s demonstrated to policymakers and politicians, as well as producers and consumers, that traditional energy policies which relied on command-and-control government regulation needed to give way to more open energy markets through regulatory restructuring. The key industries experiencing deregulation and a move to the market are the electricity and natural gas industries. In both cases the Federal Energy Regulatory Commission (FERC) has initiated the move to more competitive environments by opening access to electricity distribution and natural gas transmissions systems.

---

[98] *See* Peter Navarro, THE DIMMING OF AMERICA: THE REAL COSTS OF ELECTRIC UTILITY REGULATORY FAILURE (1985).

<u>FERC natural gas regulation has been considered nothing short</u> of revolutionary.[99] Through a series of rulemaking orders as interpreted by the D.C. Circuit Court of Appeals, and provoked by the market dislocation in the mid-1970s caused by dual natural gas markets, the natural gas industry faced its most significant restructuring since the Natural Gas Policy Act of 1978 (NGPA).[100]

In response to the distortion in the natural gas market, pipelines, producers, and consumers petitioned FERC for relief. Pipelines tried to insure their cash flow and their access to surplus gas. Producers simply wanted to get their gas to market. Consumers, naturally, tried to avoid imposition of take-or-pay costs and wanted the cheap gas. <u>FERC reacted to these requests and to changing market conditions by attempting to loosen pricing and entry and exit controls for the purpose of letting gas flow more smoothly through the distribution system from producer to end-user or, in industry jargon, from wellhead to burnertip.</u>[101] Because pipelines were the bottleneck in the natural gas fuel cycle, they were the targets of FERC regulatory efforts through a series of rulemakings.

Regarding natural gas, FERC began addressing open access with Order No. 436[102] which was remanded to FERC by the D.C. Circuit in *Associated Gas Distributors (AGD I)*.[103] *AGD I* largely agreed with FERC's approach toward opening access but remanded because the take-or-pay problem was inadequately addressed. FERC responded with Order No. 500,[104] which largely adopted the transportation regulations of Order No. 436 with some revisions.[105]

Although Order No. 500 was remanded to FERC to comply with *Associated Gas Distributors*, especially the take-or-pay issue, <u>the non-</u>

---

[99] William J. Fox, *Transforming an Industry by Agency Rulemaking: Regulation of Natural Gas by the Federal Energy Regulatory Commission*, 23 LAND AND WATER L. REV. 113-14 (1988).

[100] Pub. L. No. 95-621, 92 Stat. 3351 (codified at 15 U.S.C. §§ 3301-3432 (1994)). *See also* Allison, *Natural Gas Pricing: The Eternal Debate*, 37 BAYLOR L. REV. 1 (1985).

[101] Richard J. Pierce, Jr., *Reconstituting the Natural Gas Industry from Wellhead to Burnertip*, 9 ENERGY L. J. 22 (1988).

[102] Order No. 436, 500 Fed. Reg. 42, 408 (1985) (codified in scattered sections of 18 C.F.R.).

[103] *Associated Gas Distributors v. Federal Energy Regulatory Comm'n*, 824 F.2d 981 (D.C. Cir. 1987).

[104] Regulation of Natural Gas Pipelines After Partial Wellhead Decontrol, 52 Fed. Reg. 30,334 (1987) (codified at 18 C.F.R. pts. 2 and 284).

[105] McManus, *supra* note 62, at 50-81 to 50-82.

discriminatory open access provisions were accepted by the reviewing court.[106] In response, FERC adopted Order No. 500-H[107] which modified some of the Commission's take-or-pay rules. Order No. 500-H was largely affirmed in *AGA II*.[108]

With Order No. 436, FERC began its efforts to make pipelines into common carriers. The Commission would authorize blanket certificates for transportation conditioned on the pipeline's acceptance of non-discrimination requirements guaranteeing equal access for all customers to the new service.

The producer sales market was completely deregulated by Congress with the Natural Gas Wellhead Decontrol Act of 1989.[109] Decontrol of wellhead prices and open access go hand in hand with the intent of moving cheaper gas to market more easily and more quickly, without discrimination. The current operating regime for open access in the natural gas market is Order No. 636[110] in which the Commission found that, despite the legislation and its prior actions, the market still had impediments to full competition and that transactions were not as unbundled as a free market would indicate.[111]

In a controversial series of proposed rulemakings, FERC began to restructure the electricity market through greater reliance on market-like competition to align more closely supply, demand, and price, rather than have prices artificially set by federal or state regulators. FERC's free market favoritism is theoretically sound. However, there are structural impediments in the electricity industry—just as there are in the natural gas industry—that make complete transition from regulation to market difficult to implement quickly. Like the natural gas industry, the electricity industry may be able to promote more competition in the generation segment of its fuel cycle, but the transmission segment exhibits monopoly characteristics, and, hence, this segment must be reviewed closely. Transmission and distribution must be carefully examined to avoid captive customers, small

---

[106] *See* American Gas Association v. FERC, 888 F2d 136 (D.C. Cir. 1989).

[107] Order No. 500-H, 54 Fed. Reg. 52, 344 (1989) (final rule with modifications).

[108] American Gas Ass'n v. FERC, 912 F.2d 1496 (D.C. Cir. 1990).

[109] Pub. L. No. 101-60, 103 Stat. 157 (codified in scattered sections of 15 U.S.C.) (1994).

[110] F.E.R.C. Stats. & Regs. (CCH) ¶39, 939 (1992).

[111] McManus, *supra* note 62, at 50-88.3; *see also* Jonathan D. Schneider, Richard M. Lorenzo & James C. Beh, *Natural Gas Transportation* in 3 ENERGY LAW & TRANSACTIONS, ch. 83 (David J. Muchow & William A. Mogel, eds., 1997).

commercial and residential users, from being forced to absorb excess utility costs.[112]

FERC's rulemaking activities aspire to achieve two goals. First, FERC wants to discontinue setting wholesale rates administratively and to have them set in a competitive market. Second, following the successful lead of PURPA, which opened up markets in co-generation and small power production, FERC proposes to even further expand generation options to encourage competition by encouraging new types of generators rather than traditional public utilities.

Later in the decade, federal legislation gave FERC limited authority for opening access to the electricity market which FERC tried to implement with Order No. 888.[113] The FERC based its authority for Order No. 888, on the finding that new generation capacity was available at lower prices, as PURPA and other actors had already demonstrated. FERC also found that non-traditional utility generators ("NUGs") were competitive and that consumers were demanding access to these new generators.

Wholesale wheeling partially restructures the industry by setting in motion a set of regulations that enable multiple generators to either pool their electricity or to enter into bilateral contracts with purchasers. The pooled electricity or contract electricity will then be moved over a distribution system. The issues that remain to be addressed involve the structure and ownership of new transmission systems, which involves state regulators. All eyes are on California to see what the restructured electricity market will look like. California's program began in early 1998 and created an independent system operator (ISO) to allow both pool-based transactions and bilateral trading. Pool-based transactions are those in which the ISO operator serves a coordinator who monitors generation committed by multiple suppliers of electricity into the pool. The ISO then dispatches it to customers. Bilateral trading occurs with negotiations between customers and generators. The transmission occurs over the ISO lines.[114]

Retail wheeling involves a wide array of legal and policy issues including legal issues such as the end use customers' right to choose

---

[112] Margaret Kriz, *Deregulation Shorts Out*, NAT'L J. 1862 (August 8, 1998).

[113] Order No. 888, 61 Fed. Reg. 21, 540 (1996) (codified at 18 C.F.R. pts. 35 and 385).

[114] Laurie M. Rodgers & Joseph F. Schuler, Jr., *Ready, Fire, Aim: California and the Nation on the Eve of Competition*, 136 PUB. UTIL. FORT. 26 (Jan. 1, 1998); William W. Hogan, *Rethinking WEPEX: What's Wrong with Leased Cost?*, 136 PUB. UTIL. FORT. 46 (Jan. 1, 1998). *See also* Leonard S. Hyman & Marija Ilik, *Gas Resource, Real Business or Threat to Profitability?* in 135 PUB. UTIL. FORT. 35 (Oct. 1, 1997).

suppliers and the right of access to the pool by competitors in unbundling services and prices. Policy issues include: What is a state to do about universal service? Should wheeling be available to all customers? Are there environmental issues involved with wheeling and more competition?[115] How quickly and in what manner should retail wheeling policies emerge? Retail wheeling also involves operational issues, such as reliability, divestiture, and the role of the transmission system operators. Should they be government run or privately run? In other words, who should administer retail wheeling systems? And finally, what to do about stranded costs? Currently, about one-half of the states are actively considering restructuring.[116]

G.   1992-Present

President Bush signed the 1992 Energy Policy Act (EPACT) to provide a comprehensive national energy policy that "gradually and steadily increases U.S. energy security in cost-effective and environmentally beneficial ways."[117] The Act consisted of over 30 titles and several major provisions, including amending the Public Utility Holding Company Act; stimulating new entrants in the electricity market; opening access to the electricity grid to non-utility generators; stimulating state regulatory authorities to think about integrated resource planning; and providing subsidies and tax credits for electric vehicles. EPACT involved deregulation of imported natural gas and liquefied natural gas and provided tax relief for independent oil and gas producers, while extending tax relief and tax credits for the production of oil from shale, tar sands, and other nonconventional sources.

The Act provided for R&D for advanced clean coal technologies; provided certain relief for coal companies under the avoided cost provisions of PURPA; provided for the export of clean coal technology; and provided some relief from the Surface Mining Control and Reclamation Act. Procedures of the Nuclear Regulatory Commission were streamlined and the United States Enrichment Corporation, a government-owned entity, was created to provide uranium enrichment services in the international market. Alternative fuel vehicles were required for government use; tax deductions for investments in clean fuel vehicles were permitted; and tax credits were

---

[115] Natural Resources Defense Council, Public Service Electric & Gas Co., & Mid-Atlantic Energy Project, BENCHMARKING AIR EMISSIONS OF ELECTRIC UTILITY GENERATIONS IN THE EASTERN UNITED STATES (April 1997).

[116] Michael K. Block, DEREGULATING ELECTRICITY: PROGRESS IN THE STATES (March 1998).

[117] H.R. Rep. No. 474 (I) (1992).

provided for wind and biomass facilities. Additionally, as part of President Bush's National Energy Policy Plan, the Secretary of Energy was directed to prepare a least cost energy strategy that was environmentally sensitive, specifically with the goal of reducing greenhouse gases. The Act also involved stimulating energy efficient construction and demand side management for electricity.[118]

The most recent National Energy Policy Plan from President Clinton is the Department of Energy National Energy Policy Plan of July 1995. The 1995 Plan has been followed by the DOE Strategic Plan in 1997 and the DOE Comprehensive National Energy Strategy of 1998.

The 1995 Plan articulates three strategic goals:

- Maximize energy productivity to strengthen the economy and improve living standards.

- Prevent pollution to reduce the adverse environmental impact associated with energy production delivery and use.

- Keep America secure by reducing vulnerability to global market shocks.[119]

To accomplish those goals for an energy policy, the Plan adopts the following strategies:

- Increase efficiency of energy.

- Develop a balanced domestic energy resource portfolio.

- Invest in science and technology.

- Reinvent environmental protection.[120]

- Engage in international markets.[121]

The 1995 Plan also announces a "new approach to environmental and energy policy." The strategies to achieve this new approach include:

- Reinventing the regulatory system to increase flexibility and adopt performance-based regulations other than command and control measures.

---

[118] See generally Energy Policy Act of 1992 (Richard D. Avil, Jr. & Edward B. Myers, eds.) in David J. Muchow & William A. Mogul, 3 ENERGY LAW AND TRANSACTION (1998).

[119] Dept. of Energy, National Energy Policy Plan 7 (1995).

[120] See e.g., Bradford C. Mank, The Environmental Protection Agency's Project XL and Other Regulatory Reform Initiatives: The Need for Legislative Authorization, 25 ECOLOGY L.Q. 1 (1998) (arguing for a more sophisticated multimedia approach to environmental regulation).

[121] Dept. of Energy, National Energy Plan 7-8 (1995).

- Encourage cost-effective pollution prevention through partnerships with industry that identify innovative methods for improving environmental performance.

- Fostering the development of technologies that will increase environmental protection as well as provide industry with new technologies for export into the global market.[122]

The basic theme in the 1995 Plan is to move energy and environmental policies together in a more coordinated fashion as well as to continue to rely heavily on private initiatives and the market with increased efficiency as a goal for both sets of policies.

The 1995 Plan was followed by a DOE Strategic Plan in September 1997.[123] The Strategic Plan had as its basic goal to promote the secure competitive and environmentally responsible energy system to serve the needs of the public. To achieve that goal, the Strategic Plan set out four objectives:

- Reduce vulnerability of the U.S. economy to disruptions in energy supplies.

- Assure the competitive electricity generation industry.

- Increase efficiency and productivity of energy while limiting environmental impacts.

- Support U.S. energy, environmental, and economic interest in global markets.

- Continue information collection, analysis, and research to facilitate the development of long term energy initiatives.[124]

The most recent comprehensive national energy strategy was promulgated in 1998 from the Department of Energy. It attempts to link the issues of sustainable development discussed at an international level with our own domestic needs. More specifically, the comprehensive national energy strategy enunciates three significant challenges: "how to maintain energy security in global energy markets; how to successfully harness competition in electricity markets; how to respond to the threat of climate change."[125] A brief overview of the Comprehensive National Energy Strategy appears in

---

[122] *Id.* at 42.

[123] U.S. Dep't of Energy Strategic Plan: Providing America with Energy Security, National Security, Environmental Quality, Science Leadership (DOE/PO-0053) (September 1997).

[124] *Id.* at 11-17.

[125] U.S. Dep't of Energy, *Comprehensive National Energy Strategy* 5 (DOE/S0124) (April, 1998).

the box[126] accompanying the text. Throughout this period, we can see a greater reliance on private markets rather than on command-and-control regulatory strategies; more conscious awareness of and more explicit articulation of linkages between energy and environmental policies; and, greater attention toward the global significance of an energy-environmental policy.

The Strategy at a Glance

Goal I. Improve the efficiency of the energy system—making more productive use of energy resources to enhance overall economic performance while protecting the environment and advancing national security.

Objective 1.   Support competitive and efficient electric systems.
Enact electric utility restructuring legislation, develop advanced coal/gas powerplants, improve existing nuclear powerplants.

Objective 2.   Significantly increase energy efficiency in the transportation, industrial, and buildings sectors by 2010.
Develop more efficient transportation, industrial and building technologies.

Objective 3.   Increase the efficiency of Federal energy use.
Adopt new/innovative energy-efficient and renewable technologies.

Goal II. Ensure against energy disruptions—protecting our economy from external threat of interrupted supplies or infrastructure failure.

Objective 1.   Reduce vulnerability of the U.S. economy to disruption in oil supply.
Stabilize domestic production, maintain readiness of Strategic Petroleum Reserve, diversify import sources, reduce consumption.

Objective 2.   Ensure energy system reliability, flexibility, and emergency response capability.
Ensure reliable electricity/gas supply, refining and emergency response.

Goal III. Promote energy production and use in ways that respect health and environmental values—improving our health and local, regional, and global environmental quality.

Objective 1.   Increase domestic energy production in an environmentally responsible manner.
Increase domestic gas production, recover oil with less environmental impact, develop renewable technologies, maintain viable nuclear option.

Objective 2.   Accelerate the development and market adoption of environmentally friendly technologies.
Increase near-term deployment, expand voluntary efforts, design domestic greenhouse gas trading program, work with developing countries, design international trading/credit system.

---

[126] *Id.* at viii.

The Strategy at a Glance

Goal IV. Expand future energy choices—pursuing continued progress in science and technology to provide future generations with a robust portfolio of clean and reasonably priced energy sources.

Objective 1.   Maintain a strong national knowledge base as the foundation for informed energy decisions, new energy systems, and enabling technologies of the future.
Pursue basic research, including research on carbon / climate; support energy science infrastructure.

Objective 2.   Develop technologies that expand long-term energy options
Develop long-term options, such as fusion, hydrogen-based systems, and methane hydrates, that can have major impacts.

Goal V. Cooperate internationally on global issues—developing the means to address global economic, security, and environmental concerns.

Objective 1.   Promote development of open, competitive international energy markets, and facilitate the adoption of clean, safe, and efficient energy systems.
Encourage adoption of favorable legal / policy framework in other countries, promote clean / efficient energy systems and science / technology collaboration.

Objective 2.   Promote foreign regional stability by reducing energy-related environmental risks in areas of U.S. security interest.
Prioritize concerns and develop cost-effective solutions.

III. DEVELOPING AN INTERNATIONAL ENERGY-ENVIRONMENTAL POLICY

Ideally, there should be a convergence between energy policy and environmental policy. After all, the exploration, production, and use of natural resources for energy have environmental consequences. Thus, energy and the environment can be seen as complementary parts of the natural resources fuel cycle. Unfortunately, that ideal has not conformed fully with reality as energy policy and environmental policy are driven by different factors. Still, policymakers are moving these two fields closer together under the umbrella of sustainable development. It is this concept of sustainable development that brings energy, the environment, and the global economy together.

We have discussed the transition from wood to fossil fuels. Environmentalists have advocated a subsequent transition away from non-renewable fossil fuels and back to renewables and conservation. The argument for doing so is compelling due to three dramatic problems with fossil fuels: climate change; air pollution; and national security[127] What is most significant about these challenges is that they involve global energy markets. No longer can energy-environmental policy be strictly a matter of domestic law. Instead, because of the transboundary consequences of pollution and due to the increasing fluidity of world financial markets and intergovernmental energy projects, international energy-environmental policy is gaining in importance.

In the last twenty-five years, we can point to four formative events in bringing energy and environmental policies closer together in an attempt to balance their disparate motivating factors and do so at an international level.

The first watershed event for the development of international energy-environmental law was the Stockholm Conference organized by the United Nations in 1972 which "legitimized environmental policy as a universal concern among nations."[128] Formally called the United Nations Conference on the Human Environment, the Stockholm Conference was an integrative and important event. It was integrative as shown in its very name, "Human Environment." The Stockholm Conference intended to reorient the way people viewed the earth. Instead of a place on which humans resided and converted natural resources to their own use, the earth became a place for which humans had to take responsibility and stewardship. The Earth's resources were not limitless and the consequences of human activity were not benign for the Earth's maintenance. The Stockholm Conference began to articulate an integrative ideal that would recognize the interdependency between earth and humans. Still, a duality persisted between protection and conservation of the earth's resources, ecosystems, and environment and the need for economic development, particularly among developing countries. The outcome of the Stockholm Conference was the Declaration on the Human Environment, the Declaration of Principles, and 109 Recommendations for action with various resolutions. The Declaration contains a set of principles to "inspire and guide the peoples of the world and the preservation and enhancement of the human environment."[129]

Among the resolutions were those involving institutional and financial arrangements. They established an Intergovernmental Governing Council for Environmental Programmes, an environmental fund for financing

---

[127] John Byrne & Daniel Rich, ENERGY AND ENVIRONMENT: THE POLICY CHALLENGE 15 (1992).

[128] Lynton Keith Caldwell, INTERNATIONAL ENVIRONMENTAL POLICY: EMERGENCE AND DIMENSIONS 21 (2d ed. 1990).

[129] Quoted in Lewis B. Sohn, *The Stockholm Declaration on the Human Environment*, 14 HARV. INT'L J. 423 (1973).

programs. An action plan was also promulgated which established Earth Watch which was an environmental assessment body and also provided education, training, and public information. The Stockholm Declaration contains 26 principles that link the protection and conservation of the earth and its resources; social and economic development; and human and civil rights in a global community.

The next significant development in the area of international environmentalism was the creation of the World Commission on Environment and Development by the United Nations. Chaired by Prime Minister Gro Brundtland of Norway, the outcome of the WCED was a seminal publication, *Our Common Future*.[130] This Commission, by its very name, linked environmental protection and economic development, and did so under the heading of sustainable development.

Our Common Future provided the popular definition of sustainable development which is "to ensure that it meets the needs of the present without compromising the ability of future generations to meet their own needs."[131] The Report goes on to discuss linkages between environmental protection and economic development within a concept of equity between rich and poor nations. A more elaborate definition of sustainable development is:

> [S]ustainable development is not a fixed state of harmony, but rather a process of change in which the exploitation of resources, the direction of investments, the orientation of technological development, and institutional change are made consistent with future as well as present needs.[132]

The body of the Report sets out six policy directions involving population and human resources; fuel security; protection of species and ecosystems; energy policy; industrial development; and urban sustainability. If nothing else, the World Commission on Environment and Development made the concept of sustainable development part of the language of a new environmental paradigm which has worked itself into U.S. energy-environmental policy. For example, President Clinton established the President's Council on Sustainable Development which issued a lengthy report entitled *Sustainable America: A New Consensus for Prosperity, Opportunity, and a Healthy Environment*.[133]

---

[130] World Commission on Environment and Development, OUR COMMON FUTURE (1987).

[131] *Id.* at 8.

[132] *Id.* at 9.

[133] President's Council on Sustainable Development, SUSTAINABLE AMERICA: A NEW CONSENSUS FOR THE FUTURE (1996); Jonathan Lash, *Toward a Sustainable*

❮The President's Council adopted the Brundtland definition of sustainable development and applied it to the United States and its role in the world.❯*Sustainable America* involved strengthening domestic sustainable community and furthering the stewardship of natural resources; applying the concept of sustainability to human population; and taking a role in international leadership.❯

The next significant event was the Earth Summit held in Rio de Janeiro in June 1992.❮The Earth Summit was the United Nations' Conference on Environment and Development and thus carried through the intent of *Our Common Future*❯Approximately 175 nations were represented at the Earth Summit which involved extensive discussion on two treaties, including the United Nations Framework Convention on Climate Change and the Convention on Biological Diversity. The Earth Summit also generated the Rio Declaration on Environment Development which consisted of 27 principles directed to further progress on the concept of sustainable development. Those principles were also directed at environmental protection, the eradication of poverty, the creation of international cooperation, and a movement toward a greater sense of global interaction. The Declaration is a rather short document that is to be implemented through a very detailed document known as Agenda 21 which runs several hundred pages and examines the social and economic dimensions of sustainable development; the conservation and management of resources for sustainable development; the role of major governmental and non-governmental groups; and the means for implementation, including financial resources as well as research and development.[134]

Finally, the most recent follow-up conference to the Earth Summit was held in Kyoto, Japan in December of 1997. The purpose of the Kyoto meeting was to bring together the parties to the United Nations Framework Convention on Climate Change for the purpose of reducing greenhouse gas emissions by creating tradeable emissions targets throughout the world. Kyoto protocol set emissions targets for different countries, for example, 8% reduction below baseline emissions for the European Union, 6% for Japan, and 7% for the United States. The primary mechanism for reducing greenhouse gas emissions would be through an emissions trading regime. At this point, the United States has not ratified the treaty, but has been an active participant in shaping the terms of the protocol. In short, global environmentalism is barely three decades old yet its significance is widely recognized. The complex inter-generational and multi-jurisdictional

Future, 12 NAT. RES. & ENV'T 83 (1997).
    [134] THE EARTH SUMMIT: THE UNITED STATES CONFERENCE ON ENVIRONMENT AND DEVELOPMENT (Stanley P. Johnson, ed., 1993).

problems it must address will demand an increasing amount of attention from world leaders and policymakers.

IV. CONCLUSION

A. Energy-Environmental Policy Overview

The key to understanding the political economy of energy is recognizing the symbiotic relationship between government and industry which is manifest by four characteristics. First, in some segments of the industry energy resources are complementary, so the regulation of one does not necessarily adversely affect the other. Oil and electricity, for example, divide the energy pie into two more or less equal shares. Electricity does not occupy much of the transportation sector, and oil is an uneconomic means of producing electricity. Therefore, federal energy policy can support both oil and electricity production. Second, other energy resources are susceptible to inter-fuel competition. A federal policy that promotes the use of coal to generate electricity simultaneously discourages the use of nuclear power for the same purpose, thus promoting competition. Third, industry and government depend on each other for the distribution and allocation of economic benefits and burdens. The federal government, for example, controls most of the new oil reserves but depends on private industry for their development. Finally, both business and government are stimulated to act by market disequilibria. Oil price controls were responses to the embargoes, and increased exploration for natural gas was the reaction to a loosening of federally established prices. This interplay between government and industry has created the dominant policy model described above.

Domestic energy policy from the late nineteenth century to the present is based on the fundamental assumption that a link exists between the level of energy production and the gross national product. As more energy is produced, prices will remain stable or relatively low and the GDP will grow. Implicit in this simple formula is that the general welfare increases in direct proportion to the GDP. Energy policy continues to rely on this fundamental assumption and continues its faith in the market.

As a consequence, domestic energy policy favors large-scale, high-technology, capital-intensive, integrated, and centralized producers of energy from fossil fuels. These archetype energy firms are favored over alternatives such as small solar or wind firms because energy policymakers believe that the larger firms can continue to realize economies of scale. Policymakers gamble that greater energy efficiencies can be achieved by archetype firms, rather than by alternative firms, through technological innovation, discovery of new reserves, and discovery of new energy sources.

Put another way, as long as energy production, consumption, and prices remain stable, the embedded policy will continue. Thus, the dominant energy policy has the following general goals:

(1)   to assure abundant supplies;

(2)   to maintain reasonable prices;

(3)   to limit the market power of archetype firms;

(4)   to promote inter- and intrafuel competition;

(5)   to support a limited number of conventional fuels (oil, natural gas, coal, hydropower, and nuclear power); and,

(6)   to allow energy decisionmaking and policymaking to develop within an active federal-state regulatory system.

This policy, developed over the last 100 years, has served the country well by providing long periods of reliable energy and respectable degrees of economic stability. In light of this historical intransigence, we can project this policy into the future.

B.   The Continuing Problem of Integrating Energy and Environmental Policies

The emergence of environmental law throughout the 1970s, together with the energy crisis of that period brought to our awareness a basic conflict at the heart of both policies. The conflict was perhaps best described in Amory Lovins' book, *Soft Energy Paths*, which contrasted a soft path of renewable, energy-efficient, small scale alternative resources with the traditional hard path of capital-intensive, large scale, conventional fossil fuels.[135] Lovins argued that soft paths were not only environmentally sensitive, but made wise economic sense and that the country should no longer rely on the belief that there was a direct positive ratio between energy growth and economic growth.

The controversy regarding an energy-GNP link is not insubstantial and the belief in a direct link is a very powerful one.[136] This debate also

---

[135] Amory Lovins, SOFT ENERGY PATHS: TOWARD A DURABLE PEACE (1979).

[136] Robert Stobaugh & Daniel Yergin, ENERGY FUTURE, 141-44 (1979) (relationship between energy and GDP is not independent but elastic); Amory Lovins, SOFT ENERGY PATHS: TOWARD A DURABLE PEACE, 7-11 (1977) (no connection); Council on Environmental Quality, GLOBAL 2000, 353-54 (1980) (likely no connection); Julian L. Simon and Herman Kahn, THE RESOURCEFUL EARTH: A RESPONSE TO GLOBAL 2000, 342 (1984) (positive correlation); S. Schurr *et al.*, ENERGY IN AMERICA'S FUTURE: THE CHOICES BEFORE US, 15-16, 84-103 (1979) (some relationship); and ENERGY IN THE AMERICAN ECONOMY, 1850-1975: AN ECONOMIC

illuminates an economic issue that we discussed earlier: the question of the price elasticity of demand. In short, will there be a direct reduction in consumption in an exact ratio to price increases? Put differently, as energy prices rise, in what proportion will people conserve energy? During the energy crisis we learned that there is not a unitary elasticity nor is there inelasticity such that price rises are not met with a reduction in consumption. During the energy crisis, the country became increasingly aware of conservation in two senses. Conservation was seen as an attempt to achieve higher energy efficiencies and greater energy use. Conservation was also seen as saving resources. Further, consumers demonstrated an interest in alternative and renewable resources as people moved toward earth homes, solar energy, and wind power in some instances. In addition, particularly through portions of the National Energy Policy Act and the Energy Security Act, policy makers encouraged the development of alternative energy in two forms. Alternative energy was seen to be both renewable and alternatives to conventional fossil fuels, such as synfuels.

After the energy crisis, energy policy makers began to talk with environmentalists about the harmful consequences of energy exploration and production. At the same time, environmentalists became aware of certain market realities, that is, the consumers would use conventional resources as long as those resources were cheaper than alternatives. In addition, environmental policy makers also realized that there is a significant role to be played by the market in curbing pollution, promoting conservation, and promoting the use of alternative resources. Policymakers then went on to advocate the use of market-based incentives, for example, emissions trading, to further environmental goals.

During this time, international environmentalism became a more significant idea for policymakers. International environmentalists had to confront an extremely difficult dilemma, however. It is one thing to argue that developed countries should impose strict environmental standards. It is quite another thing to force developing countries to adopt strict (i.e., costly) environmental standards which may retard their economic growth. From this conflict between the need for developing countries to sustain economic growth, as well as the need to recognize the harmful consequences of energy production, the concept of sustainable development was born.

STUDY OF ITS HISTORY AND PROSPECTS, 16-17, 155-90 (Sam Schurr & Bruce Carlton Netschert, eds., 1970) (long term pattern inconsistent). *See also* United States Department of Energy, INTERRELATIONSHIPS OF ENERGY AND THE ECONOMY, (DOE/PE - 0300, July 1981).

Today "sustainability" is part of the rhetoric of United States domestic energy policy. Nevertheless, the dominant model of market-based, capital-intensive, fossil fuel energy policy is still dominant. In short, the country has yet to deliver the idea of actualizing the rhetoric of sustainability in real day-to-day policies except in marginal examples. The country has exercised caution on expanding oil exploration and production in environmentally sensitive areas. The Clean Air Act amendments have paid attention to greenhouse gases. The Endangered Species Act was reenacted, conservation measures promoted, and renewables supported with research and development as examples of an environmentally sensitive energy policy.

We have yet to resolve a fundamental conflict between energy policy and environmental policy. Energy policy, regardless of its awareness of its negative environmental consequences, is firmly based in the idea that economic development and growth is of central importance to the country. Environmental policy, regardless of its awareness for market-based regulations, is firmly based in the idea of resource protection is fundamental to human happiness.

Both attitudes, of course, are correct. It may very well be the case that both attitudes are reconcilable as our earlier discussion of the optimal amount of pollution demonstrates. Nevertheless, the discussion about optimal pollution was a model, not reality. The problem remains for policy-makers to develop market-based regulations that incorporate environmental and other social costs in energy prices.[137] In other words, applying the model is extremely difficult because it is extremely difficult (we hesitate to say impossible) to quantify the benefits of environmental policy.[138] Thus, the failure to "internalize the externalities" results in economic gain at the cost of environmental degradation. ❧

---

[137] Byrne & Rich, *supra* note 127 at 9.

[138] David W. Pearce & R. Kerry Turner, ECONOMICS OF NATURAL RESOURCES AND THE ENVIRONMENT, chs. 9 and 10 (1990); Per-olov Johansson, THE ECONOMIC THEORY AND MEASUREMENT OF ENVIRONMENTAL BENEFITS (1987); Allen Kneese & John Sweeney, HANDBOOK OF NATURAL RESOURCES AND ENERGY ECONOMICS (1985) (2 vols.); A. Myrick Freeman III, *Methods for Assessing the Benefits of Environmental Programs*, in Kneese & Sweeney, vol 1., ch. 6; also Kenneth E. McConnell, *The Economics of Outdoor Recreation*, in Kneese and Sweeney, vol. 2, ch. 15; V. Kerry Smith, William H. DesVousges & Ann Fisher, *A Comparison of Direct and Indirect Methods for Estimating Environmental Benefits*, in 1986 American Agricultural Association at 68 *Amer. Journal Agr. Economics* 280, 1986); Kevin J. Boyle & Richard C. Bishop, *Welfare Measurements Using Contingent Evaluation: A Comparison of Techniques*, in 1988 American Agricultural Association at 22.

CHAPTER SEVEN

Oil

*by Marla E. Mansfield
and James E. Hickey Jr.*

I.   INTRODUCTION

This book has separate chapters on Oil and Natural Gas. In reality that separation is not so discrete. In important factual and legal respects, these two energy resources often are intertwined. Factually, for example, at the production phase of the fuel cycle, oil and natural gas are merely different states, liquid and gaseous, of petroleum. They are often found together in geologic deposits (reservoirs) and produced from the same wells. At the end use phases of the fuel cycle, both oil and natural gas are used as boiler fuel to make electricity and heat, and as fuel to run automobiles, buses and trucks.

Legally, oil and natural gas often are dealt with in similar fashion under state and federal laws on production (see below). This chapter deals with oil and with oil and natural gas where they are factually and legally tied together. Specifically, this chapter addresses the fuel cycles of oil and gas in Section II, the oil industry and oil markets in Section III, state and federal regulation in Sections IV and V, and international law in Section VI. The chapter on Natural Gas deals with the discrete regulation of natural gas.

II.   THE FUEL CYCLE[1]

The term "petroleum" often is used for oil, which is the liquid state of combustible hydrocarbons. However, petroleum technically encompasses all combustible hydrocarbons of the bitumen family whether in the gaseous, liquid, or solid states. At times, the states tend to co-exist and the amount of heat during the period of creation appears to determine whether gas or oil will be formed. The chemical formulas for petroleum range from the

---

[1] Much of the material in Sections II and IV of this chapter initially appeared, in an expanded form, in Marla E. Mansfield, Chapter 49, *Petroleum and Pipelines*, THOMPSON ON REAL PROPERTY by David A. Thomas, Editor in Chief. Copyright, 1994, Lexis Law Publishing. Reprinted with permission from Lexis Law Publishing, Charlottesville, VA, (800) 446-3410. All rights reserved.

simple gaseous methane (CH_4) to the more complex octane (C_8H_{18}), a component of crude oil. Petroleum resources are concentrated in certain sections of the United States. The major oil and gas sources in the United States include the Gulf Coast, Gulf of Mexico, Pacific Coast, the Southwest, and the North Slope of Alaska.

The predominant geologic theory of petroleum formation is the organic theory. According to this theory, pressure and heat, together with chemical and bacterial reactions, transformed organic matter from marine life in sedimentary rocks into petroleum over thousands of years. The petroleum in these "source rocks" then migrated or percolated in a generally upward movement through porous and permeable "carrier" rocks. A rock is "porous" if there are spaces between the rock material into which a fluid may go. A rock is "permeable" if the pores are connected so that fluid may be transmitted through the rock. Petroleum cannot migrate through a rock which is impermeable, that is, a rock in which the pore spaces are isolated from one another.

Impermeable rocks, however, are important in the creation of a commercial petroleum resource. An impermeable feature that stops petroleum migration is a "trap." Two types of traps exist, stratigraphic and structural. A change in rock type, from permeable to impermeable for example, often causes stratigraphic traps. Structural traps occur when folding or faulting of geologic structures moves impermeable rock over permeable rocks. When a trap stops petroleum migration, a reservoir is formed.

Despite its name, an oil or gas "reservoir" or "pool" is not an underground lake or pond. The oil and gas does not gather into a discrete body of fluid in a carved out area of rock. Rather, oil and gas fill the interstices or pores of the reservoir rock. This rock may be the carrier rock or rock adjacent to it. Important reservoir rocks are sandstones, limestones, and dolomites. In addition to being porous, reservoir rock must be permeable. Porosity allows the oil or gas to accumulate; permeability allows it to be recovered. Despite the lack of an oil or gas "lake," significant amounts of petroleum can be present in reservoir rock. For example, if a reservoir rock is 10 feet thick, covers an acre, and has a porosity of 20% (meaning 20% of the area by volume is available for fluids because it is pore space), the rock would contain 15,553 barrels of oil if the only fluid present was oil and it totally filled or "saturated" the reservoir.

---

[2] A second theory of formation is the inorganic theory, which posits that hydrogen and carbon joined deep in the earth and then migrated as petroleum to where currently located. If this is true, oil and gas could be found in places currently deemed unfavorable for their discovery.

Oil, however, normally is not the only fluid in a reservoir. Salt water often is present, either as connate water in pores along with oil or separate from the oil.[3] Natural gas may also be in the reservoir in solution. If all three fluids are present, they may layer in order of weight, with salt water on the bottom and oil and then gas above. Not all reservoirs, however, will have a free-standing "gas cap" on top. Nevertheless, gas almost always will be present in solution in the oil. This makes classification of wells as oil or gas wells problematic at times, and classification of wells may have legal importance because regulators may treat oil and gas wells differently.

The production of oil and natural gas is comprised of exploration (prospecting), drilling and recovery. Exploration takes place all over the world on land and offshore using a variety of methods from seismic detonations to satellite imagery. Typically, this work is done by a petroleum geologist. Drilling is the only sure method by which the discovery of a petroleum reservoir can be confirmed. Once a potential oil or gas pool is found, test wells are drilled. A successful drilling results in a "discovery well" while an unsuccessful drilling is called a "dry hole." More dry holes are drilled than discovery wells. The petroleum engineer, as opposed to the petroleum geologist, is responsible for drilling and for recovery of oil and gas from both discovery and production wells.

Oil and gas resources are only recoverable through wells. Two distinct processes, mechanical and natural, contribute to a well's production. The first, a mechanical pump, may be used to move oil to the surface from the bottom of a well. However, only natural reservoir energy will move the oil or gas through the permeable reservoir rock to the wellbore. Once petroleum reaches a reservoir it becomes static. It no longer migrates, and reservoir pressure builds. If a well is drilled, a low pressure area forms at the wellbore and the petroleum naturally moves from areas of high pressure to low pressure. This second important process, natural reservoir energy, thus provides the pressure differential essential to recovery of oil and gas. Three natural or "primary" energy drives exist. In descending order of efficiency, they are the water encroachment drive, the gas-cap drive, and the solution gas drive. No natural drive is sufficient to recover all the oil in a reservoir.

Avoiding wasteful dissipation of this natural reservoir pressure is a major concern to both private and government petroleum engineers. Artificial pressure can be used to increase the energy drive's recovery potential. Before reservoir pressure has significantly dissipated, main-

---

[3] Because all the water in the rock pores has not been displaced by oil, an oil well often produces salt water, which must be disposed of in an environmentally sound manner.

tenance activities may consist of re-injecting gas to keep pressure up. As the primary drive force dissipates, secondary and tertiary recovery activities will add substances to the reservoir such as water, gas, carbon dioxide, or even fire or microbes, <u>all to increase reservoir pressure and enhance recovery of oil and gas.</u>

Once produced by the combination of reservoir energy and mechanical pumps, petroleum must be transported from the production wells to a refinery (for oil) or to a processing and gathering point (for natural gas). Crude oil is refined into various products, such as gasoline, diesel fuel, heating oil, jet fuel, kerosene and petrochemical feedstocks. The ease of refining may depend on whether the crude oil is light or heavy, sweet or sour. <u>Heavy crude oils tend to be sour. That is, they contain highly undesirable contaminants such as sulfur, nitrogen and metals.</u> These must be removed. Sweet or light crude that does not contain these contaminants is preferred. Similarly, natural gas may be "sour" and require processing to remove contaminants. <u>Liquids must also be removed from natural gas before it enters a transportation pipeline</u>, which is the next step in the fuel cycle.

This step entails transportation from either refineries or processing points to various marketplaces for refined or processed products. <u>Natural gas is almost exclusively moved from gathering or processing points in pipelines, although liquefied natural gas may be transported in ocean tankers and tanker trucks.</u> Natural gas transportation regulation is discussed in Chapter Eight. Crude oil and refined oil products may also use pipelines, but also are transported in trucks, and barges and oil tanker ships. The Federal Energy Regulatory Commission regulates oil pipelines as common carriers.

Finally, the oil and gas is consumed. These energy sources are used in various ways. The major use of refined oil products is for fuel for cars, buses, trucks, ships and airplanes. According to Energy Information Forecast, *Annual Energy Outlook 1996*, the share of energy provided for transportation fuel by oil and its derivatives will decrease from 97% in 1994 to 94% in 2015. Alternative-fueled vehicles increased almost 30% from 1992 to 1994 and, according to the Energy Information Administration, were expected to increase another 30% in 1996 to a total of 421,000 vehicles. These vehicles are powered by either liquefied petroleum gases (LPG), natural gas, alcohol, or electricity.[4] <u>The primary uses of natural gas are for heating, electric generation, and as boiler fuel.</u> Oil may also be used as heating fuel or for electric generation or boiler fuel. Oil is also a feedstock for the petrochemical industries.

---

[4] *See* Chapter Thirteen on Alternative Energy Resources.

III.   THE OIL INDUSTRY AND OIL MARKETS

The oil industry is composed of large vertically-integrated oil companies (the "majors" or "multinationals" like Exxon, Royal Dutch Shell, B-P Amoco, and Texaco) and independents. The large, multinational, oil companies are involved in all stages of the fuel cycle from production to marketing and retail sales. Vertically integrated multinationals may sell gasoline from their own gas stations, from gas stations using their name or from independent gas stations that sell under their independent name. Typically, multinationals will have operations that may include production in one country, transport on the high seas using company owned or chartered tankers and supertankers, refining in another country, and marketing and sales in yet another country.

The independents vary in size and they generally are not involved in every phase of energy fuel cycles. Some independents engage only in production and sell their crude oil either to the multinational oil companies or to independent refineries. For example, in the case of gasoline, oil companies and refiners may sell to other wholesalers. Other independents engage exclusively in marketing or retailing of energy products.

In the United States, independent producers of oil and gas may begin to play a greater role in the long term development of oil and gas than the major oil producers. The 1986 collapse in the price of oil eliminated many non-major producers. However, the surviving independents are increasing in importance to the industry. Those that survived had more debt than equity through the post-collapse period and they replaced reserves at lower prices. Independents in the early 1990s invested nearly half of the total expenditure made on domestic development in the United States, up from 33% in 1988-90. The independent's share of "lower-48" production went from 45% in 1989 to 54% in 1993. Between the collapse in 1986 and 1989, foreign exploration and development expenditures by the majors doubled while expenditures in the United States declined by 14%.[5]

Oil production in the United States remains significant, but it is declining when compared with the increase in oil imported. Crude oil production in the United States was 6,470,000 barrels per day (b/d) in January of 1996; 1,455,000 b/d were produced in Alaska. Total U.S. production in January of 1995 was 6,638,000 b/d. In January of 1996, total imports of petroleum (crude oil and products) as a percentage of total U.S. domestic petroleum deliveries were 50%. The same percentage in January of 1995

---

[5] *See* Energy Information Administration, *Oil and Gas Development in the United States in the Early 1990s: An Expanded Role for Independent Producers.*

was 46.3%. In May of 1996, imports hit a near 20-year high averaging 9.98 million barrels a day, or 56.5% of the nation's total petroleum demand. The United States now imports growing amounts of refined oil products and increases to domestic refining capacity continue falling behind domestic petroleum consumption.

According to Energy Information Forecast, *Annual Energy Outlook 1996*, oil and its derivatives will continue as a primary U.S. energy source through 2015. Its share of the total energy consumed is estimated to be around 40% over the next 20 years.

IV.   STATE REGULATION OF OIL AND GAS PRODUCTION

Several factors have influenced the history of state regulation of oil and gas production. These include petroleum geology, petroleum engineering, the economic importance of oil and gas, and the problems of transporting the fluids. Courts quickly determined that oil and gas could not be treated as other minerals were treated.

The physical peculiarities of petroleum first influenced ownership rights. Although in some countries the crown owned minerals, American common law gave to the owner of the land surface the minerals beneath the land. Under the so-called *ad coelum* doctrine, ownership was from heaven to the core of the earth—*cujus est solum, ejus est usque ad coelum et infernos* ("To whomever the soil belongs, he owns also to the sky and to the depths"). This doctrine works well with stationary hard rock minerals that are easily identified and associated with a particular tract of land. However, oil and gas did not behave so predictably.

Early courts analogized oil and gas to wild animals or percolating waters. Ownership of these objects was not tied directly to ownership of land, but required "capture" to perfect possession. As late as 1921, one Texas case referred to oil and gas as "percolating restlessly about under the surface of the earth, even as the birds fly from field to field and the beasts roam from forest to forest."[6] This was, of course, incorrect. Oil and gas remained static, once a reservoir was reached, until disturbed by human activity.

Nevertheless, oil and gas *do* act differently than solid minerals because of reservoir mechanics. A well in the reservoir creates a low pressure area to which oil and gas will migrate, much like air in an inflated balloon will migrate to the balloon mouth. The well will "drain" the reservoir. For example, a well drilled near a boundary line may recover oil and gas initially residing

---

[6] Medina Oil Developing Co. v. Murphy, 233 S.W. 333 (Tex. Civ. App. 1921).

under the land of another. Experts may dispute the exact area any well could drain and the interrelationship between specific wells. Nevertheless, activities by one party owning interests in a reservoir will affect others who also own interests in the reservoir. Because natural reservoir energy is so important for production, the overall efficiency of an oil and gas pool or reservoir may be affected by the number of wells drilled and the activities of all those owning interests in a common pool. State oil and gas law had to accommodate to the realities of petroleum engineering.

The limitations of petroleum geology also made their mark on legal developments. The geologist uses knowledge of the surface and makes inferences about the subsurface from geophysical exploration to predict whether there are geologic structures likely to contain oil or gas. Those predictions may only be confirmed by drilling an expensive well. Developers, of course, want to control when and where development dollars are spent and often desire to spread their risks. Many of the contracts that evolved in the oil and gas industry, including the basic oil and gas lease, reflect this reality.

Oil and gas law also responded to oil and gas's status as a finite resource of important economic consequence, imbued with a public interest. Oil and gas production states have passed conservation laws to protect the public's interest in preventing waste of the resource. These statutes were first concerned with preventing physical waste. Many now also address economic waste. Federal statutes have been enacted to supplement state law.

Finally, the difficulties of transporting the product influence oil and gas law. The most efficient way to transport oil is by pipeline. Oil also may be stored on site in tanks and transported by truck. The marketing and transportation problem is more acute for gas. Natural gas in the open air diffuses and escapes upward because it is lighter than air. Storage above ground is difficult. Additionally, natural gas may be moved only by pipeline. Marketing considerations have affected not only the regulation of pipelines, but also the duties of the lessee under an oil and gas lease.

Because of these physical, and practical influences, oil and gas law tends to be a separate field of law. Both private and public law responded to the unique characteristics of petroleum. The legal regime that evolved differs from both general property law and the law governing hard rock minerals.

A.   Oil and Gas Development on Private Land

Oil and gas development on private land is primarily a matter of state law. Although oil and gas law diverged from general mineral law, oil and gas are almost universally considered to be "minerals." Therefore, general mineral law provides a starting place to determine private property rights in oil and gas. Unless otherwise stated, a conveyance of land includes the minerals in the land. A deed, however, may convey minerals separately or by reservation or exception remove them from a grant. When one of these activities has taken place, it is said that the minerals are severed from the surface. Generally, if the minerals are truly severed, then two estates in land are created. One is the surface estate and the other the mineral estate. The owner of a mineral estate has the right to develop the minerals, the right of access and use of the surface for this purpose, and the right to lease the minerals and receive the proceeds of a mineral lease.[7]

A common law evolved to govern the relationship between the holders of the two estates. As noted, the owner of a severed mineral estate has the right to use so much of the surface as is reasonably necessary for the production of minerals. This is an implied right, one which exists even without an express grant in the document severing the mineral estate. Implied rights, however, may be expanded or contracted by agreement of the parties. The rights also may respond to new technology. Moreover, the mineral estate is deemed dominant over the surface estate. Therefore, the mineral owner generally is only liable for damages caused by negligent or unreasonable use of the surface.[8] A surface owner, however, does not merely own the soil covering the surface. The surface estate includes all rights not part of the mineral estate. Therefore, the owner of the surface may make such uses of it that do not unreasonably interfere with the extraction of minerals.

As explained earlier, oil and gas law diverged from the law governing minerals in general. The basic premise in this divergence is explained by considering the nature of the landowner's interest in oil and gas in place. The so-called "Rule of Capture" is an overriding concept that colors ownership rights to oil and gas in place. Its origin lies in an error about the nature of oil and gas. Because early courts believed oil and gas to be constantly moving, courts analogized oil and gas to wild animals or subterranean water.[9] Rights to possess wild animals—*ferae naturae*—only become fixed upon "capture." Moreover, a wild animal, once it escaped from the possessor

---

[7] There is an exception: in Louisiana, a separate estate in minerals cannot be created in fee, although two separate ownerships in the same property may be created. A severance creates a servitude in the nature of an easement. This servitude is defeasible; it will end, or to use the proper jargon, it will "prescribe" if it is not used.

[8] Nevertheless, some doctrines have evolved at common law and by statute to protect the surface owner. These include the right to subjacent and lateral support. Moreover, statutes may require oil developers to pay surface damages regardless of the right to use the surface in a reasonable manner.

[9] Current cases reject the analogies to wild animals or water. *See, e.g.*, Lone Star Gas Co. v. Murchinson, 353 S.W.2d 870 (Tex. Civ. App. 1962). Nevertheless, the idea's imprint remains.

back to its natural habitat, would become unowned and subject to capture again. The one restraint on this system of ownership which recognized a landowner's rights was that it was trespass to enter another's property to capture a wild animal.

The *ferae naturae* analogy was the first stirring of oil and gas law, but oil and gas differ from wild animals. Oil and gas do not move without some human intervention and, even more importantly for a property regime, oil and gas exists in a closed system. A reservoir is finite in area and underlies a finite amount of surface acreage. Owners of mineral rights in lands not overlying the reservoir could not recover oil or gas by drilling vertically upon their own lands. They could only enter into the reservoir through trespass. As between parties with mineral rights to lands overlying the reservoir, however, the activities of one party in the reservoir can affect oil or gas originally beneath the land of another. Human interference causes drainage as reservoir energy drives oil and gas to areas of lower pressure. Therefore, the reservoir is physically a "common pool" beneath the lands. A well could "capture" oil and gas and potentially drain any area of the common pool.

The Rule of Capture, which was adopted from other settings, has been translated in some jurisdictions into a direct rule of real property.[10] However,

---

[10] The logical extension of the Rule of Capture would be to declare that the owner of the land (or owner of the minerals if severed) would have no rights to the oil and gas in place at all. Ownership would come to fruition only upon production or "capture." This view is espoused in several major producing states, including Oklahoma, California, Louisiana, and Wyoming. Other states also follow this theory but it is, nevertheless, the minority view. The non-ownership theory does not mean that the landowner or mineral owner is devoid of rights to the oil and gas prior to production. An owner has the exclusive right to explore for, develop and produce the oil and gas from specified lands. Therefore, the theory is also referred to as the "exclusive right to take" theory. Many courts characterize these rights as a profit a prendre, which is a right to go upon land and take some part of the land or a product of the land. The owner's right is an interest in land that will be protected from interference by others.

A majority of states adopt the theory of ownership that begins with the *ad coelum* doctrine and considers oil and gas part of the real property. Under the *ad coelum* doctrine, the owner of the soil owns the oil and gas while they are a part of it. In addition to ownership, the landowner (or owner of the minerals if severed) would have the exclusive right to explore for, develop and produce the oil and gas from the lands. The ownership in place theory has been adopted by Texas, Colorado, Kansas and New Mexico, among others. The ownership in place theory recognizes a fee simple estate in the land, but physical reality tempers the ownership rights. An owner does not receive an absolute right to each molecule of oil or gas that is present beneath the land either prior to initial disturbance by man or at any particular time. Rights are

the Rule of Capture has another aspect, one which is relevant in all jurisdictions. The "Rule of Capture" is a negative rule of liability: the owner of an
interest in the common pool will have no liability for draining oil or gas from
beneath the land of another through a well on the interest-owner's property.
The draining well cannot bottom on lands to which the developer does not have
mineral rights or it would be a trespass.)If the well is properly located, however,
the drainage is *damnum absque injuria*, which cannot be the subject of an
action. The drained owner's recourse is self-help, namely to drill a well. This is
so even if artificial stimulation has increased drainage.

The non-liability provided by the Rule of Capture influences property
rights regardless of what theory of oil and gas ownership is adopted.
Because of it, anyone with mineral rights in land overlying the reservoir
may develop the reservoir from such land. The draining mineral developer
gains ownership of the produced oil or gas. Many parties potentially may
own the oil and gas while it is in the reservoir; oil and gas until produced
are the "common" property of those with the right to develop the reservoir.
The undeveloped reservoir is thus not only a common pool physically, but
also from a legal perspective. Under a pure Rule of Capture, there are no
controls on the number and location of wells that a mineral interest owner
may drill in the common pool. Every owner of a right to the common pool
has a right to produce the oil or gas and cannot prevent others from
exercising similar rights. Therefore, a race to develop the minerals ensues.

Historically, this race induced mass production that not only lowered the
price of the product, but forced expenditures on wells that were not required
to drain the reservoir efficiently.(Moreover, when the only concern of any
particular developer is speedy recovery to avoid oil or gas "capture" by
another, reservoir energy is not conserved.)Recovery of the maximum amount
of the resource is therefore impossible. Because of these examples of both
physical and economic waste, limitations on the Rule of Capture arose.

Current limitations on the Rule of Capture are of two types: judge-
made and statutory. The first restraints primarily adjust private rights
through the judge-made doctrine of correlative rights. Under it, each owner
of rights in the common pool has the right to have an opportunity to recover
the owner's fair share of the oil in the pool, but the owner has also the duty
to develop in a non-negligent and non-wasteful manner in accord with
conservation laws.[11] These conservation laws of the producing state are the
second type of limits on the Rule of Capture. They have dual objectives. The
statutes protect private rights and preserve public interests in the finite

---

subject to the Rule of Capture and its non-liability function.

[11] Elliff v. Texon Drilling Co., 210 S.W.2d 558, 562 (Tex. 1948).

resource. The interrelationship of statutory and judge-made tenets is obvious in *Elliff*: "These laws and regulations are designed to afford each owner a reasonable opportunity to produce his proportionate part of the oil and gas from the entire pool and to prevent operating practices injurious to the common reservoir. In this manner, if all operators exercise the same degree of skill and diligence, each owner will recover in most instances his fair share of the oil and gas."[12] In other words, these second, statutory restraints are justified partially as protection of correlative rights. Therefore, a conservation statute does not divest private property without compensation but rather is a statute "protecting private property and preventing it from being taken by one of the common owners without regard to the enjoyment of the others."[13]

In addition to protecting correlative rights, a second rationale of such statutes is to prevent waste, not only because waste would impact correlative rights, but because waste injures the public. Oil and gas is a limited, but necessary resource.

Generally, waste of oil and gas refers to production techniques or practices that fail to maximize the natural reservoir forces necessary to obtain the greatest ultimate recovery of oil and gas. It is thus concerned with physical waste of the hydrocarbons by not allowing for their recovery, by damaging reservoir energy, or by otherwise not conforming with proper engineering practices. Waste can take place underground or on the surface. Surface waste occurs by spillage, venting or flaring of gas, or by evaporation.

"Waste" is further defined in the various statutes of producing states. Statutory definitions may also seek to prevent "waste" of the surface itself through unnecessary drill sites. "Economic" waste may also be an element of concern. There are two aspects to economic waste. First, economic waste comes from allowing the oil or gas to be sold for too low a price, which encourages overproduction and improvident use of the resource. A second aspect of economic waste is forcing an operator to unnecessarily expend funds.

Common techniques authorized by the various statutes to protect correlative rights and prevent waste may be summarized as follows:

1. *Regulation of drilling through well permits*. Operators are required to obtain a permit that will specify proper drilling, completion, and abandonment techniques. After drilling, subject

---

[12] *Id.*
[13] Ohio Oil Co. v. Indiana, 177 U.S. 190, 210 (1900).

to some confidentiality rights, pertinent information about the subsurface will have to be filed with the agency.

2. *Regulation of drilling through well spacing.* Limiting the number of wells in a reservoir is one of the primary ways to moderate the effects of the Rule of Capture. One method is to specify the distance generally to be allowed between wells and from the boundaries of individual tracts. A second method, more specific to the geology of a particular field, is to specify the size of a drilling or spacing unit. Ideally, the unit size should be that area which one well can efficiently and effectively drain. Only one well is allowed per unit. Because the drillsite is also specified, this technique controls both the number and location of wells and creates an orderly pattern of development. However, to prevent waste and protect correlative rights, exceptions will allow wells in different locations if necessary. Additionally, to develop small tracts that do not equal the minimum unit size, almost all producing states allow "forced pooling," which is a statutory method for combining interests to share both the costs of drilling and the proceeds of production.[14]

3. *Regulation of Production and Marketing Through Market Demand Prorating and Ratable Taking.* One controversial technique to prevent overproduction is to limit total state-wide production to the amount set by either statute or the state conservation agency.[15] In the latter situation, production amounts would be based on specified criteria, often the amount of market demand as determined by the agency or by nominations by purchasers. The total statewide demand for various categories of oil and gas would then be prorated among the various producing reservoirs. Each producer in the field would receive an "allowable" enabling it to produce its fair share. In order to assure a market for each producer, purchasers of oil and gas from a field are ordered to "ratably take" from each producer.

---

[14] Kansas is the sole state without forced pooling. It adjusts well allowables in accordance with the size of a tract. *See* Mobil Oil Corp. v. State Corp. Comm., 227 Kan. 594, 608 P.2d 1325 (1980). Texas was a latecomer and its pooling statute is limited. Tex. Nat. Res. Code Ann. §§ 102.0001-.112 (West 1978); Tex. Nat. Res. Code, ch. 102 (Vernon 1993).

[15] Texas, Oklahoma and Kansas allow this technique. Among states that expressly or impliedly prohibit market demand prorating are California, Colorado, Illinois, Kentucky, Mississippi, Montana, Ohio, Utah, and Wyoming.

4. *Regulation of Production Through Water/Oil and Gas/Oil Ratios.*
    Gas or water is often the drive mechanism in a reservoir. Both
    may be produced along with oil. In order to preserve the reservoir
    energy, a conservation agency may specify the amount of water or
    gas that may be produced per barrel of oil. In combination with
    limitations on oil production known as "allowables," production is
    further limited if the gas or water production will exceed what
    would have been produced at the specified ratio.[16]

5. *Regulation of Unitization.* Secondary and tertiary recovery
    techniques require substances to be injected into the formation to
    enhance recovery when primary energy has dissipated. In order
    to do so efficiently, an entire reservoir or a sufficiently large
    portion of one must be operated as a "unit" without regard to lease
    or individual tract boundaries. If parties cannot voluntarily agree
    on such development, many conservation statutes allow for forced
    unitization.

This list is illustrative, not exhaustive. Moreover, not all conservation
agencies are allowed by statute to employ all the techniques.

B.   Oil and Gas Transactions Between Private Parties

Many issues in the private development of oil and gas deal with conflicts
between oil and gas lessors and the oil and gas companies to which they have
leased the minerals for development. Many of the tensions between a lessor and
lessee are reflected in the typical oil and gas lease. These transactions, like
private land development, are governed by state law.

The basic nature of the lease is revealed in its habendum clause, which
displays the sometimes conflicting interests of the lessor and lessee. These
conflicts are rooted in the fact that the lessee bears the financial risk of the
venture. The lessee wants to control the pace of expensive development and
to maintain the lease so long as it is either profitable to operate or has
speculative value. The lessor, who does not bear the costs of exploration and
production, wants quick oil and gas production, which will generate income
to the lessor in the form of royalties. The modern lease attempts to reconcile
the competing interests of the lessor and the lessee.

---

[16] For example, if the normal allowable for a well is 100 barrels of oil per day
and the gas/oil ratio is set at 2,000 cubic feet of gas per barrel, the well must cease
production when either 100 barrels of oil or 200,000 cubic feet of gas is produced.
Therefore, a well producing 4,000 cubic feet of gas per barrel of oil will only be able
to produce 50 barrels of oil per day.

The reconciliation is obvious in one of the first provisions of a lease, namely the habendum clause, which defines the lease's term. A typical clause reads:

> Subject to other provisions herein contained, the term of this lease is for X years from this date (the "primary term") and so long thereafter as oil, gas, or other hydrocarbons are being produced from said land.

The primary term is the definite time period specified in the lease as a number of years. During this period, the lessee has the right, but not the obligation to drill a well. The lessee therefore may pace development to the lessee's needs.

The secondary term of an oil and gas lease is that period in which the lease is kept alive by production. It is the defeasible aspect of the lease: it will last "for so long as oil or gas is produced." Production, therefore, is necessary to propel a lease into the secondary term and necessary to maintain the lease in the secondary term. In most jurisdictions, the habendum clause forms a special limitation on the estate; the lease term is not an interest subject to a condition or right of re-entry. Because the term has a special limitation, a lease terminates automatically at the end of the primary term or during the secondary term if there is no production.

Generally, the habendum clause itself requires production from the leased land, but other provisions of the lease may expand where production could occur. Additionally, other provisions of the lease may provide for substitutes for production. These substitutes are of two types. They may define an activity as constructive production or declare that, if certain circumstances happen, a lease will not cease. The latter types of provisions buy time to obtain production. These savings clauses and other doctrines such as the "temporary cessation" rule operate to modify the harsh results of an automatic termination of a lease.

In addition to the compromise revealed in the habendum clause, the manner of compensating the lessor reveals some of the same underlying tension. The lessor, who does not bear the expenses of drilling and thus generally wants prompt development, receives recompense in three ways.

The first consideration generally paid to the lessor is called the "bonus," which is a payment made upon execution of the lease. The lessor also may receive miscellaneous payments that substitute for other performance by the lessee throughout the lease term. The most important of these are the delay rental payments, which are discussed below. The potentially most lucrative remuneration to the lessor, however, is the royalty. It is therefore addressed first.

Unlike coal or other minerals, the extent or even the existence of oil or gas in the leased tract is not known until after the lessee has drilled. Therefore, the royalty evolved as a percentage of actual production, rather than as a fixed sum per unit of oil or gas produced. The lessee retains the remainder of the production as its return. The majority of leases have a fixed royalty. Prior to the 1970s, the generally accepted royalty was ⅛ in all but California, where 1/6 (or 16-2/3%) was usual. The royalty, however, is negotiable. During the last boom cycle, royalties of 1/6 and 3/16 were common. Competitive areas could command higher royalties. The percentage formula hedges against uncertainty; return for the lessor is tied to production.

Because royalties are viewed as the primary consideration given to the lessor, courts implied a duty on the lessee to drill an exploratory well so as to generate royalties for the lessor. In order to control the pace of development and avoid this drilling duty, the lessees developed the delay rental clause. The clause provides alternative consideration to the lessor to compensate for postponing drilling.

Two basic forms of delay rental clauses developed. The "or" form was developed first and obligates the lessee to "drill or pay."[17] The second form of delay rental clause is an "unless" clause. Under this form, the lease will automatically terminate "unless" a well is commenced or delay rentals are paid.[18] Therefore, the implications for the lessee from failing to pay rentals differ under the two forms.

With an "unless" clause, the lessee is neither obligated to pay the rentals nor drill. The lessee has the option to either drill, pay rentals, or let the lease lapse. The lessor may neither sue to collect rentals nor to compel drilling. The clause's most distinctive feature, however, is its self-operative

---

[17] A typical clause may read: "Commencing with the first day of the second year of the term hereof, if the lessee has not theretofore commenced drilling operations on said land or terminated the lease as herein provided, the lessee shall pay or tender to lessor annually, in advance, the sum of ___ per acre per year for so much of said land as may then be held under this lease, until drilling operations are commenced or this lease is terminated as herein provided."

[18] "If no well is commenced on said land on or before one year from the date hereof, this lease shall terminate as to both parties, unless the lessee on or before that date shall pay or tender to the lessor . . . the sum of _____ Dollars, herein called rentals, which shall cover the privilege of deferring commencement of drilling operations for a period of twelve months. In like manner and upon like payment or tender annually, the commencement of drilling operations may be deferred for successive periods of twelve months each during the primary term hereof."

nature. Under the majority view, the "unless" clause creates a special limitation on the lessee's estate. The lease terminates automatically upon the happening of the condition, which is the non-payment of rentals when there is no drilling.

Non-payment of rentals under the "drill or pay" clause is never grounds for an automatic termination of the lease. Under this formulation, the payment of rentals is not a condition, but a covenant. The lessee will have a firm obligation to pay rentals. Therefore, most "or" leases provide that the lessee may surrender the lease and avoid rentals. Initially, such clauses were viewed as creating an estate terminable at the will of one party and therefore terminable by both. However, the surrender clause was later recognized as valid. Nevertheless, because the "or" lease required the lessee to act to avoid liability for rentals, the "unless" clause was developed. The automatic termination under the clause, which is desirable when a lessee intends a lease to lapse, may be harsh when non-payment occurs for other reasons. On the other hand, a lessor's sole remedy under an unmodified "or" lease is to sue for rentals due and unpaid. Therefore, lessors revised these forms to allow the lessor to forfeit the lease if the lessee fails to pay rentals. Before forfeiture may result, however, the lessor frequently is required under the lease to give the lessee notice of default and an opportunity to cure. The lessor must act and object to non-payment, making this type of "or" estate analogous to a fee simple on condition subsequent.

The habendum clause, the delay rental clause, and the royalty provisions are involved in many of the controversies under leases. They are not, however, the only bones of contention.   In addition to the express terms of an oil and gas lease, courts generally imply obligations on the oil and gas company. Implied covenants to be undertaken by the lessor are less frequently recognized. Courts, however, regularly enforce the lessee's implied obligations unless the lessee has clearly negated them in the lease.

The lessee's implied covenants have been classified in several ways. For example, some duties deal with development and are so labeled. These include covenants to drill an initial exploratory well and to reasonably develop known formations. All jurisdictions recognize these covenants. Some jurisdictions also recognize a third independent development covenant, which requires further exploration into unproven formations or acreage. A second category contains covenants designed to protect the leasehold. The primary, basic covenant is the covenant to protect from drainage. Some jurisdictions additionally seem to require the lessee not to depreciate the lessor's interest. Finally, some covenants deal with the duty to manage and administer the leasehold. The most important of these covenants is the duty to produce and market hydrocarbons. Generally, the lessee must operate with reasonable care and seek favorable administrative action from government bodies with regulatory power over the reservoir.

These categories of duties are not hard and fast. A particular complaint may involve overlapping duties. For example, in order to protect a lease from drainage, a lessee may need to seek a favorable ruling from a conservation agency for a drilling unit or an exception location. Despite the fluidity of labeling, some of the lessee's covenants have well defined elements and the classification may be useful. At the heart of all the covenants, however, is the requirement that the lessee act as a "reasonable and prudent operator" would act under all the circumstances. This is a fact-dependent inquiry and generally requires that there be some prospect for success or profit before the lessee would be required to act.

V.   FEDERAL REGULATION OF OIL

The oil industry is subject to the full range of federal laws and regulations that govern other industries and commodities, like the antitrust and securities laws, interstate commerce laws, import and export laws and the like. This section addresses two areas of federal regulation that have particular significance for the oil industry—leasing for production from federal lands (onshore and offshore) and environmental regulation.

A.   Oil Leasing on Federal Lands

1.   Onshore

Federally-owned lands in the United States comprise about 662 million acres, which is about 29% of the land in the United States.[19] Additionally, the United States owns severed mineral interests. Most federal lands and minerals are located in the eleven contiguous western states and Alaska. Of these lands and minerals, those located in National Forests and those administered by the Bureau of Land Management (technically referred to as "public lands") are most significant for oil and gas development.

Prior to 1920, oil and gas was acquired on federal lands under the Mining Law of 1872.[20] The Mining Law of 1872 allows the miner to "stake a claim" and eventually gain title to not only the minerals discovered, but

---

[19] *See* George C. Coggins, Charles F. Wilkinson, and John D. Leshy, FEDERAL PUBLIC LAND AND RESOURCES LAW (3d ed. 1992).

[20] 30 U.S.C. §§ 21-54.

also to the land that contains the minerals. The Law is summarized in *United States v. Curtis-Nevada Mines, Inc.*[21]:

❮Under the general mining law enacted in 1872, individuals were encouraged to prospect, explore and develop the mineral resources of the public domain through an assurance of ultimate private ownership of the minerals and the lands so developed.❯The system envisaged by the mining law was that the prospector could go out into the public domain, search for minerals and upon discovery establish a claim to the lands upon which the discovery was made. This required location of the claim, which involved staking the corners of the claim, posting a notice of location thereon and complying with the state laws concerning the filing or recording of the claim in the appropriate office. A placer mining claim cannot exceed 20 acres and a lode claim cannot be larger than 1500 feet by 600 feet (which is slightly over 20 acres). The locator thus obtained "the exclusive right of possession and enjoyment of all the surface included within the lines of their locations."

[T]he claimant thus had the present and exclusive possession for the purpose of mining, but the federal government retained fee title and could protect the land and the surface resources from trespass, waste or from uses other than those associated with mining.❮The claimant could apply for a patent to the land under 30 U.S.C. § 29, and, upon meeting the statutory requirements, would be granted a patent which usually conveyed the full fee title to the land. ❯

❮In order to obtain the patent the claimant would have to establish that there was a legitimate discovery of a valuable mineral deposit on the land which a prudent man would be justified in developing.❯In many instances an investigation and hearing would be required prior to granting a patent. However, claimants could continue mining activities on the claims, without ever obtaining a patent. As a practical matter, mining claimants could remain in exclusive possession of the claim without ever proving a valid discovery or actually conducting mining operations. This led to abuses of the mining laws when mining claims were located with no real intent to prospect or mine but rather to gain possession of the surface resources. Furthermore, even persons who did have the

---

[21] 611 F.2d 1277 (9th Cir. 1980).

legitimate intent to utilize the claim for the development of the mineral content at the time of the location often did not proceed to do so, and thus large areas of the public domain were withdrawn, and as a result these surface resources could not be utilized by the general public for other purposes.[22]

The Mining Law of 1872 was the product of an era in which population of the West was encouraged and entrepreneurial spirit rewarded, especially when the government did not have the ability to monitor and protect its resources. Although the Mining Law still applies to some minerals, including uranium, it seemed untoward to allow energy minerals and the associated land to be brought into private ownership merely by staking a claim and applying for a patent. During World War I, the President and Congress began to view this system as a threat to national security and to the ability to fuel the nation's navy and army.

As a result, the Mineral Lands Leasing Act of 1920[23] withdrew oil and gas (among other minerals) from the purview of the 1872 Mining Law and instituted a system of leasing oil and gas. Oil and gas leasing onshore has gone through three systems. Initially, a party could get an exploration permit in areas that were not known to be valuable for oil and gas; if a discovery of petroleum was made, then the party would enter a lease with the federal government. Competitive bidding was required in geological areas known for oil and gas resources. This first system did not remain in place for long. The modern leasing era has been dominated by two leasing systems, which may be labeled the pre-1987 and post-1987 systems.

Before the Federal Onshore Oil and Gas Leasing Reform Act of 1987 (Leasing Reform Act),[24] lands in "Known Geological Structures" (KGSs) were leased by competitive bid. Lands outside a KGS were leased non-competitively, that is, to the first qualified applicant, without bidding or market value appraisal. Such lands could be valuable prospects for development because lands were placed in a KGS very conservatively. Alternatively, these lands could be rank wildcat acreage.

Two methods were used to determine who was the first qualified applicant for a non-competitive lease. For some lands, it would simply be the first person who filed an application "over the counter." Other lands, such as

---

[22] In 1955 Congress gave the federal government greater control of the surface resources; see 30 U.S.C. § 612(b).

[23] Now known as the Mineral Leasing Act and codified, as amended, at 30 U.S.C. §§ 181 et seq.

[24] Part of Title V of the Omnibus Budget Reconciliation Act of 1987 (P.L. 100-203), 101 Stat. 1330-256 et seq. (Leasing Reform Act).

those covered by an expiring lease that would become available for a new lease, could draw a crowd of potential applicants. These lands were placed in the simultaneous system. Their availability would be noted and all offers received by a specified date would be considered simultaneously filed. Each interested person, of course, wanted to be "first" at the magic moment of availability. A computer drawing would determine which application was to be deemed "first." This system was referred to as a "lottery," but because no one could have an interest in more than one offer to lease, the simultaneous system was not a true lottery.

To implement the various systems, the Mineral Leasing Act vests the Secretary of the Interior with lease issuance authority. The Bureau of Land Management (BLM) is the agency within the Department designated to carry out these functions. The BLM not only issued competitive leases, but issued many noncompetitive leases each year. For fiscal year 1987, it issued 576 over-the-counter leases and 5781 simultaneous system leases.[25] Competitive leases numbered 890.[26] These leases not only covered oil and gas underlying the public lands managed by the BLM, but also minerals in lands under the jurisdiction of the Forest Service, an agency of the Department of Agriculture. In these instances, the BLM maintained it had to be the final arbiter of the terms and conditions of leases impacting National Forests, but generally accepted recommendations from the Forest Service about the propriety of leasing and any necessary lease provisions. In the 1987 Leasing Reform Act, Congress declared that the BLM may not issue an oil and gas lease within a national forest over the objections of the Secretary of Agriculture.[27] Additionally, the Forest Service gained explicit control over surface-disturbing activities conducted pursuant to an oil and gas lease.

Other changes made by the Leasing Reform Act were more general and applied to leases outside of National Forests as well as within them. The Act abolished the distinction between lands within and without a KGS. All land must now be put up for competitive bidding before it can be leased noncompetitively.[28] Congress established a minimum bid of $2 per acre, which could be raised by regulation. The minimum bid would be deemed acceptable

---

[25] Bureau of Land Management, U.S. Department of the Interior, Public Land Statistics 1987, Table 39 at 60-63 (1988).

[26] *Id.* Table 38 at 58-59.

[27] 30 U.S.C. § 226(h). Prior to this, only if the lands in the forests were "acquired," as opposed to having never been privately owned, would the Forest Service have had a veto power. The terms of the special act dealing with leasing of acquired lands provided this limitation on BLM actions. 30 U.S.C. § 352.

[28] 30 U.S.C. §§ 226 (b)(1) and (c).

without reference to the lands' actual value. Market interest presumably would bring bids of the appropriate value if it would exceed the minimum. If no lease issues as the result of an auction, the first qualified applicant after 30 days may receive a lease.

Not all lands that might contain oil and gas must be leased by the federal government. The Secretary of the Interior has discretion not to lease particular lands for oil and gas exploration. The operative word in the enabling statute is "may": "All lands subject to disposition under [this Act] which are known or believed to contain oil and gas deposits may be leased by the Secretary."[29] The Leasing Reform Act did not change this provision. The discretionary wording affects not only initial leasing decisions, but also can affect subsequent lease development. If a lease is to be granted, the BLM may insert conditions in it to protect against degradation of surface or other resources. The Mineral Leasing Act, however, does not statutorily provide for phased development. Therefore, unless the Department of the Interior in the lease expressly retains the right to veto all proposed development, some oil and gas development must be allowed.[30]

2. Offshore

The greatest promise for continued domestic production of oil and natural gas lies in the offshore areas of the coastal United States in the continental shelf. The area of the United States continental shelf exceeds one billion acres. At the same time the potential for serious adverse environmental effects in the continental shelf from drilling leaks and accidents is also great.

The physical continental shelf is part of the sea bed adjacent to the coast called the continental margin. The continental margin is comprised of three distinct, geologic sections extending seaward from the coast: (1) the Continental Shelf proper, which descends gradually from the low-water mark of the coast to about 130 meters; (2) the Continental Slope, which borders the shelf and descends steeply to a depth of between 1,200 and 3,500 meters; (3) the Continental Rise beyond the slope, which is a less steep descend to depths of between 3,500 to 5,000 meters. The continental margin takes up about 20 percent of the world's ocean floor. Beyond the continental margin lies the deep seabed. Most oil production occurs in the geological

---

[29] 30 U.S.C. § 226(a).

[30] Sierra Club v. Peterson, 717 F.2d 1409 (D.C.C.A. 1983). See Marla E. Mansfield, *Through the Forest of the Onshore Oil and Gas Leasing Controversy Toward a Paradigm of NEPA Compliance*, 24 LAND & WATER L. REV. 85 (1989).

continental shelf, although the practical technology to drill in the deep seabed is becoming a reality.

The present generally accepted legal definition of the continental shelf is different from the physical definition. The 1982 Law of the Sea Convention in Article 76(1) sets out the present legal definition as follows (21 I.L.M. 1245, 1285 (1982)):

> The continental shelf of a coastal State comprises the sea-bed and subsoil of the submarine areas that extend beyond its territorial sea throughout the natural prolongation of its land territory to the outer edge of the continental margin, or to a distance of 200 nautical miles . . . [measured from the low-water mark of the coast in most cases] where the outer edge of the continental margin does not extend up to that distance.

Thus, portions of the sea-bed which lie beyond the continental margin but within 200 miles of the coast are included in the legal definition of the continental shelf as are areas beyond 200 miles that constitute the natural prolongation of the land territory. The United States in 1983 claimed a 200 mile exclusive economic zone in which the United States has exclusive natural resources jurisdiction of all waters and seabed extending 200 miles from shore.[31] The continental shelf in places is rich in oil and gas reserves. Commercial exploration of oil and natural gas offshore did not begin until just before World War II. However, by 1981 almost one fourth of the total world oil production came from offshore sources. In the United States, substantial continental shelf production occurs in the Gulf of Mexico, the Pacific Coast, and the areas offshore Alaska.

The leasing of oil and gas resources on the Outer Continental Shelf is governed by the Outer Continental Shelf Lands Act. The first OCS Act of 1953 did not provide a comprehensive leasing mechanism. It was mostly concerned with jurisdictional issues. The 1978 amendments substantially updated the Act to recognize intervening economic and environmental concerns.

---

[31] Presidential Proclamation No. 5030, March 10, 1983, THE LAW OF THE SEA: NATIONAL LEGISLATION OF THE EXCLUSIVE ECONOMIC ZONE, THE ECONOMIC ZONE, AND THE EXCLUSIVE FISHERIES ZONE (United Nations 1986). The Outer Continental Shelf Lands Leasing Act defines the "outer continental shelf" as "all submerged lands seaward [of lands ceded to the state in 43 U.S.C. § 1301] and of which the subsoil and seabed appertain to the United States and are subject to its jurisdiction and control. 43 U.S.C. § 1331.

The Supreme Court concluded that the entire Shelf, including coastal waters, was under federal control.[32] Congress, however, in 1953 passed the Submerged Lands Act which "released and relinquished" to the coastal states the part of the Shelf that extended out from the mean high tide line for three miles or to their historic boundaries. The companion OCS Lands Act of 1953 affirmed President Truman's jurisdictional declaration and provided a basic framework for mineral leasing.

In time, this framework was deemed insufficient. In 1978, Congress amended the Outer Continental Shelf Lands Act. 43 U.S.C. § 1331 *et seq.* Prior to the 1978 Amendments, an OCS lease was viewed as giving the lessee the right to eventually develop the resources, albeit subject to continuing supervision by the Department of the Interior for the protection of the environment. If the Department were to "suspend" drilling authorization necessary to the recovery of the mineral for an unreasonable time, however, it would be a "taking" of a property right, one which would require compensation.[33] The 1978 amendments introduced "phased" development, as explained in *Secretary of the Interior v. California*:[34]

> OCSLA was enacted in 1953 to authorize federal leasing of the OCS for oil and gas development. The Act was amended in 1978 to provide for the "expeditious and orderly development, subject to environmental safeguards," of resources on the OCS. 43 U.S.C. 1332(3) (1976 ed., Supp. III). As amended, OCSLA confirms that at least since 1978 the sale of a lease has been a distinct stage of the OCS administrative process, carefully separated from the issuance of a federal license or permit to explore, develop, or produce gas or oil on the OCS.
>
> Before 1978, OCSLA did not define the terms "exploration," "development," or "production." But it did define a "mineral lease" to be "any form of authorization for the exploration for, or development or removal of deposits of, oil, gas, or other minerals. . . ." 43 U.S.C. § 1331(c). The pre-1978 OCSLA did not specify what, if any, rights to explore, develop, or produce were transferred to the purchaser of a lease; the Act simply stated that a lease should "contain such rental provisions and such other terms and provisions as the Secretary may prescribe at the time of offering the area for lease." 43 U.S.C. § 1337(b)(4). . . .

---

[32] U.S. v. Louisiana, 339 U.S. 699 (1950), U.S. v. Texas, 339 U.S. 707 (1950), United States v. California, 332 U.S. 19 (1947).

[33] Union Oil Company of California v. Morton, 512 F.2d 743 (9th Cir. 1975).

[34] 464 U.S. 312 (1984)

The leases in dispute here, however, were sold in 1981. By then it was quite clear that a lease sale by Interior did not involve the submission or approval of "any plan for the exploration or development of, or production from" the leased tract. Under the amended OCSLA, the purchase of a lease entitles the purchaser only to priority over other interested parties in submitting for federal approval a plan for exploration, production, or development. Actual submission and approval or disapproval of such plans occurs separately and later.

Since 1978 there have been four distinct statutory stages to developing an offshore oil well: (1) formulation of a five year leasing plan by the Department of the Interior; (2) lease sales; (3) exploration by the lessees; (4) development and production. Each stage involves separate regulatory review that may, but need not, conclude in the transfer to lease purchasers of rights to conduct additional activities on the OCS. And each stage includes specific requirements for consultation with Congress, between federal agencies, or with the States.

The OCSLA expressly provides that the federal government could disapprove a plan for exploration if such a plan is not consistent with an applicable state coastal zone management plan unless the Secretary of Commerce finds that the plan is consistent with CZMA goals or in the interest of national security. The plan must also be disapproved if it would "probably cause serious harm or damage . . . to the marine, coastal, or human environment. . . ."[35] If a plan is disapproved for the latter reason, the Secretary may "cancel such lease and the lessee shall be entitled to compensation. . . ."[36] As for the production and development phase, the same provisions for and limitations on disapproval and cancellation apply. The reasons for cancellation are not as broad as the discretionary ability to reject leasing initially.[37] If the Department of the Interior fails to consider seriously a plan for exploration, it may be in breach of the lease terms.[38]

---

[35] 43 U.S.C. §§ 1334(a)(2)(A)(I), 1340(c)(1) (1976 ed., Supp. III).

[36] 43 U.S.C. § 1340(c)(1).

[37] Village of False Pass v. Clark, 733 F.2d 605 (9th Cir. 1984) (Canby, J., concurring in part and dissenting in part).

[38] Conoco Inc. v. United States, 35 Fed.Cl. 309 (1996), *reversed on other grounds*, Marathon Oil Co. v. U.S., 158 F.3d 1253 (Fed.Cir. 1998), *opinion withdrawn and superseded on rehearing*, 177 F.3d 1331 (Fed.Cir. 1999) (lack of consistency with the state's coastal management plan precluded development).

B.   Environmental Regulation of Oil and Gas[39]

A comprehensive discussion of the environmental regulation of the oil and gas industry in the United States is beyond the scope of this book.[40] The primary reason for this is that the United States has neither a national environmental policy nor a national energy policy that guides the formation and application of a uniform body of regulatory law. Governmental regulation of energy development (including oil and gas) and of the environment is often uncoordinated and in conflict. When viewed from a policy perspective, the adoption of statutes by Congress and state legislatures, the issuance of regulations by executive branch agencies and the rendering of federal and state court decisions appear rather aimless and haphazard.

The law and regulation of the petroleum industry that does exist in the United States, for the most part, has arisen in response to isolated factual events like oil spills, abrupt changes in petroleum prices, or dramatic changes in governmental power caused by elections. For example, the Oil Pollution Act (OPA) of 1990, which is addressed in more detail below, was a direct federal legislative response to the March 1989 Exxon Valdez eleven million gallon crude oil spill in Prince William Sound Alaska.[41] Similarly, the fuel economy standards imposed by federal government regulators on automobiles in 1975 were a direct response to the dramatic upward spike in oil prices caused by the 1973 Arab oil embargo (imposed on the United States as a result of its support for Israel during the Arab-Israeli war). Here, crude oil prices increased more than sixfold from $1.77 per barrel near the end of 1973 to $11.65 per barrel at the start of 1974. This prompted price and allocation regulation of petroleum.[42] The calls for a legislative rollback of federal environmental laws in the mid-1990s were a direct consequence of the Republican landslide victory in the 1994 Congressional elections. The regulatory result has been a confusing, incomplete, web of laws, regulations, and court decisions that sometimes bear little relation to

---

[39] This section is drawn directly from: James E. Hickey, Jr. *Environmental Regulation of The Oil and Gas Industry in the U.S.A.*, Chapter 8 of ENVIRONMENTAL REGULATION OF OIL AND GAS (GAO ed.1998).

[40] *See* Chapter Five on Environmental Protection and Energy Development.

[41] Paul S. Edelman, *The Oil Pollution Act of 1990*, NYLJ, Sept. 7, 1990 at 3; John H. Cushman, Jr., *Conferees Agree on Bill to Cover Cost of Oil Spills: Passage Expected in July*, N.Y. TIMES, June 29, 1990, at A1.

[42] *See* the Emergency Petroleum Allocation Act of 1973, P.L. 93-159, 87 Stat. 626; the Energy Policy and Conservation Act of 1975 and of 1976, P.L. 94-163, 89 Stat. 871 and P.L. 94-385, 90 Stat. 1125; *see also* Joseph P. Tomain and James E. Hickey, Jr. ENERGY LAW AND POLICY (1989) at 231-257 (hereinafter Tomain and Hickey).

one another, that often leave serious gaps in energy and environmental regulation, and that occasionally may produce results not intended by the lawmakers.

❬ The picture of environmental regulation of the petroleum industry is confused further by the intrusion of American common law principles like the rule of capture,[43] the public trust doctrine,[44] and the correlative rights doctrine.[45] Still other relevant law comes from state statutes concerned with financial conservation but which nevertheless affect environmental conservation. That state law includes statutes on spacing of oil and gas wells, on unitization of oil fields[46] and on real estate zoning.

❬ The federal environmental statute that has created the greatest recent stir in the petroleum industry is the federal Oil Pollution Act of 1990 (OPA).[47] The OPA establishes for the first time in the United States a more

---

[43] *Supra* note 10, and Tomain and Hickey, *supra* note 39, at 225-229. The rule of capture in its broadest form recognized no legal right by a landowner to protect petroleum in common pools underneath the land surface other than by extracting it before anyone else.

[44] The public trust doctrine generally refers to a state's duty to protect the natural resource interests of its citizens by means that include the imposition of limits on environmental damage, and the establishment of public access to various resources, such as water. *See generally*, Joseph L. Sax, *The Public Trust Doctrine in Natural Resource Law: Effective Judicial Intervention*, 68 MICH.LREV. 471 (1970).

[45] The correlative rights doctrine first emerged in the oil and gas setting to reconcile rights to a truly common resource, an underground oil and gas reservoir from which all owners of minerals overlying the pool have rights to remove oil and gas. As the Supreme Court in Ohio Oil Co. v. Indiana explained: "It follows from the essence of their right and from the situation of the things, as to which it can be exerted, that the use by one of his power to seek to convert a part of the common fund to actual possession may result in an undue proportion being attributed to one of the possessors of the right to the detriment of the others, or by waste by one or more to the annihilation of the rights of the remainder." Marla E. Mansfield, *Private Rights Meet Public Rights: The Problems of Labeling and Regulatory Takings*, 65 U. COLO. L. REV. 193, 207 (1994) (footnotes omitted). *See* Phillips Petroleum v. Mississippi, 484 U.S. 469 (1988).

[46] *Supra* notes 14-16, and Tomain and Hickey, *supra* note 39 at 228. Under state unitization leases common petroleum pools were consolidated to assure each producer a proportional share in the oil produced from a common pool without regard to the particular well from which it was received.

[47] 33 U.S.C.A. § 2701-2761 (West Supp. 1995). This discussion of the OPA was drawn substantially from James E. Hickey, Jr., *Environmental Regulation of the Oil and Gas Industry in the U.S.A.* in ENVIRONMENTAL REGULATION OF THE OIL AND GAS INDUSTRY (1998) 215, 223-7. *See also* William H. Rodgers, Jr., ENVIRONMENTAL LAW (2d ed. 1994) at 375-92; Celia Campbell-Mohn, et al, ENVIRONMENTAL LAW FROM

or less comprehensive scheme governing oil pollution of United States waters. It addresses, among other things, legal liability, payments for monitoring and responses to oil spills, federal authority to order removal of oil, licensing standards for tanker personnel (the so-called "drunken captain" problem), double-hull construction for tankers, pollution prevention plans for onshore and offshore locations, and criminal and civil penalties for the failure of those responsible to obey its provisions.

1.   *The Scope of Liability*

Before the OPA was passed, government regulation of oil spills was minimal and U.S. environmental laws did not address oil spills in a comprehensive or systematic way. The legal liability of the industry for the harm done by oil spills from tankers, barges and offshore facilities was extremely limited. Liability had been limited in part to protect the U.S. shipping industry as a matter of maritime law, in part because of restrictive common law requirements on parties' standing to sue, and in part because the petroleum industry had, for various reasons, escaped the brunt of most statutory environmental schemes that generally broadened the liability of polluters.[48]

With some notable exceptions, this meant that liability of the owners of oil tankers and offshore oil facilities was limited to the after-spill value of the vessel, which could be very little.[49] The owners of the oil cargo that was spilled generally were not liable.[50] In addition, the only persons capable of suing successfully for oil spill damages were those that experienced actual physical harm to legal property interests.[51] If an oil spill tainted fish in the ocean, and killed sea birds, marine mammals and marine vegetation, there was no liability because these were unowned "wild animals" in which no one had a property interest until actually caught.[52] Similarly, because lost

---

RESOURCES TO RECOVERY (West 1993); Jeffery D. Morgan, *The Oil Pollution Act of 1990: A Look at Its Impact on the Oil Industry*, 6 FORDHAM ENVT'L. L.J. 1 (1994).

[48] For example, the enactment of the sweeping 1980 CERCLA statute, 42 U.S.C.A. §§ 9601-9675 (West 1995), exempted oil from its definition of "hazardous substances" in § 9601 (14).

[49] Compensation for the $8,000,000 of clean-up costs in the Torrey Canyon oil spill was limited to the value of one lifeboat that survived the accident.

[50] 42 U.S.C.A. § 9607(a) (West 1995).

[51] *See generally* Union Oil Company v. Oppen, 501 F.2d 558 (9th Cir.1974).

[52] *See* Pierson v. Post, (1805), N.Y. Sup. Ct., 3 Caines 175 and Hammonds v. Central Kentucky Natural Gas Co., 256 Ky. 685, 75 S.W.2d 204 (1934). A special exception to this rule of capture was established in the 1970s by the United States courts which permitted commercial fishermen to sue for economic losses caused by the Santa Barbara, California oil spill of 1969. *See* Union Oil Company v. Oppen,

profits or economic harm were not grounds upon which a lawsuit could rest, recovery was denied for the loss of income by, for example, shipping interests that were unable to traverse an oil spill area, or businesses that lost money like coastal bait and tackle shops, seafood restaurants, and marina owners and boat lessors.

Some inroads were made to this limited liability scheme by selected statutes that addressed specific locations or specific activities (e.g., the Deepwater Port Act[53] and the TransAlaska Pipeline Authorization Act[54]). For the most part, however, liability for oil spills in the United States remained very limited.

The OPA now greatly expands the number and types of parties that can sue for oil spills and the parties that can be sued. It also substantially increases the amounts that can be recovered under oil spill law suits.

Under the OPA, parties who suffer only economic losses from oil pollution, like owners of hotels, seaside restaurants, bait and tackle shops, and pleasure boat lessors, may now all sue for damages resulting from an oil spill in United States waters.[55] This is in addition to property owners suffering direct physical damage from oil spills. Even members of Native American tribes may sue if they can establish that the natural resources upon which they rely for subsistence are damaged even though those subsistence resources are unowned wild animals or natural habitat.

Federal and state governments also may sue for damages for the loss of taxes, royalties, rents, fees, or profits brought about by injury to property or natural resources.[56] States also may sue for damages for the costs of providing additional public services in response to an oil spill such as protection of the public from fire, safety, or health hazards.

Under the OPA, any "responsible party" may be sued for the consequences of an oil spill.[57] This includes "any person owning, operating, or demise chartering a vessel."[58] With respect to offshore oil facilities, the OPA defines "responsible party" as the "lessee or permittee of the area in which

---

noted above.

[53] 33 U.S.C.A. §§ 1501-1524 (West 1986 & Supp. 1995).

[54] 43 U.S.C.A. §§ 1651-1656 (West 1986 & Supp. 1995).

[55] 33 U.S.C.A. § 2702(a)(b)(2)(B) (West Supp. 1995).

[56] 33 U.S.C.A. § 2702(b)(2)(D) (West Supp. 1995).

[57] 33 U.S.C.A. § 2702(a) (West Supp. 1995).

[58] 33 U.S.C.A. § 2701 (32)(A) (West Supp. 1995). "Demise chartering" is a form of bareboat charter under which the charterer takes a fully outfitted and equipped vessel and takes full responsibility for operating, maintaining, repairing and insuring costs, as if the charterer were the owner of the vessel.

the facility is located or the holder of a right of use and easement."[59] (As before the OPA, the owner of the oil cargo aboard the vessel is not a "responsible party" and cannot be sued for oil spill damages.[60] A responsible party is strictly liable both for damages and for oil removal costs.[61] A responsible party may establish a defense to liability only if it can be proved that the sole cause of the discharge was an act of God, an act of war, or an act or omission of a third party.[62] Thus, oil cargo owners now have a statutory incentive both not to own the tankers that carry their cargo,[63] and not to transport into the United States crude oil or heavy fuel products that cause more harm than clean oil products if a spill occurs.

Not only is the scope of persons who can sue and be sued for oil spills expanded under the OPA, but the limits on liability are greatly increased.[64] For tankers greater than 3,000 gross tons, the limit on liability is the greater of $1,200 per gross ton or $10 million.[65] For tankers between 300 and 3000 gross tons, the limit is the greater of $1,200 per gross ton or $2 million.[66] For all other vessels, the limit is the greater of $600 per gross ton or $500,000.[67] The liability limit for offshore facilities is $75 million plus the cost of cleanup.

(Notwithstanding the OPA's liability limits, potentially responsible parties may not rest assured that they will be entitled to invoke those liability limits.) The statute provides for unlimited liability in the event of gross negligence, wilful misconduct, failure to report a spill, failure to cooperate in connection with spill clean-up, or violation of an applicable federal safety, construction, or operating regulation.[68] In the Exxon Valdez case, a federal jury found that the Exxon Corporation was reckless when it permitted Captain Hazelwood, who had a history of alcohol abuse, to

---

[59] 33 U.S.C.A. § 2701(32)(C) (West Supp. 1995).

[60] 33 U.S.C.A.§§ 2701(32)(A)-(F) and (West Supp. 1995).

[61] 33 U.S.C.A. § 2702(a) (West Supp. 1995).

[62] 33 U.S.C.A. § 2703(a)(l)-(4) (West Supp. 1995).

[63] See Matthew L. Wald, Oil Companies Rethink Risks of Having Tankers, N.Y. TIMES, June 13, 1990 at A27.

[64] 33 U.S.C.A. § 2704(a) (West Supp. 1995).

[65] 33 U.S.C.A. § 2704(a)(1)(A)(B)(I) (West Supp. 1995).

[66] 33 U.S.C.A. § 2704(a)(1)(A)(B)(ii) (West Supp. 1995).

[67] 33 U.S.C.A. § 2704(a)(1) and (2) (West Supp. 1995).

[68] 33 U.S.C.A. § 2704(c)(1)(A)(B) (West Supp. 1995).

command a supertanker.[69] Such a finding under the OPA opens the door to unlimited liability.

∠In addition, the OPA does not pre-empt the authority of individual states to impose additional liability on parties responsible for discharging oil.[70] Indeed, the OPA specifically provides that the pre-existing Limitation of Liability Act does not pre-empt state law.[71] Thus, the OPA provides no guaranteed liability limits protection for responsible parties sued under state law.

2. Certification of Financial Responsibility

Owners of vessels and offshore facilities must obtain a Certificate of Responsibility (COFR) from the United States Coast Guard.[72] To get a COFR, owners must show their ability to pay the clean-up costs and damages for which they are responsible under the OPA.[73] If vessels do not have a COFR, they may be seized by the Coast Guard and may be fined $25,000 per day.[74] Specifically, owners of vessels over 300 gross tons must be able to prove financial responsibility in an amount equal to their maximum liability exposure which now can be very great indeed (as explained above).[75] Owners of offshore facilities must maintain evidence of financial responsibility equaling $150 million.[76] This is a dramatic increase of $115 million for facilities located in the outer continental shell. For independent oil producers operating in United States offshore waters, this presents a serious and inhibiting financial burden.

Insurance has been the standard means by which financial responsibility has been established to get a COFR prior to the OPA. If financial

---

[69] See Keith Schneider, *Jury Finds Exxon Acted Reckless in Valdez Oil Spill*, N.Y. TIMES, June 14, 1994, at A1; see In re Exxon Valdez, no. CIV.A. 89-0095 (HRH), 1995 WL 527988 (D. Alaska, 27 January 1995), Order no. 267, in which the Court denied Exxon Corporation's attempt to have a new trial on a jury's award of $5 billion in punitive damages as a result of the reckless conduct that caused the Exxon Valdez oil spill in Prince William Sound, Alaska.

[70] 33 U.S.C.A. § 2718(a)(1)(A) (West Supp. 1995).

[71] *Id.*

[72] 33 U.S.C.A. § 2716 (West Supp. 1995).

[73] 33 U.S.C.A. § 2716(a).

[74] 33 U.S.C.A. § 2716(b)(3) and s. 2716a(a) (West Supp. 1995).

[75] 33 U.S.C.A. § 2716(a)(1) (West Supp. 1995).

[76] 33 U.S.C.A. § 2716(c)(1) (West Supp. 1995). The definition of "offshore facilities" under the OPA is broad and the COFR requirements might apply to secondary structures like pipelines, fuel docks and storage tanks.

responsibility is accomplished through insurance, the insurer must become a "guarantor" and may be sued directly by injured parties.

The implications for an insurer-guarantor are far greater than they have been in the past, because under the OPA the liability of a responsible party is now potentially unlimited (as mentioned above). That is, the potential dollar liability of insurers as "guarantors" now of a responsible party is not limited, as is usually the case, by the policies that they write or by the amount paid by the parties they insure. This creates an understandable reluctance on the part of insurers to insure oil tankers sailing to the United States. Of course, if a vessel owner cannot get insurance, it cannot show financial responsibility and cannot obtain a COFR. If vessel owners have no COFR, they cannot enter United States waters. At the time the OPA was enacted, some feared that the flow of imported oil would be hampered.

3.   Double-Hull Tanker Requirements[77]

The OPA double-hull tanker requirements have been summarized as follows:

> all newly constructed tank vessels must have double hulls; existing single hull tankers must be phased out beginning in 1995; and by 2010, all vessels over 5,000 gross tons with single hulls will be prohibited from operating until they are converted to double hulls.[78]

There are exceptions to the double-hull tanker requirements, the most notable of which is that vessels unloading oil at a deepwater port more than 60 miles from shore may be single-hulled.[79] The issue of double-hull tankers was hotly debated during the enactment process of the OPA in part because they are more expensive to build, in part because it was charged that they will increase the price of oil and oil products, and in part because some charged that a double-hull requirement would adversely affect the spot market for oil where cheap, old, tankers tend to operate.[80] There also was concern expressed that the OPA's potential unlimited liability for owners

---

[77] 46 U.S.C.A. § 3703a (West Pamphlet 1995).

[78] Russell V. Randle, *The Oil Pollution Act of 1990: Its Provisions, Intent, and Effects*, 21 ENVT'L LAW REP. 10119, 10132 (March 1991).

[79] 46 U.S.C.A. § 3703a(b)(3)(A)(B)(ii) (West Supp. 1995).

[80] *See* Jeffrey D. Morgan, *The Oil Pollution Act of 1990: A Look at Its Impact on the Oil Industry*, 6 FORDHAM ENV'TL L.J. 1 (1994).

would "chill" mortgage lending to finance the new tankers because lenders would fear being classified as a owner.

The OPA at the time of enactment was characterized variously as a self-inflicted "oil blockade," a "train wreck" piece of legislation that will stop all shipping activity in United States waters, a statute that will lead to an epidemic of oil spills, and a law that will cause a drastic corporate restructuring of the oil industry.[81] However, an assessment of the OPA after five years does not bear out those dire predictions.

(a)   Oil imports to the United States did not stop. In the five years after enactment the flow of oil imports into the United States increased, not decreased, to at or near 50 per cent of all oil used.[82]

(b)   Oil spills from vessels and offshore facilities did not increase. There were a lower number of spills and those were of lesser magnitude per year in United States waters than prior to 1990.[83]

(c)   Vessel owners did not boycott United States waters. With some exceptions, most vessel owners continue to carry oil to the United States.[84]

(d)   Some corporate restructuring of the oil industry has occurred in response to the OPA (especially the double-hull tanker require-ments), but it does not seem to have seriously affected the flow of oil into the United States.[85]

(e)   The number of tankers receiving COFRs increased from a few hundred in mid-November 1994 to about 12,000 by January 1995.[86]

(f)   It is likely that over the long term more tankers will have double-hulls and meet the construction standards under the OPA. Along the way, construction deadlines may be adjusted and enforcement may have to be temporarily relaxed.

---

[81] *Id.* 13, 16-17. *See also* Matthew L. Wald, *Oil Companies Rethink Risks of Having Tankers*, N.Y. TIMES, June 13, 1990, at A27.

[82] At the end of June 1999, The United States was importing well over half of its crude oil supply <http://www.eia.doe.gov>.

[83] *Decline Listed for Spills Off the United States*, OIL & GAS J., October 5, 1992 at 30.

[84] Morgan, *supra* note 77 at 7-9.

[85] *Id.* at 9-11.

[86] Mark Morrison, *The United States Oil Pollution Act 1990: Certificates of Financial Responsibility—What Was the Problem?* 13 OIL & GAS L. AND TAXATION REV., May 1995, at 204-206.

VI. INTERNATIONAL LAW

Transnational elements of the oil and gas fuel cycle including concession contracts, joint operating agreements, joint venture agreements and other international contracts may involve private international law and both "hard" and "soft" public international law.[87] The public international law involvement is most pervasive in the areas of pollution and environmental quality.[88]

A. Hard Law

There are a number of global[89] international treaties that affect the environment and various phases of the oil and gas fuel cycle including the following:

1. *The 1992 United Nations Convention on Biological Diversity*[90]

This treaty potentially may affect the phases of the fuel cycle that interfere with preservation of the planet's biodiversity. In Articles 7 and 8 the treaty requires the identification and monitoring of activities likely to have significant adverse effects on conservation of biodiversity. It may require establishment of protected areas to conserve biological diversity. Thus, production, transportation, refining and end use of oil and gas that threatens biodiversity by disturbing land (onshore or offshore) plants, trees, atmosphere and climate may run afoul of the Biodiversity treaty.

---

[87] *See* Chapter Four on International Law.

[88] *See* the partial listing of international law treaties affecting oil pollution, *supra* at V-25 to V-27.

[89] There are a number of regional international treaties that also address the environment and oil and gas fuel cycles including: the 1994 Energy Charter Treaty 33 I.L.M. 360 (1995); the 1992 OSPAR Convention (North East Atlantic Marine Pollution Treaty), 32 I.L.M. 1069 (1993), entered into force March 25, 1998) replacing the 1972 Oslo and 1974 Paris Conventions, 11 I.L.M. 262 (1972) and 13 I.L.M. 352 (1974); and the UNEP regional seas conventions comprised of 13 regional seas and 29 treaties (*see* Johnson and Enomoto, *Regional Approaches to the Protection and Conservation of the Marine Environment*, THE ENVIRONMENTAL LAW OF THE SEA, 324-37 (D. Johnson ed. 1981).

[90] 31 I.L.M. 822 (1992). (Not in force).

2. The 1992 United Nations Framework Convention on Climate Change[91]

This framework treaty specifically addresses global warming and the need to cut greenhouse gas emissions coming from such sources as oil and gas fired power plants and from car, truck and airplane "tailpipe" emissions. This treaty requires the development of national inventories of greenhouse gas emissions and programs to reduce or stop them. It also contemplates more detailed measures such as the Kyoto Protocol discussed below.

3. The 1997 Kyoto Protocol[92]

The Kyoto Protocol represents an attempt to enforce with specific timetables and commitments the voluntary general commitments of the Climate Change Convention. The United States signed the Protocol but has not yet ratified it primarily because developing nations have not, in its view, meaningfully participated in the Protocol's obligations and commitments.

The Protocol commits ratifying industrialized nations to cut anthropogenic (human-produced) emissions of carbon dioxide, methane, nitrous oxide, hydroflurocarbons, perfluorocarbons and sulfur hexaflouride by 2012. This would require industrialized nations like the United States to reduce fossil fuel used by the equivalent of around 20 to 30 million barrels of oil a day.[93] This would in turn require, among other things, greater power plant efficiency, fuel conversion at power plants from coal to natural gas, and conservation efforts to reduce demand.

Developing countries, like Mexico or Thailand, are not obligated to limit greenhouse gases at all. Energy consumption in these countries is rapidly increasing with increased industrialization, increased economic growth, increases in population, and increases in energy demand.

4. The 1982 United Nations Convention on the Law of the Sea

This treaty affects both offshore oil and gas production in the continental shelf, pollution by oil tankers through discharges and spills, and

---

[91] 31 I.L.M. 849 (1992).

[92] 37 I.L.M. 22 (1998). For a concise discussion of the Kyoto Protocol, see William L. Thomas, *The Kyoto Protocol: A Factor in Foreign Investment in Mexico*, 137 (No. 8) PUB. UTIL. FORT. 40 (April 15, 1999) and *The Kyoto Protocol: History, Facts, Figures and Projections*, 137 (No. 8) PUB. UTIL. FORT. 48 (April 15, 1999).

[93] Energy Information Agency, INTERNATIONAL ENERGY OUTLOOK 2 (1998).

land-based pollution from the use of oil and gas that reaches the marine environment through the air, run-off and pipeline discharges.[94] For example, it requires, in article 194, the prevention, reduction and control of pollution of the oceans from "installations and devices used in exploration of the natural resources of the seabed and subsoil" (ie., oil and gas in the continental shelf).

5. *The 1973 MARPOL and the 1978 MARPOL Protocol*

These treaties address the ocean transportation of oil and gas by prohibiting discharges of oil and oil mixtures into the marine environment.

6. *The 1972 Convention on the Prevention of Marine Pollution by Dumping of Wastes and Other Matter (The London Dumping Convention)*[95]

This treaty applies to all ocean areas except internal waters and aims to protect the marine environment from certain kinds of pollutants. It affects in particular the offshore production phase of the oil and gas fuel cycle. It includes disposal of offshore oil installations and platforms by decommissioning or abandonment within the definition of dumping.[96]

7. *The 1958 Geneva Conventions on the Continental Shelf,*[97] *and the High Seas*[98]

The High Seas Convention sets a broad mandate in Article 24 that requires states to prevent pollution of oil by discharges from pipelines or from oil platforms and installations. The Continental Shelf Convention prohibits oil and gas wells offshore from unjustifiably interfering with marine conservation efforts. It calls for the establishment of 500 meter safety zones

---

[94] 21 I.L.M. 1261 (1982). The United States is not a party. However, it can be expected to become a party in the foreseeable future. In 1994, the United States signed an agreement that would resolve its objections to the Law of the Sea Treaty. *See* Jonathan Charney, Bernard Oxman, and Louis Sohn, *Law of the Sea Forum: 1994 Agreement On Implementation of the Seabed Provisions On The Law of The Sea*, 8 AM. J. INT'L L. 687 (1994).

[95] 11 I.L.M. 1291 (1972).

[96] *See* discussion of the Brent Spar in Chapter Four on International Law.

[97] 15 UST 499. The United States is a Party.

[98] 13 UST 2312. The United States is a Party.

around drilling platforms and calls for the removal of abandoned oil and gas installations.

These provisions now are replaced by the 1982 Law of Sea Treaty for states that become parties to it.

B.   Soft Law[99]

There are numerous international soft law instruments that relate to the oil and gas fuel cycles and the environment. Some of the more note-worthy soft law instruments include the 1972 Stockholm Declaration,[100] the Rio Declaration and Agenda 21,[101] UNEP Guidelines on Offshore Mining and Drilling,[102] and the IMO Guidelines and Codes on offshore installations.[103]

Hard law and soft law may work in tandem to address the rights and duties of international actors. A good example of this relates to the trans-portation phase of the oil fuel cycles dealing specifically with international law answers to crude oil pollution from ocean tanker accidents.

For over 20 years, coastal states, oil tanker owners and oil companies have addressed liability and compensation for oil pollution damage through the 1969 International Convention on Civil Liability for Oil Pollution Dam-age (CLC),[104] which constitutes hard law agreed to by states, and through two soft law instruments agreed to by oil tanker owners and oil companies. The two soft law instruments were TOVALOP (The Tankers Owners Voluntary Agreement Concerning Liability for Oil Pollution) and CRISTAL (Contract Regarding an Interim Supplement to Tanker Liability for Oil Pollution) (oil companies.) These voluntary agreements were intended to fill the gaps in the CLC by mitigating oil pollution from tankers and by compensating for damage done by oil pollution from tankers. TOVALOP and CRYSTAL ended with the conclusion of two treaties, the 1992 protocol to the

---

[99] *See* Chapter Four on International Law.

[100] *See* Chapter Five on Environmental Protection and Energy Development.

[101] *Id.*

[102] UNITED NATIONS ENVIRONMENT PROGRAMME, ENVIRONMENTAL LAW GUIDELINES AND PRINCIPLES: OFFSHORE MINING AND DRILLING (1982).

[103] *See* Chapter Four on International Law.

[104] 9 I.L.M. 45 (entered into force June 19, 1975). The United States is not a party. *See generally* Wu Chao, POLLUTION FROM THE CARRIAGE OF OIL BY SEA: LIABILITY AND COMPENSATION (1996).

CLC and the 1992 protocol to the International Convention on the Establishment of an International Fund for Oil Pollution Damage.[105] ✌

---

[105] The United States is not a party to either protocol. *See* Susan Bloodworth, *Death On the High Seas: The Demise of TOVALOP and CRISTAL*, 13 J. LAND USE & ENVTL. L. 443 (1998); Wu Chao, *supra* note 101 at 387-398.

CHAPTER EIGHT

Natural Gas

by Suedeen G. Kelly

I. INTRODUCTION TO NATURAL GAS

Natural gas is a desirable energy source today because it is inexpensive and clean, when compared with other energy sources, and is currently plentiful in the U.S. Proved natural gas reserves in the U.S. rose to 167.2 trillion cubic feet (Tcf) in 1997 for the fourth consecutive year of increase in reserves in spite of four consecutive years of increased production.[1] Domestic production was about <u>19 trillion cubic feet</u>.[2] Proved reserve additions come from unproven volumes of gas in known fields or new fields through the exploration and development process. The majority of proved reserves are located in the Gulf Coast area. The U.S. Department of Energy reports that the U.S. has a <u>technically recoverable resource base of 1,156 Tcf of natural gas</u>, exclusive of Alaskan gas.[3] The U.S. Department of Energy projects that natural gas will increase from its current share of 24% of the energy consumed in the U.S. to about 28% in the next twenty years (see Figure 1). An increase in consumption is expected because natural gas is lower in cost and greater in supply than other fossil fuels, the infrastructure needed to produce and transport it already exists, and it emits fewer air pollutants than most other fossil fuels.[4]

The natural gas industry has been transformed over the last twenty years from a highly regulated industry to one based on competitive markets. The energy crises of the 1970s propelled significant deregulation and restructuring of the industry and the emergence of a market that sets price and quantity of natural gas supplies.

---

[1] Energy Information Administration (EIA), NATURAL GAS 1998: ISSUES AND TRENDS 11 (1999).

[2] EIA, *Annual Energy Review 1998: Natural Gas, Table 6.1 Natural Gas Overview, 1949-1998* (visited July 29, 1999) <http://www.eia.doe.gov/pub/energy. overview/aer98/txt/aer0601.txt>.

[3] EIA, *supra* note 1.

[4] See EIA, *supra* note 1, at 49.

Figure 1: Energy Flow, 1998 (Quadrillion Btu)
Source: EIA, Annual Energy Review 1998 www.eia.doe.gov

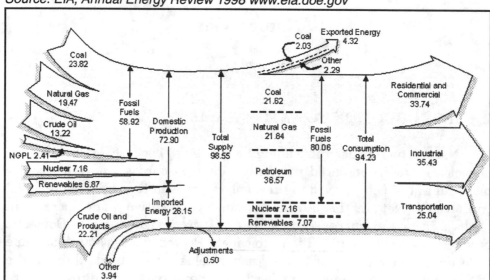

This transition began with the 1978 phase-out of price controls on gas at the wellhead. The next phase of change involved operation of interstate pipeline companies in the mid-1980s as common carriers. Previously, pipelines operated as private carriers. This change allowed the unbundling of the interstate sale of transportation from the sale of the gas itself, thus facilitating the growth of the natural gas market. Numerous states have followed this lead, providing for the unbundling of the distribution of gas from the sale of gas. Pipelines and local distribution companies still have a monopoly on the transportation of gas, and remain subject to economic regulation. However, even in this regulatory arena, the federal and state governments are moving from traditional rate of return regulation, with its comprehensive price control, to greater reliance on market mechanisms and alternative regulation.

II. THE NATURAL GAS FUEL CYCLE

Although gas is usually found with oil, the development of the gas industry lagged behind that of oil. In the early stages of American oil exploration, natural gas was considered a nuisance. It was dangerously explosive and required expensive separate pipelines or other capital intensive systems to move it or to store it. No valuable use of it could be made at the wellhead. Consequently, petroleum producers proceeded to eliminate it by flaring it, or simply venting it, at the wellhead. Not until the states passed laws prohibiting flaring and pipeline technology advanced, could the natural gas industry develop.

By the 1940s, gas was moving by pipeline from Texas and Louisiana to the population centers of the Midwest, the Atlantic Coast and the Northeast. Initially, a three-part gas industry developed: the producers, the long-distance transporters (pipeline companies), and the local distributors (gas utility companies). The pipeline companies were the lynch-pins of the industry. Typically, they entered into long-term contracts upstream with producers to buy gas, and entered into contracts downstream with local distribution companies to sell gas and deliver it to them.

The gas industry was restructured in the mid-1980s by Congressional and regulatory actions. Congress eliminated price controls on gas at the wellhead. The Federal Energy Regulatory Commission required interstate pipelines to sell transportation of gas separately from the sale of gas itself ("unbundling" of services), transforming pipeline companies into common carriers. Many states have followed the federal lead and required their local distribution companies to unbundle distribution and gas sales services. As a result, many wholesale and large retail gas consumers are now buying gas directly from producers or gas marketers. Concomitantly, the natural gas industry has evolved into one with four phases to its fuel cycle: production, pipeline transportation, local distribution, and marketing.

A.   Production

Gas is commonly found with oil in subsurface reservoirs and, therefore, its exploration and production is similar to that discussed earlier for oil.[5] Gas is found in the interstices of porous reservoir rocks—commonly sandstones, limestones, and dolomites. Gas is almost always found in solution with oil, and will sometimes form a "gas cap" within the reservoir, due to the weight differential between gas and oil. It is recovered through drilling a well into the reservoir. Low pressure at the wellbore initiates the movement of the gas or oil through the permeable reservoir rock toward the well. While there are thousands of gas producers, the major ones are the major oil companies.

Today, all but nineteen of the states produce natural gas. The major gas-producing states are Texas, Oklahoma, Louisiana, New Mexico, Kansas,

---

[5] *See* the Fuel Cycle section of Chapter Seven, *supra*.

and Alaska.[6] Three states, Texas, Oklahoma, and Louisiana, account for over half of the total natural gas produced in the U.S.[7] Texas itself produced about 37% of total U.S. production in 1998.[8] Offshore well drilling technology has made offshore sites more important over the last twenty years, and about one-fifth of domestic production today comes from offshore wells.[9] About half of the U.S.'s technically recoverable reserves of gas, exclusive of Alaskan gas, lies under federal lands, evenly divided between onshore and offshore lands. Environmental concerns about drilling have led to moratoria in drilling on many federal lands. For example, drilling is prohibited off the U.S. East and West coasts (except for a few areas off the Southern California coast), and the West coast of Florida. Drilling is permitted off the Arctic coast in the Gulf of Alaska and in Cook Inlet.

Since the mid-1980s when the strict price regulation of imported gas was lifted, foreign gas producers have sold significant volumes of gas in the U.S. Imports accounted for about 14% of total U.S. consumption in 1998.[10]

By far the largest exporter of gas to the U.S. is Canada. Import levels from Canada have steadily risen along with total imports over the last ten years, but Canada has consistently provided about 98% of the total imported gas supply due to its competitiveness with U.S. market prices. Algeria and Mexico have played minor roles. From 1984 to 1992, Mexico did not export any natural gas to the U.S. Mexico resumed minor levels of export in 1993. Import of Algerian liquefied natural gas (LNG) increased during the energy crisis of the 1970s, but ceased by 1987 due to its high prices. Algerian imports resumed in 1988 and have continued at modest levels. Australia and the United Arab Emirates recently started exporting very small amounts of gas to the U.S.[11]

---

[6] EIA, NATURAL GAS PRODUCTIVE CAPACITY FOR THE LOWER 48 STATES 1986 THROUGH 1998, at 6 (1997). *See also* EIA, HISTORICAL NATURAL GAS ANNUAL 1930 THROUGH 1998, *Table 5, Gross Withdrawals and Marketed Production of Natural Gas by State, 1967-1997 (1998).*

[7] EIA, *Energy in the United States: A Brief History and Current Trends* (visited July 23, 1999) <http://www.eia.gov/emeu/aer/eh1998/eh1998.html>.

[8] *Id. See also* EIA, *Annual Energy Review 1998: Natural Gas, Table 6.4: Natural Gas Withdrawals by State and Location and Gas Well Productivity, 1960-1998* (visited July 29, 1999) <http://www.eia.doe.gov/pub/energy.overview/aer98/txt/aer0604.txt>.

[9] EIA, *supra* note 2.

[10] EIA, *Annual Energy Review 1998: Natural Gas, Table 6.3 Natural Gas Imports, Exports, and Net Imports, 1949-1998* (visited July 29, 1999) <http://www.eia.doe.gov/pub/energy.overview/aer98/txt/aer0603.txt>.

[11] *Id.*

B. Pipeline Transportation

Natural gas is usually transported by pipeline. It can be liquefied and transported by tanker if necessary, but this process is expensive and dangerous. In the U.S., liquefied natural gas accounts for only a small fraction of total gas consumption.

Gas is gathered from wells through "gathering lines," processed as necessary,[12] and then transmitted by pipeline from the field to the consumers. Long-haul trunk lines take the gas from the field to the population centers where gas then enters the local distribution system. The point of entry of gas into the local distribution system is commonly called the "city gate."

About fifty major pipeline companies move most of the interstate gas in the U.S.[13] Pipelines are categorized for regulatory purposes as either interstate or intrastate. Interstate pipelines are those that are engaged in the transportation of natural gas in interstate commerce, or in the sale in interstate commerce of gas for resale. Intrastate pipelines are those that transport gas solely within the borders of a state, or into a foreign state, without at any point crossing the border of another state of the U.S. Interstate pipelines are regulated by the Federal Energy Regulatory Commission (FERC), while intrastate pipelines are subject to regulation by the state in which they are located.[14]

The gas industry is not vertically integrated. Generally, production, pipeline, and distribution companies are separately owned;[15] however, consolidation within the industry has begun to occur. There are 41 major pipeline systems within ten major transportation corridors within the U.S. and Canada (see Figure 2).[16]

Traditionally, a single pipeline, owned by one company, linked a producing field with a city gate. Today, pipeline companies have evolved into a highly connected network. The interstate pipeline network has grown 15% since 1990, primarily through greater interconnection, allowing for smoother operation and greater competition.[17] Market centers have grown up at points

---

[12] Typically, gas at the wellhead is processed to remove contaminants and hydrocarbon compounds other than methane.

[13] EIA, DELIVERABILITY ON THE INTERSTATE NATURAL GAS PIPELINE SYSTEM 31 (1998).

[14] Suedeen G. Kelly, *Regulatory Reform of the U.S. Natural Gas Industry: A Summing Up*, 27 NAT. RES. J. 841, 842 (1987).

[15] Arthur S. De Vany & W. David Walls, THE EMERGING NEW ORDER IN NATURAL GAS: MARKETS VERSUS REGULATION 5 (1995).

[16] EIA, *supra* note 13, at 34-48.

[17] EIA, *supra* note 13, at 31.

where multiple pipelines intersect and are supported by access to underground storage. This makes multiple routing of gas possible. Today, at least 39 market centers operate as pipeline hubs in the U.S. and Canada. The Henry Hub in Louisiana is the major natural gas market center in the U.S. Others such as the Chicago Hub are growing.[18]

Figure 2
Source: EIA, Natural Gas Issues & Trends 1998

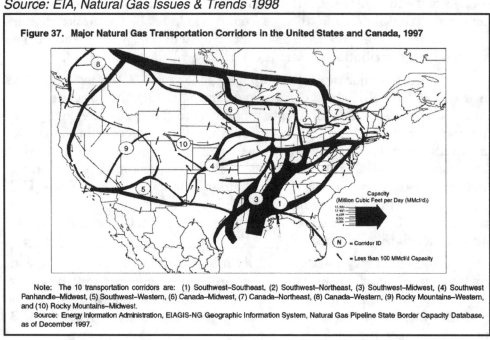

Figure 37.   Major Natural Gas Transportation Corridors in the United States and Canada, 1997

Note: The 10 transportation corridors are: (1) Southwest–Southeast, (2) Southwest–Northeast, (3) Southwest–Midwest, (4) Southwest Panhandle–Midwest, (5) Southwest–Western, (6) Canada–Midwest, (7) Canada–Northeast, (8) Canada–Western, (9) Rocky Mountains–Western, and (10) Rocky Mountains–Midwest.
    Source: Energy Information Administration, EIAGIS-NG Geographic Information System, Natural Gas Pipeline State Border Capacity Database, as of December 1997.

C.   Local Distribution

When the gas in the pipeline reaches the city gate, it flows into the local distribution system to the point of consumption ("the burner tip"). There are 1400 local distribution companies (LDCs) in the U.S. Typically the LDC purchases the gas from producers, pipelines, or marketers and delivers and resells it to its customers within the local distribution area. Sometimes large consumers of gas, such as electric utilities and industries using gas as a feedstock in their manufacturing process, physically bypass the LDC by building their own, private distribution lines from the pipeline to their facilities. In some states, consumers can buy their gas directly from producers or marketers and pay the LDC only for its distribution service.

---

[18] EIA, *supra* note 2 at 111. *See also* Figure 2, Pipeline Corridors.

D.   Marketing

With the advent of regulatory reform and increased competition in the price and sources of natural gas, the gas marketer has emerged as a new member of the natural gas industry. Prior to regulatory reform, the purchase and reselling of gas was performed almost entirely by pipeline companies. Today, there are gas marketing companies, which may or may not be affiliated with a pipeline, that purchase and resell gas and contract with pipelines and holders of excess firm transportation capacity on pipelines to transport gas. To date, marketers have primarily served large customers with fuel-switching capability.

Independent marketers are able to procure gas and ship it because of federal regulatory reform that required interstate pipelines to open access to their transportation service separately from their gas service. Not all states have required their LDCs to unbundle their services and to operate as open access transporters. Even so, most city gates are now open to at least some bypass of the LDC as merchant; however, most small gas consumers still use their LDC to sell them both transportation and the gas itself.

Gas marketers are not subject to economic regulation by the federal government or the states. However, the FERC does impose standards of conduct on interstate pipelines with marketing affiliates to ensure that they do not unfairly advantage their affiliates with transportation rates or services.[19]

III. NATURAL GAS MARKETS

A.   The Modern Gas Market

Prior to the regulatory changes of the mid-1980s, the gas market was quite rigid. Natural gas was bought and sold at the wellhead through long-term contracts, typically ten to twenty year terms, and most gas sold in interstate commerce was subject to regulatorily-imposed price ceilings. The producers sold to the pipelines, which in turn sold to the LDCs, which resold to consumers, with no contact between producers and consumers. Gas was not sold separately from its transportation. Today, the price of gas is unregulated, and gas sales are unbundled from transportation, at least to the city gate. Many states have also unbundled the sale of gas from its local

---

[19] *See* 18 C.F.R. §§ 161.1-161.3 (1999).

distribution. As a result, today's natural gas and transportation markets are more robust.

U.S. domestic gas producers are clearly in competition with each other and with foreign producers to sell their gas at "market price." Today's contracts for gas sales vary in length of time and have market sensitive pricing provisions. Wholesale consumers, like LDCs, contract directly with producers and marketers. With increasing frequency, large retail consumers, such as industrial users of gas and electric utilities, also contract directly with producers or marketers for gas. Wholesale and retail gas consumers who buy gas from a seller other than their LDC, purchase transportation separately from gas. Small consumers, even if they reside in states which permit them to buy gas from marketers, typically still rely on their LDCs for both gas and its transportation.

Regulatory reform has also changed the nature of the gas transportation market. The terms and costs of interstate transportation are regulated by FERC and specified in contracts between pipeline companies and shippers. Shippers include LDCs (which still hold a majority of the nation's supply of firm capacity), interstate pipeline companies themselves, electric utilities, industrial businesses, marketers, and others, including producers, gatherers and storage operators. In 1993, FERC gave the holders of firm transportation contracts the right to sell all or part of their transportation capacity for any length of time during the contract at a rate not to exceed the rate paid by the holder of the capacity to the pipeline itself.[20] Holders of excess firm transportation can sell capacity outright for a period of time or sell it subject to recall. Thus, today there is a "capacity release market." Between 1993 and 1998, firm transportation holders released capacity amounting to 8.0 Tcf, or the equivalent of 40% of the gas delivered to U.S. markets annually, to "replacement shippers."[21] The capacity release market is a way for shippers to change their transportation portfolios. It provides a mechanism to improve transportation flexibility to meet changing gas supply and demand conditions. At the initiation of the market, released capacity was selling for only about 10% of the price being paid by the holder to the pipeline. However, discounts for the year ending March 31, 1998, averaged about 50%.[22]

Shippers continue to prefer long-term contracts for firm transportation capacity, but "long-term" has become shorter over the years. For example, the average length of the contracts decreased from 10.9 to 7.0 years between

---

[20] FERC Order No. 636, 57 Fed. Reg. 13267 (1992).

[21] EIA, *supra* note 1, at 27.

[22] *Id.* at 27.

1994 and 1998, a decrease in length of 36%.[23] In 1998, LDCs held 55 to 57% of total firm capacity.[24] Because LDCs have traditionally had an obligation to serve all consumers in their distribution area, they typically reserve enough capacity to ensure they can meet their obligation even on a day of peak demand. Because of this contracting practice, LDCs tend to have a lower rate of utilization of their capacity than do other shippers.

Each year a substantial amount of firm capacity is up for renewal. Some shippers are choosing not to renew these contracts when they expire and instead are turning back some or all of the capacity to the pipeline. This "turned back" capacity can be remarketed by the pipeline. A study undertaken by the U.S. Department of Energy of capacity turned back between April 1996 and March 31, 1998, showed that some of this capacity had been remarketed, but at much lower rates.[25]

The changes in capacity contracting relate to the transition to more competition in the natural gas commodity and transportation markets. The increasingly important role marketers are playing in the gas industry is underscored by the fact that they are increasing not only the amount of long-term firm transportation capacity they hold, but also the overall amount of capacity they have under contract. In 1998 marketers held 24% of the total U.S. contracted capacity.[26]

B. The Current State of Supply

Five geologic regions in the U.S. account for 81% of the total domestic gas production, which accounts for 86% of domestic consumption. The largest producer is the offshore Gulf Coast area, followed by the inshore Gulf Coast, the Anadarko/Arkoma Basins, the Permian Basin, and the Rockies (see Figures 3 and 4).[27] Canada is the major supplier of imported gas to the U.S., and its market share is rapidly increasing consistent with growing availability of new gas production in Canada. The U.S. Department of Energy projects that in 2000, Canada will supply 16% of U.S. gas supplies, doubling its 1990 share.[28]

---

[23] *Id.* at 137.

[24] *Id.* at 129.

[25] *Id.* at 129.

[26] *Id.*

[27] EIA, *supra* note 13.

[28] *Id.*

Figure 3
Source: EIA, Deliverability on the Interstate Natural Gas Pipeline System

Figure 2. Major Natural Gas Producing Basins and Transportation Routes to Market Areas

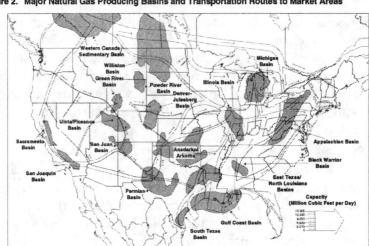

Correspondence to Major Natural Gas Producing Regions

Producing Region	State or Substate Regions	Basins Contained Whole or in Part
Gulf Coast	South Louisiana (onshore) Texas RRC Districts 1, 2, 3, 4	Gulf Coast and South Texas Basins
Anadarko/Arkoma	Arkansas Kansas Oklahoma Texas RRC District 10	Anadarko/Arkoma Basin
Permian Basin	New Mexico, East Texas RRC Districts 7B, 7C, 8, 8A, 9	Permian Basin
Rockies	Colorado Utah Wyoming	Uinta/Piceance, Julesberg, Powder River, and Green River Basins
East Texas	North Louisiana Texas RRC Districts 5, 6	East Texas/North Louisiana Basins
San Juan Basin	New Mexico, West	San Juan Basin
Appalachian	New York Ohio Pennsylvania Virginia West Virginia	Appalachian Basin
Other Onshore	Alabama, California (onshore), Florida, Kentucky, Michigan, Mississippi, Arizona, Illinois, Indiana, Maryland, Missouri, Montana, Nebraska, Nevada, North Dakota, Oregon, South Dakota, and Tennessee	Williston, Sacramento, San Joaquin, Illinois, Michigan, and Black Warrior Basins
Offshore	Federal waters of the Gulf of Mexico, and State waters of California, Alabama, Louisiana, and Texas	

Source: Energy Information Administration, EIAGIS-NG Geographic Information System, Natural Gas Pipeline State Border Capacity Database, as of December 1997.

Figure 4
Source: EIA, Deliverability on the Interstate Natural Gas Pipeline System

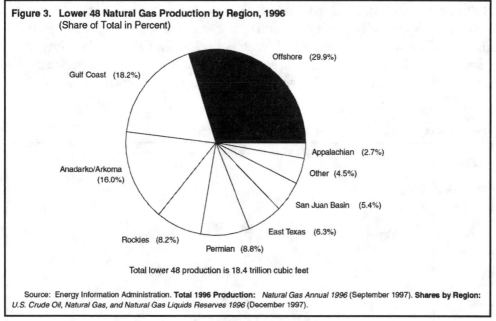

Figure 3. Lower 48 Natural Gas Production by Region, 1996
(Share of Total in Percent)

Offshore (29.9%)

Gulf Coast (18.2%)

Appalachian (2.7%)

Other (4.5%)

Anadarko/Arkoma (16.0%)

San Juan Basin (5.4%)

East Texas (6.3%)

Rockies (8.2%)

Permian (8.8%)

Total lower 48 production is 18.4 trillion cubic feet

Source: Energy Information Administration. **Total 1996 Production:** *Natural Gas Annual 1996* (September 1997). **Shares by Region:** *U.S. Crude Oil, Natural Gas, and Natural Gas Liquids Reserves 1996* (December 1997).

C.   The Current State of Demand

Industry is by far the largest consumer of natural gas in the U.S., accounting for about 44% of all end-use consumption in 1998.[29] Residential use accounts for about 23% of consumption, and commercial use accounts for about 15%. Use of gas for electricity generation, while accounting for only 15% of current consumption, is expected to increase rapidly in the next decade. Gas is an appealing fuel for new electricity generation. Its price is relatively low, and it is least polluting of all the fossil fuels. Natural gas is more easily fully combustible and has fewer impurities than other fossil fuels. Therefore, when it is burned, it emits pollutants far fewer in volume and number than any other fossil fuel. Gas can also be used to fuel distributed generation, i.e., small (50 Mw or less) generating units sited near the end-user. Distributed generation is being looked to as a way to provide greater electricity reliability in a region without building new, unpopular transmission lines.

---

[29] Consumption data is from Energy Information Administration, *Annual Energy Review 1998: Natural Gas, Table 6.5: Natural Gas Consumption by Sector, 1949-1998* (visited July 29, 1999) <http://www.eia.doe.gov/pub/energy.overview/ aer98/txt/aer0605.txt>.

Several foreign countries have been consuming U.S.-produced natural gas. The U.S. exported 157 billion cubic feet (Bcf) of natural gas in 1997, 52 Bcf to Canada, 62 Bcf to Japan, and 38 Bcf to Mexico.[30] The Southwest region of the U.S. is typically the largest consumer of natural gas, even though total energy consumption in the Southwest is far lower than in the Northeast region.[31] The Midwest is also a large consumer of natural gas. The Southeast and Western regions are relatively small consumers of natural gas.

Figure 5
Source: EIA, Historical Natural Gas Annual 1930-1997

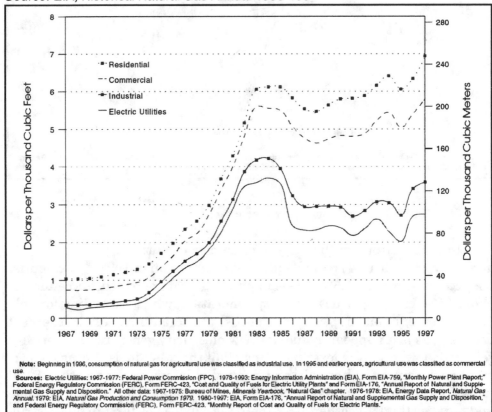

Note: Beginning in 1996, consumption of natural gas for agricultural use was classified as industrial use. In 1995 and earlier years, agricultural use was classified as commercial use

Sources: Electric Utilities: 1967-1977: Federal Power Commission (FPC). 1978-1993: Energy Information Administration (EIA). Form EIA-759, "Monthly Power Plant Report;" Federal Energy Regulatory Commission (FERC), Form FERC-423, "Cost and Quality of Fuels for Electric Utility Plants" and Form EIA-176, "Annual Report of Natural and Supplemental Gas Supply and Disposition." All other data: 1967-1975: Bureau of Mines, *Minerals Yearbook*, "Natural Gas" chapter. 1976-1978: EIA, Energy Data Report, *Natural Gas Annual.* 1979: EIA, *Natural Gas Production and Consumption 1979.* 1980-1997: EIA, Form EIA-176, "Annual Report of Natural and Supplemental Gas Supply and Disposition," and Federal Energy Regulatory Commission (FERC), Form FERC-423, "Monthly Report of Cost and Quality of Fuels for Electric Plants."

D. Prices

The price of natural gas delivered to the consumer consists of three components: transmission cost, distribution cost, and the cost of the gas itself. Interstate transmission rates are set by FERC. Intrastate trans-

---

[30] EIA, *supra* note 10.

[31] For a full discussion of regional consumption trends, *see* EIA, *supra* n. 13.

mission and local distribution rates are set by state regulators. The price of gas is set by the market.

The price of gas at the wellhead fluctuates and is affected by weather-sensitive, seasonal demand, the amount of gas in reserve and operational constraints. In 1998 the average price of gas at the wellhead was $1.74 per thousand cubic feet (mcf).[32] The wellhead price has steadily declined from its 1983 peak of $3.54 per mcf. Prices at the city gate have also declined since 1984, standing at $2.68 per mcf in 1998.[33] The decline in prices resulted from greater competition after the phase out of price controls initiated in 1978, increased production after 1978, an expanding transmission network, and improved drilling and transmission technology. The decrease in prices since 1984 is notable in that it has occurred despite the increase in demand and consumption over the same period (see Figures 5 and 6).

The price of natural gas is competitive with oil and lower than electricity for end-users. For example, the average cost of natural gas delivered to residential consumers in 1996 was $3.93 per million btu, compared with $4.54 for heating oil, and $15.62 for electricity.[34] For the month of March 1999, the average cost for natural gas delivered to residential consumers was $3.55 per million btu, compared to $3.54 for heating oil, and $14.03 for electricity.

A spot market has developed for natural gas, spurred by the emergence of market centers at pipeline hubs, or intersection points. With the advent of open access to pipelines, these markets have become more integrated. However, prices continue to be volatile, especially during the winter heating season (see Figure 7). The most important factor in spot pricing appears to be volume and accessibility of gas storage leading up to the heating season.[35]

The price volatility of the spot market can be offset somewhat by the futures market, allowing suppliers and users a hedge against risks of future price changes. A futures market in natural gas opened in 1990. A futures market is successful if it reliably predicts future spot prices at the point of delivery. So far, the natural gas futures market appears to be performing this function well.[36]

---

[32] EIA, *Annual Energy Review 1998: Natural Gas, Table 6.8: Natural Gas Wellhead, City Gate, and Imports Prices, 1949-1998* (visited July 29, 1999) <http://www.eia.doe.gov/pub/energy.overview/aer98/txt/aer0608.txt>.

[33] *Id.*

[34] EIA, *Monthly Energy Review, July 1999* (visited July 30, 1999) <http://www.eia.doe.gov/pub/energy.overview/monthly.energy/mer1-7>.

[35] John Herbert, James Thompson & James Todaro, NATURAL GAS MONTHLY, Dec. 1997, at vii, ix-xi.

[36] De Vany & Walls, *supra* note 15, at 83-92.

Figure 6: Natural Gas Delivered to Consumers in the United States, 1930-1997
Source: EIA, Historical Natural Gas Annual 1930-1997, Fig. 2

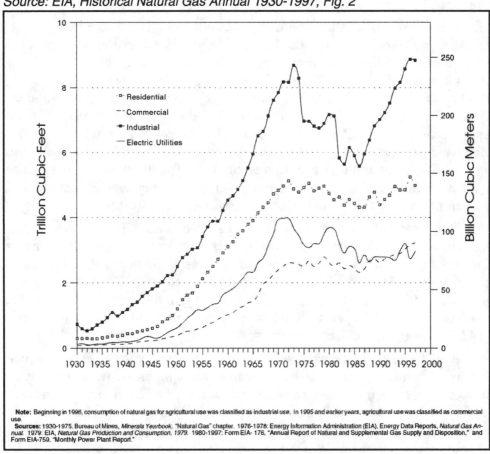

Note: Beginning in 1996, consumption of natural gas for agricultural use was classified as industrial use. In 1995 and earlier years, agricultural use was classified as commercial use.

Sources: 1930-1975. Bureau of Mines, *Minerals Yearbook*, "Natural Gas" chapter. 1976-1978: Energy Information Administration (EIA). Energy Data Reports, *Natural Gas Annual*. 1979: EIA, *Natural Gas Production and Consumption, 1979*. 1980-1997: Form EIA- 176, "Annual Report of Natural and Supplemental Gas Supply and Disposition," and Form EIA-759, "Monthly Power Plant Report."

E.   Future Trends

The prospects for the future use of gas are favorable. The U.S. Department of Energy projects that natural gas consumption will increase by 50% by 2020 over the 1997 level of 22 Tcf.[37] Natural gas is expected to become more attractive to consumers because of its cost, availability and environmental qualities. It emits lower quantities of greenhouse gases (particularly carbon dioxide) and criteria pollutants per unit of energy produced than do other fossil fuels. If technology, manpower, investment, and exploration can keep pace with increased demand, as expected, then natural gas has an expanding future.

---

[37] EIA, ANNUAL ENERGY OUTLOOK 1999, WITH PROJECTIONS TO 2020, at 20-22 (1998).

Figure 7

Source: EIA – Herbert, Thompson & Todaro, Recent Trends in Natural Gas Spot Prices. EIA, Natural Gas Monthly Dec. 1997

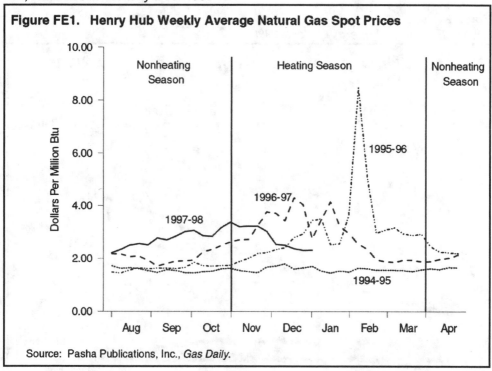

Figure FE1. Henry Hub Weekly Average Natural Gas Spot Prices

Source: Pasha Publications, Inc., *Gas Daily*.

Increased use of natural gas for electric consumption is expected to account for a significant share of the overall increase in natural gas consumption. Natural gas is expected to keep pace with petroleum consumption, and to exceed demand for coal (see Figure 8). In order to supply the projected increase in demand, the government projects that a significant increase in production will be necessary as well as expansion of infrastructure. Offshore production is expected to increase by 14%, onshore production is expected to increase by 57%, and pipeline capacity must increase by 32% over 1997 levels.[38] Increased demand is expected to increase prices. The U.S. Department of Energy projects that the industry is in a favorable position to meet the expected increase in demand because the price increase should stimulate investment in infrastructure, exploration, and production. If the Kyoto Protocol's requirement to reduce carbon emissions is adopted by the U.S., the U.S.

---

[38] *Id.*

Department of Energy predicts that demand for natural gas will be 2 to 12% higher than previous estimates.[39]

Figure 8
Source: EIA, Annual Energy Outlook 1999

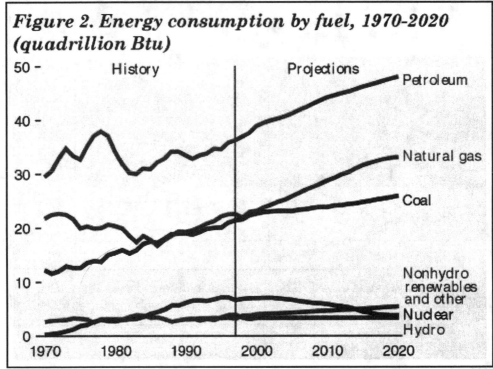

Figure 2. Energy consumption by fuel, 1970-2020 (quadrillion Btu)

IV. NATURAL GAS REGULATION

A.   Regulation in the States

In the 1920s and 1930s, states enacted oil and gas conservation legislation to prevent the economic waste of natural gas through flaring or venting. Up until that time, producing states were brightly illuminated at night by the huge natural gas flares burning in the petroleum fields. As a result of the laws eliminating the flaring and venting of gas, the natural gas business was born.

Soon after enactment of conservation laws, large pipelines were built to transport the natural gas from the producing fields to developing

---

[39] EIA, IMPACTS OF THE KYOTO PROTOCOL ON U.S. ENERGY MARKETS AND ECONOMIC ACTIVITY, at xix and 95 (1998).

markets. By the 1940s, with the improvements made in long-distance gas pipelines, the modern gas industry developed.

The configuration of natural gas pipelines was such that it put pipelines in both a monopsony and a monopoly position. At one end of the fuel cycle, the pipeline was the only buyer that gas and oil producers had available in the field for their gas. Thus, pipelines held a monopsony on the purchase of gas. At the other end of the fuel cycle, the natural gas pipeline was the only seller and transporter of natural gas available to a local distribution company or an industrial end-user. As such, the pipeline held a monopoly on the sale of gas. These characteristics made the pipelines ripe for utility-like economic regulation. Local distribution companies were also likely candidates for economic regulation because they held a monopoly on the sale and distribution of gas to the ultimate end-users.

The states initiated regulation of local gas distribution companies in the 1910s and 1920s. LDCs were found to be businesses affected with a public interest and, thus, subject to public utility regulation. Even today state commissions typically require LDCs to obtain certificates of public convenience and necessity to do business and build pipelines and distribution lines. State regulators also oversee LDCs in setting just and reasonable transportation rates, providing reasonably priced gas, affording adequate service, and ensuring service to all customers without discrimination. State regulation, therefore, has controlled most business aspects of the investor-owned gas distribution company since its infancy. The legitimacy of this regulation was upheld by the U.S. Supreme Court in two landmark cases. *Public Utilities Commission v. Landon*[40] and *Pennsylvania Gas Co. v. Public Service Commission of New York*,[41] authorized state regulation of natural gas matters deemed essentially local and for which Congress had not attempted to legislate.[42]

The limits of state regulation were explained by the U.S. Supreme Court in *Missouri ex rel. Barrett v. Kansas Natural Gas Co.*[43] Kansas Natural Gas was a production and interstate pipeline company. It sold gas wholesale to local distribution companies, which in turn, distributed and resold the gas to consumers. When Kansas Natural Gas raised its rates for sales to distribution companies in the states of Missouri and Kansas, the public utility commissions of those states were concerned that the price increase would be passed on to their consumers, and asserted jurisdiction

---

[40] 249 U.S. 236, *vacated and modified*, 249 U.S. 590 (1919).

[41] 252 U.S. 23 (1920).

[42] The Pennsylvania Gas opinion was later limited in *East Ohio Gas Co. v. Tax Commission*, 283 U.S. 465 (1931).

[43] 265 U.S. 298 (1924).

over Kansas Natural Gas for the purpose of approving the increase. Kansas Natural Gas objected, arguing that the states' attempted regulation would unconstitutionally impinge on the free movement of interstate commerce. The states responded that their actions were legitimate exercises of their police power to regulate local concerns. The Supreme Court rejected the states' assertion of jurisdiction over the interstate pipeline company as violative of the Constitution's interstate commerce clause. In its opinion the Court set out its view of the regulatory power of the state commissions. The commissions could regulate the activities of local distribution companies (primarily sale and distribution of gas to local customers). State regulation would also be allowed where the interstate gas company sold directly to consumers without an intermediate sale to a distribution company. In *Kansas Natural Gas*, however, the activity was "fundamentally interstate from beginning to end," and the states were prohibited from exerting jurisdiction over it even though Congress had not acted to provide for federal regulation. Uniformity in the treatment of interstate commerce was required "even though it be the uniformity of governmental nonaction." Three years later the *Kansas Natural Gas* principle was reaffirmed in the context of interstate sales of electricity in *Public Utility Commission of Rhode Island v. Attleboro Steam Electric Co.*[44]

Kansas Natural Gas emphasized the limit of state regulatory power over natural gas transactions. A state utility commission could impose the requirement of just and reasonable prices on a local distribution company's sale to the consumer. A major part of the distribution company's costs were the costs of purchased gas; however, when this gas was gas that had moved in interstate commerce, its cost was beyond state regulatory power. If the distribution company was forced to pay unreasonably high prices for its supply of gas, the state commission typically was forced to allow those charges to be passed on to the customer as one of the distribution company's costs of service. This problem invited solution by federal regulation, which ultimately occurred, but not for fourteen years.

States have not been constitutionally prohibited from regulating the purchasing practices of interstate and intrastate pipelines. Under "common purchaser" statutes, states have required a pipeline wishing to buy gas from a particular well to take gas ratably from all other wells in the same pool. The purpose of this requirement is to protect the owners of wells in a common pool from having gas drained from under their wells by a neighboring well and to mitigate the monopsony power of pipelines.

---

[44] 273 U.S. 83 (1927).

Major gas producing states have also regulated gas production prac-tices through prorationing statutes.[45] Pursuant to a typical statute, state regulatory agencies set monthly allowable volumes for each well. Although a producer is allowed to produce above or below this level in any given month, over a set period of time he must balance his production so as to produce the "allowable" level. If a producer consistently overproduces a well, it can be shut in. A consistently under-produced well can lose its right to make up that underproduction. The oft-stated purpose of this regulation is to conserve gas and protect correlative rights. There is evidence that some states have sometimes used their prorationing authority to set production levels at volumes below the true demand for gas, thereby raising its market price. As discussed *infra*, the Supreme Court has limited states' ability to regulate, even indirectly, the price of gas.

B. The Natural Gas Act of 1938

In 1935, the Federal Trade Commission issued a study concluding that the natural gas pipeline industry was indeed a natural monopoly, and recommending that the industry be regulated.[46] In light of that study and the inability of states to regulate interstate pipeline transactions, the U.S. Congress passed the Natural Gas Act (NGA) in 1938.[47] The statute, which is still in force today, provides for comprehensive federal regulation of interstate natural gas companies. The constitutionality of the act was sustained in *FPC v. Natural Gas Pipeline Co.*[48] Chief Justice Stone found the "sale of natural gas originating in one State and its transportation and delivery to distributors in any other State constitutes interstate commerce, which is subject to regulation by Congress."

Initially, the Federal Power Commission (FPC) was charged with implementing the NGA. Today's Federal Energy Regulatory Commission (FERC) is the successor agency to the FPC. The FPC focused its regulation of "natural gas companies" on the interstate pipeline companies. The NGA allowed the pipelines to remain private carriers of gas, thus permitting them to keep their monopsony on the purchase of gas at the wellhead. However, the price they paid for gas, as well as the price they charged for transportation, was subject to the FPC's jurisdiction to ensure "just and reasonable" rates.

---

[45] *See* Kelly, *supra* note 14, at 843.

[46] Joseph Fagan, *From Regulation to Deregulation: The Diminishing Role of the Small Consumer Within the Natural Gas Industry*, 29 TULSA L.J. 707 (1994).

[47] 15 U.S.C. §§ 717-717z (1994).

[48] 315 U.S. 575 (1942).

The flexibility of the "just and reasonable" standard, as applied to the natural gas industry, was highlighted by Justice Robert Jackson in *Federal Power Commission v. Hope Natural Gas Co.*[49] Justice Jackson pointed out that the amount and quality of service rendered by a utility will, at least roughly, be measured by the amount of capital it puts into the enterprise. However, the "elusive, exhaustible, and irreplaceable" nature of natural gas results in the possession of an adequate supply being more erratic, irregular, and unpredictable in relation to investment than any phase of any other utility business. Conventional rate-base formulas bear no rational relationship to natural gas production. Therefore, the Court held that the Commission was not bound to use any single formula or combination of formulas in determining natural gas rates.

Under the NGA, pipelines were given certificates of public convenience and necessity to provide exclusive gas and transportation services to a particular geographic area of consumers, but in return, they had an obligation to provide reliable, non-discriminatory service. Companies wishing to construct new pipelines also need to obtain certificates of public convenience and necessity under the NGA. To assure the stability of service to consumers, as well as to limit the financial risk of pipelines, regulators routinely required pipelines, as part of the certificate process, to enter into long term contracts with gas producers for a reliable supply of gas prior to selling to a new market or constructing a new pipeline. Typically, a pipeline's contract with a gas producer was for twenty years. Sometimes, however, the contracts were for the "life of the lease," or for as long as the well was capable of producing gas. In some gas basins, such as the San Juan Basin in Northwest New Mexico, the wells produce for forty years. This requirement guaranteed LDCs and their customers an adequate and reliable gas supply and assured the pipelines and their regulator that investments in pipeline construction could be recovered. This regulatory approach also resulted in a highly structured industry which, nevertheless, worked fairly well for twenty years until the FPC was required to extend price regulation to gas producers.

C.   The Natural Gas Act Applied to Gas Producers

The Supreme Court extended FPC jurisdiction to producers in 1954 in *Phillips Petroleum v. Wisconsin*.[50] In that case, the Court overturned an FPC decision and held that a producer selling gas for resale in interstate commerce fell within the regulatory jurisdiction of the NGA. Prior to *Phillips*, the subjects of FPC gas rate regulation were the small number of interstate

---

[49] 320 U.S. 591 (1944).
[50] 347 U.S. 672 (1954), *reh'g denied*, 348 U.S. 851 (1954).

pipelines. After *Phillips*, the Commission's jurisdiction suddenly included thousands of producers of gas for resale in the interstate market. The subsequent attempt by some members of Congress to enact legislation to change this interpretation of the NGA failed. The FPC was left with the unappealing task of regulating the price of a product not produced by monopolists. At first, the Commission attempted case-by-case determinations of just and reasonable producer rates, as it had done with the pipelines. Within a decade, however, the Commission was overwhelmed. It was estimated that if the Commission continued at its pace, it would have taken 83 years to clear its rate-making backlog.

The Commission moved from single-company rate regulation to the setting of area rates for producers within a geographic location. It used composite cost information in setting one rate for many sales in an area. Exceptions for individual producers were allowed on a showing of cost justification. Area rate regulation was sustained by the Supreme Court in *Permian Basin Area Rate Cases*.[51] The *Permian Basin Cases* also sustained a two-part rate system that allowed higher prices for newly discovered gas in order to encourage the development of new gas.

In the 1970s, the Commission moved from area rates to nationwide rates for new gas. Rates for previously discovered wells were also allowed to escalate. Rates for new gas, which were more than seven times as high as the rate under many existing contracts, brought objections from both gas producers and consumers. The producers urged deregulation of interstate rates. The consumers complained that the large increases in rates for new gas were allowing exorbitant profits to the gas industry. In 1977, the Court of Appeals for the District of Columbia Circuit rejected both arguments and affirmed the new nationwide rates in *American Public Gas Association v. FPC*.[52]

Price regulation thus relied on a "vintaging" system, causing a division of gas into "old" and "new." The "old" gas, which had already been discovered and was in production, was subject to low price ceilings. The "new" gas, which had not yet been discovered and was thus not available for production, was allowed a high price to encourage exploration of untapped reserves. The result was that established gas producers, who had mostly "old" gas to sell, were induced to confine their gas to the intrastate market, which was not subject to FPC authority, so they could charge higher prices. Pipeline customers also encouraged producers to make intrastate sales by balking at paying for higher priced "new" gas.

---

[51] 390 U.S. 747 (1968).
[52] 567 F.2d 1016 (D.C. Cir. 1977).

Interstate sales of gas were suppressed as a result of the federal price controls. Although the price of intrastate gas was unregulated by the federal government, it generally tracked the interstate price, at a slightly higher rate. Thus, the overall price of gas was artificially low, which led to decreased investment in new production, and, ultimately a shortage of natural gas in the United States. At the same time, the low prices also led to an increase in demand for natural gas.

The adoption of wellhead price controls also added to the complexity of certification of pipeline construction and services. The FPC was particularly concerned that low-price old gas would not be made available on the interstate market and the interstate gas supply would thus be jeopardized. The Commission was faced with prioritizing end-users in a time of shortage, and was forced to spend more time scrutinizing pipeline certificates and balancing the needs of all the purchasers in the industry—the pipelines, the LDCs, and the customers.[53]

By 1974, there was substantial discontent with price controls on producer sales in the interstate market.[54] Public criticism was also leveled at the regulatory overload effects of the *Phillips* decision on the supply of and demand for natural gas. The widespread political consensus, which had initially supported regulatory control of the natural gas industry, began to fade and political dissatisfaction with regulation rose.

D.　The Energy Crisis Spurs Gas Price Deregulation and Interstate Pipeline Regulatory Reform

The American public felt the full impact of shortages in the interstate natural gas market during the mid-1970s. The OPEC oil embargo of 1973 and record-cold winters in the later half of the decade produced a steep rise in demand for gas. This effected a price increase in the unregulated intrastate market but not in the regulated interstate market. To the extent producers had new gas, they had no incentive to dedicate it to the interstate market. The intrastate market had a surplus of the high-priced "new" gas. The discrepancy in price between the intrastate and interstate markets for gas widened, as did the discrepancy between the price of oil and interstate gas. Not surprisingly, consumers demanded more interstate gas, which was just not available. The severe shortage of gas, combined with the jump in

---

[53] *Id.*

[54] *See* Federal Power Commission v. Texaco, 417 U.S. 380 (1974).

price for unregulated gas, rendered producer price regulation under the NGA even more controversial.[55]

Congress sought to address these problems with the passage of the Natural Gas Policy Act of 1978 (NPGA).[56] First, the NGPA raised the price allowed to be charged for all gas, except old gas. Second, the NGPA provided for the phasing out of the regulation of gas prices. By July 1, 1987, the price of all gas, except old gas, was to be set by the marketplace.

The NGPA also addressed a number of other gas regulation issues that had been debated since the *Phillips* decision and effected a compromise between the wishes of producers and consumers. Federal price controls, and ultimately decontrol, was extended to the intrastate as well as the interstate market. Congress set maximum prices in the NGPA for a wide variety of categories of gas. As noted, price controls on most types and vintages of gas were to be removed by 1987. Newly discovered gas and gases with high extraction costs were initially deregulated. Prior to decontrol, gradual escalation of gas prices was allowed to reflect inflation and to bring gas prices in line with current and projected petroleum prices. An "incremental pricing" program required that most of the initial gas price increases be passed on to major industrial, rather than residential and small commercial, consumers of gas. Priorities were established to respond to curtailment of gas services.

The NPGA represented a major Congressional policy shift in natural gas regulation. By first raising the price ceilings that had discouraged production, Congress hoped to encourage producers to supply more gas. At the same time, it sought to protect residential consumers from part of the price increase by continuing to regulate the more plentiful "old" gas. Pipelines typically bought gas of many vintages and resold it to LDCs at the average price of the mix. After a transition period of eight years, Congress envisioned an unregulated, competitive market in natural gas.

At first, the NGPA had its desired effect. Gas producers across the country increased production capacity in response to the higher wellhead prices specified in the NGPA. The deregulated prices for certain categories of new gas also reduced the dichotomy between gas prices in interstate and intrastate markets, and gas supplies evened out between the markets.

However, by the mid-1980s, different and unforeseen problems arose. The higher gas prices had a classic, predictable effect on consumers: they steadily scaled back gas consumption. Then the country experienced a recession in 1981 which also caused a drop in the demand for natural gas.

---

[55] *Id.*

[56] 15 U.S.C. §§ 3301-3432 (1994).

This effect was compounded by the break up of OPEC and the resulting drop in the price of oil between 1980 and 1983. As the price of oil, an acceptable alternative fuel for many large gas users, fell below that of gas in 1983, the stage was set for fuel switching among industrial users.[57] In 1983, it was estimated that between 23 and 35% of total U.S. gas consumption could easily switch to fuel oil.[58] This was a particularly ominous scenario for pipelines.

The pipelines' problem stemmed from their long-term contracting practices with producers, which had been in place from the early days of NGA regulation. In the 1970s, to assure adequate supplies of gas to meet the extraordinary demand of the times, pipelines had contracted long-term with producers for large volumes of gas and agreed to take a high percentage of the gas the well was capable of producing on a daily basis. If the pipelines did not physically take the gas they nevertheless agreed to pay for it. These take-or-pay clauses became a problem for pipelines as the price of gas rose and demand for it fell off. The problem was exacerbated by the fact that many of the take-or-pay contracts also contained automatic price escalation clauses. As large users switched to oil and the pipelines' sales fell off, they had to pay take-or-pay penalties. Numerous pipelines were without the cash to pay the penalties and faced bankruptcy. Large producers who could wait to be paid had little incentive to renegotiate their advantageous contracts. However, by 1984, many gas producers with excess production capacity were interested in selling more gas even if they had to lower their prices to do so. Pipelines already had too much gas under contract, albeit at high prices. Producers began to talk directly with consumers. This situation helped motivate the FERC to experiment with regulatory reform of interstate pipelines. FERC issued Order No. 319-A which permitted interstate pipelines to transport gas owned by others to large users capable of switching to alternative fuels.[59] In *Maryland People's Counsel v. FERC*,[60] the D.C. Circuit approved this concept but vacated FERC's order for failure to consider the anticompetitive effects of limiting the availability of unbundled transportation of gas to large users. FERC responded to the *Maryland People's Counsel* decision with Order 436 issued in 1985, which provided a comprehensive regulatory scheme that gave pipelines strong incentives to allow any person access to their unused pipeline capacity.[61]

---

[57] Suedeen G. Kelly, *Intrastate Natural Gas Regulation: Finding Order in the Chaos,* 9 YALE J. ON REG. 355, 361 (1992).

[58] *Id.* at 361, n. 18.

[59] FERC Order No. 319-A, 48 Fed. Reg. 51,436 (1983).

[60] 761 F.2d 780 (D.C. Cir. 1985).

[61] FERC Order No. 436, 50 Fed. Reg. 42,408 (1985).

Order 436 was an historic step toward unbundling pipelines' gas sales service from their transportation service. FERC realized that the goal of the NGPA to have supply, demand and price of gas set by the marketplace could not be fully realized unless the many sellers of gas (producers) could deal directly with the many consumers of gas. This could not happen unless the parties could be assured that the gas bought could be transported from the producer to the consumer.

FERC did not have the authority to directly order pipelines to carry gas for others. However, Order 436 provided incentives that enticed most pipelines to "voluntarily" begin transporting gas for others. First, Order 436, known as the "open access" order, simplified the "convenience and necessity" certification requirements. If the pipeline agreed to provide nondiscriminatory access, or transportation, to whomever requested it, the pipeline could obtain a pre-approved "blanket" certification for new services or facilities. By agreeing to act as a common carrier, the pipeline was better able to access new end-use markets.

Second, Order 436 gave pipelines the right to convert their sales obligations under their wellhead contracts to transportation-only contracts. This allowed the pipelines to lessen their take-or-pay liabilities somewhat by agreeing to surrender their sales monopoly to the downstream market. Additionally, Order 436 permitted customers to purchase gas from any available supplier.

The Court of Appeals affirmed most aspects of Order 436 in *Associated Gas Distributors v. FERC*,[62] but remanded it to the Commission to address take-or-pay problems. The competitive incentives were retained. In response, FERC issued Order 500, establishing "acceptable passthrough mechanisms" by which pipelines could recover take-or-pay buyout or buydown costs by passing the costs through to customers. The D.C. Circuit also remanded Order 500 as unnecessarily harmful to consumers. The FERC subsequently issued Order 528 allowing pipelines to develop new methods of allocating their take-or-pay costs to spread them over all segments of the industry, so that residential and small industrial users did not bear a disproportionate share.

In 1992, FERC issued Order 636,[63] known as the "comparability" order, which it characterized as a final restructuring of the natural gas industry. This order set the stage for a competitive national market in the sale of

---

[62] 824 F.2d 981 (D.C. Cir. 1987).

[63] *See* FERC Statutes and Regulations Preamble 30,939 (1992). Final regulations for FERC Order No. 636 were not published until 1999. *See* 64 Fed. Reg. 43506 (1999).

natural gas by allowing buyers to access the pipeline transportation grid on equal terms with all other buyers and, thereby, connect with sellers nationwide. Order 636 requires pipelines to completely unbundle gas sales from transportation, and to provide "comparable" transportation services, with the same rates, terms, and conditions, to all customers. In short, Order 636 requires pipelines to be equal access common carriers of natural gas.

Even though pipelines are allowed to continue selling gas on an unbundled basis, a pipeline's sales division must be strictly separated from its transportation division, and the pipeline may not provide any services to its sales division that it does not provide to third-party sellers. As a result, most pipelines have abandoned the sales business, so that sales are made by either independent sellers or marketing affiliates, rather than by the pipeline itself.

Order 636 also contained a number of other major components. First, pipelines must provide "no-notice" service to distributors to meet severe peak-day requirements. Second, pipelines are required to use the straight fixed-variable (SFV) rate design methodology that allocates all fixed costs to the reservation component of two-part rates. Third, pipeline transportation contracts receive pre-granted abandonment authorization at the expiration of the contract, subject to a right of first refusal by the shipper. Fourth, holders of firm capacity may release that capacity to other shippers on the secondary market at any price up to the maximum rate paid by the releasing shipper. Existing buy-sell arrangements were grandfathered, but future buy-sell arrangements were prohibited. Fifth, pipelines may recover 100% of all their prudently incurred "transition costs," including take-or- pay costs, costs of new facilities installed to comply with the order and gas supply realignment costs incurred to unbundle the sales function.

Pursuant to federal regulation today, interstate pipelines are equal access common carriers of gas whose rates, terms and conditions of service are subject to regulation by FERC under the NGA. The price of natural gas is not regulated. This is so whether the gas is sold into interstate or intrastate commerce. In 1986, the U.S. Supreme Court clarified that the federal government has preempted the states from regulating intrastate gas prices. In *Transcontinental Gas Pipeline Corp. v. Mississippi Oil and Gas Board*,[64] the Court invalidated a Mississippi regulatory order issued pursuant to its common purchaser act. The Order in question required a pipeline to take ratably from a well interest owner with which it did not have a contract. The well interest owner's gas was in a common pool with other wells with which the pipeline company did have a contract and from which it was taking gas.

---

[64] 474 U.S. 409 (1986).

The noncontracted for gas was being sold at a higher rate than the gas which the pipeline company had contracted for. The Court found that the enforcement of the Mississippi Order would have an effect on the price being paid for gas. The Court also found that Congress' intent in passing the NGPA was to have the marketplace determine the price of gas. Thus, the Court concluded, Congress not only prohibited the federal government from regulating the price of gas, but also prohibited state governments from directly or indirectly regulating the price of gas.

By 1987, the federal price caps on all gas, except old gas, had expired pursuant to the NGPA. In 1989, Congress passed the Natural Gas Wellhead Decontrol Act,[65] which ended the remaining federal price controls as of January 1, 1993.

E. The States Reform Their Natural Gas Regulatory Policies

Most states have followed FERC's lead and reformed their regulation of LDCs and intrastate pipelines to require them to carry gas owned by others—at least for large customers. As of mid-1998, five states had implemented complete unbundling programs for small customers. Another thirteen states and the District of Columbia have pilot programs in place that give residential and small business customers the right to choose their own gas supplier. Twelve more states are considering doing the same.

In order to open up competition among gas suppliers to retail consumers, state regulators must require the LDC to unbundle its gas sales and transportation services and offer them separately. New York was the first state to reform its regulation of LDCs in this manner in 1984. Other states quickly followed suit.[66] They acted to maintain the health of their local distribution systems, which were threatened with the loss of their large gas consumers. As discussed earlier, at this time the delivered price of gas began to increase relative to that of oil. Large gas users threatened to switch to oil unless their gas prices were lowered. If these consumers bypassed the natural gas transportation and distribution system, the cost of maintaining the system would fall to the small, "captive" customers. Faced with the unappealing prospect of raising rates to these customers, state regulators had an incentive to find ways to lower the delivered cost of gas to potential bypassers. They were supported in this quest by many gas producers who had been shut out of existing markets and were clamoring to sell their gas, even at lower than prevailing prices. Regulators saw that

---

[65] Pub. L. No. 101-60, 103 Stat. 157, repealing 15 U.S.C. §§ 3311 to 3320, 3331 to 3333.

[66] *See,* Kelly, *supra* note 57, at 366-69.

the easiest way to lower gas costs to potential bypassers was simply to let willing producers sell them cheaper gas. However, direct retailing of natural gas to customers by a seller other than the LDC was a significant break with tradition. Change can be difficult in any industry, but it is particularly so in one guarded by longtime economic regulation. Nevertheless, over the last fifteen years, state regulators have increasingly required gas utilities under their jurisdiction to provide gas distribution service to customers wanting to buy gas from non-LDC vendors. As a result, many large industrial consumers, including electric utilities, are buying gas in the competitive market.

Even though states have required their LDCs to unbundle services, they have not prohibited their LDCs from offering bundled service. In other words, they have preserved the LDCs' traditional obligation to serve all customers within their service territories with gas. This is unlike the federal reform of interstate pipelines where FERC prohibited pipelines from selling transportation bundled with gas. As a result, in the states, customers have not *had* to find a non-LDC gas supplier and, not surprisingly, most small customers have not even considered switching from their LDC as gas supplier. The current cost of finding a lower-priced supplier and negotiating a contract far outweighs the benefit for small consumers. The U.S. Department of Energy reports that only 2% of eligible small customers actually participate in programs allowing them to choose a non-LDC provider of gas.[67] This situation has motivated a few states to affirmatively enact regulatory programs designed to make it less costly for small consumers to choose a non-LDC gas supplier. These "customer choice" programs typically require the LDC to advertise the availability of other gas suppliers' programs and handle the administrative responsibilities associated with signing up consumers for the various gas suppliers.

F.   Future Issues

1.   *State Initiatives*

State regulators are developing customer choice programs and customer information campaigns designed to make it easier for small gas consumers to switch from their LDC to a gas marketer for future gas supply.

State regulators are also reviewing their traditional regulation of LDCs as gas suppliers to see whether they need to revamp their regulatory approach to ensure that their LDCs obtain the best-priced gas in the competi-

---

[67] EIA, *supra* note 1, at 35.

tive wholesale gas market. Some of the issues include whether LDCs should be given an incentive to purchase lower-priced gas and whether LDCs should be encouraged or required to participate in the gas futures market.

The fact that LDCs are now buying gas in a deregulated gas market and having it transported by pipelines in a restructured transportation market has also raised new issues for state regulators. These include, for example, what type of gas contract portfolio is reasonable for each LDC to hold, what amount of long-term firm transportation capacity is reasonable for each LDC to keep under contract, and whether the LDC should be selling capacity in the capacity release market.

2. *Federal Reconsideration of Interstate Pipeline Regulation*

Today's interstate transportation of gas occurs through both long-term contracts and short-term arrangements. FERC is reviewing whether its regulation of transportation in either of these arenas should change.

Although the movement of gas pursuant to long-term pipeline contracts has been a staple of the industry from the beginning, today's long-term arrangements are different from yesterday's. Today's long-term contracts are shorter in length. When these long-term contracts expire, some are not being renewed; others are being renewed at lower prices. These changes underscore the fact that transportation of gas is responding to a more competitive market. These changes are also evidence that the pipeline industry is a riskier one than in the past. In light of this, FERC is asking the question whether its regulation should be reformed in order to provide the correct incentives for pipelines to offer optimal transportation services and facilities for tomorrow's market, to provide appropriate price signals, and to eliminate any regulatory bias toward either long-term or short-term transportation.[68] This inquiry is occurring against the backdrop of FERC's responsibility under the Natural Gas Act to protect consumers of natural gas from the exercise of monopoly power by interstate pipelines and to assure that rates for interstate transportation are just and reasonable.

FERC has made it clear that it will retain cost-based rate regulation for long-term transportation, but it is considering whether other types of cost-based ratemaking, such as index rates or incentive rates should be adopted. Index rates are rates based on factors other than only the pipeline's costs and volumes, such as the supply and demand characteristics of the

---

[68] FERC Notice of Inquiry regarding Regulation of Interstate Natural Gas Transportation Services, 63 Fed. Reg. 42,974 (1998).

market being served. For example, in its regulation of oil pipelines, FERC has adopted an index method of ratemaking that uses the producer price index for finished goods and an industry cost-based efficiency adjustment to modify existing pipeline rates initially set on the basis of cost factors.[69] Incentive regulation is used in lieu of, or in addition to, traditional cost-based regulation to provide an incentive to regulated entities to provide better service at lower cost, usually by giving the company a share of the costs saved.

FERC is also seeking comments on whether the trend toward shorter term contracts is a natural consequence of the evolution of competition or whether it has been unduly affected by FERC's pipeline pricing policies. Additionally, FERC is considering whether it should change its ratemaking policies affecting capacity turned back to the pipelines after the expiration of unrenewed contracts with shippers. One question FERC is asking is whether this capacity might be susceptible to market-based ratemaking. Finally, FERC is considering whether long-term firm capacity contracts should be allowed to be offered at fixed rates. This is different from what happens today where the price of this capacity is subject to changes during the term of the contract resulting from rate cases brought by the pipelines at FERC. FERC realizes that now is the time to grapple with the issue of how new pipeline capacity should be priced, before a significant amount of new capacity is actually built.

Since 1993, when FERC issued Order No. 636, active short-term transportation of gas on both a firm and interruptible basis has developed. Currently, transportation can be sold short-term as long as it is sold at a price below the maximum rate set by FERC. FERC has announced a proposed rule which would eliminate cost-based regulation for short-term transportation, including the maximum price cap on short-term transportation and require, instead, that all short-term capacity be sold through capacity auctions.[70] FERC is interested in the development of a competitive short-term transportation market where capacity is freely traded so that shippers have a large number of capacity alternatives from which to choose, thereby reducing the number of captive customers. FERC also wants to see opportunity for greater flexibility in pipeline contracting practices so that pipelines can design services that better meet the needs of existing and new entrants in the gas marketplace. Some pipelines are concerned about the

---

[69] FERC Order No. 561, FERC Stats. and Regs., Regulations Preambles, January 1991-June 1996, 30,985 (1993).

[70] FERC Proposed Rule regarding Regulation of Short-Term Natural Gas Transportation Services, 63 Fed. Reg. 42,982, FERC Docket No. RM98-10-000 (August 11, 1998) (affecting 18 CFR Parts 161, 250, 284).

risk this change would entail for them, and some LDCs are concerned that the auction will eliminate their ability to contract, in advance, for short-term capacity.

3.   *Mergers and Acquisitions*

Mergers and acquisitions in the natural gas industry are occurring as the industry responds to the competitive initiatives of the federal and state governments in both the natural gas and electricity industries. Mergers in the natural gas industry increased 400% between 1990 and 1997. Mergers or acquisitions involving regulated gas companies must be approved by their regulators, including FERC and each state having jurisdiction over any LDC involved in the corporate recombination.

As the gas industry continues to adjust to the changes brought by increased competition into both the gas sales and transportation segments of the business, corporate changes will continue to occur to enable the industry to reposition itself to achieve lower costs, economies of scale, new expertise as needed in new market conditions, and access to new markets. State and federal regulators will also continue to adjust their regulatory policies to the changes in the industry. Because much of the transportation and local distribution segments of the industry are still monopolies, regulatory jurisdiction in FERC and the states remains substantial. ❧

CHAPTER NINE

Coal

by Marla E. Mansfield

I. THE COAL FUEL CYCLE

The coal fuel cycle consists of mining, processing, transportation, and combustion. Examination of this cycle reveals that mere abundance of a resource does not translate to an unbounded source of energy to do the work of humans. Environmental concerns may constrain a fuel's desirability.

Nevertheless, coal is the non-renewable fossil fuel that is most plentiful in the United States. It is found in thirty-eight states and underlies about 13% of the nation's land. The United States has an estimated 3.9 trillion tons of coal.[1] Of this tonnage, 1.7 trillion tons are classified as "identified resources," which means they are deposits of coal in beds of a specified minimum thickness and depth. Although not all of these tons are mineable, at least 438 billion tons are included in the "demonstrated reserve base," which is the coal considered capable of being mined from both technological and economic vantage points. Coal comprises 90% of the nation's fossil fuel reserves. Proven reserves could meet current coal needs for about 600 years.

---

[1] In addition to coal itself, another potential energy source is associated with coal seams. Methane is a gaseous hydrocarbon, created at about the rate of 5,000 cubic feet for every ton of anthracite formed out of peat. Methane traditionally had been considered a safety hazard and nuisance; it is poisonous and combustible. Therefore, it was vented from underground mines. After energy price surges in the wake of the 1970s energy crises, methane was re-examined. Improved recovery technology and federal tax credits encouraged recovery of the resource. One problem was that ownership of methane became an issue when mineral estates were divided. Most courts have concluded that methane is not part of the coal estate if coal was reserved or granted alone. *See* Carbon County v. Union Reserve Coal Co., Inc., 898 P.2d 680 (Mont. 1995); Amoco Production Co. v. Southern Ute Indian Tribe, 119 S.Ct. 1719, 144 L.Ed.2d 22 (interpreting statute that reserved coal to the United States); *but see In re* Hillsborough Holdings, 207 B.R. 299 (1997) (Alabama assigns methane to coal estate if it has not migrated). The Energy Policy Act of 1992 has provisions to simplify methane development, especially in states that lack binding legal precedent clarifying ownership. § 1339 of 106 Stat. 2776, codifed at 42 U.S.C. § 13368.

The United States sometimes is referred to as the "Saudi Arabia of coal." This is not simply because of the amount of reserves, which equals one-fifth to one-third of the world's accessible and usable coal, but also because approximately half of the reserves are owned federally.

Mining is the beginning of the fuel cycle, which ultimately transforms these reserves into useful energy. Coal is mined in two general manners: underground mining and surface mining. Surface mining consists of removing the overburden or earth above a coal seam that is relatively near the surface so that the coal itself may be blasted loose and removed. Strip mining is a more value-laden term for the process. The term "surface mining" encompasses three methods: contour, area, and open pit. Contour or its variant, mountaintop mining, is used on steep terrain, most commonly in Appalachia. To use this technique, the miner cuts out a bench from the steep hillside and then removes the seam, going into the hillside. The spoil bank goes down the slope. In area mining, which is employed on flat or rolling terrain with contiguous tracts, the removal of overburden results in a spoil pile to the side of the area from which the coal is removed. The spoil can then backfill the hole. The technique is prevalent in the Western Appalachians and the Midwest. The final method, open-pit mining, is similar to area mining, but is employed where the overburden is thinner than the coal to be removed. Therefore, the overburden is insufficient to fill in the pit mining creates. The High Plains area contains most of these open pit mines.

In addition to these types of surface mines, coal also is mined in two types of underground mines. In the first type of underground mine, referred to as a room and pillar mine, coal is removed but "pillars" of coal remain to support the overlying strata. About 70% percent of the coal is removed by primary room-and-pillar mining. In a variant of this technique, miners return to remove the pillars as the mine is exhausted. This is referred to as "retreat mining." The second main type of underground mining is longwall mining. This technique recovers more coal initially because pillars are not left in place to support the surface and upper strata. The coal simply is removed from the entire face of the seam at once. Roof support is provided artificially and temporarily in the form of hydraulic jacks or shields above the miners. As mining progresses along the face of the seam, the supports are removed. The unsupported roof then caves in. The cave-in in a long-wall mine happens rapidly. Subsidence may be evident on the surface within months after the support is removed. Subsidence also occurs with room and pillar mining, but less quickly. Longwall mining was a concern of the legislators in Pennsylvania when they passed the legislation at issue in

Keystone Bituminous Coal Association v. DeBenedictis. In addition to generally being more expensive, underground mining is more dangerous to the miners than surface mining.

After mining, the next stage in the fuel cycle is processing. To understand this stage requires comprehending how coal was formed. Coal originated in prehistoric swamps. Unlike oil, coal is a sedimentary rock itself. Like oil, it is an organic substance, primarily carbon, but it is not derived from marine organisms like oil. Instead, it comes from land based vegetation. This accumulated vegetation, which eventually became coal, did not decompose completely in the swamps' oxygen-deficient waters. Rather, it first was transformed into peat, which is used as an energy source in some areas of the world but is not technically coal. The weight and pressure of sediments overlying the peat, and the resultant heat, transformed peat into coal. The amount of heat, compression, and resultant "cooking" of the coal creates different types of coal, referred to as "ranks." The second step in the coal fuel cycle is processing the coal, during which it is sorted, screened and cleaned depending on its rank, type and grade.

There are four major ranks of coal, which correspond to differing heating values expressed in British Thermal Units (BTUs) per pound of coal burned. Lignite is the least mature and lowest ranked coal and produces only 7000 BTUs. Next, there is sub-bituminous coal (9500 BTUs), bituminous coal (13,500 BTUs), and anthracite (14,000 BTUs). Anthracite is the rarest of coal and is only a very small percentage of the coal produced, primarily from eastern Pennsylvania. Lignite and bituminous coals are the primary coals mined in the United States. Bituminous is found throughout the eastern and Midwestern producing states as well as in Utah, western Colorado, and Texas. The Rocky Mountain region is home to sub-bituminous coal. It is the prevalent coal in Wyoming, western Montana, and eastern Colorado. Lignite in large quantities is located in North Dakota, western Montana, and Texas.

Ranking provides the calorific or heating value of the coal produced, which is an important factor in a coal's value, but two other classifications can influence what coal is purchased. In addition to being ranked, coal is classified by *type* and *grade*. *Type* is determined based on the proportion of various macerals that are present in the coal as well as the coal's mineral content. Macerals are simply the identifiable units of the remains of differing types of vegetation that went into the creation of the coal, such as woody material or resins. Microscopic examination determines type. *Grade* as

---

[2] 480 U.S. 470 (1987) (holding that forbidding mining under certain structures and public improvements was not an unconstitutional "taking").

applied to coal refers to whether it has the properties needed for a specific use. To determine grade, coal must be tested. For example, "metallurgical grade" coal refers to that bituminous coal that makes superior "coke," the fuel that is used to smelt steel. The ash and sulfur content of coal are two important considerations in determining the grade of coal. These two components are undesirable, because they create either environmental externalities or difficulties in boilers.

Many of the western bituminous and lignite coals are in flatter and thicker beds that are amenable to surface mining techniques. These generally are cheaper and can remove more of the coal than underground techniques. For example, the Powder River Basin has coal seams of sixty to seventy feet, as compared to typical eastern coal seams of six to seven feet. Cheaper mining costs (estimated in 1996 at $3 to $4 a ton as opposed to $15-20 costs for eastern coal) and lower sulfur contents make the western coals of the Powder River Basin attractive. Greater transportation costs and lower BTU values, however, might sometimes offset these benefits.

Transportation, an issue in obtaining low sulfur coal, is the third step in the fuel cycle. Bringing coal to its place of use has comprised at times 35-50% of the cost of coal for the consumer. Costs have recently decreased, but in 1994, the cost of transportation was still nearly $7 billion of the $23 billion utilities spent on coal. To get coal to the plants that burn it requires a vast transportation network, which is primarily composed of trains, barges, and ships. The two modes of transport, rail and barge, have separate benefits and limitations.[3] A third alternative, coal slurry pipelines, has not taken its place among the transporters.

Barge or ship transportation, naturally, is not feasible without water, but does move 16% of the nation's coal. On the Great Lakes, coal carriers are ships 700 feet long and 70 feet wide. On the Ohio or Mississippi River, barges in groups of 15 to 20 per tow together could carry 20-30,000 tons, which is more than 200 times the amount of coal contained in a single railroad car. On the lower Mississippi, super barge tows of 40 or more barges may carry 70-80,000 tons each. Barge transport, however, is limited by the system of about 150 locks and dams on the 8,500 miles of navigable inland waters. The water-works are aging and can create bottlenecks. Moreover, severe droughts—and conversely, severe floods—may reduce the ability of even the Mississippi River to be an effective highway. Nevertheless, barge transport can be efficient. Coal can be transported from

---

[3] Truck transport is the least efficient method of transport, but is used for hauls of less than 50 miles. Trucks are used in West Virginia and eastern Kentucky. All told, trucks moved 12% of the coal transported in 1997.

Pittsburgh to Cincinnati in a week and could arrive in Brownsville, Texas in four weeks. The inland water system can also reach Florida. Barges are tied together for towing and, as of 1993, barge haulage fees on a per ton basis were between a quarter to a third of rail charges for similar hauls. Recent rail cost decreases may have eliminated some, but not all, of the price differential.

Most coal, about two-thirds of it, is transported by rail. Conversely, coal is the single largest commodity transported by rail. If all freight tonnage on United States railroads were accumulated, coal would account for about 38% of it. A railroad car generally can carry slightly less than 100 tons of coal, but would be part of a train with a number of cars. Railroad trains comprised of a hundred cars dedicated to coal transport are not uncommon. Massive capital must be invested in rail lines and in specialized handling equipment and rail cars. In the eastern United States, there has long been some competition between rail carriers that could serve a coal mine and the purchasing utility. In the West, however, most coal mines are "captive" to one railroad. A mine, or a purchasing utility, is captive if the only mode of transport is a particular railroad.

The final step in the fuel cycle is combustion, which is the manner in which coal is consumed. The end-uses of coal have changed over time. Currently, about 85% of the coal produced in the United States is used for electrical generation. In determining what energy source will be used for this task, the abundance of coal is weighed against the environmental concerns arising out of the mining and combustion of the resource. Nevertheless, coal provides the fuel for 54.6% of the nation's electric generation. Other uses of coal include the steel industry and the synthetic fuels "industry." The latter industry has been more a source of technological progress than commercial success. Through various methods, synthetic fuel technology converts coal to gaseous or liquid fuels that would substitute for petroleum and natural gas in the energy field and also as petrochemical feedstocks. During World War II, Germany relied on synfuels. The Republic of South Africa did so more recently. In the United States, the last coal synfuels plant, the Dakota Company's Great Plains gasification plant in Beulah, North Dakota may not be in operation when this is read; its prices exceed those which would be charged to rate-payers if natural gas was employed in energy service.

To put current coal use in perspective, as of 1994 coal provided 22% of the energy consumed in this country. Coal was 31% of the energy produced, which reflects that the United States is an exporter of coal. In 1997, a record amount of coal was produced in the United States: 1.09 billion short tons.[4] Production increased both in the east and west; Wyoming was the largest producer followed by West Virginia and Kentucky. All of this coal is low-to-medium in sulfur content.

II. COAL MARKETS

Coal is produced all over the world, including the United States,[5] South Africa, the United Kingdom, the former U.S.S.R. and China. Coal, unlike oil, tends to be used in the region where it is produced, so that coal is primarily a regional or national market, rather than a global one. Nevertheless, the United States does export coal and on occasion, has imported coal when transportation problems in the United States have created supply problems for utilities.

Coal at one point provided 90% of the energy needs of the United States. Its users ranged from the railroads that burned it for fuel to the families who heated their houses with individual furnaces in basements. Additionally, industry directly burned coal in boilers. Coal's bulk and dirt, however, made it less desirable as a direct source of energy in residential and commercial settings. By 1945, petroleum and natural gas had displaced many of these coal uses. After 1945, the consolidation of coal use in a relatively few industries continued. These phenomena led to changes in the nature in which coal was marketed.

The Supreme Court, in deciding an anti-trust case, provided the following summary of the coal industry in *United States v. General Dynamics Corp.*, 415 U.S. 486, 498-501 (1974):

> Much of the District Court's opinion was devoted to a description of the changes that have affected the coal industry since World War II. On the basis of more than three weeks of testimony and a voluminous record, the court discerned a number of clear and significant developments in the industry. First, it found that coal had become increasingly less able to compete with other

---

[4] National Mining Association, *Facts About Coal, 1999-2000*, at 2, quoting the Energy Information Association. Preliminary figures for 1998 show an increase to 1.118 billion short tons produced. *Id.*

[5] In the United States, economically valuable coals occur in the several regions, often referred to as follows: 1) Appalachia, from Pennsylvania to Alabama; 2) Mid-continental region, especially Michigan, Indiana, Illinois, Oklahoma, Kansas, Missouri, and Iowa; 3) High Plains, including North Dakota, eastern Montana, parts of Wyoming, eastern Colorado, and Texas; and 4) Rocky Mountains, including Utah, parts of Wyoming, western Montana, parts of Colorado, and New Mexico.

sources of energy in many segments of the energy market. Following [World War II] the industry entirely lost its largest single purchaser of coal—the railroads—and faced increasingly stiffer competition from oil and natural gas as sources of energy for industrial and residential uses. Because of these changes in consumption patterns, coal's share of the energy resources consumed in this country fell from 78.4% in 1920 to 21.4% in 1968. The court reviewed evidence attributing this decline not only to the changing relative economies of alternative fuels and to new distribution and consumption patterns, but also to more recent concern with the effect of coal use on the environment and consequent regulation of the extent and means of such coal consumption.

Second, the court found that to a growing extent since 1954, the electric utility industry has become the mainstay of coal consumption. While electric utilities consumed only 15.76% of the coal produced nationally in 1947, their share of total consumption increased every year thereafter, and in 1968 amounted to more than 59% of all the coal consumed throughout the Nation.

Third, and most significantly, the court found that to an increasing degree, nearly all coal sold to utilities is transferred under long-term requirements contracts, under which coal producers promise to meet utilities' coal consumption requirements for a fixed period of time, and at predetermined prices. The court described the mutual benefits accruing to both producers and consumers of coal from such long-term contracts in the following terms:

"This major investment (in electric utility equipment) can be jeopardized by a disruption in the supply of coal. Utilities are, therefore, concerned with assuring the supply of coal to such a plant over its life. In addition, utilities desire to establish in advance, as closely as possible, what fuel costs will be for the life of the plant. For these reasons, utilities typically arrange long-term contracts for all or at least a major portion of the total fuel requirements for the life of the plant. . . ."

"The long-term contractual commitments are not only required from the consumer's standpoint, but are also necessary from the viewpoint of the coal supplier. Such commitments may require the development of new mining capacity. . . . Coal producers have been reluctant to invest in new mining capacity in the absence of long-term contractual commitments for the major portion of the mine's capacity.

> Furthermore, such long-term contractual commitments are
> often required before financing for the development of new
> capacity can be obtained by the producer. . . ."

As a result of this trend to long-term contracts, the Supreme Court noted
that less coal was available on a spot market in 1974 then previously.

Another important phenomenon in the interim between World War II
and the 1970s was that coal prices were stable in current dollars, but
decreasing in constant dollars. The average price of coal in 1969 was $4.99
a ton in the United States, which was the exact same price as was prevalent
in 1948. However, expressed in 1948 dollars, the 1969 ton suffered a forty
percent decrease to $3.06 a ton. Coal companies, however, were not neces-
sarily pushed to bankruptcy. The drop in demand for coal eliminated the
need to expend capital on new mines. Also, worker productivity increases
dropped costs. Therefore, inflationary trends were offset.

The price of coal, however, increased in the 1970s for several reasons.
Among the various upward pressures on the price of coal was the increased
price of oil and gas, which allowed coal prices to rise but also increased
mining costs because oil is not only a competitor of coal, but is used in
mining it. More importantly, environmental and worker safety statutes
forced coal mining companies to internalize some of these costs. Traditional
productivity gains could no longer keep pace. Additionally, when coal
demand increased in the late 1960s, coal companies found that they would
have to open new mines. Because much of the easily accessible, and thus
cheaply mined coal, had already been mined, the newer mines had the
potential for higher capital and operational costs. Prices for some types of
coal, mostly high sulfur coals, have undergone some downward pressures in
the late 1980s and 1990s.

Because coal prices have failed to be stable since the 1970s, pricing of
coal under a long-term contract is problematical. Few mining companies
would want to guarantee a price for twenty years. It is possible to have a
contract without a price term, which would require the price to be the
"reasonable" price at the time of delivery. Uniform Commercial Code,
§ 2-305 (Open Price Term). The utility purchasing the coal, however, might
desire some more limited parameters. To this end, a common pricing
technique in coal contracts is to set a base price, which could be subject to
change if various indicators change. Often, these provisions call for the price
of coal to "escalate" if indexes or other indicia show various costs to have
increased. For the coal company, it would be important to include all
possible increases to all elements of production. However, crystal balls have
sometimes been cloudy and unable to anticipate all potential increases. For
example, costs of unanticipated environmental requirements could destroy

the coal company's predicted margin of profit if the costs are not reflected in the escalators.

Conversely, the price of coal under these types of provisions could escalate above a then current market price. If the contract provides for a fixed price and a fixed amount to be purchased by the utility, courts have not been quick to release the utility from the deal which, in retrospect, was not advantageous. A fixed price contract—or one that only escalates upward—assigns the risk of the market price falling to the buyer. Doctrines such as force majeure, commercial impracticability, or frustration of purpose have not been found to excuse the buyer.[6] To avoid some of these problems, long term contracts sometimes have market opener provisions, which allow for renegotiation of the price at set intervals. If the parties cannot agree, often the seller has the option of meeting a competitive market bid or abandoning a contract.[7]

Coal production currently is being concentrated in larger and larger companies. Mergers have been prevalent, with producers believing they must be big to take on utilities. The playing field has changed not only because of these consolidations, but because there also has been an exodus of oil companies from the coal industry. Oil producers had gone into coal in the late 1970s and early 1980s. The only remaining big player is Chevron, which operates through its Pittsburg and Midway Coal Mining subsidiary. An additional change in coal markets since the *General Dynamic* decision is that current events have brought back some life to the spot market as well as a nascent futures market in coal. Some of this is traceable to deregulation and competition in the electric generation market.

---

[6] Northern Indiana Public Service Co. v. Carbon County Coal Co., 799 F.2d 265 (7th Cir. 1986). *Compare* Missouri Public Service Co. v. Peabody Coal, 483 S.W.2d 721 (Mo. Ct. App. 1979). In the *Missouri Public Service* case, the coal company claimed that the price in the fixed price contract was too low because the costs of mining had increased. Comments to U.C.C. § 2-615 note increased costs do not allow relief for impracticability unless an "unforeseeable" contingency caused the increase. Peabody tried to use the Arab oil embargo as an excuse, but the court said this was foreseeable. As Judge Posner noted at the end of *Northern Indiana*, the rise in oil prices had made some coal economical to mine because of the higher price of oil, which competes with coal in the electric generation market. If the oil price is high, coal which otherwise would be too costly to compete may compete.

[7] For the saga of one such contract, *see* PSI Energy, Inc. v. Exxon Coal USA, Inc., 991 F.2d 1265 (7th Cir. 1993) and 17 F.3d 969 (7th Cir. 1994).

III.   COAL REGULATION

A.   Development of Coal in Private Ownership: The Issue of Severed Coal

One of the biggest factors determining development of coal on private lands is ascertaining who has the right to mine coal by what methods. Naturally, if the owner of the land did not sever the minerals from the surface, that owner could develop the coal without question; the old maxim is that *cujus est solum, ejus est usque as coelum et infernos*, or "To whomever the soil belongs, he owns also to the sky and to the depths." A deed, however, may convey minerals separately or by reservation or exception seek to remove them from a grant. When one of these activities has taken place, it is said that the minerals are severed from the surface. Very often a coal company acquires or retains not the entire property, but only the severed coal. Therefore, arguments arise about what may be done to remove the coal.

Certain basic premises govern the respective rights of the owners of the coal and surface. First, if the minerals are truly severed, two estates in land are created. The mineral interest will be in the nature of a corporeal fee.[8] The owner of a mineral estate has the right to develop the minerals, the right of access and use of the surface for this purpose, and the right to lease the minerals and receive the proceeds of a mineral lease. The right to use so much of the surface as is reasonably necessary for the production of minerals is an implied right, one which exists even without an express grant in the document severing the mineral estate. The agreement of the parties, however, may expand or contract the implied rights. The rights may also respond to new technology.

Generally, the severed mineral estate is deemed dominant over the surface estate. Therefore, the mineral owner would only be liable for negligent damage or for an unreasonable use of the surface. Nevertheless, some doctrines have evolved at common law and by legislation to protect the surface owner. For example, courts note that the surface estate includes all rights not part of the mineral estate. Therefore, the owner of the surface may make such uses of it that do not unreasonably interfere with the extraction of minerals. To this end, some states statutorily require the miner to post security for the benefit of the surface owner before com-

---

[8] In Louisiana, a separate estate in minerals cannot be created in fee, although two separate ownerships in the same property may be created. A severance creates a servitude in the nature of an easement. This servitude is defeasible; it will end or "prescribe" for non-use.

mencing surface disturbance. Additionally, two common law doctrines temper the ability of the mineral owner to extract all the minerals beneath or in the property.

These two doctrines require protection of the surface. The first doctrine, that of the right to subjacent support, gives the surface owner the right to have the surface supported in its natural state by the underlying mineral estate. Therefore, subjacent support looks at property as if physically divided on a horizontal plane. The right to subjacent support is an absolute right: the mineral estate owner would be liable for subsidence[9] even if its mining operations were not negligent. A cause of action for subsidence generally does not arise until the supporting earth begins to fall and cause damage. Nevertheless, because of the absolute nature of the right to subjacent support, some cases have granted injunctions against proposed mining. Others, however, have limited the cause of action to damages, at least in the absence of threats of appreciable damage to the surface. The right to subjacent support however, may be waived.[10]

The surface estate also has a right to lateral support. Lateral, or side, support looks to property as if physically divided vertically. Property must support adjoining property. Removal of minerals cannot make adjoining property subside because of sideward and downward movement.

Because of the impact of some mining methods, the issue of whether the document creating a severed mineral interest authorized that method is often controverted. At one level, the issue is whether or not the surface owner waived the right to demand subjacent and lateral support. Nevertheless, for surface and strip mining concerns, because the surface is rendered totally unusable, some courts treat whether either method is authorized as an issue separate from whether the right to support has been waived. Kentucky is a jurisdiction with voluminous case law on the subject. In essence, it explained that the judicial question is "whether the `parties to

---

[9] Subsidence is the downward movement of earth that results from removal of lower strata that had supported the subsided earth. *See* Keystone Bituminous Coal Co. v. DeBenedictis, 480 U.S. 470 (1987). For the current federal regulatory authority for controlling subsidence, *see* National Mining Association v. Babbitt, 172 F.3d 906 (D.C. Cir. 1999).

[10] Pennsylvania views the right of subjacent support as a separate right that could be owned by the surface estate or the mineral estate. Additionally, the support estate may adhere to individual veins of coal, creating rights and duties between competing coal companies. In theory, the separate right could be owned by a party without either the surface or mineral estate, but in practice this does not occur. In the event this type of ownership existed, the holder of the right to subjacent support would have a right violated if support is removed, but no damages.

the deed intended that the mineral owner's right to use the surface in removal of minerals would be superior to any competing right of the surface owner."[11] Kentucky also tried to limit surface mining for severed coal in the face of a silent deed to areas where such mining was common on the date of the deed. The Kentucky Supreme Court found such a statute to be unconstitutional as a violation of separation of powers.[12] In response to the ruling, the legislature proposed and the voters ratified (by an 83% vote) an amendment to the Kentucky constitution that essentially tracked the statute. Federal constitutional questions could remain. A similar statute was found constitutional in Tennessee.[13] Comparable statutes have been passed in Colorado, Montana, and Wyoming.

The basic concern behind these court cases and statutes is that coal mining often leaves the surface heavily impacted unless reclamation is required. Problems of reclamation will be examined in conjunction with the federal Surface Mining Control and Reclamation Act (SMCRA), *infra*.[14] SMCRA has not rendered the problems of private deed interpretation unimportant, but in some circumstances has even emphasized them. For example, under SMCRA, surface mining in some locales is prohibited unless the miner had a "valid existing right." More generally, in order for a mining company to get a permit, they must obtain the consent of the surface owner to surface mining unless the company had the right to surface mine under state law. Therefore, surface and coal owners will continue to litigate whether the coal developer has the authority to mine.

B.   Development of Coal in Federal Ownership

Coal resources in the United States are not completely in private hands. The federal government owns much of the coal in the western United States. Even if the federal government has patented the surface of the land to a private party, under many statutes the federal government reserved the coal. Additionally, state and tribal governments also own minerals. While the governmental entities are similar to private mineral owners in one respect, they may have concerns that the private owner does not. Like the private mineral owner, governments rarely have the desire to directly develop their minerals; they seek a return from the minerals by enticing

---

[11] *See* United State v. Stearns Coal and Lumber Co., 816 F.2d 279 (6th Cir. 1987), quoting Martin v. Kentucky Oak Mining Co., 429 S.W.2d 395 (Ken. App. 1968).

[12] Akers v. Baldwin, 736 S.W.2d 294 (Ky. 1987).

[13] Doochin v. Rackley, 610 S.W.2d 715 (Tenn. 1981).

[14] Codified at 30 U.S.C. §§ 1201-1328.

others to mine. Unlike their private counterparts, however, the governmental concerns may be more numerous than seeking a dollar return and avoiding injury to a particular surface. Governments may want to foster energy independence, local entrepreneurs, regional equity, or other societal goals. Because of the abundance of federal coal, the regime governing its development must be addressed.

Up until 1920, coal and the lands containing it that were owned by the government were subject to purchase. This was changed by the Mineral Lands Leasing Act of 1920, currently known as the Mineral Leasing Act and codified at 30 U.S. § 121 *et seq.* Importantly, lands would no longer be transferred to private parties. The right to mine coal would come through a lease and the producer would owe the federal government a royalty on every ton of coal mined. Leases were for an indeterminate time period and provided for a yearly rental, escalating from 25 cents an acre for the first year up to one dollar per acre for the sixth and subsequent years. Rentals were credited against royalties. The Act also limited the number of leases any company could hold and provided that the Secretary of the Interior could regulate development and act to protect workers as long as such regulations did not conflict with state law. A significant percentage of the proceeds of the leases went to the state in which the leasehold was.

Initially, the Act provided a two-tier system for leasing. In lands known to have coal in commercial quantities, coal was leased by competitive bid. In lands in which coal was not known to be in commercial quantities, a party could apply for an exploration permit. If coal was found in commercial quantities, a lease would ensue. These leases were referred to as "preference right leases," with an emphasis on "right." If the private explorer found coal in commercial quantities, there was no discretion on the part of the Secretary of the Interior; a lease would have to be issued. Environmental concerns could not foreclose the lease. However, the federal government could consider environmental problems at other junctures: at issuance of the prospecting permit, in setting lease terms, and in determining if "commercial quantities" existed in light of the cost of complying with environmental laws.[15]

This state of affairs was not deemed satisfactory for several reasons. Congress therefore amended the statute governing acquisition of federal coal leases with the Coal Leasing Act Amendments of 1975 (Public Law 94-277), enacted August 4, 1976. Some of the concerns driving Congress were fiscal. With the large backlog of preference right leases, there would be little market interest in competitive leases. The government received no signifi-

---

[15] Natural Resources Defense Council, Inc. v. Berklund, 609 F.2d 553 (D.C. Cir. 1980).

cant bonuses from the preference right leases. The amount of coal under
lease was staggering, but very little was actually being mined. A 1975 House
Report revealed that the federal government owned 50% of the nation's coal
reserves, and 60% of those in the west. There were 533 active leases and
numerous pending preference right lease applications. All told, 28 billion
tons of coal were effectively leased. Production, however, was minimal: only
59 of the 533 active leases were in production. Despite the immensity of the
federal reserves, in 1974, only 3% of production came from federal lands.[16]
There was a sense that coal was being hoarded, with speculation rather
than development the goal of the lessees. Additionally, the tonnage was
concentrated in a few companies.

There were additional problems. The coal that was developed yielded
little return to the government because, regardless of the price of coal,
royalty was set at a fixed priced per ton, often only five cents. Moreover, as
revealed in *NRDC v. Berklund,* there were limited opportunities to provide
environmental protection. The Department of the Interior administratively
tried to remedy some problems and passed a moratorium on exploration
permits to allow Congress to act. Congress reacted both by directly amending the Mineral Leasing Act and by passing the Surface Mining Control and
Reclamation Act.

The most visible change to the Mineral Leasing Act was the repeal of
the provisions for preference right leases. Prospecting permission under the
new rules would not give rise to any lease entitlement. In addition, Congress
addressed other problems that prompted legislative action.[17] Most leases
were to be issued competitively and "fair market value" bonuses were
required. Additional economic concerns were met by requiring a royalty of
at least 12% of value for surface mined coal. Coal mined underground could,
if determined by the Secretary, have a lower royalty. To solve the speculation problem, leases would no longer be of indeterminate length. Leases
would have a primary term of twenty years and continue for so long as coal
is produced commercially. Lease terms, however, could be readjusted at the
end of the first twenty years and every ten years thereafter. In order to
foster diligence, leases not producing in ten years could be canceled if issued
under the amendments; parties holding old leases for more than ten years
without production would not be able to receive any federal mineral leases
under the Mineral Leasing Act, which also governs oil and gas leasing.

---

[16] Some of this could be explained by the fact that most of the coal consumers
were still east of the Mississippi River. As of 1965, only 5% of U.S. coal production
occurred west of the Mississippi. This included mining of both government-owned
and private coal.

[17] *See* 30 U.S.C. §§ 201 and 207.

Finally, environmental concerns were addressed by requiring land use planning before lease issuance; operation and reclamation plans were required before mining.

C.   Coal Combustion and the Environment

Coal combustion results in four major pollutants: particulates (small particles, primarily unburned material and ash), sulfur dioxides, nitrogen oxides, and carbon dioxide. Additionally, the Environmental Protection Agency has recently sought monitoring of a fifth pollutant, namely mercury. Research into the impacts of the first four regulated pollutants reveal that smaller particulates may present more health risks than the more visible "soot." Additionally, sulfur dioxide (SO_2) contributes to acid rain. Nitrogen oxide, like SO_2, is a poisonous gas and contributes to smog and is a "greenhouse" gas.[18] Similarly, carbon dioxide is also poisonous and contributes to the "greenhouse" effect. Control of sulfur dioxide emissions has been central to the story of coal use. Therefore, its regulation will be the subject of an examination of the Clean Air Act.

Generally, the amount of SO_2 produced during coal combustion is directly proportional to the sulfur content of the raw fuel. The variation in sulfur content could lead to divergent sulfur emissions from an uncontrolled 500-megawatt electric generating plant. Based on the coal's sulfur content, the plant could emit SO_2 at rates ranging from less than 0.5 to more than 6 pounds of the gas per one million British thermal units (Btus) of coal burned. Over a year, this would translate to a range extending from less than 7,665 up to more than 91,980 tons of SO_2. The Clean Air Act approached this problem in several ways.

The Act directly regulated coal-powered generating plants first through the New Source Performance Standards. As the name indicates, they applied to new "sources" of pollution, which in simplified terms, include new

---

[18] A "greenhouse gas" is one that allows visible light to pass through, but that blocks much of the heat reflected from the earth's surface, much as the glass in a greenhouse operates. Without the greenhouse effect, the world's temperature would be colder by 35 degrees Celsius. In such a case, most of the oceans would freeze and life would cease or take a very different form. According to the theory of global warming, an increase in greenhouse gases in the atmosphere could cause unacceptable temperature rises. The CO_2 in the atmosphere before the industrial revolution was 280 parts per million. With the increased use of fossil fuels, that figure is now 350 parts per million. The United States in 1992 produced 23% of the emissions. Although carbon dioxide emissions have more than tripled in the last 40 years, there were signs of leveling off in the late 1980s and early 1990s.

plants and major modifications of old plants.[19] The Environmental Protection Agency would promulgate the standards, which provided *uniform* emission standards. An example of such a standard would be "1.2 pounds of SO_2 for every million BTU's of heat coal would produce when burned." Similar standards were set for nitrogen oxides and particulates. These standards would apply to all sources wherever located, unless more stringent standards applied under other Clean Air Act programs, such as the Prevention of Significant Deterioration or Non-Attainment programs. The New Source Performance standards are technologically based. They are what would result if the company used the best technology "adequately demonstrated." This technology need not be available on the date of regulation, but is one shown to be available when the source came on line, albeit, available with a "margin of striving." The source is not required to use the specified technology; it must simply meet the resulting limits on emissions as if the technology had been employed.

The 1977 Amendments to the Clean Air Act modified the New Source Performance Standards. They required scrubbing regardless of the cleanliness of the coal. "Scrubbing" removes the SO_2 from the air stream *after* combustion. The amendments required a percentage reduction of sulfur. A higher percentage (90%) would be required if the natural emissions would have been higher, sliding down to a required 70% reduction for lower natural emissions. It was estimated that the modified standards would reduce emissions by half over what they would have been without the percentage reduction. The 1990 Amendments removed the percentage reduction requirements when the national cap on SO_2 emissions goes into effect in the year 2000.

Federal action did not affect existing sources directly in the original Clean Air Act. This dichotomy between types of sources could create an incentive to keep old, otherwise inefficient plants in operation to avoid "new source" requirements. Existing sources, however, could be directed to lessen their emissions by the states in their State Implementation Plans. Additionally, after 1977, states were to require "major" sources to use state-defined RACT, or "Reasonably Available Control Technology."

Federal mandates on existing sources also appear in the Acid Rain provisions of the 1990 Amendments, which are found in Title IV of the Amendments. The Amendments are designed to lower the overall emissions of both SO_2 and nitrogen oxides. Congress specified a total reduction for the entire contiguous United States. There are to be 10 million fewer tons of SO_2

---

[19] The definition of the word "source" has a long statutory and regulatory history, which is beyond the scope of this text.

and 2 million fewer tons of nitrogen oxides emitted. To achieve the SO_2 reduction by 1995, the EPA implemented a unique program. First, Phase I provided that the EPA would allocate marketable pollution "allowances" to fossil burning power plants according to a statutory formula, which is partly based on past emissions and fuel rates. An "allowance" is permission to emit a ton of the pollutant. If a plant does not have sufficient "allowances" when the EPA counts up its yearly emissions, the plant will be fined. However, those who reduce emissions and do not need their "allowances" may sell them to others. No matter how many credits a utility may buy, it is not allowed to cause a violation of the basic National Ambient Air Quality Standards, or NAAQS, set by the Environmental Protection Agency for each pollutant. Phase II will have a nation-wide cap on emissions of 8.9 million tons of sulfur dioxide, which is 10 million tons less than the levels of emissions in 1980. Sources other than utilities will be involved in Phase II, which begins in the year 2000. Any new source of the pollutant will have to offset its emissions by reducing emissions elsewhere.

Reductions since 1980 have created levels 39% below what was required for 1995; utilities were emitting 10.9 million tons of SO_2 in 1980 and were at 5.3 million in 1995. The 1995 target was to reduce emissions to 8.7 million tons. Marketable allowances were an innovation in policy. The price of the credit or allowance was set by the market at somewhere between the fine and the cost of reducing emissions. In 1995, 23 million allowances were traded in a market valued at $2 billion. As of the end of March 1996, the price paid per SO_2 credit plunged; the price of a credit dropped from $250 in 1992 to $68 in 1996. The prices were lower because scrubber technology prices have decreased (they are 50% cheaper) and deregulation of railroads made transport of low-sulfur coal cheaper. Therefore, it became easier to comply with the reduction requirements. In fact, in 1996, there were 25,000 credits for sale that no one bought.

Most utilities complied by fuel switching or blending. Only 10% of the utilities installed scrubbers (which accounted for 28% of the SO_2 reductions). Because of increasing competition in the electricity market, there was less desire to make capital expenditures. The Energy Information Administration (EIA) estimated industry-wide, annualized compliance costs as being $836 million in 1995 dollars; this amount is only 0.6 percent of the $151 billion of electric operating expenses investor owned utilities incurred. The EIA estimated that using scrubbers cost $322 per ton of SO_2 removed and was thus the most expensive method of compliance. By contrast, the cheapest method was modifying a high sulfur bituminous coal-fired plant to burn lower sulfur sub-bituminous coal. It was estimated to cost $113 per ton of SO_2 removed.

The current move towards a restructured, competitive electric market has raised concerns about increased pollution from coal-fired generating plants. About 700 plants, primarily in the midwest, were built before the 1970 and 1977 Amendments to the Clean Air Act. Although the 1990 Amendment's caps apply, these "old source" generating plants are not subject to caps for nitrogen oxides and carbon dioxide. In exempting these old facilities in 1970 and 1977, Congress anticipated their retirement at the end of their natural 20-30 year useful lives. The exemptions, together with the high capital cost of replacements, kept these facilities on line longer than anticipated. With a surplus of generating capacity, however, many of these "dirty" facilities had not been operating, or, if operating, were not at full capacity. But, as generators come to compete for customers, these facilities will become more attractive to use because they have some of the lowest operating costs in the country, thus making their electricity output cheaper. These facilities may emit four to ten times more pollution per kilowatt-hour of energy produced than newer generating plants.

D.   Transportation of Coal

Most coal, about two-thirds of it, is transported by rail. Massive capital must be invested in rail lines and in specialized handling equipment and rail cars. In the eastern United States, there has long been some competition between rail carriers that could serve a coal mine and the purchasing utility. In the West, however, most coal mines are "captive" to one railroad. A mine, or a purchasing utility, is captive if the only mode of transport is a particular railroad. Because of the potential for monopolistic bottlenecks, the federal government had regulated rail rates. The Interstate Commerce Commission had long been required to assure that rates were "just and reasonable." Generally, this meant traditional cost-of-service rates, requiring shippers to pay the transport costs plus a reasonable rate of return. Two statutes changed this formulaic reliance on cost-of-service rates.

The first statute in response to difficulties in the railroad industry was the Railroad Revitalization and Regulatory Reform Act of 1976 (P.L. 94-210, 90 Stat. 31). This Act, referred to as the 4-R Act, allowed the ICC to set rates that would allow the railroads in competitive areas to earn "adequate revenues." Additionally, in areas where one railroad dominated the market, the ICC could investigate whether rates were reasonable or derived from monopolistic power. The second major revision in railroad regulation was the Staggers Act of 1980.[20] Under it, the ICC could set "rate flexibility zones," so railroads would not have to have rate hearings for every proposed

---

[20] P.L. 96-448, 94 Stat. 1895.

tariff revision. Comparative industry costs may be considered in setting rates. Additionally, so-called "Ramsey rates," or differential rates, became prevalent. In such a rate, captive customers pay a greater share of fixed costs than those customers that have competitive options. The theory behind such a scheme is that all users benefit from keeping the non-captive shippers on the system. So long as the non-captive shippers pay their variable costs and some percentage of fixed costs, the load of the captive shipper is lightened. To a certain extent, the non-captive customer is charged based on cost of service and the captive customer's rate would be based on the value of the service. The ICC, however, had remained in the background to prevent monopolistic blackmail. Nevertheless, the trend was towards deregulation, especially where some competition existed. This trend culminated in the dissolution of the ICC. This was effectuated by the ICC Termination Act of 1995.[21] Having terminated the Interstate Commerce Commission, the Act sets up the Surface Transportation Board in the Department of Transportation to perform the Act's regulatory duties. The agency is colloquially referred to as the "Surf Board." It will look at mergers and provide relief from monopolistic pricing if necessary.

Transportation costs for coal haulage have lessened after regulatory relaxation. This decrease in cost took place despite the current trend of transporting coal longer distances. According to the Energy Information Administration's study, the *Energy Policy Act Transportation Study: Interim Report on Coal Transportation*, the Clean Air Act and other changes led to more utilities purchasing coal from the Powder River Region, which produces so called "compliance coal," or very low-sulfur coal, coal which meets not only the Phase I requirements of the 1990 Act Amendments but also the Phase II requirements. This resulted in a greater hauling distance, namely an 11% increase in the average from 604 to 671 miles. Nevertheless, the average cost of transporting the coal to the plant decreased from $11.08 to $8.93 per short ton in constant 1987 dollars, which represents a 19% decrease. The study found the cause of this reduction to be competition and change in the railroad industry. Within the railroads themselves, more powerful locomotives, cars that can hold more coal, and organizational improvements allowed railroads to lower their costs. The study also noted that if the costs of transport by barge, truck, and other modes were also entered into the equation, there also would be lower costs from 1979 to 1993. Combining all modes, there was a 23% decrease in transportation costs.

Nevertheless, a series of railroad mergers has led some utility executives to worry about the potential for re-emerging monopoly power that the

---

[21] P.L. 104-88, 109 Stat. 803, effective January 1, 1996. 49 U.S.C. §§ 10101 *et seq.*

Surface Transportation Board will not control. For example, the Powder River Basin is served by only two major railroads, the Burlington Northern Santa Fe and the Union Pacific.[22] The first railroad resulted from the merger in 1995 of the Burlington Northern and Santa Fe railroads. When the Union Pacific, which merged with the Chicago and North Western in 1995, merged with Southern Pacific Rail Corporation, the resulting railroad controlled 37,000 miles of track crossing two-thirds of the nation. The track is in 25 states, Canada, and Mexico. Only three additional major railroad companies exist. After the merger, two companies—Burlington Northern Santa Fe and the Union Pacific—carry 90% of the freight west of the Mississippi. The Surface Transportation Board approved the merger over the objections of the Departments of Justice, Transportation, and Agriculture. Benefits noted were shortened routes that would save shippers money and the ability to infuse money into the Southern Pacific lines; Southern Pacific had been losing money. Some conditions include "trackage rights," which allow customers access to Burlington Northern lines. In light of these mergers, some spokesmen for coal purchasers have taken this concept further and generally sought "open access railroads." Railroad track would, in a manner similar to electric transmission lines or natural gas pipelines, be available to transport the rail cars owned by others.

Given concerns about railroads and barges, a third mode of coal transport with potential is the coal slurry pipeline. In this technology, coal is pulverized and mixed with water and moved through a pipeline. At the coal's destination, it is de-watered. The most successful coal slurry pipeline is a 273 mile line running from the Black Mesa mine in northeastern Arizona to the Mohave power plant in southern Nevada. The pipeline is owned by the Union Pacific Railway Company. A shorter pipeline in Ohio operated briefly and then fell prey to lower railroad prices that were made possible by the railroad using "unit trains," dedicated trains of 100 car-length. In 1979, testimony at Congressional hearings praised the technology as price-competitive with rail. In the 1980s, there was a flurry of promotional activity on behalf of several lines, yet none was built. The most controversial (and litigious) line was that proposed by Energy Transportation Systems, Inc. (ETSI). The slurry would originate in Wyoming and, as originally conceived, would proceed 1400 miles to utilities in Arkansas and Louisiana. Eventually, service to Texas was also envisioned.

The ETSI pipeline ran into many roadblocks. First, it had to cross railroad tracks and federal lands. Additionally, it had to acquire water to use where the coal was mined. Wyoming is not a water-logged state.

---

[22] A third company, the Dakota, Minnesota & Eastern Railroad, announced plans in the summer of 1997 to try to compete in the Basin.

Although Wyoming passed a statute that could allow use of water from the Madison or Bell Sand formations, South Dakota objected to use of the Madison formation and attempted to entice ETSI to use unused water from an Army Corps of Engineers dam. One of ETSI's principal potential customers, Arkansas Power & Light, was finally convinced rail traffic would be more cost-effective and signed a thirty year contract with the Union Pacific System and Chicago & North Western Railway. The coal slurry project finally was abandoned.

E.   Health and Safety Regulation

Coal mining is considered one of the riskiest of occupations. Mining in general is hazardous. Fatalities in mining, however, are decreasing; they have gone from a total of over 200 fatalities in 1984 to a record low of 84 in 1996. Thirty-nine of those fatalities were in coal mines.[23] Moreover, in addition to the immediate and direct threats to life from blasting problems and methane explosions in underground mines, coal miners are subject to the risk of Black Lung disease. Congress has reacted both to basic mining hazards and the peculiar problem of Black Lung disease.

The Federal Mine Safety and Health Act of 1969, and the Federal Mine Safety and Health Amendments of 1977, as amended,[24] address general mine safety concerns. The amended act provides for comprehensive standards and inspections, as discussed in the Supreme Court case of *Donovan v. Dewey*,[25] which upheld warrantless administrative searches under the Act:

> Because a warrant requirement clearly might impede the "specific enforcement needs" of the Act, the only real issue before us is whether the statute's inspection program, in terms of the certainty and regularity of its application, provides a constitutionally adequate substitute for a warrant. We believe that it does. Unlike the statute at issue in *Barlow's*, [Marshall v. Barlow's, Inc., 436 U.S. 307 (1978)] the Mine Safety and Health Act applies to industrial activity with a notorious history of serious accidents and unhealthful working conditions The Act is specifically tailored to address those concerns, and the regulation of mines it imposes is sufficiently pervasive and defined that the owner of such a facility cannot help but be aware that he "will be subject to effec-

---

[23] Fatality totals for coal mining numbered 30 in 1997 and preliminary figures for 1998 are 29 fatalities. National Mining Association, Facts About Coal, 1999-2000, at p. 38.

[24] 30 U.S.C. §§ 801 *et seq.*

[25] 452 U.S. 594 (1981).

tive inspection." First, the Act requires inspection of *all* mines and specifically defines the frequency of inspection. Representatives of the Secretary must inspect all surface mines at least twice annually and all underground mines at least four times annually. Similarly, all mining operations that generate explosive gases must be inspected at irregular 5-, 10-, or 15-day intervals. Moreover, the Secretary must conduct follow-up inspections of mines where violations of the Act have previously been discovered, and must inspect a mine immediately if notified by a miner or a miner's representative that a violation of the Act or an imminently dangerous condition exists. Second, the standards with which a mine operator is required to comply are all specifically set forth in the Act or in Title 30 of the Code of Federal Regulations. Indeed, the Act requires that the Secretary inform mine operators of all standards proposed pursuant to the Act. Thus, rather than leaving the frequency and purpose of inspections to the unchecked discretion of Government officers, the Act establishes a predictable and guided federal regulatory presence. Like the gun dealer in *Biswell*, the operator of a mine "is not left to wonder about the purposes of the inspector or the limits of his task."

Coal mine safety is heavily regulated. The Acts and agency actions implementing them specify various command and control regulations concerning the safe operation of a mine. Sanctions include civil fines, criminal penalties, and closure orders. Most enforcement is through correction orders and fines.

Another aspect of the regulation of coal mining are special provisions to recompense miners afflicted with pneumoconiosis or "black lung" disease. Black lung had affected a high percentage of American coal miners, resulting in severe, and frequently crippling, chronic respiratory impairment. Long-term inhalation of coal dust can cause the ailment. Beginning in 1969,[26] Congress mandated provisions whereby the federal government, together with coal companies, would provide compensation for disabled miners and their survivors. The plan survived initial legal attack. The Supreme Court, in *Usery v. Turner Elkhorn Mining Co.*,[27] found that requiring companies to provide benefits for workers who had retired prior to passage of the compensation law was not retroactive rule-making. Making companies liable for past workers, although newer companies would not

---

[26] Title IV of the Federal Coal Mine Health and Safety Act of 1969, as amended by the Black Lung Benefits Act of 1972, 30 U.S.C. §§ 901 *et seq.* (1970 ed. and Supp. IV).

[27] 428 U.S. 1 (1976)

have such liabilities, was a logical way of spreading the cost of protection. "Orphaned" workers would be protected by the federal government. Moreover, because company doctors often controlled medical records and proving the cause of a lung ailment might be problematic, the *Usery* court held that Congress could employ reasonable presumptions that coal dust was the cause of ailments after certain exposure times. The Act has been amended in particulars since the *Usery* opinion, but the general thrust remains.

More recently, lifetime health benefits for coal miners subject to union contracts had been promised under private agreements. When the funds to fulfill this promise became jeopardized, Congress passed the Coal Industry Retiree Benefit Act of 1992.[28] The Act survived similar challenges as were made against the constitutionality of the Black Lung Benefits Act of 1972,[29] but in *Eastern Enterprises v. Apfel*,[30] the Supreme Court found portions of the Act, which apportioned liability for retirees to a company that had done no mining since 1965, to be invalid as applied to that company. Four justices (O'Connor, Rehnquist, Scalia and Thomas) found the Act's provision placed a severe, disproportionate, and retroactive burden on the company and thus created an unconstitutional taking of the company's property. Justice Kennedy concurred in the judgment, but thought a takings analysis was inappropriate; he found the provision violated due process. The dissenting justices (Stevens, Breyer, Souter, and Ginsburg) also found a takings analysis to be unwarranted. They noted that takings cases had dealt with an impact on specific property, be it personal or real. This act merely required a payment of money by the company. They opined that to apply a takings analysis to general money obligations would enlarge the scope of the constitutional provision.

F.   Land Reclamation Requirements

Coal mining, especially by surface mining techniques, can greatly impact the land if it is not properly reclaimed after mining. State regulation was ineffective in many areas because the need for the economic benefits of coal mining and the financial clout of mining companies tended to weaken regulatory resolve. Congress repeatedly addressed the issue, taking from 1968 to 1977 to complete legislation. President Ford twice vetoed regulatory activity. Finally, under President Carter, the Surface Mining Control and Reclamation Act of 1977 was born.[31]

---

[28] P.L. 102-486 § 19142; 26 U.S.C. §§ 9701 *et seq.*

[29] *See* In re Blue Diamond Coal Co., 79 F.3d 516 (6th Cir. 1996).

[30] 524 U.S. 498 (1998).

[31] Public Law 95-87, codified at 30 U.S.C. §§ 1201 *et seq.*

The Act regulates the surface impacts of all mining, be it surface mining or underground mining. The Supreme Court detailed some of the concerns to be addressed:

> [T]he Senate Report explained that "[s]urface coal mining activities have imposed large social costs on the public . . . in many areas of the country in the form of unreclaimed lands, water pollution, erosion, floods, slope failures, loss of fish and wildlife resources, and a decline in natural beauty." S. Rep. No. 95-128, p. 50 (1977).
>
> Similarly, the House Committee documented the adverse effects of surface coal mining on interstate commerce as including: " 'Acid drainage which has ruined an estimated 11,000 miles of streams; the loss of prime hardwood forest and the destruction of wildlife habitat by strip mining; the degrading of productive farmland; recurrent landslides; siltation and sedimentation of river systems. . . .' " And in discussing how surface coal mining affects water resources and in turn interstate commerce, the House Committee explained: "The most widespread damages . . . are environmental in nature. Water users and developers incur significant economic and financial losses as well. "Reduced recreational values, fishkills, reductions in normal waste assimilation capacity, impaired water supplies, metals and masonry corrosion and deterioration, increased flood frequencies and flood damages, reductions in designed water storage capacities at impoundments, and higher operating costs for commercial waterway users are some of the most obvious economic effects that stem from mining-related pollution and sedimentation."[32]

The Supreme Court also noted the Congressional finding that federal regulation was required to maintain uniform minimum nationwide standards and to address inadequacies in state law.

A useful overview of SMCRA is found in footnote three of National Wildlife Federation v. Lujan (NWF III, Round III):[33]

> [S]MCRA is codified as Chapter 25, Surface Mining Control and Reclamation, of U.S.C.A. Title 30, Mineral Lands and Mining. The key part of the Act for this opinion is Subchapter V, Control of the Environmental Impacts of Surface Coal Mining. SMCRA

---

[32] Hodel v. Virginia Surface Mining and Reclamation Association, Inc., 452 U.S. 264, 278-280 (1981).

[33] 31 ERC 2069, 21 ENVTL. L. REP. 20,143, 1990 WL 134826 (D.D.C. 1990)

§§ 501-529. Certain important definitions appear in SMCRA § 701. The corresponding regulations appear at Title 30 C.F.R., Mineral Resources, Chapter VII, Office of Surface Mining Reclamation and Enforcement, Department of Interior, Parts 700-955.

In establishing a comprehensive program to regulate surface mining, and the surface impacts of underground mining, Congress directed the Secretary of Interior to devise an "interim" program to regulate surface mining within 90 days from the date of the Act, August 3, 1977. SMCRA § 501(a). Congress directed the Secretary to put together a permanent regulatory program within a year from the date of the Act.

A key SMCRA feature was to create a "federalist" regulatory regime assigning certain roles to the federal government and others to state agencies. Principally, Congress gave to the Secretary of the Interior, through the Office of Surface Mining Reclamation and Enforcement (OSMRE), the power to set national standards for carrying out the Act. To accommodate the widely varying conditions of coal mining throughout the country, and particularly between the eastern and western parts of the U.S., Congress gave individual states the power, if they chose, to create state agencies charged with implementing the Act and enforcing it locally. Some states had already established their own entities to do this job under state law. These state agencies are referred to in the Act and rules as "regulatory authorities."

Under the interim program, the Secretary regulated mining operations directly, unless the state already had a regulatory program. Existing state programs had to comply with the Act's interim standards and rules for an interim program. The minimum statutory standards for the interim program are set forth in SMCRA § 502(c), referring to certain permanent standards set forth in § 515. The rules for the interim program are set out in Subchapter B of the SMCRA rules, 30 C.F.R. Parts 710-725. Congress set up the interim program both to give the Secretary time to devise a permanent program, and to enable states to set up their own program. The Act itself sets out detailed requirements for a full scheme of permanent regulation that the federal and all state programs must meet.

The statutory regulatory scheme contains four key features:

First, anyone intending to conduct a surface coal mining operation must apply for and obtain a permit to do so. SMCRA § 507. SMCRA defines surface coal mining operations broadly.

The definition goes beyond just the site of a strip mine. <u>For example, it reaches activities such as underground mining with surface impacts and coal processing.</u> In addition to covering activities, the definition encompasses the areas where those activities take place. SMCRA § 701(28). The Act requires anyone seeking a permit for any of these to submit a large amount of information in the application, including a detailed plan to reclaim the area of the mining operation. Requirements of the reclamation plan are spelled out at SMCRA § 508. The Secretary has fleshed out the statutory permit and reclamation plan requirements further in Subchapter G, Parts 773-785. The key rules are: minimum requirements for information on environmental resources for surface and underground mining . . .; minimum requirements for reclamation and operation plan for surface and underground mining . . .; and requirements for permits for special categories of mining, such as that done on farmland, mountaintops, and steep slopes, and for coal preparation plants not at a mine site.

Second, the Act <u>also requires mine operators to post a bond or to indemnify the regulatory</u> authority in the amount of the cost of reclaiming the operation to the full extent that SMCRA requires. SMCRA § 509. The bond must remain in place for the time necessary to reclaim the operation. The Secretary's rules on bonding requirements are at Subchapter J, Part 800.

<u>Third, perhaps most important, the Act spells out</u> highly <u>detailed performance standards governing</u> how the operation <u>must be conducted</u> and to what degree reclamation must take place. SMCRA § 515 contains 25 performance standards, many with several sub-parts, for surface mining operations generally, and others for special kinds of surface operations, such as steep-slope mining. Underground mining performance standards almost as numerous are spelled out at SMCRA § 516. The Secretary has fleshed these out in Subchapter K, Parts 800-828. Probably the two most important are Parts 816 and 817, governing surface and underground mining, respectively. Other standards cover auger mining, mining in alluvial valley floors, and mining on prime farmland.

<u>Fourth,</u> the Act gives the Secretary and state <u>regulatory authorities the power to enforce the Act's provisions through inspections and orders to cease operations.</u> SMCRA § 521.

At the conclusion of the interim or initial program, as noted, states had the option of submitting their own programs to the

Secretary to be implemented in lieu of the permanent program of direct federal regulation. SMCRA requires the Secretary to approve these programs before they may replace the federal effort. While the state programs may differ from the federal one, the Secretary may not approve a state program unless he determines that the state effort meets all of the federal minimum standards. SMCRA § 503. The rules for various individual state programs are contained at Parts 901-950. Some 35 states have their own programs. In the other states, and on certain federal lands, the direct federal permanent program is in effect.

Even when a state has its own program, the Secretary retains the power to oversee the program, to approve amendments, to carry out his own enforcement in certain instances, and ultimately to "seize" or federalize a state program and resume a direct regulatory role.

The judge who wrote this opinion, Judge Thomas Flannery, has perhaps heard more SMCRA litigation, and therefore had a greater impact on the scope of SMCRA regulation, than any other judge.

In sum, SMCRA seeks to regulate coal mining by requiring permits before surface mining can take place. Among the detailed performance standards referred to in Judge Flannery's opinion are the following requirements:

1. to restore the land "to a condition capable of supporting the [prior] uses . . . or higher or better uses;"

2. to backfill, compact, and grade "to restore the approximate original contour of the land;"

3. to "stabilize and protect all surface areas including spoil piles;"

4. to "restore the topsoil;"

5. to minimize the disturbance of the hydrological balance to avoid acid or toxic mine drainage;

6. to avoid the dangerous use of explosives; and

7. to provide for the revegetation of regraded areas. 30 U.S.C. § 1265.

The presence of these Congressionally written standards plus the requirement of interim regulations demonstrate the urgent nature of the problem as well as Congressional distrust of the industry and state regulators.

Nevertheless, the crux of SMCRA is permitting and very rarely does SMCRA outrightly forbid mining, although it does so in limited circumstances. No surface mining will be allowed in National Parks, Wildlife

Refuges, some National Forests, and within certain distances of homes, streets, public buildings, churches, and cemeteries.[34] These prohibitions are "subject to valid existing rights," a term the Secretary of the Interior has had great difficulty in defining. Additionally, states, or the federal government in regard to its lands, may designate lands unsuitable for surface mining. Congress also prohibited mining in alluvial valley floors west of the 100th principal meridian.[35]

Opponents of SMCRA litigated each attempt to regulate the industry. In addition to industry opponents, often environmental groups challenged regulations because they believed that the regulations were too lenient. The Office of Surface Mining rarely could please anyone. Industry opponents also attempted to have Congress repeal the Act or diminish OSM's budget to the point of ineffectiveness. They also made wholesale attacks on the Act itself.

Two of these challenges made their way to the Supreme Court. Both were facial or pre-enforcement challenges to the Act. One was concerned primarily with the requirement to restore steep slopes absent a variance[36] and the second considered the prohibition against mining on prime farmland.[37] In both cases, the Supreme Court found that the passage of SMCRA itself did not constitute a "taking" of private property. Even if some coal might have been rendered uneconomical to mine, none of the plaintiffs identified particular property that may have been impacted.[38] The *Virginia Surface Mining and Reclamation Assoc.* case also had the following to say about the federal government's authority to regulate surface mining under the Commerce Clause:

> Appellees do not, in general, dispute the validity of the congressional findings [about the interstate impacts of surface

(margin note: Const. Concerns)

---

[34] SMCRA § 522(e), 30 U.S.C. § 1272(e).

[35] SMCRA § 510(b)(5).

[36] Hodel v. Virginia Surface Mining and Reclamation Association, Inc., 452 U.S. 264 (1981).

[37] *Hodel v. Indiana*, 452 U.S. 314 (1981).

[38] Another result occurred when a specific mine was prohibited because of the presence of an alluvial valley floor. A taking was found in that instance. Whitney Benefits, Inc. v. United States, 926 F.2d 1169 (Fed. Cir. 1991), *cert. denied*, 112 S. Ct. 406 (1991). This case should be compared with a post-*Lucas* takings case that upheld an Office of Surface Mining cessation order. *M & J. Coal Co. v. United States*, 47 F.3d 1148 (Fed. Cir. 1995) (mining in manner that could put the public at risk of injury not part of coal company's property right). *See also* Eastern Minerals International, Inc. v. United States, 36 Fed.Cl. 541 (1996) (finding an unreasonable delay in deciding whether or not to grant a permit created a permanent taking).

mining]. Rather, appellees' contention is that the "rational basis" test should not apply in this case because the Act regulates land use, a local activity not affecting interstate commerce. But even assuming that appellees correctly characterize the land use regulated by the Act as a "local" activity, their argument is unpersuasive.

The denomination of an activity as a "local" or "intrastate" activity does not resolve the question whether Congress may regulate it under the Commerce Clause. . . . This Court has long held that Congress may regulate the conditions under which goods shipped in interstate commerce are produced where the "local" activity of producing these goods itself affects interstate commerce. Appellees do not dispute that coal is a commodity that moves in interstate commerce. Here, Congress rationally determined that regulation of surface coal mining is necessary to protect interstate commerce from adverse effects that may result from that activity. This congressional finding is sufficient to sustain the Act as a valid exercise of Congress' power under the Commerce Clause.

Moreover, the Act responds to a congressional finding that nationwide "surface mining and reclamation standards are essential in order to insure that competition in interstate commerce among sellers of coal produced in different States will not be used to undermine the ability of the several States to improve and maintain adequate standards on coal mining operations within their borders." 30 U.S.C. § 1201(g) (1976 ed., Supp. III). The prevention of this sort of destructive interstate competition is a traditional role for congressional action under the Commerce Clause. . . .

Finally, we agree with the lower federal courts that have uniformly found the power conferred by the Commerce Clause broad enough to permit congressional regulation of activities causing air or water pollution, or other environmental hazards that may have effects in more than one State. . . .[39]

The Supreme Court also found no violation of the Tenth Amendment: what SMCRA regulated was not the states, but the industry. Additionally, any state involvement in regulating would be at the individual state's option. If

---

[39] *Virginia Surface Mining and Reclamation Association, Inc.*, 452 U.S. at 281-82.

a state did not want to develop a state program, the federal government would regulate.[40]

Another interesting aspect of SMCRA is its surface owner consent provisions, which apply to split-estate lands. On private coal lands, the coal company must have the consent of the surface owner to surface mining before a permit could be had unless the property right held by the coal company clearly allowed surface mining.[41] If the federal government owned coal but patented the surface to another, a "qualified surface owner" would have to give consent before surface mining could proceed. A "qualified surface owner" is essentially one who resides on the land or is a bona fide rancher or farmer of the land.[42] These provisions requiring consent may change the economics of coal mining and, to a certain extent, surface owners of land overlying federal coal have been given a property interest in the coal.

IV. PUBLIC POLICY CONSIDERATIONS

The policy goals that often determine a choice of energy source include environmental protection, public health, energy independence, job creation or preservation, national security, and global equity. No one energy source can necessarily further all goals. Coal's abundance in the United States creates a conflict among some of these policy goals and even raises ethical concerns, partly because coal can be used for many energy applications. Coal can generate electricity and thus substitute directly for oil, natural gas, and nuclear fuel for this use. Moreover, as a synthetic fuel, coal could be employed for other oil usages. This plentitude can be a mixed blessing.

On one hand, energy independence is a positive goal. Price fluctuations on the world market have wreaked havoc on the domestic energy scene and can threaten national security. This was especially true when cooperative action by members of the Organization of Petroleum Exporting Countries raised oil prices in the 1970s. Additionally, wars or other turmoil in countries exporting to the United States can disrupt supplies. Therefore, due to abundant domestic supplies, coal promotes the goal of energy independence. Lowering energy imports would also lower our nation's trade deficits.

Similarly, development of a domestic energy source means domestic jobs. These jobs would not only be in electricity generating and distribution, but would be throughout the fuel cycle, including mining. However, given

---

[40] *Id.* at 289.

[41] 30 U.S.C. § 1260(b)(6).

[42] 30 U.S.C. § 1304.

the dangers of coal mining, individual workers may be exposed to more risk than if the worker was employed elsewhere.

Perhaps the greatest drawback to dependency on coal, however, is environmental degradation, absent significant technological advances. First, strip-mining is often done in areas with delicate hydrological regimes or other difficulties in reclamation. More generally, combustion of coal creates air pollution: sulfur dioxides, nitrogen dioxides, particulates and carbon dioxide. These pollutants have local impact, but they also have international affect.

Increased coal use could also endanger regional and global relations. Canada traces the source of some of its acid rain and other air pollution woes to coal-burning in the United States. Carbon dioxide, as a greenhouse gas, is a subject of global concern, as evidenced by the Kyoto Protocol of the Global Climate Change Convention.[43] If the United States increases its use of coal, it would be difficult politically and ethically to insist that developing nations with abundant coal, such as China, forego its use. Given the global commons, all the efforts the United States makes to reduce the effect of coal-burning in the United States would be rendered nugatory if China increases its use of coal. China currently burns 1.2 billion tons a year of high sulfur coal, with estimates going to 1.6 billion tons early in the next century.[44] Therefore, policy choices must include considerations of equity among nations. Additionally, because of the long-term consequences of global warming and the lifespan of carbon in the atmosphere, equity among and between generations is also an issue.

As with all the energy sources, coal presents the question of how to strike a balance between its positive attributes and those that are negative. Laws, such as environmental treaties and domestic statutes, may drive some choices, but the other questions must also be answered. ❦

---

[43] The Protocol calls for nations to reduce their carbon dioxide emissions. The United States has signed the Protocol, but the Senate has not ratified it.

[44] Homer Sun, *Controlling the Environmental Consequences of Power Development in the People's Republic of China*, 17 MICH. J. INT'L. L. 1015, 1919 (1996). China's Ministry of Power estimated that China needs to install 15,000 to 17,000 megawatts of electricity for ten years, which would equal putting on line each year the total generating capacity of Southern California Edison. Coal is expected to contribute 80% of this total. *Id.* at 1021, n. 35.

CHAPTER TEN

Nuclear Power

by Donald N. Zillman

I. INTRODUCTION

Nuclear power has become the great unpredictable in United States energy policy. In the 1950s and 1960s, nuclear power, with its potential to generate large amounts of electricity, was seen as the hope for America's energy future. A nuclear power advocate of the time spoke of "electricity too cheap to meter" as the end product of the nuclear revolution. By the 1970s and 1980s, however, stories about nuclear power more often emphasized bad news than good. Despite the operation of about 105 nuclear electric units in the United States (which provide about 20% of total American electricity generation), nuclear power's public image is one of cost-overruns, indecision about waste disposal, and real (Three Mile Island and Chernobyl) and hypothetical fears of catastrophic accidents. The harshest fact about nuclear power's future in the United States is that no utility had ordered a new nuclear unit since 1978. The utility CEO proposing such a multi-billion dollar investment probably would put his or her job at risk with the shareholders and invite widespread public criticism. Symbolic of the changes from the 1950s to the 1980s were the visible public symbols of nuclear power. In the 1950s, nuclear power was personified by Admiral Hyman Rickover, the father of the nuclear Navy, and a fanatic for technological perfection, whose disciples included nuclear Navy veteran President Jimmy Carter. By the late 1980s nuclear power was more likely to be associated in the popular mind with the bumbling cartoon figure Homer Simpson whose blue collar employment in a nuclear plant suggested anything but technical excellence.

As we approach the turn of the century nuclear power's future in the United States hangs in the balance. Opponents of nuclear power (or supporters of nuclear power, but pessimists about its future) point to the continuing failure to invest in new nuclear electric plants, to the continuing high costs and regulatory problems of the nuclear technology, to the cost-sensitive new world of deregulated electricity sales, and to the politically influential minority of the population that is strongly anti-nuclear. They also mention the premature closure of some existing plants due to cost or regulatory problems. While immediate closure of all plants commands neither economic or political support, the pessimist can point to a scenario unfolding over the next two decades in which no new plants are ordered or constructed and many existing plants reach the end of their useful lives or are closed prematurely. American nuclear expertise and leadership will continue to decline. What bright young American scientist or engineer would want to commit to a nuclear future? The major emphasis in the American nuclear field in 2010 will not be the construction or operation of plants but their decommissioning.

An alternative scenario exists. Recall that nuclear power does provide 20% of total electricity use in the United States. Electricity continues to be in demand for the 21st century. Easy replacements may not be available especially as the United States and the world begin to pay serious attention to global warming and the environmental costs of burning the fossil fuels (usually for energy purposes). Global warming can produce as catastrophic harms to the earth as significant radiation release from a nuclear accident. Increased use of nuclear energy may be the most practical current method of reducing consumption of the fossil fuels. Further, forty years of experience is offering better nuclear plant performance.[1] It is unlikely nuclear electricity will ever be "too cheap to meter," but for some markets it may be the best option considering both cost and safety. Having been overpraised in the 1950s and over-condemned in the 1980s, nuclear power may take its place as a technology in which the real risks are outweighed by the benefits in the new century.

Worldwide attitudes towards nuclear power vary. Some nations such as France and Russia remain committed to nuclear power as a principal solution to energy needs. Other countries, Germany and the United Kingdom, for example, reflect schizophrenia toward the technology. Worldwide, there are over 425 nuclear electric generating units located in most of the

---

[1] Statement of James Howard, Chairman, Nuclear Energy Institute, PROCEEDINGS OF THE NUCLEAR ENERGY ASSEMBLY, May 13-15, 1998. Mr. Howard reported at p. 2: "[O]perating U.S. nuclear plants achieved a record capacity factor of 77.8 percent in 1997. That's up nearly 10 percent since 1992 and it's about 40 percent better than the industry average in 1980." Further, "[a]verage production costs have also dropped—from 2.63 cents per kilowatt-hour to 1.91 cents per kilowatt-hour."

major economic powers.[2] As in the United States, costs, alternatives, public opinion, regulatory practices, and environmental threats will determine nuclear power's future.

II. THE NUCLEAR PROCESS

Some basic facts about nuclear energy place the subject in context.[3] The major energy use of nuclear power is for the generation of large amounts of electricity. The nuclear reaction (the splitting of the atom) produces large amounts of heat from small amounts of uranium based fuel. That thermal energy warms water to produce steam. The steam, in turn, operates a turbine which drives an electric generator. In essence, the nuclear fission process serves the same purpose as the combustion of fossil fuel in a coal, petroleum, or gas fired electric generating facility.

Uranium, an element found in nature, provides the raw material for the nuclear chain reaction. Uranium is mined in a fashion similar to coal or other hard minerals. The uranium found in nature is not useful for either electric generation or weapons purposes. A series of steps known as the nuclear fuel cycle prepares the raw uranium for use in an electric generating plant.

Private industry has performed two essential roles in the development of the nuclear electric industry. First, a handful of companies have specialized in the manufacture of nuclear reactors. Westinghouse, General Electric, Babcock and Wilcox and Combustion Engineering have made most of the American (and many foreign) reactors. Second, investor-owned public utility companies have purchased the nuclear plants to add to their generating mix. Often, a consortia of utility companies have joined to fund and operate the massive plants. Many major American electric utility companies have

---

[2] *See Testimony of NRC Chairman Shirley Jackson at 29, Reauthorization of the Nuclear Regulatory Commission, Hearing before Subcommittee on Energy and Power, House Commerce Committee*, 105th Cong., Second Sess., March 25, 1998, Serial No. 105-83 (Chairman Jackson observed that 60-65% of reactors outside the U.S. were based on U.S. technology); INTERNATIONAL ATOMIC ENERGY AGENCY, CHOOSING THE NUCLEAR POWER OPTION: FACTORS TO BE CONSIDERED (1998) at 3 notes reactors operating in over 30 countries provide 17% of the world's electricity. In countries with nuclear plants, about half draw more than 25% of their electricity from nuclear power.

[3] Material in this section is drawn from *Nuclear Regulatory Commission, Radioactive Waste: Production, Storage, Disposal (July 1996); Frequently Asked Questions about Nuclear Energy* <http://www-formal.stanford.edu/jmc/progress/nuclear-faq.html>.

made some investment in nuclear electric development over the past four decades.

The multiple manufacturers and multiple users of American nuclear power discouraged standardization in the nuclear electric industry. Congress itself viewed this as a plus. A new technology would best be advanced by allowing a competitive market to identify successful and unsuccessful designs. While plants shared common features and were subject to uniform minimum acceptable safety standards, plants were not identical.

Various types of nuclear reactors are used. Different countries favor different technologies. The United States has consistently used the light water reactor in either the pressurized-water or the boiling water form. Water serves as the coolant for both reactors.

The reactor vessel contains the nuclear fuel—the end product of the mining, milling, and enrichment processes. This uranium oxide, which contains about 3% U-235 is arranged in fuel rods. Small cylinders of uranium oxide are stacked in each 12 foot long fuel rod. The rods are grouped in bundles of 60 rods each. A reactor may have 500 or more bundles that form the reactor core. Cooling water (coolant) is pumped through this core and heated by nuclear fission. The entire reactor is housed in a reinforced concrete enclosure, called the reactor containment. The containment protects the reactor and is designed to prevent the escape of radioactive products should a rupture occur. The need for the containment was illustrated at the Chernobyl plant in the former Soviet Union. There, a plant without a containment ruptured resulting in a disastrous release of radioactivity outside the plant.

In the reactor core uranium 235 reacts with slow neutrons to undergo fission and release more neutrons. These neutrons in turn cause additional fission. The fission of one gram of uranium 235 produces the equivalent of 21,9000 kilowatt hours of thermal energy. This is thousands of times more thermal energy than produced by the combustion of an equivalent amount of one of the hydrocarbon fuels.

The water coolant circulating through the nuclear core is heated by the energy released by fission. In the boiling-water reactor, steam is generated in the reactor and is under a pressure of about 1100 pounds per square inch and an exit temperature of 550 degrees Fahrenheit. This steam is separated from the boiling water, dried, and sent to the turbines to allow the production of electricity. In the pressurized-water reactor, the reactor is filled entirely with hot water at a pressure of about 2,250 pounds per square inch and an exit temperature of about 605 degrees Fahrenheit. This pressurized water is drawn off and passed through the steam generator where it produces the desired steam by heating other feedwater.

In both types of reactors, the nuclear fission process, the chain reaction, is controlled to harness the energy produced in the core. This is done by controlling the rate of neutron reaction with uranium 235. The primary method of controlling fission is by including in the reactor core rods of neutron absorbing material. In addition, in a pressurized water reactor, neutron absorbers such as boron may be added to the water to control fission. A balanced rate of fission occurs when, for each fission only one neutron is said to be "critical." Water must be present for a reactor to be critical because the water molecules slow down the fast neutrons produced by fission. This gives the slow neutrons the opportunity to cause further fission. The power output of the reactor is thus controlled by careful movement of the control rods in the core. The operator may insert or withdraw these rods to control the amount of neutrons available to cause fission.

A bundle of nuclear fuel rods will exhaust their productive potential within a year or two. They then must be replaced and the reactor refueled. The spent fuel rods remain highly radioactive. The challenge of what to do with the spent fuel has perplexed the nuclear industry and government for several decades. The topic will be treated in a separate section of the chapter.

An assessment of nuclear power must consider the risks of the technology, the benefits of the technology, and the risks and benefits of alternatives to the nuclear process for the generation of electricity. In some respects, the nuclear process scores well on an environmental protection scale. The uranium mining fatality rate has been far below that of coal per kilowatt-hour of electricity produced. Nuclear fission avoids much of the unattractive air pollution produced by burning fossil fuels. As the worldwide control of fossil fuel consumption becomes a high public priority given concerns about global warming, this feature of nuclear power could give it new life.

The primary hazards of the nuclear process involve the undesired release of radiation. Several facts about radiation help put the debate in context. First, people are exposed to radiation in food and the surrounding environment even where there are no nuclear plants. Medical exposures (e.g., chest and dental x-rays) add to the exposure. Second, in concentrated doses radiation can kill quickly. About thirty immediate fatalities resulted from the Chernobyl plant accident primarily among workers exposed to the massive releases of radiation at the plant. They joined victims of the Hiroshima and Nagasaki bombs and a few other persons closely exposed to weapons tests and other massive radiation releases. Third, at lower doses radiation can cause near-term illness and death, longer-term cancers and genetic deformation. It remains a hotly debated topic whether there is any minimal safe level for radiation exposure. It goes without saying, however, that the release of a massive amount of radiation in a highly populated area offers the prospect of a mass disaster several times worse than any the world has seen.

Radiation exposure is a concern in all parts of the nuclear cycle. Miners and millers are exposed to some radiation in their work. The same is true of fuel fabricators. The nuclear electric plant itself is designed to prevent the exposure of workers and visitors to radiation produced in the reactor core. A trip through a nuclear plant is accompanied by regular checks to see that the visitor has not inadvertently been contaminated by radiation. Lastly, even after its useful life, the uranium fuel rods remain dangerously radio-active. A Nuclear Regulatory Commission publication summarizes: "Ten years after removal of spent fuel from a reactor, the radiation dose one meter away from a typical spent fuel assembly exceeds 20,000 rems per hour. A dose of 5,000 rems would be expected to cause immediate incapacitation and death with one week."[4]

Initially, it was assumed that the spent fuel would be reprocessed. For the time being, spend fuel was stored, usually in water, at the plant site. After the late 1970s when the United States abandoned plans to reprocess the spent fuel, the focus turned to places of long-term storage since individual plants would eventually run out of storage space. Suffice it to say that only modest progress has been made to date on a solution to the waste disposal problem.

III. FEDERAL REGULATION OF THE NUCLEAR PROCESS

In the beginning, there was the bomb. Much of the development of the American nuclear industry resulted from the fact that the first major use of nuclear fission was the Manhattan Project in World War II. The enormous investment of dollars and talent produced what was envisioned—a new weapon of massive destructive capability. Once the bomb was produced and tested, President Truman ordered its use at Hiroshima and Nagasaki in August 1945 to end the Pacific War. The awesome destructive power of those primitive atomic weapons ended the war and informed the world that warfare was forever changed.

The post-war Congress faced serious decisions regarding nuclear technology. Congress responded by passing the Atomic Energy Act of 1946.[5] The statute would shape the development of the nuclear industry for the next fifty years.

---

[4] Nuclear Regulatory Commission, RADIOACTIVE WASTE: PRODUCTION, STORAGE, DISPOSAL (July 1996) at 7.

[5] LAWS OF 1946, ch. 724, 60 Stat. 755.

The United States had a monopoly on the most potent weapon of war the world had ever known. Section 1 of the Atomic Energy Act of 1946 accurately referred to the "profound changes in our present way of life" offered by the nuclear revolution. Warfare now had the potential to destroy civilization. What was less certain were the non-military impacts. Congress equivocated: "The effect of the use of atomic energy for civilian purposes upon the social, economic, and political structures of today cannot now be determined." However, "subject at all times to the paramount objective of assuring the common defense and security, the development and utilization of atomic energy shall, so far as practicable, be directed toward improving the public welfare, increasing the standard of living, strengthening free competition in private enterprise, and promoting world peace."[6] An elaboration of the purposes of the Act identified the development of governmental and private research on nuclear matters. It further encouraged dissemination of "information concerning the practical industrial application of atomic energy."[7]

Given this prospect, Congress faced a number of critical choices:

1. Should the national government or the states regulate the nuclear process? Military and national security concerns dominated any suggestions that a potential peaceful energy technology should be left to development and regulation by individual states. The legislative history of the Atomic Energy Act put it concisely. "An absolute Government [national] monopoly of production of fissionable materials is indispensable . . ."[8]

2. Should national nuclear policy be in the hands of the civilians or the military? A serious case was made that the most awesome weapon required military control. Concerns about security (other countries learning our atomic secrets and building their own bombs) also argued for military control. Witness the remarks of Congressman Martin of Iowa: "I cannot surrender completely the whole field of atomic energy policy making to the scientist or the manufacturers, and bar absolutely only one class of people, namely those who know something about military application of any super weapon such as the atomic bomb."[9] However, what the legislative history called the "established traditions of our

---

[6] *Id.* at § 1(a).

[7] *Id.* at § 1(b)(2).

[8] S. REP. NO. 1211, Analysis of S. 1717 by Sections, Sect. 4, *reprinted* in 1946 U.S.C.C.S. 1330.

[9] CONG. REC., July 26, 1946, at 10197.

Government" won out.[10] The civilian authorities were to control the nuclear process. They would be closely involved with the military in national security issues. But, the prospect of military control of the atomic process troubled even a Congress immensely respectful of the performance of the military in winning World War II.

3.   What was the future of nuclear power? While it seems implausible in retrospect, Congress could have taken the view that the splitting of the atom had proven such a horror for humanity that every effort should be made to put the genie back in the bottle. Congress could have enacted legislation that discouraged any further research in or use of nuclear fission and attempted to see that other nations, individuals, and corporations followed suit.

Congress and the Executive Branch did have hopes of preventing a nuclear arms race. Proposals to share secrets and to demilitarize surfaced as the forty year Cold War between the Soviet bloc and the United States and Western Europe began. However, within five years of the passage of the 1946 Act, the Soviet Union had "the bomb" and both countries were engaged in an arms race that would make the Hiroshima and Nagasaki bombs look primitive in their destructive power. Under those circumstances only a strong pacifist could discourage federal expenditures on nuclear weapons technology. And, few strong pacifists were elected to Congress in the early decades of the Cold War. The federal commitment to regulate the nuclear process soon became a commitment to contribute billions of dollars to explore nuclear technology.

Even in the late 1940s the horrors of nuclear weapons research and testing encouraged a "peaceful" use of the fissioning of the atom. In the 1946 Atomic Energy Act government was instructed to assist "private research and development to encourage maximum scientific progress" while pursuing "federally conducted research and development."[11] The hope was that the enormous energy potential of the nuclear process could replace other energy sources to the benefit of all humanity. Economics drove some of the thinking—the nuclear process allowed the creation of vast amounts of energy compared with combustion of a fossil fuel. However, the desire for the "peaceful use of the atom" also reflected a desire to atone for the destructive horror of the bomb. Mankind's most awesome "sword" could be beaten into plowshares of cheap and infinite energy.

---

[10] S. REP. NO. 1211, Analysis of S. 1717 by Sections, Sect. 2, *reprinted* in 1946 U.S.C.C.S. 1328.
    [11] LAWS OF 1946, ch. 724, 60 Stat. 755, § 1(b)(1)(3).

While the Congress of 1946 could envision a future role for private enterprise in the nuclear realm, its immediate objectives reflected national security aspects of the weapons program. The federal government was to "control" the "production, ownership, and use of fissionable material to assure the common defense and security and to insure the broadest possible exploitation of the fields."[12] The federal government either owned or licensed the source material, special nuclear material and byproduct material that would be involved in a fission reaction.[13] The Atomic Energy Act required federal approval from the newly created Atomic Energy Commission (AEC) to handle nuclear material. In present form, the statute requires federal permission to "transfer or receive in interstate commerce, transfer, deliver, receive possession of or title to, or import into or export from the United States any source material after removal from its place of deposit in nature . . ."[14]

The 1946 Act also created two bodies that were to play a large role in nuclear development. The first was the Atomic Energy Commission (AEC) which was created to promote and regulate the uses of nuclear energy.[15] The second was the Congressional Joint Committee on Atomic Energy.[16] The creation of the Joint Committee permitted a far closer legislative examination of nuclear decisions than in other areas of federal oversight. Both the AEC and the Joint Committee became strong promoters of the peaceful commercial use of nuclear energy. Both bodies lasted until the 1970s. The AEC eventually fell victim to doubts about whether an agency could be both promoter of a technology and the regulator of that technology's health and safety aspects. In 1974 the AEC was abolished by Congress and its duties divided between the newly created Nuclear Regulatory Commission (NRC) and the Energy Research and Development Administration (ERDA). The NRC took over the regulatory duties of the AEC and retains that role today. The ERDA was made a part of the new Department of Energy in 1977. The Administration and Department retained the promotional role for nuclear power. Also in 1977, the Joint Committee was abolished and its responsibilities given to other committees.

In 1954 Congress enacted a major amendment to the Atomic Energy Act that still sets the contours of the use of nuclear power for electric generation in the United States. The acquisition of nuclear weapons by the Soviet Union changed the national security aspects of atomic energy law.

---

[12] *Id.* at § 1(b)(4).

[13] *Id.* at § 5.

[14] 42 U.S.C. § 2092.

[15] Law of 1946, ch. 724, 60 Stat. 755, § 2.

[16] *Id.* at § 15.

President Eisenhower's proposal before the United Nations of an Atoms for Peace program in December 1953 had stirred popular imagination around the world. At a time when nuclear power was primarily dedicated to weaponry, the President raised the hopes of turning swords to plowshares:

> The United States knows that peaceful power from atomic energy is no dream of the future. That capability, already proved, is here-now-today. Who can doubt, if the entire body of the world's scientists and engineers had adequate amounts of fissionable material with which to test and develop their ideas, that this capability would rapidly be transformed into universal, efficient, and economic usage.[17]

Private industry in the United States appeared cautiously interested in the commercial use of nuclear power, particularly for the generation of large amounts of electric energy. Or at least, they were fearful of government operation of nuclear electric plants that might compete with their businesses. The Legislative History of the 1954 Act summarized the early promise of peaceful use of the atom.

> Moreover, the atomic-reactor art has already reached the point where atomic power at prices competitive with electricity devised from conventional fuels is on the horizon, though not within our immediate reach. For more than two and a half years, the experimental breeder reactor has actually been producing relatively small amounts of electricity at the national reactor testing station in Idaho. The land-based prototype of the atomic engine propelling the U.S.S. Nautilus has already produced more than enough power to send an atomic submarine around the world, fully submerged and at full speed. The Westinghouse Electric Corp. and Duquesne Power and Light Co. are now constructing the Nation's first large-scale atomic-power reactor which will generate 60,000 kilowatts of electricity—an amount sufficient to furnish light and power for a sizable city.[18]

Some legislators were prepared to envision nuclear power as not just competitive but dominant. Rep. Hosmer cautioned "It is not probable that all conventional electric power sources such as steam and power dams will be outmoded by nuclear developments but some of them are sure to be. . . .

---

[17] *Atomic Power for Peace Address by the President*, Dec. 8, 1953, reprinted in CONG. REC., Jan. 7, 1954, at 61.

[18] S. REP. NO. 1699, *reprinted* in 1954, U.S.C.C.S. 3458-59.

We must avoid spending any millions, or billions, on projects of a conventional nature which would be made obsolete by nuclear advances."[19]

In 1954, as in 1946, Congress faced a series of choices about how to advance the peaceful commercial use of the atom. There was little doubt that federal research dollars should continue to flow to nuclear technology. Research remained essential to the nuclear weapons program, an undoubted responsibility of the national government. That combined with the attraction of advancement of peaceful uses of nuclear fission served to make a case for federal funding that cut across party or ideological lines. The multibillion dollar federal investment in nuclear development that had already taken place encouraged some legislators to propose keeping much or all of peaceful nuclear development in federal hands. Private enterprise would play only a limited role. These sentiments reflected earlier and continuing battles between public and private electric power that often centered around hydropower development.

In 1954, however, sentiment was ripe to give private enterprise a leading role. President Eisenhower was the first Republican elected since the Depression. His Cabinet drew heavily on business expertise. A Republican and conservative Congress also reflected a national mood of respect for private enterprise not seen for a quarter century.

A paragraph from the legislative history of the 1954 Act captures the prevailing sentiment:

> It is our firmly held conviction that increased private participation in atomic power development, under the terms stipulated in this proposed legislation, will measurably accelerate our progress toward the day when economic atomic power will be a fact. It is likewise our conviction that the safeguards written into this legislation will prevent special interests from winning undue advantages at the expense of the national interest.[20]

The 1954 legislation retained federal ownership over fuel production facilities and the fuel produced.[21] The Atomic Energy Commission was authorized to license such fuel for industrial uses.[22] The Commission also was given licensing authority over the nuclear facilities that would make use of the fissionable fuel.[23] The current version of statute gives the Nuclear

---

[19] CONG. REC., March 11, 1954, at 3153.

[20] S. REP. NO. 1699, *reprinted* in 1954 U.S.C.C.S. 3464.

[21] LAWS OF 1954, ch. 1073, 68 Stat. 919, §§ 41 and 52.

[22] *Id.* at § 53.

[23] *Id.* at §§ 101 and 103.

Regulatory Commission authority: "to issue licenses to persons [including corporations] applying therefor to transfer and receive in interstate commerce, manufacture, produce, transfer, acquire, possess, use, import or export . . . utilization or production facilities for industrial or commercial purposes."[24]

In the decade following 1954, it became clear that the primary commercial use of nuclear power would be for generating large amounts of electricity. The major impact of the 1954 Amendments on the Atomic Energy Act therefore involved federal regulatory approval of utility company plans to build and operate nuclear power plants.

The brief statutory mandate for federal licensing of private nuclear ventures enacted in 1954 has given rise to a highly detailed licensing process. Its core appears as Part 50, Domestic Licensing of Production and Utilization Facilities, of Title 10 of the Code of Federal Regulations. One hundred and seventy pages of closely spaced regulations lay out the licensing process for a new nuclear plant or for the significant modification of an existing nuclear license.

Further sections of Title 10 cover other matters that are relevant to the operation of a nuclear facility. These include such matters as the licensing of nuclear plant operators,[25] packaging and transportation of radioactive materials,[26] storage of high level waste,[27] and physical protection for nuclear plants and materials.[28]

A further lengthy section of the Code, Part 51, addresses compliance with a set of laws not envisioned by Congress in 1954. These are the environmental planning laws, most particularly the National Environmental Policy Act of 1969.[29] This statute requires preparation of an environmental impact statement for any "major Federal action significantly affecting the quality of the human environment."[30] The federal licensing requirement classifies construction of a nuclear plant as a "Federal action." The size and complexity of the average nuclear plant assures that it will have a significant environmental effect.

---

[24] 42 U.S. Code § 2133.

[25] 10 C.F.R. Part 55 (1988).

[26] *Id.* at Part 71.

[27] *Id.* at Part 60.

[28] *Id.* at Part 73.

[29] 42 U.S.C. §§ 4321 *et seq.*

[30] 42 U.S.C. § 4322(c).

Nuclear licensing gave rise to one of the landmark cases of the environmental movement, *Calvert Cliffs Coordinating Committee v. AEC*.[31] The litigation challenged the AEC's application of the new National Environmental Policy Act. The court, in an opinion by Judge Skelly Wright, held that the initial AEC regulations gave far too narrow an application to the NEPA and generally discouraged an independent examination of the environmental impacts of the nuclear license under review. Judge Wright detailed the faults of the AEC regulations:

> We believe the Commission's rule is in fundamental conflict with the basic purpose of the act. NEPA mandates a case-by-case balancing judgment on the part of federal agencies. In each individual case, the particular economic and technical benefits of the action must be assessed and then weighed against the environmental costs; alternatives must be considered which would affect the balance of values. . . . The magnitude of possible benefits and possible costs may lie anywhere on a broad spectrum. Much will depend on the particular magnitudes involved in particular cases. In some cases, the benefits will be great enough to justify a certain quantum of environmental costs; in other cases, they will not be so great and the proposed action may have to be abandoned or significantly altered so as to bring the benefits and costs into a proper balance. The point of the individualized balancing analysis is to ensure that, with possible alterations, the optimally beneficial action is finally taken.[32]

The court invalidated the existing AEC regulations. The decision prompted the current NEPA regulations which require the nuclear operator to detail the impact of the nuclear plant on a wide range of environmental values including water quality, air quality, radiation exposure, threats to other life forms, disruption of public services and aesthetic quality.

The major concern of the nuclear licensing process as reflected in Part 50 is human health and safety. Much, though not all, of the regulatory process is directed to seeing that the worst case scenario (massive release of radiation outside the plant) never occurs and that lesser disasters are controlled. The regulations further reflect the fact that the United States did not adopt a single design for its nuclear plants. Historians will debate the virtues and vices of this approach. But, one clear consequence was that each licensing needed to be viewed as a unique experience.

---

[31] 449 F.2d 1109 (D.C. Cir. 1971).
[32] *Id*. at 1123.

The burden is on the license applicant (typically an investor-owned utility or consortium of utilities) to provide the necessary information to the Nuclear Regulatory Commission. The NRC emphasizes that the responsibility to build and operate the plant safely remains on the operator, not the Commission. However, statute and regulation make clear that the NRC is a close participant in all operations. NRC staff, outside professional evaluators, and the Commission itself play an active role in how plants are built and operated.

The initial statute and regulations encouraged a two step licensing process. Initially, the applicants needed to secure a construction permit to begin significant work on the plant.[33] Upon completion of the construction and satisfaction of necessary conditions, the NRC would issue an operating license to allow the plant to begin to serve its purpose—the generation of electricity.[34] The typical license term was forty years.[35]

Separate sections of Part 50 detail types of licensing information needed by the NRC. The overall objective is summarized: "It is expected that reactors will reflect through their design, construction and operation an extremely low probability for accidents that could result in the release of significant quantities of radioactive fission products."[36] A further subsection describes reactor licensing requirements. "For nuclear reactors, such items as the reactor core, reactor coolant system, instrumentation and control systems, electrical systems, containment system, other engineered safety features, auxiliary and emergency systems, radioactive waste handling systems, and fuel handling systems shall be discussed insofar as they are pertinent."[37]

Other sections demand attention to such health and safety matters such as physical security,[38] fire protection,[39] technical specifications[40], and the emergency core cooling systems.[41] Some of these more detailed provisions have been the result of lessons learned from prior nuclear accidents like the Three Mile Island accident in 1979.

---

[33] 10 C.F.R. §§ 50.10(b) and 50.22.
[34] *Id.* at § 50.57.
[35] *Id.* at § 50.51.
[36] *Id.* at § 50.34(a)(1)(ii).
[37] *Id.* § 50.34(b)(2)(I).
[38] *Id.* at § 50.34(c).
[39] *Id.* at § 50.48.
[40] *Id.* at § 50.36.
[41] *Id.* at § 50.46.

A controversial set of specifications requires planning for the nuclear accident that releases radiation outside of the plant's containment.[42] In broad terms, the regulations seek a defense in depth. Initially, good plant equipment and operations should prevent radiation release. If a release occurs, the containment structure should keep the radiation from the general public. If some off-site release occurs, standards for plant location keep the nuclear facility at a distance from the civilian population. Lastly, the emergency plans seek mitigation of radiation exposure or escape from it to reduce the harm to the community.

In addition to licensing new nuclear electric plants, the statutes and regulations give the NRC authority over a wide variety of changes in equipment or operations of an already licensed plant. The laws also mandate NRC monitoring of the operations of licensed nuclear plants. The typical nuclear electric company will have a portion of the workforce dedicated to regulatory compliance. This work will be monitored by NRC employees who are resident at the plant and other NRC employees located in regional and national offices who take a regular interest in plant operations. While the nuclear plant may be privately owned, it operates under a constant government supervision that exceeds that required for any other energy source.

Until the mid-1960s, most nuclear licensing activity drew only limited public attention. Nuclear power was strongly supported by most of the American population. Further, the complexity of the nuclear process encouraged an attitude of "leave it to the experts." Those experts seemed well represented on the Atomic Energy Commission and the technical staff of the utilities who chose to enter the nuclear realm. From 1962 to 1966 only three of 26 applications for construction permits were contested. In the following four years 24 of 74 applications were contested.[43] After 1970, however, it was the rare nuclear license that was not vigorously contested.

A century from now, objective historians will assess the reasons for vehement opposition to nuclear power by a substantial minority of the American people. Looking back from a quarter-century we can discern that nuclear power had been oversold as providing limitless, cheap energy with no serious health and safety risks. The people were asked to trust the government that this was so. By the mid-1970s discontents over environmental harms, Vietnam, and government corruption changed the climate that earlier had been so accepting of nuclear power. Nuclear power itself

---

[42] *Id.* at § 50.47.

[43] E. Rolph, NUCLEAR POWER AND THE PUBLIC SAFETY (1979) at 102.

showed signs of not being able to live up to its promise.[44] As a consequence, while electoral referenda and public opinion polls demonstrated a majority support for the continuation of nuclear power, a solid and influential minority objected vehemently to any nuclear activity and a portion of the nuclear majority was immensely troubled by accidents like Three Mile Island in the United States in 1979 and Chernobyl in the former Soviet Union in 1986. Nuclear licensing was no longer just a technical and legal concern, it was a political concern as well.

While Congress had envisioned the AEC and the Joint Committee as exercising enormous control over nuclear development, it did provide for judicial review of Commission decisions in a fashion similar to the review of other administrative agencies. The Supreme Court's first review of a nuclear licensing decision came in 1961, well before nuclear power had become the controversial issue it later became. In *Power Reactor Development Co. v. International Union*,[45] the Atomic Energy Commission had approved a provisional construction permit for Power Reactor to construct an experimental fast-neutron breeder reactor for the generation of electric power.

Opponents of the project argued that the Commission must "make the same definitive findings of safety of operation [in order to grant the construction permit] as it admittedly will have to make before it licenses actual operation of the facility."[46] In practical terms, the opponents contended that once an enormous investment in construction had been made, the Commission would not impose higher safety standards that might preclude the plant from ever operating. Without expressing a judgment on the merits of the "safety now or safety later" debate, a majority of the Supreme Court backed the Commission. It found that "the responsibility for safeguarding . . . health and safety belongs under the statute to the Commission."[47] The AEC regulations that elaborated the "step-by-step" licensing procedure had been contemplated by Congress and received the implicit approval of the powerful Joint Committee. Power Reactor understood that they faced further, and stricter, licensing reviews at the operating stage.

Justices Black and Douglas dissented. They read the statute to require the ultimate safety decision to be made at the construction permit stage. They somberly observed: "The construction given the Act by the Commission

---

[44] S. Cohn, TOO CHEAP TO METER AN ECONOMIC AND PHILOSOPHICAL ANALYSIS OF THE NUCLEAR DREAM (1997), presents a non-polemical case for the failure of the nuclear option. He notes: "In fact, more than two-thirds of all nuclear plants ordered after January 1970 were subsequently cancelled" at 127.

[45] 367 U.S. 396 (1961).

[46] *Id.* at 398.

[47] *Id.* at 404.

(and today approved) is, with all deference, a light-hearted approach to the most awesome, the most deadly, the most dangerous process that man has ever conceived."[48]

Nearly two decades later the Supreme Court returned to the licensing issue in *Vermont Yankee Nuclear Power Corp. v. NRDC*.[49] The Court reviewed two licensing procedures—one granting an operating license and the other a construction permit. Intervenors insisted that the NRC had given inadequate consideration to such issues as energy conservation, fuel reprocessing, and disposing of spent fuel in approving the two licenses.

The Supreme Court viewed the cases as ones in which the lower courts reviewing the NRC licensing decisions had imposed standards on the licensees that neither statute nor NRC regulation authorized. The Supreme Court summarized: "But this much is absolutely clear. Absent constitutional constraints or extremely compelling circumstances the administrative agencies should be free to fashion their own rules of procedure and to pursue methods of inquiry capable of permitting them to discharge their multitudinous duties."[50]

The Court summarized the role of the courts in nuclear licensing:

> Nuclear energy may some day be a cheap, safe source of power or it may not. But Congress has made a choice to at least try nuclear energy, establishing a reasonable review process in which courts are to play only a limited role. The fundamental policy questions appropriately resolved in Congress and in the state legislatures are not subject to reexamination in the federal courts under the guise of judicial review of agency action. Time may prove wrong the decision to develop nuclear energy, but it is Congress or the States within their appropriate agencies which must eventually make that judgment.[51]

Five years later, in 1983, the Court reaffirmed its deference to the Nuclear Regulatory Commission. In *Baltimore Gas & Electric v. NRDC*,[52] the Court sustained an NRC rule that allowed licensing decisions to be made without a specific assessment of nuclear waste disposition in the environmental impact statement for the plant. In essence, the Court concluded that the NRC had given appropriate attention to the waste disposal

---

[48] *Id.* at 419.

[49] 435 U.S. 519 (1978).

[50] *Id.* at 543.

[51] *Id.* at 557-58.

[52] 462 U.S. 176 (1983).

issue in its overall licensing process. The fact that this did not satisfy nuclear opponents did not invalidate the NRC's action.

Earlier in 1983 the Court had rejected another challenge to a licensing decision that relied on compliance with environmental protection laws.[53] At issue was the re-opening of the undamaged Unit 1 of the Three Mile Island plant. The 1979 accident at its sister unit 2 was, at the time, the most visible nuclear plant accident in history. The People Against Nuclear Energy group sought to require the NRC to assess the impact from a reopening on the psychological health and well-being of the residents living near the plant. PANE's legal authority was the requirement of the National Environmental Policy Act for an "impact statement" of the consequences of reopening.

The Supreme Court looked to Congress' understanding of the word "environment" to reject the PANE argument. The Court found the term required a "reasonably close causal relationship between a change in the physical environment and the effect at issue."[54] In short, "a risk of an accident is not an effect on the physical environment."[55]

In the years since *PANE* and *Baltimore Gas*, the Supreme Court has not returned to the review of NRC licensing decisions. The point has been made. There is nothing so unusual about the regulation of the nuclear process that ordinary rules of judicial deference to Congress and the regulatory agencies should be changed to allow a more intensive or policy focused review. Where Congress has set standards and detailed procedures and where the NRC has implemented these standards, the courts have limited authority. The complexity of the NRC regulations and the substantial Congressional regulation of the nuclear process and the environment provide ample ground for error on the part of the nuclear utilities or the NRC regulators. Where such errors are shown, courts have been quite prepared to invalidate actions or at least insist that a correct proceeding be held.[56] But, Justice Rehnquist's language from *Vermont Yankee* accurately

---

[53] Metropolitan Edison v. People Against Nuclear Energy, 460 U.S. 766 (1983).

[54] *Id.* at 774.

[55] *Id.* at 775.

[56] *See, e.g.*, Ohio v. NRC, 868 F.2d 810 (6th Cir. 1989) (NRC discretion in setting evacuation plan); Union of Concerned Scientists v. NRC, 824 F.2d 108 (D.C. Cir. 1987) (consideration of costs in ordering safety improvements to previously licensed plants); San Luis Obispo Mothers for Peace v. NRC, 799 F.2d 1268 (9th Cir. 1986) (failure to grant public hearing on expansion of spent fuel storage); Limerick Ecology Action v. NRC, 869 F.2d 719 (3d Cir. 1989) (assessment of accident consequences); Sierra Club v. NRC, 862 F.2d 222 (9th Cir. 1988) (expansion of spent fuel storage capacity); Massachusetts v. NRC, 924 F.2d 311 (D.C. Cir. 1991) (evacuation

summarizes the area. Congress has authorized nuclear electric activity subject to reasonable regulation. The fundamental policy issues are for the legislature and the agencies, not the courts.

Forty years of nuclear regulatory experience advises us that there is no magic in the word regulation. All problems are not solved simply because a regulatory structure exists to review the decisions of private industry in the operation of nuclear plants. We need to ask are the right matters being regulated? How competent are the regulators? How should they interact with the officers of the private business being regulated?

More regulation is not always better. Consider the conclusion of the primary commission that investigated the 1979 Three Mile Island accident.

> We note a preoccupation with regulations. It is, of course, the responsibility of the Nuclear Regulatory Commission to issue regulations to assure the safety of nuclear power plants. However, we are convinced that regulations alone cannot assure safety. Indeed, once regulations become as voluminous and complex as those regulations now in place, they can serve as a negative factor in nuclear safety. The satisfaction of regulatory requirements is equated with safety. This Commission believes that it is an absorbing concern with safety that will bring about safety—not just the meeting of narrowly prescribed and complex regulations.[57]

As an example of regulatory overload the Report noted that in the first minutes of the TMI accident "more than 100 alarms went off, and there was no system for suppressing the unimportant signals so that operators could concentrate on the significant alarms."[58]

A second example of regulatory unreality was disclosed at a 1979 legislative oversight hearing. Regulations required the preparation of evacuation plans in case of a nuclear accident that released radiation offsite. The Bailly nuclear plant near Gary, Indiana was a short distance from Bethlehem Steel's Burns Harbor plant. A union representative at the steel plant explained that the steel plant would take a week to shut down. He noted:

> That evacuation plan [in case of nuclear accident] also called for approximately 300 people to stay behind for a period of from days to over a week in order to insure the orderly shutdown of the

---

plans); Citizens Awareness Network v. NRC, 59 F.3d 284 (1st Cir. 1995) (decommissioning practices).

[57] *Kemeny Commission Report* at 93.

[58] *Id.* at 95.

steelmaking facilities, which is absolutely essential to prevent the destruction of those facilities. The company admits, in its evacuation plan, that it does not know how it could keep those people, or encourage those people to stay behind. This is what is commonly referred to as the suicide squad . . .[59]

Congress' most recent major initiatives on nuclear energy appear as parts of the Energy Policy Act of 1992.[60] The overall goal of the Act, passed with memories of Operation Desert Storm and disruption of Middle Eastern oil imports still fresh, was a "comprehensive national energy policy that gradually and steadily increases United States energy security in cost-effective and environmentally beneficial ways."[61] The actual legislative product was a more modest collection of regulatory modifications and government subsidies that involved the energy resources.

The nuclear provisions reflected a Congress still sympathetic to a nuclear future but cautious about overinvestment in the technology. One section of the Act sought to revitalize and eventually privatize uranium enrichment activity in the United States. The Act created the United States Enrichment Corporation which was to serve as the "exclusive marketing agent" for United States enrichment activity.[62] The legislation also offered a plan for the privatization of the Corporation after it had shown its capacity to generate a profit.[63]

A further section of statute addressed concerns over delays in licensing. The section gave statutory authorization for combined licensing. This practice would allow a licensing decision to combine elements of the construction permit and operating license procedures.[64] A third innovation provided a variety of federal incentives to promote research and development of an advanced generation of nuclear reactors. One goal of the initiative was a standard reactor design.[65] Few legislators expected the Energy Policy Act initiatives to jumpstart the industry. Economics and politics, more than law, would drive that decision. However, Congress was willing to provide modest help if an industry revival appeared possible.

---

[59] *Nuclear Regulatory Process, Oversight Hearings Before the Subcommittee on Energy and the Environment of the Committee on Interior and Insular Affairs*, H.R., 96th Cong., 1st Sess., Series No. 96-8, Part III, at 107-08.

[60] Pub. L. 102-486, 106 Stat. 2776.

[61] H.R. REP. NO. 102-474 (I), *reprinted* in 1992 U.S.C.C.A.N. 1955.

[62] Pub. L. 102-474, Title IX, § 1401.

[63] *Id*. at §§ 1501 *et seq.*

[64] *Id*. at § 2801.

[65] *Id*. at § 2121.

IV. STATE AND LOCAL GOVERNMENT INVOLVEMENT IN NUCLEAR REGULATION

The 1946 Atomic Energy Act placed primary regulatory responsibility on federal, rather than state or local, authorities. When Congress opened nuclear technology to the private sector in 1954, the federal government remained the primary regulator. In effect, this legislative approach reversed the normal regulatory pattern for energy resources.

In 1959, Congress gave the states some responsibility for nuclear regulation. Public Law 86-373, Atomic Energy—Cooperation With States, created the concept of the "agreement state." The approach would later characterize much federal environmental legislation. The statute authorized an agreement between the Atomic Energy Commission and the governor of a state by which the AEC could turn over some licensing responsibility to the state. Subjects of state regulation were typically sources of low-level radiation. The AEC retained regulatory control over weapons programs and over the licensing of nuclear electric generating plants. A majority of states have entered into agreements under the Agreement State program. One consequence has been to create state agencies and state employees with some degree of sophistication in nuclear issues.

During the placid 1950s, most states, municipalities, and citizens endorsed the federal commercial nuclear program. A nuclear plant in the neighborhood was seen as a valuable new technology and a sign of economic growth. This pro-nuclear attitude encouraged plans to locate nuclear plants close to many of America's major cities since this would reduce the cost of long-distance transmission of the power from the place of generation to the place of use.

The growth of the anti-nuclear movement changed this peaceful picture of state-federal relations. By the mid-1970s the nuclear plant was one of the most visible examples of the NIMBY (Not In My Back Yard) phenomenon. Nuclear power suggested a classic situation in which benefits and risks would not be evenly shared. The electricity generated by the nuclear plant could be used hundreds or even thousands of miles from the plant site. By contrast, the primary harm of a major radiation accident would fall on the people living in close proximity to the plant.

Individual nuclear controversies addressed such matters as the shipment of nuclear waste through populated areas, the short or long term storage of spent nuclear fuel, radiation releases from nuclear plant operations, evacuation plans in case of radiation accidents, and the construction and operation of nuclear plants.

While national anti-nuclear campaigns and groups arose, much anti-nuclear activity took place at the grass roots—local citizens objecting to some aspect of the existing or proposed local nuclear plant. A number of statewide initiatives opposing nuclear power were held. Nuclear supporters consistently won at the ballot box. But, anti-nuclear advocates typically demonstrated that at least one third of voters opposed any or further nuclear development.

A second form of activism used the NRC licensing procedures and rule-makings to challenge nuclear activity. These matters often ended up in the federal courts. Even if the nuclear supporters won at the agencies and the courts, the victories could be phyric. Nuclear licensing was delayed, costs were increased, and media coverage of the dispute often brought new supporters to the anti-nuclear camp.

A third citizen challenge to nuclear power development called on the state or local legislative authorities to enact anti-nuclear legislation. Many of these laws invited challenges to the intrusion of state and local laws on federal prerogatives protected by the negative Commerce Clause and the Supremacy Clause.

The 1983 Supreme Court decision in *Pacific Gas & Electric Co. v. State Energy Resources Conservation and Development Commission*,[66] sets the contours of state and local involvement in nuclear power decision making. Resistance to nuclear operations in the State of California took several approaches in the late 1970s and early 1980s. A citizen initiative, Proposition 15, which sought to retard nuclear operations because of safety concerns was defeated at the polls. The California Legislature then enacted the Warren-Alquist Act addressing a number of issues in nuclear licensing. A crucial provision sought to control the licensing of any new nuclear plants. Before a new plant could be licensed in California, the state Energy Commission had to certify to the California Legislature that the federal government had approved a method of disposing of nuclear waste produced by the plant. The California Legislature had the ability to disaffirm such a finding. Supporters of nuclear power raised constitutional challenges to the statute. In essence, they argued that California had impermissibly intruded on the federal government's regulatory authority over nuclear power. As a practical matter, both supporters and opponents of nuclear power believed that the federal government would not be able to certify that the waste disposal problem had been solved for a number of years. In practice, then, the statute had the effect of precluding new nuclear construction in California.

---

[66] 461 U.S. 190 (1983).

The Supreme Court began its opinion by observing that the case dealt with the intersection of established federal and state powers.[67] Federal authority controlled the safety of nuclear operations under the Atomic Energy Act. The states could offer an even lengthier history of authority over the "generation and sale of electricity."

The Court agreed that "the radiological and safety aspects involved in the construction and operation of a nuclear plant" remained the province of the federal government.[68] State or local intrusion on these functions would most probably be unconstitutional. However, from the Atomic Energy Act of 1946 to the present, Congress had never "expressly require[d] the States to construct or authorize nuclear powerplants or prohibit[ed] the States from deciding . . . not to permit construction of any further reactors."[69] The States (and localities) "retain[ed] their traditional responsibility in the field of regulating electric utilities for determining questions of need, of reliability, cost, and other related state concerns."[70]

The Court then addressed what the California statute intended to do. A determination that it was focused on safety would have caused it to be held unconstitutional since "the Federal Government has occupied the entire field of nuclear safety concerns, except the limited powers expressly ceded to the States."[71] However, the Court accepted California's contention that economic, rather than safety, reasons prompted the statute.

Pacific Gas and Electric has been reaffirmed in a series of Supreme Court decisions addressing state law damage remedies for nuclear accidents.[72] Quite clearly, the line of decisions requires the states and localities to defer to the NRC in much of its regulation of nuclear safety. The existing nuclear plant that is deemed "safe enough" by the NRC is generally immune from a state regulatory authority demanding more. New plant licensing, however, clearly faces the prospect of California-type legislation. It does not take a very adept state legal counsel to advise the Legislature how to draft a "no more nukes" statute that would be based on economic or planning reasons rather than on safety concerns.

Both law and politics suggest that state and local governments must be taken into account in the operation of a nuclear plant. *Pacific Gas &*

---

[67] *Id.* at 194.

[68] *Id.* at 205.

[69] *Id.*

[70] *Id.*

[71] *Id.* at 212.

[72] Silkwood v. Kerr-McGee Corp., 464 U.S. 238 (1984); Goodyear Atomic Corp. v. Miller, 486 U.S. 174 (1988); English v. General Electric Co., 496 U.S. 72 (1990).

Electric makes clear that the states and localities have the power to prevent a new nuclear activity. Should economics and politics ever allow a return to nuclear development, states would need to assess their policy toward further nuclear development. In dealings with licensed plants (the present generation), political realities, if not the constitutional law of federalism, suggest that interested states can play a considerable role in plant activity. The nuclear plant management that draws the ire of a Governor, state legislature, or both puts itself at serious risk. The *Pacific Gas and Electric* precedent may prevent the states from imposing additional safety standards on the plant. However, the plant and its utility management engage in a variety of relationships with state government. The utility will continue to need the state utility commission. A hostile governor or influential state legislator with ready access to the media can be harmful to the nuclear plant's continued financial and political success.

V.   THE LEGAL RESPONSE TO NUCLEAR ACCIDENTS

The 1954 Amendments to the Atomic Energy Act encouraged private industry activity in the nuclear field, particularly in the operation of electric generating plants fueled by the fission process. However, the initial response from industry was cautious. Hard-eyed utility business managers were doubtful about the prospects for near-term nuclear profits and cautious about longer-term hopes. One concern was the fear of tort liability resulting from a serious nuclear accident.

Congress attempted to address this problem in 1957 with a further amendment of the Atomic Energy Act.[73] The Act soon became known as the Price-Anderson Act for its primary sponsors.

The Act's legislative history spoke of the "primary concern of the Federal Government . . . with the protection to the people who might suffer damages from the new atomic energy industry."[74] A separate section of the amendment advanced public safety by providing statutory authority for the Advisory Committee on Reactor Safeguards, one of the primary reviewing authorities over health and safety issues in nuclear licensing.[75] However, the Act's language and origins suggest that Congress was at least as interested in encouraging the fledgling nuclear industry by controlling the liability it might face from a serious accident.[76]

---

[73] Pub. L. 85-256, 71 Stat 576.

[74] S. REP. NO. 296, *reprinted* in 1957 U.S.C.C.A.N. 1816.

[75] Pub. L. 85-256, § 5 at 71 Stat. 579 (1957).

[76] S. REP. NO. 296, *reprinted* in 1957 U.S.C.C.A.N. 1803, 1804.

The legislation was also tied to the national defense uses of atomic power. As the legislative history explained:

> Since many of the reactors which will be built will be producing special nuclear material which is vital for the defense of the country, it is in the interest of the common defense and security to see that these companies are protected in their operations by having moneys available to them for payment of public liability claims and having limitations of liability proceedings available when those funds are insufficient. Since title to special nuclear material is in the United States, Congress has special powers and duties with respect to the use of that material.[77]

The Atomic Energy Commission and the Congress recognized the dilemma of peaceful nuclear technology:

> The possibility of dangerous materials escaping and causing damage outside the reactor facilities is infinitesimal. However, the possibility does still exist. . . .

> Since radioactive materials are many times more toxic and poisonous than other substances, the companies which are interested in participating in the reactor program are hesitant about assuming the liabilities which could ensue in the remote event of a reactor meltdown with the resulting release of fission products and radioactive materials into the air. At this stage of development of atomic energy these companies do not envision any profit for many years from the research and development efforts that have to be put into the program. Yet, in the unlikely event of a runaway reactor they may be subjected to damage claims which have been estimated in the testimony before the committee at sums ranging from several hundred thousand dollars . . . to sums up to a billion dollars, and somewhat beyond in a few estimates.[78]

Congress faced the problem of how to account for a potentially massive liability that might never be incurred. The Senate Report on the Price-Anderson Act summarized the concern:

> A system of indemnification is established rather than an insurance system, since there is no way to establish any actuarial basis for the full protection required. The chance that a reactor

---

[77] *Id.* at 1816.
[78] *Id.* at 1804.

will run away is too small and the foreseeable possible damages of the reactor are too great to allow the accumulation of a fund which would be adequate. If this unlikely event were to occur, the contributions of the companies protected are likely to be too small by far to protect the public, so Federal action is going to be required anyway. If the payments are made large enough to insure that there is an adequate fund available, the operation of the reactors will be made even more uneconomic. On the other hand, if, as the Joint Committee anticipates, there never will be any call on the fund for payments, the funds will have been accumulated to no purpose.[79]

A Senate Report summarized the structure of the original Price-Anderson Act in 1987 just prior to the most recent amendment of the Act.[80]

The original Price-Anderson Act contained three central features. First, the Act established a limit on the aggregate liability of those who wished to undertake activities involving the handling or use of radioactive materials, either through contract with the Federal Government or under a license issued by the Federal Government for the private development of such activities. The limit on liability was initially set at the sum of $500,000,000 plus the amount of financial protection that a licensee or contractor could obtain under reasonable terms and conditions from private sources. In 1957, the amount of insurance available through private sources was $60,000,000.

Second, the 1957 Act provided that any person who might be held liable for public liability resulting from a nuclear incident, including not only the party directly engaged in the activity that results in the nuclear incident but any other person as well, was to be indemnified under the Price-Anderson system—the so-called "channeling of liability" or "omnibus coverage" provisions of the Act.

And third, the 1957 Act provided that all public liability claims that exceeded the required level of private financial protection would be indemnified by the Federal Government, up to the aggregate limit on liability.

In order to carry out the objectives of this Act, the Atomic Energy Commission (AEC) was authorized to enter into indemnity

---

[79] *Id.* at 1811.
[80] S. REP. NO. 100-218, *reprinted* in 1988 U.S.C.C.A.N. 1477.

agreements with AEC licensees or contractors for a 10-year period, beginning in 1957.

The original Act had a 10 year life. It was extended and modified in 1966, extended and modified again in 1975, and most recently amended in 1988 for a period that runs until 2002.

The amendments have had several objectives. One goal has been to bring all of the probable major radiation related accidents within the coverage of the Price-Anderson Act. The Act now addresses the "nuclear incident" liability of the nuclear electric generating facilities, the liability of the major government contractors (e.g. major research facilities like Los Alamos or Lawrence Livermore National Laboratories), and the liability of parties involved in the transport and disposal of high level nuclear waste.[81]

Second, the statute seeks to consolidate nuclear claims and provide a plan for prompt adjudication and fair payment of claims.[82] Various defenses arising from state law are rejected.[83] Strict liability principles are applied. Consolidation of all claims in the local federal district court is encouraged.[84] That court is encouraged to make a fair distribution of compensatory dollars if the total amount of damages exceeds the compensation available.[85]

Third, the amendments (most notably that of 1988) increased the dollars available to compensate for the nuclear mass disaster, a consideration that the accidents at Three Mile Island and Chernobyl had shown could be of more than theoretical concern.[86] Presently the large nuclear power plant accident could generate statutory compensation in the range of $6-7 billion.[87]

The liability limits reflect a graduated sharing of risk. The initial responsibility is on the individual nuclear plant at which the accident occurs and its private insurers. Damages up to about $160 million are paid from that source. If damages exceed that amount, the secondary coverage kicks in. Those revenues are drawn from an assessment imposed on each operating nuclear plant of an inflation-adjustable amount set in 1988 at $63

---

[81] 42 U.S.C. § 2210(a), (b), (d), (n).

[82] *Id.* at § 2210(i), (m).

[83] *Id.* at § 2210(n).

[84] *Id.*

[85] *Id.* at § 2210(o).

[86] L. Hoegberg, Director General of the Swedish Nuclear Power Inspectorate, provides concise summaries of the two accidents at 372 and 375-76. INTERNATIONAL ATOMIC ENERGY AGENCY SYMPOSIUM PROCEEDINGS, *Reviewing the Safety of Existing Nuclear Power Plants*, Vienna, October 8-11, 1996 (1997).

[87] *Id.* at § 2210(e).

million.[88] That "deferred premium" is only collected if an accident requires it. In effect, this system spreads the risk of a major nuclear accident among all major nuclear electric plants regardless of their "fault" for the accident. The last tier is, of course, the Federal Government.[89] The statute now recognizes, what may always have been assumed—that in case of nuclear disaster the federal government would commit its personnel and dollars to providing help for the citizens harmed in a fashion similar to other natural disasters.

This tiering of liability received Supreme Court approval in the major constitutional challenge to the Price-Anderson legislation. Plaintiffs in *Duke Power Co. v. Carolina Environmental Study Group, Inc.*[90] contended the limitation of liability in case of nuclear accident was inadequate to compensate for the plausible harms. They contended the potential for uncompensated harm to their property deprived them of their rights under the takings, due process, and equal protection clauses.

The Supreme Court showed little sympathy for plaintiffs and sustained Price-Anderson as constitutional against all challenges. The statutory limit on damages was needed to "encourage private industry participation" and bore "a rational relationship to Congress' concern for stimulating the involvement of private enterprise in the production of electric energy through the use of atomic power . . ."[91] Congress' estimate of maximum damages (then $560 million) was a legitimate "working hypothesis" and joined with the recognition that Congress "would likely enact extraordinary relief provisions to provide additional relief, in accord with prior practice."[92] The Court further recognized that the Price-Anderson remedy provided advantages over reliance on the common-law tort jurisprudence of the state.

> The Price-Anderson Act not only provides a reasonable, prompt, and equitable mechanism for compensating victims of a catastrophic nuclear incident, it also guarantees a level of net compensation generally exceeding that recoverable in private litigation. This panoply of remedies and guarantees is at the least a reasonably just substitute for the common-law rights replaced

---

[88] *Id.* at § 2210(b)(1).

[89] *Id.* at § 2210(e)(2). Congress will "take whatever action is determined to be necessary . . . to provide full and prompt compensation to the public for all public liability claims resulting from a disaster of such magnitude."

[90] 438 U.S. 59 (1978).

[91] *Id.* at 84.

[92] *Id.* at 85.

by the Price-Anderson Act. Nothing more is required by the Due Process Clause."[93]

VI. NUCLEAR CLEAN-UP

All of the major energy sources cause environmental harms. These include pollutants released into the air from the burning of fossil fuels, land surfaces disrupted by the construction of hydroelectric facilities or the opening of a coal mine, water polluted by intentional or accidental oil spills, or oil platforms or dams still standing after their energy-useful life has expired. A considerable portion of energy and environmental law deals with the question—to what extent should government require the energy business to clean up and return the environment to the condition preceding the energy project?

The purist will insist that every environmental harm should be corrected. He or she might point out that unless the "polluter pays," society will not properly value the energy product that is offered. However, economics and politics play a role in environmental clean up as well. The economist will insist on an accurate measure of costs and benefits of any clean-up effort. Is an expensive reclamation appropriate if it adds little to the value of the land after reclamation? The politician will weigh costs and benefits to constituents. The clean-up effort that will add substantially to the cost of a product may put a local employer out of business with its impact on jobs and tax revenues.

Nuclear energy law has been especially concerned with clean-up efforts. The rational and irrational fears of nuclear power, more exactly, of nuclear radiation, have encouraged popular attention to nuclear waste issues. The ample federal regulatory authority also has stimulated a federal interest in clean up issues.

From the first days of the civilian nuclear program nuclear wastes accumulated. This waste joined the defense related wastes that had been accumulated since the Manhattan Project during World War II. For a variety of reasons, the initial commitment to peaceful nuclear uses did not include a comprehensive program to deal with the waste material. By the 1970s the topic of waste disposal began to reach the public consciousness. Early federal efforts to locate a permanent storage place (a repository) for the waste went badly. An initially promising site in rural Kansas failed tests of geologic stability. At the same time leaks from the Hanford, Washington

---

[93] *Id.* at 93.

defense storage facility further undercut federal leadership in the area.[94] In 1977 President Jimmy Carter abandoned plans for significant reprocessing of spent nuclear fuel in part because of fears of unauthorized use of the reprocessed fuel for weapons manufacture. As the Supreme Court litigation in *Vermont Yankee*[95] suggested, by the late 1970s, the nuclear waste problem had become a major impediment to the peaceful use of the atom.

A 1982 Congressional Report was blunt:

> The need for legislation to address problems besetting nuclear waste management, and Congressional efforts to address these problems, has increased and become urgent since the early 1970's. Prior to this time, the inventory of wastes from nuclear activities grew with little public notice and minor Congressional concern. An opiate of confidence that the technical issues effecting nuclear waste disposal were easily resolvable for decades rendered Federal officials responsible for providing the facilities apathetic towards addressing those technical issues, and unprepared for the immense social and political problems which would obstruct implementation of a serious repository development program.[96]

Many nuclear plant owners of the early 1980s faced an unappealing prospect. Waste storage capacity at the reactor site would be occupied before the expiration of the useful life of the plant. Realistic hope that much of the "waste" would be removed for commercially attractive reprocessing now looked unlikely. Nuclear opponents were ready to use the waste disposal issue as a basis to stop nuclear activity altogether. Prospects for a near-term solution appeared unlikely. Lastly, an emerging public consensus appeared to be: We should have a safe, permanent storage place for past and future nuclear waste. It should be located nowhere near me.

Congress responded with the Nuclear Waste Policy Act of 1982.[97] The Findings and Purposes section recognized the nuclear waste problem "requires safe and environmentally acceptable methods of disposal."[98] While the federal government "has the responsibility to provide for the permanent disposal" of the waste "the costs of such disposal should be the responsibility of the generators and owners of such waste and spent fuel."[99] The Findings

---

[94] H.R. REP. No. 97-491, Part I, *reprinted* in 1982 U.S.C.C.A.N. 3792-93.

[95] Vermont Yankee Nuclear Power Co. v. NRDC, 435 U.S. 519 (1978).

[96] H.R. REP. No. 97-491, Part I, *reprinted* in 1982 U.S.C.C.A.N. 3792-93.

[97] Pub. L. 97-425, 96 Stat. 2201.

[98] *Id.* at § 111(a)(1).

[99] *Id.* at § 111(a)(4).

also recognized the need for "[s]tate and public participation in the planning and development of repositories."[100]

The major focus of the Act was a program for the identification, investigation, and eventual operation of one or more permanent storage repositories for high level nuclear waste and spent nuclear fuel.[101] While Congress left many of the details of selection of sites to the Secretary of Energy, it made clear its expectations that the repository would be in a geologically stable area remote from significant population and minimally impinging on environmentally sensitive areas. The program also made a commitment to "the disposal of high level nuclear waste which do not rely on human monitoring and maintenance to keep the wastes from entering the biosphere."[102]

The Kansas experience of too prompt a commitment to a geologic site encouraged a thorough scientific study of potential sites. The hypothetical discovery that an active earthquake fault ran through the repository site provided the makings of a public relations nightmare. However, Congress also knew that even a geologically perfect site would likely face political opposition.

Accordingly, the statute went to great lengths to involve the Secretary, the President, the Congress, states and Indian tribes, and the general public in the selection process. Initially the Secretary of Energy was to recommend three prospective sites to the President.[103] The President would then recommend one site to Congress.[104] As this process was advancing, a second selection process would be underway that would identify further prospective sites and give rise to a second site designation.[105]

During this process, the Governors and legislatures of states under consideration were to be kept informed. Public hearings were scheduled at different times in the process.[106] Federal dollars for exploratory work were offered to assist site characterization.

At the extreme a Legislature or Governor could disapprove of a State's selection for a repository.[107] That veto, however, could be overridden by a

---

[100] *Id.* at § 111(a)(6).

[101] *Id.* at § 112.

[102] H.R. REP. NO. 97-491, Part I, *reprinted* in 1982 U.S.C.C.A.N. 3795-96.

[103] Pub. L. 97-425, 96 Stat. 2201, § 112.

[104] *Id.* at § 114.

[105] *Id.* at §§ 112 and 114.

[106] *Id.* at § 112.

[107] *Id.* at § 116.

resolution of both houses of Congress.[108] Therefore, even if no State wanted a repository, Congress could claim it had tried its best to provide a process that mixed ample scientific study, opportunity for public and local political comment, and involvement at the highest levels of state and national government.

Another important provision of the lengthy statute addressed the opportunities for interim storage of waste[109] while the permanent repositories advanced towards what was speculated as completion "around 1995".[110] A further provision set up a Nuclear Waste Fund to assure nuclear industry funding of the costs of the waste disposal project.[111]

The Department of Energy began implementing the complex procedures of the Nuclear Waste Policy Act. A handful of sites for the first repository soon moved center stage. By the time the Secretary had cut the list to three sites—Yucca Mountain in Nevada, Deaf Smith County in Texas, and Hanford in Washington State—it appeared clear that no state government and few local governments were eager to house the repository. Despite, or because of, this reaction, the Secretary of Energy recommended the Yucca Mountain site to President Reagan on May 26, 1986.[112]

Nevada, which had already served as the site of most military nuclear testing by the federal government, reacted with outrage. Congress, having attempted in 1982 to spread the burdens of waste storage among the states, now in 1987 attempted to make 49 states and their representatives happy and Nevada angry. The Nuclear Waste Policy Amendments of 1987 were enacted as part of the 1987 Omnibus Budget Reconciliation Act.[113] The initial substantive section ordered a phase out of site selection activities at other than Yucca Mountain.[114] A following section stopped study of a second repository site and ordered the Secretary of Energy to report to Congress on the need for such a site between 2007 and 2010.[115] Site characterization at Yucca Mountain was to continue. If the Secretary found the site unacceptable, work was to terminate and the Secretary report the bad news to Congress. Congress did offer a number of financial incentives to Nevada.[116]

---

[108] *Id.* at § 114.

[109] *Id.* at § 131.

[110] H.R. REP. NO. 97-491, Part I, *reprinted* in 1982 U.S.C.C.A.N. 3797.

[111] Pub. L. 97-425, 96 Stat. 2201, § 302.

[112] Omnibus Budget Reconciliation Act, Pub. L. 100-203, 101 Stat. 1330, § 5002.

[113] *Id.* Title VA.

[114] *Id.* at § 5011.

[115] *Id.* at § 5012.

[116] *Id.* at § 5031.

It also created a waste site negotiator who was given a five year commission to try to find a State or tribe willing to host the repository.[117]

The Nevada Legislature passed resolutions opposing site characterization activities. In more confrontational fashion it attempted to prohibit federal activity in Nevada in connection with the waste site. It also brought suit in federal court.

In *Nevada v. Watkins*,[118] the Ninth Circuit rejected a broad ranging challenge to Congressional authority. Nevada offered a constitutional smorgasbord in its attempt to avoid the site designation. The United States defeated assertions under the Property Clause, the Privileges and Immunities Clause, the Supremacy Clause, the Port Preference Clause, the Equal Footing Doctrine, and the 10th Amendment. If one sentence summarized the court's position it was the one that found that "[T]he tenth amendment does not protect a State from being outvoted in Congress."[119]

Supreme Court denial of review in *Watkins* probably marked an end to serious judicial challenge to the Nevada location. It by no means marked an end to political guerilla warfare over the site location. As recently as 1996 Congress asked the Secretary of Energy to provide it and the President with "a viability assessment of the Yucca Mountain site."[120] Work goes on. Added waste accumulates. Every Nevada candidate for national or statewide office in 1998 opposed the Yucca Mountain location. Best estimates envision a completed nuclear waste repository no earlier than 2010.

In 1996, another portion of the Waste Policy Act reached the federal courts.[121] The original Act of 1982 had created the trust fund to pay for the repository. Nuclear utilities had been contributing to the fund on the statutory representation that "beginning not later than January 31, 1998, [the Secretary] will dispose of the high-level radioactive waste . . . involved."[122] The Secretary defended on the grounds that no active repository had been completed. The court adopted the utilities' interpretation of the word "dispose" in the 1982 Act. The plain meaning of the word meant that the statute "create[d] an obligation in DOE, reciprocal to the utilities' obligation to pay, to start disposing of the [waste] no later than January 31, 1998."[123]

---

[117] *Id*. at 5041.

[118] 914 F.2d 1545 (9th Cir. 1990).

[119] *Id*. at 1556.

[120] Energy and Water Development Appropriations Act 1997, Pub. L. 104-206, 110 Stat. 2984, Title III.

[121] Indiana Michigan Power Co. v. DOE, 88 F.3d 1272 (D.C. Cir. 1996).

[122] *Citing* 42 U.S.C. § 10222(a)(5)(B).

[123] Indiana Michigan Power Co. v. DOE, 88 F.3d 1272, 1277 (D.C. Cir. 1996).

A second nuclear clean-up issue involves so-called low-level wastes. A 1980 legislative report estimated that approximately 3 million cubic feet of such waste were generated yearly in the United States.[124] A 1985 report elaborated on the nature of low-level waste.

> Low-level radioactive waste is material which has been contamin-ated by radioactive elements or radionuclides. Low-level radio-active waste is often defined by what it is not. It is not spent reactor fuel, wastes from reprocessed reactor fuel, uranium mine and mill tailings or items contaminated with specified levels of transuranic elements. . . . Nationwide, utilities accounted for 64 percent of the total waste stream in 1983, with industrials at 28 percent, academic institutions at 3 percent, medical at 3 percent and the Federal Government at 2 percent. Although medical waste generated directly from medical procedures amounts to 3 percent of the nations waste, the waste produced by industrials which service the medical community boosts the total amount of waste produced as a result of medical activities to 25 percent. Low-level radioactive waste is generated from a variety of sources and comes in a variety of forms. Forms of such waste common to all generators include paper trash, used protective clothing, discarded glassware, tools and equipment. In addition, each generator produces wastes reflective of their unique operations. For instance, nuclear power plants produce used chemical ion exchange resins, filters, lubricating oil and greases.[125]

While these wastes typically lacked the toxicity of spent nuclear fuel or by-products of the nuclear weapons program, they were radioactive and needed careful disposal and storage.

The Low-Level Radioactive Waste Policy Act of 1980,[126] structured a federal policy towards this form of nuclear waste. Section 4(a)(1) made "each State . . . responsible for providing for the availability of capacity either within or outside the State" for low-level waste generated within its borders. The following subsection encouraged states to enter into multistate compacts to provide for regional waste disposal facilities. Under the Constitution the compacts required Congressional consent. Congressional consent, however, offered protection against claims that the state activities violated the interstate commerce clause. As the statute indicated: "After January 1, 1986, any such compact may restrict the use of the regional

---

[124] S. REP. NO. 96-548, *reprinted* at 1980 U.S.C.C.A.N. 6938.
[125] H.R. REP. NO. 99-314, Part 2; *reprinted* at 1985 U.S.C.C.A.N. 3004-05.
[126] Pub. L. 96-573, 94 Stat. 3347.

disposal facilities under the compact to the disposal of low-level radioactive waste generated within the region."[127]

The 1980 Act entered a real world in which several low-level waste sites had closed. Remaining sites at Barnwell, South Carolina, Richland, Washington, and Beatty, Nevada showed little enthusiasm for providing access to low-level waste in any amount and from any destination.[128] Studies prior to the 1985 Amendments to the Low-Level Waste Act indicated that compacts were well on their way to formation, but that new disposal sites were not being constructed.[129]

The 1985 Amendments[130] presented a more specific package of carrots and sticks in this interesting example of state-federal collaboration. In broad terms, the objective of the statute was 1) to encourage the creation of compacts or a clear recognition of individual state responsibility for low-level nuclear waste 2) to encourage the construction of additional storage sites to augment the Nevada, South Carolina, and Washington sites 3) to provide for necessary interim storage while the compact site program moved to completion and 4) to provide a series of sanctions for states or compact areas that were not advancing the completion of the program.

This exercise in creative federalism met constitutional challenge in *New York v. United States*.[131] Despite the fact that state governments had been a major proponent of the Act, the Court reviewed the case in the posture of the federal government infringing on states' rights under the 10th Amendment and the Guarantee Clause of Article IV ("The United States shall guarantee to every State in this Union a Republican Form of Government . . .").

There was little disagreement that Congress had the power to regulate low-level waste under the Commerce Clause. What was at issue were "the circumstances under which Congress may use the States as implements of regulation; that is, whether Congress may direct or otherwise motivate the States to regulate in a particular field or a particular way."[132]

The Court recognized its "cases have identified a variety of methods, short of outright coercion, by which Congress may urge a State to adopt a

---

[127] *Id.* at § 4(a)(2)(B).

[128] S. REP. NO. 96-548, *reprinted* at 1980 U.S.C.C.A.N. 6938; H.R. REP. NO. 99-314, Part 1, *reprinted* at 1985 U.S.C.C.A.N. 2976.

[129] H.R. REP. NO. 99-314, Part 2, *reprinted* at 1985 U.S.C.C.A.N. 3003.

[130] Low-Level Radioactive Waste Policy Amendments Act of 1985, Pub. L. 99-240, 99 Stat. 1842.

[131] 505 U.S. 144 (1992).

[132] *Id.* at 161.

legislative program consistent with federal interests."[133] Two aspects of the low-level waste program passed muster. The first offered federal financial incentives to states complying with the federal objectives. The second allowed waste sites to eventually deny access to states not complying with the federal objectives. The states were free not to participate if they chose. However, Congress could constitutionally imposed consequences on that choice.

A third provision did cross the line to impermissible coercion. That provision required the states to "take title" to the low-level waste generated within the State if they did not meet the federal standards. The Court found the provision "unique."

> No other federal statute has been cited which offers a state government no option other than that of implementing legislation enacted by Congress. Whether one views the take title provision as lying outside Congress' enumerated powers, or as infringing upon the core of state sovereignty reserved by the Tenth Amendment, the provision is inconsistent with the federal structure of our Government established by the Constitution.[134]

The high-level and low-level nuclear waste programs described above focus on waste products created at the nuclear electric plant. A separate radiation hazard stems from the mill tailings produced as part of the processing of the uranium for fabrication into nuclear fuel for reactor use.

A 1978 House Report describes the nature of the waste. "Uranium mill tailings are the sandy waste produced by the uranium ore milling process. Because only 1 to 5 pounds of useable uranium is extracted from each 2,000 pounds of ore, tremendous quantities of waste are produced as a result of milling operations."[135] Until the 1970s the radioactive mill tailings stimulated little concern on the part of the private companies producing them, the Federal Government that had contracted for most of the uranium under the Manhattan Project and subsequent defense programs, and the state and local governments that had geographic jurisdiction over the mill sites.

Serious concern about the hazards began with the discovery that mill tailings had been used as construction material in Grand Junction, Colorado. Legislation in 1972 sought to clean-up this environmental blunder.[136]

---

[133] *Id.* at 166.
[134] *Id.* at 177.
[135] H.R. REP. NO. 95-1480, Part 1, *reprinted* in 1978 U.S.C.C.A.N. 7433.
[136] *Id.* at 7434.

It also called attention to the potential hazards from the tailings. These were summarized in a 1985 Congressional Report:

> Mill tailings present a potential long-term health hazard principally because they emit small amounts of radon. Radon is a colorless, inert, radioactive gas formed by the radioactive decay of radium, an element found with the uranium in the ore. Radon, with a half-life of four days, decays to form products that are also radioactive. Although radon is found in many rocks and minerals, it is more readily released from uranium mill tailings because they have been finely crushed, and tend to contain high concentrations of radium. The tailings piles may also contain other radioactive and nonradioactive contaminants.
>
> Remedial action is necessary to limit human exposure to radiation and other contaminants associated with tailings. The level of human exposure to radon and other radioactive substances in the tailings pile is quite low. Nevertheless, there is concern that even low levels of radiation may pose health hazards to those who might be exposed over long periods of time. There is also concern that future generations may misuse the tailings for construction materials or for other purposes.[137]

The Grand Junction fiasco encouraged study of the entire uranium milling waste problem. By 1978, Congress estimated that the federally encouraged milling programs had generated nearly 90 million tons of tailings. Of this amount, 27 million tons were located "at sites where no commercial milling has taken place and which are not the responsibility of any active milling company."[138] Congress sought to remedy the problem with the Uranium Mill Tailings Radiation Control Act of 1978.[139] The two major parts of the statute addressed the past and the future. How do we clean up abandoned tailings sites? How do we properly regulate ongoing milling activity to avoid a recurrence of the abandoned site problem?

Title I of the Act addressed the abandoned site clean-up. Despite its doubts about Federal Government "responsibility" for causing the problem, Congress was willing to be the lead actor in cleaning up the mess. Congress identified 22 areas in which a tailings waste problem appeared to exist.[140] Congress directed the Secretary of Energy to review the problem areas, consider adjacent areas that might also be contaminated, and prioritize a

---

[137] S. REP. NO. 100-543, *reprinted* in 1985 U.S.C.C.A.N. 4329.

[138] H. REP. NO. 95-1480, Part 1, *reprinted* in U.S.C.C.A.N. 7434.

[139] Pub. L. 95-604, 92 Stat. 3021.

[140] *Id.* at § 102.

clean-up program.[141] State governments were to be consulted during the process and encouraged to share financial responsibility for the clean-up.[142] The Administrator of the Environmental Protection Agency was to identify appropriate clean-up techniques to "assure the safe and environmentally sound stabilization of residual radioactive materials . . ."[143] While the States would exercise much control during the clean-up, the stabilized radioactive sites were to be turned over to the Secretary of Energy to allow permanent control over the waste site.

Title II of the Act took a number of steps to tighten federal regulatory control over uranium milling operations. States could continue to regulate under the agreement state program. But, the statute made clear that federal standards were to control. As in the abandoned site program, the federal authorities would also control the eventual stabilized sites.

In familiar fashion, the site remediation program has faced delays, errors, and cost overruns. However, solid progress has been made in cleaning up the initial designated sites. It is reasonable to predict that most of the worst sites will have been stabilized within another decade.

A last, and quite significant, part of the nuclear cleanup involves the plant itself. Statute and regulation authorized forty year licenses for plant operation. The forty years approximated the expected life of the nuclear plant, a life expectancy similar to that for fossil-fueled electric plants. Actual nuclear plant operation has shown that some components (steam generators, for example) last less than forty years. Other parts of the plant may well survive in good working order well beyond forty years.

Whatever the wear and tear during operation, the replacement or abandonment of nuclear plants involves radiation hazards. Important plant components are highly radioactive and must be treated as such. Closure of the nuclear plant demands far more than simply ceasing power production and locking the gates.

Several American nuclear electric plants are nearing the end of their licensed life. Most are showing signs of wear and tear. A decision to refurbish an old plant to current standards may require an investment in the hundreds of millions of dollars, serious money to a cost-conscious electric generating company. Beyond individual plants is the larger issue of whether nuclear electric generation has a future in the United States. A negative answer to that question could force us to recognize that the next twenty

---

[141] *Id.*

[142] *Id.* at § 103.

[143] *Id.* at § 108.

years will be dedicated to the expensive and environmentally sensitive task of closing out a technology whose time has come and gone.

Unlike high and low level waste and mill tailings, Congress has not written specific legislation to address the closure of nuclear plants. The broad licensing authority of the Atomic Energy Act has encompassed closure of plants as well as their opening. Various portions of Part 50 of Title 10 of the Code of Federal Regulations address closure issues. The original licensing process should address the plans for decommissioning.[144] A crucial requirement is the provision of funds to decommission the plant—an amount estimated in the hundreds of millions of dollars.[145] The regulations anticipate that no business will be excited about spending money on an abandoned facility or technology. Therefore, the Nuclear Regulatory Commission insists on financial assurances up-front. The regulations offer the options of prepayment of decommissioning costs, an accumulating sinking fund, or the provision of some form of surety agreement or insurance.[146]

Licensees are expected to complete decommissioning within 60 years after the permanent cessation of operations at the plant.[147] The NRC offers several decommissioning options including mothballing the plant in a fashion that prevents leakage of radiation and full dismantling and decontamination or safe storage of radioactive plant components.

Aside from the radioactive hazards, a wealth of other considerations accompany the closure of a plant. A plant located in a small town or rural area may provide a large portion of the tax base for the local residents. Closure of the facility may work a sea change in local government. Full-scale dismantling of the plant, however, may open up a geographic area for new development.

VII. CONCLUSION

A 1997 General Accounting Office Report summarizes the challenges facing the Nuclear Regulatory Commission in the coming decade:

> NRC faces significant challenges as it begins to plan for its future. Many nuclear power plants are cutting costs to stay competitive in the face of deregulation. The safety consequences of these actions will likely result in NRC's reassessing its regulatory program in the future. Furthermore an aging nuclear industry is

---

[144] 10 C.F.R. § 50.33 (4).

[145] *Id.* at §§ 50.33(k)(1), 50.75.

[146] *Id.* at § 50.75.

[147] *Id.* at § 50.82 (3).

challenging NRC's ability to ensure that adequate funds are available for decommissioning plants that have closed prematurely. Finally, the prospect of NRC's assuming oversight over the Department of Energy's (DOE) laboratories and weapons plants would dramatically affect NRC's resources, structure, and strategies.[148]

Despite statements about the death of the nuclear option in the United States, it is too soon to write off nuclear power as a failed technology. Legislation like the 1992 Energy Act indicates that Congress is still willing to encourage a nuclear option. A few utilities are seeking relicensing of existing plants.[149] New technologies may yet make nuclear power sufficiently safe and cost-competitive to stimulate investors and consumer-voters. The environmental harms from fossil fuel consumption may also make nuclear power the best of options for generating electric power.

Even if the United States has built its last nuclear electric generating plant, the phasing out and cleaning up of nuclear power offers a half-century of difficult legal and policy problems. Monitoring the safe closure of a failed technology doesn't inspire workers or leaders. But, it is work that will need to be done with competence and consistency. ❦

---

[148] General Accounting Office, B-277583, *Results Act; Observations on the Nuclear Regulatory Commission's Draft Strategic Plan*, July 31, 1997 at 1.

[149] The CEO of one such utility observed: "We had to examine everything in the plant that might be affected by age. There were some 334 activities that we thought needed age management practices, but in reviewing what we have been doing, 68 percent of those already existed. Another 27 percent existed but had to be modified a little bit. Only 5 percent of that 334 needed some new inspection program or age management practice to be put into place." Christian Poindexter, CEO of Baltimore Gas and Electric, PROCEEDINGS OF NUCLEAR ENERGY ASSEMBLY, San Francisco, May 13-15, 1998 at 3.

CHAPTER ELEVEN

Hydroelectric Power

by Marla E. Mansfield

I.   THE HYDROELECTRIC FUEL CYCLE

The power of water has been harnessed throughout history; for many centuries the mill wheel turning was the symbol of industrial activity. Hydropower today does not use moving water to power machinery by mechanical energy directly. Rather, the water is used to turn turbines, which then create electricity. The water power may come simply from a river's flow. Projects such as these are known as "run of the river" generation. Water falls, such as Niagara Falls, also may provide energy. More often, however, in a conventional hydropower facility, water is stored behind a dam.

The process of generating electricity from the stored water illustrates the conversion of energy from one type to another. The water at the top of the dam has potential energy. When it falls, it has kinetic energy. The dam allows the operator to store water for release when needed. It also allows control of water fluctuation in nature. More human intervention is obvious in the third type of project, namely, those hydroelectric plants that do not merely store the river's flow. These "pumped storage plants" use electricity when it is at a surplus to pump water to the top of the dam. The water can be released to generate electricity at times of peak need. Thus, energy is "stored." Any one of these methods to use water to generate electricity has various limitations and benefits.

One benefit is the fact that the "fuel" is essentially free, except for the cost of pumping in a pumped storage project. Therefore, the electric generator is not subject to fluctuating costs as with fossil fuels or nuclear reactors. This reliance on nature is, of course, a two-edged sword. Although the generator need not pay to get the water each year, the amount of water available may vary due to drought and flood. Even with a dam, the generator cannot be assured of an ever-present energy source.

Despite potential vagaries of nature, compared to some other energy sources, hydroelectric power seems environmentally friendly. There are no problems of air pollution from combustion of carbons nor is there the problem of disposal of wastes as there is in the nuclear industry. Nevertheless, the environmental impacts from building a dam may be great. A free-flowing river becomes a lake, inundating wildlife habitat and human endeavors. Siltation behind the dam changes the nature of the water going downstream. Moreover, water temperature changes may make the re-conformed river suitable for different aquatic life than before. Additionally, fish that once traveled up or down stream may find passage blocked. Therefore, new hydroelectric plants can be controversial and some plants have been controversial in the past.

Although there have been dams, such as the Hoover Dam, that have been viewed as architectural wonders, the damming of the Hetch-Hetchy River in Yosemite Park was one of the outrages to John Muir and fellow preservationists that led to the vitalization of the Sierra Club. In the United States, it is possible that there will be no new large-scale projects for both economic and environmental reasons. First, most of the best sites from an economic standpoint have already been used. As an example of environmental pressures brought to bear on projects, the last large proposal, that of the City and County of Denver to build the Two Forks Dam for municipal water supply, was killed when the Environmental Protection Agency vetoed the decision to grant it a necessary permit.[1]

Nevertheless, hydroelectricity plays a role in the current electric generation mix and may play a role in the future. Low head dams that will produce localized electricity are a viable choice. These dams are not the huge Hoover Dams, but are smaller and less intrusive. Other alternatives to boost hydro-electric generation include adding electric generation equipment to an existing dam. Dams built primarily for irrigation, navigation, or flood control may easily be modified by this addition. Although perhaps individually insignificant, these small projects may cumulatively add to the nation's electricity base. In 1978, as part of the Carter Administration's emphasis on energy conservation and renewables, Congress passed the Public Utility Regulatory Policies Act of 1978 (PURPA).[2] It requires the Department of Energy to establish a program to encourage small hydroelectric facilities. The Federal Energy Regulatory Commission (FERC) is to seek expeditious licensing for small projects employing existing dams. The statute defines a small project as one with not more than 30,000 kilowatts of installed capacity. These projects also benefit under PURPA's economic provisions for co-generation and small power production facilities; electric utilities must purchase excess power generated by such facilities at the

---

[1] Alameda Water & Sanitation District v. Reilly, 930 F. Supp. 486 (D. Colo. 1996).

[2] 16 U.S.C. §§ 2701 et seq.

utility's "avoided cost" (i.e., cost to generate it alternatively) and must supply back up power at "reasonable cost."[3]

II. THE HYDROELECTRICITY MARKET

Some recent data on hydroelectric production and consumption reveal its significance. Hydroelectricity as of 1996 supplied 11% of the United States' electricity and in 1995 constituted 3.36% of total energy use. Hydroelectricity production grew 6.1% in 1993, in which year it supplied 9% of the nation's electricity. In certain parts of the nation, such as the Pacific Northwest, hydroelectricity is a very significant player, supplying 62% of electricity as of 1991. Figures from 1994 reveal that the United States produced 2.6 quads of hydroelectric power, but consumed 3.1 quads, which was 3.5% of total energy use. The gap between production and consumption of hydroelectric power was met by importing electricity from Canada. Internationally, some nations generate a higher percentage of their electricity in this manner than either the United States or Canada. Hydroelectricity is more than 50% of the electricity of Austria, Sweden, Switzerland, and New Zealand; Norway generates 99.6% of its electricity by hydroelectric power.

Hydroelectric power can be used as a source of base power or peak power. Generally, utilities prefer base generation to have low operating costs because of its near-constant use. Peak power generation, used during seasons or times-of-day when demand increases, could have higher operating costs because it is used less often and often its product could command higher rates. Pumped storage hydroelectric plants are well-suited to provide such peak power. During non-peak times, excess electricity can be used to pump water to the storage facility.

One unusual aspect of the domestic hydroelectric market is that the federal government generates and then sells hydroelectricity in several settings. Responding to regional pressures and to forward various goals, dams have been built for irrigation, flood control, navigation, and directly for power generation. Naturally, dams built for one purpose can serve the other purposes.

Six regional marketers were formed under federal law with electric generation as part of their specific mandates. These include the most famous, the Tennessee Valley Authority, which was created during the New Deal.[4] Additionally, there are regional marketers that are part of the Department of Energy: the Bonneville Power Administration, Southeastern

---

[3] Section 210 of PURPA, 16 U.S.C. § 824a-3.
[4] 16 U.S.C. § 831c(j).

Power Administration, Southwestern Power Administration and the Western Area Power Administration. In 1995, a sixth marketer, the Alaska Power Administration, was sold to the state of Alaska for $84 million. The Alaska Energy Authority will run its two small projects, which provide a significant proportion of Alaska's electricity and 80% of the needs of Juneau. Congress considered selling other power marketers, but met with objections from local cooperatives and others dependent on the relatively cheap power. Also at issue in the sales proposal was what to do with shoreline development around the lakes. Therefore, sale of these regional electricity marketers was not an easy deficit reducer.

 In addition to these marketers, the federal government more generally ends up with power to sell as a by-product of dams built primarily for other purposes. The Bureau of Reclamation, an agency within the Department of the Interior, builds dams for irrigation and the Army Corp of Engineers has flood control and navigation within its dam-building mandate. The two agencies are often bitter rivals for dam sites. Statutes such as Section 9(c) of the Reclamation Project Act of 1939,[5] and Section 5 of the Flood Control Act of 1944,[6] authorize the sale of power from federal projects. The cost of federal hydro-power is generally lower than that produced by alternative generation employing fossil fuels or nuclear power. Competition for the power is therefore great.

The acts implementing federal sales authority do not merely seek a return for the federal government, but also attempt to forward social objectives. For example, Section 9(c) of the Reclamation Project Act of 1939 provides that in sales or leases of electric power or power privileges, made by the Secretary, "preference shall be given to municipalities and other public corporations" and to cooperatives financed under the Rural Electric Act.[7] This preference requires that the preference parties be served first, but does not prohibit the Secretary of the Interior from discriminating amongst equally preferred purchasers.[8] Therefore, a preferred costumer would have a "property interest" in its entitlement for power for due process purposes vis-a-vis non-preference parties, but not in reference to other preference parties.[9] An over-riding concern for irrigation, however, makes it impossible for the Secretary to sell power to a preference entity if, in the Secretary's

---

[5] 43 U.S.C. § 485h(c).

[6] 16 U.S.C. § 825s.

[7] 43 U.S.C. § 485h(c).

[8] Arizona Power Authority v. Morton, 527 F.2d 721 (9th Cir. 1975), *cert. denied*, 425 U.S. 911 (1976).

[9] City of Santa Clara v. Andrus, 572 F.2d 660, 667 (9th Cir. 1978).

estimation, to do so would have the effect of cutting back on the power necessary to operate the federal dam's pumping facilities.[10]

The policy regarding sales from Corps of Engineer dams is less clear. One court has labeled its guidance " too vague and general to provide law to apply":

> The Flood Control Act's directive to market power in such a way as to "encourage the most widespread use thereof" [Section 5 of the Flood Control Act of 1944, 16 U.S.C. § 825s] could be interpreted in many different ways, such as to require that power be sold to as many different preference entities as possible, thereby fostering the most widespread geographic use of the power, or to mandate sale of the power to those preference entities whose customers present the most diversified mix of agricultural, industrial or residential users, or to require sale of federal power to those preference entities which serve the largest number of ultimate consumers.[11]

Therefore, the Secretary of the Army has wide discretion in sales.

Other laws also may impact on the federal government's ability to sell hydroelectricity. As noted in *Tennessee Valley Authority v. Hill*,[12] the Endangered Species Act may prevent the building of a dam because federal agencies must ensure that their actions are not likely either to jeopardize the continued existence of a threatened or endangered species nor modify or destroy critical habit. In addition, the ESA may affect the operation of dams. In *O'Neill v. United States*,[13] the Bureau of Reclamation was excused from delivery of water when the water was required to assist endangered species. According to the court, the provision of the water services contract stating that government would not be held liable for damages arising from shortage in water supplied on account of errors in operation, drought, or "any other causes," unambiguously relieved the government from liability in connection with the unavailability of water resulting from mandates of valid legislation. Moreover, even if the contract did obligate the government to supply a specified amount of water without exception, the contract was not immune from subsequently enacted statutes.

The second major quirk in the hydroelectric market is obvious: any hydroelectricity development requires a right to impound and then use

---

[10] 43 U.S.C. § 485 h(c).
[11] *City of Santa Clara*, 572 F.2d at 667.
[12] 437 U.S. 153 (1978).
[13] 50 F.3d 677 (9th Cir. 1995).

water to turn turbines. Therefore, a broad overview of water law, concentrating on surface water, is necessary to understand the hydroelectric market.[14] On the physical side, water usage generally is measured by the term "acre feet." One acre foot is the amount of water it takes to cover an acre one foot deep, or, in more familiar terms, 325,851 gallons of water. As to the law, there are two major water law regimes, the riparian and prior appropriation systems.

The first of the two major water rights regimes is dominant in the more humid eastern portion of the country. This system, the riparian system, allocates the right to use water to the owners of land adjoining, or riparian, to the waters. In the English riparian system, all riparian right holders had the right to the natural flow of the water in the watercourse. Therefore, except for domestic and husbandry uses of water, this brand of riparian law did not envision consumptive water uses. Water could drive the mill wheel, with the water then returned to the river, but water could not be permanently removed from the basin. Most jurisdictions in the United States follow the so called American rule, under which each riparian may make "reasonable use" of the water. The riparian doctrine gives the owner of land the right to divert the water flowing by the riparian land for use upon that land, without regard to the extent of such use or priority in time. All riparians on a stream system have similar, common rights so that when water is short, all riparians must reduce their usage proportionately.

The second major American system, the law of prior appropriation, substitutes water use and priority in time for land ownership as the arbiters of rights. The doctrine arose in the more arid western states, most directly in response to the mining industry's need to use water where the ore was

---

[14] Groundwater is not always treated in the same way as surface waters even in the same state. Some states apply appropriation law to ground water. Others use the English rule of absolute ownership. Under the English rule, ownership of land over the ground water gives a right to consume the water for any purpose except malice. Therefore, a rule of capture phenomenon results. An alternative way of managing underground waters is the so-called American rule, which limits rights of landowners to reasonable uses, generally on the overlying land. A fourth method used by some states is a balancing or correlative rights regime. Under it, each landowner has co-equal rights to the resource and each has a right to a fair and equitable share. Texas historically followed the English Rule, but is re-thinking it in light of water shortages and environmental concerns in the Edwards Aquifer. A statutory modification of the absolute ground water rights by the Edwards Aquifer Act was upheld in *Barshop v. Medina County Underground Water Conservation District*, 925 S.W.2d 618 (Tex. 1996), but the Texas Supreme Court refused to abandon the English Rule generally without a statute. Sipriano v. Great Spring Water of America, Inc., 1 S.W.3d 75 (Tex. 1999).

located, which might be distant from the shores of a water body. The appropriation doctrine confers upon one who actually diverts and uses water the right to do so with some limitations: the water must be used for reasonable and beneficial uses and the water must be surplus to that used by earlier appropriators. States often specify that certain uses, such as domestic uses, may have priority over less favored uses, but within the same class of uses, the rule of priority is "first in time, first in right."[15] The senior appropriator is entitled to fulfill the appropriator's needs before a junior appropriator is entitled to use any water. Moreover, no new use can be initiated that would impair a senior appropriator's rights.

Users of a particular water source are bound together in appropriative law. In order to get full beneficial use of a water source, an appropriator has some right to expect the watercourse to remain in the form it was in when the appropriation was made. Therefore, if an appropriator seeks to change either the place of diversion or the type of beneficial use made of a water right, regulatory officials would not approve the change of use unless it did not impair both senior and junior appropriators. For example, an agricultural water right might be for 6 acre feet, of which 4 are either used by the plants or lost to evaporation. Two acre feet would return to the stream. If the farmer desired to change the use of the water, the return flow would have to be maintained (or less diverted) if to not do so would impair the rights of either senior or junior appropriators.[16]

In addition to these two water law regimes, a third system of water law blends riparian and appropriative systems. This blend is the law in the coastal states of Oregon, California and Washington and the states that straddle the 100th principal meridian, which separates the relatively wet Eastern part of the nation from the arid west, namely: Kansas, Nebraska, Oklahoma, Texas, North Dakota, and South Dakota. Mississippi is the tenth blended state. California began with a dual system; the remaining states

---

[15] Under most modern systems, priority is judged not from the time of actual water use, but from the date of permit application or first public steps toward use, provided the project is completed with diligence. The rationale behind this is to prevent untoward races to privatize the common property and to allow for orderly development, especially when many water projects require substantial investments.

[16] Why should the junior appropriator be protected against a change of point of diversion or use? Suppose that A had an appropriative right to divert 20 cfs (cubic feet a second) for a 120 day growing season. B, knowing this, then gets a right to divert 10 cfs from a downstream headgate. B might not have realized that A's return flow was equivalent to the 10 cfs B was to appropriate. If A, in selling A's right, would be able to move the entire 20 cfs, there would be no water for B. What would happen to B's expectations if this were allowed to occur? Would people tend to invest in partially developed streams? Would water be efficiently used?

originally followed riparian law and then added appropriative systems. In most blended states, riparian rights have been modified and adopted into the system of prior appropriation by requiring the rights to be registered. No new uses other than domestic could be asserted outside of the more general system.[17]

Common to all these legal regimes is the idea that rights to use water are simply that—namely, usufructuary rights to divert and employ the water. In fact, many states, especially in the west, declare that water is the property of the people of the state. A private "water right," although a species of property right, consists not of ownership of the fluid itself, but of owning the advantage of water's use, and is limited by the uncertainties of nature as to its amount. Therefore, the concept is not one of water "ownership," but of obtaining and holding the right to use the water. Such a right is protected against trespass by others and from uncompensated governmental taking. However, the nature of the right does allow for governmental regulation.

All of the water law systems contain within them the possibility of police power regulation. By their very nature, they curb any claim to an inviolable "absolute" right to do with one's water what one may desire. At the heart of modern riparian law is the doctrine that use must be reasonable;[18] hence one individual's use may not be viewed in isolation because all other riparians have correlative rights. The concept of beneficial use in and of itself limits an appropriative right: no water right exists if the use is not beneficial. Moreover, in appropriative systems, the various state systems require permits to be acquired. Once a permit for an appropriative water right is issued, the permit holder has the right to take and use the water according to the terms of the permit.

The California Supreme Court underscored a further significant limitation on water rights: the "public trust" doctrine. The court in *National*

---

[17] *But see* Franco-American Charolaise, Ltd. v. City of Ada and Oklahoma Water Resources Bd., 855 P.2d 568 (Okla. 1993) (holding that Oklahoma's statute modifying riparian rights was an unconstitutional taking of property).

[18] *But see* Herminghaus v. South. California Edison Co., 252 P. 607 (1926), *appeal dismissed*, 275 U.S. 486 (under riparian doctrine, an owner is entitled to the full flow of stream even though that owner was to use water wastefully to flood lands; an upstream appropriator could thus not store water for power plant). In response to *Herminghaus*, a constitutional amendment was enacted in 1928 subjecting all water users—riparians and appropriators alike—to the universal limitation that water use must be reasonable and for a beneficial purpose. (Cal. Const., art. X, § 2.)

Audubon Society v. Superior Court[19] held that the state's navigable waters are subject to a public trust and that the state, as trustee, has a duty to preserve this trust property from harmful diversions by water rights holders. Under this doctrine, no one has a vested right to use water in a manner harmful to the state's waters and public attributes of them. In addition to recognizing the public trust doctrine, California also authorizes its Water Board to consider the public interest in granting or denying a private right to initiate a water right. Not all such agencies are empowered to consider the public interest at this juncture. For example, in Colorado, if the state water agency identifies a public need for water, the agency must initiate a water right on the public's behalf and that right can be an instream right.[20] Moreover, not all states recognize and use the public trust doctrine as a limitation on private rights.

III. HYDROELECTRICITY REGULATION

The federal government has always taken an interest in navigable waters. Control of navigation was one of the core functions of Congress's interstate commerce power. Related to this interest, Congress passed the Water Power Act in 1920, which required licenses for construction of certain hydroelectric facilities. In 1935, these provisions were imported into the Federal Power Act.[21] The Federal Power Commission implemented the Act until the Federal Energy Regulatory Commission took over in 1977. Section 23(b) of the Power Act reads:

> It shall be unlawful for any person * * * for the purpose of developing electric power, to construct, operate, or maintain any dam, water conduit, reservoir, power house, or other works incidental thereto across, along, or in any of the navigable waters of the United States, or upon any part of the public lands or reservations of the United States (including the Territories), or utilize the surplus water or water power from any Government dam, except under and in accordance with * * * a license granted pursuant to this Act. Any person * * * intending to construct a dam or other project works across, along, over, or in any stream or part thereof, other than those defined herein as navigable waters, and over which Congress has jurisdiction under its au-

---

[19] 33 Cal.3d 419, 189 CAL.RPTR. 346, 658 P.2d 709 (1983).

[20] Board of County Commissioners v. United States, 891 P.2d 952 (Colo. 1995).

[21] The Act was also modified in 1935. Prior to such date, those building on non-navigable waters simply had an option, but not an obligation, to file an application for a license. Farmington River Power Co. v. F.P.C., 455 F.2d 86 (2d Cir. 1992)

thority to regulate commerce with foreign nations and among the several States shall before such construction file declaration of such intention with the Commission, whereupon the Commission shall cause immediate investigation of such proposed construction to be made, and if upon investigation it shall find that the interests of interstate or foreign commerce would be affected by such proposed construction, such person * * * shall not construct, maintain, or operate such dam or other project works until it shall have applied for and shall have received a license under the provisions of this Act. If the Commission shall not so find, and if no public lands or reservations are affected, permission is hereby granted to construct such dam or other project works in such stream upon compliance with State laws.

To understand the federal licensing procedure, several questions must be addressed. First, when is a license required? Second, what must be considered in granting a license? Finally, what other statutes are relevant in the licensing decision? The first question is addressed in the so-called *Taum Sauk* decision.[22]

The statute's first sentence clearly requires a license for works on navigable streams or on federally owned lands. The *Taum Sauk* case, however, involved the licensing scenario broached in the second sentence of § 23(b) of the Act, which has two tests. The first determines when someone must file a "notice of intent" to build and the second test determines which of these "notice" projects would require a license. The case arose out of a development on the East Fork of the Black River, which is a non-navigable tributary of the Black River. The Black River is a navigable stream, as is the White River into which it flows. Because of the East Fork's connection to a navigable stream, it was a water "over which Congress has jurisdiction under its authority to regulate commerce with foreign nations and among the several States." Therefore, a notice of intent to build had to be filed. The main issue in the case was the meaning of the phrase, "the interests of interstate or foreign commerce would be affected by such proposed construction," which was the test to require a license. Two possible interpretations were posed: first, that commerce in the shape of navigation must be impacted; or, second, that any impact on interstate or foreign commerce would require a license. The Supreme Court sided with the Federal Power Commission and opted for the latter interpretation:

> To focus the inquiry, it is well to state what is not involved in this case. There is no question that the interstate transmission

---

[22] Federal Power Commission v. Union Electric Company, 381 U.S. 90 (1965).

of electric energy is fully subject to the commerce powers of Congress. Nor is there any doubt today that projects generating energy for such transmission, such as Taum Sauk, affect commerce among the States and therefore are within the purview of the commerce power, quite without regard to the federal control of tributary streams and navigation. Thus, there are no constitutional doubts or barriers to the FPC's interpretation. The only question is whether Congress has required a license for a water power project utilizing the headwaters of a navigable river to generate energy for an interstate power system. We think an affirmative answer is required by both the language and purposes of the Act.

The language of the Act, in our view, plainly requires a license in the circumstances of this case. Section 23(b) prohibits construction of nonlicensed hydroelectric projects on navigable streams, regardless of any effect, detrimental or beneficial, on navigation or commerce by water and requires those proposing a project on a nonnavigable stream to file a declaration of intention and to come before the Commission for a determination of whether the "interests of interstate or foreign commerce would be affected," a determination which obviously does not speak in terms of the interests of navigation or water commerce. Plainly the provision does not require a license only where "the interests of interstate or foreign commerce *on navigable waters* would be affected." Although transportation on interstate waterways is interstate commerce, the phrase "affect the interests of commerce" on its face hardly supports any claim that Congress sought to regulate only such transportation. Rather, it strongly implies that Congress drew upon its full authority under the Commerce Clause, including but not limited to its power over water commerce. . . .

***

The central purpose of the Federal Water Power Act was to provide for the comprehensive control over those uses of the Nation's water resources in which the Federal Government had a legitimate interest; these uses included navigation, irrigation, flood control, and, very prominently, hydroelectric power—uses which, while unregulated, might well be contradictory rather than harmonious. Prior legislation in 1890 and the Rivers and Harbors Act of 1899, [33 U.S.C. §§ 401, 403 (1958) ed.] prohibiting the erection of any obstruction to navigation, including those on nonnavigable feeders, and requiring the consent of Congress and approval of the Secretary of War before constructing a bridge, dam, or dike along or in navigable waters, was thought inadequate, for it accommodated only the federal interest in navigation. As this Court has had occasion to note before, the 1920 Federal Water Power Act "was the outgrowth of a widely supported effort of the conservationists to secure enactment of a complete scheme of national regulation which would promote the comprehensive development of the water resources of the Nation, in so far as it was within the reach of the federal power to do so * * *." *First Iowa Hydro-Electric Coop. v. Federal Power Commission*, 328 U.S. 152, 180. The principal use to be developed and regulated in the Act, as its title indicates, was that of hydroelectric power to meet the needs of an expanding economy.[23]

Licenses are required only on such *Taum Sauk* facilities if construction occurred after August 26, 1935, the date of the FPA amendment.[24]

There are other limits to federal jurisdiction. The Supreme Court ruled that the breadth of the licensing power does not extend to any facility that generates electricity for interstate commerce and which affects a navigable river. Therefore, a fossil fuel plant that uses cooling water from a navigable river did not need a license because the plant was not a "project works" under FPA § 4(e), which refers to licenses for "constructing, operating, and maintaining dams . . . power houses, transmission lines, or other project works . . . across . . . any of the streams or other bodies of water over which Congress has jurisdiction . . . or upon any part of the public lands and reservations of the United States."[25]

If, however, the project was a traditional hydroelectric facility, FERC construed "affect interstate commerce" broadly when dealing with installations on non-navigable waters. For example, a small hydroelectric plant that did not sell electricity could affect the power load or demand of an electric company with interstate ties. A small plant might not individually have an impact, but might have a cumulative impact when considered with similarly situated plants.[26] A recent FERC decision, however, found no license was

---

[23] *Id.* at 94-97 (emphasis in original).

[24] Hodgson v. FERC, 49 F.3d 822 (1st Cir. 1995). *See generally*, Max J. Mizejewski, Comment, *FERC's Abdication of Jurisdiction over Hydroelectric Dams on Nonnavigable Rivers: A Potential Setback for Comprehensive Stream Management*, 27 ENVTL. L. 741 (1997).

[25] Chemeheuvi Tribe of Indians v. FPC, 420 U.S. 395 (1975).

[26] Habersham Mills v. FERC, 976 F.2d 1381 (11th Cir. 1992).

required for a project totally on private land that would generate electricity for the owner's private use and remain unconnected to the interstate power grid. The Commission did not require a license despite the project's impact on anadromous fish. The majority of the Commissioners read *Taum Sauk* as requiring an impact on interstate electricity.[27]

Once federal jurisdiction is established, the Federal Power Act provides the first basic commands on what should be considered in licensing. There are two fundamental but separate concerns: *Who* should build and *whether* a project should be built. Both subjects were broached in *Udall v. Federal Power Commission.*[28] The Federal Power Commission had awarded a private company a license to build a hydroelectric project on the Snake River, near the Salmon River. Eight federal dams existed and one additional federal dam had been planned for the area. The Supreme Court characterized the primary issue as

> an interpretation of § 7(b) of the Federal Water Power Act of 1920, as amended by the Federal Power Act, 16 U.S.C. § 800(b), which provides: "Whenever, in the judgment of the Commission, the development of any water resources for public purposes should be undertaken by the United States itself, the Commission shall not approve any application for any project affecting such development, but shall cause to be made such examinations, surveys, reports, plans, and estimates of the cost of the proposed development as it may find necessary, and shall submit its findings to Congress with such recommendations as it may find appropriate concerning such development."[29]

The Court found that the provision required the Commission to make a finding on the appropriateness of federal development, especially if the Department of the Interior had raised the question.

The Court also looked at the requirements Section 10a of the Act, which in its basic form provided that "the project adopted" shall be such `as in the judgment of the Commission will be best adapted to a comprehensive plan for improving or developing a waterway [for interstate and foreign commerce] * * * and for other beneficial public uses, including recreational purposes." The applicants had argued the public interest would be served because electricity was needed. The Court responded:

---

[27] *Guy M. Carlson*, 62 FERC ¶ 61,009, 1993 WL 27840 (1993).
[28] 387 U.S. 428 (1967).
[29] *Id.* at 431.

The question whether the proponents of a project "will be able to use" the power supplied is relevant to the issue of the public interest. So too is the regional need for the additional power. But the inquiry should not stop there. A license under the Act empowers the licensee to construct, for its own use and benefit, hydroelectric projects utilizing the flow of navigable waters and thus, in effect, to appropriate water resources from the public domain. The grant of authority to the Commission to alienate federal water resources does not, of course, turn simply on whether the project will be beneficial to the licensee. Nor is the test solely whether the region will be able to use the additional power. The test is whether the project will be in the public interest. And that determination can be made only after an exploration of all issues relevant to the "public interest," including future power demand and supply, alternate sources of power, the public interest in preserving reaches of wild rivers and wilderness areas, the preservation of anadromous fish for commercial and recreational purposes, and the protection of wildlife.

The need to destroy the river as a waterway, the desirability of its demise, the choices available to satisfy future demands for energy—these are all relevant to a decision under § 7 and § 10 but they were largely untouched by the Commission.[30]

The Act as initially envisioned required the Commission to broadly balance the various public needs a river could serve.

In 1986, Congress passed the Electric Consumers Protection Act, which in part emphasized the need to consider the environment in licensing decisions. It amended Sections 4(e) and 10(a) of the FPA as follows:

In deciding whether to issue any license under [the FPA] for any project, the Commission, in addition to the power and development purposes for which licenses are issued, shall give equal consideration to the purposes of energy conservation, the protection, mitigation of damage to, and enhancement of, fish and wildlife (including related spawning grounds and habitat), the protection of recreational opportunities, and the preservation of other aspects of environmental quality.[31]

---

[30] *Id.* at 450.
[31] 16 U.S.C. §§ 797(e), § 4(e) of the FPA, as amended by the Electric Consumers Protection Act (ECPA), Pub. L. No. 99-495, 100 Stat. 1243 (1986).

All licenses issued under this subchapter shall be on the following conditions: That the project adopted . . . will be best adapted to a comprehensive plan . . . for the adequate protection, mitigation, and enhancement of fish and wildlife (including related spawning grounds and habitat) . . .[32]

The ECPA's admonition to give "equal consideration" in the licensing process to varied aspects of environmental concern, however, has been interpreted to simply require the FERC to take note of these issues, not to force environmentally sensitive decision-making.[33]

Other provisions of the FPA mandate other consultation and consideration of additional issues. For fisheries, under section 10(j) of the FPA,[34] FERC must impose conditions on licenses "based on recommendations received pursuant to the Fish and Wildlife Coordination Act[35] from the National Marine Fisheries Service, the United States Fish and Wildlife Service, and State fish and wildlife agencies." The FERC retains ultimate authority, however, to decide whether any recommended conditions are "inconsistent with the purposes of" the FPA or other laws.[36] When the FERC acts contrary to a recommendation received from a wildlife agency, however, FERC must make an appropriate finding on the record to justify its decision.[37] Additionally, Section 18 of the FPA also provides the following special consideration of fish:

> The Commission shall require the construction, maintenance, and operation by a licensee at its expense of . . . such fishways as may be prescribed by the Secretary of the Interior or the Secretary of Commerce, as appropriate.

FERC is simply a conduit for these last requirements. Nevertheless, if the relevant department does not provide support in the record for a requirement in a particular case, the condition will be deemed arbitrary and

---

[32] 16 U.S.C. § 803(a) (1988), § 10(a) of the FPA, as amended by the Electric Consumers Protection Act (ECPA), Pub. L. No. 99-495, 100 Stat. 1243 (1986).

[33] United States Department of the Interior v. Federal Energy Regulatory Commission, 952 F.2d 538 (D.C. Cir. 1992).

[34] 16 U.S.C. § 803(j).

[35] 16 U.S.C. §§ 661 *et seq.*

[36] 16 U.S.C. § 803(j)(2).

[37] *See* American Rivers v. Federal Energy Regulatory Commission, 187 F.3d 1007 (9th Cir. 1999) (FERC has discretion to reclassify, reject, or modify such recommendations, including power to determine that recommendation does not fit within the section).

capricious. In one case, the court accused the agency record of revealing a " 'Field of Dreams' justification: 'If you build it, they will come.' "[38]

Other constraints are placed upon FERC if the proposed hydro-electric license is in a "reservation" of public lands. In such a case, "licenses shall be issued within any reservation only after a finding by the Commission that the license will not interfere or be inconsistent with the purpose for which such reservation was created or acquired." FPA § 4(e).[39] A National Forest is such a reservation. In a controversy over development in the Olympic National Forest, the Ninth Circuit found that the provisions of ECPA requiring equal consideration of developmental and non-developmental values apply in this situation; therefore, a finding of consistency or non-consistency with the Forest's purposes can only be made after this balancing occurs. The FERC, in determining the Forest's purposes, may place great reliance on the views of the Forest Service, but both agencies should look to the statutory purposes of the forest, not merely a forest plan.[40]

If a license is issued, § 4(e) provides that the license shall include conditions deemed necessary by the Department having jurisdiction over the reservation "for the adequate protection and utilization of [that] reservation." FERC will not have discretion over whether or not to include the condition, but the rationale will have to be supported in the record.[41] These provisions apply to re-licensing as well as initial construction.[42]

Other statutes also affect the licensing process. The National Environmental Policy Act of 1969[43] requires interdisciplinary analysis of a hydro project and consideration of alternatives. The Endangered Species Act (ESA)[44] caused the judicial blockage of the Tellico Dam in Tennessee. Tellico was begun in 1967 as a multipurpose project designed to stimulate development, provide recreation, and generate electricity. Opponents of the dam cited many negatives, but the presence of the snail darter became the cause celebre, because the darter was protected by the ESA.[45] The ESA is a

---

[38] Bangor Hydro-Electric Co. v. FERC, 78 F.3d 659 (D.C. Cir. 1996). *See also* *American Rivers*, 187 F.2d at 1007 (concurring on the mandatory inclusion of § 18 conditions in a license).

[39] 16 U.S.C. § 797e.

[40] Rainsong Co. v. FERC, 78 F.3d 1435 (9th Cir. 1996).

[41] Escondido Mutual Water Co. v. La Jolla Band of Mission Indians, 466 U.S. 765 (1984)

[42] Southern California Edison v. FERC, 116 F.3d 507 (D.C. Cir. 1997).

[43] 42 U.S.C. §§ 4331 *et seq.*

[44] 16 U.S.C. §§ 1630 *et seq.*

[45] Tennessee Valley Authority v. Hill, 437 U.S. 153 (1978).

continuing presence in hydroelectric development, especially in light of the endangered status of some salmon (e.g., the Snake River sockeye salmon is endangered and the Snake River spring/summer and fall chinook are threatened). The problem of salmon, however, is even more complex than the normal endangered species problem. In the Pacific Northwest, three different planners seek to replenish the plunging salmon stocks. To further confuse matters, three different goals motivate the three planning groups.[46]

First, the National Marine Fisheries Service is the agency charged with implementation of the ESA for salmon. Its 1993 Biological Opinion for the continued operation of dams in the Columbia River basin was found to be substantively insufficient to prevent jeopardy.[47] Two additional Biological Opinions have been rendered. The 1995-99 Opinion was litigated and upheld; a major objection to it was the reliance on trucking and barging of immature salmon around obstacles rather than improving river conditions.[48] A Biological Opinion seeks reasonable and prudent alternatives to proposed actions so as to avoid jeopardy to the species.

Second, even before the species were listed, Congress especially addressed the fish problem in the Pacific Northwest Electric Power Planning

---

[46] See generally, Michael C. Blumm, Michael A. Schoessler & R. Christopher Beckwith, Beyond the Parity Promise: Struggling to Save Columbia Basin Salmon in the Mid-1990s, 27 ENVTL. L. 21 (1997); John M. Volkman, The Endangered Species Act and the Ecosystem of Columbia River Salmon, 4 HASTINGS W.-N.W. J. ENVTL. L. & POL'Y 51 (1997); Michael C. Blumm, The Amphibious Salmon: The Evolution of Ecosystem Management in the Columbia River Basin, 24 ECOLOGY L.Q. 653 (1997); and Michael Mirande, Sustainable Natural Resource Development, Legal Dispute, and Indigenous Peoples: Problem-Solving Across Cultures, 11 TUL. ENVTL. L.J. 33 (1997).

[47] Idaho Dept of Fish & Game v. National Marine Fisheries Service, 850 F. Supp. 886 (D. Or. 1994), vacated as moot, 56 F.3d 1071 (9th Cir. 1995).

[48] See American Rivers v. National Marine Fisheries Services, 126 F.3d 1118 (9th Cir. 1997) and American Rivers v. National Marine Fisheries Service, No. 97-36159 (9th Cir. March 8, 1999). In late 1995, the National Academy of Science said the most biologically effective and cost-effective way to help salmon on the Columbia and Snake Rivers is to barge them around dams. This finding pleased the hydroelectric industry, which did not want what the environmental community wanted as the solution. Environmentalists wanted to increase river flows at certain times, which would mean drawing down reservoirs. The Corps of Engineers collected 24.5 million salmon in 1995 and transported about 18.5 million past dams. It is considering increasing 6 barges to 15. Other impediments to salmon health are ocean conditions and land use decisions that impact watersheds and riparian areas, thereby altering stream conditions. See generally, Michael C. Blumm & Greg D. Corbin, Salmon and the Endangered Species Act: Lessons from the Columbia Basin, 74 WASH. L. REV. 519 (1999).

and Conservation Act.[49] The act was initially passed in 1980 and amended in 1996.[50] Under this Act, referred to as the Northwest Power Act, fish were to be considered equal to hydropower in operations. The Power Planning Council called for in the Act adopted a Strategy for Salmon in December of 1994. Pursuant to it, the Bonneville Power Administration plans to significantly reduce the output of certain hydroelectric plants and will spend about $427 million annually on fish recovery and protection programs for the Columbia River Basin.[51] An earlier Strategy was deemed legally insufficient.[52] The goal of the Council is to double the size of salmon runs without the loss of biological diversity.

Third, a coalition of Columbia Basin Indian tribes championed a more aggressive salmon management regime in 1995. These tribes have treaty rights to fish for salmon. Typical wording give the tribes rights to fish "in common" with the white settlers.[53] Courts have interpreted these provisions as giving the Native Americans rights to one-half of the harvest and to "a livelihood—that is to say, a moderate living. . . ."[54] The goal of the tribes is more ambitious that either of the other two groups, namely, to restore historical runs of salmon.

IV.   THE INTERSECTION OF FEDERAL AND STATE AUTHORITY

In addition to the environmental and treaty concerns noted in the licensing material, major public policy considerations involve ascertaining the appropriate government to respond to these concerns. Furthermore, with hydroelectric generating costs often lower than alternative power sources, competition for the electricity often pits local governments against private companies and can have international trading implications.

As noted in the licensing section, the FPA provides for a federal "first option" to build. In addition to the question of whether the federal govern-

---

[49] 16 U.S.C. §§ 839-839h (1994).

[50] 110 Stat. 2984, 3005.

[51] The coming of competition in the electric industry has left the Bonneville Power Administration concerned about its ability to fund the salmon restoration project. Timothy A. Johnson, *Coping with Change: Energy, Fish, and the Bonneville Power Administration*, 26 ENVTL. L. 589 (1996).

[52] Northwest Resource Information Center v. Northwest Power Planning Council, 35 F.3d 1371 (9th Cir. 1994).

[53] Nez Perce Tribe v. Idaho Power Co ., 847 F.Supp. 791, 805-06 (D. Idaho 1994).

[54] Washington v. Washington State Commercial Passenger Fishing Vessel Association, 443 U.S. 658, 686 (1979).

ment should build a project, there is a second "who" question, which involves another statutory preference. If the federal government decides not to build, then a state or municipal government has a preference for an initial license. Most licenses under the Water Power Act were for fifty years. At the end of this time, the question was who should get to re-license the facility. An existing private generator generally wanted to keep a facility that was providing good service at generation costs lower than alternatives. The privately owned existing licensees claimed that they should be given priority in the re-licensing of "their" facility. State and municipal power companies claimed their statutory preference applied, allowing them to trump even the original licensee. The 1920 Act was not clear on this point. FERC opinions and court cases reached different results. The FERC also changed its position with different administrations.

Finally, Congress resolved the issue in the Electric Consumers Protection Act of 1986.[55] If there are competing re-licensing proposals, FERC must select the proposal "best adapted to serve the public interest." The statutory considerations include: 1) the applicant's plans, 2) its ability to comply with the plan, 3) the efficiency and reliability of electric service, 4) the need for the electricity generated, 5) the applicant's proposed transmission services, and 6) the proposal's cost effectiveness. If the existing licensee is an applicant, FERC must consider its prior record of service. The existing licensee receives a preference; the Act requires FERC to "ensure that insignificant differences . . . between competing applications are not determinative and shall not result in the transfer of a project."[56]

In other sections, the ECPA set the re-licensed term at between 30 and 50 years and provides for negotiations between an existing and new licensee if a change of license ownership takes place. A FERC decision that it need not give preference to municipal license applicants when an existing licensee seeks re-licensing has been upheld.[57] The lack of a right to a re-license has led one court to conclude that in a condemnation award, the value of plant license renewal expectation could be excluded.[58]

Between 1993 and 2010, the licenses for 419 projects have expired or will expire. Many of the largest projects will expire between 2005 and 2010. In the "class of 1993" alone, 173 licenses were subject to re-licensing. For this reason, many environmentalists were disappointed that President Clinton did not appoint any commissioners to FERC with either special ex-

---

[55] P.L. 99-495, 100 Stat. 1244 (1986) (ECPA).

[56] *Id.*

[57] Clark-Cowlitz Joint Operating Agency v. FERC, 826 F.2d 1074 (D.C. Cir. 1987) (*en banc*).

[58] U.S. v. 42.13 Acres of Land, 73 F.3d 953 (9th Cir. 1996).

pertise in hydroelectric or environmental matters. Some re-licenses have been granted and some projects are operating on annual permits pending decision. One question being considered by FERC is whether, if it decides to not re-license a facility, FERC may require the holder of the expiring license to remove the facility and rehabilitate the river. Industry spokesmen maintain that this is beyond FERC's authority, but FERC claims it may order such a removal with a decommissioning.[59] It so ruled in regard to a dam in Maine, the Edwards Dam.[60] The case settled with the state agreeing to pay some of the costs of removing the dam.[61] A court test of the theory was therefore avoided. FERC also maintains that even if license provisions to protect the environment make a project uneconomical, if the cost of decommissioning would be more than running the project with mitigation, a license would be granted. To a large extent, environmental concerns have become the new competition for hydropower licensees.[62] Additionally the FERC and relevant state governments may differ on how to address these concerns.

To understand the tension in hydroelectric licensing between the federal government and various states requires an understanding of the federal government's relationship to water law. The federal government is the owner of much of the western United States today and was the owner of almost all of it in the past. It could have also asserted rights to all the water in the west as a riparian owner and controlled the waters' disposition when it disposed of federally-owned lands. The United States, however, decided to divorce water rights from the land to a certain extent: a patent of land from the United States would not entail the grant or transfer of water rights.[63] The private party would gain water rights through state law and be regulated by that law. The federal government, therefore, began to defer to state law for water regulation.

This trend continued in 1902, when the federal government passed the Reclamation Act, which enabled large projects for irrigation to be built. The law provided that:

---

[59] *See* Swiger, Southwick & Mairs, *Paying for the Change: Can the FERC Force Dam Decommissioning at Relicensing?*, 17 ENERGY L.J. 163 (1996) (arguing against the authority).

[60] *Edwards Manufacturing Co., Inc.,* 81 F.E.R.C. ¶ 61,255 (1997).

[61] *Edwards Manufacturing Co., Inc.,* 83 F.E.R.C. ¶ 61,269 (1998).

[62] Donald H. Clarke, *Relicensing Hydropower: The Many Faces of Competition*, 11 NAT. RESOURCES & ENV'T 8 (1996).

[63] *See* Desert Land Act of 1877, 19 Stat. 377.

> Nothing . . . shall be construed as affecting or intending to affect
> or to in any way interfere with the laws of any State or Territory
> relating to the control, appropriation, use, or distribution of water
> used in irrigation, and the Secretary of Interior, in carrying out
> the provisions of this Act, shall proceed in conformity with such
> laws. . . . [64]

The Supreme Court in *California v. United States*[65] interpreted this provision as allowing states to condition water rights held in connection with federal projects, so long as the conditions do not destroy the federal purpose. Specific federal statutory provisions, such as those limiting the use of the water to specific acreage amounts, would have precedence over state law. A state requirement specifying a specific instream flow for a federally-licensed hydroelectric plant could also conflict if asserted under the state's power to grant water rights.[66] The federal interest in power regulation would have priority.[67]

The Supreme Court, however, continued to examine the relationship between federal hydropower licensing authority and the states. This time, the context in *PUD No. 1 of Jefferson County v. Washington Department of Ecology* was the Clean Water Act.[68] At first glance, *California v. FERC* would seem controlling: a state was seeking to put an instream flow requirement on a federal hydroelectric license. However, the state was proceeding

---

[64] Section 8, codified at 43 U.S.C. § 383.

[65] 438 U.S. 645 (1978).

[66] *California v. FERC,* 495 U.S. 490 (1990).

[67] The concept of federal purposes "trumping" state law leads to the second major strand in federal intervention in water law. Although the federal government generally defers to state law for water right adjudication, federal purposes may override restraints in state law or provide access into the state system that differs from the route of private parties. The major manifestation of this is the doctrine of "federal reserved water rights." The Supreme Court summarized this doctrine in this manner: "Congress, in giving the President the power to reserve portions of the federal domain for specific federal purposes, *impliedly* authorized him to reserve "appurtenant water then unappropriated *to the extent needed to accomplish the purpose of the reservation.*" United States v. New Mexico, 438 U.S. 696 (1978), citing Cappaert v. United States, 426 U.S. 128, 138 (1976). The reserved water rights are given a priority as of the date the land was reserved, not the date water was put to use.

[68] 511 U.S. 700 (1994). In another important Clean Water Act case, the D.C. Circuit Court of Appeals found that changes in water quality brought about by dam operations were not "discharges of pollutants," and therefore did not need a National Pollution Discharge Elimination System Permit (NPDES). National Wildlife Federation v. Gorsuch, 693 F.2d 156 (D.C. Cir. 1982).

under the §401 of the Clean Water Act. The Supreme Court in *PUD No. 1* described the law in this manner:

> States are responsible for enforcing water quality standards on intrastate waters. 33 U.S.C. § 1319(a). In addition to these primary enforcement responsibilities, § 401 of the Act requires States to provide a water quality certification before a federal license or permit can be issued for activities that may result in any discharge into intrastate navigable waters. 33 U.S.C. § 1341. Specifically, § 401 requires an applicant for a federal license or permit to conduct any activity "which may result in any discharge into the navigable waters" to obtain from the state a certification "that any such discharge will comply with the applicable provisions of sections 1311, 1312, 1313, 1316, and 1317 of this title." 33 U.S.C. § 1341(a). Section 401(d) further provides that "[a]ny certification . . . shall set forth any effluent limitations and other limitations, and monitoring requirements necessary to assure that any applicant . . . will comply with any applicable effluent limitations and other limitations, under section 1311 or 1312 of this title . . . and with any other appropriate requirement of State law set forth in such certification." 33 U.S.C. § 1341(d). The limitations included in the certification become a condition on any Federal license. *Ibid.*[69]

The State of Washington had previously set water quality standards for the affected river. It was to be used for recreation and fisheries purposes. Moreover, it had set a general antidegradation standard, which meant that no new activity should worsen water quality.

Washington's minimum flow requirement was attacked on several grounds. The Court rejected the petitioners' assertion that the Clean Water Act is only concerned with water quality, not quantity. This would be an artificial distinction for two reasons. First, a sufficient lowering of quantity could destroy all of a river's designated uses. Second, the CWA recognizes that reduced stream flow can constitute water pollution. The Court also noted that the "applicant" was to "comply" with appropriate state law; therefore conditions were not limited to the "discharge" activity. The majority of the Court brushed aside potential conflicts with FERC authority:

> The FPA empowers FERC to issue licenses for projects "necessary or convenient . . . for the development, transmission, and utilization of power across, along, from, or in any of the

---

[69] *Id.* at 707.

streams . . . over which Congress has jurisdiction." § 797(e). The FPA also requires FERC to consider a project's effect on fish and wildlife. §§ 797(e), 803(a)(1). In *California v. FERC*, we held that the California Water Resources Control Board, acting pursuant to state law, could not impose a minimum stream flow which conflicted with minimum stream flows contained in a FERC license. We concluded that the FPA did not "save" to the States this authority.

No such conflict with any FERC licensing activity is presented here. FERC has not yet acted on petitioners' license application, and it is possible that FERC will eventually deny petitioners' application altogether. Alternatively, it is quite possible, given that FERC is required to give equal consideration to the protection of fish habitat when deciding whether to issue a license, that any FERC license would contain the same conditions as the State § 401 certification. Indeed, at oral argument the Solicitor General stated that both EPA and FERC were represented in this proceeding, and that the Government has no objection to the stream flow condition contained in the § 401 certification.

Finally, the requirement for a state certification applies not only to applications for licenses from FERC, but to all federal licenses and permits for activities which may result in a discharge into the Nation's navigable waters. . . . Because § 401's certification requirement applies to other statutes and regulatory schemes, and because any conflict with FERC's authority under the FPA is hypothetical, we are unwilling to read implied limitations into § 401. If FERC issues a license containing a stream flow condition with which petitioners disagree, they may pursue judicial remedies at that time.[70]

A state could therefore mandate a condition in a hydroelectric license requiring an instream flow to maintain a designated use under a state's water quality standards.

Justice Thomas wrote a dissent, in which Justice Scalia joined. He argued that the majority's decision undermined the more particularized Congressional structure for hydroelectric licensing:

The Court's interpretation of § 401 significantly disrupts the careful balance between state and federal interests that Congress struck in the Federal Power Act (FPA), 16 U.S.C. §§ 791a *et seq.*

---

[70] *PUD No. 1*, 511 U.S. at 721-22.

. . . Section 10(a) empowers FERC to impose on a license such conditions, including minimum stream flow requirements, as it deems best suited for power development and other public uses of the waters. . . .

Today, the Court gives the States precisely the veto power over hydroelectric projects that we determined in *California v. FERC* and *First Iowa* they did not possess. As the language of § 401(d) expressly states, any condition placed in a § 401 certification, including, in the Court's view, a stream flow requirement, "*shall* become a condition on any Federal license or permit." 33 U.S.C. § 1341(d) (emphasis added). Any condition imposed by a State under § 401(d) thus becomes a "ter[m] . . . of the license as a matter of law," *Department of Interior v. FERC*, 952 F.2d 538, 548 (CADC 1992) (citation and internal quotation marks omitted), regardless of whether FERC favors the limitation. Because of § 401(d)'s mandatory language, federal courts have uniformly held that FERC has no power to alter or review § 401 conditions, and that the proper forum for review of those conditions is state court. Section 401(d) conditions imposed by States are therefore binding on FERC. Under the Court's interpretation, then, it appears that the mistake of the State in *California v. FERC* was not that it had trespassed into territory exclusively reserved to FERC; rather, it simply had not hit upon the proper device—that is, the § 401 certification—through which to achieve its objectives.

***

The Court's observations simply miss the point. Even if FERC might have no objection to the stream flow condition established by respondents in this case, such a happy coincidence will likely prove to be the exception, rather than the rule. . . .

Moreover, the Court ignores the fact that its decision nullifies the congressionally mandated process for resolving such state-federal disputes when they develop. Section 10(j)(1) of the FPA, 16 U.S.C. § 803(j)(1), which was added as part of the Electric Consumers Protection Act of 1986 (ECPA), provides that every FERC license must include conditions to "protect, mitigate damag[e] to, and enhance" fish and wildlife, including "related spawning grounds and habitat," and that such conditions "shall be based on recommendations" received from various agencies, including state fish and wildlife agencies. If FERC believes that a recommendation from a state agency is inconsistent with the FPA—that is, inconsistent with what FERC views as the proper balance between the Nation's power needs and environmental concerns—it must "attempt to resolve any such inconsistency, giving due weight to the recommendations, expertise, and statutory responsibilities" of the state agency. § 803(j)(2). If, after such an attempt, FERC "does not adopt in whole or in part a recommendation of any [state] agency," it must publish its reasons for rejecting that recommendation. After today's decision, these procedures are a dead letter with regard to stream flow levels, because a State's "recommendation" concerning stream flow "shall" be included in the license when it is imposed as a condition under § 401(d).[71]

Congress has not enacted legislation to restore the pre-*PUD* understanding of the balance of power.[72] Moreover, courts have held that FERC does not even have the jurisdiction to ascertain if the conditions proposed by a state are within the state's CWA authority.[73]

In addition to conflicts between state sovereignty and federal power in licensing, hydroelectricity has raised federalism questions in other settings. For example, the Supreme Court invalidated a state's attempt to restrict interstate transportation of hydroelectric power generated within its borders. The Court found that New Hampshire's attempt was not consistent with the Commerce Clause and that the Federal Power Act did not provide an affirmative grant of authority to New Hampshire to so restrict transportation. Section 201(b) of the Act, which in part provides that it "shall not ... deprive a State or State commission of its lawful authority now exercised over the exportation of hydroelectric energy which is transmitted across a State line," was not an affirmative grant of power to the states to burden interstate commerce; it merely preserved whatever laws that might previously have been lawful.[74]

V.　INTERNATIONAL JURISDICTIONAL ISSUES

A third level of potential jurisdictional conflict is in the international arena. Hydroelectric power can be transmitted across national borders. The most likely trading partner for the United States is Canada. Salmon, which has garnered attention in the domestic arena, have also engendered competitive concerns with international dimensions. A petition under the

---

[71] *Id.* at 732-35 (Thomas, J. dissenting).

[72] George William Sherk, *Approaching A Gordian Knot: The Ongoing State / Federal Conflict Over Hydropower*, 31 LAND & WATER L. REV. 349 (1996).

[73] American Rivers, Inc. v. Federal Energy Regulatory Commission, 129 F.3d 99 (2d Cir. 1997).

[74] New England Power Co. v. New Hampshire, 455 U.S. 331 (1982).

environmental side-agreement protocols of the North American Free Trade Agreement alleged that Canada was not enforcing fish habitat protection laws in regard to hydroelectric generation by B.C. Hydro. The allegation included an assertion that the environmental costs imposed on producers in the United States created an uneven playing field and Canadian generators should also comply.[75]

In addition to trade questions, the building of hydroelectric facilities in one nation can have direct impacts on another nation. In the international arena, the law of waterways that span more than one country has evolved from the so-called "Harmon Doctrine," under which a riparian country could, under the guise of sovereignty, do anything it wanted without being answerable to downstream riparian countries. Currently, most nations subscribe to the 1966 Helsinki Rules on the Uses of the Waters of International Rivers, which refers to using water in an "equitable and reasonable matter," and to the theory that a country can only use water in a manner that will cause "no harm" to another country. These two rules can conflict, because an "equitable and reasonable" test requires balancing of benefits and costs, whereby [not by] the latter test forbids any use that crosses a certain threshold of harm.[76] The 1997 United Nations Convention on International Watercourses speaks of "equitable and reasonable utilization" and also of "optimal and sustainable utilization" in a manner "consistent with adequate protection of the watercourse;" these provisions are to be read together with an additional provision in the Convention that requires a using party to "take all appropriate measures" to mitigate and prevent harm.[77] Hydroelectric development is one use of a watercourse that could trigger disputes between two nations.

One such dispute is the Gabcivkovo-Nagymaros project on the Danube. Once envisioned as a model of communist cooperation between Hungary and Czechoslovakia, it turned into a clash between Slovakia and Hungary. The project consisted of a large reservoir upstream in Slovakia, an asphalt-lined canal to divert the river flow to the Gabcikovo power station in Slovakia,

---

[75] *See* Greg M. Block, *NAFTA's Environmental Provisions: Are They Working as Intended? Are They Adequate?—A View from Canada*, 23 CAN-U.S. L.J. 409, 412-413 (1997). *Compare* Carel H. V. De Villeneuve, *Western Europe's Artery: The Rhine*, 36 NAT. RESOURCES J. 441, 442 (1996) (discussing loss of salmon from the Rhine despite a Salmon Convention dated 1886 and current desire to have salmon runs return).

[76] *See generally* Naveen Tadros, Comment, *Shrinking Water Resources: The National Security Issue of This Century*, 17 Nw. J. INT'L L. & BUS. 1091 (1996-97).

[77] Stephen C. McCaffrey and Mpazi S injela, *The 1997 United Nations Convention on International Watercourses*, 92 AM. J. INT'L L. 97 (1998).

and an additional dam in Hungary at Nagymaros to control flooding from peak-time use of the power plant and to provide for shipping on the diverted Danube River. Most of the economic benefit was to Slovakia. Hungary alleged environmental damage in the form of a lowered groundwater level in the undiverted stretch of the Danube, which affected drinking water, agriculture, forestry, fishing, and wildlife. Hungary backed out of the earlier agreement, but Slovakia continued and diverted the river in 1992 to feed the hydroelectric plant. A thirty mile stretch of the Danube, which formerly marked the border between the two nations, is now in Slovakia. The International Court of Justice in the Hague found that Hungary's abrogation of the agreement was not proper under customary international law and the countries must meet to work out an agreement.[78]

In developing countries, which need international funding, the rules of the World Bank can influence whether or not a hydroelectric project will be completed. For example, Nepal planned the Arun III Project. This project would have had a large impact on Nepal's debt structure, making the country forego other projects. Although Nepal needed energy and revenue, opponents argued the energy would be too costly for the average Nepalese and that the project would displace people and cause environmental harm. The project was brought to the attention of the Inspection Panel of the World Bank. The allegations against the project included violations of three Bank rules: 1) lack of an adequate environmental assessment; 2) failure to determine adequate compensation for those involuntarily resettled because of the project, and 3) failure to ensure that the project would aid the indigenous people. Ultimately, the World Bank withdrew funding from the project and it was not built.[79]

Another controversial project is proceeding in the Peoples Republic of China. The United States is not participating in the Three Gorges Dam, but other foreign investors are. The project will include a dam on the Yangtze River 600 feet high and one and a quarter miles wide. The dam will create a reservoir that is 360 miles long and will inundate 150,000 acres. It is slotted for completion in 2003. The project will moderate flooding and

---

[78] *See* Joanne Linnerooth-Bayer and Susan Murcott, *The Danube River Basin: International Cooperation or Sustainable Development*, 36 NAT. RESOURCES J. 521 (1996).

[79] *See* Daniel D. Bradlow, *A Test Case for the World Bank*, 11 AM. U. J. INT'L L. & POLICY 247 (1996). The Narmada Valley Project and Tehri Project in India faced similar human rights concerns about displacement of people, but continued to be built. *See* Armin Ronsencranz and Kathleen D. Yurchak, *Progress on the Environmental Front: the Regulation of Industry and Development in India*, 19 HASTINGS INT'L & COMP. L. REV. 489, 510-17 (1996)

generate much-needed electricity, substituting for electricity produced from coal, the most readily available source in China. Nevertheless, many oppose the project because it will displace 1.3 million people, destroy scenic treasures, flood archeological sites, and interfere with wildlife. 🍎

CHAPTER TWELVE

Electricity

by Suedeen G. Kelly

I. THE ELECTRICITY FUEL CYCLE

Electricity represents approximately one-half of the energy used and produced in the United States. Electricity is not a natural resource, rather it is generated from oil, coal, natural gas, nuclear power, and falling water (hydropower) for the most part, with a small portion generated by alternative resources such as wind, biomass, geothermal energy, and the sun. This book is being written during a period of major restructuring in the electricity industry and later in the chapter we indicate the direction of that restructuring. We begin, however, by describing the traditional structure of the industry and the fuel cycle and then go on to describe the market for electricity. The three major components of the electricity fuel cycle are: generation, transmission, and distribution.

A. Electric Generation

The generation of electricity occurs internationally, nationally, and regionally and is the largest sector in the electricity business. Generation accounts for half of an electric utility's assets and can amount to half of the cost of producing and delivering electricity to consumers.[1]

As noted, electricity is generated from a variety of natural resources. Yet, whatever source is used, the production is similar. In a basic steam turbine, fossil fuel is burned to produce steam, which in turn rotates a shaft, which with the help of generators converts mechanical energy into electric energy. A magnet is placed on the shaft and as it rotates its magnetic lines cross a wire to generate electricity. Similarly, in a gas engine a hot jet turns the turbine, and in the case of hydroelectricity, the shaft is rotated by falling water. Ultimately, as the rotations increase, the angles of the magnetic lines

---

[1] Leonard S. Hyman, AMERICA'S ELECTRIC UTILITIES: PAST, PRESENT, AND FUTURE 19 (6th ed. 1997). *See also* Ronald D. Jones, Jeffrey W. Meyers & Robert J. Glasser, *Electricity,* 2 ENERGY LAW & TRANSACTIONS, ch. 52 (David J. Muchow & William A. Mogel, eds., 1998).

of force in relation to the wire change directions thus increasing or decreasing the number of force lines cut with wire. Consequently, the electric current generated gets stronger or weaker and reverses direction producing an alternating current (AC).

The combination of turbines, electric generators, and necessary auxiliary equipment comprises a generating station. The ability of a generator to produce a given output of electricity at an instant in time is known as the generator's capacity. Capacity ratings of an electric generator are measured by watts and are expressed in kilowatts (1000 watts) (kw), megawatts (million watts) (Mw), or gigawatts (billion watts) (gw). A kilowatt used for an hour is a kilowatt hour (kWh).

The generation process is incapable of capturing all of the heat that is produced. Consequently, electricity generation produces waste heat. Utilities attempt to capture as much of the excess heat as possible and have developed two procedures to do so: *cogeneration* and *combined cycle generation.* Through *cogeneration*, waste heat is used by the utility or sold to an end user. *Combined cycle generation*, on the other hand, combines a gas turbine and a steam turbine. The gas turbine produces electricity and its waste heat is passed on to the steam turbine which also produces electricity. Such a procedure can reach 50% efficiency whereas a traditional steam turbine generally has a 35% efficiency.

Once electricity is generated it cannot be stored effectively. The closest utilities come to storing electricity is the *pumped storage plant* where water is stored in a reservoir until water is released turning electrical turbines below. For the most part, electricity must be produced at the generator at the time the customer demands it.

Fluctuation in customer demand requires an electric utility to raise or lower its output instantaneously. For that purpose, electric utilities must have a mix of capabilities. First, electric utilities must have power plants which are operated at a constant output to serve the minimum demand on the system. These are called *base load* plants. Second, electric utilities must have sufficient production facilities available to meet the maximum demand on its system. As a result, electric utilities maintain *spinning reserves* plants. Spinning reserves are kept in low level operation and are ready to be switched on to serve increased load changes above the base load. Finally, other plants, referred to as *cold reserves*, are available for service but require some lead time to "fire up."

Utilities will use their most efficient and least expensive power plants first to meet base load and their more expensive power sources to meet peak load. Base load plants are typically large and expensive to build. Once they are built, it is efficient for utilities to to keep the plants in continuous operation. Thus, the utility is able to spread the fixed costs of operating the plant over a long period of time. Peaking units are typically less expensive to build but their operating costs are often higher—because of higher fuel costs. Therefore, a utility is better off using these plants to meet peak load.

Utilities attempt to keep generators idle as little as possible. How the load is spread and whether there is a difference between the average demand on the system and demand at peak is measured by the *load factor* which is defined as the average load in a period of time as a percentage of peak load. The higher the load factor the better positioned the electric utility is to maximize the use of its generation. A load factor can also be too high when a utility uses its generators so much that it does not have enough reserve in order to allow for maintenance of its base load plants. An electric utility's ability to meet its reserve needs is normally measured by the *reserve margin*. A reserve margin is the difference between peak load and capacity as a percentage of peak load. Reserve margin is generally 20% or more.

In the traditional regulatory environment, utilities have tried to ensure that their capacity is available to meet the peak load, and constructed a sufficient number of plants to meet that expected demand. In today's more competitive and cost conscious regulatory environment, utilities and regulators experiment with alternative approaches. *Demand side management* is a technique by which utilities cut down peak load by charging more for power at certain times of the day or year depending on peak demand. Other devices, such a marginal cost ratemaking or incentive pricing also allow utilities to manage load by having rates more closely reflect competitive prices rather than historic costs.

B. Electric Transmission

Once generated, electricity is transmitted to either a distributor or to an end-user through transmission lines. Electricity is transmitted across large distance using high voltage transmission lines. Typically, substations increase voltage over long distances and then decrease it before it reach the end-users at home.

Throughout the process, transmission losses reduce the amount of electricity available for consumers and increase electromagnetic radiation. While recent technological development of better conductors may reduce transmission losses, the process remains inefficient. Furthermore, because transmission lines form a regional grid which are connected in a network, electricity does not flow directly from point A to point B. As a result of the way intervening lines are loaded, the flow may loop around, loading some lines more than others. In short, selecting the appropriate voltage level for a transmission line involves tradeoffs among cost, electric line losses, and space and distance considerations. Conversely, higher voltage lines are more costly and require some separation of conductors and more space.

Electric transmission and supply in the United States today is coordinated and synchronized among the many electric systems and companies through the physical interconnection of electric facilities, regional reliability councils, and power pools. Through *interconnections*, every utility is either connected or capable of being connected with its neighbor. The United States and Canada have four large interconnected power systems. While it is technically accurate to say that there is a national electric grid, there are basically three large grids throughout the united States. One grid operates west of the Rocky Mountains, one operates east of the Rocky Mountains, and one operates in Texas.

Electric reliability councils maintain and improve the reliability of interconnected electric operations and ensure the adequacy of regional electricity supplies. Voluntary regional electrical reliability were formed in the later half of the 1960s. In 1968 the National Electric Reliability Council was formed in response to a massive blackout in New York City. Today there are nine voluntary regional councils which formulate strategies to deal with the effect on reliability of mergers in the industry.

Electric utilities also rely on *power pools* to coordinate electric supply. Power pools are formal and informal agreements by groups of utilities to operate and plan their respective electric systems. A formal power pool is defined as two or more electric systems which coordinate the planning and/or operation of their bulk power facilities for the purpose of achieving greater economy and reliability in accordance with a contractual agreement that establishes each member's responsibilities. There are two kinds of power pools: tight and loose. In a tight power pool, reserve requirements are enforced by penalties and system operation is assured by a central dispatch system. A loose power pool provides both operating and planning coordination but generally does not include penalties or central dispatch provisions. Informal power pools are coordination arrangements which are chiefly characterized by the absence of contractual commitments. A grouping of utilities generally agree to establish principles and practices for interconnected operation, to jointly review area power supply adequacy, to exchange generation and transmission construction plans, and to seek coordinated action for best economy and reliability. The informal grouping relies on voluntary adherence by members to pool principles and criteria.

C.   Electric Distribution

The distribution of electricity is made through direct purchases from producers and through local distribution companies (LDCs). An LDC is a local utility such as Pacific Gas and Electric or Pennsylvania Power and Light. These local utilities are regulated by state public utility commissions (PUCs) as well as by federal regulators. Regulatory responsibilities will be discussed in more detail later. The distribution function is generally carried out by a utility that is given a set territory and has the obligation to serve all customers in that territory.

There are basically three consumer classes: residential, commercial, and industrial. Each customer class puts different demands on the system for the amount of electricity that it consumes, the amount of plants necessary to generate that electricity, and the amount of service required from the LDC. The significance of these customer classes is addressed when we discuss electricity rates.

II.   ELECTRICITY MARKETS

A.   History

The history of the electric industry dates back to 1831, when Michael Faraday invented the dynamo which converted mechanical energy into electric energy. That technology was put to use to power batteries for telegraphs. Thomas Edison, a telegrapher, began improving the instrument when in 1879 he managed to develop the first incandescent lamp.[2]

Edison expanded the use of electricity for both lighting and power, replacing candles and gas. In 1879, he patented an electric distribution system, formed the Edison Electric Light Co., and organized the Pearl Street Station in New York City in 1882. The Pearl Street station was the first commercial plant for generating electricity.

While Edison was building central plants in New York, the English firm of Gaulard and Gibbs developed the *alternating current*. In 1886, George Westinghouse bought the Gaulard and Gibbs rights and formed the Westinghouse Electric Company. AC current was less expensive to transport than direct current which enabled a utility to transport electricity across long distances. Eventually, AC systems and DC systems were linked.

In the late 19th and early 20th centuries, central station plants served local areas and were competitive. Still, a franchise from the local municipality was necessary to run electrical wires over public streets. In the beginning, franchises were non-exclusive, thus allowing competition. As technology developed and electric systems found widespread use, and

---

[2] *See generally*, Joseph P. Tomain, *Electricity Restructuring: A Case Study in Government Regulation*, 33 TULSA L.J. 827 (1998).

utilities began to show a profit, there was a proliferation of electric power companies. In addition, municipalities entered the electricity business. In fact, municipally owned utilities outnumbered privately owned utilities until the mid 1920s.

As the number of independent electricity generating plants grew, the technology of transmission also grew. In turn, this led to an increase in networks, which with advanced technology, allowed interconnections into a grid. Finally, there was no operational reason to have independent generating stations and the industry began to consolidate in order to capitalize on economies of scale and to avoid inefficiencies.

Eventually, individual central stations gave way to corporate holding companies which owned some or all of the shares of stock or assets of other companies and thereby controlled them. Holding companies developed complex structures containing many subsidiaries and combinations of unrelated business. In 1932, almost half of the investor-owned electric utility industry was controlled by three holding companies and another 35 percent was controlled by the twelve next largest systems. The eight largest holding companies controlled 73% of the investor-owned business.[3]

The growth of the holding companies also led to widespread abuses. Securities companies were selling stocks to employees and customers who did not understand what they were buying. The continued expansion of the holding companies created liabilities that the system could not meet and the practices of some companies' management reduced investor confidence in the market.

In an effort to curb the abuses of holding companies, Congress enacted the Public Utility Act of 1935 Title I (Public Utility Holding Company Act)(PUHCA) and Title II (amendments to the Federal Water Power Act of 1920, also known as the Federal Power Act.)[4] The PUHCA was passed in response to concerns that while local regulatory agencies supervised electric utilities, nobody was regulating the holding companies which owned those utilities. The PUHCA defined a holding company and required them to register with the Securities and Exchange Commission and conform to its rules. In addition, the Act broke up holding companies that did not satisfy their regulation. After passage of the Act, most holding companies were dismembered. In fact, since 1935, only one holding company had been formed.

---

[3] Hyman, *supra* note 1 at 106.
[4] *Id*. at 116; Public Utility Holding Company Act of 1935, 15 U.S.C. §§ 79-79z-6 (1994 & Supp. II 1996); Federal Power Act of 1920, 16 U.S.C. § 791a-823b (1994 & Supp. II 1996).

B.   Market Structure and Demand

The electric industry is comprised of integrated and non-integrated producers, mostly privately owned, with some federal generation and some municipal or locally owned distribution. Several government agencies such as the Tennessee Valley Authority are in the business of generating and selling electricity. Five federal power marketing authorities supply power from federally owned projects developed in large part by the Corps of Engineers. In 1995, 68.9% of electric generating capacity was owned by investor owned systems[5] and approximately 11.8% by rural electric cooperatives, largely through umbrella combinations of cooperatives known as generation and transmission companies. The remaining 19.3% was generated by government entities. Most investor owned systems are vertically integrated. Vertical integration has been driven by the difficulty of storing electricity and the need to produce it continuously as well as the utilities' continuous search for economies of scale.

From the turn of the century, electricity markets grew rapidly through the mid 1960s. After World War II, the annual growth rate of electricity was a predictable 7%. Energy consumption grew with the economy in 1945-65, but electricity sales rose much faster because the real price of electricity was dropping relative to the prices of other fuels.[6] Continuous improvement in the generation process led to reduced prices. The industry opted for larger generating stations in order to realize economies of scale. In transmission, construction cost per mile increased. However, that was offset by increasing the voltage of the lines, resulting in more capacity per mile. The industry overall also had sufficient reserve capacity, in 1945-1965, to encourage new demand without fear of being unable to meet demand. Most notably, from the late 1950s to the early 1970s investment in and construction of nuclear power plants grew to approximately 20% of the nation's generation capacity. In 1973, the Organization of Petroleum Exporting Countries (OPEC) began embargoes of crude oil shipments to the United States causing supply shortages and fuel price increases. Utilities passed the increase in fuel prices on to consumers, and Americans reduced their consumption of electricity. In 1974, the public's faith in investment in the utility industry, particularly in nuclear plants, declined significantly. To complicate matters further, in 1979, the Three Mile Island accident dampened post OPEC embargo efforts to switch to nuclear energy. Eventually, the industry's overall reserve margins rose sharply, indicating its over-capacity.

---

[5] Hyman, *supra* note 1.
[6] *Id.* at 120.

In an effort to encourage more efficient pricing of electricity, reduce the consumption of foreign oil, help energy conservation, and develop competition, Congress passed the Public Utility Regulatory Policies Act of 1978[7] (PURPA) as part of a comprehensive package of national energy legislation. Title I required utilities to develop information about their rate structure. Title II created a new class of generators, qualifying facilities, that could sell electricity to electric companies. (QFs were mostly cogenerators.) In addition a new entity called independent power producer (IPP) emerged. IPPs do not enjoy the financial advantages of PURPA and do not own transmission or distribution facilities.

In 1992 Congress enacted the Energy Policy Act (EPAct) of 1992.[8] The Act was designed to allow newcomers to enter the electric supply industry. The law opened the utility's transmission lines for use by competing generators. The Act also created a new nontraditional generator called the *exempt wholesale generator* (EWG), which was exempt from PUHCA requirements. In 1996, FERC articulated its open access policy by issuing Orders 888 and 889, which together formed the "Open Access Rule." Through those orders utilities could receive wholesale power sold by distant generators through the national transmission grid (called wholesale wheeling). Today, a number of utilities are meeting increased demand for electricity by purchasing power from others rather than building their own new generating plants. EPAct prohibits the Federal government from ordering retail wheeling. However, states can order this and many are doing so. These changes to the electricity fuel cycle are being accompanied by a restructuring of the industry. Mergers among investor-owned utilities have accelerated dramatically. In 1996, in an attempt to facilitate the process, FERC issued its Merger Policy, stating how it intended to evaluate mergers among public utilities. FERC promised to speed up the process, deciding cases on a summary basis if it finds no problems with the paperwork. Municipal systems have so far resisted the merger trend.

III.   ELECTRIC POWER REGULATION

A.   Electric Companies Compete (1882-1920)

As noted, the electricity industry began in 1882 in New York City with Thomas Edison's Pearl Street Station. This station generated electricity that was distributed to 85 customers. Over the next several decades cities grew

---

[7] Public Utility Regulatory Policies Act of 1978, Pub. L. 95-617, 92 Stat. 317 (codified as amended in scattered sections of titles 15, 16, 42 & 43 U.S.C.).

[8] Energy Policy Act of 1992, Pub. L. No. 102-486, 100 Stat. 2776 (1992).

interested in bringing electricity to their residents; entrepreneurs had a similar interest. Competition to serve municipalities and their residents began. Initially, about half the cities decided to provide electric service themselves. The other half typically entered into franchise agreements with private, investor-owned utilities (IOUs) that allowed the IOUs to use city streets and rights-of-way for distribution and transmission lines to provide city residents with electricity. Some franchise agreements also required the IOU to provide service and gave the IOU an exclusive franchise to serve for a period of years.[9]

In the early stages of the industry, power stations were constrained by existing technologies and did not exceed 10 MW. With increasing demand for electricity, producers entered the market with a multiplicity of electricity generation and distribution stations. It was also common for a large business, e.g., hospital, university or even resort, to build its own small power plant.[10] By 1922, there were 3,774 privately owned electric utilities.[11] Faced with growing demand and vigorous competition, these firms sought greater market share through technological innovation and corporate restructuring. They vertically integrated from generation to transmission and distribution and expanded their capacities in each area of the business to try to capture economies of scale and a greater share of the market. The larger firms even built generators, ground conductors and electric fixtures, including light bulbs. For example, Edison's company merged with others to become the General Electric Company.[12]

B.   Electric Companies Concentrate—and Become Regulated (1921-1934)

As the electric industry pursued economies of scale, larger entities absorbed smaller ones. The states responded by passing legislation authorizing economic regulation of utilities. From 1922 to 1927, over 1600

---

[9] Once states began regulating the electric industry, they usually assumed the responsibility of granting an IOU the right to serve particular areas or customers. So, today a typical franchise agreement between a municipality and an IOU does not include a right to serve the residents of the city with electricity.

[10] Jon R. Mostel, *Overview of Electric Industry Bypass Issues*, 37 NAT. RE-SOURCES J. 141, 142 n. 2 (1997).

[11] Peter C. Christensen, *Overview of Electricity Generation and the Industry,* THE ELECTRIC INDUSTRY: OPPORTUNITIES AND IMPACTS FOR RESOURCE PRODUCERS, POWER GENERATORS, MARKETERS, AND CONSUMERS at 1-2 (Rocky Mtn. Min. Law Fdn. 1996).

[12] TECHNOLOGY FUTURES, INC. & SCIENTIFIC FORESIGHT, INC., PRINCIPLES FOR ELECTRIC POWER POLICY 231 (1984).

privately-owned electric systems were absorbed, and many companies were consolidated into holding companies. By 1927, sixteen holding companies controlled 85 percent of the nation's electric industry. These holding companies helped advance the capture of scale economies but at a real cost to consumers. The electric trusts, like the oil trusts before them, were susceptible to stock manipulation and shareholder abuses. The public clamored for more effective regulation, and Congress responded.[13]

1. States Regulate the Rates and Activities of Electric Utilities

The first general steps taken by state legislatures were to provide for regulation of electric utilities to protect consumers in cases where there was no competition. Expansive power to regulate rates, entry and exit, and terms and conditions of electric utility service was granted to public utility commissions in all the states. A jurisdiction grant typically looked something like this:

> The commission shall have general and exclusive power and jurisdiction to regulate and supervise every public utility[14] in respect to its rates and service regulations and in respect to its securities, taking into account the public interest, the interest of consumers and the interest of investors, to the end that reasonable and proper services shall be available at fair, just and reasonable rates, and to the end that capital and investment may be encouraged and attracted so as to provide for the construction, development and extension, without unnecessary duplication and

---

[13] Joseph P. Tomain, *Electricity Restructuring: A Case Study in Government Regulation*, 33 TULSA L. J. 827, 830-31 (1998).

[14] Numerous states exempt cooperatively owned and municipally owned utilities from state rate regulation, or even from all state regulation. In the case of cooperatives, the rationale for exemption is that the consumers are also the owners and elect the board of directors that operates the cooperative and sets its rates. Thus, the consumers can protect themselves from any monopoly abuse through their power to elect their board. Likewise with municipally owned utilities, the residents of the municipality elect the city's governing body, which is responsible for operating the municipal utility and setting its rates. Even when states exempt municipally owned utilities from state rate regulation, they might empower the state commission to supervise the rates the municipal utility sets for persons it might serve residing outside the municipal boundaries who do not have the right to vote for municipal officials.

economic waste, of proper plants and facilities for the rendition of service to the general public and to industry.

This broad authority to regulate electric utilities continues in force in states today.

State regulators also used their power to prescribe electric rates in regions where electric utilities initially did compete. Inevitably rate wars ensued between competing utilities and resulted in the destruction of one of them, or a division of the territory between them. As the Idaho Supreme Court explained in a 1914 decision, "experience shows that there can never be any permanent competition in matters of [supplying electricity]."[15] This type of competition was judged unsatisfactory by both utility investors, who wished investment stability, and consumers, who wished to be served at the lowest cost—"and such an end cannot be reached if the community is served by duplicate plants, [which is] a waste of resources and an extra tax on the people."[16] As a result, state regulators fixed a specific rate, instead of a rate maximum. This took away the opportunity for rate-cutting, one of the principal instruments of warfare between competing utilities. In addition, state regulators exercised their authority to determine which utilities could serve which areas. The general rule was that one utility serving an area could continue to do so unless the public convenience and necessity, as determined by the state commission, required an additional utility. State regulators also have taken on the responsibilities of assuring adequate service by the utility, protecting the parties who furnish the money for utility construction, and supervising the utility's service "in every material particular."[17]

2. The Federal Government Regulates the Rates and Activities of Electric Utilities

a. The "Attleboro Gap" in Regulation

In 1927, the U.S. Supreme Court limited the power of states to regulate interstate sales and transmission of electricity. A Massachusetts electric utility, Attleboro Steam & Electric Company, had been purchasing all its electricity from a Rhode Island electric utility, Narragansett Electric Lighting Co., under a twenty year contract at a specified special rate. In 1924, Narragansett sought a rate increase. It filed a new rate schedule that

---

[15] Idaho Power and Light Co. v. Blomquist, 26 Idaho 222, 141 P. 1083 (1914).
[16] Id.
[17] Id.

applied only to its sales to Attleboro with its regulator, the Public Utilities Commission of Rhode Island (PUC). The PUC approved the new rate schedule and ordered it replace the rate in the Narragansett-Attleboro contract.

Attleboro sued the PUC, arguing that its order imposed an unconstitutional burden on interstate commerce. The U.S. Supreme Court agreed. In *Public Utilities Commission of Rhode Island v. Attleboro Steam & Electric Co.*,[18] the Court found that (1) the sale of electricity by Narragansett to Attleboro was "a transaction in interstate commerce, notwithstanding the fact that the current is delivered at the State line," and (2) state regulation of this interstate service placed a direct burden upon interstate commerce in violation of the Commerce Clause. The Court noted that if Rhode Island could constitutionally raise the rate of this transaction to benefit Narragansett's Rhode Island customers, then Massachusetts could legitimately argue it could constitutionally lower the rate of this transaction to benefit Attleboro's Massachusetts customers. The Court concluded that the "rate is therefore not subject to regulation by either of the two States in the guise of protection to their respective local interests; but, if such regulation is required it can only be attained by the exercise of the power vested in Congress."[19]

From the *Attleboro* decision in 1927 until 1935, the interstate transmission and wholesale sale of electricity went unregulated and came to be called the "Attleboro Gap" in regulation. Initially, there were few interstate electric transactions. However, as small utilities became consolidated into large interstate holding companies, a significant portion of the nation's electric business was conducted by holding companies and was unregulated.

b.   *The Federal Power Act of 1935 Fills the Gap*

In 1935, Congress filled the regulatory gap with passage of the Federal Power Act,[20] which regulates electric utility companies in their engagement in interstate commerce. Like the states that had regulated electric utilities before it, Congress sought to regulate the interstate business of these utilities in order to control the economic power they had as monopolies. The federal agency that implements the Federal Power Act today is the Federal

---

[18] 273 U.S. 83 (1927).

[19] *Id.* at 90.

[20] Title II of the Public Utility Act of 1935, 16 U.S.C. §§ 791a-825r (1994 & Supp. II 1996), made the Federal Water Power Act (which was enacted in 1920 to create the Federal Power Commission and provide it with authority to license private hydroelectric projects located on navigable waters of the U.S.) Part I of the Federal Power Act and added Parts II and III to the Federal Power Act.

Energy Regulatory Commission (FERC), the successor to the Federal Power Commission.

The Federal Power Act and, thus, federal regulation, applies to most, but not all, (1) transmission of electric energy in interstate commerce, (2) sale of electric energy at wholesale in interstate commerce, (3) facilities used for interstate transmission and wholesale sales of electricity, and (4) public utilities that own or operate facilities subject to the jurisdiction of FERC.[21] The Act does not apply to the United States, or any State, or any political subdivision, agency, authority or instrumentality of the United States or any State. These governmental bodies can engage in transmission and wholesale sales of electricity without being subject to FERC's jurisdiction.[22]

Except as specifically provided in the Act, the Federal Power Act does not give FERC jurisdiction over facilities: (1) used for generation of electricity, (2) used in local distribution, (3) used only for transmission of electricity in intrastate commerce, or (4) for transmission of electricity consumed wholly by the transmitter.[23] Typically, the states take regulatory jurisdiction over these facilities. However, few, if any, states regulate facilities in the last category, i.e., private transmission facilities for transmission of electricity consumed wholly by the transmitter.

Under the Federal Power Act, the Federal Energy Regulatory Commission, and its predecessor the Federal Power Commission, has exercised traditional economic regulatory control over the transmission and wholesale sale of electricity in interstate commerce, consistent with the monopoly nature of the electric business. It regulates rates for interstate transmission and wholesale sales of electricity.[24] It assures adequate interstate electric service.[25] It authorizes purchase and abandonment of utility assets.[26] It regulates the securities issued by public utilities under its jurisdiction.[27] It

---

[21] Federal Power Act §§ 201(b), (e); 16 U.S.C. §§ 824(b), (e) (1994). FERC has found that it does not have jurisdiction to regulate rural electric cooperatives under the regulatory authority of the Rural Utilities Service. Judith M. Matlock, *Federal Regulation and Wholesale Wheeling,* THE ELECTRIC INDUSTRY: OPPORTUNITIES AND IMPACTS FOR RESOURCE PRODUCERS, POWER GENERATORS, MARKETERS, AND CONSUMERS at 2-6 (Rocky Mtn. Min. Law Fdn. 1996) (discussing Dairyland Power Cooperative, 37 F.P.C. 12, 67 P.U.R.3d 340 (1967)).

[22] Federal Power Act § 201(f); 16 U.S.C. § 824(f) (1994).

[23] Federal Power Act § 201(b); 16 U.S.C. § 824(b) (1994).

[24] Federal Power Act § 205; 16 U.S.C. § 824d (1994).

[25] Federal Power Act § 207; 16 U.S.C. § 824f (1994).

[26] Federal Power Act § 203; 16 U.S.C. § 824b (1994).

[27] Federal Power Act § 204; 16 U.S.C. § 824c (1994).

approves mergers and acquisitions.[28] It is also responsible for directing the interconnection and coordination of electric facilities, such as transmission lines, across the United States.[29]

c.   The Line between Federal and State Jurisdiction over the Rates and Activities of Electric Utilities

The Federal Power Act notes that the federal regulation of the transmission of electricity and sale of electricity at wholesale in interstate commerce shall "extend only to those matters which are not subject to regulation by the States."[30] However, the dividing line between federal and state jurisdiction acknowledged by this provision is not always a clear one. The courts have been called upon numerous times to clarify it in the context of different electricity transactions.

All wholesale sales of electricity are subject to plenary federal regulatory jurisdiction pursuant to section 201(b) of the Federal Power Act, except those which Congress has made explicitly subject to regulation by the states. This was the holding in *Federal Power Commission v. Southern California Edison Co.*,[31] where the U.S. Supreme Court rejected the argument that states should be allowed to regulate these sales in the first instance subject to superintending federal jurisdiction.

The U.S. Supreme Court has also upheld broad federal regulatory jurisdiction under the "transmission of electric energy in interstate commerce" provision of the Federal Power Act. In *Federal Power Commission v. Florida Power & Light Co.*,[32] the Court sustained the Federal Power Commission's assertion of jurisdiction over Florida Power & Light Co. (FP&L). All of FP&L's generation and transmission lines were confined to Florida, with none of its transmission lines being directly connected to any lines of out-of-state companies. However, FP&L's lines were connected with the lines of other Florida utilities in the Florida Pool, including the Florida Power Corp., which in turn connected with the lines of the Georgia Power Company. Through the connection between Florida Power Corp. and Georgia Power, the utilities in the Florida Pool were also members of the

---

[28] Federal Power Act § 203; 16 U.S.C. § 824b (1994).

[29] Federal Power Act § 213; 16 U.S.C. § 824a (1994).

[30] Federal Power Act § 201(a); 16 U.S.C. § 824(a) (1994).

[31] 376 U.S. 205 (1964) (finding that federal, not California, jurisdiction attached to a ten-year contract between the City of Colton, California and the Southern California Edison Co. under which Edison would supply Colton with its full wholesale requirements for electricity).

[32] 404 U.S. 453 (1972).

Interconnected System Group, a national interlocking of utilities that automatically provided power in emergencies. Although there was no evidence that at any time Georgia drew electricity from the Florida Pool that came solely from FP&L, there was evidence that sometimes when Georgia was drawing power from the Florida Pool, FP&L was contributing power to the Pool. The Court found that this was sufficient to establish transmission in interstate commerce. Specifically, the Court said, if FP&L power enters the Florida-Georgia bus (a transmission line of three conductors into which a number of subsidiary lines connect) at the same moment that power leaves the bus for out-of-state destinations, then one can conclude that some FP&L power goes out of state.

The dividing line between federal and state jurisdiction has historically been a contentious issue in the context of which jurisdiction has ratemaking authority. The Narragansett doctrine[33] holds that the Supremacy Clause demands that when a utility reasonably incurs a cost to serve retail customers arising from a rate approved by the FERC, state utility regulators must pass this cost on to retail consumers in the utility's retail rates. In other words, the state utility regulator is bound by the FERC approval and has no jurisdiction to find it to be an unreasonable cost. To allow otherwise would expose the utility to unrecoverable or "trapped" costs. The state regulator does, however, maintain jurisdiction to determine whether the FERC-approved cost was reasonably *incurred* by its utility. For example, if Utility A buys wholesale power from Utility B at 4 cents per kWh and resells the power to its retail customers, the state cannot object to the 4 cents as an unreasonable price to pay. However, the state could look to see whether it was reasonable for Utility A to buy wholesale power from Utility B, given that it could have bought wholesale power from Utility C or D, at a lower price.

The U.S. Supreme Court has extended the reasoning of the Narragansett doctrine from FERC-approved rates to FERC-approved allocations of power. In *Nantahala Power and Light Co. v. Thornburg*,[34] the Court held that the Public Utility Commission of North Carolina had no jurisdiction under the Supremacy Clause to find unreasonable the amount of power one of its utilities bought from the Tennessee Valley Authority under a contract approved by the FERC. In that case, Nantahala and Tapoco were sister utilities, both wholly owned by the Aluminum Company of America (Alcoa). Nantahala served customers at wholesale as well as at retail.

---

[33] The Narragansett doctrine was first enunciated in Narragansett Electric Co. v. Burke, 119 R.I. 559, 381 A.2d 1358 (1977), *cert. denied*, 435 U.S. 972 (1978). It is an extension of the "filed rate doctrine."

[34] 476 U.S. 953 (1986).

Tapoco served only Alcoa. Nantahala and Tapoco jointly received from the Tennessee Valley Authority a fixed supply of low-cost "entitlement" power pursuant to a contract filed with FERC. They also purchased higher-cost power from TVA when the low-cost entitlement power was insufficient for their needs. When the North Carolina Commission set Nantahala's retail rates, it determined that Nantahala should be receiving a greater share, and Tapoco a lesser share, of the low-cost TVA entitlement power. This change to the allocation would mean Nantahala's costs would be lower and its retail rates would be lower. The Commission set Nantahala's retail rates based on the imputation of the lower costs. The U.S. Supreme Court held this action was preempted by the FERC-approved power allocation, pointing out that to allow the North Carolina Commission to impose a different power allocation would expose Nantahala to trapped costs just as surely as allowing the commission to impose a different rate for that power—already forbidden by the Narragansett doctrine.

Two years later, the U.S. Supreme Court extended the reasoning in *Nantahala* in another case where it held a state commission was preempted from undertaking an inquiry into whether its utility had imprudently incurred costs in the exceedingly expensive Grand Gulf Unit 1 nuclear power plant. In *Mississippi Power & Light Co. v. Mississippi,*[35] Mississippi Power & Light (MP&L) was one of four utilities owned by a public utility holding company, Middle South Utilities (MSU). MSU had another subsidiary, Middle South Energy, Inc., which constructed and owned Grand Gulf to meet the power needs of MSU's utilities. Middle South had agreements with the four utilities that entitled them to wholesale power generated by Grand Gulf and allocated Grand Gulf's capacity and costs among them. These agreements were filed with FERC which approved an allocation of 33% of Grand Gulf's capacity costs to MP&L as just and reasonable. The cost of building Grand Gulf had greatly exceeded projected construction costs and thus the cost of the power produced was greater than that of MP&L's other generating facilities.

MP&L filed for a retail rate increase with the Mississippi Public Service Commission to cover its increased costs associated with Grand Gulf. The Commission eventually approved a retail rate increase to cover MP&L's 33% of the costs of Grand Gulf. The Attorney General of Mississippi, representing consumers, appealed this decision to the Mississippi Supreme Court on the grounds that the Commission should have investigated the prudence

---

[35] 487 U.S. 354 (1988). *See* James E. Hickey, Jr., *Mississippi Power & Light Company: A Departure Point for Extension of the 'Bright Line' Between Federal and State Regulatory Jurisdiction Over Public Utilities*, 10 J. ENERGY L. & POL'Y 57 (1989), reprinted in PUBLIC UTILITIES LAW ANTHOLOGY 1989, vol. XII (1990).

of the expenses associated with constructing Grand Gulf. The Mississippi Supreme Court agreed and ordered the commission to examine the prudence of the management decisions that led to the construction of Grand Gulf before ordering a retail rate increase. On appeal, the U.S. Supreme Court reversed the Mississippi Supreme Court, finding that the reasoning in *Nantahala* applied to preempt the state from conducting proceedings to determine whether some or all of the costs were not prudently incurred.

The Mississippi Supreme Court had reasoned that the state was not preempted by the FERC proceedings because FERC had not litigated the issue of the prudence of the costs of Grand Gulf. The U.S. Supreme Court disagreed with this reasoning, characterizing it as the sort of case-by-case analysis of the impact of state regulation upon the national interest rejected in *FPC v. Southern California Edison Co.* and analogizing MP&L's situation to that of Nantahala. Just as Nantahala had no right to obtain any more low-cost TVA entitlement power than the amount allocated by FERC, MP&L may not pay for less Grand Gulf power than the amount allocated by FERC. The practical message of this decision is that the Attorney General of Mississippi should have intervened in the FERC proceeding for approval of the MSU agreements in order to raise the issue of the prudence of the costs of constructing Grand Gulf.

3.   PUHCA Regulates Public Utility Holding Companies

In 1935, Congress enacted the Public Utility Holding Company Act (PUHCA).[36] It was designed to eliminate holding company abuses. A holding company is a business enterprise which owns all or a controlling amount of the shares of stock or assets of other companies. Organizing businesses into a holding company can enable them to reduce their costs by putting them in a position to take advantage of economies of scale. The organization of electric utilities into holding companies in the 1920s and 1930s enabled them to construct large, central station electric generation plants which could supply electricity in several service territories at a significantly lower cost than that same amount of electricity could be generated by more, smaller generating plants. It also enabled utilities to lower their supplies and equipment costs because the holding company could purchase bulk amounts at a discount. These were all positive developments for consumers. However, they were also accompanied by some negative developments.

---

[36] 15 U.S.C. §§ 79-79z (1994).

Because the company at the top of the pyramid of electric utilities organized into a holding company does not itself directly own or operate facilities used for electricity generation, transmission or distribution, it was not regulated as a public utility by the states in the 1920s and 1930s. Also, many of the transactions undertaken by the utilities within the holding company were interstate in nature, so they went unregulated because of the "Attleboro Gap" in regulation. These regulatory voids allowed financial abuses within the holding company to go unchecked. These abuses included excessive financial charges made by one company to another, extraction of exorbitant profits from the electric operations to the parent holding company, distorted write-ups of properties, stock manipulation, and even control of the holding company by banks for their own benefit. These abuses weakened the financial strength of the companies within the holding company structure and resulted in unfair costs being passed on to ratepayers. As the Great Depression deepened in the 1930s, the financial weaknesses were exposed and the other abuses came to light. Congress passed PUHCA to reform and regulate the holding company structure and eliminate the abuses.

PUHCA achieved a major reorganization of the electric industry as holding companies reformed themselves to come into compliance with the Act, which was aggressively enforced by the Securities and Exchange Commission (SEC) and the courts. PUHCA effectively abolished the pyramiding of electric utility companies in holding companies by requiring that any electric enterprise within a holding company be limited to operating a single integrated public utility system located in a single operating area.[37] A holding company can operate more than one integrated public utility system only if it can show that this arrangement will produce substantial economies of scale, that the systems are confined to one state or its immediate neighbors, and that the systems will assure local management, efficient operation and effective regulation.[38] Furthermore, the public utility holding company cannot engage in other businesses unless they are "reasonably incidental or economically necessary or appropriate to the operations of" the utility.[39] Most of the extant public utility holding companies could not meet these tests and had to restructure themselves. PUHCA also had a broad reach because it expansively defined a holding company to include any company directly or indirectly holding ten percent or more of the voting stock of a public utility company, or of another holding company. Today, while there are thirteen public utility holding companies, they do only about fifteen percent of the country's electricity generation business.

---

[37] 15 U.S.C. § 79k(b) (1994).

[38] 15 U.S.C. § 79k(b)(1) (1994).

[39] 15 U.S.C. § 79k(b)(1) (1994).

The reform of public utility holding company behavior since the enactment of PUHCA has been so dramatic that many, including even the SEC itself, have recommended its repeal.[40] Congress is currently considering this as part of its overall review of the desirability of restructuring the electric industry again through federal legislation.

C. The Golden Age of the Electric Industry and Its Regulation (1935-1965)

The thirty years between 1935 and 1965 has been called the "golden age" of the electric industry.[41] For privately owned, vertically integrated utilities, economies of scale continued as the size of generation units grew. Growth and demand for electricity also grew steadily, doubling every ten years at a rate of roughly seven percent annually. Continued technological advances, together with reliable and predictable growth, caused the average cost of production to stay relatively flat for a period of time. Utility investments were safe ones. Consumers saw their rates rise slightly or not at all. Regulators held non-controversial hearings. All the stakeholders in the industry were content. Utilities were pleased with their continued growth and growth in earnings. Shareholders were pleased with their predictable returns on investment. Consumers were pleased with the stable, or even decreasing, rates. And regulators were pleased with the absence of pressure to change regulation or the industry structure. However, this all changed as technological advances and economies of scale flattened and the energy crises of the 1970s unfolded.

D. The Energy Crises of the 1970s Stimulates the Reintroduction of Competition into Electric Generation

The regulatory compact, establishing a government protected monopoly operating essentially under a cost plus rate formula, works well in an expanding economy with accompanying technological advances. Under such circumstances, industry growth occurs and prices stabilize or fall. However, when economies of scale and technological advances flatten, the cost of doing business increases. An increased cost of doing business can have negative effects on any business. It can have disastrous effects on a regulated monopoly. These problems began for the U.S. electric industry in approximately

---

[40] Douglas Hawes, *Public Utility Holding Company Act of 1935—Fossil or Foil?* 30 VAND. L. REV. 605 (1977).

[41] Leonard S. Hyman, AMERICA'S ELECTRIC UTILITIES: PAST, PRESENT AND FUTURE 119-130 (6th ed. 1997).

1965 when the marginal costs of producing electricity began to exceed the average cost, and electric utilities saw their profit margin begin to slide.

Traditionally, the rates of an electric utility are set on the basis of its historic average costs and include allowance for a reasonable rate of return on capital invested in utility assets. If costs are declining, steady rates mean increasing profits to the utility. However, as marginal costs increase, profits will decline, unless and until rates are set at marginal cost.

In the 1970s electric utilities saw costs increase all over the business. Labor costs rose and inflation increased. The international cartel called the Organization of Petroleum Exporting Countries in 1973 asserted its control over oil supplies. Oil supplies available to the U.S. fell, and the cost of oil soared. Electric utilities firing their boilers with oil sought to switch to gas or coal. Domestic interstate supplies of natural gas had been subject to stringent federal price caps since about 1960. Supplies had contracted in response to the low profitability of the industry. Accordingly, additional natural gas was not available. Liquified natural gas was imported at exorbitant prices. Conversion of plants to be able to burn coal was expensive and took time. Congress looked for ways to stimulate the production of U.S. natural gas and other forms of energy. One of its vehicles for achieving this, which related directly to electric utilities was the Public Utility Regulatory Policies Act, passed as one of five energy acts in 1978.

1.   *PURPA Encourages Independent Generation*

Congress passed the Public Utility Regulatory Policies Act[42] (PURPA) in part to encourage the growth of generation not owned by utility companies. PURPA sought to achieve this by requiring the local electric utility to buy the power produced by certain types of non-utility generators, which PURPA calls "qualifying facilities"[43] (QFs). There are two types of QFs: small electric generators (80 megawatts or less) powered by a renewable energy resource, and cogenerators. A cogenerator is an electric generator that also produces another form of energy (steam or heat, for example) which is put to use. A qualifying cogeneration facility is one that meets certain efficiency standards.[44] QFs could sell their power to the local utility at the price that the utility would have paid for that power had it generated or bought that power itself. This is called the utility's "avoided cost." Only a small class of generators qualified for this treatment. And, while they

---

[42] Pub. L. 95-617, 92 Stat. 3117 (codified as amended in scattered sections of titles 15, 16, 42, & 43 U.S.C.).

[43] 16 U.S.C. § 796 (1988).

[44] *Id.*

could sell their power to the local utility, they did not have access to the utility's transmission lines to wheel their power to any other utility. Nevertheless, it marked the formal reintroduction of competition into generation. Some states, such as California, adopted state regulatory policies to further this independent power development, such as requiring utilities to enter into long-term contracts with QFs. From 1989 through 1993, the number of QFs grew from 576 to 1200 and installed QF capacity increased from 27,429 megawatts to 47,774 megawatts.[45]

2. Rising Electric Costs Add to the Pressure for More Competition

Electric utility cost increases came from many places in the 1970s. Labor costs rose and inflation increased rapidly. In the 1950s and 1960s, nuclear power was touted as "too cheap too meter," but the cost of construction of nuclear plants skyrocketed. Nuclear plants under construction in the 1970s were generally over budget and behind schedule. As mentioned above, the cost of oil also ballooned. Eventually, so did the cost of gas. Another of the energy acts of 1978, the Natural Gas Policy Act, provided for high gas prices for new U.S. supplies of gas as an incentive to get U.S. gas producers to increase their production. These costs increases led to consumer conservation just at the time that new long-lead-time electric generation was coming on line and needed to be paid for too. The glut of expensive generation capacity, for which consumers had to pay much of the cost, shot prices up. Between 1970 and 1985, industrial electric rates quadrupled in nominal terms and saw an 86% increase after adjustment for inflation. Residential rates tripled in nominal terms with a 25% increase after adjustment for inflation.[46] People looked for new ways to bring rates down. New generation in the 1980s could be built for substantially less than the average price of existing generation. Political pressure mounted to expand competition in generation.

E. The Federal Energy Regulatory Commission of the 1980s Fosters Competition through Transmission Access

The development of the QF industry in the 1980s demonstrated that power could be produced reliably by sources other than traditional, vertical-

---

[45] Preamble to FERC Order No. 888, 75 F.E.R.C. ¶ 61,080, FERC Statutes and Regulations ¶¶ 31,036, 31,642, 61 Fed. Reg. 21,540 (May 10, 1996) [hereinafter Preamble to FERC Order No. 888].

[46] *Id.* at ¶ 31,640.

ly integrated public utilities. The industry also discovered that larger generation units needed greater maintenance and experienced longer downtime. As a result, the price of each incremental unit of electric power exceeded average cost. Smaller size units became cost effective. Combined cycle units, typically using natural gas, offered the advantages of lower capital costs, increased reliability and relatively minimal environmental impacts. Conventional steam units using circulating fluidized bed boilers and fueled by coal or other conventional fuels were also found to be more efficient and less polluting. As a result, the optimum size of generation plants shifted from large (e.g., 500 megawatt plants) with long lead times to build to smaller units that could be built quickly.[47] During this time, a market for non-traditional power, in addition to QF produced power, began to emerge. Independent power producers (IPPs) began to sell power in the bulk power market. These producers did not own any transmission or distribution facilities and did not have the benefit of PURPA's mandatory purchase requirement. Even some traditional utilities formed non-utility affiliates to sell power in the fledgling bulk power market. Generation owned by IPPs and affiliated power producers (APPs), exclusive of QFs, increased from 249 generators with 9,216 megawatts of capacity to 634 generators with 13,004 megawatts of capacity between 1989 and 1993.[48]

In the 1980s, IPPs needed access to transmission owned and controlled by utilities to expand their market and effectively compete with traditional utility-owned generators. FERC wanted to provide this. Some utilities provided transmission access as a result of decisions in antitrust litigation[49] or through Nuclear Regulatory Commission license conditions and voluntary preference power transmission arrangements associated with federal power marketing agencies.[50] Even though FERC did not have explicit power under the Federal Power Act to order utilities to wheel power for IPPs, FERC sought to get the utilities to provide transmission access "voluntarily." In a number of cases where utilities wanted authority for themselves and their affiliates to sell bulk power from their generators at market rates, rather than tariffed rates, FERC authorized it *if* the utility agreed to open transmission under its control to all generators on a nondiscriminatory basis.[51] FERC also approved several mergers and consolidations on condition

---

[47] *Id.* at ¶ 31,640-41
[48] *Id.* at ¶ 31,643.
[49] *See*, for example, Otter Tail Power Co. v. United States, 410 U.S. 366 (1973).
[50] Preamble to FERC Order No. 888, *supra* note 45, at ¶ 31,644.
[51] *See, for example*, Ocean State Power, 44 F.E.R.C. ¶ 61,261 (1988).

that the new utility open access to its transmission.[52] These conditions on approvals were justified, and justifiable, as necessary to offset anti-competitive effects to other generators potentially arising from the utility's new ability to sell power at market rates or from its merger. These "open access" conditions required only that the utilities provide point-to-point transmission service. They did not require that the same quality of transmission service be provided as the utility-owners themselves enjoyed. Even so, these efforts by FERC spurred on competition in generation.

F. The Energy Policy Act of 1992 Eases the Way for More Competition in Generation

By the early 1990s, it became clear that the wholesale market in electricity was not as robust as it could be. There were two limiting factors. Non-utility generators, other than QFs, found it difficult to enter the market because they had no exemption from the requirements of the PUHCA. These generators seemed particularly desirable because they could provide new generation capacity which promised to supply electricity at a lower cost.[53] The second constraint on market expansion was FERC's lack of authority to mandate wheeling over transmission lines. In 1992, Congress passed the Energy Policy Act (EPAct)[54] and eliminated both these constraints.

EPAct eliminated the PUHCA constraint by authorizing persons exclusively in the business of selling electric energy at wholesale to be exempt from PUHCA's ownership restrictions.[55] A generator can be exempted from these PUHCA restrictions if FERC finds that it is engaged exclusively in the business of owning or operating a generator that sells electric energy at wholesale.[56] These generators are called exempt wholesale generators (EWGs). By amending PUHCA to exempt electric generators selling exclusively into the wholesale electricity market from being regulated as electric monopolies, EPAct set the stage for a larger competitive, and unregulated, wholesale market to materialize. Smaller and more

---

[52] *See* discussion in Preamble to FERC Order No. 888, *supra* note 45, at ¶ 31, 644.

[53] State mandated competitive bidding processes for new electric generation capacity showed that the cost of new generation based on new technologies could supply new capacity at a lower cost than existing capacity. Robert E. Burns, Esq., *Electric Industry Restructuring: Finance, Mergers, and Acquisitions, Two Years In Review*, YEAR-IN-REVIEW (ABA Sec. of Nat'l. Res., Energy & Environment, ed., 1999).

[54] Pub. L. No. 102-486, 100 Stat. 2776 (1992).

[55] 15 U.S.C. § 79z-5a (1994).

[56] 15 U.S.C. § 79z-5a (1994).

efficient gas-fired combined-cycle generation facilities can produce power today at a cost ranging from three to five cents per kWh. Similarly, circulating fluidized bed combustion boilers, fueled by coal and other conventional fuels, can produce power at substantially lower costs than today's average cost of power.[57] Improved transmission facilities across the United States and an increase in coordination transactions[58] in electricity now permit consumption of power produced many miles distant.[59]

Second, EPAct authorized FERC to order utilities that own transmission facilities (including intrastate utilities, Federal power marketing agencies, qualifying cogeneration facilities, and qualifying small power production facilities) to transmit wholesale power over their system.[60] Significantly, EPAct prohibits FERC from ordering access to transmission for retail power sales.[61] Also, a wholesale power transaction that is merely a sham for a retail power sale does not fall within FERC's authority to order wheeling.[62] To be a legitimate reseller of electricity, the entity must buy

---

[57] Federal Energy Regulatory Commission (FERC) Final Rule Promoting Wholesale Competition Through Open Access Non-Discriminatory Transmission Services by Public Utilities, Order No. 888, 61 Fed. Reg. 21,540, 21,544 (1996) (codified at 18 C.F.R. pts. 35 and 385) [hereinafter FERC Order No. 888].

[58] Coordination transactions are voluntary sales or exchanges of specialized electricity services, e.g., sale of electricity from temporary excess capacity.

[59] FERC Order No. 888, *supra* note 57, 61 Fed. Reg. 21,544 (1996).

[60] *See* §§ 211 and 212 of the Federal Power Act, as amended by EPAct, which gives FERC authority to order "transmitting utilities" to provide requested wholesale transmission for any electric utility, Federal power marketing agency, or any other wholesale electric generator to a legitimate reseller if FERC finds this transmission is in the public interest.

[61] Section 212(h) of the Federal Power Act states that no wheeling order issued by FERC shall be conditioned upon or require the transmission of electric energy directly to an ultimate consumer. 16 U.S.C. § 824k(h)(1) (1994).

[62] EPAct's anti-sham provision, 16 U.S.C. § 824k(h) (1994), reads as follows: No order issued under this Act shall be conditioned upon or require the transmission of electric energy:
(1)   directly to an ultimate consumer, or
(2)   to, or for the benefit of, an entity if such electric energy would be sold by such entity directly to an ultimate consumer, unless
   (A)   such entity is a Federal power marketing agency, the TVA, a State or any political subdivision of a State (or an agency, authority, or instrumentality of a State or a political subdivision), a corporation or association that has ever received a loan for the purposes of providing electric service from the Administrator of the Rural Electrification Administration under the Rural Electrification Act of 1936, a person having

power wholesale and use "transmission or distribution facilities that it owns or controls" to "deliver all" the power to the ultimate electric consumers.[63] This requirement is designed to prohibit retail customers from gaining access to cheaper wholesale electric power by owning less than all of the distribution or transmission facilities.

G. FERC Order Nos. 888 and 889 Mandate Open Access Across the Country's Transmission Grid for Wholesale Power Sales

FERC used its wholesale wheeling authority under EPAct aggressively between 1993 and 1996, ordering wholesale transmission in most of the applications it acted on.[64] Then, in 1996, FERC effectively ended case-by-case wholesale transmission orders by promulgating a rule requiring all public utilities that own, control or operate facilities used for transmitting electric energy in interstate commerce to have on file open access non-discriminatory transmission tariffs that contain minimum terms and conditions of non-discriminatory service.[65] This rule is commonly called "FERC Order 888." Order 888 also requires utilities to unbundle their transmission service function from their generation and power marketing functions, and to provide unbundled ancillary transmission services. It also

---

an obligation arising under State or local law (exclusive of an obligation arising solely from a contract entered into by such person) to provide electric service to the public, or any corporation or association which is wholly owned, directly or indirectly, by any one or more of the foregoing, and

(B) such entity was providing electric service to such ultimate consumer on the date of enactment of this subsection or would utilize transmission or distribution facilities that it owns or controls to deliver all such electric energy to such electric consumer.

[63] Section 212 of the Federal Power Act, 16 U.S.C. § 824k(h) (1994).

[64] In one of these, Tex-La Electric Cooperative of Texas, Inc., 67 F.E.R.C. ¶ 61,019 (1994) order on rehearing, FERC even found that it had the authority to order wholesale transmission over local distribution facilities. In doing so, FERC recognized that section 201(b) of the Federal Power Act excludes local distribution facilities from its jurisdiction. However, FERC reasoned that interpreting section 201(b) to preclude it from ordering wholesale wheeling whenever *any* local distribution facilities were involved would mean that most future applications for transmission services would have to be denied. This result, FERC concluded, would be contrary to the intent of Congress expressed in EPAct to expand the Commission's authority to order wheeling. *Id*. at ¶ 61,055.

[65] FERC Order No. 888, *supra* note 58.

allows utilities the opportunity to recover their wholesale stranded costs. Order 888 was accompanied by Order 889, that requires public utilities to participate in an open access same-time information system (OASIS) and promulgates standards of conduct designed to prevent anticompetitive activities.

1.   Order No. 888

In Order No. 888, FERC mandated open access transmission of wholesale electric power. The goal was to create a more robust competitive market in wholesale power by allowing more customers more access to more wholesale electricity generators. FERC estimated that open access transmission would achieve two goals: increase the availability of competitively priced electricity, saving U.S. electric consumers between $3.8 and $5.4 billion a year, and encourage more technical innovation in the industry.[66] At the same time, FERC wanted to ensure that the nation's power supply reliability would not be adversely affected and that utilities losing customers because of the new market in wholesale electricity would have a fair opportunity to recover past prudently incurred costs as well as the costs of making the transition to a competitive wholesale market.

Between March 29, 1995, when FERC proposed its open access rule and May 10, 1996, when FERC adopted the final rule as Order 888, 106 of the approximately 166 public utilities owning, controlling, or operating transmission facilities used in interstate commerce offered some form of wholesale open access. FERC noted that it was imperative that all wholesale buyers and sellers of electricity be able to obtain non-discriminatory transmission access. FERC relied on its statutory obligation under sections 205 and 206 of the Federal Power Act to remedy undue discrimination as its authority for ordering mandatory open access. Sections 205 and 206 require the FERC to ensure that, with respect to any transmission in interstate commerce or any sale of electric energy for resale in interstate commerce by a public utility, no person is subject to any undue prejudice or disadvantage.[67] Order 888 also provided for the recovery of stranded costs associated

---

[66] Preamble to FERC Order No. 888, *supra* note 45, at ¶ 31,652.

[67] FERC also analyzed the cases it deemed relevant to its authority to remedy undue discrimination by ordering industry-wide non-discriminatory open access. The primary case it relied on was Associated Gas Distributors v. FERC, 824 F.2d 981 (D.C. Cir. 1987), *cert. denied*, 485 U.S. 1006 (1988) [hereinafter AGD]. The AGD case upheld FERC's authority to order access as a remedy for undue discrimination under the Natural Gas Act of 1938, 15 U.S.C. §§ 717-717w (1994). The Natural Gas Act is patterned after the Federal Power Act.

with providing open access and explained FERC's assessment of the boundary delineating federal and state jurisdiction over transmission and local distribution of electricity.

a. *Open Access*

Traditionally, public utilities provided electricity at wholesale and the transmission of that electricity as a bundled service at a single price. Order 888 requires that these services be unbundled and sold separately. FERC found that this functional unbundling of services was necessary to achieve non-discriminatory open access transmission. Specifically, utilities must file separate tariffs with separate rates, terms, and conditions for wholesale generation service, transmission service and any ancillary services. Ancillary services range from actions taken to effect the transmission, such as scheduling and dispatching, to services that are necessary to maintain the integrity of the transmission system during a transaction, such as load following and reactive power support. Other ancillary services are needed to correct for the effects associated with undertaking the transmission, such as energy imbalance reckoning. Under Order 888, to ensure that a utility does not favor itself with its own transmission facilities, a utility must take transmission service and ancillary services for all its new wholesale sales and purchases of electricity under the same tariff that applies to outside users of its transmission.

FERC did not require that public utilities establish separate corporate affiliates to manage the utilities' unbundled services. However, FERC indicated it was interested in accommodating voluntary utility corporate restructuring, including divestiture of generation or transmission assets. In its companion rule to Order 888 (i.e., Order 889), FERC set out a code of conduct applicable to utilities to ensure that the transmission owner's wholesale marketing personnel and the transmission customer's marketing personnel have comparable access to information about the transmission system.

Neither did FERC require utilities to set up independent system operators (ISOs) of their transmission systems to prevent undue discrimination or mitigate the market power of utility-owned wholesale generators. FERC promised that it would monitor the emerging wholesale electricity market to ensure the transmission customers were adequately protected and, if necessary, require ISOs or other mechanisms to assure non-discriminatory open access transmission.

Neither did FERC generically provide for market-based rates for the wholesale sale of electricity. Utility requests to sell wholesale power at market-based rates are still decided by FERC on a case-by-case basis.

However, FERC announced in Order 888 that it would no longer require a utility wishing to sell wholesale power from new generating facilities to prove that it lacks market power in new generation capacity. FERC based this on the fact that it had "examined generation dominance in many different cases over the years" and had "yet to find an instance of generation dominance in long-run bulk power markets."[68] FERC ascribed this to industry and legal changes which have allowed ease of market entry in new generation. However, this will not prevent parties objecting to market-based rates from raising generation dominance issues related to new capacity. To obtain market-based rates for wholesale sales from existing generation, FERC continues to require public utilities to show that there is no generation dominance in existing capacity. In all market-based rate cases, FERC will look at whether an applicant or its affiliates could erect other barriers to entry and whether there may be problems due to affiliate abuse or reciprocal dealing.

b.   Stranded Costs

Under Order 888, if a utility's pre-existing retail or wholesale customer is able to reach a new generation supplier because of the new open access, any "legitimate, prudent and verifiable" costs stranded as a result of the new wholesale transmission access will be recoverable. However, if a utility's pre-existing customer ceases to purchase power from it through self-generation or use of another utility's transmission system, costs stranded by this event would not be recoverable. These costs would not be stranded as a result of the new open access order.

FERC's approach to stranded cost recovery is based on the philosophy that because utilities entered into contracts to make sales under an entirely different regulatory regime, they should have an opportunity to recover stranded costs that occur as a result of the change in law. FERC did not believe utilities should be held responsible for failing to foresee the actions FERC would take to alter the use of their transmission systems.

In order to recover stranded costs, the utility must demonstrate that it had a reasonable expectation of continuing to serve the customer, and for how long. In calculating recoverable stranded costs, FERC will use a "revenues lost" approach. Under this approach, stranded costs are calculated by subtracting the competitive market value of the power the customer would have purchased from the revenues that the customer would have paid had it stayed on the utility's generation system.

---

[68] Kansas City Power and Light, 67 F.E.R.C. ¶¶ 61,183, 61,557 (1994).

c. *Federal/State Jurisdiction*

Jurisdiction over the transmission of electricity includes both the authority to order transmission and the authority to set the rates, terms and conditions of transmission. The dividing line between federal and state authority to order transmission is clearly set out in the Federal Power Act. FERC has the authority to order the transmission of wholesale electricity and is prohibited from ordering the transmission of retail electricity.[69] Opponents of state authority to order the transmission of retail electricity have argued that the federal government has preempted state authority to order retail transmission of electricity by occupying the field of interstate commerce in electricity in the FPA. They add that the retail transmission of electricity affects interstate commerce in electricity even when it is limited to the transmission and distribution facilities of the local utility.[70] Nevertheless, as discussed below, numerous states have assumed they have such jurisdiction and passed legislation mandating transmission of retail electricity.

Congress has also clearly given FERC the authority to set rates, terms and conditions for the transmission of wholesale electricity.[71] However, the law governing the division of authority between the federal government and the states to set the rates, terms and conditions of transmission of retail electricity is unclear because, having prohibited FERC from ordering retail transmission, the FPA does not speak to any authority FERC might have regarding the rates, terms and conditions of retail transmission. Nevertheless, in Order 888, FERC asserted its exclusive authority over the rates, terms and conditions of any transmission in interstate commerce associated

---

[69] Section 721 of EPAct amended § 211 of the Federal Power Act to provide that any electric utility (including intrastate utilities), Federal power marketing agency, or any other person generating electric energy for sale for resale, i.e., wholesale electricity, may apply to FERC for a wholesale transmission order. Section 212(h) of the Federal Power Act, as amended by EPAct, states that no wheeling order issued by FERC shall be conditioned upon or require the transmission of electric energy directly to an ultimate consumer. 16 U.S.C. § 824k(h)(1) (1994).

[70] These arguments were made in *In the Matter of the Application of the Association of Businesses Advocating Tariff Equity for Approval of an Experimental Retail Wheeling Tariff for Consumers Power Co.*, Nos. U-10143 and U-10176, Opinion and Interim Order Remanding to the Administrative Law Judge for Further Proceedings, 150 P.U.R.4th 409 (Mich. Pub. Serv. Comm'n Apr. 11, 1994), *appeal dismissed for lack of jurisdiction*, Attorney General v. Michigan Pub. Serv. Comm'n, No. 175245 (Mich. Ct. App. June 15, 1994).

[71] Federal Power Act, §§ 201, 205, 206, 212; 16 U.S.C. §§ 824(a), 824(d), 824(e), 824k (1994).

with retail transmission, whether it occurs voluntarily or pursuant to state order. FERC reasoned that when Congress enacted the FPA, it gave the Commission exclusive jurisdiction over the rates, terms and conditions of transmission in interstate commerce by public utilities and did not limit, by any words, FERC's jurisdiction to only the transmission in interstate commerce of electricity sold at wholesale. Therefore, FERC concluded, it should also take jurisdiction over the transmission in interstate commerce of electricity sold at retail. In so doing, FERC went out of its way to explain that it did not intend to exercise any jurisdiction over the local distribution facilities associated with retail transmission—which have historically been under state jurisdiction. However, FERC declined to propose the "precise demarcation" between transmission in interstate commerce and local distribution and stated that it was a factual matter "to be decided in the first instance by the Commission." Nevertheless, FERC indicated that it thinks its jurisdiction will be extensive because the courts have construed "in interstate commerce" broadly. FERC concluded that because of the highly integrated nature of the electric system, "most transmission of electricity is in interstate commerce." In summary, FERC contends that it has jurisdiction over the transmission in interstate commerce of electricity sold at retail and the states have jurisdiction over the transmission over local distribution facilities of electricity sold at retail. FERC declined to propose where the dividing line between these activities is located. This issue will ultimately be resolved by the courts or Congress.

2.   *Order No. 889*

Order No. 889 established an electronic information system to aid the competitiveness of the wholesale market made possible by open access to transmission. This system, called OASIS (open access same-time information system), provides existing and potential transmission users the same access to transmission information that the transmission owner enjoys.

Order No. 889 also requires public utilities to comply with standards of conduct intended to preclude anticompetitive conduct by transmission owners, such as favoring affiliated generators or power marketers with transmission services.

H.   CONCERNS ABOUT UNDUE MARKET POWER IN A RESTRUCTURED ELECTRIC INDUSTRY REMAIN

One of the significant issues implicated by the establishment of wholesale open access is the future competitiveness of the wholesale market. There are more than 3,000 electric utilities in the United States. More than

75% of these are vertically integrated, meaning they own generation as well as transmission facilities. The vertically integrated utilities serve over 75% of the retail customers in the United States. Once wholesale generation is deregulated, the concern arises whether utilities owning transmission will favor their own generation with special access. The other concern is whether utilities already owning generation will acquire additional market share in generation when they are allowed to compete unrestrained outside their existing service areas to the extent they will gain undue horizontal market power.

When FERC first proposed Orders 888 and 889, many commenters asked it either to order transmission-owning utilities to divest their generation assets or to impose structural institutional arrangements to better assure non-discrimination in the transmission and sale of electricity. Possible structural arrangements include regional independent system operators (ISOs) or other regional transmission organizations (RTOs). ISOs and RTOs are entities that are independent of the owners of transmission but, nevertheless, manage the transmission systems. FERC did not accede to these requests, preferring instead only to require utilities to "functionally unbundle" the transmission function of the utility from its generation and power marketing functions. Functional unbundling means that the activities are functionally separated within the corporation; they need not even be put into separate corporate entities.

FERC promulgated standards of conduct to reinforce its principle of separation of competitive and monopoly functions. Under these standards, a utility must take transmission services under the same tariff of general applicability as do others; state separate rates for wholesale generation, transmission and ancillary services; and rely on the same electronic information network that its transmission customers rely on to obtain information about its transmission system when buying or selling power.

Although FERC did not require utilities to develop independent system operators in Orders 888 and 889, FERC strongly encouraged utilities and power pools to form them voluntarily.[72] Now, FERC is formally looking at the desirability of creating them.[73] In addition to structurally separating

---

[72] FERC approves the formation of ISOs. FERC has announced eleven ISO principles; its goal is to ensure that the ISO is sufficiently independent and operational to fulfill its responsibilities. It has approved the California ISO and Power Exchange, the PJM Group (i.e., Pennsylvania-New Jersey-Maryland Interconnection), the New York Power Pool. It has conditionally approved ISO New England, Inc. (ISO/NE) for the New England Power Pool (NEPOOL).

[73] FERC Notice of Intent to Consult With State Commissions, 63 Fed. Reg. 66158 (1998).

transmission from generation and marketing functions, ISOs, or RTOs, with authority to operate the transmission system within a region can address loop flow issues, eliminate pancaked transmission rates within the system, manage short-term transmission reliability, manage congestion, and plan transmission expansion. Under Section 202(a) of the Federal Power Act, FERC is "empowered and directed to divide the country into regional districts for the voluntary interconnection and coordination of facilities for the generation, transmission, and sale of electric energy." However, before FERC can exercise this authority it must notify the regulatory commission of each State to be affected.[74] Currently, FERC is holding conferences with the states to receive their input on how these entities should be developed, if FERC decides to require them, and what role the states should have in their formation and governance.

I.   COMPETITION HAS BEEN EXTENDED TO THE RETAIL MARKET IN SOME STATES

About one-third of the states have passed legislation to extend competition in electricity to the retail level by requiring their public utilities to wheel power to the end user over their distribution and transmission lines.[75] Most of these states have postponed the opening day of competition to a few years hence. However, California's entire retail market has been open to competition since 1997. Connecticut's entire market opened in 1998, as did New Hampshire's.[76] Many states are phasing in competition. For example, Pennsylvania has opened one-third of the peak load in each customer class to competition; Arizona has opened twenty percent of its IOUs' load to competition; and Montana allows competition for the retail load of large customers (greater than one megawatt).

1.   *Stranded Cost Recovery*

In deciding to open the state to retail competition, one of the first issues the state must address is whether to allow the incumbent utilities to recover

---

[74] Federal Power Act, § 202(a).

[75] These states include Arizona, California, Connecticut, Illinois, Massachusetts, Maine, Maryland, Montana, Nevada, New Hampshire, New Jersey, New Mexico, New York, Oklahoma, Oregon, Pennsylvania, Rhode Island, and Virginia.

[76] New Hampshire's market was subsequently closed by order of the federal district court in Public Service Co. of New Hampshire v. Patch, 167 F.3d 15 (1st Cir. 1998) (affirming preliminary injunction), where the legality of some of the actions taken by the New Hampshire Public Utilities Commission in implementing retail competition is being litigated.

their stranded costs. To date, most states have allowed their utilities the opportunity to collect all their stranded costs. Typically, stranded costs are recovered through a temporary surcharge levied on the distribution of kilowatt hours of electricity to all consumers in the jurisdiction. A few states allow some customers to bypass this surcharge if they generate their own electricity.[77]

In some states the actual recovery of stranded costs is more difficult than in others. For example, in some states only "unmitigable" stranded costs can be recovered.[78] Illinois' statute takes this a step further by pre-determining what percentage of stranded costs are "mitigable." New Hampshire's stranded cost recovery provision is arguably the most stringent for utilities, and has given rise to litigation challenging it. New Hampshire will allow full recovery only in those situations where utility management's discretion to invest in generation which has now proven to be above market value was significantly reduced or eliminated by government mandate.[79] Furthermore, New Hampshire will not allow full recovery in any event where to do so would result in a rate above the regional average. New Hampshire's Public Utility Commission has interpreted these terms strictly and disallowed recovery of much of Public Service Co. of New Hampshire's ill-fated investment in Seabrook Nuclear Generating Station. This regulatory order is currently stayed while its legality is being determined by the courts.

Several states have conditioned stranded cost recovery on divestiture of some or all of the utility's generation.[80] Requiring a utility to sell its generation aids in the certainty of calculating the cost that is stranded.[81] Some critics of this approach argue that the advantage of a certain price is outweighed by the risk that putting a utility's generation on the auction block all at once and on a legislatively imposed date will reduce the price buyers are willing to pay for it, thereby increasing the stranded cost.

---

[77] See, for example, Montana and Maine. Maine also allows customers to bypass the stranded cost surcharge in certain fuel conversion situations or with the adoption of demand side management programs. Other states require customers leaving the system to self-generate to pay an exit fee designed to recover their estimated stranded costs repayment "liability." See, for example, Arizona.

[78] See, for example, Connecticut, Maine, Massachusetts.

[79] Pennsylvania's stranded cost recovery provision is similar.

[80] See, for example, Connecticut, which required its utilities to divest all non-nuclear generation. In Rhode Island, utilities must divest fifteen percent of their generation assets within three years. Maine will require its utilities to divest all their generation by 2001. California required Pacific Gas and Electric and Southern California Edison to divest at least 50% of their generation.

[81] If a market value is not arrived at through an actual price paid for the asset, then it must be estimated in an administrative proceeding.

2.   *Amelioration of Incumbent Utilities' Market Power*

Requiring utilities to divest their generation assets also has the effect of reducing or eliminating the utilities' market power in the newly formed retail electricity market. In spite of its advantage for aiding the development of a retail competitive market, divestiture of generation assets is not being required in many states. Often it is opposed by the incumbent utilities which may have significant economic and political strength in their states. Their opposition to forced divestiture is frequently matched by the labor unions and non-unionized utility employees who have been securely employed and wish to see the same ownership continue. Maintenance of the status quo also appeals to many in the public who, while they want the lower electric rates held out by the prospect of competition, are anxious about what new electricity providers means for the reliability of their service and the level of solicitude for them as consumers.

Most states that do not require their utilities to divest generation assets set up codes of conduct designed to prevent discrimination by the utility against new entrants in the generation market. Several states are investigating the possible formation of an independent system operator to manage the distribution and transmission facilities within the state or region.[82] California has already formed one, which has been approved by FERC.

3.   *Non-market Efforts to Assure Lower Rates*

One of the primary political forces behind the passage of legislation in the states to open electricity to retail competition is the belief that it will result in lower electric rates. Some states are reluctant to rely on a nascent competitive market to achieve this and have enacted programs and temporary regulatory controls designed to assure it. For example, California, Connecticut and Illinois have made state bonds available to the incumbent utilities owning generation assets to allow them to refinance at a lower interest rate. The states require this cost savings to be passed on to the utilities' traditional retail customers in the form of a rate decrease. At least in California, the rate decrease seems to have had the effect of lowering the

---

[82] Texas effectively has one in its Electric Reliability Council of Texas (ERCOT) which has been in existence for decades. Massachusetts calls for an ISO and perhaps a power exchange to operate with a reformed NEPOOL. New Hampshire and Rhode Island seek a regional power pool, a reformed NEPOOL. Arizona, Oklahoma, and Virginia have also called for the formation of an ISO.

price for retail electricity for residential customers below the point where new entrants can effectively compete for a share of the market.[83]

Massachusetts has phased in a mandatory, temporary rate decrease. It required its utilities to offer to sell unbundled electricity at 2.8 cents per kWh in 1998. When the utilities divest their generation they can raise this to 3.2 cents and in 2004 they can raise it again to 5.1 cents. After 2005, they are free to offer electricity at the price they see fit.

In at least a few other states, the incumbent utilities have been prohibited from recovering any stranded costs if to do so would require them to raise their retail electric rates.[84]

At least one state has authorized its political subdivisions to aggregate load, in competition with private load aggregators, for purposes of contracting with competitive generators.[85]

4. Regulating Externalities

About half of the states that have introduced retail electric competition have set up programs to enable them to continue to have jurisdiction over the externalities associated with the generation and distribution of electricity. Most of these states have imposed a surcharge on the distribution of electricity, usually called a competition transition charge (CTC), to fund programs variously designed to promote electricity efficiency, demand side management programs, research and development of renewable fuels, environmental improvement, universal electricity service, low income assistance, and utility employee health, retirement and retraining programs.[86] Connecticut has announced that it will establish uniform state standards for generation facilities to improve air quality.

Some states have a renewable resource portfolio requirement that must be met by electricity providers seeking to be licensed to do business in their jurisdictions. For example, Maine will require licensed power marketers to generate a minimum of thirty percent of the power offered for sale in Maine from renewable energy resources. Connecticut's minimum is six percent. Nevada's minimum is 0.2 percent beginning in 2000 and increasing annually

---

[83] See the press release of Enron which pulled out of the California residential market, citing an inability to lower its prices below that of the incumbent utilities.

[84] See, for example, Montana and Oklahoma.

[85] See Massachusetts, for example.

[86] See, for example, California, Connecticut, Maine, Massachusetts, New Hampshire, Pennsylvania, Rhode Island. On the other hand, Virginia Corporation Commission has recommended to the legislature that it institute no CTC.

by 0.2 percent until it reaches one percent. However, Nevada has authorized its public utility commission to establish a system of tradable renewables credits.

At least one state has required all power marketers doing business in its jurisdiction to follow a standard format for all their disclosures, explanations and sales information in order to enable consumers to better compare prices and offerings.[87]

5.   *Publicly and Cooperatively Owned Utilities*

Only a few states that have provided for retail competition have mandated that their publicly and cooperatively owned utilities participate. Arizona is one of these states. Arizona has made retail wheeling applicable to its rural electric cooperatives and the Salt River Project, a publicly owned water and electric utility, although Arizona has exempted municipally owned utilities from the program. Oklahoma and Pennsylvania have required their rural electric cooperatives to open their transmission and distribution lines to competitive power, but they have allowed their publicly owned utilities to opt into the program at their discretion. Most states allow their cooperatives and publicly owned utilities to opt into competition, although Montana requires its coops to participate unless they opt out. Many of the states that decline to force their publicly and cooperatively owned utilities to open their customer base to retail competition also prohibit these non-participating utilities from participating in the competitive market by selling power at retail outside their service territories. Those states that allow non-participating utilities to nevertheless sell power at retail in other utilities' historic customer service areas have been criticized by investor-owned utilities on the ground that publicly owned utilities have an unfair advantage because of the tax exempt bonds they use to finance the purchase of generation.

6.   *Competition in Ancillary Services*

Several states have announced that they will require their utilities to open up their ancillary services to competition in the future. For example, in 2000, Massachusetts utilities must open up their billing and collections, metering and meter reading services to competition. In Maine this will occur after March 2002. In Arizona it is scheduled to be phased in by 2000 for large industrial customers and for all others in 2001.

---

[87] *See* Nevada, for example.

7.   *Consumer Protection*

Many states have authorized their state regulatory commissions to educate the public about electricity choice. Many have also enacted anti-slamming legislation. Interestingly, this legislation has sometimes been criticized by new entrants for making switching electricity providers so burdensome that it will be a barrier to choice.

J.   The Electric Industry is Restructuring Itself Through Mergers and Acquisitions in Response to the Changing Marketplace

1.   *FERC's Merger Policy*

FERC has the authority and obligation to approve mergers and acquisitions under the Federal Power Act. FERC must ensure that a proposed merger is "consistent with the public interest."[88] In 1969, FERC's predecessor, the Federal Power Commission, devised a six factor test for evaluating mergers.[89] This test was followed until relatively recently. By 1996, the wholesale electricity market had become increasingly competitive. FERC was authorizing market-based rates for wholesale electricity sales when it found that the utilities lacked market power. States were contemplating retail competition. FERC decided the 1969 test needed to be updated to account for changing market structures, the effect of a merger on competitive bulk power markets and the consequent effects on ratepayers. FERC announced its new test as a policy rather than a rule and rather than developing it on a case-by-case basis. FERC wanted to give the public greater certainty about what the profile of an acceptable merger would be, yet retain its flexibility to adjust the test over time.

FERC's new merger policy is a three factor test. FERC looks at the effects of the proposed merger on competition, on rates, and on regulation. In analyzing the effect on competition, FERC has adopted the Department

---

[88] Federal Power Act, § 203(a), 16 U.S.C. § 824b(a) (1994).

[89] These factors included the effect of the proposed merger on competition and on the applicants' operating costs and rate levels; the reasonableness of the purchase price; whether the acquiring utility has coerced the to-be-acquired utility into acceptance of the merger; the impact of the merger on the effectiveness of state and federal regulation; and the contemplated accounting treatment. Commonwealth Edison Company, Opinion No. 507, 36 F.P.C. 927, 936-42 (1966), *aff'd sub nom.* Utility Users League V. FPC, 394 F.2d 16 (7th Cir. 1968), *cert. denied*, 393 U.S. 953 (1969).

of Justice/Federal Trade Commission Merger Guidelines as its analytical framework. The Guidelines involve five steps. First, FERC will assess whether the merger would significantly increase concentration and result in a concentrated market. In light of this, FERC will then assess whether the merger raises concerns about potential adverse competitive effects. Third, FERC will look at whether entry would likely deter or counteract the competitive effects of concern. Next, FERC will assess the efficiency gains that reasonably cannot be achieved by the parties through other means. Finally, FERC will assess whether, but for the merger, either party would be likely to fail, causing its assets to exit the market. By apply an analytic "screen" based on these assessments early in the merger review process, FERC expects to identify proposed mergers that clearly will not harm competition. Applicants who demonstrate that their merger passes this market power screen will have a presumption that the merger raises no market power concerns and, therefore, will not require a trial-type hearing on the issue. In order to be approved, the post-merger market power wielded by the new company must be within acceptable thresholds or be satisfactorily mitigated.

In assessing the effect of a proposed merger on rates, FERC will require applicants to propose appropriate rate protection for customers. FERC encourages the parties to the case to settle this issue through pre-filing consensus-building efforts. In order for the merger to be approved, acceptable customer protections must be in place.

With regard to the effect of the merger on regulation, FERC adopted the approach it had used in recent cases. Where regulatory authority will shift to the Securities and Exchange Commission because the new company will be part of a registered public utility holding company, FERC nevertheless requires it to commit to abide by FERC's policies regarding affiliate transactions. Where the merger is also subject to state approval, FERC will leave the issue of the merger's effect on state regulation to the state commissions. In order to be approved, any adverse effect on regulation must be satisfactorily addressed.

2.   *State Approvals*

Most states require public utilities doing business in their jurisdictions to receive approval from the state commission prior to any merger or acquisition. To date, few states have explicitly developed a merger approval policy for restructurings in the newly competitive electric industry.[90] The usual approach is for states to ask whether the merger is "in the public interest" by looking at whether the benefits exceed the costs. State regulators are typically concerned that the merger not result in a loss of state jurisdiction over the new entity, that the merger result in real economic benefits to customers (lower rates for example), and that the merger not jeopardize economic development or utility-related jobs in the state.[91] Commentators suggest that state regulators should also be particularly concerned that mergers not create excess capacity and energy which can be used to prevent new entrants into electricity markets. ॐ

---

[90] *But see,* Robert J. Graniere and Robert E. Burns, MERGERS AND ACQUISITIONS: GUIDELINES FOR CONSIDERATION BY STATE PUBLIC UTILITY COMMISSION (National Regulatory Research Institute, ed. 1996), which propose some presumptions states might adopt for merger reviews.

[91] *Id.* at 23.

CHAPTER THIRTEEN

Alternative Energy Sources

by Suedeen G. Kelly

I. INTRODUCTION

Although America has diversified its mixture of energy sources, as we approach the year 2000, almost all of the United States' energy continues to come from the traditional sources of coal, petroleum, natural gas, hydro-power, and nuclear power. In 1996, fossil fuels were the source of 80% of the energy produced in the U.S. and 85% of the energy consumed while hydro-power and nuclear power, together, constituted 15% of production and 12% of consumption. Twenty-three percent of the energy consumed in the U.S. in 1996 was imported, primarily in the form of petroleum and natural gas.[1] These traditional sources of energy accounted for 99.8% of the electricity generated in the U.S. during the same year.[2]

Traditional sources of energy, particularly fossil fuels, are subject to uncertainties of supply, fluctuations in global markets, and changes in federal policy that render them vulnerable as long-term reliable fuels sufficient to meet the nation's energy needs. The eventual scarcity of fossil fuels will undoubtedly increase prices. Additionally, all traditional energy sources cause some harm to the human and natural environment. There are pollutant effects associated with all fossil fuels, and the energy industries have given rise to some of the most blatant examples of pollution in American society. Today, energy pollution is a worldwide problem. Acid rain and the "greenhouse" effect promoting global warming may demand serious international pollution control. Finally, nuclear power growth has stopped in the wake of the Three Mile Island accident and the Chernobyl disaster. All of these factors create an interest in displacing these traditional sources of energy and particularly in decreasing U.S. dependence on foreign petroleum. There are a variety of old and new technologies that constitute

---

[1] Energy Information Administration (EIA), ANNUAL REPORT TO CONGRESS 1980, Vol. 2, p. 5; and EIA/Coal Industry Annual 1996. *See also* Introduction to this Text, pp. 7-8.

[2] EIA, ANNUAL REPORT—COAL EIA FORM—759. *See also* Introduction to Text, p. 4.

"alternatives" to the traditional sources of energy. They presently amount to a small percentage of current U.S. energy production and consumption. The most common alternative energy source is renewable resources, such as solar and geothermal energy. Renewable resources accounted for 5% of the energy produced and 3% of that consumed in the U.S. in 1996. Additional alternatives to traditional energy sources include conservation, fuel cells, and synthetic fuels.

Solar energy, a renewable resource, is generally described to include all sources that gain some energy from the sun. This includes not only direct solar energy, such as passive or active solar heating, but also wind energy produced by varying air temperatures, ocean thermal energy created by differing ocean temperatures, and biomass energy, such as wood heat or gasohol, since the sun is involved in photosythesis. This chapter will discuss each of these forms of solar energy as distinct renewable resources. Geothermal energy, also a renewable resource, is created by heat generated from within the earth in the form of drysteam, hot water, and hot rocks.

Conservation, while not a direct source of energy, is considered an alternative source because it reduces the consumption and depletion of primary energy sources. Conservation includes not only a reduction in energy dependence but also the more efficient use of energy. Energy efficiency can be realized through such things as improved machinery design, co-generation of energy through the use of steam or heat created by one activity to power another, or elimination of heat waste through the use of insulation.

Fuel cells are electrochemical devices that generate DC electricity similar to batteries. However, unlike batteries, they take their energy from a fuel that is supplied from the outside. The best fuel for many types of fuel cells is hydrogen but a variety of other fuels—methanol, ethanol, natural gas, and liquefied petroleum gas—can be used. Energy can also be supplied by biomass, wind and solar energy. While not a primary source of energy, fuel cells produce electricity more efficiently than conventional methods of power generation and, thus, are considered an alternative energy source.

The last category of alternative energy sources discussed in this chapter is synthetic fuels, or "synfuels." Synfuel energy is essentially the creation of a fuel resembling natural gas or petroleum from something other than traditional oil and gas resources. Synfuels include the conversion of coal (both gasification and liquification), oil shale, and tar sands.

While the cost of production of some of these alternatives is higher than traditional energy sources, the advancement of technologies typically lower costs. Additionally, even though some of the alternative sources can only be used in on-site, small-scale operations, such applications have the potential to eliminate or reduce the need for large-scale transmission and distribution systems. Economic, environmental, or political changes may push these technologies to the forefront within the foreseeable future.

II. FUEL CYCLES OF ALTERNATIVE ENERGY RESOURCES

A. Renewables

1. *Solar Energy*

Solar energy is probably the most widely publicized alternative energy source. Solar enthusiasts note that energy from the sun was responsible millions of years ago for the photosynthetic process that provided the raw materials for what are now the fossil fuels. From this perspective, solar energy provides more than 90% of current energy resources and, even more fundamentally, without sunlight life on the planet would not exist. Further, although it is not counted in most energy use calculations, the world's population receives much free heat, light, wind, and drying capacity from the sun.

Legal definitions of solar energy have included matters not intuitively thought of as being solar. The Solar Energy Research Development and Demonstration Act of 1974, defines solar energy in Section 3(1) as including both direct and indirect solar sources. The direct uses of the sun's rays are clearly solar and primarily include photovoltaic cells, solar thermal systems, and solar buildings. Indirect solar sources include biomass energy which relies on the sun's role in the photosynthetic process and wind energy and ocean thermal energy derived from differential solar heating of the land and water surfaces. These indirect solar sources of energy will be discussed as distinct renewable resources.

The energy available from the sun is enormous. The problem is to use a reasonable part of it. In the United States, solar energy falls on the surface, day in and day out, at an average rate of about 4.76 kilowatt-hours (kWh) per square kilometer per day or 1.7 billion kWh per square kilometer per year. If all the energy from the sun that reaches the United States were harnessed, it has been estimated that it would provide about 500 times the nation's present energy demands.

Photovoltaic (PV) solar cells convert sunlight directly to electricity. A solar cell is based upon the long-known principle that many materials, especially semi-conductors, produce free electrons when photons from sunlight strike them. These free electrons flow, thereby producing an electric current, in an electric field that is formed by a junction of two different materials. The usual solar cell is made of silicon and a layer of another substance, such as phosphorous. When exposed to sunlight, its electrons are excited and migrate toward the junction between the two. On arrival, they generate direct current (DC) electricity. The electrical current produced is proportional to the area of the cell. For greater power levels, cells are interconnected. Photovoltaic systems come in a near infinite number of sizes, ranging from a single solar cell to power a calculator or a single module (containing multiple cells) to power a light, to multiple modules to power a water pump or home, to large arrays of modules to provide industrial-scale power.

The majority of PV cells in use today are crystalline silicon flat plate collectors. These utilize single crystal silicon (more efficient but more expensive) and polycrystalline silicon, (cheaper but less efficient). The crystals are grown or cast from molten silicon and then sliced into the appropriate size and shape. The cells are then assembled onto a flat surface. Research continues into improving silicon solar cells and developing other materials.

Another kind of PV cell, the "thin film" system, is less expensive than crystalline but also less efficient. It is manufactured by placing a thin layer of PV material onto glass or metal. The silicon used includes the amorphous type rather than crystalline. Yet another manner of PV cell use involves "concentrators." Lenses or reflectors are configured in such a way as to focus sunlight on the cell and thus increase the amount of electricity it produces.

Although technology is improving, the cost for large scale generation of electricity by solar cells remains high. The manufacture of polycrystalline PV cells, for example, still has a way to go to achieve profitable efficiency as it typically produces cells with only 12% to 15% efficiencies. In 1975, the industry could produce photovoltaic cells for $30,000 a kilowatt. In 1987, the city of Austin installed a unit for peak power generation at a cost of $10,000 a kilowatt, approximately double the cost of conventional generation at that time.

While solar cells can be utilized in any area of the country and even on overcast days, the power output is maximized by keeping the PV array pointed at the sun. The amount of solar energy received in a given area over time varies daily and seasonally because of the changing relation of the earth to the sun. Single-axis tracking of the array will increase the energy production in some locations by up to 50% for some months and by as much as 35% over the course of a year. The greatest benefit comes in the early morning and late afternoon when the tracking array will be pointing more nearly at the sun than a fixed array. Generally, tracking is more beneficial at sites between 30° latitude North and 30° latitude South. For higher latitudes the benefit is less because the sun drops low on the horizon during winter months. Thus, to maximize effectiveness, it is necessary to have accurate solar data for the locale.

Not all solar energy generates electricity. Solar thermal systems operate by transferring solar generated heat to a fluid. The heated fluid is then used for any number of purposes. A relatively simple solar thermal system uses water, or water with anti-freeze in it, which is piped through a box having a glass front. The heat in this liquid is transferred to another liquid in another set of pipes and is employed for hot water use or to run through a radiator for space heating. Solar water heaters are the most common use of solar energy by home owners and are available and relatively easy to retrofit to existing homes.

A more complex mode of solar thermal energy involves concentrators. There are three basic system designs, the trough, power tower, and dish systems. Trough systems use parabolic reflectors in a trough configuration and are the most mature solar thermal technology. Troughs concentrate the sun up to 100 times onto a fluid-filled receiver tube positioned along the line of focus in the trough. Heat can be produced efficiently up to 400°C (750°F) and used as heat or to generate electricity by providing heat for boilers that power steam turbine generators. Troughs are modular, and can be grouped together to produce more heat or power.

Power tower systems, also called central receivers, use heliostats (highly reflective mirrors) to track the sun and reflect it to a central receiver atop a tower. The sunlight is concentrated on the receiver up to 800 times its normal intensity. The sun heats a fluid in the receiver typically to temperatures up to 650°C (1200°F). The heated fluid is converted to steam that drives a turbine to produce electric power. The most noteworthy example of this system is Solar Two, a 10 megawatt utility-scale solar power plant near Barstow, CA. It cost $50 million to build and consists of 2,000 computer-controlled metal and glass heliostats spread over 95 acres. These direct sunlight at a 300-foot tower, on whose top rests a tank containing molten salt. The salt is heated to over 1000°F and pumped through a steam-generating system. The salt retains enough warmth so that its energy can be transformed into electricity up to 12 hours after sunset. Scientists are hopeful that such plants can eventually produce from 30 to 200 megawatts.

Dish systems use parabolic reflectors in the shape of a dish to focus the sun's solar rays onto a receiver mounted above the dish at its focal point. The solar energy ultimately heats a fluid powering a small engine/generator mounted at the focal point of the dish. Operating at about 800°C (1500°F), a single dish module can generate up to 50 kilowatts of electric power. Like trough systems, dishes can be grouped together to produce more power. Dishes achieve the highest performance of all concentrator types in terms of annual collected energy and peak solar concentration.

Solar building technology includes both passive and active systems to provide heating, cooling, and daylight for buildings. A passive system achieves the flow of heat by natural means such as radiation, conduction, and convection. An active system uses mechanical means, such as a fan or pump, to distribute the heat. Passive systems control the transmission of solar radiation through glass, for use as lighting, and by storing heat within the building mass, for use in space heating. Passive solar buildings are well-insulated, have south-facing glass, and thick floors to absorb heat. Double or triple pane windows are used for greater insulation and the space between panes can be filled with argon to prevent heat loss. Another technique of passive heating is the thermal storage wall. The wall may be of massive masonry painted black on the outside to absorb solar radiation. Space heating is accomplished by radiation and convection from inside the wall. In other cases, the wall may be double with the outer wall of glass or black painted masonry. Air circulating within this double wall is thus heated and heats the building. Water may also be stored within the double wall to retain the heat.

In addition to these primary types of solar energy, another way to use solar energy is solar cooking. There are two basic kinds of solar cook stoves. One, more complicated and expensive, is a wooden box with a glass top and a mirrored lid. Food is placed in a black pot underneath the glass. The second, simpler and cheaper, consists of a mirrored parabolic panel. A black pot is placed at the panel's focal point and covered with plastic.

2. Wind Energy   Most promising

Wind is an indirect form of solar energy caused by differential heating of the earth's surface and by the earth's rotation. Wind flow patterns are modified by the earth's terrain, bodies of water, and vegetative cover. This wind flow, or motion energy, when "harvested" by wind turbines can be used to generate electricity. Windmills have been useful for hundreds of years, primarily as a water pump to bring water from underground wells to the surface. The use of wind systems to generate electricity did not come into being until the early twentieth century.

Conversion of wind energy to electricity is simple. A set of turbine blades, like airplane propeller blades, driven by the wind turns a mechanical shaft coupling to a generator that then produces electricity. Wind turbines are often grouped together into a single wind power plant, also know as a wind farm, to generate bulk electrical power. Electricity from these turbines is fed into the local utility grid and distributed to customers just as with conventional power plants.

Wind turbines are available in a variety of sizes, and therefore power ratings. The largest machine, such as one built in Hawaii, has propellers that span more than the length of a football field and stand 20 stories high.

It produces enough electricity to power 1,400 homes. A small home-sized wind machine has rotors between 8 and 25 feet in diameter. It stands upward of 30 feet and can supply the power needs of an all-electric home or small business. All electric-generating wind turbines, no matter what size, are comprised of a few basic components: the rotor (or blade), the electrical generator, a speed control system, and a tower. Some wind machines have fail-safe shutdown systems for the event of a mechanical failure.

Wind energy is very abundant in many parts of the United States, but wind speed is a critical factor because the energy in wind is proportional to the cube of the wind speed. Wind resources are categorized by wind-power density classes, ranging from class 1 (the lowest) to class 7. Good wind resources (class 3 and above), which have an average annual wind speed of at least 13 miles per hour, are found along the east coast, the Appalachian Mountain chain, the Great Plains, the Pacific Northwest, and some other locations. North Dakota, alone, has enough energy from class 4 and higher winds to supply 30% of the electricity of the lower 48 states. It is estimated that there is enough wind potential in the U.S. to displace at least 45 quads of primary energy used annually to generate electricity (one Quad, a quadrillion BTUs, is equivalent to the energy produced by 167,000,000 barrels of oil).[3]

Unlike conventional power plants, wind plants emit no air pollutants or greenhouse gases. In 1990, California's wind power plants offset the emission of more than 2.5 billion pounds of carbon dioxide, and 15 million pounds of other pollutants that would have otherwise been produced. There is, however, some concern over the noise produced by the rotor blades and possible interference with television reception. Also, birds are sometimes killed by flying into the rotors.

The major challenge to using wind as a source of power is that it is intermittent and it does not always blow when electricity is needed. Wind cannot be stored, unless batteries are used, and not all winds can be harnessed to meet the timing of electricity demands. Good wind sites are often situated in remote locations far from areas of electric power demand. Finally, wind resource development may compete with other uses for the land and those alternative uses may be more highly valued than electricity generation. However, wind turbines can be located on land that is also used for grazing or even farming.

---

[3] D.L. Elliot, L.L. Wendell, and G.L. Gower, *U.S. Aerial Wind Resource Estimates Considering Environmental and Land-Use Exclusions*, presented at Windpower '90 Conference, Washington, D.C., September 1990.

3. Geothermal Energy

Geothermal energy is heat from beneath the earth's surface. Most of the earth's heat resides in the earth's molten core and mantle below the earth's crust at depths presently incapable of being tapped by drilling. However, in certain parts of the world there are areas called "hot spots" where the earth's protective crust is shallow and access to geothermal heat by man is possible. In some areas molten or very hot rock is located very close to the earth's surface. Hot springs and geysers, like Old Faithful in Yellowstone National Park, are areas where geothermal energy has actually reached the earth's surface. In other areas, wells can be drilled from the surface into the geothermal reservoir. In the United States, including Alaska and Hawaii, as much as 1.3 million acres of land have potential for power production from geothermal energy.

Depending on the geology, geothermal energy may be available as dry steam, hot water, or hot rocks. Dry steam resources are the easiest to find and use, and are the least expensive to exploit. Wells are drilled into the steam reservoir. Steam then travels up the well pipe directly into a turbine that runs a generator. Once the steam is used, it is piped into a condenser, converted to water and returned by another pipe to the reservoir.

The problem with steam systems is basically threefold: First, some of the condensed water often contains boron and hydrogen sulfide and, since excess heat must be disposed of on the surface, there are environmental concerns. Second, the dry steam system is inefficient. It requires significantly more energy from the reservoir to produce one kilowatt in contrast to fossil fuel plants. Third, the number of sites are limited and are smaller than the other geothermal resources.

Hot water geothermal deposits are larger and some twenty times more abundant than dry steam deposits. Although there are no commercial hot water power plants in operation in the United States, the basic technology exists to tap this resource. The problems again are the disposal of mineral rich hot water and efficiency. Hot water is at a lower temperature than dry steam, which produces low conversion efficiencies and requires, in turn, very large turbines.

Hot rock systems have a larger power potential than the other two systems. Unlike the other systems, which depend upon steam or hot water from natural underground reservoirs, hot rock systems can be located anywhere. In a hot rock system two wells are drilled to form a closed-loop system from the surface to the hot rocks. Water is injected down one well, superheated by the hot rocks and, under high pressure, comes back to the surface through the second well to drive steam turbines or provide space heating.

4. Biomass Energy

Biomass is a form of alternative energy technology that includes the use of organic materials such as wood from trees, and agricultural crops such as beets and corn, and waste such as garbage or sewage. Wood may be used as a direct substitute for petroleum to provide residential heating.

Agricultural crops may be grown and converted into usable fuel such as ethane and methane which can be substituted directly for petroleum-based fuels or can be mixed with gasoline to form gasohol. Ethane normally is a colorless gas recovered as a liquid at refineries and natural gas processing plants. However, it may also be derived from agricultural products that contain sugar or starch such as corn, wheat or beets. Ethane's primary use is as petrochemical feedstocks to make chemicals and plastics. Methane is a colorless, odorless flammable gas that forms the major component of natural gas. It can also be derived from a variety of sources ranging from coal to biomass substances such as wood and waste materials (garbage and sewage). One problem with methanol is that it also produces formaldehyde, which the EPA has found to be a probable cancer-causing agent in humans.

Energy production in the form of gas from agricultural and municipal waste is a proven technology. Energy is produced from the action of microorganisms that eat decomposing garbage and sewage and excrete carbon dioxide and methane. The methane gas is collected by covering a site with a clay and soil mix, inserting a pipe into a drill hole and collecting the gas from a valve attached to the pipe at the surface. Many companies already capture and sell methane as a byproduct from the decomposition of materials like food and papers. For example, Brooklyn Union Gas uses methane recovered from the Fresh Kills landfill on Staten Island, New York, to provide heating and cooking gas to 10,000 households. Potentially, bioconversion of waste into energy could produce the usable energy equivalent of up to 3 million barrels of oil a day.

5. Ocean Thermal Energy

Oceans provide two potential alternative sources of energy—ocean thermal energy conversion (OTEC) and wave energy. OTEC is really a form of solar energy since water temperature differences are created by the sun's rays and then utilized to produce energy. In tropical seas the water temperature at the surface and to a depth of 100 feet can be up to 40°F warmer than the water temperature at lower depths. The warmer surface water potentially can be used to vaporize liquid ammonia or freon contained in a piping system connected to a generator. The resulting gas from vaporization turns an electric turbine generator located at the surface. Heat is removed from the gas. The gas is then pumped into the deep or colder water, causing it to liquefy through a condenser and then the cycle is repeated. The electricity produced could be used at the ocean site by industrial facilities located there to use the electricity. It could also be transmitted to shore via electric cable or used to electrolyze water to hydrogen, which would then be shipped to shore by pipeline to be burned like natural gas.

Wave energy has a more limited application than OTEC. Although waves—the natural rise and fall of ocean waters—occur everywhere, their employment for useful energy production is thought to be quite limited. First, wave energy must be utilized near shoreline areas that are configured in a way that maximizes the wave energy and sufficiently focuses the waves on the energy system deployed. The most successful method of harnessing wave energy is by a water tower system. Here, a hollow tower is erected near shore. When a wave arrives on shore, it forces water up inside the tower, displacing air, which passes upward through a turbine at the top of the tower. When the wave recedes, the water in the tower falls, sucking air back into the tower through the turbine. (The turbine is designed to rotate in only one direction.) There are no such wave energy plants in the United States. However, the French and the Norwegians have experimented with small tidal wave power plants. One problem with a wave energy system is that it produces a very disturbing siren-like noise, but technological improvements in reducing the rotor speeds of the turbines could reduce the noise to acceptable levels.

B. Conservation

The term "energy conservation" is not consistently defined. Most people understand energy conservation to mean reduction in energy production and consumption. To some, it means primarily a reduction in dependence on traditional energy sources, especially the fossil fuels. To others, conservation means a change in life style and reduced dependence on all energy. To still others, it means more efficient use of energy and hence reduction in use without major social or economic changes. The most broadly accepted use of the term "energy conservation" implies the wise use of energy, an increased reliance on more plentiful and dependable sources, and the making of certain social and economic changes to minimize the impact of short- and long-range changes in supply. The ultimate aim is to reduce energy consumption while maintaining acceptable social and economic patterns. Thus, conservation is considered an energy source because it displaces the need for other sources.

1. Buildings

A major use of energy in the United States is for heating buildings. This space heating consumes about 16% of all energy produced. If water heating, air conditioning, lighting, cooking, and refrigeration are added, a total of over 20% of energy used in the United States goes into domestic and commercial building uses. For this reason a reduction in energy use in buildings would have a far-reaching effect on conservation efforts.

Many studies have shown that conservation measures taken in new home construction or in retrofitting older homes are economically justifiable. Depending on the part of the country in which the building is located, important conservation measures are the insulation of walls and roofs, the installation of storm windows and automatic thermostats, and the use of tight, leak-free construction throughout the house. As the cost of gas and oil heating rises, there will be increased attention paid to more efficient furnaces in residential buildings. Most experts agree that use of insulated ducting, the use of heat recovery in the stack, and the replacement of pilot lights with electric ignitions could reduce gas consumption of domestic furnaces by as much as one-third. Water heating in buildings consumes significant energy, an indication of why solar water heating has received considerable attention in many parts of the country. Commercial buildings can also reduce their energy consumption using the same general principles that apply to conservation in residences.

2. Transportation

The automobile consumes 13% of all the energy used in the United States. Trucks use another 6%. Transportation used about one-half of all petroleum (domestic and imported) consumed in this country. Of all the energy used for transportation, the automobile used about 50%, trucks about 24%, and air transport about 7%. The sharp increase in gasoline prices throughout the 1970s spurred a trend toward cars that use less fuel. The major technique for reducing fuel consumption was to reduce the weight of the car, which also allowed the use of smaller engines. As fuel use in cars is essentially proportional to vehicle weight, this was far more valuable than attempts to increase the efficiency of gasoline engines. Diesel engines are typically 20 to 30% more efficient than gasoline engines. However, they produce more pollutants, especially nitrogen oxide, create more noise, and are somewhat heavier and more costly. Other forms of transportation such as rail, truck, barge, and airplane are all undergoing studies aimed at reduced energy use. This effort is primarily driven by the high cost of fuel.

3.   Industrial Use

The industrial sector uses about 25% of the energy produced in the Untied States. The major energy consumers are the chemical, iron and steel, and paper industries, followed by industries that support agricultural production. One-third of industrial energy is used in the form of steam, while about one-half is used as heated gases. There is considerable interest in solar energy as a source of heat for low temperature steam and gas generation. High temperature applications require sources other than solar energy.

The cost of energy as a function of industrial production has been slowly declining since World War II. This is due to better technology, increased interest by companies in management of electric consumption, and relocation and new plant development in milder climates. Other efforts to conserve industrial energy use include more efficient processes, recycling (resource recovery), and co-generation, a method of using process steam to create an energy source. Of these, co-generation has perhaps the greatest immediate potential.

Co-generation is the use of a single fuel source such as coal, oil or gas to make sequentially two usable forms of energy, usually electricity and heat. For example, oil or gas is used first in a boiler to fuel a turbine, which produces electricity. The boiler also gives off excess or reject heat in the form of steam and the steam is then used to provide heating. There are two basic types of co-generation facilities depending on the sequence of the process. A topping cycle co-generation facility generates electricity first and then uses the waste thermal energy in some way, usually to provide heating. A bottoming cycle co-generation facility operates in reverse sequence. That is, it produces thermal energy first and then uses the waste heat to generate electricity.

The primary aim of co-generation facilities is conservation of energy. It is the reuse of reject heat that conserves oil or gas. Not all industrial operations benefit equally from co-generation. Process and space requirements or fluctuating energy needs may make co-generation difficult. Co-generation was boosted by the Public Utility Regulatory Policies Act of 1978 (PURPA). PURPA, among other things, created a market for the sale and purchase of electric power produced by certain facilities that meet the statute's requirements as qualifying co-generation or small power production facilities. However, many of the prices established in long-term contracts exceed the current market price of electricity and, therefore, potentially block competition.

Food production, processing, and distribution systems also account for a significant amount of United States energy usage, with food transportation, field equipment, and chemicals (pesticide, fertilizer, container) production using the most. Increased conservation efforts in agriculture are especially directed toward the fertilizer industry and pesticide production. Conservation measures are receiving a great deal of emphasis throughout the United States. Present and anticipated rises in energy costs, concerns over dependability of supply, international marketing competition, and other factors, are causing residential, commercial, industrial, and agricultural energy users to design more energy efficient operations and installations. The wise use of energy is the basis of conservation and is likely to be an important part of our thinking for many years to come.

4.   Limitations on Conservation

It is important to emphasize that conservation is influenced by technological and economic factors. Many of our energy conversion processes operate at far less than 100% efficiency. One unit of coal burned in the plant does not produce one equivalent unit of electricity. Some energy can be saved through the use of a cleaner raw material, a more efficient combustion process, or improved transmission of the electricity. However, present technologies have their efficiency limitations.

Economic factors also influence conservation. An economist's view of waste will consider whether the value of a conserved resource will exceed the full cost of its conservation. The economist may not regard it as wasteful to fail to extract all of the oil and gas that could be extracted from a reservoir by the most advanced technological process. If the return on the production does not pay for the added cost of extraction, the economist denies that waste has occurred. A legislator or regulator, however, may disagree. The same applies to residential energy efficiency. The layperson may regard it as wasteful to allow any heat to escape a home. Conservation would be promoted by insulating, caulking, and weather stripping every dwelling to the maximum degree. However, in many situations the cost of the process may not pay off for the homeowner.

Conservation measures must also consider the rational and irrational preferences of human beings. A mandatory 55 miles per hour speed limit, if enforced, saves gasoline and reduces highway fatalities. However, it will also slow the delivery of goods, persuade some families to fly rather than drive on vacation, and frustrate citizens who regard putting the pedal to the metal as part of the pursuit of happiness.

C.   Fuel Cells

Fuel cells, which convert liquid fuel into electricity through a chemical reaction rather than combustion, have been around for more than 100 years.

But until recently, fuel cells were so expensive that they were practical only for specialized use on space missions. Due to technological and scientific improvements, however, fuel cells now appear to be a serious option for widespread use.

Fuel cells are electrochemical devices that generate DC electricity similar to batteries. However, unlike batteries, they take their energy from a fuel that is supplied from the outside. While hydrogen appears to be the best fuel for many types of fuel cells, a variety of other fuels—methanol, ethanol, natural gas, and liquefied petroleum gas—can also be used. Biomass, wind and solar energy can also supply the energy needed, thus promoting energy diversity and a transition to renewable energy sources. There are several types of fuel cell, each differing in its operating characteristics, temperatures, power densities and, therefore, in the most suitable end uses.

In principle, a fuel cell operates like a battery. Unlike a battery, a fuel cell does not run down or require recharging. It will produce energy in the form of electricity and heat as long as fuel is supplied. A fuel cell consists of two electrodes sandwiched around an electrolyte. Oxygen passes over one electrode and hydrogen passes over the other, generating electricity, water and heat. Hydrogen fuel is fed into the anode of the fuel cell. Oxygen (or air) enters the fuel cell through the cathode. Encouraged by a catalyst, the hydrogen atom splits into a proton and an electron, which take different paths to the cathode. The proton passes through the electrolyte. The electrons create a separate current that can be utilized before they return to the cathode, to be reunited with the hydrogen and oxygen in a molecule of water. A fuel cell system that includes a "fuel reformer" can utilize the hydrogen from any hydrocarbon fuel, including natural gas, methanol, and even gasoline.

Fuel cell automobiles are at an earlier stage of development than battery-powered cars, but could be an attractive alternative. They offer the advantages of battery-powered vehicles but can also be refueled quickly and could go longer between refueling. Since the fuel cell relies on chemistry, not combustion, emissions from this type of system would be much smaller than emissions from the cleanest fuel combustion processes, thereby decreasing the release of "greenhouse" gases.

Proton exchange membrane fuel cells (PEMFC) operate at relatively low temperatures (about 200°F), have high power density, can vary their output quickly to meet shifts in power demand, and are suited for applications, such as automobiles, where quick startup is required. Direct methanol fuel cells (DMFC) are similar to the PEM cells in that they both use a polymer membrane as the electrolyte. However, in the DMFC, the anode catalyst itself draws the hydrogen from the liquid methanol, eliminating the need for a fuel reformer. Efficiencies of about 40% are expected with this type of fuel cell, which would typically operate at a temperature between 120-190°F. Higher efficiencies are achieved at higher temperatures.

The phosphoric acid fuel cell (PAFC) is the most commercially developed type of fuel cell. It is already being used in such diverse applications as hospitals, nursing homes, hotels, office buildings, schools, utility power plants, and airport terminals. PAFCs generate electricity at more than 40% efficiency, and nearly 85% if steam produced by the fuel cell is used for co-generation. This compares to 30% for the most efficient internal combustion engine. Operating temperatures are in the range of 400°F. These cells can also be used in larger vehicles, such as buses and trains.

Another type of fuel cell is the molten carbonate (MCFC), which is able to consume coal-based fuels. MCFC promises high fuel-to-electricity efficiencies. This cell operates at about 1200°F. Also promising is the solid oxide fuel cell (SOFC), which uses a hard ceramic material instead of a liquid electrolyte, allowing temperatures to reach 1800°F. Power generating efficiencies could reach 60% and it is anticipated that the SOFC could be used in big, high-power applications, including industrial and large-scale central electricity generating stations. Long used by NASA, alkaline fuel cells (AFC) can achieve power generating efficiencies of up to 70%. They use alkaline potassium hydroxide as the electrolyte. Until recently, however, they were too costly for commercial applications.

In spite of advances in fuel cell technology, fuel cells are still too expensive for everyday use. The cost for automobiles, which would probably be the biggest users of a cost-effective fuel cell, is roughly 100 times more per horsepower than an internal combustion engine. Running houses on fuel cells is also substantially more expensive than relying on power from conventional utility plants. A big part of the expense is that fuel cells are hand-assembled, mostly by scientists, because there is still no mass market. Components, as well, are expensive. However, fuel cells are beginning to look like a serious contender to conventional power generation technologies and research and development is widespread in the private sector as well as the government.

D. Synthetic Fuels

"Synthetic fuel" is a term covering a number of alternative energy sources. It is commonly referred to as synfuel. The Energy Security Act of 1980 defines synthetic fuel to mean "[a]ny solid, liquid, or gas, or combination thereof, which can be used, as a substitute for petroleum or natural gas (or any derivatives thereof, including chemical feedstocks) and which is produced by chemical or physical transformation (other than washing, cooking, or desulfurizing) of domestic sources of coal, including lignite and peat; shale; tar sands . . .; and water, as a source of hydrogen only through electrolysis." Tar sands include heavy oil resources where the cost, technical, and economic risks make extraction and processing uneconomical without federal financial assistance.

Coal gasification is the most advanced synthetic fuels technology. In this process coal is heated together with steam in a "gasifier." The gasifier causes some of the hydrogen in the steam to join with the carbon in the coal to form methane, the primary ingredient of natural gas. As the carbon to hydrogen ratio in the coal is reduced, by addition of hydrogen and/or removal of carbon, various types of gases and liquids of different properties and heating values are produced. These include low, medium, and high BTU fuel gases and heavy and light liquid fuels.

Coal gasification has certain environmental and distribution advantages, as it removes harmful sulfur, other particulates, and heavy metals to produce a clean burning gas. In addition, there already exists a network of natural gas pipelines to transport the gas to end-users; and coal is widely distributed throughout the United States. However, there are also a number of environmental concerns associated with synfuel production. Sulfur emissions are a primary concern. The disposal of wet ash produced by the coal gasification process is an additional problem. Water consumption and pollution are also major concerns, particularly in the western United States where water is often a scarce resource. Air and water pollution and water consumption are of even greater concern with the production of synfuel from oil shale or tar sands, making these technologies even less attractive.

III. ALTERNATIVE ENERGY MARKETS

The alternative energy sources addressed in this chapter vary but share a common attribute—they are not widely available presently to energy markets. There are several reasons for their lack of general availability. First, there are significant technological impediments to the full development of particular alternatives. Second, many alternatives are not financially feasible because traditional energy sources continue to be less expensive. Thus, alternative energy markets tend to be small-scale with the energy being produced and used locally. Examples are photovoltaic cells used on-site for electricity, windmills constructed on farms and ranches, and conservation efforts undertaken in a particular facility. There are, however, more and more alternative energy markets producing energy on a larger-scale, such as large wind farms in California. Following is a summary of the current state of supply, demand, and cost of the various alternative energy sources as well as the future prospects for each.

A. Renewables

1. Solar Energy

All life on earth is supported by the sun, which produces an amazing amount of energy. On any given day the solar radiation varies continuously from sunup to sundown and depends on cloud cover, sun position, and content and turbidity of the atmosphere. The atmosphere is a powerful absorber and reduces the solar power reaching the earth at certain wavelengths. Only a very small percentage of the sun's energy strikes the earth but, even so, it is still more than enough to provide all our needs.

The solar energy market is currently the world's second fastest growing energy source. Since 1990, the average growth rate has been 16% per year. Solar markets are even expanding at ten times the rate of the oil industry. Sales of solar cells alone have increased more than 40% in 1997.[4] Solar energy has the advantage of being plentiful, non-polluting, and reliable. However, there are also disadvantages such as the current high cost, space needed, and legal restraints.

In this country and in Europe, environmental concerns offer a paramount reason for pursuing solar options. The Kyoto Protocol calls for the U.S. and the European Community to reduce emission of greenhouse gases.[5] Switching from fossil fuels to readily available and renewable energy sources such as solar would help accomplish this. Today, powering the typical American household produces 23,380 pounds of greenhouse gases.[6] Placing a million U.S. homes on solar energy would eliminate 5 million tons of carbon dioxide per year.[7]

---

[4] *See Solar Power Markets Boom*, WORLDWATCH INSTITUTE PRESS BRIEFING, July 16, 1998.

[5] *See* U.N. REPORT OF THE CONFERENCE OF THE PARTIES ON ITS THIRD SESSION, HELD AT KYOTO FROM 1 TO 11 DECEMBER 1997—ADDENDUM—PART TWO: ACTION TAKEN BY THE CONFERENCE OF THE PARTIES AT ITS THIRD SESSION, Article 3, Clause 3; Annex B (1998).

[6] *See* James Udall, *Global Climate Change Mitigation Can Start at Home*, SOLAR TODAY, November/December 1998) (visited Feb. 3, 1999) <http://<www. sustainablebusiness.com/insider/jan--/1-climate.cfm>.

[7] Dep't of Energy, *Vice President Gore Announces $2,000 Solar Tax Credit* (visited Feb. 3, 1999).

On June 27, 1997, Secretary of Energy Federico F. Peña outlined a "Million Solar Roofs Initiative."[8] This initiative calls for the Department of Energy to spearhead an attempt to install one million solar energy systems on the roofs of buildings and homes across the U.S. by the year 2010. Federal and state programs, local communities, businesses and utilities will all be employed in an effort to increase the use of such systems. The federal government alone owns more than 500,000 rooftops and, for its part, can rely on Executive Order 12902 (1994), which urged the purchase of solar systems for federal buildings. The initiative will also involve federal grant programs in the Environmental Protection Agency and Departments of Commerce, Defense, and Energy. Participation will also include eight federal lending programs overseen by the Small Business Administration, the Department of Agriculture, and the Department of Housing and Urban Development.

There are numerous examples of solar energy projects across the country. Sun Power Electric of Boston, MA (a non-profit organization), in December, 1998, dedicated 60 of the 156 PV panels that will comprise a 50 kW system. The energy generated is sold to consumers who wish to switch their electricity usage from fossil fuels to renewables.[9] In 1995, the EPA installed a solar thermal system to meet the hot water needs of its twelve-story headquarters in Washington, D.C. The system saves 33,000 kWh and $3,000 per year, along with 22,000 pounds of greenhouse gases.[10] CIA Headquarters in Langley, Virginia uses a solar water heating system, passive solar heating, and photovoltaic cells.[11]

Although the cost of energy produced by photovoltaic systems continues to drop, kilowatt-hour for kilowatt-hour, the cost of PV energy is still generally higher than energy bought from a local utility company. Also, the initial cost of PV equipment is higher than an engine generator. Yet, there are many applications where a PV system is the most cost-effective long-

---

[8] *See* Dep't of Energy, *Peña Outlines Plan to Send Solar Sales Through the Roof* (June 27, 1997) (visited Feb. 3, 1999) <http://www.eren.doe.gov/millionroofs/press.html>.

[9] *See* Dep't of Energy, *Power Starts to Flow at First Solar Electric Plant Built for Deregulated Market Announces Sun Power Electric* (Dec. 10, 1998) (visited Feb. 3, 1999) <http://www/eren/gov/greenpower/sol_ma_1298_pr.html>.

[10] *See* Dep't of Energy, *EPA Helps Protect the Environment by Using Solar Hot Water* (visited Feb. 3, 1999) <http://www.eren.doe.gov/femp/newsevents/femp_focus/apr96_epa.html>.

[11] *See* National Renewable Energy Laboratories, *CIA Headquarters Complex: A Renewable Energy Assessment* (visited Feb. 3, 1999) <http://www.nrel.gov./femp/cia_headquarters.html>.

term option. This is particularly true if the application is in a remote location where accessing an electrical grid is infeasible or expensive. In that case, there are many cost advantages to a PV system. A well-designed system will operate unattended for more than 20 years and requires minimum maintenance since there are no moving parts. Other advantages include the fact that it is modular (allowing easy expandability); there is no cost to supply and store conventional fuels since solar energy is delivered free; and PV systems do not create pollution or waste products.

PV systems have proven a reliable source of power in an ever-growing number of applications. Lighting is one common use for these systems. Cost-effective applications of lighting powered by PVs include small garden lights, street lights, lighting for recreational areas, highway signs, warning signs and signals, and businesses and homes both in the developed and developing world. PVs are ideal and commonly used for water pumping because water can be pumped into a storage tank during daylight hours, then distributed by gravity whenever it is needed. PV systems commonly pump water for remote livestock watering tanks, and in the developing world, entire village water supplies are powered by PVs.

An interesting low-tech version of the dish-type solar thermal system is currently operating in Gujarat, India. Two shallow dishes roughly 15 feet in diameter beam light into a simple structure where the energy is used to heat water and cook for over 250 persons each day.[12] Another, somewhat modified low-tech version is underway at San Juan Pueblo, New Mexico. The pueblo uses a solar oven which has reflecting panels arranged in a bowl-like pattern so as to focus sunlight on the oven itself.[13] San Juan Pueblo also has an interesting example of a solar building. A village co-operative is drying, packaging, and selling fruits and vegetables grown on the pueblo. The drying process includes a 1,200 square-foot greenhouse to which a black floor was added, resulting in internal temperatures that reach 120-140°F. If solar cooking can be successfully propagated throughout the poorest parts of the Third World, the practice could have a significant effect on deforestation, which is a serious problem where wood is used for cooking.

On a larger scale, Solar Two, the "power tower" solar thermal power plant in Southern California, was inaugurated in June 1996 and is scheduled to produce power through 1999. During this time, Solar Two will undergo continuous testing and evaluation. By testing Solar Two in a power production setting, engineers can increase confidence in the reliability and

---

[12] *See* <http://www.accessone.com/~sbcn/images/gujarat1.jpg>.

[13] *See Past and Future Meet in San Juan Pueblo Solar Project* (visited Feb. 12, 1999) <http://www.accessone,com/~sbcn/sanjuan1.html>.

cost of future commercial power towers. Using the experience of Solar Two, U.S. industry can position itself to take advantage of what DOE and the International Energy Agency predict will become a multibillion dollar market for power towers during the next 10 to 20 years.

It appears likely that solar power will become a more and more significant player on the global energy scene in years to come. Deregulation of electricity generation in the U.S. will allow environmentally concerned customers of utility companies the option of paying a modest surcharge for "green" energy of the sort delivered by Sun Power. Disenchantment with nuclear power may grow rather than diminish, leaving solar as an important path to pursue. Technological advances will continue and bring solar ever closer to competitive equality with fossil fuels, for both small and large-scale production and application.

2. *Wind Energy*

Worldwide, wind energy has become the fastest growing energy source, with global installed generating capacity estimated to have grown by 35% during 1998. The world wind industry added 2100 Mw to reach a total of 9600 Mw at year's end, an amount of capacity that is sufficient to generate approximately 21 billion kilowatt-hours of electricity, or enough power for 3.5 million suburban U.S. homes.[14] The most significant growth has occurred in Europe, an example of which is the north German state of Schleswig-Holstein where wind power provides 10% of the region's electricity. In the United States, wind capacity grew by more than 230 Mw in 1998, with major new wind plants built in Minnesota, Oregon, Wyoming and Iowa.

The state of California is the largest producer of wind energy with 16,000 wind turbines and a total generating capacity approaching 1700 Mw. These privately owned wind farms generate more than 3 billion kWh of electricity per year, enough to meet the residential requirements of a city of about 1 million.[15] This combined capacity is equivalent to a medium sized nuclear plant. The incredible amount of wind energy produced in California pales in comparison to the huge untapped potential found on the Great Plains between North Dakota and Texas, and running east from Colorado to Iowa. The states of North Dakota, South Dakota and Texas alone have sufficient wind resources to provide electricity for the entire nation.

---

[14] *See* American Wind Energy Association <http://www.econet.org/awea>.

[15] Gerald R. Nix, National Renewable Energy Laboratory, *Wind Energy as a Significant Source of Electricity*, prepared for the 18th World Energy Engineering Conference, Atlanta, Georgia (November 8-10, 1995) <http://www.nrel.gov/wind/database.html>.

Despite the fact that the U.S. leads the world in wind power potential with the Great Plains alone able to provide one-fifth of its current power needs, several countries throughout the world are far ahead in the development of the resource. There are many reasons for the United States' slow response to developing this resource, the most prominent of which is that, at this time, wind energy is not cost-competitive with electricity produced by coal or natural gas.

Even though the cost of wind power has decreased dramatically in the past 10 years, the technology requires a higher initial investment than fossil-fueled generators. Roughly 80% of the cost is the machinery, with the balance being the site preparation and installation. If wind generating systems are compared with fossil-fuel systems on a "life-cycle" cost basis, however, wind costs are much more competitive with other generating technologies because there is no fuel to purchase. Technological development in design and manufacture of parts is also decreasing mechanical failure rates and, therefore, maintenance costs.

Technology innovations are also being adapted for remote and stand-alone power applications with smaller wind turbines. Hybrid power systems are being developed for non-grid connected generation applications. These village power systems typically use a combination of wind energy, solar, PV cell, battery storage, and conventional diesel generators to supply power for remote, small village communities. In areas without electric utility service and with good wind resources, a single wind turbine can provide electricity at lower costs than diesel generation. Larger "mini-grid" village power systems incorporating multiple wind turbines and other generation sources are often more economical than transmission line extension for communities in remote, but windy regions. Smaller wind turbines are also being explored for application on utility grids to supply power during periods of peak demand, avoiding costly upgrades in distribution equipment.

New, utility-scale, wind projects are being built all around the U.S. today with energy costs ranging from 3.9 cents per kilowatt-hour (at the very windy sites in Texas) to 5 cents or more in the Pacific Northwest. In most areas, 5 cents per kilowatt-hour is not cost-competitive with coal or natural gas produced electricity for the bulk electricity market. However, prices are expected to drop even further over the next 10 years. As a result, wind is expected to be one of the least expensive forms of new electric generation in the next century.

The wind energy industry has grown steadily over the last 10 years and American companies are now competing aggressively in energy markets across the nation and around the world. The industry, in partnership with the U.S. Department of Energy, continues to expand and develop a full range of highly reliable, efficient wind turbines. These new-generation turbines, when installed, perform at 98% reliability in the field, representing remarkable progress since the technology was first introduced in the early 1980s. Up to 5% of the new generating plant capacity in the next decade, an immense amount of electricity in practical terms, could be fueled by wind. Wind power now produces less than 1% of the nation's electricity. The Department of Energy forecasts a 600% increase in wind energy use in the nation in the next 15 years. By the middle of the next century, the wind could be producing 10% of U.S. electricity—as much as hydroelectric dams do today.[16]

3.   Geothermal Energy

Geothermal energy, used primarily in the western U.S., is not expected to contribute much to the national energy supply. Geothermal electricity generation fell to about 14.7 million kWh in 1995 from 17.1 million the prior year. Even though total geothermal electricity generation has been decreasing, there are facilities that continue to produce steady amounts of electricity. Additionally, over the period of 1994 through 1997, over 53,000 geothermal heat pumps were manufactured and shipped worldwide. The U.S. Army's Fort Polk military base in Leesville, Louisiana has the largest installation of geothermal heat pumps in the world. A significant event in the U.S. geothermal industry was the startup, in 1996, of a new 40 Mw power plant in California, Salton Sea Unit IV. The U.S. Department of Energy continues to sponsor research aimed at developing the science and technology necessary for tapping the geothermal energy resource to the greatest extent possible.

Priority is given to projects that address the most challenging hurdles to future commercial development of geothermal energy, namely, cost barriers and environmental concerns. Principle research and development thrusts are aimed at reducing development costs, increasing efficiency of production, cutting maintenance expenses, reducing air and water emissions, producing useful by-products, and reducing water loss. In addition, since the most intense heat and steam is found below the surface

---

[16] *See* U.S. Dep't of Energy Wind Energy Program (visited June 22, 1999) <http://www.eren.doe.gov/wind.html>.

of the earth, practical solutions are being sought to the challenges associated with drilling through many kinds of materials to tap these heat sources.[17]

4. Biomass Energy

The earth's abundant plant life is nature's storehouse of solar energy. Biomass is the largest of the non-hydroelectric renewable energy sectors, with wood being the largest part of biomass energy. While there are many uses for biomass besides fuel, available biomass, in terms of its energy content, is estimated at a total annual production of 2,740 Quads. This level of energy production is approximately eight times the total annual world consumption of energy from all sources (about 340 Quads). At present, the world uses only about 7% of the annual production of biomass.

Biomass energy consumption in the U.S. increased by 3.1% from 1994 to 1995, somewhat more than the 2.6% annual growth rate seen from 1991 to 1994. Excluding hydropower, biomass accounted for 87% of the remaining renewable energy consumption in the U.S. in 1995. Wood pellets, manufactured from finely ground wood fiber, represent a fast-growing biomass fuel market. In the residential and commercial sectors, an increase in residential wood use for heating resulted in a 10% increase in renewable energy consumption in 1995, while pellet production increased by 18%. Fuel ethanol production, however, dropped because of short corn supplies and high prices.

Production of energy from municipal solid waste (MSW) supplies, which grew rapidly during the 1980s as a result of public policy that promoted construction of waste-to-energy (WTE) facilities, has been curtailed during the 1990s. Current environmental policies encourage recycling and require costly pollution control at WTE facilities. The WTE industry is also feeling the competitive pressures of deregulation. Electricity prices are dropping, and waste streams are going to the cheapest disposal option, which in many cases is landfills. The use of landfills as a waste disposal option is likely to increase in the near term; however, it is unlikely that many landfills will begin converting waste to energy because of the unfavorable economics.[18]

---

[17] *See* U.S. Dep't of Energy Geothermal Technologies Program (visited June 22, 1999) <http://www.eren.doe.gov/geothermal/program.html>. *See also* Sandia National Labs Geothermal Technology (visited June 22, 1999) <http://www.sandia.gov/ Renewable_Energy/geothermal/geo.html>. *See also* U.S. Dep't of Energy Renewable Energy 1998: Issues and Trends Executive Summary (visited June 22, 1999) <http://www.eia.doe.gov/cneat/solar.rnewables/rea_issues/rea/rea_issues_sum.html>.

[18] *See* U.S. Dep't of Energy Renewable Energy Annual 1996 (visited June 23, 1999) <www.eia.doe.gov/cneaf/solar.renewables/renewable.energy.annual/hilites.html>.

5. Ocean Thermal Energy

The oceans cover 70% of the earth's surface, making them the world's largest solar energy collector and energy storage system. On an average day, 60 million square kilometers (23 million square miles) of tropical seas absorb an amount of solar radiation equal in heat content to about 250 billion barrels of oil. If less than one-tenth of one percent of this stored solar energy could be converted into electric power, it would supply more than 20 times the total amount of electricity consumed in the United States on any given day.

The economics of energy production today have delayed the financing of a permanent, continuously operating OTEC plant. However, OTEC is very promising as an alternative energy resource for tropical island communities that rely heavily on imported fuel. OTEC plants in these markets could provide islanders with much needed power, as well as desalinated water and a variety of mariculture products.

The most likely markets in which a land-based OTEC plant, coupled with a second-stage desalinated water production system, may be competitive include the small island nations in the South Pacific, Hawaii, Guam and American Samoa. An additional potential market for floating plants, that house a factory or transmit electricity to shore via a submarine power cable, include Puerto Rico, the Gulf of Mexico, and the Pacific, Atlantic, and Indian Oceans. However, OTEC's greatest potential is to supply a significant fraction of the fuel the world needs by using large, grazing plantships to produce hydrogen, ammonia, and methanol.[19]

B. Conservation

The single largest conservation program in the U.S. is a result of the National Energy Conservation Policy Act, as amended by the Energy Policy Act of 1992. As a requirement of the Act, each federal agency is to achieve a 10% reduction in Btu consumption per gross square foot by 1995, a 20% reduction by 2000, and a 35% reduction by 2010. The Federal Government is the largest energy consumer in the U.S., providing energy to approximately 500,000 buildings, comprising over 3 billion square feet of floor area and consuming 1.7% of the total energy used in the U.S. in 1996. In addition to direct energy usage in these buildings, the Government consumes energy

---

[19] *See* National Renewable Energy Laboratory Ocean Thermal Energy Conservation (visited June 22, 1999) <http://www.nrel.gov/otec>.

in vehicles and equipment, including aircraft and naval fuels and automotive gasoline.

As a result of the Federal Energy Management Program, the Government's total net energy consumption in 1996 decreased 23.4% from base year 1985. This total decrease was attributed to a decrease of 24% in buildings and facilities energy usage and a 27.7% decrease in consumption of vehicle and equipment fuels. In 1996, the Government's energy bill was $7.7 billion, representing approximately 0.5% of total Federal expenditures for the year. In real dollars, the Government spent $6.9 billion less than in 1985 with an accumulated savings of almost $44.3 billion.[20] As part of the Federal Energy Management Program, the Government also participates in new technology demonstration projects. These demonstrations, located at various Federal host sites, include cooperative research and development agreements, through which public and private collaborators share the costs and results of the projects.

Secondarily contributing to conservation in the electric power industry was the advent of utility demand-side management (DSM) programs. Electric utility DSM refers to programs implemented by utilities to modify customer load profiles. The Public Utility Regulatory Policies Act of 1978 (PURPA) helped to focus attention on the benefits of "increased conservation of electric energy" and "load management techniques." Responding to the large potential to increase efficiency of energy use, state regulators supported, and utilities implemented, a variety of DSM programs, including programs to reduce energy use, both during peak and off-peak periods. Many of these DSM programs are viewed as energy resources because they capture cost-effective energy savings that would not otherwise be achieved. However, when utility companies lose potential sales as a result of using energy more efficiently, revenues and profits go down, creating an obvious dilemma for the industry. To counteract these effects on the utilities, state commissions had to institute various financial incentive programs. The potential for restructuring in the electric power industry, however, could further affect the utilities' interest in energy savings.[21]

Despite these advances in energy conservation, energy efficiency has not sold well in the marketplace. In 1995, the Energy Information Administration of the U.S. Department of Energy collected information on specific

---

[20] *See* Federal Energy Management Program Overview (visited June 22, 1999) <http://www.eren.doe.gov/femp/aboutfemp/fempoverview.html>

[21] *See* U.S. Electric Utility Demand-Side Management: Trends and Analysis (visited June 22, 1999) <http://www.eia.doe.gov/cneaf/pubs_html/feat_dsm/contents.html>.

conservation features or practices for commercial buildings.[22] They found that, while most commercial buildings have some type of building shell conservation (insulation), lighting and HVAC (heating, ventilation, and air-conditioning) features are, in general, less common. Both HVAC and lighting system conservation features are more often installed in larger than average commercial buildings, where the cost benefits are greater. In addition, information was collected on the use and sponsorship of renewable energy sources or features (besides wood). Those features were: passive solar, photovotaic arrays that convert sunlight directly to energy, geothermal or ground source heat pumps, wind generation, and well water used for cooling. Of those, passive solar was the only type that was found in a sufficient number of buildings to even report data.

Before undertaking research and development of new energy-efficient technologies and design tools, a better understanding needs to be gained of the motivation and forces that lead designers and building owners to adopt energy-efficient measures. Buildings are not built to be energy efficient; they are built or retrofitted to meet the housing or business needs of the occupants and owners. Furthermore, energy is consumed not by buildings, but by the users of buildings, the millions of individuals who turn up thermostats, turn on lights and appliances, and manipulate the environmental conditions of the spaces they occupy. By focusing on individual buildings, sight is lost of opportunities for energy efficiency at community-wide levels. The economies of scale can be lost when individuals must learn about and purchase energy conservation products. Thus, research and development must look at human factors and community systems to address the societal opportunities and barriers to implementing energy efficiency. Social scientists, urban planners, and architects must work closely with community residents, real estate professionals, public health officials, and building developers.

C. Fuel Cells

Fuel cells have been known since the 1800s but only recently have technological and scientific improvements made them an option for wide-spread introduction. Fuel cells are beginning to look like a real contender to conventional power generation technologies and an interesting possibility in the automotive sector. Major energy companies and most vehicle manufacturers have some form of fuel cell development program.

---

[22] *See* Commercial Buildings Characteristics 1995—Energy Conservation Features (visited June 22, 1999) <http://www.eia.doe.gov/emeu/cbecs/char95/conserve.html>.

In the very short term the first applications of fuel cells are in niche markets. Mobile power sources, such as replacements for bulky battery packs are tempting for the military, where cost is not as much of an issue. The Department of Energy is involved in research in molten carbonate and solid oxide fuel cells for stationary power and has invested in demonstration fuel cell power plants that provide heat and power at selected military bases around the country. The first such plant was installed at Vandenberg Air Force Base in California. The efficiency of power output from fuel cells also makes them attractive for IT companies, where power surges have to be protected for data security and equipment preservation.

The Department of Energy further recognized the potential of fuel cells for transportation applications and began development of a phosphoric acid fuel cell (PAFC) powered bus in 1987. By 1990, the proton-exchange membrane (PEM) fuel cell had demonstrated sufficient progress in performance, and thus a light-duty fuel cell vehicle program was launched in partnership with General Motors. Methanol was selected as the fuel because of its availability, simplicity of storage, rapid refueling, high energy density, and ability to be easily reformed. In 1994, DOE initiated programs with industry leaders to develop direct hydrogen-fueled PEM fuel cell propulsion systems. In 1995, a program was initiated to develop a flexible-fuel processor capable of reforming gasoline and other common transportation fuels.

Throughout this short history, DOE has actively supported research on critical fuel cell components and materials to address technical barriers to commercialization for vehicle application. In order for fuel cell propulsion systems to reach their potential, significant technical challenges must be met, including: size and weight reduction, rapid start-up and transient response capability, fuel processing development, manufacturing cost reduction, complete fuel cell system integration, and durability and reliability. Non-technical barriers to fuel cell vehicle commercialization include capital investment for large-scale fuel cell vehicle production, an alternative fuel infrastructure, consumer awareness, industry standards for mass production and servicing, and the lack of safety regulations.[23]

In 1998, for the first time, a fuel cell began supplying all the power to a suburban house in Latham, New York, another sign that the innovation is on the verge of breakthrough as an alternative to traditional energy sources.[24] The device looked more like a home air-conditioning unit than the

---

[23] *See* Office of Transportation Technologies Fuel Cell Program (visited June 22, 1999) <http://www.ott.doe.gov/oaat/fuelcell.html>.

[24] *See* Matthew L. Wald, *Fuel Cell Will Supply All Power to a Test House*, N.Y. TIMES, June 17, 1998, at A28.

small chemical plant that it was. Officials at the Department of Energy, which helped to pay for the test in Latham, say they have high hopes that within a few years thousands of homes will be drawing electric power from fuel cells, cutting pollution and fuel consumption.

Other recent developments in fuel cells include the first commercial sale of a fuel cell for remote power (to the New Jersey Department of Transportation, for a traffic warning sign) and the first street-ready car powered by a fuel cell (built by students at Humboldt State University in California). A scientist at Los Alamos National Laboratory in New Mexico is also experimenting with a tiny cell that converts methanol into enough current to run a laptop computer or a cellular telephone. What has made experts even more optimistic is the progress scientists are making in refinement of the fuel cell's super-thin membranes, which are crucial in facilitating the basic chemical reaction and look like plastic wrap or aluminum foil. W.L. Gore & Company has taken its signature product, Gore-Tex, and put it into the membranes of fuel cells, including the one in Latham, in a way than many researchers say has great promise.[25]

But for all the breakthroughs, fuel cells are too expensive for everyday use. The cost for cars is approximately 100 times more per horsepower than an internal combustion engine. In 1998, Chrysler, for example, estimated that each car-sized fuel cell stack it bought cost $170,000. Plug Power predicts that it can commercialize fuel cells for houses by 2000, at a cost of $3,000 to $5,000 each. Although prototype costs are astronomical, the production of thousands more units will lower costs. Detroit Edison, a part-owner of Plug Power, plans to purchase 30,000 to 50,000 units. A New Jersey company, H-Power, also hopes for mass sales. In 1998, it made what it described as the first unsubsidized, fully commercial sale of a fuel cell, for a trailer-mounted highway sign, the kind than commonly warns of construction ahead. The company plans to supply sixty-five of them for $759,000.[26]

The concern for the commercial future of fuel cells is not whether they can be made to work, but whether they can be made to work cheaply enough.

D. Synfuels

The Energy Security Act of 1980 established the United States Synfuels Corporation to stimulate the commercialization of synthetic oil and gas. The stimulation was to be accomplished through a federal subsidy to

---

[25] *Id.*
[26] *Id.*

private efforts to extract liquids and gas from among other things, coal, oil shale, and tar sands. The original goals of the Synfuels Corporation were to subsidize production of 500,000 barrels a day of synfuels by 1987 and 2 million barrels by 1992. These goals were never met. Funding was slashed over the following years and, on December 12, 1985, the Synfuels Corporation was defunded and abolished. The reasons for the short-lived history of the Synfuels Corporation and the Government's well-intentioned effort to assist in the development of a synthetic fuels industry are complex and wide-ranging. Suffice it to say, the environmental concerns were enormous and the economic viability unlikely. Despite these drawbacks, however, there continues to be limited research into new and improved synfuel technologies, particularly in the area of coal liquefaction and gas-to-liquid technology.

IV. LEGAL

A. Property Rights in Alternative Energy Sources

Whenever a new energy technology is developed, it is introduced into a society that has already defined legal rights in property. At first, the new technology may find existing law not suited to its development. Later, the new technology may influence changes in the law to accommodate its distinctive features. For example, the requirements of oil and gas extraction gave rise to the distinctive body of oil and gas law. Solar energy and geo-thermal energy raise unique problems concerning property rights. Without clear property rights in alternative sources, such as sunlight and wind, development of new technologies and markets will be hindered.

1. Access to Sunlight

Basic solar energy requires direct access to sunlight. Property rights to assure access to the sun are not well developed in the United States. The doctrine of "ancient lights" adopted in England establishes a landowner's right to continued air and sun if the access had been present for twenty years. The use creates a negative easement and gives the landowner the right to prevent others from using their property to block the sun. The doctrine of ancient lights has not been adopted in the U.S.

Americans have invoked nuisance laws to define rights to and protect interests in access to sunlight. In *Fontainbleau Hotel Corp. v. Forty-Five Twenty-Five*, the Fountainbleau Hotel brought suit against a neighboring hotel for building an extension that blocked the sun from the Fountainbleau's pool and sunbathing areas.[27] The court rejected Fountainbleau's assertion of a legal right to the free flow of light and air from adjoining land, noting that "it is universally held that where a structure serves a useful and beneficial purpose, it does not give rise to a cause of action . . . even though it causes injury to another by cutting off the light and air."[28] *Fountainbleau* states the prevailing position in American law. Common law property doctrines do not recognize either an immediate or a prescriptive (acquired after the passage of a specified time) right to forbid a neighbor from a use on his property that blocks your access to sunlight. The American cases that adopted this position and rejected the contrary English doctrine of ancient lights predate the energy crisis of the 1970s, and the recognition of solar energy as a significant energy technology.

Fountainbleau recognizes two ways of obtaining solar access rights. First, landowners can agree to a solar easement that protects the solar user. One of the most common state statutes promoting solar energy recognizes the legitimacy of a solar easement and in some cases specifies the requirements for the easement. The easement can be made a matter of public record and its terms will bind parties that subsequently acquire the covered properties. Second, local zoning ordinances can recognize limits on a landowner's ability to screen the sun from a neighbor's property.[29]

The development of solar energy systems has encouraged judicial rethinking on the subject of solar property rights. *Prah v. Marreti* uses private nuisance theory to give rights to the user of solar energy.[30] In *Prah,* the plaintiff brought suit against his neighbor for building a house which blocked the sunlight from the solar panels which plaintiff had installed on his roof. He invoked a theory of private nuisance law. The Wisconsin Supreme Court held that the reasonable use doctrine of private nuisance law was applicable, and found in the plaintiff's favor because "it will promote the reasonable use and enjoyment of land in a manner suitable to the 1980s."[31]

Comparison of *Fontainbleau Hotel Corp. v. Forty Five Twenty Five, Inc.* with *Prah v. Maretti* reveals that nuisance law might evolve to protect a landowner's reasonable use of the sun from unreasonable interference by

---

[27] 114 So.2d 357 (Fla. Dist. Ct. App. 1959).

[28] *Id.* at 539.

[29] The City of Rio Rancho, New Mexico designated, by municipal ordinance, a residential area as a "solar village." The city requires setbacks and height restrictions to protect solar access. It also specifies construction and design requirements for all buildings to take advantage of solar access for domestic energy generation.

[30] 321 N.W.2d 182 (Wis. 1982).

[31] *Id.* at 191.

another's use of their property. However, reliance on this doctrine means rights are not secure until a court has intervened and balanced the interests of the respective property owners against a reasonableness standard.

Other experiments in assigning rights include actions such as those taken in New Mexico, which statutorily adopted the concept of prior appropriation of solar access as an allocative tool for sunlight in the New Mexico Solar Rights Act.[32] The doctrine of "prior appropriation" means that the first user of the resource has the use of the resource to the exclusion of others. A user initiates his right to sunlight by actual use of the sun before being blocked, or, in some instances, even after being blocked. This type of statute eliminates the "reasonableness debate" of nuisance law, but introduces a notice problem unless the act requires recordation and notice of alleged appropriations.

2. Access to Wind

Uncertainty over right to access to wind is likely to plague development of wind energy. For example, Texas law currently provides no protection for wind rights. Clusters of high technology wind farms are sprouting on the windy hills of West Texas. "Wind rights" are being bought and sold under contract for as much as $2400 per windmill.[33] As these contracts become more common, and prices wind rights continue to rise, Texas lawyers predict litigation over neighbors' blocking the wind.[34]

3. Geothermal Resources

Property rights in geothermal resources could be confused if a property has been severed into mineral and surface estates. Geothermal resources consist of heated rocks (a "dry" system) or heated liquids (a "wet" system). The liquids at least nominally resemble water. Water is generally deemed part of the surface estate.

Geothermal resources, however, have been considered part of the mineral estate because they are recovered and used in a manner similar to other energy sources that are characterized as mineral. *United States v. Union Oil* dealt with whether the United States reserved geothermal resources under a reservation of all minerals required by the Stock-Raising

---

[32] N.M. Stat. Ann. § 47-3-1 (1978).

[33] Susan Warren, *Where the Wind Blows, Landowners Find Profits*, WALL ST. J. (Texas Journal), October 30, 1996, at T1.

[34] *Id.*

Homestead Act.[35] As a matter of statutory interpretation, the desire of Congress to control energy sources influenced the court in deciding the resources were reserved to the United States. *Geothermal Kinetics v. Union Oil* involved a private dispute and reached the same result.[36]

B. Regulation to Move the Country From Traditional to Alternative Sources of Energy

Direct government regulation to stimulate use of alternative sources of energy dates from the energy crisis of the 1970s. The combination of a constrained supply of oil and skyrocketing prices forced the U.S. to recognize its reliance on foreign oil. This recognition and its implications for national security resulted in a spate of new laws encouraging conservation and development of alternative sources of energy. The crisis subsequently abated with the lifting of price controls and discovery of new petroleum supplies. Oil prices dropped and the stimulus for alternative energy abated somewhat. The 1991 Iraqi invasion of Kuwait and the Gulf War provided fresh stimulus for government to intervene and encourage the transition to alternatives. Once again, new federal policies and spending programs resulted. This crisis subsequently abated as well.

The federal government's stimulus for action in the alternative energy arena has been rising prices and constrained quantity of conventional sources. When a market pinch has occurred, the government has stepped up its stimulus, but this urge recedes when the market for traditional sources stabilizes and their prices drop. A stable, low-cost market for traditional energy presents a substantial barrier to development of new alternatives. The barriers imposed by the pre-existing legal system can also be a significant hurdle for use of unconventional energy sources. Over the last twenty-five years, federal, state, and local governments have attempted to adjust both the market and the legal system to support the development of alternative energy.

1. Efforts to Remove Unintended Consequences of Pre-Existing Laws

When new technologies and laws to promote the use of alternative sources have run into pre-existing regulatory schemes that stymie development, conflicts have usually been worked out on a case-by-case basis.

---

[35] 549 F.2d 1271 (9th Cir. 1977).
[36] 141 CAL. RPTR. 879 (Cal. Ct. App. 1977).

a.   Land Use Regulations

Local zoning measures were not prepared to deal with the interest in solar energy for domestic use spurred by the 1970s energy crisis and the resulting development of new technology. In one case from that time, *Katz v. Bodkin*, a homeowner who wanted to install a solar panel on his roof ran afoul of municipal land use ordinances limiting rooftop structures.[37] The Supreme Court of New York found that the Town Zoning Board of Appeals' refusal to approve a building permit for the homeowner was arbitrary, capricious, and contrary to both national and state policies concerning encouragement of alternative energy sources. The court chided the town by noting that "it is incumbent upon the zoning agency to adopt an attitude other than an ostrich head-in-the-sand approach, especially when adoption to changing scientific advances follows and complies with national and state interest in energy conservation."[38]

As alternative energy sources become better known, they can develop a legislative constituency that is able to promote their development through the regulatory process. Occasionally, laws will exempt alternative energy sources from the normal regulatory process. An example is an ordinance amendment to exclude solar equipment from the prohibition of rooftop structures. Several states have enacted such legislation for the development of solar energy.

b.   Other Laws

New alternative energy laws themselves have at times resulted in unintended consequences for development of these resources.

For example, a waste-to-energy plant may seem an ideal way to kill two birds with one stone, but such plants have run into unexpected statutory hurdles. Chicago operates the Northwest "Waste-to-Energy" plant, which is a municipal incinerator that burns solid waste, recovers energy, and in the process creates MWC (municipal waste combustion) ash. The plant burns about 350,000 tons of waste per year, producing energy that is subsequently used by the facility and sold to other energy users. The incineration generates about 140,000 tons of MWC ash per year. The city then disposes of the ash—in landfills licensed to accept only non-hazardous waste. In 1988, the Environmental Defense Fund (EDF) sued the city to stop this practice.

---

[37] 1 SOLAR L. RPTR. 495 (N.Y. Sup. Ct. 1979).
[38] *Id.* at 501.

EDF argued that the MWC ash was sufficiently toxic to be regulated as a hazardous waster under Subtitle C of the Resource Conservation and Recovery Act.[39] Subtitle C requirements are more stringent than those for non-hazardous waste. The Supreme Court agreed that the ash should be regulated as a hazardous waste under Subtitle C, even though the parent waste (household and non-hazardous industrial/commercial waste) was not itself hazardous under EPA's definitions. The issue boiled down to the interpretation of Section 300(i) of RCRA,[40] which attempted to clarify an earlier definition of the household waste exclusion. A majority of the Court, in an opinion authored by Justice Scalia, concluded that the statute, on its face, did not intend the generation of hazardous waste to be included in the household waste exclusion.[41] Justices Stevens and O'Connor dissented, noting that the Report of the Senate Committee that recommended the enactment of the amendment clearly stated the purpose was "to clarify the coverage of the household waste exclusion with respect to resource recovery facilities recovering energy through the mass burning of municipal solid waste."[42] The majority, however, interpreted the amendment to mean that, while the facility itself was exempt, the ash generated by the incineration and energy generation process, was not. Therefore, the ash, due to its toxic character, must be disposed of at a landfill licensed to accept hazardous waste.

The dissent comments that, while this may make good environmental policy sense, it will also fly in the face of national goals to encourage recovery of energy from municipal wastes, a major concern motivating RCRA's enactment. "Whether these purposes will be disserved by regulating municipal incinerators under Subtitle C and, if so, whether environmental benefits may nevertheless justify the costs of such additional regulation are questions of policy that we are not competent to resolve."[43]

2. Incentives

When alternative sources of energy are more expensive than traditional ones, they generally will not be consumed for their energy value in a competitive market. This resistance can be overcome if the alternatives possess other desirable characteristics that are highly valued by consumers, or consumers are given a valuable incentive to consume them despite their

---

[39] City of Chicago v. Environmental Defense Fund, 511 U.S. 328 (1994).

[40] 42 U.S.C. § 6921(i) (1994).

[41] 511 U.S. 328, 337 (1994).

[42] 511 U.S. 328, 343 (1994) (Stevens, J., dissenting).

[43] *Id.* at 348.

higher price. The federal and state governments have been active over the last twenty-five years in devising incentives to promote alternative energy sources.

a. Monetary Incentives

Government has provided monetary incentives through direct dollar payments and the tax system to promote the research, development and use of alternative energy resources. Direct monetary incentives include subsidies and grants for research of alternative energy technology or for purchase of alternative energy. Less directly, a tax credit or deduction for research or purchase of alternative energy, will influence the economics of energy choices and spur development of alternatives. Monetary incentives skew the market for alternative energy, and that is the purpose of the incentive. An incentive seeks to increase the use of the technology subject to the incentive. If use can be increased to the level where the technology can be mass produced, then the price of the technology will fall. The two objectives of government incentives in the alternative energy area have been to create a demand for it and to accelerate the development of cost-competitive technology for mass-production of alternative energy.

i. Grants or Leases of Government Property

Since the beginning of this country, government has regularly granted or leased its property at less-than-market prices to encourage certain behavior. We have previously examined the opening of the public lands for traditional energy development. The government has adopted this approach to support alternative energy development, too. For example, many attractive geothermal and synthetic fuel deposits are located on federally owned land or on land in which the federal government has reserved a mineral interest. Development of geothermal resources on federal land is governed by the Geothermal Steam Act of 1970.[44] The statute is similar to other federal energy resource leasing schemes in its invitation to the private sector to develop geothermal resources. However, the Act has been a general disappointment, and has not stimulated geothermal production on federal lands due to acreage limitations and competitive bidding requirements.

Other national resources are being devoted to the development of alternative energy. Today, with the end of the Cold War, the National Laboratories of the United States are being redirected from weapons research to research technologies for alternative energy resources. They

---

[44] 30 U.S.C. §§ 1001-27 (1994).

have also been empowered to partner with private entities to develop these technologies.[45] The latter effort has led to the development of cost-sharing plans between the labs and private industry to conduct research under Cooperative Research and Development Agreements, called the CRADA program.

The National Renewable Energy Laboratory (NREL) in Golden, Colorado, devotes its research and development efforts to solar power, wind power, biomass, and geothermal power.[46] Included within NREL are the Solar Radiation Research Laboratory and the National Wind Technology Center. Sandia National Laboratory's Renewable Energy Technologies Division focuses on developing commercially viable technologies based on solar, wind and geothermal resources.[47] Several of the other national laboratories have alternative energy research programs. These include Brookhaven National Laboratory's efforts on energy efficiency, alternative fuels such as methanol, and geothermal;[48] the Pacific Northwest National Laboratory's research on co-generation, energy efficiency, and energy conservation for buildings;[49] and Lawrence Berkeley Laboratory's[50] and Los Alamos National Laboratory's[51] research on fuel cells and batteries.

ii. Tax Credits and Deductions

Tax incentives purposely skew the market for alternative energy sources by trying to bring their costs in line with traditional fossil energy

---

[45] For a comprehensive review of all national laboratory activities, *see,* Dep't of Energy *The United States Department of Energy Laboratories and Facilities* (visited June 24, 1999) <http://www.doe.gov/people/peopnl.htm>.

[46] *See* Dep't of Energy, *NREL at a Glance* (visited June 24, 1999) <http://www.nrel.gov/lab/overview/body.html>.

[47] *See* Sandia National Laboratories, *Renewable Energy Technologies* (visited June 24, 1999) <http://www.sandia.gov/Renewable_Energy/renewable.html>.

[48] *See* Brookhaven National Laboratory, *Department of Applied Science, Energy Science and Technology Division* (visited June 24, 1999) <http://www.das.bnl.gov/est.html>.

[49] *See* Pacific Northwest National Laboratory, *Thermal Energy Storage (TES) Technologies for Utility-Scale and Industrial Applications* (visited June 24, 1999) <http://www.pnl.gov/energy/tes_ext.html>.

[50] *See* Lawrence Berkeley National Laboratory, *Advanced Energy Technology Department* (visited June 24, 1999) <http://eetd.lbl.gov/EAT.html>; and *Building Technologies Department* (visited June 24, 1999) <http://eetd.lbl.gov/EAP/buildings.html>.

[51] *See Los Alamos National Laboratory, Fuel Cell User Facility,* (visited June 23, 1999) <http://ext.lanl.gov/orgs/citpo/DTIN/open/UsrFac/userfac56.html>.

sources, in order to encourage alternative energy development and increased use. Governments have used several different tax credit programs to stimulate alternative energy.

For example, the Department of Energy initiated the "Million Solar Roofs Program" in 1997. The goal of this program is to install a million solar energy rooftop systems by 2010 by partnering with private businesses and local governments.[52] The program includes a 15%, up to $2000, solar tax credit as well as funds to support 25 partnerships with utilities, builders, local governments, and financial institutions.[53]

iii. Tax Penalties

Tax penalties on energy consumption can encourage conservation. Though many industrialized western nations utilize tax penalties, they are not in favor in the United States. President Clinton proposed a modest Btu tax in 1993 that was soundly defeated before it even got to a vote in Congress.[54] However, a 4.3 cent per gallon gasoline tax was passed.[55] The Clinton administration has not pursued tax penalties since its first year, preferring to put its efforts elsewhere to encourage alternatives.

iv. Government Spending Programs

Government spending programs include funding for public and private sector research, development and demonstration projects for alternative energy. The Department of Energy's Office of Energy Efficiency and Renewable Energy enters into private sector partnerships for development and implementation of a variety of alternative energy technologies. Many of the spending programs have been authorized by statute, prompted by the energy crisis of the 1970s. The Solar Energy Research, Development and Demonstration Act of 1974 provided funds for the study of the feasibility of development

---

[52] *See* Dep't of Energy, *Secretary Announces Million Roofs Milestones* (visited June 26, 1999) <http://www.eren.doe.gov/millionroofs/earthday.html>.

[53] For more information on the Million Solar Roofs Initiative, *see* Federal Energy Management Program, *Federal Participation in Million Solar Roofs* (visited June 25, 1999) <http://www.eren.doe.gov/femp/millionroofs/ms-ovw.html>; and *Frequently Asked Questions* (visited June 25, 1999) <http://www.eren.doe.gov/millionroofs/faq.html>.

[54] *See* Alan S. Miller, *Energy Policy from Nixon to Clinton: From Grand Provider to Market Facilitator*, 25 ENVTL. L. 715 (1995).

[55] *See* Richard Williamson, *The Clinton Administration's New Energy Policies*, 2 TULSA J. COMP. & INT'L L. 115 (1994).

of solar energy.[56] The Solar Photovoltaic Energy Research, Development, and Demonstration Act was passed in 1978 to stimulate a market for solar energy through promotion of small power production, favoring tax depreciations and research and development funding.[57] The Resource Conservation and Recovery Act (RCRA) of 1976 authorized funding for the study of the potential of waste to energy conversion.[58] The Geothermal Energy Research, Development, and Demonstration Act of 1974 provided funding to assist exploration of geothermal reservoirs.[59] The Geothermal Energy Act of 1980 tried to overcome barriers to development of geothermal energy on federal lands through a program to provide loans and insurance.[60] The Wind Energy Systems Act of 1980 provides for a research and development program as well as technology application and transfer.[61] The years of the energy crisis were capped with the passage of the comprehensive Energy Security Act of 1980.[62] This legislation encouraged the development of renewables through loans, loan guarantees, purchase agreements, and price guarantees. It included a number of smaller pieces of legislation, including the Biomass Energy and Alcohol Fuels Act,[63] the Renewable Energy Resources Act,[64] the Solar Energy and Energy Conservation Act,[65] and the Geothermal Energy Act.[66]

The overall trend in federal funding for such programs over the last two decades has been downward from its high of $1.3 billion in FY 1979 (influenced by the 1970s' energy crisis).[67] With the subsequent rise in oil supplies and decrease in prices, the priority for and funding of renewables declined throughout the 1980s, reaching a low of $132 million in 1990. Interest in renewables rebounded somewhat after the Gulf War and passage of the bipartisan Energy Policy Act in 1992 during the Bush administration, followed by a strengthened commitment to alternative energy development by the Clinton administration. Funding for renewable energy research and

---

[56] 42 U.S.C. §§ 5551-66 (1994).

[57] 42 U.S.C. §§ 5581-94 (1994).

[58] 42 U.S.C. § 6985 (1994).

[59] 30 U.S.C. §§ 1101-02, 1121-26, 1141-47, 1161-64 (1994).

[60] 30 U.S.C. §§ 1501, 1511-16, 1521-22, 1531, 1541-42 (1994).

[61] 42 U.S.C. §§ 9201-13 (1994).

[62] Pub. L. No. 96-294, 94 Stat. 611 (codified as amended in scattered sections of titles 7, 15, 30, 42 & 50 U.S.C.).

[63] Pub. L. No. 96-294, 94 Stat. 683 (codified as amended in scattered sections of Titles 15 and 42 U.S.C.).

[64] 42 U.S.C. §§ 7371-75 (1994).

[65] 42 U.S.C. §§ 8285-82866 (1994).

[66] 30 U.S.C. §§ 150, 1511-16, 1521-22, 1531, 1541-42 (1994).

[67] *See* Solstice, *Renewable Energy: A New National Outlook?* (visited June 24, 1996) <http://solstice.crest.org/renewables/crs/re/crs2.html>.

development in FY 1996 was $340 million.[68] Although DOE budget propos-
als have consistently requested increased spending levels for their research
and development programs, Congress has continued the downsizing trend,
and even (unsuccessfully) proposed closing the National Renewable Energy
Laboratory in 1996. Congress authorized $251 million for the solar and
renewable energy program in FY 1997 and $268 million in FY 1998.[69]
However, related efforts in market stimulation are carried under various
accounts, such as the Climate Change Technology Initiative, which is funded
separately as part of the Research Fund for America. While the actual total
of federal funds spent on fostering conservation and the use of renewable
energy is therefore greater than it would first appear, it is unlikely to
approach the peak levels of funding of the late 1970s unless oil prices
skyrocket again.

Included in the Department of Energy's budget are a wide variety of
programs to encourage use of alternative energy. The National Energy
Conservation and Production Act of 1976 created the Weatherization Assistance Program (WAP) administered by the Department of Energy.[70] The
WAP still provides grants to states which distribute these and other funds
to local organizations to perform energy audits and install conservation
measures in homes of qualified low-income residents, especially the
elderly.[71] Conservation measures include insulation, caulking and weather-
stripping, and increasing heating and cooling efficiency. The Department of
Energy reports that over 5 million homes have been weatherized under this
program using federal and leveraged funds, with an average energy savings
of 18% and a favorable cost-benefit ratio of 1.6.[72]

Title XII of the Energy Policy Act of 1992 establishes additional spending programs for renewable energy.[73] Included is the Renewable Energy
Advancement Award program.[74] This program recognizes developments in

---

[68] *Id.*

[69] *See* Office of Management and Budget, *Appendix, Budget of the United States Government, Fiscal Year 2000, Energy Programs* (visited June 25, 1999) <http://frwebgate.cgi?WAISdocID=3785128791+1+0+0&WAISaction=retriev>.

[70] *See* Dep't of Energy, *History of the Weatherization Assistance Program* (visited June 25, 1999) <http://www.eren.doe.gov/buildings/weatherization_assistance/history.html>.

[71] *See* Dep't of Energy, *DOE Weatherization Assistance Program* (visited June 25, 1999) <http://www.eren.doe.gov/consumerinfo/refbriefs/la3.html>.

[72] *See* Dep't of Energy, *Weatherization Assistance Program Fact Sheet* (visited June 25, 1999) <http://www.eren.doe.gov/buildings/weatherization_assistance/fact-sheet.html>.

[73] 42 U.S.C. §§ 13311-13317 (1994).

[74] 42 U.S.C. § 13313 (1994).

practical applications of biomass, geothermal, hydroelectric, photovoltaic, solar thermal, ocean themal, and wind technologies with cash awards. The Act also calls for development of a comprehensive database and information dissemination system,[75] study of tax incentives,[76] and a comprehensive technology transfer program that encourages development of foreign and domestic markets for United States renewable energy technology and provides financial assistance to United States firms in support of market development.[77]

As mentioned previously, President Clinton established the Million Solar Roofs Initiative in 1997 to further stimulate the market for solar energy technology by providing tax credits to encourage the installation of solar rooftops systems on buildings. The Initiative also provides technical assistance grants and commits the federal government to install solar systems on 20,000 federal buildings by 2010, through the Federal Energy Management Program.[78] The Department of Energy awarded $5 million in grants under this program in 1998.[79] In April 1999, Energy Secretary Bill Richardson announced the award of $600,000 in grants to 18 partnerships.[80] That money will be leveraged with private funds to support the installation of a minimum of 500 solar systems per partnership. The total number of partnerships to date is 36, bringing the total number of solar roof systems committed to 900,000.[81]

Fuel cells are also a focus of the Department of Energy. The Department is helping to fund a demonstration project in Latham, New York, where a refrigerator-sized fuel cell is supplying all the power to a suburban home.[82] However, the private sector is in the forefront of development of fuel cells for vehicles, with DaimlerChrysler and a Toyota-General Motors partnership both pursuing marketing within five years.[83]

---

[75] 42 U.S.C. § 13315 (1994).

[76] 42 U.S.C. § 13314 (1994).

[77] 42 U.S.C. § 13316 (1994).

[78] *See*, Dep't of Energy, *Million Solar Roofs: Frequently Asked Questions* (visited June 25, 1999) <http://www.eren.doe.gov/millionroofs/faq.html>.

[79] *See* Dep't of Energy, *Press Release: Sunny Day for Million Solar Roofs* (visited June 22, 1999) <http://www.doe.gov/html/doe/whatsnew/pressrel/pr98052.html>.

[80] *See* Dep't of Energy, *Press Release: Secretary Announces Million Roofs Milestones* (visited June 26, 1999) <http://www.eren.doe.gov/millionroofs/earthday.html>.

[81] *Id.*

[82] *See* Matthew L. Wald, *Fuel Cell Will Supply All Power to a Test House*, N.Y. TIMES, June 17, 1998, at A28.

[83] *See* Jeffrey Ball, *To Define Future Car, GM, Toyota Say Bigger is Better*, WALL ST. J., April 20, 1999, at B4.

The Wind Energy Systems Act of 1980 established a research and development program to increase the use of wind energy systems as a source of electricity.[84] The Act calls for federal assistance in research, development, and technology application. Although funding for wind systems research and development within the Department of Energy has fallen short of requested amounts, the budget for FY 97 was $29 million, and for FY 98 was $33 million. This money was primarily used to support wind turbine efficiency research.[85]

The Energy Security Act of 1980 established the Synfuels Corporation to encourage development of synthetic oil and gas.[86] Federal subsidies in the form of loans, price guarantees, purchase agreements and joint ventures were provided. The Corporation's initial budget was $24 billion, but was eventually slashed to $8 billion. Because synfuels are economically non-competitive with conventional oil and gas, there was little pressure to develop synfuels, and the Synfuels Corporation was eventually abolished. States have funded research and development of alternative energy sources as well. With the advent of electricity deregulation and rate re-structuring, numerous states have taken the opportunity to enact "wire charges." Such charges are a tax on consumption of electricity that, balanced against the expected decrease in costs with greater competition, are not expected to raise electricity prices, but will provide additional moneys to be used to fund research and development of renewable energy sources.

b.   Market Creation

Government has also "created a market" for alternative energy by requiring itself and public utilities to consume energy specifically from alternative sources. The Public Utility Regulatory Policies Act of 1978 (PURPA) required utilities to purchase power generated by "qualifying facilities (QFs)," primarily small, independent generators of power that used alternative sources of energy, such as solar, wind and biomass.[87] The objective of PURPA was to stimulate a market for alternative sources of energy. It did so, although it has had some unanticipated consequences. PURPA required utilities to purchase the electricity generated by qualifying facilities at their "avoided cost," that is, the cost that the utilities would have had to pay to

---

[84] 42 U.S.C. § 9204 (1994).

[85] *See* American Wind Energy Association, *How Much Funding is Provided for Federal Wind Energy Research and Development?* (visited June 26, 1999) <http://www.awea.org/faq/fedrfnd.html>.

[86] 42 U.S.C. § 8702 (1994).

[87] 16 U.S.C. § 796(17) (1994).

generate the electricity themselves. Some utilities entered into long-term contracts with QFs at those anticipated avoided cost levels. With the subsequent plunge in oil and gas prices, these contracts became expensive ones for the utilities and their customers. These utilities fear the trend of deregulation of electricity generation will leave them in a non-competitive position in comparison with start-up companies that do not carry such contracts.[88] California, a leader in the deregulation movement, has allowed utilities to impose a "competition transition charge" to help pay down the stranded costs associated with these contracts over a number of years.[89]

The Energy Policy Act of 1992 requires the federal government to purchase alternative fueled vehicles as part of their fleet.[90] President Clinton noted in 1998 that the federal fleet included 180 electric vehicles and hoped to increase that to 500 by 1999.[91] The Act also requires federal agencies to increase energy efficiency in federal buildings.[92] Increasing efficiency at the federal government's 500,000 plus buildings nationwide is seen as a significant contribution to national energy savings.

Executive Order 13123, signed by President Clinton on June 3, 1999 further establishes the federal government's role in energy conservation and use of alternative energy sources.[93] Executive Order 13123 superseded Executive Order 12902, which encouraged the use of solar systems for federal buildings. Executive Order 13123 requires each agency to reduce its greenhouse gas emissions by 30% by 2010 and to reduce energy consumption by 30% by 2005 and 35% by 2010. It also encourages each agency to use renewable energy sources and to participate in the Million Solar Roofs Initiative by installing 2000 solar energy systems at federal facilities by 2000 and 20,000 solar energy systems by 2010. Even the National Christmas Tree is being powered by solar energy.[94]

---

[88] See Jeff Bailey, 'PURPA' Power: Carter-Era Law Keeps Price of Electricity Up in Spite of a Surplus, WALL ST. J., May 17, 1995, at A1.

[89] See Benjamin A. Holden, Electricity Savings to be Short-Circuited, WALL ST. J., September 24, 1997, at A2.

[90] 42 U.S.C. §§ 13211-19 (1994).

[91] See Dep't of Energy, Press Release: Feds Get Charged Up Over Electric Vehicles (visited June 22, 1996) <http://www.doe.gov/html/doe/whatsnew/pressrel/pr98068.html>.

[92] 42 U.S.C. §§ 8253-62 (1994).

[93] 64 Fed. Reg. 30,851 (1999).

[94] See Dep't of Energy, Press Release: Oh Christmas Tree, Oh Christmas Tree, How Solar Are Your Branches? (visited June 22, 1999) <http://www.doe.gov/html/doe/whatsnew/pressrel/pr97136.html>.

Individual agencies have energy management plans tailored to their needs. The Department of the Interior has an Energy Management Program policy that includes six goals: 1) use energy-efficient and cost-effective technology to reduce energy costs, eliminate waste, and conserve energy resources; 2) design and acquire buildings, facilities, and transportation systems with energy efficiency in mind, especially using renewable energy sources; 3) encourage vehicle efficiency and decrease the consumption of petroleum; 4) use capital investment and improved operations to increase energy efficiency; 5) partner with other government and non-governmental organizations to furnish technical aid and to allot costs on initiatives in order to conserve energy; and 6) encourage achievements in promoting energy conservation, advancing Federal and Departmental energy policy, and saving money.

3. State Regulation of Public Utilities and Electric Generators

Some state utility regulators have required their electric utilities to engage in integrated resource management and, through this process, to bring on-line electric generators fueled by alternative sources, similar to federal requirements under PURPA. States have also used incentive regulation to encourage their public utilities to engage in demand-side management. There are two categories of demand-side management: conservation measures and load-shifting measures. Conservation measures are techniques used to reduce total demand for electricity over all periods of consumption. Load management measures are techniques used to shift demand from daily or seasonal peak periods to other times (total demand is spread out over a longer period of time, but not decreased overall). By decreasing peak demand for electricity, fewer generators need be built to supply peaking power. This power instead can be supplied by cheaper, more efficient baseload generation. At least half the states have some type of conservation incentive program in place.[95]

---

[95] A study by the National Association of Regulatory Utility Commissioners reports that 37 states allow their utilities to recover conservation costs in rates in one form or another, 11 states allow their utilities to recover revenues due to decreased sales caused by conservation, and 26 states have additional shareholder incentives in place to encourage their utilities to actively seek conservation among their customers. *See* Michael W. Reid, Julia B. Brown & Jack C. Deem, INCENTIVES FOR DEMAND-SIDE MANAGEMENT (2d ed. 1993), reprinted in 14 NATIONAL REGULATORY RESEARCH INSTITUTE QUARTERLY BULLETIN 349 (1993). (Executive Summary only).

Some states are deregulating electricity generation, and have enacted renewables portfolio requirements for electric generators wishing to do business in the state. This typically takes the form of specifying that a minimum percentage of power sold in the state be generated from renewable sources. Maine's minimum is 30%; Connecticut's is 6%; Nevada's is .2% in 2000 and increasing annually by .2% until it reaches 1%.

V.   PUBLIC POLICY CONSIDERATIONS AND NOTES

A.   Market Economics

In the United States today, market economics primarily dictates the success of alternative energy. When oil prices skyrocketed during the energy crisis of the 1970s, and rose again when supply was threatened during the Gulf War, the price of alternative energy was more competitive. Today, with the price of oil less than the price for designer water,[96] the immediate future for alternatives does not look as rosy.

However, one oil company executive noted the importance of other factors in addition to price in his prediction that the world was entering "the last days of the age of oil."[97] Arco's chief executive predicted that the next 15 years would see a substantial shift away from oil to cleaner and greener alternative fuels, due to problems and perceptions of environmental pollution. Only time will tell.

1.   Electricity Deregulation: Preferences and Willingness to Pay

Deregulation and initiation of retail competition in electricity has the potential to hurt or help the development of alternative energy. Many small, independent generators, which were fostered by the requirements of PURPA, are anticipating that price competition will put them out of business.[98] As utilities are freed from PURPA's requirements to purchase electricity from qualifying facilities which use alternative energy sources, the higher prices of the alternatives may spell doom for many of the independent generators. However, some states are adding requirements for

---

[96] *See* Michelle Krebs, *Planting the Seeds for a Crop of Lean, Green Machines*, N.Y. TIMES, March 15, 1998, at 12-1.

[97] *See Arco Chief Warns of Shift from Oil to Other Energy*, WALL ST. J., February 10, 1999.

[98] *See* Ross Kerber, *Independent Electric Producers Losing Power Struggle*, WALL ST. J., August 7, 1996, at B4.

specified percentages of fuel to be derived from alternative sources, (i.e., portfolio requirements). In addition, people's preferences and willingness to pay for cleaner energy sources is a critical factor in determining the market competitiveness of alternative energy. There is emerging evidence that people are willing to pay more for "green" electricity.[99] One researcher estimates that 11 million California households may be willing to pay $5.50 more per month for electricity generated from a mix of conventional and alternative, renewable fuels. Sacramento utilities have found that about 600 customers each year are willing to pay $4.00 more per month for rooftop solar panels. In addition, a pricing experiment in Massachusetts found that 1,457 households out of 4,745 would be willing to pay 16% more for energy that offered environmental benefits. People in Traverse City, Michigan pay 20% more in order to get their electricity from a clean source of energy.[100] These preferences signal people's willingness to internalize the cost of negative externalities associated with energy use. This may be a permanent change sweeping the country, or it could be more mercurial—a willingness to spend money in such a way only during healthy economic times.

In any event, some energy companies have climbed aboard what they perceive as a "green" bandwagon, and are actively pursuing customers with "green marketing" strategies, advertising their electricity as a product of alternative energy. The Environmental Protection Agency and the Federal Trade Commission are already looking into ways to ensure that customers are getting what they are promised by such offers, by requiring utilities to print with their bills a breakdown of generation sources and resulting air pollutants.[101]

2. *Emission Allowance Trading*

In an effort to reduce air pollution as well as achieve greater economic efficiency, the EPA introduced an emission allowance trading system pursuant to the Clean Air Act Amendments of 1990.[102] The trading system allows units of emissions of particular pollutants to be issued like permits to companies, which can then sell or exchange the units they do not need.[103] If

---

[99] *See* Ross Kerber, *Energy: For Sale: Environmentally Correct Electricity*, WALL ST. J., July 23, 1997, at B1.

[100] *See* Keith Schneider, *Utility Customers Put a Premium on Wind Energy*, N.Y. TIMES, July 13, 1996, at A1.

[101] *See* Ross Kerber, *id.*

[102] *See* 42 U.S.C. § 7651b (1994).

[103] *See* USEPA, *The Clean Air Act Amendments of 1990: Summary Materials*, U.S. Gov't Printing Office, Washington, D.C., 1990.

the sale price of a unit is greater than the cost of reducing pollution, then the generator will opt to reduce pollution and sell the extra units of emission allowance at a profit. Assuming that the sale price of emission units is sufficiently high, the trading system offers a tremendous market-based incentive to reduce pollution in an economically efficient manner. This has been an attractive alternative to the conventional command-and-control regulatory approach to lower emissions.

A major controversy associated with such systems is the initial allocation of units to generators, which establishes the total supply of tradable units, and necessarily influences demand for and price of the units. The success of market establishment depends on successful initial allocation. Tension is inevitably set up between established utilities and new companies seeking to reap the rewards of deregulation and increased competition. Under a proposal by existing utilities in Georgia, 100% of the tradable pollution allowances would be distributed among utilities already in operation in the state, thereby cutting out new market entrants.[104] New companies hoping to enter the Georgia power market complain that such an allocation would be anticompetitive and have proposed that some credits be set aside for future companies. The established companies counter that new companies can build new plants more cheaply than they can refurbish their existing equipment to meet pollution standards, and thus the new companies already have a competitive advantage. Such tensions are common in other states' experiences with tradable allowances. Tennessee decided to give new generators 4.3% of the state's total allowances. Other states are awaiting the outcome of a legal challenge to EPA rulemaking on nitrogen-oxide emission standards.

B. The Global Economy and Increases in Alternative Sources of Energy

1. Developing Countries

Developing countries, with their increasing demand for energy, will determine how much of their increased demand will be met by alternative sources rather than conventional fuels. The United States has adopted a policy of encouraging foreign countries to shift to alternative energy. Title XII of the Energy Policy Act of 1992 includes the establishment of a renewable energy export technology training program.[105] The Act also

---

[104] *See* Motoko Rich, *Utilities Battle for Georgia Credits on Emissions*, WALL ST. J., May 5, 1999, at S1.

[105] 42 U.S.C. § 13312 (1994).

establishes an interagency working group to coordinate federal activities regarding the export of renewables, a data base on other countries' energy technology needs, a program to encourage the export of renewables to other countries and develop overseas markets for them through financial assistance, and development of opportunities for U.S. firms to compete in foreign markets.

2.   *The Kyoto Protocol of 1997*

The Kyoto Protocol has the potential to spur world growth of renewable energy sources and conservation efforts. The Protocol's objective is to reduce worldwide greenhouse gas emissions. Shifting from fossil fuels to alternative sources is seen as a critical step in this direction.

The success of the Kyoto Protocol and its objectives rest with the will of governments to implement its provisions. President Clinton signed the Protocol, but to date, the United States Congress has not ratified it. The scientific basis of the Protocol and need for the specific emission reductions continues to be debated.[106]

The U.S. Department of Energy predicts that if the Kyoto Protocol becomes law, U.S. energy markets will respond by expanding wind and biomass energy production.[107] Internationally, Germany has been the leader in production of wind energy since 1997, when it overtook the U.S. Spain and Denmark also have significant wind energy production capacity, spurred by higher electricity prices and government subsidies. If energy production from biomass increases, it is likely to be in the area of ethanol production for the transportation sector. The Protocol would also likely stimulate increased capacity for solar energy production, but the Department of Energy predicts it would not be significant until 2020.[108] Should the Protocol be ratified by Congress, the persistence with which the U.S. government has supported development of alternative energy will likely translate into greater technological readiness for its implementation.

In response to the Kyoto Protocol, the Clinton Administration's 1998 Comprehensive National Energy Strategy included specific goals of increasing use of renewable energy sources, designing an international greenhouse

---

[106] *See* Henry S. Rowen and John P. Weyant, *The Greenhouse Follies*, WALL ST. J., December 2, 1997, at A22; and Dolly Setton, *Some Like it Cold*, FORBES, June 14, 1999, at 152.

[107] *See* Dep't of Energy, *Impacts of the Kyoto Protocol on U.S. Energy Markets and Economic Activity*, prepared for the U.S. House of Representatives Committee on Science (October 1998).

[108] *Id.*

gas trading and credit system, and pursuing further research and development efforts to expand energy choices.[109] The strategy called for a doubling of nonhydroelectric, renewable energy production capacity in such sources as photovoltaics and solar thermal to 25,000 megawatts by 2010. It also proposed extending the government's previous efforts in stimulating development of alternative energy sources, described throughout this chapter. However, the strategy puts more emphasis on tracking milestones and relying on free markets, competition, and public/private partnerships—a direction seen as imperative to win congressional and public support. ❦

---

[109] *See* Dep't of Energy, *Press Release: Energy Secretary Peña Announces Comprehensive National Energy Strategy* (visited June 22, 1999) <http:// www.doe.gov/html/doe/whatsnew/pressrel/pr98041.html>.

Index

References are to chapter-page